NATIVE AMERICANS TODAY

NATIVE AMERICANS TODAY:

SOCIOLOGICAL PERSPECTIVES

edited by
Howard M. Bahr, Bruce A. Chadwick,
Robert C. Day
Washington State University

HARPER & ROW, PUBLISHERS
New York   Evanston   San Francisco   London

Standard Book Number: 06-040443-4
Library of Congress Catalog Card Number: 76-179065

CONTENTS

PREFACE   ix

CHAPTER 1: THE SETTING   1

Indian-White Relations in Early America: A Review Essay
   Bernard W. Sheehan   7

Rural Indian Americans in Poverty
   Helen W. Johnson   24

American Indians and White People
   Rosalie H. Wax and Robert K. Thomas   31

CHAPTER 2: PATTERNS OF PREJUDICE AND DISCRIMINATION   43

The Red Man's Burden
   Peter Collier   51

*The Influence of Differential Community Perceptions on the Provision of
      Equal Educational Opportunities*
   James G. Anderson and Dwight Safar   69

Renaissance and Repression: The Oklahoma Cherokee
   Albert L. Wahrhaftig and Robert K. Thomas   80

Prejudice and Discrimination Against Navahos in a Mining Community
   Ralph A. Luebben   89

*Red and Black in Contemporary American History Texts: A Content
      Analysis*
   Lee H. Bowker   101

Stereotyping of Indians and Blacks in Magazine Cartoons
   Kathleen C. Houts and Rosemary S. Bahr   110

Red, White, and Gray: *Equal Protection and the American Indian*
   Daniel H. MacMeekin   115

CHAPTER 3: INDIAN EDUCATION   128

The Inedible Feast
  Bruce A. Chadwick   131
The Warrior Dropouts
  Rosalie H. Wax   146
White Rites Versus Indian Rights
  A. D. Fisher   155
Indian Children and the Reading Program
  William L. E. Philion and Charles G. Galloway   162
Achievement Motivation in Navaho and White Students
  Roland Reboussin and Joel W. Goldstein   172
The Enemies of the People
  Murray L. Wax and Rosalie H. Wax   177

CHAPTER 4: ACCULTURATION AND IDENTITY   193

American Indians, White and Black: The Phenomenon of Transculturalization
  A. Irving Hallowell   200
The Measurement of Assimilation: The Spokane Indians
  Prodipto Roy   225
Urban Residence, Assimilation and Identity of the Spokane Indian
  Lynn C. White and Bruce A. Chadwick   239
From American Indian to Indian American: The Changing Identity of the
    Hupa
  John H. Bushnell   249
Ethnic Identity and Acculturation in Two Eskimo Villages
  Seymour Parker   261
The Cowboy and the Lady: Models as a Determinant of the Rate of Accul-
    turation Among the Piñon Navajo
  James F. Downs   275
Health Practices and Educational Aspirations as Indicators of Acculturation
    and Social Class Among the Eastern Cherokee
  Harriet J. Kupferer   291
The 150% Man, a Product of Blackfeet Acculturation
  Malcolm McFee   303

CHAPTER 5: CRIME AND DEVIANT BEHAVIOR   313

Crime and the American Indian
  Charles Reasons   319

The Relationship of the Social Structure of an Indian Community to Adult and Juvenile Delinquency
  Mhyra S. Minnis   327

Report on Legal Services to the Indians: A Study in Desperation
  Lowell K. Halverson   338

Navaho Drinking: Some Tentative Hypotheses
  Frances Northend Ferguson   345

The Extent and Costs of Excessive Drinking Among the Uintah-Ouray Indians
  Arthur D. Slater and Stan L. Albrecht   358

Suicide and the American Indian: An Analysis of Recent Trends
  Jack Bynum   367

Some Thoughts on the Formation of Personality Disorder: Study of an Indian Boarding School Population
  Thaddeus P. Krush, John W. Bjork, Peter S. Sindell and Joanna Nelle 377

Mental Health of Eastern Oklahoma Indians: An Exploration
  Harry W. Martin, Sara Smith Sutker, Robert L. Leon, and William M. Hales   389

CHAPTER 6: THE URBAN INDIAN   401

An End to Invisibility
  Howard M. Bahr   404

Relocated American Indians in the San Francisco Bay Area: Social Interaction and Indian Identity
  Joan Ablon   412

The Migration and Adaptation of American Indians to Los Angeles
  John A. Price   428

The Personal Adjustment of Navajo Indian Migrants to Denver, Colorado
  Theodore D. Graves   440

Some Aspects of American Indian Migration
  Alan L. Sorkin   467

A "Rural" Indian Community in an Urban Setting
  John H. Dowling   478

CHAPTER 7: RED POWER, ACTION PROGRAMS, AND THE
    FUTURE   485

The New Indian
    Roy Bongartz   490

This Country Was a Lot Better Off When the Indians Were Running It
    Vine Deloria, Jr.   498

The Emergence of Activism as a Social Movement
    Robert C. Day   506

Let the Indians Run Indian Policy
    Senator Edward M. Kennedy   532

INDEX   537

PREFACE

A few years ago, in preparation for a course on American minorities, one of the editors of this volume reviewed a number of texts, including several collections of readings, in an attempt to find material for a lecture on "American Indians Today." He was startled to find a virtual vacuum. In five of the most popular texts on the sociology of minority relations, the Native American was almost totally ignored. The most substantial treatment occurred in a 400-page text in which nine pages were devoted to Indians.

The situation at present is considerably better than it was when that review of available materials was conducted. The past five years have seen a tremendous increase in publications about Indian people, and many of these works, while not explicitly sociological, are near enough to the mark to serve as supplementary reading in social science courses. At least descriptions of the modern urban Indian by competent journalists are now available.

The initial stimulus for this book was the frustration deriving from that attempt to include the sociology of Native Americans in a course on minority-majority relations. Having discovered the sociologists' lack of interest, in Indians either as subjects of research or as topics for discussion, we reasoned that the extensive study of the American Indian by anthropologists and historians must have produced some articles that dealt with theories or concepts commonly designated as sociological and began a search to uncover them.

Many of the articles discovered are included in this volume. However, one of the great voids that was still evident following our search was the almost incredible dearth of information about Indian people *today*. Much of the anthropological work has to do with Indians of the past, or with present-day Indians who most closely approximate the "pure" Indian cultures of yesterday. The historians, by definition, are somewhat out of touch with the present. The economists, psychologists, political scientists, and, to repeat, the sociologists have been almost complete in their professional neglect of the Native American. Consequently, we do not know how many Indian people there are, where they live, nor what their characteristics may be.

It is estimated that between 50 and 60 percent of all Indian people live in urban areas, yet the sociologists, those students of the urban scene *par excellence*, have somehow overlooked them. There are innumerable volumes about Custer's last stand, yet not more than a handful of books about city Indians. Critics have argued that Indian history is biased and sketchy. At least the history is there, to be reviewed, corrected, recast with the changing historical perspectives. The sociology of the Native American remains to be created.

Thus, sociologically speaking, the field of Indian-white relations is still a no-man's-land. The vast historical and anthropological literature about Indian people in white America (or even white people in Indian America) has no counterpart in sociology. As a consequence, this anthology illustrating "sociological perspectives" draws heavily upon the work of anthropologists, historians, educators, and other nonsociological types. And if it is an embarrassment for us to admit that most of the previously published pieces herein are by anthropologists or others even further removed from the province of formal sociology, we take comfort in noting that many are the kinds of things sociologists *might* have done, had they not acquired in their professionalization a trained incapacity to observe the Indian at all. We also take some small comfort from the fact that nine of the ten previously unpublished pieces in this volume are by sociologists.

Perhaps we should not lament too loudly about the sociologist's absence from the field. In *Custer Died for Your Sins*, Vine Deloria singled out the anthropologist as one of the chief burdens of Indian people, and it is probable that if the sociologists had been out collecting data in their usual way they, too, would be *personae non gratae* with the Native Americans of today. As it stands, however, perhaps sociologists can profit from the experience of the anthropologists and force themselves to design and conduct research that has immediate payoffs for the people being studied as well as for the researchers and the nebulous posterity of jargon junkies at whom much of the stuff we squirrel away in soon-musty journals seems to be aimed. Such payoffs for those who participate as research subjects might range from simply providing direct employment in the research enterprise to the accumulation of data *specifically designed* to improve the delivery of certain services, or to illustrate particular problems. The project could be designed with the specific, formal intent, *as part of the research program*, of creating conditions which would bring pressure to bear so that inequities or other problems revealed or highlighted by the researchers might be resolved.

In selecting works for this anthology, we were guided by a number of criteria. Obviously we were influenced by the length of a work, and by our personal evaluations of the author's style. Other things being equal, we favored short pieces over more lengthy ones, and as for style, we can only say that all of the works included were pieces that we "liked" in the sense that the ideas conveyed were packaged in language that carried us along without distracting. Undoubtedly some readers will question our judgment on this matter, especially with reference to a few of the more statistical pieces. To answer in advance, let us point out that the major aim was to assemble examples of empirical studies of Indian people, and the language of even the best empirical research often is a far cry from the lilting song of the novel.

In addition to the criteria of length and style, we were concerned about a work's relevance to sociological interpretation. Accordingly, we asked ourselves whether the piece demonstrated, or could be adapted to demonstrate, principles or variables relevant to the sociology of minority-majority relations.

Another important factor was the methodological expertise manifested in a piece of work. Of course, in the end the pieces had to be judged in terms of what the author set out to do, rather than what we wished he had done. In general, works which reported the testing of hypotheses, either implicitly or explicitly, were given preference over more descriptive reports. However, this criterion was not applied uniformly. In Chapter 1 ("The Setting"), for example, our purpose was primarily to describe, and no hypothesis-testing works are included. The final chapter, "Red Power, Action Programs, and the Future," also has little empirical work, but for a different reason. Most of the events and movements considered in that chapter have not been systematically scrutinized by social scientists of any type, and we had to fall back upon journalistic accounts or perceptive essays. In the remainder of the book we have tried to include enough illustrative material in the form of case histories, essays, or literate qualitative analyses to supplement and "flesh out" the picture created by the research studies.

Two final criteria guiding the selection process were currency of the material and geographic scope. Items published recently were given preference over older material, and articles about present-day Indian people were preferred over historical analyses. All of the selections reprinted were published after 1960. As for geographic scope, within chapters we attempted to represent as wide a variety of tribal or geographic settings as possible.

The process of choosing works for this volume led us to identify with many of the selections. Our "handling" them in comparing, evaluating, and arranging created a sense of easy familiarity and pride in a "good" piece of work. Initially we divided up the chapters among us, and the sense of possession of another man's creation was marvelous to behold as we argued over the merits of including or setting aside a favorite piece. Our greatest debt is to the authors and publishers of the selections included here, who have graciously allowed us to use their work in constructing chapters organized about topics or illustrating perspectives that they have not approved in advance. We are grateful for their trust and hope that they are not disappointed at the context in which their work appears.

We are indebted to many others who have provided advice and assistance during the preparation of this work. We wish to acknowledge the research assistance of Marcia Switzer, Grant Childers, and Ruth Thompson. Valuable clerical assistance was provided by Lonna Hopkins, Cheryl Roper, and Alison Olson. We have profited from the

use of bibliographies assembled by Lynn White. A special thanks is
due the authors of works published here for the first time. Several of
them prepared pieces "made to order" for this book, and others
consented to undertake substantial (and often painful) revisions to
make their work fit our notions about the format of particular
chapters. Also, we wish to express appreciation to Professor Donald
Cressey, who supplied much-needed encouragement at a time when
we had almost abandoned the project. Finally, it should be
mentioned that a considerable portion of the bibliographic work and
literature review was accomplished under a grant from the National
Institute of Mental Health (MH-15582-01) as part of the program for
the establishment, maintenance, and evaluation of an experimental
education program for Indian children.

In assembling the works in this volume, we have been impressed
with the need for careful, relevant, program-oriented social research
about Indian people in modern America. One of the trends of our
time is a movement toward the establishment and monitoring of
"social indicators" of all kinds, and in calling for special attention to,
or the creation of, social indicators that pertain to Indians and to the
whites who interact with them, we are not merely echoing the
popular refrain in a slightly different key. Social scientists have
ignored the Native American too long. Regardless of how modest or
massive the indicator systems that monitor the society as a whole
come to be, the experience of the past decades of social scientific
research suggests that Indian people, especially those who do not live
on reservations, may continue to be members of a forgotten
minority. Social research can illuminate the interplay of attitudes,
values, and behavior, the nature of intergroup relations, the establishment and maintenance of social cohesion, the comparative utility of
programs for directed social change or the adequacy of existing
institutional mechanisms for delivery of social services in ways
beyond the reach of the journalist or historian. The problem, as we
see it, is not that the Native American needs the social scientist, but
rather that the white man needs to know the Native American. The
social scientist as creator and purveyor of valid, replicable observations about what is going on "out there," say, with reference to the
adjustment of Indian people to urban life and the concomitant
maintenance and even strengthening of their tribal ties, can
communicate insights and alternative modes of problem solving which
will enrich the larger society, and perhaps improve its viability. It is
our hope that the present volume will be a small step toward
developing the sociology of Native Americans into a substantial
specialty, rather than an oddity, in the sociology of the 1970s.

H. M. B., B. A. C., R. C. D.

CHAPTER 1

THE SETTING

This chapter is an attempt to provide a general background against which the more specialized selections in future chapters may be viewed. It is not a definitive introduction to the study of Indian-white relations. Instead, we have selected a few pieces which treat topics we consider critical, and have placed them here as a "setting" in the hope that the remainder of the book will take on greater meaning in the light of the insights and information here assembled and identified as preliminary material. The general areas covered in this introductory chapter include a review of the assumptions and perspectives modern writers have tended to bring to the study of Indian-white relations and a brief overview of the economic status of the Indian people. We conclude with an essay which illustrates the nature of culture contact and conflict at the interpersonal level.

If the culture of the Native Americans is to be taken seriously, as Bernard Sheehan suggests in "Indian-White Relations in Early America," then the process of Indian-white relations must be defined as more than victimization of Indians by whites. Instead, it is the complex interplay between (at least) two cultures, and to the extent that the interplay is defined in moralistic terms (white man as "conscienceless aggressor," Indian as "unwitting victim"), we blind ourselves to many aspects of the culture conflict. Accordingly, Sheehan urges that we move from the "guilt-ridden accounts of the past" to studies which emphasize both Indian and white cultures as contributing to the outcome of the conflict.

The conflict was a cultural one, not subject to the control of any one man or group of men. The disintegration of the Indian cultures was not due merely to "a shortage of governmental or philanthropic goodwill" but partly due to rapid social change in white America, a nation "bursting out of the constrictions of its social bonds" and incapable of establishing collective rules for protecting the culture of its "fragile neighbor," the Indian, whose society was "virtually devoid of the resources for serious competition." Given the nature of the two cultures, the transformation, if not the annihilation, of the Indian was assured.

Sheehan does not approve the self-righteousness of white society or the "disheveled individualism that underlay its rush for conquest." But to assert that the whites are guilty does not illuminate the process of the Indian's decline. The essential thing is to understand Indian

culture and to emphasize the special character of that culture. The
Indian was not merely a "hapless victim"; the real crime, if there was
one, was "the inexorable breakdown of the native's cultural integrity,
in part the result of conscious policy and in part the inevitable consequence of competition between two disparate ways of life." Nor
was the Native American the object of a single "despicable act," but
rather he was the victim of a process, and the fact that it was a
process diffuses the guilt. The process was one of cultural intermingling, and one cannot define an entire society as guilty. Individuals may have committed criminal acts; but the process was one of
culture contact and conflict, and, to be judged fairly, it must be
judged in relativistic terms, that is, in terms of the values of the
persons involved in the process. The Native Americans were victims
of their cultural values; those who judge them by hindsight are
victims of their own, rather different, cultural values, and no one can
say that the latter-day judges are more "right" than those involved in
the process.

Thus, Sheehan insists that the Indian-white confrontation must
be interpreted in the light of the cultural integrity of both the white
and Native cultures, and of their essential incompatibility and the
social consequences of that incompatibility quite independently of
the personal motives of the actors involved. He pleads for a cultural
analysis, a setting aside of the moralizing in favor of assessing what
actually occurred as "civilized" manners infiltrated into Native American society, and, to some extent, as the whites were influenced by
Indian culture. The white man's way of life might operate as a culture-dissolving ideology, but the outcome of that ideology in culture-
contact situations depended in part on the unique character of the
culture of the Native Americans, and to overlook the *active* role of
Indian culture in the process and outcome is to distort and over-
simplify the process. Those who define the white man as guilty are
still telling the story from the white man's point of view, still denying the Indian identity as an Indian; he is, instead, anonymous
opponent or victim, and hence, in his apology to the Indian, the
moralist tends to continue the stereotype, rather than treating the
Indian culture on an equal basis with the white.

The consequence of the moralizing historian's approach frequently is that "civilization simply sweeps across the pages in triumph or
ignominy and the Indian fights or dies with no more identity than
any other expendable resource." The essential point is that whatever
side one takes, whether the onrush of European civilization is seen as
a moral victory or as hypocritical genocide, the integrity of Indian
culture is ignored. The Indian remains passive, acted upon rather than
acting, a mere target for the beneficent or malevolent actions of the
whites.

Sheehan also makes the point that part of the seductiveness of
the guilt-assigning approach to history is that it allows the writer to
impose his own values on events and to enhance (or attenuate) the

prestige of the Indian by removing him from his "cultural maelstrom." The Indian is stereotyped in one of the older white myths,
that of the noble savage who was spoiled by the white man, rather
than being viewed as a participant, as was the white man, in a peculiar complex culture. The myth of natural innocence adds nothing to
the understanding of the contact process. The white authors produce
Indians who are impersonations of white men; and again the cultural identity of the Indian is denied.

A central element in the history of contact between whites and
Indians is the Bureau of Indian Affairs, located in the Department of
the Interior. Space limitations have prevented the inclusion of descriptive material about the BIA in this chapter. However, let us
mention three readily available sources for readers who wish to pursue the matter. Brophy and Aberle's *The Indian: America's Unfinished Business* (Norman: University of Oklahoma Press, 1966)
contains a chapter on the purpose and structure of the BIA and considers possible measures for improving its services. Another useful
source is an official publication of the Department of the Interior,
American Indians and the Federal Government, which outlines the
priorities and policies of the department with respect to Indian
people. It is pointed out that the BIA's greatest single expenditure is
for education; it operates boarding and day schools, subsidizes public
schools, and conducts educational programs for adults, including
vocational training. A second important area of BIA activity is industrial and commercial development of Indian resources. This involves
providing loans for Indian enterprises and attracting industrial and
recreational development to reservation lands. The stated purpose of
BIA development activity is to create additional jobs and income for
Indians living on the reservations.

The BIA works with other governmental agencies to provide two
additional special services to Indians. Indian health is the responsibility of the Public Health Service, and usually free medical and
dental services are available to reservation Indians. In addition, Public
Housing and the BIA are working together to provide better housing
for Indians. The fact that 75 percent of Indian housing is below the
minimum government standards indicates the need for greater effort
in this area.

A contrasting point of view is available in Edgar Cahn's *Our
Brother's Keeper: The Indian in White America*. In a section entitled
"The BIA's Three Lessons" there is a scathing denunciation of the
BIA and its failure to help the Indian people.[1] According to Cahn,
Indian people learn three basic lessons from the BIA. The first lesson
is that the Indian's attempts at self-realization are almost always
frustrated. In "fulfilling its stewardship" the BIA denies the Indians,
individually and as a group, the right to make decisions that affect
their immediate lives. Cahn provides examples of land usage, water
rights, claims money, and so forth that are controlled by the BIA
officials without regard to the plans or wishes of the Indian to whom

the resources rightfully belong. To make matters worse, the Indian
has no means or procedures for appealing decisions of BIA officials.
The results are feelings of powerlessness and frustration, and acceptance of the futility of planning for the future.

The second lesson Cahn accuses the BIA of teaching the Indian is
that dependency is a virtue. The most dramatic example of this process is the act of terminating reservation status of the most progressive
Indian tribes. The results of such experiments have been disastrous
both for the Indians concerned and for the surrounding white communities.

The third and final lesson is that alienation is rewarded. In
other words, Indians who reject their language, birthplace, people, and
culture in favor of white culture are rewarded with economic security. One important consequence of this process of rewarding "assimilation" into white culture is that potential Indian leadership is co-
opted out of Indian organizations and passes into the BIA and other
white organizations.

Despite its flaws the Indians vigorously defend the continued
existence of the BIA. A recent Presidential suggestion that the functions of the BIA be transferred to the Department of Health, Education and Welfare met with strong opposition from Indian people.
Some Indians who criticize the BIA explain their paradoxical defense
of the status quo by asserting that with the BIA the Indian "knows
his enemy," and thus is able to cope with him. This attitude is often
coupled with the belief that as bad as the BIA is, anything new
would probably be worse. Whatever the answer, the BIA remains a
central element in the life of the Native American.

Another dominant aspect of Indian life is poverty. Indian poverty
far exceeds that of other minority groups. In 1967 the average Indian
income was $1500, 75 percent below the national average, and three-
fourths of the Indian families had an annual income below $3000.[2]
At a time when the median family income for the nation as a whole
was $5952, rural Navaho families reported a median family income of
less than $750 per year and the highest median annual family income
for any tribe was the $2928 reported for the Chippewa in Bertram
County, Minnesota.[3]

The unemployment level for American Indians is incredibly high.
In 1967 the unemployment rate for reservation Indians was 37.3
percent, 12 times greater than the non-Indian rate of 3.1 percent.[4]
Moreover, since 1955 the disparity between Indian and non-Indian
unemployment rate has been increasing.[5] Surveys of particular reservations have provided evidence that corroborate the national statistics
and, in fact, suggest that things may be even worse than the national
figures would indicate. During the middle and late 1960s, the unemployment rate for the Choctaw of Mississippi was 86 percent,[6] and
among the Pueblos of New Mexico, the Blackfoot of Montana, and
the Cheyenne and Arapaho of the plains states, unemployment rates
were over 70 percent.[7] The Cherokees of Oklahoma estimated that

between 50 and 60 percent of their males over the age of 16 and not in school were unemployed. The lowest rate we discovered was 33 percent for the Sioux in South Dakota.[8]

One finds the same dismal situation when looking at housing. It is estimated that three-fourths of all reservation housing is below minimum standards as defined by the Census Bureau, and that half of the houses are so badly dilapidated that repair is impossible.[9] These conditions exist despite government efforts to provide low-cost housing on the reservations.

Further dramatic indicators of Indian poverty are their high morbidity and mortality rates. Testimony before the Senate Subcommittee on Indian Education revealed that among Indian people the infant mortality rate was twice the national average, that the tuberculosis rate was seven times the national average, and that the average Indian lived at least ten years less than his non-Indian counterpart.[10] In some tribes the situation was even worse. Among the White Mountain Apache the life expectancy was 40 to 46 years, compared to over 70 for non-Indians.[11]

A unique characteristic of Indian poverty is that poverty may become a way of life that some accept as a tribal virtue necessary to protect their Indian traditions. Many Indian people view attacks on poverty with suspicion, defining them as attempts to force the acculturation of Indian people. This suspicion was expressed by Mel Thom, a tribal Office of Economic Opportunity director: "Another move by our opposition and protector is the declared 'War on Poverty.' War has been declared on our condition. To many of us poverty is a way of life. We do not like to be miserable, but our poor conditions have preserved a way of life for awhile. Is this just stepping up efforts to absorb us into the mainstream of American life?"[12]

The selection by Helen Johnson, "Rural Indian Americans in Poverty," is adapted from a recent report published by the U.S. Department of Agriculture. Demographic characteristics of rural Indians in the 1960s are summarized, and details about their family income, health, and occupational distribution are given. Following her review of the dimensions of poverty among Indian people, Johnson comments that in comparison to the numbers of urban poor, the rural Indians are a very small population. At the same time, however, their poverty is much more serious than that of most of the nation's poor people. Given the relatively small number of Indians, it would seem that the costs of reducing or removing their poverty should not be too severe:

Considering the depth of distress of the rural Indians, the task of ameliorating the poverty of the great majority of them would not be an insuperable undertaking for an affluent country like the United States. . . . It has been estimated that "the basic economic problem of the Indian communities could be solved by the provision of 40,000 jobs." This would seem a small demand for a nation where civilian employment has increased an average of 723,000 each year from 1955 to 1965. . . .

The final selection in this chapter, "American Indians and White People" by Rosalie H. Wax and Robert K. Thomas, is an attempt to explain why Indians and whites may have trouble talking to each other. When they meet in the course of day-to-day activities, Indians and white people bring different sets of expectations, values, and ideas about "proper" behavior. Friction or embarrassment may result as the expectations of one party are violated, or as the other behaves "improperly." For example, when a white individual confronts a novel situation the normal behavior is to try a wide range of responses with the expectation that one of them will be appropriate. The white motto is "Try and try again." The authors contrast this response pattern with the Indian pattern of "freezing" and not responding until cues as to the appropriate behavior have been picked up from other actors in the situation. When these two cultural patterns meet, the results are predictable. The white will commence to pepper the Indian with small talk in hopes that one of the questions or comments will elicit a response in the other. The Indian is puzzled or put off by this onslaught of questions and remains silent. "His practiced silence will spur the white to even more extreme exertions; and the more frantic the one becomes the less response he is likely to elicit from the other."

Wax and Thomas contrast the norm of noninterference among Indian people with the "meddling" ways of the white man. Among Indians the noninterference is said to extend even to the behavior of passengers in automobiles: "If the car is the property of the driver, no passenger ever considers giving him suggestions or directions." The development of the norm of noninterference among Indian children is described; like the white norm of interference, it is deeply ingrained early in childhood. When white interferers and Indian noninterferers get together, trouble is likely to develop. One way to minimize the chances for such trouble is to teach white people who deal with Indians to practice noninterference in Indian matters.

NOTES

1 In other sections of *Our Brother's Keeper*, Cahn attacks the BIA as "a terminal case of bureaucracy" and "the compromised advocate." See Edgar Cahn (ed.) *Our Brother's Keeper: The Indian in White America* (New York: New Community Press, 1969), pp. 146-162.

2 Statement by Wayne Morse, U.S. Senator from the State of Oregon. *Indian Education Subcommittee Hearings, 90th Congress*, First and Second Sessions, Part V, May 1968, p. 1909.

3 Alfred L. Wahrhaftig, "Social and Economic Characteristics of the Cherokee Population of Eastern Oklahoma: Report of a Survey of four Cherokee Settlements in the Cherokee Nation," *Indian Education Subcommittee Hearings, 90th Congress*, First and Second Sessions, Part II, February 1968, p. 937.

4 Alan Sorkin, "Education and Manpower Programs for Indian Americans," *Indian Education 1969, Hearing before the Subcom-*

mittee on Labor and Public Welfare, U.S. Senate, 91st Congress, First Session, Part II, p. 1593.

5 *Ibid.,* p. 1593.

6 Stan Steiner, *The New Indians* (New York: Dell Publishing Co., 1968), p. 199.

7 *Ibid.,* pp. 199-200.

8 Statement by Dr. Carl Mindell, U.S. Public Health Service Psychiatrist, Pine Ridge, South Dakota, *Indian Education Subcommittee Hearings, 90th Congress,* First and Second Sessions, Part IV, April 1968, p. 1273.

9 Herbert E. Striner, "Toward a Fundamental Program for the Training, Employment, and Economic Equality of the American Indian," prepared for the W. R. Upjohn Institute for Employment Research and reprinted in *Indian Education Subcommittee Hearings, 90th Congress,* First and Second Sessions, Part II, February 1968, p. 628.

10 Wayne Morse, *op. cit.,* p. 1909.

11 Statement by Mr. Ronnie Lape, Chairman of White Mountain Apache. *Indian Education Subcommittee Hearings, 90th Congress,* First and Second Sessions, Part III, March 1968, p. 1009.

12 Steiner, *op. cit.,* pp. 194-195.

BERNARD W. SHEEHAN: INDIAN-WHITE RELATIONS IN EARLY AMERICA: A REVIEW ESSAY

The white man is guilty. He has been charged with the destruction of the American Indian, the evidence has been presented, and the verdict returned for all to see. The sorry remnants of the American aborigine in our own day, beneficiaries and victims of the government's largess, testify to the overwhelming culpability of the civilized intruder in the Indian's domain. No doubt the objective fact is true: the modern Indian does, at least in the white man's mind, present a depressing contrast to his past eminence; and the occupation of the American continent by the European settler is surely the cause of his decline. The story has been recounted often enough to be part of the American folklore. Whether the settler out of sheer viciousness or unconquerable greed drove the native population from its ancestral home, decimating tribe after tribe until the pathetic survivors were herded onto reservations in the late nineteenth century, or merely brought to the new land the trappings of a foreign environment,

Source: Reprinted by permission from *William and Mary Quarterly* 26 (April 1969), 267-287.

liquor and disease, hostile to the Indian's continued existence, the result was the same. And the criminal was still the civilized European.

The archetypal historical definition of the white man's guilt was presented in 1881 by Helen Hunt Jackson in her *Century of Dishonor.* Though frankly polemical (the cover of the second edition in 1886 was stamped in red with a quotation from Benjamin Franklin: "Look upon your hands! They are stained with the blood of your relations."), the volume also made historical pretensions. But more important, it revealed the deep sense of guilt many white men felt at the fate of the Indian, and it contrived to formulate a scheme that would portray the native as a hapless victim and the white man as a merciless aggressor. In tone sentimental, it was in substance a moral tract whose purpose was to convict civilization of its crimes against the aborigine; and history was subordinate to this greater object.

Besides the melodrama of murder, robbery, cruelty, perfidy, and the white man's generally outrageous behavior, the burden of Mrs. Jackson's book conveyed a basic interpretation of Indian-white relations. In the first pages she spelled out her conviction that the Indians were organized into sovereign nations and that the whites were obliged under international law to treat them as such. The natives had a right to the soil that should have been honored and their agreements carried the force of sovereign contracts. In repeatedly violating treaties, the whites had set themselves outside the law and were thereby subject to arbitrary punishment by any civilized nation that should see fit to call them to account.[1] Indian negotiators behaved not in the manner of "ignorant barbarians" but as "clear-headed, statesman-like rulers, insisting on the rights of their nation."[2] The whites, especially on the frontier, were largely responsible for the violence that repeatedly flared between the two societies. And the conflict was not merely the fortuitous meeting of two groups of people with different interests. On the white man's side there was a measure of calculation. "Thus early in our history was the ingenious plan evolved of first maddening the Indians into war, and then falling upon them with exterminating punishment." Indian violence was the exception in the sum of frontier conflict and then it was either in response to the white man's aggression or instigated by the white for his own interests.[3] The Indian was depicted as the innocent victim of a hostile and unprincipled civilization and, adding pathos to his decline, as the possessor of a public order and private virtues not dissimilar to those supposedly characteristic of civilization.

To be sure, later historians, though deeply sympathetic to the Indian's cause, were neither so sentimental nor so one-sided in their treatment of Indian-white relations. Yet the Indian seemed consistently to manifest the qualities of national independence and most poignantly to suffer from the crass aggressiveness of the whites. For example, in her treatment of Indian removal, the culminating event of Indian-white relations in the early period, Annie H. Abel described with admirable detachment the process through which the Indians were induced to move west of the Mississippi.[4] Throughout the Indians performed as any other sovereign people, carrying on long and difficult negotiations with a power of equal independence. The other segment of the story was told by Grant Foreman in two studies, both dwelling on the actual process of removal.[5] Here the Indians "with bitter sorrow in their hearts, weakened by hardship and privation, decimated by disease, oppressed by penury, despondent and disheartened," struggled over their "trail of tears" to exile in the west.[6] In Annie Abel's account the native was scarcely recognizable as an Indian and in Foreman's two volumes, though solid and moderate works, the victimized aborigine could not but cast his shadow on the overwhelming guilt of the white man.

The white man's crime, however, was not an abrupt or even readily definable act. After all, whatever the Indian suffered as a consequence of the advent of the European on the American continent took a long time to reach its ghastly conclusion—has yet, in fact, to do so. In truth, as a historical phenomenon, the Indian disintegrated; as an Indian he was not annihilated but he faded culturally into another entity. The crime, if there was one, was the inexorable breakdown of the native's cultural integrity, in part the result of conscious policy and in part the inevitable consequence of competition between two disparate ways of life. Rather than the singular clarity of one despicable act, the American aborigine was the victim of a process. Perhaps process can be criminal but its natural complexity diffuses the locus of guilt. Criminality tends to be individual and guilt is much more easily imputed when the criminal and his victim can be seen apart from circumstance or the slow, dissolving force of cultural breakdown. The moralistic impact falls more exactingly when the demarcation between the opposing forces is set off clearly. When Indian and white meet on equal terms and the white man brazenly violates most of the rules, or when the Indian, helpless before the overpowering force of civilization, is portrayed as the pitiable victim of aggression, the simplistic duality makes the assignment of guilt an easy task; but when the conflict is submerged in the process of cultural intermingling, the moralistic dichotomy dissolves. If only because it is virtually impossible to declare a whole society guilty, the moralistic approach requires an implicit denial of the integrity of culture, in effect, a shattering of the wholeness of that complex of experience and rational judgment from which men inevitably construct a style of life peculiar to themselves.

As a formalizing conception, the notion of integral culture[7] is freighted with the dangers of moral relativism. Anthropologists, ethnologists, and sociologists have long argued the matter to no great satisfaction. Historians seem even more open to the apparent dilemma of scholarly detachment and moral involvement. Certainly the conflict between Indian and white, deeply associated with civilized man's misgivings in the face of his primitive antithesis, has always conjured in the historical mind oppression and hypocrisy and has demanded a moral accounting. Robert Berkhofer, in his recent study of missionary activities among the Indians, carries the relativist perspective beyond the subject perceived into the very eye of the perceiver. "Current indictments of past American conduct," he writes, "are on the same plane as earlier American condemnations of savage society. The Americans of the past were victims of their cultural values just as their latter-day judges are victims of today's beliefs."[8] We are all, one supposes, witting or not, in one degree or another, victims of our nurture, but at least we recognize it, thus saving the historian's capacity for judgment from the epistemological dead end of consistent relativism. The concept of integral culture should not reduce the historian to a mere recorder; it should only insure that judgments be qualified by the peculiar circumstances of a distinct cultural definition. Ethics, the imputing of guilt or innocence, must not be excluded from the process of historical judgement but it must become much less obtrusive. The issue of right or wrong must give way to an understanding of the process of cultural conflict that characterized the meeting of European and Indian in the New World. Cultural analysis should be relativist only in the sense that it is an inclusive conception, in the sense that it allows the historian to see all the intricate permeations of the intermeshing of disparate cultures rather than the one-to-one moral dichotomy of oppressor and oppressed.

Practically, it should be enough to refurbish William N. Fenton's plea in 1953 that Indian-white relations be treated as a common ground of history and ethnology. Little had been done when he wrote to combine the two sources of knowledge, that is, to examine Indian-white conflict as a clash of culture, and little has been done since. According to one historian of the frontier, recent work in anthropology and ethnology "has brought us much closer to a satisfactory understanding" of the character of native reaction to white intrusion. Another makes the determined pledge "to understand the life, the societies, the cultures, the thinking and feeling of the Indians."[9] The intentions are the best and even the performance is solid and enlightening. But it cannot be said in any broad sense that Fenton's hope has been fulfilled. We still await an account of Indian-white relations in the early period that will bring to bear the full weight of the knowledge of human culture.

The best of the recent literature does indeed make use of cultural analysis though not usually to the extent of excluding the moralistic disjunction. A notable exception is Wilbur R. Jacobs's examination of frontier diplomacy in the light of the native tradition of gift giving. By centering upon the major form of official contact between white and Indian and pointing out its ceremonial significance for the native society, Jacobs adds the sinews of culture to the bland confrontation between native and civilized negotiators. Though perhaps the broad subject of cultural conflict cannot be interpreted on the basis of so limited a theme, the volume remains one of the few recent efforts to lay out some of the intricacies of Indian-white relations while taking seriously the character of the native way of life. Surely, however, the most successful attempt in the past generation, describing the consequences of the infiltration of civilized manners into primitive America, is Anthony F. C. Wallace's biographical study of the Delaware leader Teedyuscung. Through a personality fatally undermined but rich in historical implications, Wallace examines the effect of civilization on the delicate structure of Indian culture.[10]

Of course there is much evidence in the recent literature that historians do take the integrity of the Indian's culture seriously. Reginald Horsman notes in more than one place the Indian's conscious determination to defend his own way of doing things against the inexorable push of advancing America. Louis De Vorsey, while conceding the rudimentary character of tribal political organization, maintains that "the Indians evinced a passionate desire to retain their territorial bases which they identified as vital to their continued existence as a people." In his account of New England frontier, Alden Vaughan refers to the barriers of custom and language over which the Puritan missionaries could not prevail. But it is perhaps Berkhofer who sees most distinctly the Indian as a cultural entity. In perceiving that the cultural clash between missionary and native was total, that the missionary demanded nothing less from the Indian than a complete ethnic capitulation ("To become truly Christian was to become anti-Indian."), he broaches the question of the dynamics of cultural interplay. Though the white man's way of life operates, in this case as a culture-dissolving ideology, the Indian's manners and mores, in their gradual dissolution, are conceded a unique definition. The Indian and the white man are different because their experience and historical adjustment to the surrounding world have been different. They come together in the inevitable clash and denouement and just as certain decline of the weaker, less resilient party. The totality of the conflict sharpens the conception of cultural differentiation.[11]

Paradoxically, the successes illustrate the failures. Though virtually every historian of Indian-white relations would agree to the need for a recognition of cultural distinctness as an essential part of his conceptual apparatus, few have been able to bring the idea into the actual complexities of cultural competition. It is virtually de rigueur for an author to make some formal pronouncement on the subject, but there seems to be no requirement that the ideas reach fruition. What one comes to expect still is a history of Indian-white contact told from the white man's side, the Indian playing the role of anonymous opponent or victim. Disintegration or acculturation is often noted, and approved or regretted, but there is seldom any deep analysis of the processes. Civilization simply sweeps across the pages in triumph or ignominy and the Indian fights or dies with no more identity than any other expendable resource. If the conceptualization need not produce an extensive ethnological examination, it should at least qualify the tendency for moralistic division and manifest some sense of the consequences of cultural conflict.

Berkhofer, having laid down the most solid base for cultural relativism, suffers most patently from the failure. As he writes, "psychologically speaking, there seemed to be no halfway point" for the Indians in their confrontation with civilization. The missionaries' ideology paid little heed to the complications of cultural transformation. They "did not know ... that basic values change very slowly."[12] In taking his cue from the white man's mental disposition, Berkhofer never enters the arena in which the two societies meet. The missionaries try to supplant the native social order and fail because, as he aptly points out, their ideology takes no cognizance of the relative imperviousness of culture to change. Just so the historian, even though he is aware of the importance of cultural analysis, is unable to move beyond the sterile detachment of the white man's anti-cultural ideology. Cultural relativism, unless it leads to an analysis of the processes of societal transformation, will do more than trace the outlines of a historiographical problem. It will not fill the empty space.

The older approach to Indian-white relations, which on principle paid little attention to cultural interplay, and portrayed the Indian as unwitting victim and the white man as conscienceless aggressor, apparently still has some steam left in it. It is well enough that Leach should maintain that "we are now less interested in pointing the finger of guilt at one race or the other" or that Jacobs should caution us that in its own time the confrontation was not viewed "as the black-and-white moral issue which it often seems to us today." Wilcomb E. Washburn, however, will have none of such pussyfooting. In a vigorous and knowledgeable defense, he proclaims his strong sympathy for the American Indian and insists that historians must judge from the sources the relative weight of guilt or innocence in the story of Indian-white conflict. One cannot, as he says, "split the difference."[13]

The historian as distributor of censure has a far easier task if he may be permitted to abstract his subject from history and therefore from cultural analysis. And such has been the most frequently used method in assigning the burden of guilt to the white man. The Indian is enhanced in prestige by the simple expedient of being plucked from the cultural maelstrom. From the beginning of Indian-white contact the convention of the noble savage has acted primarily as a criterion of moral rectitude against which the transgressions of civilization might be judged. And it has always been an explicitly ahistorical concept, posited on a pre-Adamic definition of man. Washburn reveals a sympathy for just such an understanding of the Indian. He contends particularly that the natives manifested a natural hospitality toward the Europeans on first encounter and that violence was the fault of the whites. The Indian can be blamed only for retaliating against an original aggression. Indeed the noble savage convention itself stems from the first reports of this aboriginal good will.[14] In fact noble savagism had long been a part of the paradisaic strain in Western thought and did not grow out of the observations of early explorers and settlers. They brought the idea with them but were undoubtedly pleased for a new field in which to apply it.[15] At the same time it is entirely possible that European society had a higher violence quotient than the Indian's way of life; the white man was, after all, more adept. Of far more importance is the prognosis for historical understanding on the basis of a blatantly non-historical original assumption. A history of Indian-white relations must take its beginning in the admission of the Indian's peculiar cultural composition, itself the product of history. It can gain nothing, and it might well lose everything, by proposing a mythic natural innocence and proceeding to direct thunderbolts at those who supposedly despoiled it.

Despite his predilection for moral history, however, Washburn does not propose a consistent utilization of the noble savage theme in interpreting Indian-white relations. He defines noble savagery with a list of primitive attributes, "generosity, stoic bearing of pain, dignity, loftiness of speech in council," all of which are common properties of Edenic man. But for him they are merely the norms of a noble Indian society.[16] He comes back finally to a cultural conception but his determination to assign moral blame leads him to impose on it the ends usually expected from the noble savage convention. The methodological ambiguity of such an approach can only cast doubt on the ultimate conclusions.

Though less abstracted than the primitivism of the noble savage concept, there has long been a tendency in Western thought to see human nature as a static, universal quality. Only the accidents of existence change; at the core of the human organism there remains a stable, predictable essence. Thus arguments for equality and human dignity usually have their basis in a timeless realm of moral value. In a practical sense, it is frequently difficult for the historian to see the complex of motive and action in a peculiar culture as in its root different from that of another style of existence. Besides the inhibitions of the historian's own ethnocentrism, he is usually forced to come to terms with a universalist ideology that constantly nudges him toward a static explanation of behavior.

In attempting to unravel the intricacies of the Indian-white relationship, therefore, the historian is tempted frequently to judge both sides against the same set of expectations. The Indian behaves as the white man does and for the same reasons. Of course there is some merit in the procedure. The Indian was far more affected by the white than the white by the Indian. He began absorbing the ways of civilization at first contact, sometimes even before a face-to-face meeting. But the Indian was not a blank tablet; even in the process of acculturation there remained a substratum of Indian character. He was always an Indian and the whites were frequently reminded of it. The truth of the matter will be out when the historian can tell at any given moment the level of Indianness in his subject—when, in effect, he can judge the extent of acculturation.

Doubtless such a demand is beyond the capacity of the historical science. Yet it is also questionable that analysis should be stopped at a mere recitation of the particular changes instituted in Indian society under the influence of civilization. If Berkhofer explained little about the processes of historical change in defining the totalism of the missionary ideology, Mary Young does not reveal more in listing the positive changes begun under missionary auspices. The introduction of civilized medicine, the discouragement of dancing and ball play, the elimination of elaborate and prolonged mourning, and the attack on polygamy, infanticide, whiskey drinking, and obscene conversation, all bore heavily on the alteration of native society, but, surely, not all to the same degree, and the cancellation of one white-induced habit, whiskey drinking, might well have meant a return to the old ways.[17] Breaking into a dynamic situation at a given point, without considering the subtle process of change, as in any still life, risks distortion. One is inclined, as a consequence, to weigh the quantity of change without detecting its vital quality.

Still more serious is the practice of imputing characteristics of the white man's culture to the Indians, as, for example, Francis Paul Prucha's contention that the "elemental question" between the two societies was "who was to own and control the land."[18] To be sure, the white man wanted the land and the Indian opposed him sometimes, but little has really been said about the nature of the conflict unless the position of land (even the concept takes its meaning from civilization) is laid out in the differing value systems of the two societies. The land can be accounted the basic point of conflict only if it can be shown that the Indian had a sense of spatial identity similar to the white man's. He did not, or at least there is no reason to think that he did. He did not do the same things to land that the white man did. If he sometimes manifested the jealous attachment to it that the whites were wont to expect, he certainly gave much of it up without more than a perfunctory struggle—assuming that he even understood what was meant by giving it up. Also, as the Indian came to see the white man's intense desire for the land and as he felt the effects of the civilized invasion of his own cultural sphere—which was, in effect, the white man taking the land—he came also to see that he had to preserve his territorial integrity. This, however, was more likely the consequence of acculturation than a primitive allegiance to a plot of soil. The issue was not so much the land as the disintegration of the native's culture which led finally to his sturdy defense of his territorial possessions. Whatever the explanation, it must avoid a formulation of values based on one culture without considering the interplay of different value systems.

Similarly Jacobs speaks of an Indian "war for independence" and of an essentially democratic government and individualist spirit. Allen Trelease uses such terms with reference to Indian society as "public opinion," "anarchy," and an "oligarchic body of sachems." Fenton seems to think it possible that the Iroquois federation served as archetype for the federal constitution. And Alvin M. Josephy, Jr., using Franklin's exasperated but quite conventional comparison of the supposed political accomplishments of the Indians and the ingrained divisiveness of the colonies, maintains that the Iroquois league had an "indirect" influence on the establishment of the union and the structure of the new government in 1789. Furthermore, he contends, these politically astute aborigines can be described with at least partial accuracy in the conventional wisdom of noble savagery. They believed in the "freedom and dignity of the individual" and relied on unanimous vote in their councils to preserve the "equality of individuals and respect for their rights." Such transference of the clichés of the white man's political rhetoric cannot but do violence to the Indian's cultural integrity. There is no dignity in the Indian impersonating the white man.[19]

More pertinent is the treatment of the Indian as warrior and diplomatist. Since a fair portion of the story of Indian-white relations is taken up with the proceedings of war and the making of peace, most authors are forced to commit themselves, at least implicitly, to a rationale for dealing with the subject. Indeed no problems are more difficult of explanation than the motives which impelled the savages to violence and determined their objects in ending it. The great danger to the historian is in attributing to the Indian the rational detachment in external politics that would be expected from a civilized statesman. Perhaps the two best examples are Parkman's account of Pontiac as a potential builder of a forest empire and George T. Hunt's economic explanation of Iroquois belligerence.[20]

Trelease deals with the question of Iroquois motivation in his book on seventeenth-century Indian affairs in New York. A cautious historian, he approaches the matter with some trepidation. Though the Indians, he thinks, did not necessarily have the same motives as the whites, there is as much reason to attribute economic incentive to them as there is to civilized man. Before the arrival of the European, the Indians fought for various reasons, but with the beginning of the fur trade economics became paramount.[21] Without question, then, the European demand for furs and the Indian's willingness to supply them created a convenient barter nexus between the two societies—a decidedly economic relationship. But outside of Manchester there is no purely economic condition. The key is in the cultural context, the effect of the white man's artifacts on Indian society. The Indian's dependence was not economic, it was cultural. Any explanation must deal with the peculiar ecological and cultural changes induced by the spreading of the white man's wares through the forest.

The Iroquois portrayed by Trelease are far more self-contained than might be expected, though it is difficult to deny them their continued talent in wilderness politics even after their life had been seriously affected by the inroads of a foreign culture. The Five Nations prove their independence, writes Trelease, in choosing to move into the west for their own purposes; their attack on the Huron is a conscious tribal policy. (A similar calculation can be seen in the activities of the Algonquin Indians in the Peach War of 1655.) The Iroquois' prudence is illustrated in their determination not to expand the conflict to the Abenaki when they were already at war with the French; and their diplomatic nimbleness when, at least on one occasion, they were able to outmaneuver both the French and the British.[22] Now in any of its parts it is not really an unlikely story; Trelease tells a sensible tale and he writes from the sources. However, it is the accumulation, the piling up of evidence of native ability that tends finally to draw the two societies apart. The situation changes from the subtle intermingling of disparate cultures to the confrontation of two sovereign powers, both jealous of their independence, and both fully equipped to maintain it. The treatment of Indian-white relations through the medium of foreign policy leads invariably to the neglect of the cultural process.

But, even aside from the relative emphasis on the cultural approach, it seems that the white man's policy toward the Indian is in the throes of reinterpretation. There appear still such treatments as William T. Hagan's overview of the Indian in American history, more concerned with gratuitous slures against the white than the thoughtful understanding of the meeting of the two societies, or R.S. Cotterill's essay in sarcasm on the five southern tribes.[23] In two recent volumes, however, the history of American Indian-white relations has taken an important step beyond the guilt-ridden accounts of the past. At one end of the period, Alden T. Vaughan on Puritan-Indian relations in the seventeenth century and, at the other end, Francis Paul Prucha on government Indian policy in the early national period, have provided the basis for a different perspective on the subject.

Vaughan's effort is a disarming defense of the Puritan treatment of the New England natives. On the whole the Puritans were "humane, considerate, and just," and "had a surprisingly high regard for the interests of a people who were less powerful, less civilized, less sophisticated, and—in the eyes of the New England colonists—less godly." Though doubtless their kind of violence was more intense, they employed it less frequently than the Indians. Rather than bringing chaos to New England, the Puritans were the only power capable of keeping the peace among the volatile tribes. In the two major Indian-white conflicts, with the Pequots and later against King Philip, the Puritans dealt devastating blows to Indian power but they did not cause the fighting. In the first, the Pequots, themselves intruders, must take the blame, and in the second, the impetus for war came not from the Puritans but from Philip in his fear for the loss of his prestige and power.[24]

Vaughan is not unsympathetic to the Indian. He simply believes that the Puritan attitude toward them was worthy of praise. The two societies did not really clash; it was merely that the one was "unified, visionary, disciplined, and dynamic" while the other was "self-satisfied, undisciplined, and static."[25] One knows, however, whose side he has chosen. The Puritans expanded, as was the European habit, into the sphere of the Indians. Since what the Indians did in a certain location cannot really be called occupying the land, at least not in the sense that the whites did, Puritan society gradually moved in and took over. It is not just a question of physical displacement though there was much of that; the Puritans did purchase land from the Indians. Rather the process was more an imperceptible cultural advance by the Puritans and recession by the Indians.

Thus in his conclusions Vaughan communicates a sense of the process of the Indian's cultural decline. But the bulk of his book contains no such impression. In overturning the critical view of the white man and in raising the estimation of the Puritan's intentions, he dwells on the theme of positive policy. The Indian and Puritan, finally, are treated as equals, dealing with one another over the vital issues of war, peace, trade, religion, and social conviviality. The Indian, having a sound notion of the meaning of land possession, sells it, most often willingly, to the Puritan. The law of civilization is accepted by the native people as an equitable means of arranging for a mutually satisfactory juridical condition. The Puritans introduce themselves into a complex extra-tribal political situation as one more power among equals.[26] In his recounting of the story, Vaughan does not really break into the cultural interplay of Indian-white relations. It is not merely because he willingly uses only Puritan sources (all the historical sources, after all, are the white man's) but that he fails to take the Indian on his own terms. Indian society, as he notes, is "divided, self-satisfied, undisciplined, and static": all anti-virtues in Protestant civilization's hierarchy of value. The great defect of the Puritan in dealing with the Indian (with any other people, for that matter) was his inability to see the external world through any other glass but his own, and that darkly. If on the whole the Puritan did his best for the Indian, as a good Christian it was only expected of him, but he did not concede the Indian a cultural separateness and integrity. Vaughan has disposed of the guilty white man scheme, but just as the Puritans had, he does not act on the recognition that the two societies really were different.

Culminating with the removal policy and the revision of the trade and intercourse acts of 1834, Prucha presents a compelling account of the policy of the young nation toward the natives. His sympathy for the Indian is manifest, but he offers a rounded and perceptive portrayal of the white man's struggle to deal with the confrontation of the two societies. Though his perspective is dictated by his emphasis on policy, he is sensibly aware of the clash of culture, especially of the decline of the Indian under the influence of civilization, and he is chary of distributing blame. Perhaps the major revision in the volume is contained in chapter nine: "Civilization and Removal." The very title hurls defiance at an interpretation long accepted by historians. Removal, after all, has been considered the *locus classicus* of Indian-white relations as a "suffering situation." It was the last outrage heaped by the merciless white man on the heads of the much abused eastern Indians. Prucha's motive in coupling removal with the effort to civilize the Indian is clearly to metamorphose the argument from the one-level "trail of tears" to the complicated interplay of the white man's interest and conscience on the one side and the painful acculturation of a primitive society on the other. He admits, of course, that there was a sufficiency of nefarious motives behind the decision to drive the Indians west of the Mississippi but maintains that not enough attention has been paid to the good motives of those who made government policy in the second and third decades of the nineteenth century. The crucial point is the decision of such men as Thomas L. McKenney, Lewis Cass, and William Clark that the civilizing program had failed, that the major effect of the white man on the Indian was deleterious rather than improving, and that the native could be saved only by removing him from harm's way. Beyond the Mississippi, out of reach of the corrosive elements in the white man's way of life, he could be preserved and possibly civilized before the next advance of American society rolled over him. Removal for many who approached the Indian from the highest philanthropy was "another program for the 'preservation and civilization' of the aborigines."[27]

Prucha's case is well taken; the oppressor-victim interpretation, after all, will not explain why men of generally laudable character favored removal. Placing it in the context of civilized philanthropy and Indian disintegration tells something of the way two disparate societies meet and come finally to terms with each other. But Prucha's intentions are limited. He is dealing with policy and the immediate motives leading to its formulation. Except for noting the dawning perception of the consequences of civilization on the Indian, he is not really concerned with the question of cultural interplay. And, indeed, a definition of policy without digging into the substratum of culture that rests beneath it will not yield an interpretation of Indian-white relations that brings together all the elements of cultural differentiation. Yet in showing that there was more to the white man's actions than viciousness, greed, and hypocrisy, he has opened a broad vista for historical imagination.

Horsman supplies the theme of American expansion as an introduction to his account of Indian-white relations in the early years of the nation. The Indian was overwhelmed by a new thriving people but not without a lingering sense of the wickedness of the proceeding. Americans were caught by the incompatibility of their interests (a growing population, the attraction of the fertile west, national feeling, and the need for strategic protection), and their conscience (the righteousness of the Revolution and the uniqueness of the American experiment) which in the face of Indian opposition could not produce a realistic policy.[28] The good will of the white man, then, as manifested in the civilizing program, appears as an inconsequential quirk, an aberration when the reality was removal. The pieces are all there but Horsman's division seems arbitrary. The thrust of the white man's culture, more likely, had an essential unity. The philanthropic determination to civilize the Indian was as much a part of an expanding America as greed for land and removal. The danger in assuming a contradiction between civilization and removal is that the first inevitably becomes a sham and the second merely positive evidence of the white man's callousness. Similarly, it tends to transpose the question out of the realm of cultural conflict. If the Indian was destroyed by the onrush of European culture then philanthropy must be seen as one instrument in the Indian's gradual demise. As Prucha so aptly puts it: "It was a question of civilization versus the savage state, and no one was ready to preach that savagism should be perpetuated."[29] Horsman's extension of the interpretation into an examination of the forces of American expansion together with Prucha's association of removal with the civilizing program constitute a significant move towards the understanding of Indian-white relations as a problem in cultural conflict. Both the source of the white man's overpowering influence on the fragile structure of native society and the subtle operations of civilization's best intentioned philanthropy are thrown open to scrutiny.

Implicit in the suffering-Indian, wicked white-man interpretation is the proposition that the American aborigine could have survived. The vague assumption is that things might have been different, that the white man should have been less pushy, that the Indian might have been better protected, that the treaties should have been kept, that, finally, the Indian could have endured as an Indian. As a moral injunction the idea takes on certain pristine clarity but it says little about the interplay of culture. Without drifting into the bog of historical inevitability, it must be said that any rearrangement of the forces of Indian-white relations in the early period does little to improve the native's chances. Perhaps a slowing of the white man's advance, some accomodation on median issues, even palliation of the native's suffering, a gentler demise, but whether the Indian was annihilated or transformed, he would no longer be an Indian. Short of abandoning the Mississippi Valley, says Horsman, there seems no reason to think that the problem could have been solved. The "stark realities," writes Leach, dictated that the native society had tó submit. Even Hagan, speaking of the Cherokèes, believes their case was hopeless.[30]

The consequences of Indian-white confrontation, the passing of a culture, are, however, too cosmic to be without a villain. The unruly frontiersman, fresh from years of Turnerian adulation, must now bear a major portion of the guilt for the Indian's destruction. As agent of American ex-

pansion, the wily and undisciplined pioneer, year after year, despite repeated governmental efforts to curb him, pushed the line of white settlement farther into the Indian country.[31] He was the practical surrogate of
the white man's brash and aggressive society as it met and proceeded to
accomplish the demolition of the native culture. The frontiersman could
have been curbed only if the very nature of America could have been
qualified; to stem the advance would have meant, conversely, to impair the
very vitality of the white man's society. Besides attributing to the societal
phenomenon an unrealistic level of rational discipline, the contention that
order could have been imposed on the frontier assumes the existence of a
bureaucratic and military establishment of far greater size and proficiency
than circumstances would permit. The government could not have built a
Chinese Wall, as Washington put it, to keep the whites and Indians apart.[32]
Even the supposed guilt of the frontiersman will not assuage the historiographical decisiveness of the situation; within the terms available for explanation, the Indian's transformation was inevitable.

As mere sentiment the hope for the Indian's survival removes the encounter between white and native from the dynamics of historical process,
but it reveals also an unspoken rationalism which, when applied to history,
supposes that society is capable of self-articulation far beyond realistic
expectation. A society manifesting such detachment, revealing fully its own
inner workings, and thereby judging the effect it might have on another
culture, would be a rare phenomenon. Doubtless, in every age there are
some who are able to see a fair portion of the intricate patterns of their
society and they are sometimes successful in convincing a fraction of their
fellows of the accuracy of the vision. But the limitations of rational articulation and control are compounded when the society is as lacking in co-
herence as colonial and early national America. It was not merely a
question of a shortage of governmental or philanthropic good will but of a
booming white America bursting out of the constrictions of its social
bounds, causing the decline of a native society virtually devoid of the
resources for serious competition. The white man is guilty only if one
supposes his society capable of a total transmogrification into an entity of
mature social discipline, able to establish settled and well-defined relations
with its fragile neighbor. There was as much possibility for such a cosmic
alteration as there was that the Indian would suddenly develop the cultural
muscle to withstand the effects of the white man's aggressiveness. Of
course, neither the one nor the other was conceivable. The pattern of
interrelation between white and Indian, at least in its limits, was set by the
integral nature of the two cultures and its history can be written only by
accepting its tragic implications for the Indian and proceeding to the business of analyzing the cultural clash between the two societies. One need
not sanction the self-righteousness of the white man's society or see any
merit in the disheveled individualism that underlay its rush for conquest to
understand the Indian's desperate situation. The process of his decline derives no meaning from the assertion of the white man's guilt; without the
context of cultural disintegration the accusation is gratuitous. Within that
context, however, it takes on a fitting pathos.

To be sure, the concept of integral culture is at base ethnological, but it is also historical. In the deepest sense there is no history that is not cultural history. Any other conception separates man from his existential dimension. Though a wide knowledge of ethnology would be of incalculable value in the study of Indian-white confrontation, what is more important is the sensitive perception that the human condition, civilized or savage, is always a pattern of intricately connected elements, that the pattern has its limits, and that the limits set off one society from another. For historical research the concept is self-validating. The investigation of governmental policy toward the Indian will develop against the content of American society and its political organization. An account of the native's adjustment to the influx of civilized artifacts will unfold according to the aborigine's ability to .absorb or repel them, or conversely, it will describe the eroding effects of the importation of such foreign elements. In the interweaving of the two, in the meeting of the two disparate social orders, the concept of integral culture is of supreme importance. A model of what may be done is Eric R. Wolfe's *Sons of the Shaking Earth,*[33] an account of the clash of Indian and Spanish culture in middle America. Though based on wide ethnological study, the volume is a perceptive combination of cultural analysis and historical evolution. From the very origins of the land and humankind in the New World, he carries the story to the ascendant warrior kingdoms at the arrival of the Spaniards in the sixteenth century. The native culture, tense and precarious in its grip on life, proved no match for the Europeans who came fully prepared to impose their own ways on the Indian population. Paradoxically, the Spaniards also came in search of a paradise that would fill an elusive deficiency in their own psychic makeup. In bringing together all the strands of competitive interplay between native and European culture and superimposing the anti-culture of the Spaniards' paradisaic ideology, Wolfe goes to the heart of the dynamics of human development.[34]

Above all the Indian must be perceived as an Indian. Justice can be done him historically only if his special character is admitted. If he turns out to be only a vague reflection of the white man's wish for what he sees as best in himself—an idealized white man—or even if it is assumed that his behavior as a historical character can be judged by the objective definitions applied to civilized man, then the Indian will never be portrayed with the integrity he deserves. If his death is to be tragic, it must be the death of his real self, not of a white impostor.

NOTES

1 Helen Hunt Jackson, *A Century of Dishonor: A Sketch of the United States Government's Dealings with Some of the Indian Tribes,* 2d ed. (Boston, 1886), 29.
2 *Ibid.,* 41.
3 *Ibid.,* 33-34, 40, 339, 405-406.
4 Annie H. Abel, "The History of Events Resulting in Indian Consolidation West of the Mississippi River," American Historical Association,

Annual Report for the Year 1906 (Washington, 1908), I, 233–450.

5 Grant Foreman, *Indian Removal: The Emigration of the Five Civilized Tribes of Indians,* new ed. (Norman [orig. pub., Norman, 1932], 1953); and Grant Foreman, *The Last Trek of the Indians* (Chicago, 1946).

6 Foreman, *Indian Removal,* 386.

7 My own understanding of the concept is taken in part from: A.L. Kroeber and Clyde Kluckhohn, *Culture: A Critical Review of Concepts and Definitions,* Vintage ed. (New York, 1963); Robert K. Merton, *Social Theory and Social Structure,* 3d ed., (New York, 1968), Chap. III; A.R. Radcliffe-Brown, *Structure and Function in Primitive Society: Essays and Addresses* (New York, 1952), Introduction, Chap. IX; T.S. Eliot, *Notes towards the Definition of Culture* (New York, 1949); Robert A. Nisbet, *The Sociological Tradition* (New York, 1966).

8 Robert Berkhofer, Jr., *Salvation and the Savage: An Analysis of Protestant Missions and American Indian Response, 1787-1862* (Lexington, Ky., 1965), ix.

9 William N. Fenton, *American Indian and White Relations to 1830: Needs & Opportunities for Study* (Chapel Hill, 1957), 17; Douglas Edward Leach, *The Northern Colonial Frontier, 1607-1763* (New York, 1966), 7; Louis De Vorsey, Jr., *The Indian Boundary in the Southern Colonies, 1763-1775* (Chapel Hill, 1966), 43.

10 Wilbur R. Jacobs, *Wilderness Politics and Indian Gifts: The Northern Colonial Frontier, 1748-1763* (Lincoln, Neb., 1966); originally published as *Diplomacy and Indian Gifts: Anglo-French Rivalry along the Ohio and Northwest Frontiers, 1748-1763* (Stanford, 1950); Anthony F.C. Wallace, *King of the Delawares: Teedyuscung, 1700-1763* (Philadelphia, 1949).

11 Reginald Horsman, *Expansion and American Indian Policy, 1783-1812* (East Lansing, Mich., 1967), 38, 60; Reginald Horsman, *Matthew Elliot, British Indian Agent* (Detroit, 1964), 39; De Vorsey, *The Indian Boundary,* 44; Alden T. Vaughan, *New England Frontier: Puritans and Indians, 1620-1675* (Boston, 1965), 298, 304; Berkhofer, *Salvation and the Savage,* 69, 107, 122.

12 *Ibid.,* 57, III. Similarly, Roy Harvey Pearce, *The Savages of America: A Study of the Indian and the Idea of Civilization,* rev. ed. (Baltimore, 1965), in an often brilliant exposition of the content of the white man's mind on the subject of the Indian, is not able to stretch his account to cover the interplay of the two societies. Since his thesis is that the native was perceived mainly with reference to the white man's conception of himself, he does not step over and treat the Indian on his own ground. The validity of the thesis is not in question but the assumption that ideology can be so pristine and self-contained is another problem. The direct effect of the white man's conception, as Pearce admits, is the manipulation of the Indian and, therefore, even civilization's intellectual inversions concerning native society may be seen as part of the interplay of culture.

13 Leach, *The Northern Colonial Frontier,* 7; Wilbur R. Jacobs, ed., *The Paxton Riots and the Frontier Theory* (Chicago, 1967), I; Wilcomb E. Washburn, ed., *The Indian and the White Man* (Garden City, N.Y., 1964), xi.

14 Wilcomb E. Washburn, "The Moral and Legal Justifications for Dispossessing the Indians," in James Morton Smith, ed., *Seventeenth Century*

America: Essays in Colonial History (Chapel Hill, 1959), 22; Washburn, ed., *The Indian and the White Man,* xii, 415. Nancy Oestreich Lurie, "Indian Cultural Adjustment to European Civilization," in Smith, ed., *Seventeenth Century America,* 36-38, offers an explanation of the Indians' hospitable greeting of the Virginia settlers without recourse to any version of the noble savage theme.

15 Henri Baudet, *Paradise on Earth: Some Thoughts on European Images of Non-European Man,* Elizabeth Wentholt, transl. (New Haven, 1965).

16 Wilcomb E. Washburn, "A Moral History of Indian-White Relations: Needs and Opportunities for Study," *Ethnohistory,* IV (1957), 55. An admirably perceptive treatment of relations between the Indian and one particular group of whites is in Lewis O. Saum, *The Fur Trader and the Indian* (Seattle, 1965). He contends that fur traders, frequently skirting the formulations of noble savagism (p. 80), managed to come up with a generally realistic conception of the native. "The more the trader saw of the Indian the greater were his misgivings." (p. 134).

17 Mary Elizabeth Young, *Redskins, Ruffleshirts, and Rednecks: Indian Land Allotments in Alabama and Mississippi, 1830-1860* (Norman, 1961), 24-25.

18 Francis Paul Prucha, *American Indian Policy in the Formative Years: The Indian Trade and Intercourse Acts, 1790-1834* (Cambridge, Mass., 1962), 139; Horsman, *Expansion and American Indian Policy,* Introduction, makes the same point on the relation of land to Indian-white conflict.

19 Jacobs, *Wilderness Politics and Indian Gifts,* 13-14, 185, n. 143; Allen W. Trelease, *Indian Affairs in Colonial New York: The Seventeenth Century* (Ithaca, 1960), 22; Fenton, *American Indian and White Relations to 1830,* 18, 27; Alvin M. Josephy, Jr., *The Indian Heritage of America* (New York, 1968), 34-35; see also Alvin M. Josephy, Jr., *The Patriot Chiefs: A Chronicle of American Indian Leadership* (New York, 1961), 28-29.

20 Francis Parkman, *The Conspiracy of Pontiac . . .* (Boston [orig. pub., Boston, 1851], 1898), I, 190-198; for an alternate explanation, see Howard H. Peckham, *Pontiac and the Indian Uprising,* (Chicago, 1961), 107-108, n. 12; George T. Hunt, *The Wars of the Iroquois: A Study of Intertribal Trade Relations* (Madison [orig. pub. Madison, 1940], 1960), 32-37; see the review by Fenton in *American Anthropologist, New Ser., XLII (1940),* 662-664.

21 Trelease, *Indian Affairs in Colonial New York,* 53.

22 *Ibid.,* 118-120, 141-142, 260, 266-267, 299.

23 William T. Hagan, *American Indians* (Chicago, 1961), takes every opportunity to see the worst in the white man's action. "Traders employed any tactics to make an immediate profit" (p. 16); intermarriage was intended merely to further the economic and political objectives of the whites (p. 12); a "double standard of morality" was used by whites in dealing with Indians (p. 20); Indian students at William and Mary were "supported by charity and instructed in segregated classes." (pp. 10-11) Worse yet, during the Revolution "two Indians killed were partially flayed to provide boot tops for the troops as addicted to souvenir-hunting as their twentieth century counterparts." (p. 38) And Tecumseh, so the report goes, "was flayed and his skin made into souvenir razor strops by the representatives of the higher way of life." (p. 63) The Indian is merely victim and the white man only oppressor. R.S. Cotterill, *The Southern Indians: The Story of the Civilized Tribes*

before Removal (Norman, 1954), 124, 139-140, 153, 174, 224; a particularly cavalier and simplistic description of Jeffersonian policy may
be found in Marshall Smelser, *The Democratic Republic, 1801-1815*
(New York, 1968), 132-134.

24 Vaughan, *New England Frontier,* vii-viii, 78, 136-137, 183-184,
312-313. Douglas Edward Leach, *Flintlock and Tomahawk: New
England in King Philip's War* (New York [orig. pub., New York, 1958]
1966), 14-22, blames the conflict on the Puritan pressure for land.

25 Vaughan, *New England Frontier,* 323.

26 *Ibid.,* 104-109, 155, 183, 210.

27 Prucha, *American Indian Policy* 224-227. But aside from Prucha, it is
virtually impossible to find a treatment of removal that sees it as an
extension of the civilizing effort. Most historians conceive of the two
policies as contradictory and evidence of the hypocrisy or stupidity of
the whites. See Horsman, *Expansion and American Indian Policy,*
109-111, 116-117, 140; Hagan, *American Indians,* 44, 54; Young, *Redskins, Ruffleshirts, and Rednecks,* 5-6, 9; R. Pierce Beaver, *Church,
State, and the American Indians: Two and a Half Centuries of Partnership in Missions between Churches and Government* (St. Louis, 1966),
90, 99-100, 117; Cotterill, *The Southern Indians* 225-226. A recent
Book-of-the-Month-Club Selection, Peter Farb, *Man's Rise to Civilization as Shown by the Indians of North America from Primeval Times
to the Coming of the Industrial State* (New York, 1968), 250, calls
the removal policy "genocide" and compares it to the Nuremburg
Laws.

28 Horsman, *Expansion and American Indian Policy,* Introduction,
172-173.

29 Prucha, *American Indian Policy,* 239; Pearce, *Savages of America,* ix,
3-4, 41-42, 73-74, also emphasizes the division between savagism and
civilization. He contends that after the middle of the eighteenth century the native was looked on mainly as an obstacle to civilization's
advance. And hence civilizing the Indian was one way of mastering
him, of overcoming an obstacle to progress. Leslie A. Fiedler, *The
Return of the Vanishing American* (New York, 1968), 76, offers a
typically racy but apt version of the essential unity of the white man's
treatment of the Indian:
> "Not quite destroying, really, for the act of genocide with which
> our nation began was inconclusive, imperfect, inhibited by a bad
> conscience, undercut by uncertainty of purpose. 'There's no good
> injun but a dead injun,' the really principled killers, which is to
> say, the soldiers, cried; but, 'The next best thing is a Christian
> Indian,' the softhearted castrators, which is to say, the Priests,
> reminded them; and, 'We can get along with *any* Indian, so long as
> he's on the Reservation,' the practical-minded ghetto-izers, which
> is to say, the bureaucrats and social workers, advised them both—
> having final say."

30 Horsman, *Expansion and American Indian Policy,* 173; Leach, *The
Northern Colonial Frontier,* 190; Hagan, *American Indians,* 76.

31 Prucha, *American Indian Policy,* 3, 143-144, 147, 162.

32 George Washington to Timothy Pickering, July 1, 1796, John C. Fitz-
patrick, ed., *The Writings of George Washington . . .* (Washington,
1931-1944), XXXV, 112.

33 *Eric R. Wolfe, Sons of the Shaking Earth* (Chicago, 1959).

34 *Ibid.,* Chap. VIII, IX, X.

HELEN W. JOHNSON: RURAL
INDIAN AMERICANS
IN POVERTY

INTRODUCTION

Most Indian Americans are rural residents, and they are poor. They are not attuned to the modern technological economy of America, nor are they certain in what direction their future lies—within the larger society or separate from it; on the reservation or away from it; as Indians or as Indian Americans. Somewhere between these polar points, a way will doubtless be found.

The story of why rural Indians today are in poverty has roots in their history, in the development of the industrialized American economy, and in the difficult process of assimilation of a minority culture by the dominant one in every society. There is considerable documentation of the history of this minority group vis-a-vis the U.S. Government in the long contention over land, tribal rights, relocation of living space, and redirection of occupational activity. All of these past events have a bearing on the size and vigor of the Indian population, their attitudes and present outlook, and the eventual resolution of their problems. This history will not be recounted here since its major impacts are already well-known to the American public.[1]

The critical element in the history of the U.S. economy which helps to explain the current distress of rural Indians is the development of an urbanized, technical society—a society for which rural Indians are not prepared. Nothing in their history or experience has contributed to making possible successful adjustment in a nonfarm economy—educationally, occupationally, or socially. Rural in orientation and largely separated from the rapid urbanization of the last few decades, Indians have been out of touch with industrial and technological developments now predominant in our national economy.

The cultural hiatus between Indian Americans and the society around them is equally severe in its implications for rural Indian disadvantage. Acculturation of a minority population is always a long and tortuous process. A minority group confronted with the loss of its own cultural heritage as the price of assimilation finds itself resisting new ways as long as possible. At some point in time, a choice is made—to give up the old familiar values and patterns of living, to adopt the ways of the alien culture, or to

Source: Reprinted from Helen W. Johnson, *Rural Indian Americans in Poverty,* Economic Research Service, U.S. Department of Agriculture, Agricultural Economic Report no. 167 (Washington, D.C., 1969).

effect some combination of the old and the new. Meanwhile, there is a drawing apart of the two cultures on both sides. The dominant society, not really understanding the dilemma, often manifests impatience and prejudice, or at the very least, lack of empathy. Until the gap between the two cultures is closed, the minority group suffers not only economic and social discrimination, but malaise of spirit.

Indian experience with American culture has been no exception. Rural Indians today are mostly poor, ill at ease, and largely unacculturated. They are in limbo, not at home in either world. The way to achieve an intermediate position between the familiar culture and the dominant but alien one is not at all clear. Some first steps, however, are quite apparent and apply to people in poverty wherever they are and of whatever cultural origin. Alleviation of poverty status, improvement of educational and employment opportunity, and wider participation in the society at large constitute high-priority needs for all people in distress. Rural Indians are among the most deprived groups in America today. The pages that follow will give some measure of the depth of their disadvantage.

RURAL INDIANS IN THE 1960s

Demographic Characteristics

In 1960, there were 552,000 Indians in the United States, including 28,000 Aleuts and Eskimos in Alaska.[2] Indians constituted the smallest of three minority ethnic groups, or less than 1 percent of the U.S. total population. The Spanish-surname population, by contrast, was about 2 percent of the total and Negroes were 11 percent. Indians were, however, the most rural of these groups—about 70 percent of them were classified in the 1960 Census as living in rural areas, compared with 21 percent of the Spanish-surname people and 27 percent of the Negro population. More than half the rural Indians (55 percent) were rural nonfarm residents. . . .

Family Income

More than three out of five rural Indian families had less than $3,000 income in 1959, nearly twice the proportion in the total rural population. Family income below the $1,000 level was three times as prevalent among the rural Indian population as among the total rural population. At the other end of the scale, less than 3 percent of rural Indian families had incomes of $10,000 or more, whereas nearly 12 percent of families in the total rural population reported that level of income (Table 1). The high proportion of rural Indians in a low-income position points to especially serious deprivation when the large average size of families is considered.

. . . The income of rural Indian families is not only low, but is derived largely from sources unproductive for the Indian families and for the national economy. Many families are receiving public assistance from Federal or State funds. Many reservation Indians also obtain some income from leases of land, but these rents are generally low because much of the land is of poor quality. Moreover, the share of income each family receives has

TABLE 1

Distribution of Family Income for Rural Indians and
Total Rural Population, United States, 1960

Income	Rural Indians		U.S. Rural Population	
	Families	Percentage of total	Families	Percentage of total
	NUMBER	PERCENT	NUMBER	PERCENT
Under $1,000	18,025	28.0	1,310,295	9.9
$1,000 to $2,999	22,085	34.3	3,112,294	23.6
$3,000 to $4,999	12,391	19.2	3,154,303	23.9
$5,000 to $6,999	6,557	10.2	2,670,812	20.3
$7,000 to $9,999	3,659	5.7	1,422,191	10.8
$10,000 to $14,999	1,290	2.0	1,198,998	9.1
$15,000 and over	354	0.6	319,458	2.4
Total families	64,361	100.0	13,188,351	100.0

Source: 1960 Census of Population, PC (2) 1C and PC (1) 1C.

greatly diminished over the years due to the fragmentation of property rights through generations of inheritance in large families. Income derived from employment available on and near reservations is relatively limited because of prevailing low wage rates and the seasonal or sporadic nature of the jobs. Income from all sources, therefore, still leaves most rural Indian families in poverty....

Health

Since 1955, on about 250 reservations in 23 Federal Indian Reservation States and in several hundred villages in Alaska, the Indian population has received health protection from the Public Health Service (PHS) of the U.S. Department of Health, Education, and Welfare. The service population, estimated to be 381,000 in 1965, comprises potential beneficiaries who depend in varying degrees on PHS for essential health services. These beneficiaries include some small groups for whom sanitation facilities projects are authorized, but who do not receive medical services from the Indian Health Service (in PHS). The stated goal of the Public Health Service is to "elevate the health status of Indians and Alaskan Natives (Indians, Aleuts, and Eskimos) to the highest possible level."[3]

Some aspects of Indian health have shown marked improvement in the past 10 to 15 years, but stubborn problems remain. Provision of adequate health services and facilities is complicated by the heterogeneity of the Indian tribal population and its dispersion over a very large geographic area, frequently in out-of-the-way places. Reaching these people with health assistance is difficult because of language barriers, the Indians' frequent lack of knowledge that help is available, and their high degree of social as well as physical isolation. Some of the most acute problems in safeguarding and improving the health of Indians are rooted in the environmental hazards under which they live. These include substandard, overcrowded housing; lack of adequate sanitation facilities and safe water supplies; insufficient understanding of proper hygienic practices; and often a pervading atmosphere of despair and frustration, which introduces a sense of hopelessness about improved health and well-being. In addition, there are diet deficiencies which contribute to physical and spiritual debilitation.

In an attempt to remedy the most serious problems, the Public Health Service has instituted programs to increase the number and kind of health services, to make them more accessible, and to raise their acceptance level. To supplement their own hospitals and health centers and to stretch resources, the Public Health Service has contractual arrangements with hundreds of private health practitioners, community general hospitals, State and local tuberculosis and mental hospitals, and a few nursing homes. In the PHS program to improve sanitation, Indians themselves have participated in planning and constructing facilities and have contributed more than one-third of the total program effort since 1959 by donating labor, materials, and money. There are also training programs being carried on for Indian personnel in all phases of the health field.

Considerable progress has been made in reducing mortality from communicable diseases and in lowering infant mortality rates. The most outstanding success has been in decreasing the number of deaths from tuberculosis, a disease very widespread in the Indian population. The rate had declined to 21 deaths per 100,000 population by 1964, a drop of 61 percent in 10 years (Table 2). Infant mortality rates decreased 45 percent during 1954-64. However, compared with the general population the progress has been relative. These 1964 rates, for example, are roughly comparable to those in the total population some 15 or 20 years ago and are thus still much higher than rates among non-Indians.

"Unfinished business" in the Indian health field is enormous. Life expectancy among Indians is considerably below that of the general population; infant and maternal mortality rates remain high; and environmental changes needed to bring about substantial improvement in health are far from accomplished. Unmet needs of varying dimensions cover the entire health spectrum, including not only facilities and services, but educational and environmental improvement. . . .

Occupational Distributions

There are striking similarities between the occupational patterns of rural Indians and rural people as a whole. Both populations are overwhelmingly in nonfarm occupations—63 percent for employed rural Indians and 76 percent for the total employed rural population, according to the 1960 Census of Population (Table 3). About 38 percent of both groups were in blue-collar occupations, and a slightly larger percentage of rural Indians than total rural population were in service work (13 and 9 percent, respectively). In white-collar occupations, however, the proportion of all rural

TABLE 2

Selected Vital Statistics, Indians and Total
U.S. Population, 1964 and 1954

Vital Statistics	Indians	United States (All Races)
	NUMBER	*NUMBER*
Infant deaths per 1,000 live births:		
1964	35.9	24.8
1954	65.0	26.6
Maternal deaths per 10,000 live births:		
1964	6.3	3.4
1954	18.4	5.2
Deaths per 100,000 population, by specified cause—		
Tuberculosis:		
1964	21.3	4.3
1954	54.0	10.2
Gastritis, enteritis, etc.		
1964	19.3	4.3
1954	56.0	4.9
Morbidity per 100,000 population by specified cause[1]—		
Tuberculosis:		
1964	184.1	26.6
1954	571.0	62.4
Dysentery:		
1964	417.5	8.5
1954	428.1	8.4
23 Federal Indian Reservation States—birth rate (registered live births per 1,000 population):		
1964	43.1	21.0
	YEARS	*YEARS*
Average age of death, 1964	43.8	63.6
Life expectancy at birth, 1964	63.5	70.2
Median age of population	17.3	29.5
	PERCENT	*PERCENT*
Percentage of population under 20 years	55.2	38.5

[1]Cases reported per 100,000 population.

Source: Indian Health Highlights, 1966 edition, U.S. Dept. Health, Educ., and Welfare, Pub. Health Serv., pp. xvi, 7.

people was twice as high as for rural Indians—28 percent, compared with 12 percent. This undoubtedly reflects a relative lack of nonfarm job opportunities and a lower level of educational attainment among rural Indians. The predominance of rural Indian workers in lower paid occupations also helps to account for their generally low level of income. . . .

TABLE 3

Occupational Distribution of Employed Rural Indians and Total Rural Population, United States, 1960

Occupational Category	Rural Indians		Total Rural Population	
	Total	Percentage of total	Total	Percentage of total
	NUMBER	PERCENT	NUMBER	PERCENT
White-collar workers	7,892	12.0	4,752,562	27.6
Blue-collar workers	25,241	38.3	6,707,235	38.9
Service workers	8,382	12.7	1,566,678	9.1
Farmworkers	17,506	26.5	3,604,185	20.9
Occupation not reported	6,939	10.5	618,197	3.6
Total employed	65,960	100.0	17,248,857	100.0

Source: U.S. Census of Population, 1960, PC(2) 1C and PC(1) 1c.

Note: White-collar workers: Professional and technical: managers, officials, and proprietors; clerical; and sales. Blue-collar workers: Craftsmen and foremen; operatives, and nonfarm laborers. Service workers: Private household and service. Farmworkers: Farmers and farm managers, farm laborers, and foremen.

CONCLUSIONS

Rural Indian Americans comprise a relatively small but exceptionally needy minority group. They are not only poor in material goods, they are widely impoverished in spirit. This is due to a prolonged period of dependence on society at large, as well as profound disturbance about the future. More than a century of social isolation in separate enclaves has taken its toll on initiative, creativity, and independent thought and action. The way ahead, especially for the present generation of Indian youth, abounds in difficult questions, with few positive answers to the problem of accommodating Indian culture to the surrounding society.

Although the present size of the Indian population is not known, estimates range from 600,000 to 800,000. Even accepting the latter figure as approximately correct, the Indian population in need represents a relatively small proportion of the total rural poor. Considering the depth of distress of rural Indians, the task of ameliorating the poverty of the great majority of them would not be an insuperable undertaking for an affluent country like the United States. Material poverty can be lifted primarily with money and jobs. It has been estimated that "the basic economic problem of the Indian communities could be solved by the provision of 40,000 jobs. This would seem a small demand for a nation where civilian employment has increased an average of 723,000 each year from 1955 to 1965, and where the last five years the average increase has been almost 1.5 million per year."[4]

Poverty of spirit can perhaps be lifted by releasing the energies and talents of Indians in local decision-making and by developing creative public and private relationships to work out feasible solutions to difficult problems. Some new kind of Indian-Government partnership to guide the future course of Indian communities, whether on or off of reservation lands, appears to be desirable.

It is important not only to recognize the need for Indian leadership and full participation in policy making, but also to identify specific Indian wants and desires. To remedy the unusual situation of prolonged dependent status in American society requires extraordinary effort and understanding on the part of the non-Indian population. As a recent task force report of the Chamber of Commerce of the United States said, "Indian spokesmen have stated Indian wants. They want to retain their culture. They want to be consulted and to have a real voice in decisions relating to themselves. They want to retain their reservation lands. And Indians want to enter modern economic life and enjoy its advantages. The Task Force supports these legitimate aspirations of Indian Americans. The Task Force further believes the public has a special and continuing national responsibility to see that the opportunities and rewards of society are fully extended to these citizens."[5]

Genuine acculturation of the Indian people can be promoted only when they play their full part in the life of the larger society. When rural Indian Americans come to feel they have not only a real stake in the future of America, but a responsibility, and the ability, to contribute to it, they will then be able to lift themselves out of poverty of spirit. Meanwhile, the rest of society can help by finding a way to remove the conditions that produce material poverty. Achieving these twin objectives will then lend credence to the phrase Indian *Americans.*

NOTES

1   Brandon, William, *The American Heritage Book of Indians* (Dell Publ. Co., New York, 1964). See also, "Indian, North America," *Encyclopaedia Britannica,* Vol. 12, 1957 edition and references cited therein, p. 209.

2   U.S. Census of Population, 1960, PC (2) IC, Nonwhite Population by Race, Subject Reports.

3   Statement supplied by Bureau of Indian Affairs, pp. xi-xii and p. 1.

4   Nader, Ralph, "Lo, the Poor Indian," *The New Republic,* Mar. 30, 1968, quoting Professor Gary Orfield of the Univ. of Virginia, p. 15.

5   Chamber of Commerce of the United States, Rural Poverty and Regional Progress in an Urban Society, Task Force on Economic Growth and Opportunity, Fourth Report, 1969.

ROSALIE H. WAX, ROBERT K. THOMAS: AMERICAN INDIANS AND WHITE PEOPLE

As the Hughes have pointed out, when peoples come into troublesome contact with each other, popular and scholarly attention is usually focused on only one of them. Thus the relationship between Indians and the persons of European extraction, known as whites, is commonly termed the "Indian problem." While these authors agree that such emphasis is natural,. they call attention to the fact that the unit of racial or ethnic relations is no single people, but the situation—the frontier of contact of the two or more peoples inhabiting a community or region.[1]

This paper is an attempt to describe one of the more intimate aspects of just such a frontier situation, namely, what happens when American Indians and white people meet in the course of their day-to-day activities and try to communicate with each other. It does not attempt to define the major areas of difference between Indian and white American culture or personality, nor does it discuss the major reasons for conflict and hostility between the two, but rather tries to explain how and why they find talking to each other difficult. It is, therefore, directed as much to the Indian as to the white reader.

We are aware that there are significant differences in behavior and personality among the various kinds of Indians and, likewise, among the various kinds of white men, and that interesting exceptions may possibly be found to all of our generalizations. Nevertheless, our observations have convinced us that most white men who live in the United States share ideas and practices about proper behavior that are very different from those shared by most Indians.

Social discourse is one of the areas where Indians and whites most easily misunderstand each other. Placed in an informal social gathering, such as a small party where he knows only the host, the Indian will usually sit or stand quietly, saying nothing and seeming to do nothing. He may do this so naturally that he disappears into the background, merging with the wall fixtures. If addressed directly, he will not look at the speaker; there may be considerable delay before a reply, and this may be pitched so softly as to be below the hearing threshold of the white interlocutor; he may even look deliberately away and give no response at all.

In this same situation, the white man will often become undiscourageably loquacious. A silent neighbor will be peppered with small shop talk in the hope that one of his rounds will trigger an exchange and a conversational engagement. If the neighbor happens to be an Indian, his

Source: Reprinted by permission from *Phylon* 22 (Winter 1961), 305-317.

protracted silence will spur the white to ever more extreme exertions; and the more frantic the one becomes the less the response he is likely to elicit from the other.

Ironically, both parties are trying hard to establish communication and good feeling. But, like Aesop's would-be friends, the crane and the fox, each employs devices that puzzle, alienate, and sometimes anger the other.

From childhood, white people and Indians are brought up to react to strange and dangerous situations in quite different ways. The white man who finds himself in an unstructured, anxiety-provoking situation is trained to react with a great deal of activity. He will begin action after action until he either structures the situation, or escapes from it, or simply collapses. But the Indian, put in the same situation, is brought up to remain motionless and watch. Outwardly he appears to freeze. Inwardly, he is using all of his senses to discover what is expected of him—what activities are proper, seemly, and safe. One might put it this way: in an unfamiliar situation a white man is taught to react by aggressive experimentation—he keeps moving until he finds a satisfactory pattern. His motto is "Try and try again." But the Indian puts his faith in observation. He waits and watches until the other actors show him the correct pattern.

Once he has picked up the cues and feels relatively certain that he can accomplish what is expected, the Indian may respond with a sudden energy and enthusiasm that can bewilder his white partners. For example, at a party for a group of Indian college students by the white members of a faculty, the Indian students sat and said virtually nothing. The faculty members did their best to draw out their expressionless and noncommittal guests. Even the stock questions of school and educational plans brought little response. At length in desperation, the faculty members talked to each other.

After refreshments were served the party broke into small clusters of guests, and in each cluster an Indian student did most of the talking. He delivered a modest, but well organized address describing his educational plans. From questions put to him, each had concluded that his role at the party was to paint his academic future. When opportunity offered, he gave the faculty members exactly what he thought they wanted.

The active experimenting disposition of many white men and the motionless alertness of Indians may be related to different cultural attitudes toward what white people call success or failure. Indian friends tell us that they do not praise or reward their children for doing what is proper or right; they are expected to behave well, for this is "natural" or "normal". Thus a "good" Indian child reflects no special credit on himself or on his parents. He is simply behaving as a child of his people should behave.[2] On the other hand, the "bad" or ill-intentioned child is censured and the child who makes mistakes is shamed, which, in an Indian community, is a grave punishment. As one sophisticated Indian remarked: "As a result of the way they are raised, very few Indians will try to do something at which they're not good [adept]. It takes a lot of courage."

As an example, he cited a phenomenon, common in his tribe, of men gathering to help a relative build a house.

You watch a housebuilding among my people. You see some men struggling with the work of erecting the structure, and, over there, sitting on the grass, may be a man, just watching, never lending a hand, even with the heaviest work. They get the structure up, and all of a sudden there's that man on the roof, working away, laying shingle—because what he knows how to do is lay shingle. All these men that were there are kin come to help with the housebuilding, but each person only offers his assistance in what he knows he can do.

He also reminded us of how an Indian girl who had been making tortillas at a picnic immediately stopped when two highly skilled girls began to help her. She excused herself and disappeared. But a white girl who knew nothing of Indian cookery pitched in and was quite unembarrassed by her lack of skill.

Many other examples of the Indian's reluctance to exhibit clumsiness or ineptitude before others appear in the literature. For example, Nash relates how a Maya girl learns to operate weaving or spinning machines in a factory by silently observing the operator. Only when she feels competent will the observer take over and run the machine. "She will not try her hand until she feels competent, for to fumble and make mistakes is a cause for *verguenza*—public shame. She does not ask questions because that would annoy the person teaching her, and they might also think she is stupid."[3]

Again, Macgregor mentions that an Indian school track team was reluctant to run because they knew they could not win, and a basketball team did not want their parents and neighbors to come to an interschool game for fear they would laugh at their mistakes and failure to win.[4]

Perhaps it will be reassuring to the Indian to realize that the reckless torrents of words poured out by white people are usually intended as friendly or, at least, social gestures. The more ill at ease a white man becomes, the more he is likely to talk. He is not nearly so afraid of making mistakes as is the Indian and it is almost impossible (by Indian standards) to embarrass or "shame" him. By the same token, he will rarely hold an Indian's mistakes against him. Conversely, the white person who has had little experience in talking with Indians should find it heartening to know that the silence and downcast eyes with which his first conversational gambits may be received spring from shyness and, often, from courtesy. He is not being snubbed or ignored; on the contrary, his words and actions are being observed with minute care. Once the Indian has discovered what his response ought to be, he will make it. This may take a little time, but the person who is not willing to spend a little time ought not to try to talk to Indians.

The over-sensitive white man may take comfort in the fact that the Indian who wishes to insult him will generally make his intentions quite clear. The Indian who looks away when you address him is being considerate—to stare into your face might embarrass you. But the Indian who treats you as if you were invisible is putting you beneath the notice of a highly observant man.

In every human relationship there is some element of influence, inter-ference, or downright compulsion. The white man has been and is torn between two ideals: on the one hand, he believes in freedom, in minding his own business, and in the right of people to make up their minds for themselves; but, on the other hand, he believes that he should be his brother's keeper and not abstain from advice, or even action, when his brother is speeding down the road toward perdition, death, or social isola-tion due to halitosis. The Indian society is unequivocal: interference of any form is forbidden, regardless of the folly, irresponsibility, or ignorance of your brother.

Consequently, when the white man is motivated as his brother's keeper, which is most of the time when he is dealing with Indians, he rarely says or does anything that does not sound rude or even hostile to the latter. The white, imbued with a sense of righteousness in "helping the downtrodden and backward," does not realize the nature of his conduct, and the Indian cannot tell him, for that, in itself, would be "interference" with the white's freedom to act as he sees fit.

In a general sense, coercion has been and is a fundamental element in the social orders of the Western world. Social theorists have characterized the state as that national institution that effectively claims the legitimate monopoly of violence. Lesser institutions utilize a variety of corporeal and spiritual sanctions to effect cooperative action, and the economy prides itself on utilizing the lash of need and the lure of wealth. These character-istics of Western social structure have stimulated the more idealistic to the proposal of new communities in which the elimination of brute compulsion would ensure the release of the creative energies of man; but so deeply entrenched is this system of hierarchial and enforced organization that these are ridiculed as "utopian." In contrast, many of the Indian societies were organized on principles that relied to a great extent on voluntary cooperation and lacked the military or other coercive instrumentalities of the European.

Recent years have seen a marked shift in the general American social patterns. The use of physical violence has been curtailed and the emphasis has shifted toward verbal manipulation; this has been evident is such di-verse areas as the armed services, business corporations, educational insti-tutions, and the family. Educational movies shown to children at school impress them with the fact that the admirable leader is the boy or girl who can "get other children to do what he (the leader) wants them to do by convincing them that they really want to do what he (the leader) wants them to do." Children are taught by parents and playmates that their success in most areas of life will depend on their skills as an influence on or manipulator of others. Thus white children begin to practice influencing other people very early in life and they conscientiously try to improve their skills, if we may judge by the letters sent to columnists asking for advice on how to get parents, dates, spouses, or children to do things that (one assumes) these parents, dates, spouses, or children are not particularly eager to do.

This ability is justly valued by the white people since a great deal of modern industrial and organizational work could not be carried on without it. For example, an office manager or foreman finds himself in charge of a group of people of different religious and ethnic backgrounds, different ages and temperaments, and widely varying moral and ethical views. If he is going to get the job done he must find some way of getting all of these folk to work together and he does this by being an extraordinarily flexible, agreeable, and persuasive influencer.

Perhaps because these "human relations skills" are a social replacement for physical force, white people tend to be insensitive to the simple fact that they are still interpersonally coercive. The "non-directive" teacher still wants the children to work as a group and on the project for which she has the materials and the skills. Similarly, the would-be hostess who will not listen to an excuse and interprets a refusal as a personal affront may not realize that she is forcing her guests to do what they do not wish to do. Even when white people do not wish to accomplish some end, their conversational patterns are structured along coercive lines. Thus, at a casual party, the man who remarks that he plans to buy a pear tree may anticipate that someone will immediately suggest that he buy a peach tree instead. If he remarks that he is shopping for a new car, someone will be happy to tell him exactly what kind of a car he ought to buy. The same thing happens if he ventures an opinion about music or politics. Someone is bound to inform him (in a friendly way, of course) that he ought to be listening to, reading, or attending something for which he has no particular inclination. Perhaps these patterns of conversation entertain white people because they play with the forms that are so serious in their society. The man who can out-advise the other is "one-up," and the loser is expected to take his defeat with good grace.

The Indian defines all of the above behavior, from the gentlest manipulation to the most egregious meddling, as outside the area of proper action. From earliest childhood he is trained to regard absolute non-interference in interpersonal relations as decent or normal and to react to even the mildest coercion in these areas with bewilderment, disgust, and fear.

Though most sensitive white persons who have lived with Indians are aware of this phenomenon, we have found none that have successfully described it in general terms.[5] Under these circumstances it might be wise to follow the Indian pattern of communication and describe the Indian "ethic of non-interference" by examples.

One of the more spectacular examples is the behavior of Indian passengers in an automobile. If the car is the property of the driver, no passenger ever considers giving him suggestions or direction. Even though a rock slide or a wandering steer may have blocked the right of way, no one says a word. To do so would be "interference." In consequence, accidents can occur which might have been prevented had any one of several passengers chosen to direct the attention of the driver to the hazard or obstacle. As the car rolls merrily into the ditch all that may be heard is a quiet exhalation of breath.

An example of this "ethic" was noted over thirty years ago among the Pit River Indians of California and recorded by Jaime de Angulo:

I have heard Indians say: "That's not right what he's doing, that fellow...." "What d'you mean it's not right?" "Well... you ain't supposed to do things that way....it never was done that way....there'll be trouble." "Then why don't you stop him?" "Stop him? How can I stop him? It's his way."[6]

A more personal example was given by an Indian friend. The friend was living with his wife's family and customarily drove to work every morning. One morning at breakfast he noticed that his sister-in-law, Mary, had dressed up as if she were going to town. Curious, he asked his wife: "Is Mary going any place?" "Oh yes," said his wife, "She's going to Pheonix."

"Does she have a lift to the bus station?" asked our friend. "No," said his wife.

Our friend then asked his sister-in-law if she would like him to give her a lift on his way to work and she accepted. After driving for some time, our friend suddenly became aware of the fact that he had automatically driven directly to work, passing right by the bus station without stopping. His sister-in-law was calmly looking out of the window. She had made no comment when he overshot the bus station and she made none now. Without a word, he turned the car around and took her to the bus station.

Characteristic Indian "non-interference" was shown by Mary, not only when she did not comment on the fact that her brother-in-law was passing the bus station, but also in her behavior before they set out. To have asked her brother-in-law to take her to the bus station would have constituted an indelicate attempt to influence him. Perhaps he would not wish to take her with him. By asking him she might "force" him to refuse and thus cause him embarrassment and discomfort. Again, if he took her unwillingly he would feel resentment toward her. By dressing up she could communicate her desires in a way that he could accept or reject without arousing any "bad feelings." That is, he could invite her to go along or he could "be occupied" and go without her.

Great delicacy and sensitivity of feeling are essential to even a moderate standard of Indian good manners. If one is extending invitations to a get-together one does not urge people to come; such urging would be "interfering," for, if they wish to come, they will come. Again under ordinary circumstances, one does not address another human being unless he has given some indication that he is willing to give you his attention. Thus, if one wishes to begin a conversation, even with a spouse or relative, one first puts oneself in his line of vision. If he does not acknowledge your presence this is a sign that he is occupied and you wait or go away. To address him while he is talking to someone else or meditating would be gross interference. If one is talking with a friend and he unwittingly brings up a delicate or painful subject, one lets him know this by pretending not to hear, by looking away, or by changing the subject. Most Indians follow these rules of etiquette unconsciously. Even so-called assimilated Indians follow them in part, and are not aware that they do so.[7]

A profound respect for the interests, occupations, and responsibilities of other human beings begins to show itself even in the very young Indian child. We have, for example, conversed with Indian parents for hours, while half a dozen children played around us, and, not once, did any of the children address a word to us. A little girl of three or four might leave the playgroup for a while and lean against an adult relative or sit in a lap. But, only in a grave emergency did she try to attract the attention of an adult and even then she tried not to interrupt what they were doing. Thus, if a bold child wanted to know if [he] might have a piece of the watermelon that an adult was cutting, [he] might creep up and whisper into [his] mother's ear.

We have asked a number of Indians how it is that even very young children do not bother older people. We are usually told something like this: "When I think about it, I see you're right. We never did bother grown-up people when I was a kid. It's funny because I can't remember that anybody said anything to us about it. We just didn't do it."

Such statements suggest that the Indian child is taught very early not to interfere with or bother older people who are otherwise occupied and that both instruction and learning may proceed on a subconscious level. Indeed, we have noticed that even little toddlers do not make the loud and vigorous attempts to monopolize their parent's attention which are characteristic of so many white infants.

Since the human infant must be taught to demand the attention of its parents and since Indian parents simply do not respond to "interfering" demand, it is possible that many Indian infants never learn some of the coercive and aggressive oral and verbal techniques available to children in other cultures. We do not suggest the Indian children lack aggression, but rather that their culture gives them virtually no opportunity to express it by interfering with the activities of others. On the other hand, they are taught consideration through the example of their elders, for Indian adults consistently treat children with the same respect they expect for themselves. To interrupt a child at play, or force it to do something against its will but "for its own good," are contrary to all precepts of Indian child-rearing.[8]   Indeed, Erikson tells of an Indian man reared by whites who felt that his wife ought to forbid his children to use profanity. His wife, reared as an Indian, regarded her husband's interfering attitude as evidence that he was sick in mind.[9]

Indians rarely discipline their children in a fashion noticeable to white persons. In the few cases where Rosalie Wax has seen an Indian child punished, parental disapproval was directed against "interference." In one case an Indian boy of about six who had played a great deal with white children repeatedly interrupted a conversation between Indian elders. At first he was ignored or gently set aside. When, after five or six rejections he was still persisting, his father addressed him directly: "Son," he said, "You're making it hard for all of us." This boy's father says regretfully that he thinks his son will grow up to be a white man. "When my wife or I show disapproval, it no longer makes any impression on him. He behaves just like the white boys he plays with."

In another case R. Wax was engaged in a conversation with an Indian man. His wife, a woman of notorious impatience, wished to go home. Not venturing to intrude herself, she sent her five year old daughter to tell Papa to come home. Papa, though very fond of his little girl, behaved as if he neither saw nor heard her. I noticed that the child was very distressed and frightened, but I did not realize at this time how severely her father was rebuking her.

By this time some non-Indian readers may have concluded that the upbringing of Indian children must be harsh indeed and that the little tykes creep through their days behind a wall of silence created by adults. Nothing, of course, could be farther from the truth. Indian parents are by no means "busy" all the time, and when they are unoccupied they like nothing better than to coddle, play with, and talk to little children.[10] Moreover, when an Indian gives anyone, child or adult, his attention, he gives all of it. Thus, when he is interacting with an adult, the child is not only treated with the warmth and indulgence noted by so many observers, but he is given an attention that is absolute. As we have already noted, this intense concentration on the emotional and intellectual overtones of a personal relationship also characterizes adult interaction. Thus, there really is no such thing as a casual or dilatory conversation between Indians. If they are not *en rapport* they are worlds apart; if they are giving their attention, they use every sense to the utmost.

As we have noted, the first impulse of an Indian who encounters an interferer (with whom he is on terms of friendship) is to withdraw his attention. If the ill-mannered person does not take the hint, the Indian will quietly go away. If it is impossible for him to leave, he does his best to make himself inconspicuous. By disappearing he avoids provoking the disturbed individual to further outbursts and also avoids embarrassing him by being a witness to his improper behavior. Simultaneously, he rebukes him in a socially sanctioned manner. In the past an entire community might withdraw from an incorrigible meddler and leave him quite alone.

Perhaps because these social sanctions are usually effective in an Indian community, Indians have not yet developed devices for dealing with an interferer who claims to be peaceable but aggressively refuses to permit them to withdraw. They can only marvel at his bizarre behavior and wish that he would go away. Sometimes, when prodded past endurance, Indian women will lose their self-control and try to drive out intruders with harsh words and even physical force.

Since the white man from infancy has been encouraged to defend himself and "face up" to unpleasant things, he almost invariably interprets the Indian's withdrawal from his verbal "attacks," not as an unostentatious rebuke, but as evidence of timidity, irresponsibility, or, even, as a tendency to "flee from reality."[11] This Indian trait more than any other seems to baffle the white man, for though he has been exposed to Christian doctrine for many, many centuries, he still cannot begin to understand the man who will not fight back.

We regret that some social scientists are among the least perceptive persons in this particular matter. (Perhaps their training makes them over prone to equate a disappearing informant with personal failure.) For example, we have seen a social scientist of some repute attempt to initiate a discussion with Indians by suggesting that they no longer possessed any culture of their own but were unrealistically clinging to an impoverished "reservation" culture. What they ought to do, he went on to say, was to leave the reservations and become assimilated. When this remark was received in expressionless silence the scientist suggested that this "lack of response" supported his point, for no one present had been able to defend the existence of their culture. The faces of the Indians became even more impassive, but the scientist did not notice that the feet and legs of some of the young men from the Plains tribes had begun to tremble as with the ague. A white person in the audience could no longer control his impulse to interfere, and, in the ensuing debate, much of the Indian's tension was dissipated.

On another occasion a psychiatrist whose initial overtures had been observed in silence by his Indian audience began to prod them with remarks intended to arouse their anger. The Indian men, as usual, made themselves inconspicuous. A few stole out of the meeting. But some of the women lost their tempers and the session ended in a loud and rather vulgar brawl.

After these incidents we talked with both the white and the Indian participants. Both of the social scientists assured us that they had merely been trying to elicit a response from the Indians and the second one seemed naively pleased with the "discovery" that "they'll only react if you get them mad." The Indians seemed to feel that it was best to ignore the whole thing. As one older man remarked: "You do not take the words of an insane person seriously or get angry at him."

The reader, by now, may be able to appreciate the blunt truth of a statement made by a middle-aged Apache who was attending a college class of the behavior of ethnic groups. Hoping to stimulate a discussion of accommodation and assimilation, the instructor asked: "What develops when two different peoples meet?" Laconically, the Apache replied: "Bad feelings."

One cannot examine a situation as distressing as the Indian and white frontier of sociable contact without wondering what might be done to make it less painful for both parties. To tell most white people that they can get along with Indians fairly well if they do not interfere is almost like telling them to give up breathing. It is, perhaps, equally difficult for an Indian to appreciate that the "mean" and "crazy" deeds of the white men do not necessarily have the same significance as the mean or crazy deeds of an Indian.

We have noted that there is less tension and distress in those situations in which the atmosphere of power and authority in which the Indian and the white man usually meet is mitigated or absent. Thus, the white man often finds it easier to get along with the Indian when he is gambling, trading, partying, or simply "chewing the rag." This is not because there is anything particularly friendly or brotherly in these activities but because they represent some of the few remaining social situations in which the white man cannot always immediately assume an authoritative or interfering role. In such situations the Indian learns to make allowances for or take advantage of the white man's restlessness, his incomprehensible "pride" and his reckless "courage." The white man, for his part, learns to accommodate himself to the slow pace, sudden temperamental outbursts, and unexpected disappearances of the Indian.

We have noted that most white people who have a tolerably good relationship with Indians consciously or unconsciously subscribe to the notion that white men ought to keep their noses out of Indian matters. However else they may behave seems to make little difference. Thus, one of the finest field workers known to us is an anthropologist of so gentle and unaggressive a nature that one sometimes wonders how he can maintain himself in the modern world. When he is in the field, the Indians spend a good deal of their time seeing that he comes to no harm. Another white man has no tact at all and breaks some rule of Indian decorum in almost every sentence he utters. Both men, however, subscribe to non-interference in Indian matters and both are admired and liked by Indians.

On the matter of interaction between groups composed both of Indians and whites, we have noted that "good feelings" are more likely to arise when the situation is clearly defined as one of contact. By this we mean that the participants from both groups come to realize that they are interacting in an entirely new situation, alien to both, and that their comfort, enjoyment, and accomplishment will depend on their ingenuity in inventing new forms and rules applicable to this new situation.

It is remarkable how rapidly and spontaneously new social forms comfortable to both parties may be defined, provided that both parties strongly desire to act or play together. We were, for example, unable to accomplish much in the Workshop on American Indian Affairs until we redefined the teaching-learning situation and we were obliged to do that before we could participate in picnics and dances at which both white people and Indians could have a good time. It is possible that such "accommodating" contact situations are established more frequently than social scientists realize. Their recognition and study might help to throw light on problems of great importance.

We are aware that we have presented a picture and analysis of Indian child rearing practices not entirely compatible with those of certain other observers. However, we think that the significant differences are quantitative rather than qualitative and rest on the fact that we emphasize what other scholars have overlooked.

We agree with Dorothy Lee that it is misleading to call Indian child-rearing practices "permissive" or "indulgent."[12] It might be more accurate to say that it usually does not occur to Indian parents to permit or forbid their children to do anything, much less permit or forbid them to move their bowels. White parents, on the other hand, see themselves as "permitters" and "forbidders." Nevertheless, from the Indian point of view, they leave vast and very important areas of their children's behavior completely unstructured. Thus one might suggest that in both cultures parents and elders subject infants and children to an intensive and careful training, but that they use very different methods and emphasize very different skills.

Again, we believe that Erikson has overlooked something very important when he depicts Sioux upbringing as one in which the child is introduced to social discipline "in the form of a tradition of unrelenting public opinion" only after an infancy in which he "is allowed to be an individualist" and is subjected to no frustration of impulse.[13]

According to our observations, Sioux and other Indians begin to train their children to be highly sensitive social beings long before they can talk and, perhaps, even before the age when white infants are subjected to oral and anal frustrations. Here we again agree with Lee in the view that Indian training in social sensitivity and in respect for others begins at birth, and, apparently, is reinforced with every interpersonal experience.

Perhaps, on occasion, too intense a focus on a formidable theoretical framework may serve to blur important aspects of the phenomena one intends to observe. This may be especially so with an alien culture. Thus, a people who do not practice the classic Freudian instinctual disciplines may be characterized as lacking in discipline, whereas the fact that they may practice a kind of subliminal "sleep-training" on their children (as do the Papago) may be overlooked. On the other hand, we may anticipate that, in time, cross-cultural studies will help to refine and develop our existing body of theory.

NOTES

1 Everett Cherrington Hughes and Helen MacGill Hughes, *Where Peoples Meet* (Glencoe, Illinois, 1952), pp. 18-19.
2 We have not heard an Indian use the old-fashioned term, "decent," in this context though we note that Kluckhohn used it to describe the Indian point of view (cited in Dorothy B. Lee, *Freedom and Culture* [Englewood Cliffs, New Jersey, 1959], p. 130). We find it apt since, in the white society of a generation ago, decent behavior was expected of children and brought no reward while indecent behavior was severely punished.

   The Indian conception that decent or proper behavior deserves no particular notice or praise is, nevertheless, rarely appreciated by white people. We, for example, have heard teachers and other professionals complain that their Indian students and clients never thanked them for their work and devotion. And Margaret Mead remarks that to Indians "All government employees, no matter how honest, how tireless, how enthusiastic, would be voted as merely 'doing their duty' and given neither laurels or thanks." This Indian behavior does not reflect hostility or ingratitude. It merely reflects the Indian view that medals or laurel wreaths are not given to people for doing what they ought to do (Margaret Mead, *The Changing Culture of an Indian Tribe* [New York, 1932]; cited by Erik H. Erikson in "Observations on Sioux Education," *Journal of Psychology,* VII [1939] 123).
3 Manning Nash, *Machine Age Maya*, Memoirs of the American Anthropological Association. No. 87 (1958), pp. 26-27, 46.
4 Gordon Macgregor, *Warriors Without Weapons* (Chicago, 1946), p. 137.
5 Lowie's examples of the attitude of Indian parents toward their children's property is, we think, an example of non-interference *(Primitive Society,* New York, 1925, pp. 233-34). See also, Paul Radin, *The Trickster* (New York, 1956), p. 9 and p. 55. On p. 153 Radin suggests

that part of the Trickster Cycle criticizes the chief, since "one of his functions was to interfere in all kinds of situations." Macgregor's statement that the Indian respects the individual's accountability to himself for his own actions is helpful and Lee's remarks on individual autonomy and social structure are extremely acute. Indeed, only Lee seems to see that Indian "respect for the individual" is an integral part of Indian "respect for social structure" (Macgregor, op. cit., p. 65, n. 7; Dorothy Lee, op. cit., Chap. I). Erikson (op. cit.) has made an uncommon attempt to describe how white people and Indians see each other and often notices the Indians' reaction to "interference" without quite understanding what is going on.

6 "Indians in Overalls," *Hudson Review,* III (1956), 369.

7 Some fine descriptions of the extremely delicate interaction demanded in Eskimo communities may be found in the works of Peter Freuchen.

8 White people frequently interpret this consideration as indifference or gross indulgence. As Macgregor remarks:

> [Indian] Parents do not force their children to conform because 'mother knows best' or to avoid damaging the parents' reputation or self-esteem. A child who runs away from school is usually not asked why he came home. Likewise, a grown son who leaves the reservation and is not heard from in years is rarely questioned on his return about what he has been doing. *(Op. cit., p. 67, n. 7.)*

9 Erikson, *op. cit.,* p. 130.

10 The men of some tribes do not play with little children but they usually seem to enjoy talking to them.

11 Even Erikson, who is far more aware of the withdrawing disposition of the Indian than are most other white men, does not see that it is, to the Indian, a matter of self-evident good manners. See for example, his complex discussion in *op. cit.,* 124-25.

12 *Op. cit.,* p. 6.

13 *Op. cit.,* pp. 152-53.

CHAPTER 2

PATTERNS OF PREJUDICE
AND DISCRIMINATION

It is a startling and disturbing experience to discover that only a handful of the innumerable sociological investigations of prejudice and discrimination have dealt with treatment of the American Indian.[1] The great majority of studies have focused on the attitudes of whites toward blacks, Jews, and Spanish-speaking minorities, presumably because of their greater numbers and "visibility" as minorities in segregated urban ghettos. Among the rationalizations that can be offered to "explain" the paucity of sociological studies of anti-Indian prejudice and discrimination are the lack of Indian-white contact in the urban scene and the relative "invisibility" of Indians to sociologists oriented to urban problems. These rationalizations are somewhat weakened by the fact that during the last 20 years Indians have migrated to the cities and now form sizable minorities in Los Angeles, San Francisco, Phoenix, Seattle, Denver, Minneapolis, Chicago, and other metropolitan areas. In recent years, especially during the past decade, sociologists and psychologists have had ample opportunity to study Indian-white relations, but have not done so. It may be that they have feared to "trespass" on territory traditionally claimed by the anthropologists. More probably, they have simply been insensitive to or unaware of the problems of discrimination and poverty faced by Indian-Americans.

This paucity of studies on prejudice and discrimination against Indians is even more startling when viewed in historical perspective, because Indians as a group have experienced as much systematic discrimination as any minority in American history, if not more. Estimates of the Indian population within the current boundaries of the United States in 1492 range from 700,000 to 1 million. By 1871, when they became official wards of the nation, their numbers had been reduced by the most radical forms of discrimination, war, and genocide, to less than half a million. Further decline occurred under the early reservation system. The Indian population reached a low point of approximately 240,000 persons during the first few years after 1900. The following official census figures for Indians in the United States reflect population trends since 1890:[2]

1890	248,253
1920	244,437
1940	333,369

1950   357,499
1960   523,591

An analysis of the ill-conceived and sometimes genocidal actions of the United States government during the period which history texts euphemistically call the "western expansion" will not be undertaken here. Excellent historical accounts are available which provide details of white relations with individual tribes or groups of tribes.[3] Such reports might serve as a solid base for more extensive analysis of the social pressures and structural constraints which affected Indian-white relations during the entire period of white expansion (1607-1870) and the systematic decimation of Indian tribes that accompanied it. The current concern and debate in United States society over institutional discrimination and the related crime, civil disorder, and escalating urban violence would be put in greater perspective by careful studies of earlier forms of "institutional violence" enacted against Indians for so long a period.

Progress for the Indian toward "equal opportunity" relative to whites and blacks has not been very rapid by any set of criteria. Much of the responsibility for the rate of progress must be laid to the Bureau of Indian Affairs, the official bureaucracy for implementing federal Indian policy. Accounts of the forms of discrimination practiced by local agencies and schools of the BIA are included in the first selection reprinted in this chapter, Peter Collier's "The Red Man's Burden." Despite an exceedingly high ratio of staff to clients, the overall effect of many BIA programs is continued poverty and deprivation. Yet the Indian tolerates the agency because he sees it as the lesser of two evils: "The BIA is all he has, and every promise to replace it with something better has been broken."[4] The revealed discrepancy between official policy, stated as self-help and self-control for Indians, and the allegations that BIA policies are restrictive and coercive is cause for serious examination of the situation and, where required, alteration of current institutional practices.

Empirical studies of anti-Indian prejudice began with the pioneering work of Emory S. Bogardus, who, in 1926, 1946, and 1956 directed studies of the attitudes toward minorities held by college students in the United States.[5] These surveys provide a unique opportunity to gauge changes in attitudes over a 30-year span. His original "social distance scale," used in all three studies, asked subjects to rank members of 30 minority groups on a seven-point scale, ranging from rank 1 ("Would marry into group") to 7 ("Would debar from my nation"). The results of the three surveys, taken together, indicate that while the ranking of at least one-third of the minority groups shifted substantially from study to study, the attitudes toward Indians remained remarkably stable. The degree of social-distance-type prejudice toward Indians increased from a rank of 18th in 1926 to 20th in 1946 and 1956. Similar results were found with Mexican-Americans, reflecting the generally quiescent, stable status and degree of visibility of the two groups during the period involved. Other researchers have utilized the Bogardus scaling technique in studies of attitudes toward various ethnic and racial groups, including Indians, but the reports have not included analyses of the extent to which Indians, in particular, are the objects of prejudice and discrimination.

Given the dearth of studies focusing directly on the extent and results of anti-Indian prejudice and discrimination, the researcher is forced to consider indirect indicators and infer consequences. Unemployment, low occupational attainment, low educational achievement, inadequate housing, and high rates of deviant behavior have been presented by some analysts as direct results of prejudice and institutional discrimination (i.e., the discrimination hypothesis). An alternate theory states that Indian norms and values stressing group sharing and affiliation over competitive striving for achievement, leadership and material advantages (i.e., the culture hypothesis) is the primary cause of Indian poverty and maladjustment. There is some supportive evidence for each of these perspectives and for others as well, but the only reasonable position at this juncture is that there is far too little evidence to justify taking a definite stand either way. A multitude of factors, including white descrimination and Indian cultural imperatives, may be acting in combination to produce the visible patterns of Indian response within a context of relative social and economic deprivation.

As of the fall of 1970, the various government agencies responsible for the collection and distribution of information about employment and housing (e.g., the Labor Department, the Equal Employment Opportunity Commission) were a good deal more aggressive, systematic and thorough in obtaining and disseminating data on blacks than they were in dealing with information on Indians and Mexican-Americans. It is true that the Indian people are a much smaller minority than the black population (650,000 versus nearly 23 million), but, as a group, the Indians experience significantly greater poverty and deprivation. The large concentrations of Indian people in metropolitan areas are as accessible and economically deprived as other urban minorities and deserve equal attention and services. But in statistical reports they tend to be placed in the "nonwhite" category and "buried" there, and they suffer a similar lack of official attention in the provision of social services.

Despite this neglect there are available general indicators of the deprivation experienced by Indians. The unemployment rate among them is ten times that of the rest of the nation. The average annual income of Indians on reservations is $1500 or less, a figure only one-third as high as the median for urban blacks.[6] In terms of sanitation and health facilities, conditions on reservations are among the worst in the nation. Estimates of the extent of substandard housing run as high as 90 percent. Health statistics are appalling: Indians experience 49 times more amoebic and bacillary dysentery than the national average, 7 times as much tuberculosis, and 4 times the death rate from influenza.[7] Infant mortality rates among Indians are the highest in the nation; the life expectancy is 10 years less than that of the average American. The median number of years of schooling is 5.5, well behind that for blacks, and ranges as low as 2.7 years in Arizona and 4.3 years in New Mexico (see Chapter 3 for additional information about the education of Indian students). Finally, the suicide rate among Indian teenagers is 3 times the national average, and on some reservations it soars to 10 times the national rate.[8]

One of the most systematic studies of alleged institutional discrimination against Indian-Americans is the massive assessment of factors influencing educational achievement of whites, blacks, Indians, and other groups directed by James S. Coleman and his associates. Information about facilities, curriculum, personnel training and attitudes toward teaching minority-group students, students' performance, social background, attitudes toward self, and future occupational goals was gathered from a random sample of 4,000 schools in the United States.[9] The results clearly and emphatically demonstrate that Indian scores on tests of verbal skills, reading, general information, and mathematics are substantially below scores for whites. On tests of verbal skill, Indians in 1st grade start with a moderate deficit in relation to whites and, on the basis of group averages, appear to fall further behind each year. Coleman's data show conclusively that the physical facilities and access to textbooks afforded Indian students are not significantly different from those of whites, despite glaring exceptions such as those described by Cahn.[10] However, it does appear that minority students' perceptions and attitudes concerning their chances for controlling outcomes in the white system (e.g., for obtaining and advancing in good jobs) exert a marked effect on their achievement levels. The school performance of Indian students seems to be rather strongly influenced by personal and group assessments of the "openness" of the community institutions to be entered after graduation. More data are now required to test these ideas, but Coleman's evidence seems to suggest that Indians who succeed in the student role tend to perceive their chances for success in future jobs or further education as relatively good.

The Bogardus studies are the most extensive national or regional surveys on prejudice toward Indian people. However, a few community surveys have included questions about attitudes toward Indians. One such study, Anderson and Safar's "The Influence of Differential Community Perceptions on the Provision of Equal Educational Opportunities," is reprinted in this chapter. The authors report that a survey of citizens' attitudes toward Anglo, Spanish-American, and Indian children showed that members of all groups defined the whites as most capable of achieving educational and occupational success, and the Indian students least capable. The lack of ability of the Indian students was perceived as innate or due to lack of family support rather than due to a lack of compensatory education to make up for the disadvantages attending early life in cultural settings different from those of the school. More importantly, it was found that members of the minority groups themselves had internalized these notions about their own inferiority, with predictable consequences for their children. And although educators in the communities studied stated that they thought the educational programs or facilities were not adequate for Indian pupils, the members of the community did not think the school programs were inadequate; instead, they defined the minority students as inferior.

The third selection deals with the discriminatory treatment of the Cherokee in eastern Oklahoma. In "Renaissance and Repression: The Oklahoma Cherokee," Albert L. Wahrhaftig and Robert K. Thomas point out the advantages accruing to the local power structure from their maintaining the fiction that the Cherokees are a "vanishing breed." In alleging that the Cherokees have all been assimilated and thus "joined the system," the white leaders strive to rationalize and validate the prevailing economic and political discrimination, and to blunt or nullify the threat of a newly emergent Indian militancy in the region.

Considerable case study material on anti-Indian racism, common stereotypes, and institutional discrimination is available, including work by Deloria, Steiner, Kluckhohn and Leighton, Macgregor, Sasaki, and Spicer and Chesky.[11] Spicer and Chesky summarized white orientation toward the Papago in Arizona: "The general public looks upon these Indians as a lower-class group with a tendency toward drunkenness, and, though not subjected to as marked social discrimination as are Negroes, they must endure a certain amount of racial prejudice."[12] The article by Ralph A. Luebben reprinted in this chapter describes the treatment of Navaho miners working and living in "Carbonate City," Colorado. Luebben reports that the Navahos are considered to be generally "stupid," "mean and unpredictable about getting to work," "too diseased to share toilets" with Anglos in the mine, and lacking in the required initiative to handle supervisory positions adequately. Negative stereotypes about Indian drinking, reckless driving, stealing, and body odor also are common. Initially Luebben hypothesized that the Navahos in "Carbonate City" were the objects of discrimination, prejudice, and as an aggregate were accorded minority status, and his investigation supported all three hypotheses.

Among the more damaging forms of discrimination endured by Indian people has been the distortion of history in textbooks. Lee Bowker's "Red and Black in Contemporary American History Texts," is the report of an application of the technique of content analysis to grade school and high school textbooks in an attempt to identify the nature and extent of Indian representation in history books published in the 1960s. His careful tabulation of pages, sentences, and "mentions" of the Indian reveals that while "the quality and quantity of textural material about blacks was found to have improved since the early 1960s ... that of the American Indian was found to have remained static or, in some cases, to have deteriorated."

In connection with textbook distortion of Indian culture and history, two excellent works not reprinted in the present chapter deserve to be mentioned. One of these, Virgil Vogel's "The Indian in American History Textbooks"[13] illustrates four methods (obliteration, defamation, disembodiment, and disparagement) historians have used "to create or perpetuate false impressions of aboriginal Americans." The "obliterative" techniques include conscious falsification, selective reporting, or simply ignoring the Indian. Their successful application has, in a real sense, served to make an "unperson" of the Native American. Historians who have applied the "disembodiment" techniques have, to be sure, acknowledged that the Indian existed, but have treated him as part of the natural resources or as a subhuman wanderer, a "wild beast," "savage," or "brutish" man. As a consequence of their presumed savagery, the spoilation of the Indians by the advance of "civilization" has been conveniently defined as necessary to progress.

The "defamation" technique consists merely of calling attention to the Indians' faults, real or imagined, and ignoring anything that might be said in their favor. The defamers create Indians who are always on the warpath, bloodthirsty, debauched, idle, rootless, and barbaric. Finally, there are the disparagers, who minimize or deny the many contributions Indian people have made to Western culture. In refuting those who assert that the Indian has contributed little to our civilization, Vogel mentions their medical and pharmaceutical skills, the advanced civilizations manifested by the Central and South American Indians, the Indian elements in Western dress, music, literature, agriculture, art, architecture, language, and military tactics, and the Indians who have successfully participated as individuals in the "rival culture" of the United States. Vogel concludes with a discussion of "recommended books" which, in the main, avoid the sins of obliteration, disembodiment, defamation, and disparagement.

Another excellent qualitative discussion of the biased treatment of Indian people in history books is Jeannette Henry's "Textbook Distortion of the Indian."[14] Members of the Indian Historical Society evaluated 43 textbooks at 4th, 5th, and 8th grade levels, and concluded that the Indian was rarely mentioned in connection with the Colonial period, that his contributions to the nation's economy were ignored, that his role in many important historical periods or events tended to be minimized, and that where Indian-white relations were reviewed, the facts were distorted, or, at best, inaccurate. Henry supports the charge of distortion with examples taken from specific texts. She concludes with a thoughtful statement about the positive benefits to be derived from teaching students the "unvarnished facts" about the role of the Indian in American history.

The negative stereotypes fostered by textbooks are sustained and elaborated by other communications media, primary culprits being television programs, movies, and novels. Less noticed as a purveyor of stereotypes is the cartoonist, yet his works also play a significant role in shaping the images held about minority persons. The selection by Houts and Bahr, "Stereotyping of Indians and Blacks in Magazine Cartoons," illustrates how cartoons in one magazine, *The Saturday Evening Post*, served to sustain the popular stereotypes. Contrary to expectations, Indian characters were *over*-represented in *Post* cartoons. However, they tended to be portrayed in a few standard stereotypes: In one-third of the cartoons containing Indians, they were shooting arrows, and in eight of every nine Indian cartoons one or more of the Indians was wearing feathers. Small wonder that tourists from the East still expect to find "wild" Indians in the West. Most striking was the absence of modern Indians and blacks in the cartoons surveyed. Judging from the cartoons, one might conclude that the modern American society included neither blacks nor Indians.

The final selection contrasts white and Indian rights with respect to a particular kind of behavior, namely the crime of rape. MacMeekin reviews the history of the discriminatory legislation which in effect places a higher penalty on the rape of a non-Indian woman than on the rape of an Indian woman. In the process, MacMeekin discusses the history of federal Indian law and the assumptions upon which it is based, and points to the unconstitutional differentials in due process which are allowed by the current statutes on rape.

NOTES

1 For general reviews of the literature see: John Harding, Harold Proshansky, Bernard Kutner, and Isidor Chein, "Prejudice and Ethnic Relations," in Gardner Lindzey and Elliot Aronson, eds., *The Handbook of Social Psychology*, vol. 5 (Reading, Mass.: Addison-Wesley, 1969), pp. 1-76; George E. Simpson and J. M. Yinger, *Racial and Cultural Minorities: An Analysis of Prejudice and Discrimination*, 3rd ed. (New York: Harper & Row, 1965); Charles F. Marden and Gladys Meyer, *Minorities in American Society*, 3rd ed. (New York: American Book, 1968), pp. 356-377; Jack D. Forbes, ed, *The Indian in America's Past*, (Englewood Cliffs, N.J.: Prentice-Hall, 1964).
2 United States Census data for 1890, 1920, 1940, 1950, 1960.
3 See, for example, David H. Cockran, *The Creek Frontier, 1540-1783* (Norman: University of Oklahoma Press, 1967); Merle H. Deardorff, *The Religion of Handsome Lake: Its Origin and Development* (Washington D.C.: Bureau of American Ethnology Bulletin 149, 1951), pp. 77-107; Edward Eggleston and Lillie Eggleston Seeyle, *Tecumseh and the Shawnee Prophet* (New York: Dodd, Mead, 1878); George T. Hunt, *The Wars of the Iroquois, A Study in Intertribal Trade Relations* (Madison: University of Wisconsin Press, 1940); Theodore Kroeber and Robert F. Heizer, *Almost Ancestors: The First Californians* (New York: Ballantine, 1970); James Mooney, *The Ghost Dance Religion and the Sioux Outbreak of 1890*, Bureau of American Ethnology 14th Annual Report, Part 2 (Washington, D.C.: U.S.

Government Printing Office, 1896); Marion L. Starkey, *The Cherokee Nation*, (New York: Knopf, 1946); Alden T. Vaughan, *New England Frontier, Puritans and Indians, 1620-1675* (Boston: Little, Brown, 1965); Anthony F. C. Wallace, *King of the Delawares: Teedyuscung, 1700-1763* (Philadelphia: University of Pennsylvania Press, 1949).

4　Edgar S. Cahn, ed., *Our Brother's Keeper: The Indian in White America* (New York: New Community Press, 1969), p. 14.

5　Emory S. Bogardus, "Measuring Social Distance," *Sociology and Social Research*, 9 (March 1925), 299-308; *Immigration and Race Attitudes* (Boston: Heath, 1928); "Changes in Racial Distance," *International Journal of Attitude and Opinion Research*, 1 (December 1947), 55-62; "Racial Distance," in Murray A. Straus and Joel I. Nelson, *Sociological Analysis: An Empirical Approach Through Replication* (New York: Harper & Row, 1968, pp. 276-281.

6　James T. Wilson, "Notes and Comments on the American Indian," *Civil Rights Digest*, 3 (Winter 1970), 19-21; United States Senate, *Hearings Before the Special Subcommittee on Indian Education of the Committee on Labor and Public Welfare, United States Senate, 90th Congress*, Part V (Washington, D.C.: U.S. Government Printing Office, 1969), p. 1909.

7　William Payne, "Food for First Citizens," *Civil Rights Digest*, 2 (Fall 1969), 2.

8　Wilson, *op. cit.*; U.S. Senate, *op. cit.*

9　James S. Coleman et al., *Equality of Educational Opportunity* (Washington, D.C.: U.S. Government Printing Office, 1966).

10　Cahn, *op. cit.*

11　Vine Deloria, Jr., *Custer Died for Your Sins* (New York: Macmillan, 1969); Vine Deloria, Jr., *We Talk, You Listen* (New York: Macmillan, 1970); Stan Steiner, *The New Indians* (New York: Harper & Row, 1968); Gordon MacGregor, *Warriors without Weapons: A Study of the Society and Personality Development of the Pine Ridge Sioux* (Chicago: University of Chicago Press, 1946); Kroeber and Heizer, *op. cit.*; Helen H. Jackson, *A Century of Dishonor* (New York: Harper & Row, 1965); Clyde Kluckhohn and Dorothea Leighton, *The Navaho* (Cambridge, Mass.: Harvard University Press, 1947); Joseph Spicer and Jane Chesky, *The Desert People* (Chicago: University of Chicago Press, 1949); Tom T. Sasaki, *Fruitland, New Mexico: A Navaho Community in Transition* (Ithaca, N.Y.: Cornell University Press, 1960); Cahn, *op. cit.*

12　Spicer and Chesky, *op. cit.*, p. 110.

13　Virgil J. Vogel, "The Indian in American History Textbooks," *Integrated Education*, 6 (May-June 1968), 16-32.

14　Jeannette Henry, "Textbook Distortion of the Indian," *Civil Rights Digest*, 1 (Summer 1968), 4-8.

PETER COLLIER: THE RED MAN'S BURDEN

When fourteen Indian college students invaded Alcatraz on a cold, foggy morning in the first part of November—claiming ownership "by right of discovery," and citing an 1868 treaty allowing the Sioux possession of unused federal lands—they seemed in a light-hearted mood. After establishing their beachhead, they told the press that they had come there because Alcatraz already had all the necessary features of a reservation: dangerously uninhabitable buildings; no fresh water; inadequate sanitation; and the certainty of total unemployment. They said they were planning to make the five full-time caretakers wards of a Bureau of Caucasian Affairs, and offered to take this troublesome real estate off the white man's hands for $24, payment to be made in glass beads. The newspapers played it up big, calling the Indians a "raiding party." When, after a 19-hour stay, the Indians were persuaded to leave the island, everyone agreed that it had been a good publicity stunt.

If the Indians had ever been joking about Alcatraz, however, it was with the bitter irony that fills colonial subjects' discourse with the mother-country. When they returned to the mainland, they didn't fall back into the cigar-store stoicism that is supposedly the red man's prime virtue. In fact, their first invasion ignited a series of meetings and strategy-sessions; two weeks later they returned to the rock, this time with a force of nearly 100 persons, a supply network, and the clear intention of staying. What had begun as a way of drawing attention to the position of the contemporary Indian, developed into a plan for doing something about it. And when the government, acting through the General Services Administration, gave them a deadline for leaving, the Indians replied with demands of their own: Alcatraz was theirs, they said, and it would take U.S. Marshals to remove them and their families; they planned to turn the island into a major cultural center and research facility; they would negotiate only the mechanics of deeding over the land, and that only with Interior Secretary Walter Hickel during a face to face meeting. The Secretary never showed up, but the government's deadlines were withdrawn.

Alcatraz is Indian territory: The old warning to "Keep Off U.S. Property" now reads "Keep off Indian Property"; security guards with red armbands stand near the docks to make sure it is obeyed. Women tend fires beneath huge iron cauldrons filled with food, while their kids play frisbee in what was once a convicts' exercise yard. Some of the men work on the prison's wiring system or try to get more cellblocks cleared out for the Indian people who are arriving daily from all over the country; others

Source: Reprinted by permission from *Ramparts* 8 (February 1970), 26-38.

sit fishing on the wharf with hand-lines, watching quietly as the rip-tides churn in the Bay. During the day, rock music plays over portable radios and a series of soap operas flit across a TV; at night, the prison is filled with the soft sounds of ceremonial drums and eerie songs in Sioux, Kiowa and Navajo.

In the few weeks of its occupation, Alcatraz has become a mecca, a sort of red man's Selma. Indian people come, stay a few days, and then leave, taking with them a sense of wonderment that it has happened. Middle-aged "establishment" Indians are there. They mix with younger insurgents like Lehman Brightman (the militant Sioux who heads a red power organization called the United Native Americans), Mad-Bear Anderson (The Iroquois traditionalist from upstate New York who fought to get the United Nations to stop the U.S. Army Corps of Engineers' flooding of precious Seneca Indian lands), Sid Mills (the young Yakima who demanded a discharge from the Army after returning from Viet-Nam so that he could fight his real war—against the state of Washington's denial of his people's fishing rights), and Al Bridges (one of the leaders of the first Washington fish-ins in 1964, who now faces a possible ten-year prison sentence for defying the state Fish and Game Commission). The composition of the ad hoc Indian community changes constantly, but the purpose remains the same: to make Alcatraz a powerful symbol of liberation springing out of the long American imprisonment.

The people enjoy themselves, spending a lot of time sitting around the campfire talking and gossiping. But there is a sense of urgency beneath the apparent lassitude. Richard Oakes, a 27-year old Mohawk who worked in high steel construction before coming West to go to college, is one of the elected spokesmen. Sitting at a desk in the old Warden's Office, he talks about the hope of beginning a new organization, the Confederacy of American Indian Nations, to weld Indian groups all over the country into one body capable of taking power away from the white bureaucracy. He acknowledges that the pan-Indian movements which have sprung up before have always been crushed. "But time is running out for us," he says. "We have everything at stake. And if we don't make it now, then we'll get trapped at the bottom of that white world out there, and wind up as some kind of Jack Jones with a social security number and that's all. Not just on Alcatraz, but every place else, the Indian is in his last stand for cultural survival."

This sentiment is reflected in the slogans lettered on walls all over the prison, the red paint bleeding down onto the concrete. One of them declares: "Better Red than Dead."

The Alcatraz occupation is still popularly regarded as the engaging fun and games of Indian college kids. In its news coverage of the U.S. Coast Guard's feeble attempt to blockade ships running supplies to the island, one local television station found amusement in showing their films to the musical accompaniment of U.S. cavalry bugle calls. It was not so amusing to the occupiers, however. The California Indians now on the Rock know that their people were decimated from a population of 100,000 in 1850 when the gold rush settlers arrived, to about 15,000 thirty years later, and that whole tribes, languages and cultures were erased from the face of the earth. There are South Dakota Indians there whose grandparents were alive in 1890 when several hundred Sioux, mostly women and children leaving the reservation to find food, were caught at Wounded Knee, killed, and buried in a common grave—the old daguerreotypes still showing heavily-mustachioed soldiers standing stiffly over the frozen bodies like hunters with their trophies. Cowboys and Indians is not a pleasant game for the Alcatraz Indians and some must wonder whether, in another 150 years, German children will be gaily playing Nazis and Jews.

But the past is not really at issue. What is at stake today, as Richard Oakes says, is cultural survival. Some of the occupiers have known Indian culture all their lives; some have been partially assimilated away from it and are now trying to return. All understand that it is in jeopardy, and they want some assurance that Indian-ness will be available to their children. It sounds like a fair request, but fairness has never ruled the destiny of the Indian in America. In fighting for survival, the Indians of Alcatraz are challenging the lies perpetuated by anthropologists and bureaucrats alike, who insist that the red man is two things: an incompetent "ward" addicted to the paternalism of government, and an anachronism whose past is imprisoned in white history and whose only future is as an invisible swimmer in the American mainstream. The people on Alcatraz have entered a struggle on a large scale that parallels the smaller, individual struggles for survival that many of them have known themselves; it is the will to exist as individuals that brought them together in determination to exist as a people.

One of the original 14 on Alcatraz was a pretty 22-year-old Shoshone-Bannock girl named La Nada Means. Her hair is long and reddish-black; her nose arches slightly and prominent cheekbones square out her face. Her walk is slightly pidgeon-toed, the result of a childhood disease for which she never received treatment. If you tell her that she looks very Indian, she will thank you, but with a searching look that suggests she has heard the same comment before, and not as a compliment.

"When I was little," she says, "I remember my family as being very poor. There were 12 of us kids, and we were always hungry. I remember sometimes getting to the point where I'd eat anything I could get my hands on—leaves, small pieces of wood, anything. The other thing I remember is the meanness of the small towns around the reservation. Blackfoot, Pocatello—they all had signs in the store windows to keep Indians out. One of them I'll never forget; it said, 'No Indians or Dogs Allowed.' There were Indian stalls in the public bathrooms; Indians weren't served in a lot of the restaurants; and we just naturally all sat in the balcony of the theatres. You learn early what all that means. It becomes part of the way you look at yourself."

She grew up on the Fort Hall reservation in southern Idaho. The Jim Crow atmosphere of the surrounding small towns has lessened somewhat with the passage of time and the coming of the civil-rights bills, but it is still very much present in the attitude of white townsfolk towards Indians. And while there are no longer the small outbreaks of famine that occurred on the reservation when La Nada was growing up in the '50s, Fort Hall is still one of the bleakest areas in the country, and the people there are among the poorest.

Like most Indian children of her generation (and like a great many today), La Nada Means was sent away to school. Her youth became a series of separations from home and family, each more traumatic than the one before. The first school she attended was St. Mary's School for Indian Girls in Springfield, South Dakota. "I took a lot of classes in subjects like 'Laundry,'" she remembers, "where the classwork was washing the headmaster's clothes. All Indian people are supposed to be good with their hands, you know, and also hard workers, so we didn't do too much regular schoolwork at St. Mary's. They also had what they called a Summer Home Program where you're sent out during the summer break to live with a white family. It was supposed to teach you white etiquette and things like that, and make you forget your savage Indian ways. When I was 13, I was sent up to Minnesota where I became a sort of housekeeper for the summer. I don't remember too much about it, except that the wages I got, about $5 a week, were sent back to St. Mary's and I never saw them. After being at that school a little while, I got all upset. They said I was 'too outspoken,' and expelled me. After I got back to Fort Hall, I had my first breakdown."

For awhile she attended public school in Blackfoot, the small town bordering the reservation. She was suspended because she objected to the racial slurs against Indians which were built into the curriculum. She was 15 when the Bureau of Indian Affairs (BIA) sent her to its boarding school in Chilocco, Oklahoma. On her first day there, the matrons ordered her to lower the hems on the two dresses she owned. She refused and was immediately classified as a troublemaker. "At Chilocco, you're either a 'good girl' or a 'bad girl,'" she says. "They put me in the bad girls' dormitory right away with Indians mainly from the Northwest. The Oklahoma Indians were in the good girls' dorm, and the matrons constantly tried to keep us agitated by setting the tribes to fighting with each other. Everything was like the Army. There were bells, drills and set hours for everything. The food was called 'GI Chow.' There was a lot of brutality, but it was used mainly on the boys, who lived in another wing. Occasionally they'd let the boys and girls get together. You all stood in this big square; you could hold hands, but if the matrons saw you getting too close, they'd blow a whistle and then you'd have to march back to the dorm."

La Nada made the honor roll, but was expelled from Chilocco after a two-month stay for being involved in a fight. "The matrons just had it in for me, I guess. They got about 100 other Indian girls against me and a few other 'bad girls.' They put us in a small room and when the fight was ready to begin, they turned out the lights and walked out, locking the doors behind them. We had a 'riot,' and I got beat up. The next day, the head of the school called me into his office and said that I didn't fit in."

She was sent off with one dollar, a sack lunch, and a one-way bus ticket from Chilocco back to Idaho. She lived with her family for a few months, helping her father collect data about conditions at Fort Hall, and then was sent by the BIA to another of its boarding schools, Stewart Institute, in Carson City, Nevada. Her reputation as a "difficult Indian" followed her, and she was again sent home after being at Stewart for less than a day. The BIA threatened to send her to "reform" school; then it forgot about her. "I stayed around the reservation for awhile," she says, "and when I got to be 17, I took GED [high school equivalent] exams. I only had about nine real years of schooling, but I scored pretty well and got into Idaho State College. I lasted there for a semester, and then quit. I didn't really know what to do. At Fort Hall, you either work in some kind of menial job with the BIA agency there, or you go off the reservation to find a job in one of the towns. If you choose the BIA, you know that they'll try to drill a subservient mentality into you; and in the towns, the discrimination is pretty bad."

La Nada again spent time working with her father, a former tribal chairman. They sent out letters to congressmen and senators describing conditions on the reservations, and tried to get the Bureau of Indian Affairs office to respond. As a result, her father was harassed by local law enforcement officials. La Nada drifted for a time and then asked the BIA for "relocation" off the reservation. Many of the Fort Hall Indians have taken this route and 80 per cent of them return to the reservation, because, as La Nada says, "things in the slums where you wind up are even worse than on the reservation, and you don't have your people to support you."

The BIA gave her a one-way ticket to San Francisco, one of eight major relocation centers in the country. When she first arrived, she sat in the local BIA office from 8 to 5 for a few days, waiting for them to help her find a job. They didn't, and she found a series of temporary clerk jobs by herself. As soon as she found work, the BIA cut off her $140 a month relocation payment. She wound up spending a lot of time in the "Indian bars" which are found in San Francisco and every other relocation town. She worked as a housekeeper in the private home for Indian girls where the BIA had first sent her, and as a barmaid in a beer parlor. She was "drunk most of the time," and she became pregnant. She was 17 years old.

"After I had the baby," she says, "my mother came out from the reservation and got him. She said they'd take care of him back home until I got on my feet. I really didn't know what to do. The only programs the BIA has are vocational training for menial jobs, and I didn't especially want to be a beautician. Actually, I wanted to try college again, but when I told this to a BIA counselor, he said they didn't have any money for that and told me I was being 'irrational and unrealistic.'

"All types of problems develop when you're on relocation. The Indian who has come to the city is like a man without a country. Whose jurisdiction are you under, the BIA's or the state's? You go to a county hospital when you're sick and they say, 'Aren't you taken care of by the Indian Affairs people?' It's very confusing. You hang around with other Indians, but they are as bad off as you are. Anyway, I started sinking lower and lower. I married this Sioux and lived with his family awhile. I got pregnant again. But things didn't work out in the marriage, and I left. After I had the baby, I ended up in the San Francisco General psychiatric ward for a few weeks. I was at the bottom, really at the bottom. Indian people get to this point all the time, especially when they're relocated into the big city and are living in the slums. At that point, you've got two choices: either kill yourself and get it all over with—a lot of Indians do this—or try to go all the way up, and this is almost impossible."

As she looks at it now, La Nada feels she was "lucky." She tried to get admitted to the local colleges, but was refused because of her school record. Finally, because the University of California "needed a token Indian in its Economic Opportunity Program for minority students," she was admitted in the fall of 1968. She did well in her class and became increasingly active, helping to found the United Native Americans organization and working to get more Indian students admitted into the EOP program. "After my first year there," she says, "everything was going along all right. I liked school and everything, and I felt I was doing some good. But I felt myself getting swallowed up by something that was bigger than me. The thing was that I didn't want to stop being an Indian, and there were all these pressures, very hidden ones, that were trying to make me white." At the summer break she went back to the reservation and spent some time with her family. The next quarter she became involved in the Third World Liberation Front strike at Berkeley, fighting for a school of Ethnic Studies, including a Native American program. She was suspended by the University.

La Nada's experiences, far from being extreme cases, are like those of most young Indians. If she is unique at all, it is because she learned the value of fighting back.

Each generation of Americans rediscovers for itself what is fashionably called the "plight" of the Indian. The American Indian today has a life expectancy of approximately 44 years, more than 25 years below the national average. He has the highest infant mortality rate in the country (among the more than 50,000 Alaskan natives, one of every four babies dies before reaching his first birthday). He suffers from epidemics of diseases which were supposed to have disappeared from America long ago.

A recent Department of Public Health report states that among California Indians, "water from contaminated sources is used in 38 to 42 per cent of the homes, and water must be hauled under unsanitary conditions by 40 to 50 per cent of all Indian families." Conditions are similar in other states. A high proportion of reservation housing throughout the country is officially classified as "substandard," an antiseptic term which fails to conjure up a tiny, two-room log cabin holding a family of 13 at Fort Hall; a crumbling Navajo hogan surrounded by broken plumbing fixtures hauled in to serve as woodbins; or a gutted automobile body in which a Pine Ridge Sioux family huddles against the South Dakota winter.

On most reservations, a 50 per cent unemployment rate is not considered high. Income per family among Indian people is just over $1500 per year—the lowest of any group in the country. But this, like the other figures, is deceptive. It does not suggest, for instance, the quality of the daily life of families on the Navajo reservation who live on $600 per year (exchanging sheep's wool and hand-woven rugs with white traders for beans and flour), who never have real money and who are perpetually sinking a little further into credit debt.

To most Americans, the conditions under which the Indian is forced to live are a perennial revelation. On one level, the symptoms are always being tinkered with half-heartedly and the causes ignored; on another level, the whole thrust of the Government's Indian policy appears calculated to perpetuate the Indians' "plight." This is why La Nada Means and the other Indians have joined what Janet McCloud, a leader of the Washington fishing protests, calls "the last, continuing Indian War." The enemies are legion, and they press in from every side: the studiously ignorant politicians, the continuously negligent Department of the Interior, and the white business interests who are allowed to prey upon the reservations' manpower and resources. But as the Indian has struggled to free himself from the suffocating embrace of white history, no enemy has held the death grip more tightly than has his supposed guardian, in effect his "keeper": the Bureau of Indian Affairs.

The Bureau came into being in 1834 as a division of the War Department. Fifteen years later it was shifted to the Department of the Interior, the transition symbolizing the fact that the Indian was beginning to be seen not as a member of a sovereign, independent nation, but as a "ward," his land and life requiring constant management. This is the view that has informed the BIA for over a century. With its 16,000 employees and its outposts all over the country, the Bureau has become what Cherokee anthropologist Robert Thomas calls "the most complete colonial system in the world."

It is also a classic bureaucratic miasma. A recent book on Indian Affairs, *Our Brother's Keeper,* notes that on the large Pine Ridge reservation, "$8040 a year is spent per family to help the Oglala Sioux Indians out of poverty. Yet median income among these Indians is $1910 per family. At last count there was nearly one bureaucrat for each and every family on the reservation."

The paternalism of the BIA, endless and debilitating, is calculated to keep the Indian in a state of perpetual juvenilization, without rights, dependent upon the meagre and capricious beneficence of power. The Bureau's power over its "wards," whom it defines and treats as children, seems limitless. The BIA takes care of the Indian's money, doling it out to him when it considers his requests worthy; it determines the use of the Indian's land; it is in charge of the development of his natural resources; it relocates him from the reservation to the big city ghetto; it educates his children. It relinquishes its hold over him only reluctantly, even deciding whether or not his will is valid after he dies.

This bureaucratic paternalism hems the Indian in with an incomprehensible maze of procedures and regulations, never allowing him to know quite where he stands or what he can demand and how. Over 5000 laws, statutes and court decisions apply to the Indians alone. As one Indian student says, "Our people have to go to law school just to live a daily life."

The BIA is the Indian's point of contact with the white world, the concrete expression of this society's attitude towards him. The BIA manifests both stupidity and malice; but it is purely neither. It is guided by something more elusive, a whole world view regarding the Indian and what is good for him. Thus the BIA's overseership of human devastation begins by teaching bright-eyed youngsters the first formative lessons in what it is to be an Indian.

The Darwinian educational system which La Nada Means endured is not a thing of the past. Last spring, for instance, the BIA's own Educational Division studied Chilocco and came to the following conclusions: "There is evidence of criminal malpractice, not to mention physical and mental perversion, by certain staff members." The report went on to outline the disastrous conditions at the school, noting among other things that "youngsters reported they were handcuffed for as long as 18 hours in the dormitory . . . or chained to a basement pillar or from a suspended pipe. One team member . . . verified a youngster's hurt arms, the deformed hands of another boy, and an obviously broken rib of another . . . ."

The BIA responded to this report by suppressing it and transferring the investigators who submitted it. The principal of Chilocco was fired, but more as punishment for letting such things be discovered than for the conditions themselves. The same story is repeated at other BIA boarding schools. At the Intermountain Indian School in Utah, Indian children suspected of drinking have their heads ducked into filthy toilets by school disciplinarians. At Sherman Institute in Riverside, California, students of high school age are fed on a budget of 76 cents a day.

But there is a far more damaging and subtle kind of violence at work in the school as well. It is, in the jargon of educational psychology, the initiation of a "failure-orientation," and it derives from the fact that the children and their culture are held in such obviously low regard. Twenty-five per cent of all BIA teachers admit that they would rather be teaching whites; up to 70 per cent leave the BIA schools after one year. If a teacher has any knowledge at all of his student's needs and backgrounds, he gets it from a two-week non-compulsory course offered at the beginning of the year. One teacher, a former Peace Corps volunteer who returned to teach at the Navajo reservation, told the Senate Subcommittee on Indian Education that the principal of her BIA school habitually made statements such as "All Navajos are brain-damaged," and "Navajo culture belongs in a museum."

The results of the Indian's education, whether it be supervised by the BIA or by the public school system, indicates how greatly the system fails him. Twenty per cent of all Indian men have less than five years of schooling. According to a recent report to the Carnegie Foundation, there is a 60 per cent drop-out rate among Indian children as a whole, and those who do manage to stay in school fall further behind the longer they attend. A study of the Stewart Institute in Carson City, Nevada, for instance, shows that Indian sixth graders score 5.2 on the California Achievement Test. Six years later, at graduation, their achievement level is 8.4.

In a strange sense, the Indian student's education does prepare him for what lies ahead. What it teaches him is that he is powerless and inferior, and that he was destined to be so when he was born an Indian. Having spent his youth being managed and manhandled, the Indian is accustomed to the notion that his business must be taken care of for him. He is thus ideally equipped to stand by and watch the BIA collect mortgages on his future.

The Indians of California have more than their share of troubles—in part because they never received an adequate land base by government treaty. They are scattered up and down the state on reservations which are rarely larger than 10,000 acres and on rancherias as small as one acre. It takes a special determination to find these Indians, for most of them live in backwoods shacks, hidden from view as well as from water and electricity.

They have to struggle for every bit of federal service they get; disservice, however, comes easy. In 1969 the only irrigation money the BIA spent in all of Southern California, where water is an especially precious commodity to the Indians, was not for an Indian at all, but for a white farmer who had bought an Indian's land on the Pala reservation. The BIA spent $2500—of money appropriated by Congress for the Indians—to run a 900-foot pipeline to this white man's land. The Indians at Pala have been asking for irrigation lines for years, but less than one-half of their lands have them.

At the Resighini rancheria, a 228-acre reservation in Northern California, the Simpson Timber Company had been paying the Indians 25 cents per 1000 feet for the lumber it transported across their land. The total paid to the Indians in 1964 was $4725, and the right of way was increasing in value every year. Then the BIA, acting without warning, sold the right of way outright to Simpson Timber Company for $2500, or something less than one-half its yearly value.

The tiny Agua Caliente band of Indians sits on top of some of the most valuable land in the country: over 600 acres in the heart of Palm Springs. In the late '50s, the BIA, reacting to pressure from developers, obligingly transferred its jurisdiction over the Agua Caliente to a judge of the State Superior Court in the Palm Springs area who appointed "conservators" and "guardians" to make sure that the Indians would not be swindled as development took place. Ten years later, in 1967, a Riverside Press Enterprise reporter wrote a devastating series of articles showing the incredible fees collected for "protecting" the Agua Calientes. One conservator collected a fee of $9000 from his Indian's $9170 bank account; an Indian minor wound up with $3000 out of a $23,000 income, his guardian taking the rest. The "abdication of responsibility" with which the BIA was charged is surely a mild discription of what happened to the Agua Calientes, who are supposedly the "richest Indians in the world" living on what is regarded as "an ermine-lined reservation."

The Indian Claims Commission was set up in the 1940's to compensate tribes for the lands stolen during the period of white conquest. In the California claims award of 1964, the Indians were given 47 cents an acre, based on the land's fair market value in 1851. The total sum, $29 million, less "offsets" for the BIA's services over the years, still has not been distributed. When it is, the per capita payout will come to about $600, and the poorest Indians in the state, will have to go off welfare to spend it. The BIA opposed an amendment to the Claims Award which would have exempted this money in determining welfare eligibility. The BIA testified that such an amendment constituted preferential treatment, and that it had been struggling for years to get *equal* treatment for the Indian. The amendment failed, and California's Indians will have to pay for a few months bread and rent with the money they are getting in return for the land that was taken from them.

Cases such as these exist in every state where Indian people live. If the Indian is the Vanishing American, it is the BIA's magic which makes him so. California Indians are fortunate only in one respect: they have an OEO-funded legal rights organization, the California Indian Legal Services, which attempts to minimize the depredations. Most Indians have no one to protect them from the agency which is supposed to be their advocate.

At the entrance to the Fort Hall reservation, where La Nada Means grew up, there is a plaque which commemorates the appearance in 1834 of the first white traders and indicates that the Hudson Bay Company later acquired the Fort and made it into an important stopover on the Oregon Trail. But other aspects of the history of Fort Hall are left unmentioned. It is not noted, for instance, that by the time a formal treaty was signed with the Bannock and Northern Shoshone in 1868, the whites who settled this part of Southern Idaho were paying between $25 and $100 for a good Indian scalp.

Today, the approximately 2800 Shoshone-Bannocks live on the 520,000-acre reservation, all that remains of the 1.8 million acres of their land which the treaty originally set aside for their ancestors to keep. The largest single reduction came in 1900, when the government took over 416,000 acres, paying the Indians a little more than $1 an acre for the land. As late as the beginning of World War II, the government took over another 3000 acres to make an airfield. It paid the Indians $10 an acre; after the war, it deeded the land to the city of Pocatello for $1 an acre, for use as a municipal airport. Each acre is now worth $500.

But the big problem on the Fort Hall reservation today is not the loss of large sections of land; rather it is the slow and steady attrition of Indian holdings and their absolute powerlessness to do anything about it. In 1887, the Dawes Allotment Act was passed as a major piece of "progressive" Indian legisation, providing for the break-up of community held reservation land so that each individual Indian would receive his plot of irrigable farming land and some grazing land. The federal government would still hold the land in trust, so it could be sold only with BIA approval, the assumption being that an individual holding would give the Indian incentive to be a farmer and thus ease him into American agricultural patterns. Fort Hall shows that the law had quite different effects.

Today, some of these orginal allotments are owned by anywhere from two to 40 heirs. Because of the complexity of kinship relationships, some Indian people own fractional interests in several of these "heirship lands" but have no ground that is all their own. These lands are one of the symbols of the ambiguity and inertia that rule at Fort Hall. As Edward Boyer, a former chairman of the tribal council, says, "Some of the people, they might want to exchange interest in the land or buy some of the other heirs out so they can have a piece of ground to build a house on and do some farming. Also, a lot of us would like the tribe to buy these lands up and then assign them to the young people who don't have any place of their own. But the BIA has this policy of leasing out these lands to the white farmers. A lot of the time the owners don't even know about it."

The BIA at Fort Hall doesn't like the idea of any Indian lands laying idle. And the land is rich, some of the best potato-growing land there is. Its value and its yield are increasing every year. Driving through the reservation, you can't avoid being struck by the green symmetry of the long cultivated rows and by the efficiency of the army of men and machinery working them. The only trouble is that the men are white, and the profits from Fort Hall's rich land all flow out of the Indian community. The BIA is like any technocracy: it is more interested in "efficient" use than in proper use. The most "efficient" way for Fort Hall's land to be used is by white industrialist-farmers with capital. Thus the pattern has been established: white lessees using Indian land, irrigating with Indian water, and then harvesting with bracero workers.

All leases must be approved by the BIA Superintendent's office; they may be and are given without the consent of the Indians who own the land. The BIA has also allowed white lessees to seek "consents" from the Indians, which in effect provide for blank leases, the specific terms to be filled in later on. The BIA authorizes extremely long leases of the land. This leads to what a recent field study of Fort Hall, conducted by the Senate Subcommittee on Indian Education, calls "small fortunes" for white developers: "One non-Indian in 1964 leased a large tract of Indian land for 13 years at \$.30-\$.50/acre/year. While the lease did stipulate that once the lessee installed sprinkler irrigation the annual rent would rise to \$1.50-\$2.00/acre, Indians in 1968 could have demanded \$20-\$30 for such land. Meanwhile, the independent University Agriculture Extension Service estimates that such potato operations bring the non-Indian lessee an annual *net* profit of \$200 per acre." In addition, these leases are usually given by the BIA on a non-competitive, non-bidding basis to assure "the good will of the surrounding community." Fort Hall has rich and loamy land, but Indian people now work less than 17 per cent of it themselves and the figure is declining.

The power of white farmer-developers and businessmen within the local Bureau of Indian Affairs office is a sore point with most people at Fort Hall. They have rich lands, but theirs is one of the poorest reservations. They are told that much revenue comes both to the tribe and to individuals as a result of the BIA farm and mine leasing program, yet they know that if all the revenues were divided up the yield would be about \$300 per capita a year. But for some of them, men like Joseph "Frank" Thorpe, Jr., the question of farming and mining leases is academic. Thorpe was a successful cattleman until BIA policies cut down the herds; now he is in the business of letting other people's cattle graze on his land.

Livestock are something of a fixation with Thorpe. He comes from a people who were proud horesemen, and he owns an Apaloosa mare and a couple of other horses. As he drives over the reservation, he often stops to look at others' cattle. In the basement of his home are several scrapbooks filled with documents tracing the destruction of the cattle business at Fort Hall. There is a yellowing clipping from the Salt Lake City Tribune of November 4, 1950, which says: "Fort Hall Indians have been more successful in cattle raising then any other activity. Theirs is the oldest Indian Cattleman's Association in the country. Association members raise more than 10,000 head of purebred herefords, and plan gradually to increase the herd . . . ." That was how it was 20 years ago. Thorpe, just back from war-time duty with the Marines, worked his herd and provided jobs for many of his kinsmen; the future was promising. Yet by 1958, there were only 3000 head of Indian owned cattle left, and today there are only ten families still involved in full-time cattle operation.

"Around the early '50s," Thorpe says, "the BIA decided that the Indians who'd been using tribal grazing lands without paying a grazing fee were going to be charged. The BIA also made us cattle people set up a sinking fund to pay grazing fees in advance. The bills just got higher and higher, and pretty soon we found we had to start selling off our seed stock to pay them."

Less than 30 per cent of all Fort Hall Indians are permanently employed today. Men like Frank Thorpe once had a going business that harked back to the old times and also provided jobs on the reservation. The BIA had decided that the best use for Fort Hall land was farming; it removed the Indians' cattle from trust status, which meant they could be sold, and began the accelerated program of leasing Indian lands to whites that is still in effect today.

Thorpe spends a good deal of time driving his dust-covered station wagon along the reservation's unpaved roads. A former tribal chairman, he spends much time checking up on the BIA and trying to function as a sort of ombudsman. He drives slowly down the dirt highways where magpies pick at the remains of rabbits slaughtered by cars. He points out where white farmers have begun to crop-dust their leased fields from airplanes. "The game, rabbits and pheasants and all, is disappearing," he says. "Our Indian people here rely on them for food, but the animals are dying out because of the sprays. And sometimes our kids get real sick. These sprays, they drift over and get in the swimming holes. The kids get real bad coughs and sometimes rashes all over their bodies."

Near the BIA agency office on the reservation sits a squat, weathered concrete building. "That's the old blouse factory," he says. "The BIA cooked up this deal where some outfit from Salt Lake City came in here to start a garment plant. The tribe put up the money for the factory, about $30,000, and in return the Salt Lake people were going to hire Indians and train them to sew. It lasted for about a year, and now we've still got the building. The last few years, they've used it to store the government surplus food that a lot of Indians get."

The old blouse factory is one symbol of the despair that has seized Fort

Hall. Thorpe points out another one nearby. It is known as a "holding center," and it is a place for Fort Hall Indians who are suspected of being suicidal. The reservation has one of the highest suicide rates in the nation. Last year there were 35 attempts, mostly among the 18-25 age group. Many of them occurred in the nearby Blackfoot City Jail.

Blackfoot town authorities, embarrassed by the number of Indian suicides which have occurred in their jail, now use the holding facility at Fort Hall. It is headed by John Bopp, a former Navy man who is the public health officer on the reservation. "I guess kids here just feel that their future is cut off," he says. "A lot of them are dropouts and rejects from schools. They look around and see their elders pretty down-trodden. They get angry, but the only thing they can do is take it out on themselves. From reading some of their suicide notes, I'd say that they see it as an honorable way out of a bad situation."

"The young people," says Thorpe, "they're our only hope. They've got to clean things up here. But a lot of our young guys, they've just given up." The human resources at Fort Hall, like the land, seem to be slipping away. The best interpretation that could be placed on the BIA's role in it all is to use the words of a teacher at nearby Idaho State College who says that they are "guardians of the poorhouse."

There are other reservations that seem to be in better shape. One is the mammoth Navajo reservation, whose 25,000 square miles reach into portions of Arizona, New Mexico, Utah and Colorado. On the one hand, it too is a place of despair: many of the 120,000 Navajos live in shocking poverty, doing a little subsistence farming and sheep-raising, suffering severe discrimination when they go outside the reservation for a job, and being preyed upon by the white traders and the exotic diseases which infest the reservation. But it is also a place of hope: Navajo-land is rich in resources—coal, oil, uranium, and other minerals—and the tribe gets about $30 million a year from rents and royalties. While this would come to less than $1000 a year if distributed to each family, the Navajos have tried, and to some extent succeeded, in using it as seed money to begin a small but growing series of tribal industries—a sawmill, a handcrafts center, a tourist motel—which provide valuable jobs and income organized around the tribal community.

Private enterprise has also come onto the reservation, epitomized by the large Fairchild Industries plant. There has been much discussion of giving tax incentives to get industry to locate on reservations all over the country, but in general little has come of it. Of an estimated 10,000 jobs opened up by industries on Indian lands, more than half of them have been filled by whites. On the Navajo reservation, however, the tribe has seen to it that practically all the employees hired are Indian, and it seems like a good beginning. Everything there, in fact, appears to be on the upswing; the Navajos seem to be the one tribe that is beginning to solve its problems. This, however, is an oversimplification.

As far as private enterprise is concerned, the plants are mainly defense-oriented: they use federal money for job training and then work on a cost-plus basis. In effect, the government is underwriting private profit, when the same money could have gone into setting up community business. The Navajos do get about 1000 jobs, but they are generally low-paying and are given to women, thus destroying the ecology of the Indian family.

Roughly the same thing applies to the rapid development of their natural resources. The way in which these resources are exploited—be it strip-mining or otherwise—depends on the desires of the businesses exploiting them, not on what the Navajos want or need. One result is that the Navajos have no way of planning the development of resources for their own future needs as a community. Navajos get royalties, but private concerns off the reservation get the profits (as well as the depletion allowances, though it is Navajo resources which are being depleted). Indian people have often brought up the possibility of joint economic development of their reservation with the help of private firms. This is always rejected by the BIA, which has an age-old bias against "socialistic" tribal enterprise as well as a very contemporary regard for big business.

The Navajos are seemingly doing well, but their environment is in the hands of others who are interested only in revenue, and not in the Indians' future. The Navajos are thankful, however, for short-term gains, which most tribes don't have; and they have no choice but to leave tomorrow up to the BIA. As anthropologist David Aberle has pointed out, "Let us suppose that we cut a cross-section through the reservation territory . . . and make a rapid-motion picture of the flow of population, money and resources . . . . We would see oil, helium, coal, uranium, and vanadium draining off into the surrounding economy; we would see rents and royalties flowing into the tribal treasury, but, of course, major profits accruing to the corporations exploiting the reservation. We would see the slow development of roads, water for stock and drinking, government facilities, and so forth, and a flow of welfare funds coming in, to go out again via the trader. The net flow of many physical resources would be outward; the flow of profits would be outward; and the only major increases to be seen would be population, with a minor increment in physical facilities and consumer goods. This is the picture of a colony."

The BIA is an easy organization to whip. Its abuses are flagrant, and the Indians it is charged with protecting are in great jeopardy. But if places like the Navajo reservation resemble a colony, the BIA is no more than a corps of colonial officers whose role is not to make policy but rather to carry it out. It is impossible not to feel that the Bureau itself has, over the years, taken on the most outstanding feature of the Indians it administers: their utter lack of power. It could make life on the reservation less complicated and cruel and establish some provisions for the Indians' cultural future, but it could never solve the larger issues that lie behind federal Indian policy. The BIA is only a unit within the Department of Interior, and not a very important one at that—certainly nothing like the powerful Bureaus of Land Management and Reclamation. It is the Department of Interior itself which is involved in the big power moves in Indian affairs. As trustees both for the Indians' private trust lands and for public trust lands, it is involved in an irremediable conflict of interst which it solves by taking from the red man's vanishing domains.

The Navajo reservation is mainly arid, and alkaline deposits gather at the foot of the small hills like snowdrifts. Here, as on other reservations, water is a precious asset, and groundwater is minimal. And when the tribal council recently almost gave away the Navajo's rights to the Colorado River, it didn't do so willingly or with forethought; it was conned.

The population of the Colorado River Basin has exploded during this century, and there has been much feuding among the various states over water. The 1922 Colorado River Compact apportioned the Colorado River water between the Upper Basin states (Colorado, Utah, Wyoming, New Mexico and Arizona) and those of the Lower Basin (California, Nevada, and again, Arizona). After the Supreme Court water decision of 1963, Arizona conceived an ingenious plan to use the water it had been allotted: the annual 50,000 acre-feet of Upper Basin it had been awarded would be used for power to pump its Lower Basin water (2.8 million acre-feet per year), into the gigantic Central Arizona Project, thus irrigating much of the state and providing for its industrial development. The only thing standing in the way of this plan was the Navajos.

Water rights are one of the few Indian prerogatives laid out in clear judicial terms. They are considered an intrinsic part of the reservation the Indians occupy, and the so-called Winters Doctrine, most recently validated in *California vs. Arizona,* specifies that Indians have priority in the use of waters adjacent to, surrounding, or underneath their land, and that upstream and downstream non-Indian users can have only that which is left over after Indian needs are fulfilled. These rights are guaranteed, and not subject to some "use it or lose it" free for all.

The Navajos have never yet asserted a claim to the Colorado River because their underdevelopment has not required it. But if and when they do, most water lawyers feel that their award could be very large, especially since a much smaller group of Indian tribes on the lower Colorado was awarded one million annual acre-feet in 1963 in *California vs Arizona.* The Navajos could, in fact, probably get enough of the Colorado to turn their reservation into an oasis. For this reason, and because their potential rights could destroy Arizona's plan for using the water it had been awarded (not to mention the whole basis for the apportionment of water among the Upper and Lower basin states), the Navajo tribal council was persuaded, in December 1968, to waive virtually all rights to the River "for the lifetime of the [pumping] plant, or for the next 50 years, whichever occurs first." In return for passing this resolution, the council received some minor considerations, including a $125,000 grant for its new Navajo Community College. The deal was presented casually as an administrative courtesy with adequate compensation, and the tribe was not aware of what lay behind it.

Actually, the Navajos were caught in the middle of some high level maneuvers. Wayne Aspinal, congressman from Colorado and chairman of the House Subcommittee on Interior and Insular Affairs, had made it clear to the Department of Interior that he would kill legislation funding the Central Arizona Project unless this waiver of the Navajos' Upper Basin Claim—which could affect his own state—was obtained. By the same token, then Secretary of the Interior Stuart Udall was committed to the Central

Arizona Project which, among other things, would benefit his own home state. Thus it was he who had the resolution drafted and sent to the tribal council via the local BIA superintendent's office.

All of this would probably have gone unchallenged, perhaps to be discovered several years later, if it hadn't been for the OEO-funded legal rights organization on the reservation. This group, the DNA (the acronym derived from the Navajo phrase meaning "economic revitalization of the people"), has been a constant irritation to those who are accustomed to raiding Navajo resources, and it has earned both a large grassroots following and the enmity of the BIA-influenced tribal hierarchy. The DNA found out about the politics behind the waiver last Spring, documented its implication for the Navajos' future, and by early summer was able to persuade the tribal council to rescind its resolution.

The Fort Mojaves of California are currently involved in another fight related to the Colorado River. They have learned, over the last few months, the truth of the maxim widely quoted in California parapolitics: "Water is the name of the game." The Fort Mojaves woke up one morning to find that the State of California, working in concert with the Interior Department Bureau of Land Management, had swindled them out of 1500 acres of invaluable river frontage.

The state had had its eyes on this acreage for many years. It first tried to grab it in 1910, using provisions of the Swamp and Overflow Act of 1850 (which allows swampland created by a river to be placed under state jurisdiction). This initial attempt failed, as did others over the years. Then, early in 1967, the state, supported by the Bureau of Land management, finally succeeded in obtaining the land, again citing the Swamp and Overflow Act because its regular powers of eminent domain did not apply to tribal land. The Mojaves didn't even know that hearings on the matter were taking place; they found out that their land had been confiscated only several months afterward, and then it was by accident.

The acreage claimed by California is clearly too high to have ever been a swamp. Moreover, in 1850 when the Swamp and Overflow Act applied, the wild Colorado River's course ran nowhere near the 1500 supposedly swampy acres, having been "channelized" into its present regular course only in the early 1940's. Independent hydrologists' studies have proven conclusively that the contested area was never part of the river bed.

The state is driven to assert fraudulent claims to land in this apparently low-value desert area, just as Interior is bound to back them up, because of their fear that the Mojaves will develop the area. Private developers are eager to come in: they feel that the Colorado River area will become invaluable, especially as Southern California's population spills outward in search of recreation space. Indian water rights are the prime water rights and developers know that even if there is a water shortage, the Indians will get their allotment first because of the Winters Doctrine, spelled out in *California vs. Arizona.*

The state of California and the Bureau of Land Management, reacting to pressure from the powerful Metropolitan Water District of Southern California, do not want this development to take place, even though it is a key to the Indians' future survival. They fear a water shortage and they are fighting it in the easiest way—by confiscating the prior water rights attached to Indian land out of the Indians' hands.

Behind the machinations of the BIA and the grander larcenies of the Department of Interior stands the Indians' final enemy, that vague sense of doom called federal policy. It has always been sinister, and no less so today than in the days when Indian tribes were nearly annihilated by the white man's gifts of blankets saturated in smallpox. The current mode of attack began in the 1950's, with by far the most ominous title in the lexicon of Indian affairs: termination. Its objectives were stated innocuously in a 1953 act of Congress: "It is the policy of Congress, as rapidly as possible to make the Indians within the United States subject to the same privileges and responsibilities as are applicable to other citizens of the United States, to end their status as wards of the United States, and to grant them all of the rights and prerogatives pertaining to American citizenship . . . ." Cultural assassination always comes cloaked in such altruisms, and the crucial phrase, "to end their status as wards of the United States," was neatly circumscribed by florid rhetoric. But that phrase was the heart of the resolution, and its impact was disastrous.

Over the last two decades, the Indian has learned that he must fear most those who want to eliminate the Bureau of Indian Affairs and who make pompous statements about it being time "for this country to get out of the Indian business." A hundred and fifty years ago, perhaps, attaining such equilibrium with the red man would have been laudable; but America got into the Indian business for good when it stole a continent and put its inhabitants in land-locked jails. While the Indian knows that the BIA works against him most of the time, he also realizes its symbolic value as the embodiment of promises made in the treaties which secure his land and culture. Indian people and lands have been, and continue to be, terribly damaged by their relationship to the federal government. But their federal trust status guarantees their Indian-ness. And if it is terminated, they know there will be nothing left to mismanage.

The reservations which were actually terminated as a result of this sudden shift in federal policy in the '50s provide ample warning. The Minominees of Wisconsin, for instance, whose termination began in 1954 and was completed in 1961, had a stable pattern of life which was destroyed. They owned a thriving tribally-run sawmill. They had a hospital and other community services; they had a fairly large tribal bank account. Then came termination, which made the Minominees citizens of Wisconsin and nothing more. The hospital had to close down because it didn't meet state standards; the tribal bank account was doled out to the tribesmen in per capita payments, which were quickly dissipated. The sawmill became a corporation and floundered because of mismanagement, thereby no longer providing the Minominees with jobs. The Indians were supposed to become just like everyone else in Wisconsin, but today they still stand apart as among the poorest people in the state. Much of their land, which was not taxable when held in trust, has been sold at forced auctions to make up defaulted state property taxes.

Another classic case of termination is that of the Klamaths of Oregon. As part of the proceedings in 1954, their richly—forested reservation was sold off and the receipts distributed equally among enrolled members of the tribe. The payout came to over $40,000 per person, and even before it was made the predators began to descend, offering high-interest loans and a treasure house of consumer goods. A few years after termination was accomplished, many of the Klamaths were destitute and on welfare; they had no land left, no money and no future. As one member of the tribe said, "My grandchildren won't have anything, not even the right to call themselves Indian."

Because of the disasters it caused, termination is now "voluntary," although the Congressional resolution which authorized it has yet to be rescinded. Temporarily, at least, it has taken a backseat to the New Frontierish strategies like luring private enterprise onto the reservation and allocating meager OEO funds. However, today there are still tribes in the process of termination—several small ones in California and the Colvilles of Washington—and no attempt is made to stop the misinformation given Indians about the benefits that will result from such an option. Nor will termination ever disappear for good until Indians hold in their own hands the life and death powers over their communities which others now wield. Every time an Indian is "successfully" relocated in a city far from his people, it is a kind of termination, as it is when a plot of ground or the rights to water slip out of his hands. It is not necessary for Indian people to have Secretary of Interior Hickel tell them that they should "cut the cord" that binds them to their reservation, to know that termination exists as the final solution to the Indian Problem.

Strangled in bureaucracy, swindled out of lands, forcibly alienated from his own culture, the Indian continues to be victimized by the white man's symbolism: he has been both loved and hated to death. On the one hand, the white looked out at him from his own constricted universe of acquisition and grasping egocentrism and saw a Noble Savage, an innocent at peace with his world. Here was a relic of a better time, to be protected and preserved. But on the other hand the white saw an uncivilized creature possessing, but not exploiting, great riches; the vision was conjured up of the Murdering Redskin whose bestiality provided the justification for wiping him out and taking his land. The Indian's "plight" has always inspired recurrent orgies of remorse, but never has it forced us to digest the implications of a nation and culture conceived in genocide. We act as if the blood-debt of the past cannot be canceled until the Indian has no future; the guiltier he has made us, the more frantic have been the attempts to make him disappear.

Yet, having paid out almost everything he has, the Indian has survived the long exercise in white schizophrenia. And there are some, like Hopi mystic Thomas Banyaka, who give out prophecies that the red man will still be here long after whites have been destroyed in a holocaust of their own making.

JAMES G. ANDERSON, DWIGHT SAFAR: THE INFLUENCE OF DIFFERENTIAL COMMUNITY PERCEPTIONS ON THE PROVISION OF EQUAL EDUCATIONAL OPPORTUNITIES

ABSTRACT

Through extensive interviews with community members and school personnel in two multicultural Southwestern communities, the authors of this study attempt to demonstrate the importance of perceptions and attitudes in the provision of equal educational opportunity for Spanish-American and Indian children. The findings demonstrate a ubiquitous feeling that Spanish-American and Indian children are less capable of achieving desirable goals than are their Anglo contemporaries. This lack of achievement of the minority groups appears, in a large part, to be perceived as a lack of innate ability and support rather than as the fault of inadequate school programs. Moreover, this feeling of inferiority appears to be internalized by the minority groups themselves, thus creating an insidious negative climate for their children.

EQUAL EDUCATIONAL OPPORTUNITIES[1]

Two recent studies commissioned by the United States Office of Education in response to Section 402 of the Civil Rights Act of 1964[2] were designed to assess the availability of equal educational opportunities for children from the various racial, ethnic, and religious groups. These and other studies show that four distinct criteria have been employed to assess inequality of educational opportunity.[3]

First, the availability of equal educational opportunities for children from various minority groups has been determined by comparing physical facilities, curricula offered, characteristics of the instructional and administrative staffs, teacher-pupil ratios, per pupil expenditures, teachers' salaries, etc.[4]

A second approach has been to ascertain the degree of compliance with the Supreme Court decision of 1954[5] by determining the proportion of each minority group presently attending desegregated schools.[6]

With the belated realization of the extent to which a student's background drastically affects his performance in school, a third approach has been adopted, namely, to assume that students from culturally impoverished homes are *de facto* subject to unequal educational opportunities.[7]

Finally, a number of authors state that equality of educational opportunity will exist only when the graduates of the schools are equally well prepared to compete for jobs, income, status, and housing.[8]

Source: Reprinted by permission from *Sociology of Education* 40 (Summer 1967), 219-230.

These last two approaches at best call attention to the difficulties encountered by minority group children in the schools; at worst add little to our understanding as to why such *de facto* inequality exists. On the other hand, the quantitative approach, while enlightening in many respects, neglects less tangible phenomena such as differential attitudes and perceptions of members of the community and of educators regarding racial or ethnic characteristics and the efficacy of educational programs. Although intangible, these attitudes and perceptions may have a significant bearing upon the school's ability to provide equal educational opportunities.

Perceptions of a phenomenon or condition often play a more important role in determining the behavior of the perceiver than the conditions as they may appear to an independent observer. Furthermore, in our estimation, awareness of the perceptions held by the racial ethnic groups represented in the schools is paramount in the provision and assessment of equality of education.

The perspective draws on the thinking of perceptual psychologists such as Combs and Snygg,[9] who view behavior as based largely on an individual's perception of the situation, and of himself. The individual develops a self concept through his interaction with significant other persons in his environment and through their evaluation of him and their response to him. He then responds to his environment and to other persons with whom he has relationships in terms of this self-concept.[10]

For most children, members of their immediate family are the major socializing agents. Attitudes, values, and experiences within the family profoundly influence children's conceptions of themselves, as well as their performance in the school.[11]

After the home the school appears to have a significant effect on the development of a child's self-perception. Studies by Jersild,[12] Reeder,[13] and Stevens[14] all have demonstrated a relationship between student achievement and positive self-image. Other studies have shown that children's perceptions of their teachers' attitudes toward them is related to their self-image, academic achievement, and classroom behavior.[15] As Clark[16] has suggested and the Coleman-Campbell study demonstrates, minority group children begin school at a distinct educational disadvantage, encumbered by a lack of middle class manners and self-control, lacking adult models with whom to identify, deficient in cultural experiences that profoundly affect aptitude and achievement measures. Consequently, they perform at a much lower level than their Anglo classmates, thus fulfilling the expectations of their parents and teachers and guaranteeing their failure in the school and ultimately in society.

As a necessary precurser to the provision of equal educational opportunities, however, there must exist an awareness of the "hidden dissuaders"[17] that operate covertly and insidiously within the schools to the detriment of all but the white middle class student. In addition there must be an appreciation of the influence that a child's and his parents' perceptions of his ability and opportunities have on his behavior. Without such an awareness by the public, as well as by educators charged with the responsibility for designing and carrying out the educational program, racial and ethnic inferiority in ability and motivation are blamed for the failure of minority children rather than the inadequacies in the school's programs that subtly and covertly discourage and discriminate against children from these groups.

With these considerations in mind the present study was undertaken.[18] An attempt has been made to explore the perceptions of parents, teachers, school administrators, school board members, and the community at large as to the abilities of children from each of the racial and ethnic groups studied (in this instance Anglo, Spanish-American and Indian). Perceptions of the adequacy of the school program for each of the three groups of children was also an integral part of the study.

Major questions asked were: How does the dominant majority Anglo culture view the abilities of Spanish-American and Indian children in comparison to their own? In turn, how do the Spanish-American and the Indian parents feel about the abilities of their own children in comparison to their Anglo classmate? Is the failure of Spanish-American and Indian children, in contrast to the relative success of Anglo children in school, perceived as a result of differential treatment by teachers and school administrators?[19]   How much of this failure do the members of the three cultural groups and the educators themselves attribute to inadequacies in the school program?

In order to explore these questions, a study was conducted in two South-western communities. Community A is a rural farming community, predominantly Anglo in makeup. Spanish-speaking families and a very few Indian families constitute small minority groups (approximately 13 percent and two percent, respectively, of the total population of 6,000). The bulk of the Indian students who attend the schools reside in a dormitory in the community. The school board, school administration and all but a few teachers are Anglo. The community operates three elementary schools, one junior high school and one senior high school and employs 89 teachers.

Many of the Anglos and Spanish-Americans residing in Community B are employed by the government at one of several military installations. This community is truly biethnic in that 60 percent of the families residing in the community are Spanish-American, the other 40 percent are Anglo. The schools are attended by approximately equal numbers of Anglo, Spanish-American and Indian students who are bussed in from the reservation each day. In this case, the school board consists of one Anglo and four Spanish-American members. The superintendent is Spanish-American, but the other administrators and most of the 63 teachers are Anglo. The school system comprises two elementary, one junior high and one senior high school.

A two-stage cluster sample was drawn of families residing in each community. The relative percentages of Spanish-American and Anglo families selected reflect the ethnic composition of each community and provide evidence for the representativeness of the samples. In Community A a total sample of 73 families was drawn, composed of three percent Indians, 15 percent Spanish-Americans and 82 percent Anglos. Data from the Indian families were not reported since there were only two families

TABLE 1

Community A—Perceptions of the Abilities of Anglo, Spanish-American, and Indian Pupils

Group	N	Ability to Finish High School			Ability to Attend Trade School or College			Ability to Find a Job After High School		
		Anglo pupils	Spanish-American pupils	Indian pupils	Anglo pupils	Spanish-American pupils	Indian pupils	Anglo pupils	Spanish-American pupils	Indian pupils
Spanish-American community	11	4.3[a]	4.2	4.1	3.9	3.6	3.9	4.2	4.1	4.0
Anglo community	60	4.3	4.2	3.9	4.0	3.9	3.7	4.0	3.7	3.4
School board	2	4.0	4.0	4.0	3.5	3.5	3.5	4.0	4.0	4.0
School administration	7	4.0	4.0	3.6	4.0	3.1	3.4	3.9	3.6	3.1
Teachers	32	4.3	4.1	3.9	4.1	3.7	3.5	4.0	3.8	3.5

[a] Mean score based on: 1   2   3   4   5

Low ability   High ability

TABLE 2

Community B—Perceptions of the Abilities of Anglo, Spanish-American, and Indian Pupils

Group	N	Ability to Finish High School			Ability to Attend Trade School or College			Ability to Find a Job After High School		
		Anglo pupils	Spanish-American pupils	Indian pupils	Anglo pupils	Spanish-American pupils	Indian pupils	Anglo pupils	Spanish-American pupils	Indian pupils
Spanish-American community	45	4.4[a]	4.2	4.1	4.2	4.0	3.8	4.0	3.4	3.3
Anglo community	30	4.2	4.1	3.9	4.1	4.0	3.6	3.8	3.7	3.4
School board	5	4.4	4.0	3.6	4.0	3.6	3.0	4.4	4.0	3.8
School administration	4	4.3	4.3	4.0	4.0	4.0	3.8	3.8	3.5	3.0
Teachers	15	4.3	4.3	3.9	3.9	3.8	3.4	3.9	3.9	3.7

[a] Mean score based on: 1   2   3   4   5

Low ability   High ability

interviewed. Sixty percent of the sample of 75 families from Community B were Spanish-American; 40 percent were Anglo.

In both communities all available school board members and school administrators (the superintendent, assistant superintendent, and principals) were interviewed. Also a sample of teachers from each grade level in each school was selected and interviewed.

PERCEPTIONS OF ABILITY

To explore the hypothesis that perceptions of ability have significant effects upon educational programs and subsequent pupil behavior, we examined how different groups in the community perceived the abilities of students from different backgrounds. Members of the several cultural groups, the school board, school administrators, and teachers were asked: "In your opinion, what proportion of the (Anglo, Spanish-American, Indian) children could (finish high school, go on to trade school or college, find a job) if adequate encouragement and assistance were given?" Responses to these questions are presented in Tables 1 and 2 for Communities A and B, respectively.

Two distinct patterns emerge from the data. First, members of *all* groups perceive the Anglo child as *most* capable of achieving these goals, the Spanish-American as less capable, and the Indian as least capable.

The Anglos interviewed attributed the lower ability of the Spanish-American children to a lack of encouragement by parents and a general lack of appreciation for education. At the same time they viewed the Indian as lazy and lacking incentive. A few alluded to the language barrier faced by many of these Indian children who do not learn to speak English until they enter the elementary school.

The Spanish-American families interviewed reflected many of the same sentiments regarding members of their own culture and the Indians'. They too felt that many Spanish-American families fail to appreciate the need for formal education and, consequently, do not encourage their children. They viewed the Indian child as having inferior mental ability and as lacking incentive due to their dependency on the Federal Government.

Interpretation of these findings suggests that a "self-fulfilling prophecy" might well be operating in these communities; that is, minority group members think of themselves as inferior and subsequently fail in school, thus reinforcing their perception. Minority groups, such as the Spanish-American and the Indian, who consistently do poorly in school and who are subtly discriminated against by the present system of education (essentially designed for the high-ability, college-bound, middle class, Anglo student), may internalize their feelings of inferiority and come to feel that their failure is deserved. This phenomenon has frequently been observed among Negroes in the South; it is significant that the same pattern obtains for minority groups in the Southwest.

This hierarchical pattern of perceived pupil abilities is reflected by the school board, school administration, and teachers in both communities. In addition, school personnel are predominantly Anglo and are, in a large part, responsible for the educational programs offered in these communities. Consequently one effect of the failure of students from minority groups may be the reinforcement of a stereotyped view of the Spanish-American and Indian as inferior in ability and motivation, rather than an appreciation of the failure of the school to provide adequate programs for these children. Moreover, with both teachers and the community at large responding to the minority students as though such students are unlikely to succeed in the schools,[20] and with the minority students tending to think of themselves as others think of them, it is not surprising to find a high drop-out rate and a low level of achievement among Spanish-American and Indian children.

The second pattern that emerges is a tendency for all groups to see pupils as most capable of completing high school, less capable of attending trade school or college, and least capable of finding a job after high school. This ordering realistically reflects the current shortage of jobs in the area that do not require considerable post-high school preparation. One reaction of minority group members may well be "why complete high school when one's ability to find a job is questionable?" By contrast, the middle class Anglo values post-high school preparation and is not overly concerned about difficulties in finding a job after completing his education. The same self-assurance is not evident among the parents of pupils from minority groups.

PERCEPTIONS OF ENCOURAGEMENT GIVEN TO STUDENTS

Encouragement given to students by teachers, counselors, and school administrators is generally considered to be an important factor in their success or failure in school. However, whether or not parents and their children feel that all students receive the same assistance and encouragement may be as important an influence on pupil performance as the actual circumstances. In order to determine the extent to which persons in the community and the school staff feel that differential treatment is accorded children from the three ethnic groups, the following questions were posed: "In your opinion, to what extent are the (Anglo, Indian, Spanish-American) children encouraged by teachers, counselors, and school administrators to do well in the schools?" The responses of the various groups within Communities A and B are shown in Tables 3 and 4, respectively.

The community at large and the school personnel in Community A feel that children from Spanish-American and Indian families receive less encouragement than their Anglo classmates. The greatest disparity in encouragement is perceived by the school administration. Quite to the contrary, the school board members interviewed feel that all of the children are equally encouraged. Moreover, they believe that all students are encouraged to a much greater extent than did any of the other groups interviewed.

TABLE 3

Community A
Perceptions of Encouragement Given to Anglo, Spanish-American
and Indian Pupils by School Personnel

Group	N	Anglo Pupils	Spanish-American Pupils	Indian Pupils
Spanish-American community	11	4.4[a]	4.0	4.3
Anglo community	60	4.2	4.0	4.0
School board	2	4.5	4.5	4.5
School administration	7	4.3	3.7	3.9
Teachers	32	4.2	4.0	4.1

[a] Mean score based on:

	1	2	3	4	5	
	Little encouragement				Much encouragement	

TABLE 4

Community B
Perceptions of Encouragement Given to Anglo, Spanish-American
and Indian Pupils by School Personnel

Group	N	Anglo Pupils	Spanish-American Pupils	Indian Pupils
Spanish-American community	45	4.3[a]	4.0	3.9
Anglo community	30	4.1	4.2	4.0
School board	5	4.4	3.4	3.2
School administration	4	4.5	4.5	4.8
Teachers	15	4.3	4.2	4.3

[a] Mean score based on:

	1	2	3	4	5	
	Little encouragement				Much encouragement	

Within Community B, a quite different picture is revealed. There, the school board, four out of five of whom are Spanish-American, feels rather strongly that Spanish-American and Indian pupils are not given the encouragement that Anglo pupils get. Also in contrast with Community A, the school administrators and teachers in Community B see little difference in the encouragement given to students from different backgrounds. Where the board was sensitive to differences in the treatment afforded minority groups, the educators saw equal treatment; where the board members saw inequality, the teachers saw equality.

PERCEPTIONS OF THE ADEQUACY OF SCHOOL PROGRAMS

Educators have argued that the school reflects the Anglo middle class culture. Is this argument substantiated by perceptions held by the Anglo community, the minority communities, members of the school board, school administrators, and teaching staff? In view of the respective groups' differential perceptions of pupil ability and encouragement, what perceptions do they have concerning the adequacy of their school program?

Tables 5 and 6 contain the responses for the various groups in Communities A and B, respectively, to a set of questions which asked: "In your opinion, how adequate is the school's program of studies for (Anglo, Indian, Spanish-American) children?" The disparity in perceptions between the Anglo and Spanish-American segments of Community B is manifested again. The Spanish-Americans on the whole feel that the school program is designed more for the Anglo student, while the Anglo community sees little difference in the adequacy of the school program for the three groups of children. Generally, however, all of the community groups perceive relatively little difference in the adequacy of the educational program available to pupils from the three ethnic groups.

Moreover, the Spanish-American families interviewed in both communities evidenced the highest level of satisfaction with the present educational program despite the fact that their children do poorly in the schools in comparison with their Anglo classmates. In view of previous

TABLE 5

Community A

Perceptions of the Adequacy of the School Program for Anglo,
Spanish-American, and Indian Pupils

Group	N	Anglo Pupils	Spanish-American Pupils	Indian Pupils
Spanish-American community	11	2.6[a]	2.6	2.6
Anglo community	60	2.5	2.3	2.3
School board	2	2.0	2.0	2.0
School administration	7	2.2	2.0	1.7
Teachers	32	2.4	2.2	2.1

[a] Mean score based on: 1   2   3
                        Adequate   Inadequate

TABLE 6

Community B

Perceptions of the Adequacy of the School Program for Anglo,
Spanish-American, and Indian Pupils

Group	N	Anglo Pupils	Spanish-American Pupils	Indian Pupils
Spanish-American community	45	2.5[a]	2.3	2.2
Anglo community	30	2.4	2.4	2.4
School board	5	2.0	1.8	1.6
School administration	4	2.3	2.0	1.5
Teachers	15	2.0	1.9	1.6

[a] Mean score based on: 1   2   3
                        Adequate   Inadequate

findings that demonstrate a ubiquitous lack of confidence in the ability of Spanish-American children to achieve the same goals expected of Anglo children it may be that the Spanish-Americans and Indians in the Southwest attribute the failure of their children in the schools to a lack of ability rather than to inadequacies in the schools programs.

On the other hand, school administrators and teachers in both communities perceive considerable variance in the adequacy of the school program for students from different backgrounds. For the most part, they perceive the educational program to be most adequate for Anglo pupils, less adequate for Spanish-American pupils, and least adequate for Indian pupils. It seems obvious that members of the school administration and teaching staff have been unable to communicate their discontent with the present educational programs to the community or, in Community A, even to the school board.

CONCLUSION

In interpreting these findings, one is struck by the similarity in perceptions in two quite disparate communities at opposite ends of the state. The responses are markedly similar, even though the Spanish-Americans and Indians are a decided minority in the one community while the other is split evenly into Spanish-American and Anglo segments. In both communities, there is an almost unanimous feeling that Spanish-American and Indian children are less capable of achieving desirable goals and ultimately becoming productive members of society than are their Anglo contemporaries.

This lack of ability of the minority groups appears to be perceived by Anglo members of the communities studied as a lack of innate ability and family support rather than as the fault of an inadequate school program that provides few opportunities to compensate for the educational disadvantage of these children, many of whom can barely speak English when they enter the schools. We see again the stereotyped view of Spanish-Americans and Indians as little interested in education, as coming from families that place little value on education and do little to assist or support their children's attempts in school, and, in the case of the Indian in particular, as content to live as wards of the Federal Government.

A belief in their inferiority appears to be internalized by the minority groups themselves, with unhappy consequences for their children. With minority-group parents reflecting the same negative valuation of their children's ability to achieve at the level of the dominant Anglo child as that held by school administrators, teachers, and the public at large, is it any wonder that these children are perceived as evidencing little motivation, interest and perseverance in the schools? Are we asking too much of a child to continue working toward vague educational goals and gainful employment when most of the significant adults in his life—parents, adult friends, teachers, counselors—all evidence a lack of confidence in his ability to achieve the same goals as his Anglo classmates?[21]

Our findings in the Southwest are remarkably similar to those of Martin Deutsch in New York which he summarizes in the following statement:

> The thesis here is that the lower-class child enters the school situation so poorly prepared to produce what the school demands that initial failures are almost inevitable, and the school experience becomes negatively rather than positively reinforced. Thus the child's experience in school does nothing to counteract the invidious influence to which he is exposed in his slum, and sometimes segregated, neighborhoods.
>
> ... We know that it is difficult for all peoples to span cultural discontinuities, and yet we make little if any effort to prepare administrative personnel or teachers and guidance staff to assist the child in this transition from one cultural context to another. This transition must have serious psychological consequences for the child, and probably plays a major role in influencing his later perceptions of other social institutions as he is introduced to them.
>
> ... The frustration inherent in not understanding, not succeeding, and not being stimulated in the school—although being regulated by it, creates a basis for the further development of negative self-images and low evaluations of individual competencies.... No matter how the parents might aspire to a higher achievement level for their child, their lack of knowledge as to the operational implementation, combined with the child's early failure experiences in the school, can so effectively attenuate confidence in his ability ever to handle competently challenge in the academic area, that the child loses all motivation.[22]

In both communities the educators are less sanguine about the adequacy of the schools' programs for Spanish-American and Indian children than are either the Anglo or the minority group members of the community. For the most part, however, they seem unable to communicate their feelings to the communities at large or, in one instance, even to the school board, much less to translate this dissatisfaction into action. The result of this non-awareness of these differential community perceptions appears to be educational programs that are ill suited for Spanish-American and Indian children who enter school at a distinct educational disadvantage. Because of this gulf between the communities and their professional educators, the schools fail to assist the minority child in overcoming his educational handicaps and little is done to offer true equality of educational opportunity.

NOTES

1 We are indebted to Drs. Darrell S. Willey, Alfred M. Potts, and Glenn M. Linden for their assistance, advice, and criticism. Also we wish to express our appreciation to Miss Ann Simmons and Mr. Ellis Scott for supervising the coding of the data, and to Mrs. Ann Bixby for editing the manuscript.

2 The first of these is the massive *Equality of Educational Opportunity* by James S. Coleman and Ernest Q. Campbell (Washington, D.C.: Government Printing Office), OE–38001, 1966 which surveyed the extent to which equal educational opportunities are being provided all over the United States. The second study, an adjunct to the first one, involved a study of school integration in ten American cities by Raymond W. Mack. Portions of the data and findings are reported in the publication cited above.

3 These four criteria are identified by Ernest Q. Campbell and James S. Coleman, "Inequalities in Educational Opportunities in the United States," Paper presented at the Annual Meeting of the American Sociological Association, Miami Beach, Florida, August, 1966, pp. 2-3.

4 See, for example, *Equality of Educational Opportunity* (Washington, D.C.: Government Printing Office), OE–38000 Summary, 1966.

5 Brown v. Board of Education of Topeka (Kansas). 347 U.S. 483, 74 Sup. Ct. 686 (1954).

6 See Raymond W. Mack, "School Integration and Social Change," paper presented at the Annual Meeting of the American Sociological Association, Miami Beach, Florida, August, 1966, for details of the study mentioned earlier.

7 Frank Riessman, *The Culturally Deprived Child* (N.Y.: Harper & Row, 1962).

8 *Ibid.*

9 A. W. Combs and D. Snygg, *Individual Behavior* (N. Y.: Harper Brothers, 1959).

10 See, for example, C. R. Rogers, *Client-Centered Therapy*, (Boston: Houghton Mifflin, 1951).

11 For example, a study by Sidney M. Jourard and Richard M. Remy entitled, "Perceived Parental Attitudes, the Self, and Security," *Journal of Consulting Psychology* XIX (October, 1955), pp. 364-366, demonstrated that self-appraisals by children are highly related to their perception of their parents' appraisal of them. Also see Sarene S. Boocock, "Toward a Sociology of Learning: A Selective Review of Existing Research," *Sociology of Education*, XXXIX (Winter, 1966), pp. 1-45, for a review of the literature on the sociological factors related to student achievement in the schools.

12 A. T. Jersild, *"In Search of Self"* (N. Y.: Teachers College Bureau of Publications, Columbia University, 1952).

13 T. A. Reeder, "A Study of Some Relationships Between Level of Self Concept, Academic Achievement and Classroom Adjustment," *Dissertation Abstract*, XV (1955), p. 2472.

14 P. H. Stevens, "An Investigation of the Relationship Between Certain Aspects of Self-Concept Behavior and Students' Academic Achievement," *Dissertation Abstract*, XVI (1956), pp. 2531-2532.

15 Helen H. Davidson and Gerhard Lang, "Children's Perception of Their Teachers' Feelings Toward Them Related to Self-Perception, School Achievement and Behavior," *Journal of Experimental Education*, XXIX (December, 1960), pp. 107-118.

16 Burton Clark, *Educating the Expert Society* (San Francisco: Chandler, 1962).

17 Riessman, *op. cit.*, 19 uses this term for a number of indirect and subtle forms of discrimination in the schools many of which are totally unintentional.

18 The data for this study was collected as part of "An Interdisciplinary
    Institute for the In-Service Training of Teachers and Other School
    Personnel to Accelerate the School Acceptance of Indian, Negro, and
    Spanish-Sepaking Pupils from the Southwest," Contract No. OEC
    4-6-000201-1980, from the Office of Education, Department of
    Health, Education, and Welfare, directed by Dr. Darrell S. Willey, Pro-
    fessor and Head of the Department of Educational Administration,
    New Mexico State University.
19 Data from our own study, not reported here, illustrates the failure of
    Spanish-American and Indian children to achieve at a commensurate level
    with their Anglo classmates much as does the Coleman-Campbell study.
20 In one community, for example, all Indian children are automatically
    placed in low-ability "special education" classes upon entering junior
    high school, even though they may be entering from an elementary
    school on the reservation where their achievement is well above average
    on national norms.
21 This contention is supported by the results of a study by David P.
    Ausubel (et al.), "Perceived Parent Attitudes As Determinants of
    Children's Ego Structure," Child Development, XXV (September,
    1954), pp. 173-183 which found that the level of children's aspira-
    tions, their tolerance of frustration, ideational independence from
    parents, and the maturity of their personalities were all related to the
    children's perceptions of their parents' valuation of them. Also a study
    by Wilbur B. Brookover and Shailer Thomas, "Self-Concept of Ability
    and School Achievement," Sociology of Education, 37 (1963-1964), pp.
    271-278 demonstrated a significant positive relationship between self-
    concept of ability and grade point average. Self-concept of ability in turn
    was significantly related to the perceived evaluation of significant others.
22 Martin Deutsch, "The Disadvantaged Child and the Learning Process,"
    Education in Depressed Areas, A. Harry Passow, editor (N.Y.: Teachers
    College Press, Columbia University, 1963), pp. 163-164, 177.

---

*ALBERT L. WAHRHAFTIG, ROBERT K.
THOMAS:* RENAISSANCE AND REPRES-
SION: THE OKLAHOMA CHEROKEE

A week in eastern Oklahoma demonstrates to most outsiders that the
Cherokee Indians are a populous and lively community: Indians *par
excellence.* Still, whites in eastern Oklahoma unanimously declare the
Cherokees to be a vanishing breed. Prominent whites say with pride, "we're

all a little bit Indian here." They maintain that real Cherokees are about "bred out." Few Cherokees are left who can speak their native tongue, whites insist, and fewer still are learning their language. In twenty years, according to white myth, the Cherokee language and with it the separate and distinctive community that speaks it will fade into memory.

Astonishingly, this pervasive social fiction disguises the presence of one of the largest and most traditional tribes of American Indians. Six rural counties in northeastern Oklahoma contain more than fifty Cherokee settlements with a population of more than 9,500. An additional 2,000 Cherokees live in Indian enclaves in towns and small cities. Anthropologists visiting us in the field, men who thought their previous studies had taught them what a conservative tribe is like, were astonished by Cherokees. Seldom had they seen people who speak so little English, who are so unshakably traditional in outlook.

How can native whites overlook this very identifiable Indian community? The answers, we believe, will give us not only an intriguing insight into the nature of Oklahoma society, but also some general conclusions about the position of other ethnic groups in American society.

This myth of Cherokee assimilation gives sanction to the social system of which Cherokees are a part, and to the position Cherokees have within that system. This image of the vanishing Cherokee in some ways is reminiscent both of the conservative Southern mythology which asserts that "our colored folk are a contented and carefree lot," and of the liberal Northern mythology, which asserts that "Negroes are just like whites except for the color of their skins." The fiction serves to keep Cherokees in place as a docile and exploitable minority population; it gives an official rationale to an existing, historic social system; and it implies that when the Indian Territory, the last Indian refuge, was dissolved, no Indian was betrayed, but all were absorbed into the mainstream.

The roots of modern eastern Oklahoma are in the rural South. Cherokees, and whites, came from the South; Cherokees from Georgia and Tennessee; and whites from Tennessee, Kentucky, Arkansas and southern Illinois.

In the years immediately preceding 1840, Cherokees, forced out of their sacred homelands in Georgia and Tennessee, marched over an infamous "Trail of Tears," and relocated in a new Cherokee Nation in what is now the state of Oklahoma. They created an international wonder: an autonomous Cherokee Nation with its own national constitution, legislature, judiciary, school system, publishing house, international bilingual newspaper, and many other trappings of a prosperous Republic. The Cherokees, who as a people accomplished all this, along with their neighbors, the Creeks, Choctaws, Chicasaws and Seminoles, who followed similar paths, were called the five civilized tribes.

Promising as the Cherokee Nation's future might have seemed, it was plagued by internal controversy from birth. Bitterness between the traditional Ross Party and the Treaty Party was intense. The Ross Party resisted demands for relocating from the South until its followers were finally corralled by the Army; the Treaty Party believed cooperation with the United States Government was the more prudent course for all Cherokees.

The sons and daughters of the Ross Party kept their ancient villages together. They reestablished these in the hollows and rough "Ozark" country of the Indian territory. Hewing new log cabins and planting new garden spots, they hoped to live unmolested by their opponents. They are today's "fullbloods," that is, traditional and Cherokee-speaking Cherokees. On the other hand, descendants of the Treaty Party, who concentrated in the flat bottomlands and prairies they preferred for farming, are now assimilated and functionally white Americans, though fiercely proud of their Cherokee blood.

The Ross Party was the core of the Cherokee tribes. It was an institution which emerged from the experience of people who lived communally in settlements of kinsmen. The Treaty Party was a composite of individuals splintered from the tribal body. There were of course great differences in life style among nineteenth century Cherokee citizens. The Ross men, often well-educated, directed the Cherokee legislators from backwoods settlements. Treaty Party men were more often plantation owners, merchants, entrepreneurs, and professionals—conventional southern gentlemen. The overriding difference between the two factions, however, was between men who lived for their community and men who lived for themselves.

During the 1880's this difference came to be associated not with party but with blood. Geographically separated and ostracized by Ross men, members of the Treaty Party perforce married among the growing population of opportunistic whites who squatted on Indian land, defying U.S. and Cherokee law. The Treaty Party became known as the "mixed blood" faction of the tribe; the Ross Party as "full bloods." These terms imply that miscegenation caused a change of life style, a reversal of the historic events.

By 1907 when the Cherokee Nation was dissolved by Congressional fiat and the State of Oklahoma was created, the mixed bloods were already socially if not politically, part of the white population of the United States. The Ross Party settlements, now the whole of the functionally Cherokee population, are intact but surrounded by an assimilated population of mixed blood Cherokees integrated with white immigrants.

From the 1890s to 1920s, development of this area was astonishingly rapid. A flood of whites arrived. Land was populated by subsistence farmers, small town trade boomed, commercial farming expanded, railroads were built, timber exhausted, petroleum exploited and token industrialization established.

Already shorn of their nation, fullbloods were stunned and disadvantaged by the overnight expansion and growth. Change was rapid, the class system open. Future distinguished elders of small town society arrived as raggedy tots in the back of one-mule wagons. Not only was social mobility easy, few questions were asked about how the newly rich became rich. Incredible land swindles were commonplace. At the turn of the century, every square inch of eastern Oklahoma was alloted to Cherokees; by the 1930s little acreage remained in Indian possession.

The result of this explosive development was a remarkably stratified society, characterized by highly personal relationships, old time rural political machines, Protestant fundamentalism, reverence of free enterprise, and unscrupulous exploitation; in short, a system typical of the rural south.

Superficially, this society appears to be one with the most resourceful at the top, and the unworthy, who let opportunity slip by, at the bottom. In reality, however, the system consists of ranked ethnic groups, rather than classes. The successful old mixed-blood families, now functionally "white," whose self-identification as "Cherokee" is taken as a claim to the venerable status of "original settlers," dominate. Below them are the prosperous whites who "made something of themselves," and at the bottom, beneath the poor country whites, Cherokee "full bloods."

In primitive tribes, myth is a sacred explanation of the creation of the tribe and of its subsequent history. Myth specifies the holy design within which man was set to live. The fiction of Cherokee assimilation illustrates that modern man still uses myth, though differently. For in Oklahoma, the myth of Cherokee assimilation validates the social conditions men themselves have created, justifying the rightness and inevitability of what was done. As Oklahomans see it, the demise of the Cherokee as a people was tragic, albeit necessary. For only thus were individual Cherokees able to share in the American dream. The Oklahoman conceives of his society as an aggregate of individuals ranked by class, with unlimited opportunity for mobility regardless of individual ancestry. The high class position of the old Cherokee mixed-bloods signifies to the Oklahoman that the job of building Oklahoma was well done. The "responsible" Indians made it. The Cherokees, as a single historic people, died without heirs, and rightfully all those who settled on their estate now share in the distribution of its assets. For the culturally Indian individuals remaining, Oklahoma can only hope that they will do better in the future.

Even as the mythology serves to sanctify their high rank position, it insulates whites from the recognition of the Cherokee as a viable but low ranked ethnic community with unique collective aims and interests. Where a real community exists, Oklahomans see only a residue of low status individuals. The myth, by altering perceptions, becomes self-perpetuating.

Paradoxically, the myth of Cherokee assimilation has also contributed to the survival of the Cherokee as a people. To the extent that Cherokees believed the myth, and many did, it was not only an explanation of how the tribe came into the present but a cohesive force. Since the end of the tribal movement led by Redbird Smith, a half century ago, in response to the final pressures for Oklahoma statehood, Cherokees have seemed inert, hardly a living people. Nevertheless, Cherokee communal life persisted, and is in a surprisingly healthy state. Cherokee settlements remain isolated, and if what goes on in them is not hidden, it is calculatedly inconspicuous. For the freedom from interference that it afforded, Cherokees willingly acceded to the notion that the Cherokees no longer exist.

In addition to sanctioning the form of Oklahoma society, the myth also gives credence to basic social and economic institutions. The economy of the area depends on Cherokees and country whites as an inexpensive and permanent labor market. Cherokees are expected to do low paying manual work without complaint. In 1963, Cherokee median per capita income, approximately $500, was less than half the per capita income of neighboring rural whites. In some areas, Cherokees live in virtual peonage; in others, straw bosses recruit Cherokee laborers for irregular work at low pay. Even though Cherokee communities are relatively hidden, Cherokee labor has become an indispensable part of the local economy. Apparently one would think that daily contact of white workers and bosses with these Cherokee laborers might expose the myth of the well-off assimilated Cherokee. On the contrary, the myth prevails because the humble occupations practiced by Cherokees are seen as evidence that Cherokee character is indeed that which the myth of assimilation predicts.

WHITE BLOOD MAKES GOOD INDIANS

Imbedded in the Oklahoma concept of assimilation, is a glaring racism. Typical is the introductory page of a book published in 1938 entitled *A Political History of the Cherokee Nation,* written by Morris Wardell, a professor at the University of Oklahoma.

A selection: "Traders, soldiers, and treaty-makers came among the Cherokees to trade, compel and negotiate. Some of these visitors married Indian women and lived in the Indian villages the remainder of their days. Children born to such unions preferred the open and free life and here grew to manhood and womanhood, never going to the white settlements. This mixture of blood helped to produce strategy and cleverness which made formidable diplomats of many of the Indian leaders."

To white genes go the credit for Sequoyah's genius and John Ross's astuteness, whereas the remaining Cherokee genes contribute qualities that are endearing but less productive. Thus, in a history of the Cherokees published only six years ago, the author, an Oklahoman, says of modern "fullbloods": "They supplement their small income from farms and subsidies from the government with wage work or seasonal jobs in nearby towns or on farms belonging to white men. . . . Paid fair wages, this type of worker usually spends his money as quickly as he makes it on whisky, and on cars, washing machines, and other items that, uncared for, soon fall into necessitous dissuse."

Oklahomans divide the contemporary Cherokees into two categories: those who are progressive and those who are not. The page just quoted continues, "this progressive type of Indian will not long remain in the background of the growing and thriving, and comparatively new, State of Oklahoma." That a viable Indian tribe exists is apparently inconceivable. Either Cherokees are worthy, responsible and assimilating, or they are the dregs: irresponsible, deculturated and racially inferior.

Through mythology, the exploitation of Cherokee labor is redefined into benevolent paternalism. Some patrons have Cherokees deliver their welfare checks to them, deduct from these housing and groceries. Afterwards the remainder is handed over to Cherokee tenants. Unknown to the welfare department, these same Cherokees receive stingy wages for working land and orchards belonging to the patron or to his kin. Patrons consider that they are providing employment and a steady paternal hand for unfortunate people who they contend could never manage themselves. The same ethic enables whites in good conscience to direct vestigal Cherokee tribal affairs; including the disbursement of well over two million dollars in funds left from a tribal land claim settlement.

POLITICIANS ARE VICTIMS OF OLD FEARS

It might seem odd that no one seeking to improve his position in the local establishment has ever tried to weaken these relationships. Why has no political figure taken cognizance of those thousands of Cherokee votes, and championed their cause? Instead politicians rely on the inefficient machinery of county patronage to collect Cherokee ballots. Unfortunately no one has yet dared, because fear binds the system. Older whites remember living in fear of a blood bath. The proposal to create Oklahoma meant a new state to whites; to Cherokees it meant the end of their own national existence. Their resistance to statehood was most desperate. Cherokees were a force to be contended with. They were feared as an ominously silent, chillingly mysterious people, unpredictable and violent. And Cherokees did organize into secret societies, much akin to the committees of twenty-five delegated in days past to murder collaborators who signed treaties. The reward of public office, politicians feel, does not justify the risk of rekindling that flame. To the extent that Oklahomans are aware of the numbers of Cherokees and the force they might generate, the myth of the assimilated Cherokee is a form of wishful thinking.

Finally, the myth protects the specific relationships of rank and power which determine the stability of the present eastern Oklahoma social system. It does this in the following ways: By preventing recognition by whites and Indians alike of the Cherokees as a permanent community of people whose demands and aspirations must be taken seriously, it allows whites to direct the affairs of the region as they see fit.

By causing Cherokee aspirations to be discounted as romantic and irrelevant, it prevents the emergence of a competitive Cherokee leadership and discourages Cherokees from taking action as a community. For example, by 1904 Cherokees were given what was thought of as an opportunity to develop individualism and responsibility. The U.S. Government divided their communally owned land and each Indian was given his own piece. Thus the efforts of the present day Cherokee Four Mothers Society to piece together individual land holdings, reestablish communal title, and develop cooperative productive enterprises, is smilingly dismissed as an atavistic retreat to "clannishness."

By fostering the notion that Cherokees are an aggregate of disoriented individuals, it allows whites to plan for Cherokees, to control Cherokee resources, and to reinforce their own power by directing programs devoted to Cherokee advancement.

By denying that there is a Cherokee community with which a Cherokee middle class could identify and to which a Cherokee middle class could be responsive, it draws off educated Cherokees into "white" society and leaves an educationally impoverished pool of Cherokees to perpetuate the image of Cherokee incompetence.

The myth prevents scholars, Indian interest organizations, and the like from becoming overly curious about the area. If Cherokees are assimilated and prosperous, as the myth implies, there is neither a problem nor a culture to study. For 40 years no social scientist has completed a major study of any of the five civilized tribes. For 40 years the spread of information which might cast doubt on the myth itself has been successfully impeded.

In all, the myth stabilizes and disguises the Oklahoma social system.

The stability of a local social system, such as that of eastern Oklahoma, is heavily influenced by events in the larger society. The past decade of civil rights activity shook Oklahoma. Gradually, Oklahomans are becoming aware that their society is not as virtuous, homogeneous, attractive, and open as they may have supposed. And Oklahomans will now have to deal with the old agrarian social system of Cherokees, hillbillies, mixed-blood Cherokees, and a new urban elite grafted onto the old.

Left behind in the rush of, workers to industry and of power to industrialized areas, the Ozark east of Oklahoma is a shell, depopulated, and controlled by newly dominant cities, Tulsa and Oklahoma City. The area, quaint enough to attract tourists, is far too rustic for sophisticated Oklahoma urbanites to take seriously. Local politicians offer weak leadership. Beginning to suspect that the local establishment is no longer all powerful, Cherokees have begun to assert themselves as a tribal community. The Cherokees conceive of themselves as a civilized nation, waiting for the dark days of the foreigners' suppression and exploitation to end. Oklahomans regard Cherokees as an aggregate of disadvantaged people still in the background of an integrated state, a definition which Cherokees do not share. In fact, the Cherokees are flirting with political office and have entered the courts with a hunting rights case. In launching a "Five County Northeast Oklahoma Cherokee Organization," they are gaining recognition as a legitimate community with rights, aspirations, resources and competence.

Consequently, the reappearance of assimilated Cherokees threatens the newly emergent regional power structure. Cherokees and the local establishment have begun jousting on a field of honor extending from county welfare offices (where the welfare-sponsored jobs of suspect members of the "Five County Organizations" are in jeopardy) to annual conventions of the National Congress of American Indians. Besides threatening an already shaky white power structure, the militant Cherokees are challenging the self-esteem of the elderly and powerful "assimilated." Curiously, many white Oklahomans do not appear to be alarmed, but pleased, apparently, to relieve the tension that has developed between conflicting images of pretended assimilation and the reality of a workaday world.

The manner in which Oklahomans view their society is the manner in which American sociologists all too often view American society. Great emphasis is placed on class and on individual mobility. And, social description, in these terms, is seen very much as a product of the American ethos.

White Oklahomans consider themselves members of a class-stratified society in which any individual (Negroes excepted) has free access to any class. Descriptions of that system vary according to who is doing the describing. Generally, white Oklahomans conceive their society to be one in which the upper class is made up of prosperous whites and old Cherokee mixed-blood families, or their descendants; next in order is a layer of middle class whites and assimilated Cherokees; then, a lower class of poor, country whites, full-blood Cherokees and Negroes. Young liberals see a two-class system: A middle class of "decent" whites and Cherokees and a socially unacceptable class of poor, country whites, Cherokees and Negroes.

HOW MYTHICAL IS MOBILITY?

This latter classification suggests that younger people perceive a much more closed system than their elders. Everyone is viewed as part of the same *community*—a word Oklahomans are fond of using. Presumably all groups of people have an equal share in the life of the community. Nationality, the word Oklahomans use to denote ethnic origin, is a principal clue to class position. As evidence of how open their society is, eastern Oklahomans point to Cherokees and poor, country whites (although not yet to Negroes, to whom the system is closed) who occupy respected positions. These are store owners, bureaucrats, and entrepreneurs; Babbitts of the 1960s, though born of traditional Cherokee parents. Always, however, these have been individuals who followed the only approved channel of mobility by scrupulously conforming to standards of behavior defined by those in control of the system.

The classic sociological studies on class in America, such as those by W. Lloyd Warner and Robert Lynd, are essentially static descriptions of the rank position of aggregates of individuals similar to the native Oklahoman's conception of his society. These studies reflect a perculiarly American bias. First, they examine the system that has formed rather than study how the system was formed. Americans are phenomenologists, more concerned with the things they have created than with the lengthy processes whereby these things have developed, more interested in ends than concerned with means.

Secondly, Americans do not stress ethnic considerations. In the American dream all individuals can "make it," regardless of nationality. For sociologists, class is a phenomenon in which individuals have social rank; ethnicity is treated as no more than an important clue in determining that rank. Thus, to be Irish was to be an outcast in nineteenth century Boston; not so today.

Thirdly, Americans, envisioning themselves as a nation of individualists, have assumed that social mobility for the most part rests on individual achievement. Immigrant groups are seen as having migrated into lower class positions in 'a relatively fixed class system through which individual immigrants rapidly became mobile. By contrast, Oklahoma's rapid entry into the formative American industrial economy caused a class-like structure to form on top of pre-existing ethnic communities.

A more balanced view shows that in the parts of the United States which industrialized earlier and more gradually, whole immigrant communities were successively imported into and butted one another through a social system which was in the process of formation and closure. The ways in which entire ethnic communities achieve mobility are overlooked.

Now it is becoming obvious that this mobility has slowed, even for those ethnic communities (like Poles) already "in the system." For communities which were brought into the system late (like Puerto Ricans) or at its territorial fringe (like Mexican-Americans in the Southwest) the situation is different.

Cherokees maintained technical independence as an autonomous nation until 1907, and in fact held America at arm's length until the 1890s. They provide an example of incorporation of an ethnic group into the industrial system in an area where no earlier group has paved the way. Thus, Cherokees are a "case type" which illustrated the modern dynamics of our system in pure form. Cherokees are now caught in our "historically mature" system of rank ethnic group—a system which, for some, is rigid and closed, with little chance for individual and less for communal mobility. The total rank-structure of eastern Oklahoma is cemented by the mythology Americans use to obscure and rationalize their privileged position in a closed system.

In their conception of class, American sociologists are often as wedded to myth as are Oklahomans, and the resulting large areas of American social science they have created obediently subscribe to official fictions within the American world view.

Now, successive summers of violence have exploded some of the folk and scientific mythology shrouding the structure of our nation. The *Report of the National Advisory Commission on Civil Disorders* declares: "What white Americans have never fully understood—but what the Negro can never forget—is that white society is deeply implicated in the ghetto. White institutions created it, white institutions maintain it, and white society condones it." Yet throughout this unusually clear report the phenomenon of white racism is barely alluded to, as though it were an "attitude" born by an uninformed populace and unrelated to the core of our national social system. That system, as we see it in operation in Oklahoma, beneath its mythology of assimilation, consists of a structure of ranked ethnic groups, euphemistically called "classes" by American sociologists; a structure which is growing more stable and more rigid. This kind of structure is general in America and, of course, implied in the above quote from the Kerner report. In Oklahoma such a system of relationships has enabled aggressive entrepreneurs to harness and utilize the resources of ethnic communities which are frozen into a low ranked position by the dominant community's control over channels of mobility and by the insistence that the whole complex represents one single community differentiated only by personal capability. Thus, essentially "racist" perceptions and relationships are the "motor" driving the system and are embedded in the very day-to-day relationships of middle class Oklahoma.

FURTHER READING SUGGESTED BY THE AUTHORS:

And Still the Waters Run by Angie Debo (Princeton University Press, 1940) is a historian's meticulous account of the techniques through which the Five Civilized Tribes were stripped of their resources at the beginning of this century.

The New Indians by Stan Steiner (Harper and Row, 1968): Chapter one presents a portrait of spokesmen for the present community of traditional Cherokee Indians and an account of their efforts to buck the Oklahoma "establishment."

RALPH A. LUEBBEN: PREJUDICE AND DISCRIMINATION AGAINST NAVAHOS IN A MINING COMMUNITY

ABSTRACT

Three hypotheses concerning the socio-cultural inter-realtionships of Anglos and Navahos residing in "Carbonate City," Colorado are tested using ethnographic data. It is concluded that Navahos experience discrimination, are a target of prejudice, and have become another American minority aggregate.

INTRODUCTION

Because the resources of the Navaho Reservation are inadequate to support the growing population, continuous expansion of local resources and resettlement of a large number of Navahos in off-reservation communities is not only desirable—but is an economic necessity. The area cannot support the entire present population, even at a low subsistence level (Sub-committee 1950: 586-6). Government estimates suggest that even under the best circumstances, with all projected irrigation and other

Source: Reprinted by permission from *The Kiva* 30 (October 1964), 1-17.

economic developments in operation, the reservation can only support half of the 1952 population (Planning in Action 1952: 39).

During the World War II period, work opportunities in a number of industries throughout the West led to widespread emigration. Military depot projects and mining offered the greatest employment opportunities. Permanent off-reservation groups were founded at Belmont, Morenci, and Parker, Arizona; Wingate Village, New Mexico; Barstow, California; and Bingham Canyon, Utah. Communities adjacent to the reservation such as Gallup and Farmington, New Mexico; Cortez, Colorado; and Holbrook, Winslow, and Flagstaff, Arizona; attracted some Navaho families. Other Navahos have voluntarily settled in Albuquerque, New Mexico; Phoenix, Arizona; Salt Lake City, Utah; Los Angeles, California; Denver, Colorado; and at section points along the Santa Fe Railroad. Since World War II, when an acute labor shortage developed, the mines in "Carbonate City," Colorado, the focus of this paper, have also offered excellent opportunities for permanent off-reservation employment.

More recently, in an effort to relieve population pressure and to improve the standard of living, the Relocation Program of the Bureau of Indian Affairs was designed and initiated to facilitate voluntary resettlement of Indian families from reservations to Los Angeles, San Francisco, Oakland, and San Jose, California; Denver, Colorado; Dallas, Texas; Chicago, Illinois; and Cleveland, Ohio; where employment opportunities are more readily available. Only those candidates who supposedly meet minimum standards relating to health, education, and acculturation are accepted for relocation assistance. Necessary funds are provided to cover the expense of moving, and the program assists families to locate housing, schools, sources of medical care, and employment. By November, 1957, the scope of services was broadened to include an adult vocational training program in the above cities and in some communities adjacent to the reservation and to assist people in establishing themselves in nearby communities possessing various industries or other employment opportunities.

Under the Relocation Services Program, 3,273 persons, including 555 families and 1,029 single people, had been resettled up to 1960 (For a detailed summary of the program, see Young 1961: 333-8). About 65% (nearly 2000) of the resettled Navahos have remained in their new communities for at least one year.

Such directed, but also undirected, migration from the reservation will undoubtedly continue in the future. While the Navaho Service and Tribe encourages permanent off-reservation employment, little data relating to those Navahos already living off the reservation are available. No systematic, extended study of any of the off-reservation activities in which Navahos are engaged had been made. Regular contact should be maintained with these displaced persons in order to keep abreast of their potential problems. Hoskie Cronemeyer, member of the Navaho Tribal Council Committee on Relocation, has periodically inspected areas of relocation, met with resettled Navahos, forwarded pertinent reports to the Tribal Council, and imparted constructive criticism to the Bureau of Indian Affairs concerning the program.

Off-reservation employment is now the cornerstone of Navaho liveli-hood; and without it, life on the reservation would be impossible (Navaho Welfare 1951: 8). Both the Navajo Tribe and Bureau of Indian Affairs are optimistic about all forms of Navaho resettlement. Some economic gains probably can be claimed; but to make resettlement a real success, economic accomplishments should be complemented by socio-cultural integration of Navahos into their respective new communities. Data from "Carbonate City" indicate that the latter is not always the case. Three hypotheses, relevant to Navaho socio-cultural adjustment, are the bases for this paper. If Navahos reside in and work in an industry set in an Anglo (English-speaking Caucasoid) community (*e.g.,* the mines at "Carbonate City," Colorado), then Navahos will:

1 Experience discrimination.
2 Be a target of prejudice.
3 Become another American minority aggregate.

On November 1, 1953, the total population of "Carbonate City" numbered 335 people. One hundred seventeen Navahos comprised 35.0% of the total population. Roughly the same percentages in the various sex, age, and status subcategories were found within both the Navaho and Anglo aggregates. The only marked differences appear in the presence of some unmarried Anglo females and an overwhelming number of pre-school Navaho children.

These Navahos brought a limited educational and occupational back-ground to the Anglo-American community. Few had completed high school; most attended government elementary schools for brief periods of time, only a couple had passed beyond third grade, and another spent two years in the "Carbonate City" Public School.

Prior to arriving in "Carbonate City," some Navahos had worked for wages on and off the reservation; however, when hired by the company, most had no previous experience in either hardrock mining or other jobs that developed skills usable in mining. A few had worked in other lead and zinc mines; some had mined coal for domestic purposes on the reservation; and several were qualified to operate a caterpillar tractor. Other experience was mostly as common labor on track laying crews of the various railroad companies. Thus, initial usefulness of most Navahos, when first employed by the mining company, was quite limited.

DISCRIMINATION

One hypothesis suggests that in a predominantly Anglo-American community, like "Carbonate City," Navahos will experience discrimination. First, allow me to consider inter-personal relationships in the mines and then other facets of camp life. When available, Anglos were hired in preference to Navahos; yet the latter always represented a readily available labor pool in case of an Anglo shortage. Navahos were nearly always hired as helpers, the lowest grade, regardless of economic conditions (*i.e.,* supply and demand), mining capabilities, and previous experience. Once hired, they were usually restricted to the two lowest positions, namely underground helper and miner. Generally they did not hold any of the other skilled or supervisory positions, even though qualified; however after the author left camp, a Navaho was promoted to timberman. During World War II, one had been a shift boss in one of the mines. Rarely were Navahos maliciously exploited; however, in one case, a skilled tractor operator only drew helper's pay in contrast to his well-paid Anglo counterpart. For Navahos, promotion was slower than for Anglos, and some qualified Navahos were admittedly bypassed in promotion from helper to miner by more favored Anglos. Other discriminations also appeared in the company's policy toward Navahos. One predominantly Navaho crew was required to furnish private transportation to the mine, but the company provided a vehicle for the larger operation worked by a mixed crew. When an Anglo was hired, his rate was determined more by economic need at that particular time; so they had a better opportunity for employment at more than helper's pay. While Anglos also worked as helpers and miners, they monopolized the other hourly and salaried staff positions.

Around the mine warehouse, in transit to the mines, in the mine, and while eating, voluntary interaction soon precipitated two non-antagonistic groups. Most frequently they were physically separated, and the Anglos invariably enjoyed the preferred and most favorable location or surroundings. Even when no great physical separation existed, the members of each group usually remained mutually exclusive. While a few Navahos transgressed the physical boundaries and peripherally joined the conversation of the Anglos, the latter very rarely intruded into a Navaho group. Unless required, little verbal or physical interaction took place between members of the different groups. When an occasional Anglo and Navaho voluntarily interacted, a joking relationship followed; moreover, both men were the brunt of the other's verbal or gestural jokes. Such jesting was limited to a very few individuals. No incidents of major incompatability were ever recorded under circumstances of voluntary interaction. However members of the opposite group were deliberately ignored. On several occasions, Anglos en route to work drove their vehicles past a walking Navaho without offering the latter a ride.

If a single person of either culture was present with members of the opposite group, the individual was tolerated, but usually excluded from full participation. Under such circumstances, a lone Navaho was very uneasy; and with few exceptions, either the lone Anglo or Navaho, as the case may be, usually remained inconspicuous or took the earliest opportunity to isolate or absent himself from members of the other group.

Most Anglos collected their bimonthly pay checks at the mine office; but because Navahos and some Anglos of questionable character were credit risks, assignments of their future wages were required as an economic safeguard by the local mercantile manager. Refusal to sign the questionably legal assignment at the time of employment and at the beginning of each month meant that no credit was extended to the person or family. The store then received these pay checks directly from the company and deducted its outstanding bill from the amount earned; thus the mercantile was assured of its credits. While the mercantile personnel attempted to hold expenditures within the limitations of their next pay check, Navahos frequently overextended their earnings. If the bill exceeded the amount of the check, the amount due was carried forward against the next pay period, and the Navaho did not receive any cash. While sound economic reasons may have dictated the dispersal of Navahos' checks via assignments, state legal statutes concerning the assignment of wages were either ignored or flagrantly violated. Navahos never questioned the legality of the operation. Most Anglos thought that the assignment was legal and binding; however, the manager of the store recognized that the assignment should have been officially registered with the county clerk to make it legally binding. Actually the arrangement was an informal agreement worked out by mine management and the mercantile operator, and a convenient device for satisfying the desires of the respective parties, including the Navahos. Parenthetically, if Navahos had taken advantage of tribal resettlement facilities to cushion their arrival in "Carbonate City," they would not have had to assign their wages to the local mercantile.

The local mercantile functioned very much like a trading post on the reservation. It served as a place of business and a social center for Navahos. Instead of bartering wool, lambs, rugs, or jewelry for "imported" goods, the "Carbonate City" Navahos bartered a piece of paper representing their services to the company for goods.

Additional informal economic arrangements had been made [so that] . . . anyone who did business with Navahos (*e.g.,* coalman, public power) might use the mercantile as a billing and collection agency. The charges were added to the existing mercantile bill and were, therefore, theoretically covered by the assignment. For this service and for loaned money, regardless of time involved, the store received a 10% fee from the Navaho. Payment followed on the next payday. The mercantile served as a convenient bookkeeping agency for the Navahos and ultimately handled and claimed most of their money. Smaller discriminations against Navahos were also noted in the computation of sales tax and larger amounts required for deposits. In many ways the mercantile manager catered to Navaho preferences and desires. Low grade meat which could be sold cheaply was selected expressly for Navahos. In the process, the operator alienated some Anglos but satisfied his best customers, the Navahos. While Navahos and Anglos rubbed elbows while making purchases and loafing in the store, relatively little personal interaction took place.

Other businesses in camp and adjacent communities attempted to operate on a "cash" policy. In reality, credit was extended to a few favored Navahos and a majority of Anglos by the local liquor store and bar operators. Because Navahos depreciated cars more rapidly than Anglos, automobile sales agencies in a nearby community demanded significantly higher down payments from Navahos purchasing vehicles.

At the time of the field study, facilities for public recreation in "Carbonate City" were limited to the bar which was patronized by both Anglos and Navahos. During the initial phase of the study, the federal law restricting sale of alcoholic beverages to Indians was in effect. At that time, Navahos usually yielded more favorable booths with regard to proximity to stove and bar to Anglos, and seldom seated themselves at the bar itself. With the removal of the prohibition restrictions, Navahos increasingly encroached on the bar. On only a few occasions was voluntary interaction and joint drinking observed between Anglos and Navahos. The proprietor of the bar tolerated boisterous behavior of and permitted significant extensions of credit to Anglos, but denied these to Navahos. To discourage some Navahos from entering the establishment, the door was deliberately locked by the proprieter. This was done to "avoid trouble" if the Navaho supposedly was inebriated. Previously when a pool hall had been open, it was the scene of a number of brawls which crystalized along racial-cultural lines.

Apart from the economic pattern, no extended personal interaction between members of the two groups existed. Cross-cultural social visitation, other than for conducting business related to the mine or to buying Navaho handicraft objects, was not approved by Anglos. Aside from a missionary, the anthropologist and his wife, and one Anglo of dubious character, home visitation did not take place between either individuals, families, or groups. Even when invited, Navahos were reluctant to enter an Anglo house; moreover, some Navahos with long residence in "Carbonate City" had never been inside an Anglo home. Social life of the two groups went along independently. Interestingly, much more social life existed among the Navahos than among the Anglos.

Navaho housing in "Carbonate City" must be considered in terms of location and quality. Navaho residents were situated in two areas. One, a crescentic-shaped cluster of houses, extended across the northern periphery of the community. Part of this was a major concentration of families who lived in company-owned, segregated structures usually referred to as "Indian Village." A second scattering of Navaho houses was located at the southeast side of the camp. In both cases, the housing units were peripheral to "Carbonate City," and in the latter area Anglo residences were interspersed with those occupied by Navahos. Houses occupied by Navahos, whether owned or rented, were generally inferior to those occupied by Anglos. Relatively new houses made available to Navaho employees by the company were furnished with markedly less living space and fewer appointments than those for Anglos. Navahos living in privately owned structures utilized outhouses, and some structures did not have water piped into the house.

Within the political frame-work of the camp, Navahos, who made up a third of the population, had no political representation on the town board, on the school board, or among any of the administrative community offices. No Navaho spokesman existed or served as a representative for making requests or needs known. Navahos were permitted to vote, and no effort was made to disfranchise them. Navahos were not encouraged to register and vote. When they did cast a ballot, however, their vote was usually manipulated by some of the Anglo residents who made certain that the Navahos voted "correctly." Most Navahos did not understand voting procedure; nor did they demonstrate interest in American politics.

Incidentally, one female Anglo poll clerk, while interogating a Navaho to see whether he was eligible to vote, inquired if the Navaho was a "naturalized citizen."

In concluding these remarks relating to discrimination, field data adequately supports the proposed hypothesis: If Navahos work in an industry set in an Anglo community, then Navahos will experience discrimination. Discrimination against Navahos was present in company, mercantile, and other situations. Personal discrimination is apparent in all sorts of contexts involving a choice. Aside from necessary economic interaction, two mutually exclusive, parallel aggregates exist within but do not share the facilities of "Carbonate City."

PREJUDICE

A second proposed hypothesis suggests that a group of Navahos in an American community will be the target of Anglo prejudice. Again, I should like to first consider the mine situation. To some Anglo miners, "Carbonate City" was not attractive, because, among other reasons, it was a "Navaho camp." When other employment opportunities were available, Anglos ignored the camp. Generally, the attitude prevailed that Navahos lowered the standard of living, were satisfied with lack-luster day wage rates, and were willing to work under unsafe conditions because they were unable to conceptualize the possible consequences.

So long as Navahos were considered unskilled or only semi-skilled underground workers and were not promoted beyond miner, they were not considered economic threats by Anglos. To retain their margin of comfort, Anglo workers made every effort to deprecate the mining ability, enthusiasm, and cooperation of Navahos; were critical of the high absenteeism and turnover rates of Navahos; and cited difficulties growing out of the admitted communications problem which existed because Navahos did not speak English well. Any supervisor's comments which were critical of Navaho labor were quickly picked up by Anglo workers to assist in verifying their case against the Navahos. Although Navahos were theoretically considered for promotion on an equal basis with Anglos, the latter certainly had the advantage in promotion and preferential jobs, but Anglos rejected the idea of favored treatment. While supervisors extolled the merits of several qualified Navahos and considered them for positions apart from helpers and miners, none were promoted during the author's stay. On the basis of previous experience with only one Navaho shift boss, there was general condemnation of and reluctance to consider a Navaho for such a position. While other tangential reasons were offered, Anglo resentment of a Navaho supervisor and a threat to superior Anglo status was the key issue.

Neither Anglos nor Navahos liked working as members of racially-culturally mixed crews or, more specifically, with a partner of the opposite group. Supervisors attempted to avoid the latter arrangement as much as possible; yet such combinations did occur. Overtly the men were indifferent and accepted the mixing as inevitable, but preference for a partner with one's own background was always inferred. If a choice were available, Navahos would have preferred to associate with other Navahos and some Anglos. Only a few Navahos were viewed by most Anglos as very desirable helpers and, therefore, were quite acceptable in a work group, although Anglos categorically rejected any suggestions, regardless of quality, made by a Navaho partner because such a thinking individual was a threat to the superior position and personal security of Anglos. Any kind of Navaho flippancy was resented.

Most Anglos believed that the mining company had coddled Navahos; given them more opportunities to prove themselves than they deserved; and had been overly sympathetic. Willingness to rehire Navahos; awarding them lucrative contracts; tolerating absenteeism, drunkenness, and careless handling of explosives were cited to clinch the point concerning Navaho favoritism. To further substantiate reasons for Anglo paranoia, they referred to the case of the only person to work for less than helper's pay. This involved a young local Anglo who was quite provoked when a Navaho's son of equivalent age and no experience was hired as a regular helper. In the writer's opinion, some indulgence of Navahos had occurred; moreover, Navahos played a very subtle role in keeping Anglos alert and most productive. As an aside, prejudice may have existed in placing Navaho workers underground; but this was to their advantage because most mine accidents occurred outside the mine itself.

Sanitation in the mine was a major problem. Men were encouraged to leave the mine if feasible, and finally portable toilets were introduced. Any fecal material encountered in the mine was attributed to Navahos. Unless absolutely necessary, Anglos were reluctant to use this facility because of the supposed disease and lack of cleanliness of Navahos; moreover, one Anglo threatened to quit if he had to dispose of the refuse. Anglos also hesitated to share water facilities of various kinds with Navahos.

This Anglo attitude picturing Navahos as diseased persons and as a health menace to the community was constantly reiterated. Among Navahos, personal cleanliness and attitudes toward cleanliness varied considerably, as was the case for Anglos. Following traditional procedure, some Navahos defecated and urinated rather indiscriminately and ignored available toilet facilities. When some Navahos built outhouses rather than utilizing a central modern facility provided in "Indian Village," Anglos concluded that the structures had been built because other Navahos were dirty and diseased and that the builders did not want to share the common facilities. Convenience and privacy, so important to Navahos, were never considered as possible factors. In considering housing, Anglos agreed that Navahos permeated a structure with a nauseating, sweet odor; readily accepted poor housing; did not desire indoor plumbing or other amenities; and resisted property ownership because it restricted their freedom. If a structure was musty smelling or rodent infested, Navahos were blamed. Anglos suggested, sometimes correctly, that when Navahos got through with a building, it was ready to be destroyed.

Questionable health was cited by Anglos as the basis for reluctance to accociate with Navahos of any age, and, more specifically, to admit Navaho children into various youth organizations. In an effort to protect and develop the talents of their offspring, prejudices toward Navahos are clearly stated. Attitudes toward scouting typify this kind of thinking. When first considered, Anglo parents were opposed to the incorporation of Navahos into such an organization. Agreement was reached that if Navahos could not be segregated because of the brotherhood principle, they should not be asked; and, Anglos rationalized, since Navahos typically did not show initiative and could not financially afford membership, they would not attempt to join. When eventually parents allowed their sons to decide if Navahos should be included in the Boy Scouts, only one child voted against including them. But before the Navahos sought admission, some parents were already scheming on how to eliminate the Navahos on the basis of the health issue and for added reasons of financial, transportation, and effort burden to Anglo parents. Eventually the Cub, Boy and Girl Scouts accepted Navahos, who quite satisfactorily met the various requirements. Because of Navaho membership, some Anglo parents refused to allow their children to join the organizations. Other Anglo girls' clubs and children's parties, however, remained exclusively Anglo. In most informal, voluntary situations, data do not bear out the general claim that Anglo and Navaho children chose not to play together. Mixed groups played amiably; although snowball fights and other personal attacks usually crystalized along racial-cultural lines. Anglo girls accepted Navaho girls more readily than Anglo boys accepted their Navaho counterparts.

Within the local school system, Navahos were usually blamed for any problem which developed. Parents wished that Navaho children would reach 16 years of age so they could voluntarily leave school and suggested that the federal government should assume the responsibility for off-reservation Navaho education. Admittedly, Navaho absenteeism, age discrepancies of students in the same grade, and inability to speak much English did present real problems and delayed progress; yet some Navahos proved very adept scholars and eclipsed Anglo students (*e.g.,* one Navaho girl won the county spelling bee). In attempting to better educational conditions, Navaho parents were not encouraged to attend PTA meetings or to support the school program. A few more acculturated Navaho women did come to the meetings which were largely social in nature. As in the case of the PTA and scouting, Anglos rationalized and then assumed that Navahos did not want to participate in other community activities like the Masonic Order; Woman's Club; adult church group; and the volunteer fire company. Interestingly, Sunday School was operated for the children of the community by the missionary to the Navaho. Both Anglos and Navahos attended without any visible evidence of antagonism or overt comment by parents.

In the history of "Carbonate City," dancing played a significant role in personal entertainment. At first, Navahos were welcome; but more recently, Navahos were not invited or were discouraged from participating in order to "avoid trouble." Teen-age dances were exclusively Anglo, and no cross-cultural dating took place. At the biggest social event of the season, the Firemen's Dance, Navahos, who paid for admission and attended, did not dance. One Navaho woman refused an Anglo invitation to dance. Moreover, Anglo ladies were basically afraid of Navaho males and did not wish to dance with them. Had an Anglo woman been shown any discourtesy or been molested, some Anglo demonstration would have followed.

Whatever the context, Navahos were considered mean and not trusted. Anglos disputed Navahos' abilities to drive a vehicle safely, to interact peaceably, to drink alcoholic beverages sanely, and to not steal unguarded property. Some petty pilfering took place in camp, but no one was ever apprehended and tried in court. While Navahos were expected to retain their proper status and not intrude on Anglos, the latter believed in their prerogatives to enter a Navaho house without announcement or explanation. Firemen, who were engaged in making a safety inspection, accomplished their mission in this impetuous manner.

Enough data has been cited to indicate that Anglos in "Carbonate City" were prejudiced against the Navaho aggregate. Because of the rigid attitude, there was a ready predisposition to respond to stimuli evoked by Navahos with a highly emotional quality not found in most attitudes. Despite personal differences, all Navahos were categorically lumped together and stereotyped. Many clichés were used to describe the Navahos; simple, primitive, unemotional, irresponsible, children, etc.

Such distorted, categorical thinking misrepresented observed data, yet Anglos defended their distorted preceptions, misjudgments, and stereotypes. However, as individuals, Navahos responded quite differently to persons of the opposite social group. Some Navahos were talkative and interacted on first contact; others were quite reserved and gradually increased their responsiveness under favorable consideration and encouragement from Anglos; a few Navahos never breached the cross-cultural barriers, so even necessary associations were tagged with avoidance, or more rarely, antagonistic responses.

Actually, mine supervisors suggested that some Navahos made very fine and capable miners. Ability, as for Anglos, was limited by personal qualities and educational and experience background. The outside doctor attending the community suggested that the health of Navahos, aside from children under three years, was very good. The camp was constantly being scrutinized by the physician for communicable diseases. Thus, in reality, many of the Anglo prejudices were not verified; some few, as previously indicated, were borne out.

MINORITY STATUS

The third hypothesis suggests that Navahos would be members of a minority aggregate. In verifying this, the point of departure lies in Navahos being easily distinguished physically and socio-culturally from other members of the camp. Aside from Mongoloid racial features, clothing worn by males and females, distinctive motor habits, and culturally patterned behavior made them visibly different. More subtle roles of the extended matrifamily, attitudes, and other traditional phenomena also differentiated

Navahos from Anglos. Exclusive use of the Navaho language among themselves, intentional withdrawal from Anglos, and selection of Navahos for voluntary interaction produced a situation of self-segregation and confirmed Navaho solidarity. The significance of linguistic differences in the total picture is not to be underestimated. Generally the culture of the reservation continued to exert a strong attraction for many Navahos in "Carbonate City;" and most of them maintained continuous contact with the reservation.

The second criterion for minority status incorporates the concept of differential and unequal treatment. Previously cited data verified the hypothesis related to discrimination. Navahos were accorded such treatment; and they, as individuals and as an entity, recognized themselves as objects of personal and institutional discrimination. Thirdly, they also recognized the existence and role of a corresponding favored, dominant Anglo aggregate with different customs and expectations. Certainly Navahos were more keenly aware of Anglo culture than the reverse. Even after long contact, Anglos had only a fleeting image of Navaho culture and feeble explanations for Navaho behavior. In many subtle ways, Navahos deferred to Anglos. For example, Navahos assumed that Anglos' watches were more nearly correct. Navahos expected discrimination and prejudice; they were conditioned to hold inferior ratings, even if comparably trained and experienced. They recognized prejudice in Anglo choices and preference for Anglo associates. Thus, the criteria for the Navahos as a minority were fulfilled.

As minority members, Navahos had little recourse or forces for overt retaliation; however, the "inferior" Navahos were delighted when an Anglo made a mistake or appeared ridiculous in a situation. While Navahos were scapegoats for the Anglos in "Carbonate City," Navahos also had their own scapegoats, namely the Ute Indians. Sentiments against Anglos could be readily displaced without fear to the hapless Ute.

In reviewing the early historical relationships between Indians and Anglos in the area, one should conclude that present day contacts had bad precedents. While early contacts were infrequent, many were antagonistic.

On the other hand, the first Navaho miners, who worked in the "Carbonate City" mines, were few in number and well integrated into the camp. More recently several Indians with other tribal backgrounds, a "Mexican" woman, and a Negress were accorded the privileges of active participation in Anglo society or were at least tolerably accepted. Isolates, like the first Navahos or even members of other minority groups, bothered no one and were consequently accepted; but Navahos *en masse* presented a social problem of another order and challenged Anglo socio-cultural dominance. Even so, Navahos were considered more desirable than "Mexicans (Spanish-speaking Americans)." Considerable verbal antipathy was directed against "Mexicans" by both Anglos and Navahos as well.

CONCLUSIONS

The hypotheses which were originally proposed have been satisfied. Navahos working in the mines and residing in "Carbonate City" experienced discrimination, were a target for prejudice, and became another minority aggregate. So ultimately, Navaho status was not too different from that of many Negroes, Puerto Ricans, and other minorities in American society.

I do not wish to convey the idea that all Anglo-Navaho relationships in "Carbonate City" were antagonistic. Instead, in fact, little overt antipathy was demonstrated by either Navaho or Anglos. Data citing voluntary personal assistance and sharing are present. In the past, the "Carbonate City" baseball teams, collections for victims of circumstance, and many small personal favors suggest that racial-cultural differences could be set aside. On certain occasions, like the Labor Day Hard-Rocker's celebration, Anglos even attempted to capitalize on the presence of Navahos in the community. Navaho chants and dances received favorable billing and applause. Several Navahos were members of the planning committee, although their roles were limited to the entertainment realm.

In another paper, the author (Luebben 1964) concludes that a disproportionate number of Navahos were arrested in "Carbonate City;" yet in considering the percentage of convictions and fines assessed, data refute the suggestion that discrimination occurred against Navahos. Discrimination appears to have been at a minimum in the justices' courts; although slight, but consistent, favoritism for either Navahos or Anglos appeared in the records for different justices. To relegate the larger percentage of Navahos appearing on the police blotter to discrimination is taking a narrow view of the situation. Instead, the traditional behavior of Navahos continued to operate in this off-reservation mining camp and was in conflict with the expectations of Anglo law.

Sufficient evidence is available to suggest that the Navajo Tribe's and governmental office's goals of getting Navahos off the reservation has been met in "Carbonate City." Yet these agencies have failed to effectively prepare Navahos for and to cushion the move to the new community. None of the "Carbonate City" Navahos made use of the financing and other assistance available for relocation. The people have been uprooted physically and transplanted economically; but they now experience prejudices, discriminations, and minority status. Navahos are seldom received as equals. An unstable economic pattern has been replaced by a questionably desirable social situation. The goal of making these people good, solid "middle-class" citizens is highly commendable; but in reality, if the Navahos are converted into urban slum dwellers or second class citizens in some other context, then the solution to the dilemma which the Tribe and Navajo Service wishes to achieve has not been satisfactorily reached.

ACKNOWLEDGEMENTS

Field research was made possible by a Research Training Fellowship awarded by the Social Science Research Council, New York, for the "Field investigation of the cultural, economic, and social behavior of Navaho Indians in a Colorado mining community." The paper in abbreviated form was presented at the 62nd Annual Meeting of the American Anthropological Association which was held at San Francisco, California, November 21-24, 1963. I should like to thank Janell Luebben for assistance in collection of the data and for secretarial assistance. Miss Linda Linville also assisted in preparing the manuscript.

REFERENCES

Luebben, Ralph A. (1964), Navaho Behavior and Anglo Law. *The Kiva,* Vol. 29, No. 3, pp. 60-75. Tucson.
Navajo Welfare and Placement Division (1951), Navajo-Hopi Placement Service: Yearbook: 1950-51. Window Rock.
Planning in Action on the Navajo-Hopi Indian Reservations: A Progress Report on the Land and Its People (1952), United States Government Printing Office. Washington.
Subcommittee on Indian Affairs of the Committee on Public Lands, House of Representatives (1950), Material Relating to the Indians of the United States and the Territory of Alaska, United States Government Printing Office. Washington.
Young, Robert W. (1961), *The Navajo Yearbook,* Report Number VIII. Navajo Agency, Window Rock.

LEE H. BOWKER: RED AND BLACK IN CONTEMPORARY AMERICAN HISTORY TEXTS: A CONTENT ANALYSIS

For more than twenty years, educators and interested observers have been writing articles on the inadequacies of American history texts, and there is an extensive bibliography on the subject of historians' treatment of American minorities. Despite this obvious concern which has heightened with increased pressure from the minority groups themselves, competent studies of the treatment in public school texts of either blacks or Indians have been scarce. There are many articles which refer to only a handful of texts,[1] and usually those works which have considered a more adequate sample of publications have not quantified their findings so as to provide convincing empirical evidence for their position.[2] The present study attempts to extend previous work on this subject by systematically examining the treatment of American Indians and blacks in 67 contemporary American history texts.

METHODS

All of the texts were published in the 1960s. Text sampling was on an availability basis, initially comprising all the American history texts available in several local academic and curriculum libraries. To be selected a text had to be devoted exclusively to American history. World history, civics, and American democracy texts were excluded. Only texts which nominally dealt with American history from Columbus to the late 1950s were included. This eliminated the specialized "period" history texts now coming into vogue.

Each text was analyzed along five basic dimensions: (1) number of times Indians or blacks were mentioned, (2) total size of "mentions," (3) number of adjectives, (4) mean adjective affect, and (5) a historical item checklist.

A "mention" was defined as a textbook page on which at least one sentence described the persons or activities of one or more American Indians or blacks. Mentions were initially identified by noting all the entries in a work's index under the terms black, slavery, Negro, and Indian. Where these words in turn referred the reader to other entries, the latter were also included. Mentions about Indians had to refer to tribes living in the area which is now the United States, but items relating to the African origins of American blacks were included.

Each mention recorded in the index was then examined in context to determine whether it qualified as a "legitimate" mention. Many passages referred to a minority group in passing but described only the actions of whites. Such passages were not counted as legitimate mentions. Thus, "The prospect of meeting Apaches at night terrified the settlers," would not qualify as a mention, but "The Apaches often terrified the settlers without meaning to," would be counted.

The size of mentions was tabulated by counting the number of relevant sentences and pages. These were added together to provide a measure of the extent of the discussion about each minority within a given text.

Each adjective modifying a general (Negro, Iroquois) or specific (Martin Luther King, Chief Sitting Bull) ethnic noun was recorded. For example, in the sentence, "The honest Indian said little," the word "honest" would have been recorded. Several other constructions convey essentially the same thought and would also have been counted, even if technically they were not adjectives. Thus, the two sentences "The honestly speaking Indian said little," and "Those Indians who were honest said little," would have been coded the same as the first example.

All recorded adjectives were submitted to a panel of 15 judges, including the professors and graduate students in two sociology seminars in race and minority relations. The adjectives were rated on an affect scale running from 1 (negative) to 5 (positive) with 3 being the neutral point. The adjective-affect scale value for an adjective was the mean of the judges' ratings. In addition, an adjective-affect score was assigned to each text. It consisted of the mean of the adjective-affect scale values of all the adjectives used to modify nouns indicating Indians or blacks in that text.

Adjectives which appeared more than once were counted separately for each occurrence.

The scope of historical coverage was assessed via checklists of 20 items for blacks and 21 items for Indians. The checklists were created after a pretest survey of five texts from all grade levels and an examination of a number of specialized publications on black and Indian history.[3] They were designed to facilitate comparison of texts published at different dates and for different grade levels, and did not represent the 20 items that erudite historians might agree upon as the most significant items in each group's historical experience. The historical checklists are presented in Table 1.

TABLE 1

Checklists for Analysis of Scope of Coverage of Historical Texts

Indians	Blacks
1. Helped Puritans	1. Being slaves
2. In the fur trade	2. Description of slave life
3. Wars with early Virginians	3. Middle passage
4. British allies in War of Independence	4. Slave revolts or suicides
5. French and Indian War	5. As skilled artisans
6. Purchase of Manhattan	6. In Continental Army
7. Mad Anthony Wayne battles	7. Underground railroad
8. Quaker friendship and treaties	8. Fighting in Civil War
9. Whitman Mission events	9. In reconstruction governments
10. Indian heroes of 1850s wars	10. Crushed by Black Codes
11. Treaties of 1860s	11. Victims of KKK
12. Seminole battles in the Southeast	12. The great migration
13. Allotment policy	13. Improvement of selves after 1900
14. Reservation system explained	14. Sit-ins and freedom rides
15. Removal	15. Integration of schools
16. Red Power since 1945	16. In modern professions
17. Use of buffaloes	17. Segregation in cities
18. Made canoes, moccasins, bows, and arrows	18. General discrimination against
19. Corn growing	19. Jazz, music contributions
20. Mention further details of any Indian culture	20. Other contributions to U.S. life
21. Any non-Red Power mention since 1945	

FINDINGS

Indians or blacks were mentioned on about 50 pages of each history text surveyed. However, most of these pages contained only one or two lines relating Indian or black activities, so that the actual space devoted to these minorities was approximately 14 pages per text. Often, as much as half of the 14 pages contained concentrated units on "primitive" Indian cultures at the beginning of the text and on the "emergence" of the black man at the end of the text. In both these cases, the material on minorities

TABLE 2

Mean Number, Size,[1] and Proportionate Size[2] of Mentions of
American Indians and Blacks in 67 American History
Texts by Grade Level and Year of Publication

Minority	Year of Publication by Grade Level					
	1960-1965			1966-1970		
	Grade	Jr. High	High	Grade	Jr. High	High
MEAN NUMBER OF MENTIONS						
Indian	29.1	28.5	21.7	29.9	22.5	23.0
Black	10.8	14.3	24.5	26.8	27.5	42.8
Total	39.9	42.8	46.2	56.7	50.0	65.8
MEAN TOTAL SIZE OF MENTIONS						
Indian	7.84	6.40	6.00	8.53	4.60	4.60
Black	2.45	3.02	6.69	10.53	6.47	13.87
Total	10.29	9.42	12.69	19.06	11.07	18.47
PROPORTIONATE SIZE OF MENTIONS						
Indian	2.2	0.9	0.8	1.7	0.7	0.6
Black	0.7	0.4	0.9	2.1	0.9	1.7
Total	2.9	1.3	1.7	3.8	1.6	2.3

[1] Mean mention size is measured in pages. In cases where a mention was shorter than one page, sentences were converted into fractions of a page according to the standard, 1 page = 37 sentences. This standard was arrived at by counting the number of sentences per page of text in a nonrandom sample of 14 of the books used in this study, and computing the mean.
[2] Mean total size of mentions of American Indians and blacks in 67 American history texts as a percentage of mean book size.

was segregated from the main flow of American history rather than considered as an integral part of it.

Table 2 shows considerable variation by grade level and publication date in the number of mentions of American Indians and blacks, ranging from 21.7 for high school texts published between 1960 and 1965 to 29.9 in grade school texts published from 1966 to 1970. Black mentions show more variation, ranging from 10.8 for blacks in grade school texts published between 1960 and 1965 to 42.8 for blacks in high school texts published between 1966 and 1970.

For American Indians, the relationship of mentions to grade level is an inverse one with the highest number of mentions at the lowest grade levels. An examination of Indian mentions by period of publication shows little change from 1960-1965 to 1966-1970, the only large difference being a decrease at the junior high school level. The number of mentions of blacks rises steadily as grade level increases and sharply as the year of publication approaches 1970.

Since a mention may vary from one sentence to a full page, it is important to know the exact length of the material devoted to minorities.

The pattern of relationships between size of mention, grade level, and year of publication (see Table 2) is similar to that for mean number of mentions. The only exception is that while the number of times American Indians are mentioned in high school texts rises slightly from 21.7 in 1960-1965 to 23.0 in 1966-1970, the total size of these mentions decreases considerably from about 6 pages to slightly over 4½ pages. The average size of Indian mentions in high school texts declined from 11 to 8 sentences between these two time periods.

Table 2 also shows the mean total size of mentions of blacks and American Indians as a percentage of textbook size. Book size increases as the grade level advances, and within grade levels increased considerably from 1960-1965 to 1966-1970. By controlling for textbook size in this way, one gains a more accurate perception of changes in textbook coverage of minorities. Between 1960-1965 and 1966-1970 the proportion of space devoted to American Indians decreased at all grade levels. In contrast to this trend the proportion of space devoted to blacks in the latter period was more than double the pre-1966 coverage, although it still did not amount to more than 2.1 percent.

In describing the observed trends in treatment of minorities in texts, it may be helpful to express the relationship between Indian and black mentions as a ratio. Table 3 exhibits this ratio for the mean total size of mentions at the various grade levels and publication periods. In 1960-1965 texts, Indians received more than three times the space that blacks received at the grade school level, declining to a near balance in high school texts. The trend of a decline in the ratio of material about Indians to that about blacks as a grade level increases is repeated in 1966-1970 texts, but in that period blacks get the lion's share, culminating in a more than 2 to 1 superiority at the high school level. Some publishers seem to have decreased their Indian material at the same time that they have increased their black material, almost as if they were using a quota system for minority coverage.

Mentions of Indians and blacks are not randomly scattered over the historical spectrum. Table 4 shows that generally there was less material about Indians in 1966-1970 texts than in those published in 1960-1965. In particular, texts at various grade levels show decreases for the historical periods 1880-1945 and 1946-1960. The only substantial increase is in coverage of the pre-1777 period in grade school books, which increases from

TABLE 3

Ratio of Mean Total Size of Mentions of American Indians to Mean
Total Size of Mentions of Blacks in 67 American History
Texts, by Grade Level and Year of Publication

Year of Publication	Grade Level		
	Grade	*Jr. High*	*High*
1960-1965	3.1	2.2	0.9
1966-1970	0.8	0.8	0.4

4.31 pages to 6.10 pages between 1960-1965 and 1966-1970. Many texts surveyed devote much space to Indian cultural characteristics while ignoring the details of the historical confrontation between the Indian and the white races. There seems to be some correlation between the number of "foul deeds" perpetrated on the Indian in a given period and the length of material describing that period. Unfortunately, the correlation is inverse rather than direct.

Table 5 demonstrates that material about blacks tends to be concentrated in the period 1777-1880. The total size of black mentions has increased for 1966-1970 over 1960-1965 in all historical periods and at all grade levels. However, descriptions of black activities and culture prior to 1777 continue to be short and sparse, with African origins usually ignored. Coverage of black activities for the period of 1881-1945 is almost nil in texts published between 1960 and 1965 at all grade levels, but has increased somewhat in texts published since 1965. Material from the period

TABLE 4

Mean Size of Mentions of American Indians in 67 American History Texts, by Historical Period, Grade Level, and Year of Publication

Historical Period	Year of Publication	Grade Level		
		Grade	Jr. High	High
Before 1777	1960-1965	4.31	2.74	2.52
	1966-1970	6.10	1.88	1.81
1777-1880	1960-1965	3.02	1.34	1.81
	1966-1970	1.86	1.50	2.04
1881-1945	1960-1965	0.44	2.04	1.57
	1966-1970	0.39	1.23	0.52
1946-1960	1960-1965	0.08	0.22	0.10
	1966-1970	0.18	0.05	0.05

Note: Mean mention size is measured in pages.

TABLE 5

Mean Size of Mentions of Blacks in 67 American History Texts, by Historical Period, Grade Level, and Year of Publication

Historical Period	Year of Publication	Grade Level		
		Grade	Jr. High	High
Before 1777	1960-1965	0.39	0.34	0.69
	1966-1970	1.30	0.62	1.70
1777-1880	1960-1965	1.78	1.30	3.90
	1966-1970	4.17	3.23	6.27
1881-1945	1960-1965	0.05	0.29	0.73
	1966-1970	2.32	0.80	2.58
1946-1960	1960-1965	0.20	1.08	1.37
	1966-1970	2.74	1.81	3.38

Note: Mean mention size is measured in pages.

1946-1960 had also increased quite a bit, but the mean size masks considerable variation among texts, with some new texts having extensive sections on the modern black American and others continuing in the old tradition.

One might expect that with the increasing sensitivity of minorities to the content of public school texts, the "loading" of adjectives used to describe minority individuals would become more positive. A slight positive trend in adjective affect did appear (see Table 6) for both racial groups at the grade school and high school levels. However, the differences are too small to be significant.

Finally, the matter of extent of historical coverage was examined. The checklist scores presented in Table 7 cannot be taken as an exact rating of the coverage of historical material in the diverse texts, but they do provide general indications of the trends in depth of historical coverage present in the texts examined. Coverage of the black minority rises at all grade levels between 1960-1965 and 1966-1970, while coverage of Indian activities increases only at the high school level. At the grade school and junior high school levels the scope of the coverage of Indians actually *decreases* as the date of publication becomes more contemporary.

TABLE 6

Mean Adjective Affect Scores of American Indians and Blacks in 67
American History Texts, by Grade Level and Year of Publication

Minority	Year of Publication by Grade Level					
	1960-1965			1966-1970		
	Grade	Jr. High	High	Grade	Jr. High	High
Indian	3.2	3.0	3.0	3.8	2.9	3.3
Black	3.2	3.4	2.8	3.5	3.3	3.2
Total	3.2	3.1	2.9	3.7	3.2	3.3

Note: Adjective affect is measured on a scale of 1 to 5, positive to negative, with 3 being the neutral point.

TABLE 7

Checklist Scores of Historical Events and Cultural Characteristics of
American Indians and Blacks in 67 American History Texts,
by Grade Level and Year of Publication

Minority	Year of Publication by Grade Level					
	1960-1965			1966-1970		
	Grade	Jr. High	High	Grade	Jr. High	High
Indian	11.8	14.4	10.3	11.0	11.8	12.6
Black	5.4	9.9	12.7	12.9	14.1	18.8
Total	17.2	24.3	23.0	23.9	25.9	31.4

Note: The checklists consist of 21 items for Indians and 20 items for blacks, covering the entire span of American history. Thus, highest possible scores were 21 and 20, respectively.

For Indians, coverage and depth of coverage is inadequate at all grade levels. In fact, it appears that in many school districts students are learning less about American Indians today than they did five to ten years ago.

Black coverage has improved from totally inadequate to moderately inadequate at the grade and junior high text levels, and has become quite good at the high school level. However, many checklist items are merely referred to in a passing sentence, so that while scope of coverage in modern high school texts may be adequate, depth of coverage remains very poor.

DISCUSSION

In almost every text surveyed, there is an obvious attempt to minimize coverage of situations in which the United States government or whites in general appear to have acted poorly according to middle-class moral standards currently prevalent. As a consequence, whole periods of Indian and black history are "blocked out" and never reviewed. Indians are seen mostly as "teddy bears" at lower grade levels and not at all in the higher grades. Junior high texts are strikingly poorer than both grade school and high school texts. The Sambo myth of the nature of American blacks is on the way out but certainly is not dead. The only truly bright spots are the excellent sections on Indian culture which appear in several recent grade school texts and the greatly improved coverage of black history in a few contemporary high school texts.

Extent of coverage of Indian activities is more consistent with their proportionate size, but Indian mentions are lower in quality than black mentions. Though blacks comprise more than one-tenth of the American people, the highest proportion of material about blacks in any of the texts is about 2 percent. There is no reason why the percentage of textual material has to be exactly equal to the percentage of a minority in the population, but the extent of disparity with respect to blacks seems indefensible.

It is reasonable to expect that adjectives having a negative effect that are used in texts will be balanced with adjectives having a positive effect, and this is largely the case in the texts surveyed. However, words such as *inferior, stupid, deceitful, lecherous, murderous, selfish, treacherous, filthy, ungrateful, dumb, imcompetent, servile, unreliable, vagrant, weak,* and *unscrupulous* would probably not be missed if they were omitted from public school texts. The ethnocentrism inherent in the description of minority actions in these terms is unjustifiable. It is true that some minority individuals may be accurately described by these terms, but in American history texts, how often are the myths about white cultural heroes made realistic by the inclusion of their negative characteristics?

All of the textbooks judged poorest in coverage of minorities were published before 1967, but there is little reason for congratulations in this fact, since many of the texts now in use in public schools are doubtless of older vintage. In fact, many publishers keep older editions in print to supply "replacements" for texts used in school districts which have policies aimed at minimizing coverage of minority activities.

In a recent article, Jules Henry argues that "by leaving out and distorting information, textbooks strive for the goal of stupidity." It is possible to find much to support such a thesis in the endless minority stereotypes, distortions of historical fact, and rationalizations for self-seeking white acts that abound in American history texts. In the end, the American public gets the kind of education it wants. In Michigan, New York, and California, political pressure forced action against discriminatory texts. Apparently there are some Americans who will no longer tolerate texts that baldly omit and distort the role of Indians and blacks in American history.

Summary

A sample of American history textbooks published between 1960 and 1970 was examined to determine the nature and extent of coverage of American Indians and blacks. The texts were rated with reference to number of mentions, total size of mentions, adjective affect, and specific historical events discussed. The quality and quantity of textual material about blacks was found to have improved since the early 1960s, but that of the American Indian was found to have remained static or, in some cases, to have deteriorated.

NOTES

1   See as examples Jules Henry, "Education for Stupidity," *New York Review of Books,* 10 (May 9, 1968), 20-26; Kenneth M. Stampp et al., "Negro in American History Textbooks," *Negro History Bulletin,* 31 (October 1968), 13-16; Kenneth M. Stampp et al., *Report of University of California Professors on Newly Adopted Fourth-Grade History and Geography Books, with Respect to Their Treatment of Minority Groups* (Sacramento, California: State Department of Education, June 25, 1964); Peter Schrag, "Voices in the Classroom; The Emasculated Voice of the Textbook," *Saturday Review,* 50 (January 21, 1967), 74; and American Indian Historical Society and American Indian Committee to Discuss the Role of the Indian in State-adopted Textbooks, *Proposed Criteria as to the Role of the American Indian in State-adopted Textbooks* (Sacramento, California: State Department of Education, 1965).

2   See as examples Lloyd Marcus, *The Treatment of Minorities in Secondary School Textbooks* (New York: Anti-Defamation League of B'nai B'rith, 1961); "AJC Survey Finds Errors and Prejudice in Textbooks," *Library Journal,* 94 (September 15, 1969), 3122; and Harold J. Noah, Carl E. Prince and C. Russell Riggs, "History in High-School Textbooks," *School Review,* 70 (Winter 1962), 415-436.

3   Among the publications consulted were the following: American Indian Historical Society and American Indian Committee to Discuss the Role of the Indian in State-adopted Textbooks, *op. cit.;* Stanley Axelrod, "Treatment of the Negro in American History School Textbooks," *Negro History Bulletin,* 29 (March-April 1966), 135-136, 167; Board of Education, City of New York, *The Negro in American History* (New York, 1965); John Collier, *The Indians of the Americas* (New York: Norton, 1947); Phillip H. Drotning, *A Guide to*

Negro History in America (Garden City: Doubleday, 1968); Louis R. Harlan, *The Negro in American History* (Washington, D.C.: American Historical Association, 1965); Oliver LaFarge, *The Changing Indian* (Norman, Oklahoma: University of Oklahoma Press, 1942); Irving Sloan, *The Negro in Modern American History Textbooks* (Chicago: American Federation of Teachers, 1966); John Tebbel and Keith Jennison, *The American Indian Wars* (New York: Harper & Row, 1960); and Carter Woodson and Charles Wesley, *The Negro in Our History* (Washington, D.C.: Associated Publishers, 1962).

KATHLEEN C. HOUTS, ROSEMARY S. BAHR: STEREOTYPING OF INDIANS AND BLACKS IN MAGAZINE CARTOONS

The purpose of this paper is to illustrate the nature and extent of negative stereotyping of blacks and Indians which occurred in cartoons appearing in a popular American magazine, the *Saturday Evening Post,* during two historical periods, and to identify changes in the content and frequency of that stereotyping over time.

The popularity of cartoons is well established. They reach a wide variety of individuals because "the cartoon exacts from the reader no great amount of concentration, it supplies its own context in simple and direct form [and] its impact is swift and lasting."[1] A consideration of the popularity of cartoons and their possible effects on their audiences more than justifies an analysis of their content. Among the previous studies of cartoon content are analyses of propaganda techniques employed in political cartoons around the time of the Civil War and of the way various federal administrations have been depicted in political cartoons.[2] The thematic content of Sunday comics and characteristics of major comic strips have also been analyzed.[3]

The subject matter or content of cartoons is quite susceptible to social pressure. As early as 1930, only 25 years after cartoons were introduced in newspapers, Schoenfeld observed "A cartoonist must try to please everybody and hurt nobody."[4] For example, in 1930 a cartoonist who depicted a girl talking back to her mother was severely sanctioned; as a consequence of the negative responses of readers the offending cartoon series was dropped. As Schoenfeld explains, "A vast number of 'taboos', 'don'ts' and 'mustn'ts' surround the production of comic strips and not only explain many of the whys and wherefores of the business but furnish as illuminating a commentary on the American viewpoint as one could wish."[5] What may be quite acceptable for another media is often off limits to cartoonists, and the cost of violating a social norm of what "ought to" appear in cartoons seems to vary directly with the social power of the particular group or individual being portrayed.

The manifestation of minority stereotyping in cartoons occurs when some particular characteristic is treated as distinguishing those who manifest it from other members of society. To be identifiable in cartoons, members of a minority must be portrayed in such a way as to be recognizable by readers. For example, references to ethnic background or skin color may identify a member of a minority group. Stereotyping occurs when the group is characterized in specific ways and these characterizations are attributed to all individuals because of their membership in the group. The imputed attributes tend to be well-defined and few in number, and include both physical characteristics and behavior patterns.

One of the most popular methods of studying stereotyping in the mass media is content analysis.[6] In an analysis of short-story characters, Berelson and Salter found that "Americans" (white, Anglo-Saxon, English-speaking Protestants) were overrepresented in popular magazine fiction, while minority and foreign groups were seldom represented, and that the "Americans" appeared more often as major characters than did members of the minority groups. Moreover, characters in fiction were portrayed in standard stereotypes with "Americans" enjoying higher socioeconomic status and more desirable occupations than did the minorities.[7] On the basis of these findings from magazine fiction, we hypothesized that blacks and Indians would be underrepresented in magazine cartoons and that when they were portrayed at all it would be in terms of a few standard negative stereotypes.

It was anticipated that the extent of negative stereotyping would bear some relation to the relative numerical size and extent of political organization of racial minorities, and so initially we intended to compare the period 1900-1910 (when blacks were beginning to organize national associations) with 1960-1970 (when black organizations exerted considerable political pressure and American Indian organizations were beginning to appear). However, an inspection of early issues of the *Post* revealed that 1922 was the first year that nonpolitical cartoons appeared there, and so the decade 1922-1931 was designated as the initial period. There were also constraints in the final period, since the *Post* went out of business in 1968. Accordingly, the second interval was set at 1958-1968.

Data were collected and analyzed via usual techniques of content analysis.[8] Illustrations of fiction and feature articles were excluded from the study, as were political cartoons related to the editorial positions. In order to be included in the study, a cartoon had to show an identifiable black or Indian character or have an artifact representing either group. Cartoons containing an obvious artifact of the Indians (arrows or teepees) or the blacks (a cannibal's cooking pot) were included in the total count of cartoons for that minority, but such "artifact" cartoons were not included in some of the more detailed analyses unless Indian or black characters were portrayed.

In addition to identification of minority cartoons, the characteristics of the central figure or figures appearing in them were coded. Those character-istics included geographical location (United States or "other"), setting (ur-ban, rural, jungle, reservation, "out West," "at sea," or "other"), racial composition (native blacks only, native blacks with whites, African blacks only, African blacks and whites, Indians only, Indians and whites, or other), and behavior stereotypes manifest in the character's actions (canni-balism, rain-dancing, peace-pipe-smoking, shooting arrows, etc.)

During the first ten-year period, the *Post* printed a total of 2643 cartoons, of which 41 showed American blacks, 11 represented native blacks, and 17 included Indians. In the later period there were 5803 car-toons, including only 4 cartoons which showed American blacks, 59 with native blacks, and 56 Indian cartoons. There were 25 "artifact" cartoons, 22 of which contained Indian artifacts and 3 of which contained native black artifacts. The number and characteristics of these cartoons are given in Table 1. The most notable trends in these figures is the decrease in the number of cartoons depicting American blacks and a corresponding increase of native black cartoons.

TABLE 1

Number and Proportion of Cartoons in the Saturday Evening Post
Depicting Indians and Blacks, 1922-1931 and 1958-1968

	Period			
	1922-1931		1958-1968	
	Number	*Percent*	*Number*	*Percent*
Total	2643	100	5803	100
American blacks	41	2	4	0
Native blacks	11	0	59	1
Indians	17	1	56	1

It had been hypothesized that blacks and Indians would be under-represented in magazine cartoons. On the basis of representation in terms of population, there should have been 1 black cartoon for every 8 white cartoons both in the 1920s and the 1960s. As for Indians, in the 1920 decade there should have been 1 Indian cartoon for every 500 white car-toons, and in the 1960s one Indian cartoon for every 300 white cartoons. Table 1 indicates that the blacks were greatly underrepresented in both periods, but the Indians were *overrepresented*.

We had also anticipated that the blacks and Indians would be por-trayed in standard stereotypes, and the findings provided ample evidence of this. The most prevalent stereotypes that emerged were the Indian shooting arrows and the native black as cannibal. Table 2 shows that in the decade of the 1960s, 93 percent of the blacks in *Post* cartoons were portrayed as natives and 49 percent were portrayed as native cannibals. The Indians also were portrayed in standard stereotypes, although not quite as overwhelmingly as the blacks. In the same period about one-fifth of the cartoons where Indians were portrayed showed them shooting arrows. When the "artifact"

TABLE 2

Cannibal and Indian-Warrior Stereotypes in Cartoons Depicting
Indians and Blacks, 1922-1931 and 1958-1968

	Period			
	1922-1931		1958-1968	
	Number	*Percent*	*Number*	*Percent*
Blacks (total)	52	100	63	100
Cannibal	2	4	31	49
Other	50	96	32	51
Indians (total)	17	100	56	100
Shooting arrows	4	24	11	20
Other	13	76	45	80

cartoons were excluded, one-third of the cartoons in which Indians were represented showed Indians shooting arrows, 24 percent showed pottery, teepees, or smoke signals, and 88 percent included an Indian with feathers in his hair.

The data in Tables 1 and 2 indicate that between the 1920s and the 1960s the American black virtually disappeared as a cartoon character. In the 1960s the black in a cartoon was likely to be portrayed as a native, about half the time as a cannibalistic native. It seems probable that the apparent lack of interest in American blacks reflects an awareness of possible "costs," that is, letters to the editor, canceled subscriptions, etc., involved in including American blacks, costs easily avoided by removing them from cartoons altogether. At any rate, from the recent cartoons one would conclude that few blacks lived in the United States.

The stability of the Indian warrior as a stock character suggests that cartoonists, editors, and the public at large were less "up tight" about the Indian, either because his political organizations were not particularly powerful during either of these periods, or because the cartoons were not defined as negative stereotyping. Yet the message they convey, taken together, is that the Indian in American life is important only as a primitive, historical bow-and-arrow type who has no place in the modern society. Judging from the cartoons, neither the modern Indian nor the modern black man exists in contemporary America.

It is recognized that these conclusions derive from an analysis of cartoons in a single magazine. Yet, to the extent that the *Saturday Evening Post* shaped interracial attitudes at all, it is difficult to see how the net result of its cartoons could be anything but a perpetration of negative and unrealistic stereotypes of blacks and Native Americans. It is possible that content analyses of cartoons in other magazines would reveal more positive stereotypes, some of which might counteract the ones fostered by the *Post* cartoons. However, on the basis of an unsystematic, cursory review of cartoons in other magazines, we are not sanguine about this possibility.

NOTES

1   James K. Lively, "Propaganda Techniques of Civil War Cartoonists," *Public Opinion Quarterly,* 6 (Spring 1942), 99.

2   Robert A. Rothman and Donald W. Olmsted, "Chicago Tribune Cartoons during and after the McCormick Era," *Journalism Quarterly,* 43, (Spring 1966), 67-72.

3   Francis E. Barcus, "A Content Analysis of Trends in Sunday Comics, 1900-1959," *Journalism Quarterly,* 38 (Spring 1961), 171-180; and Marvin Spiegelman, Carl Terwilliger, and Franklin Fearing, "The Content of Comic Strips: A Study of a Mass Medium of Communication," *Journal of Social Psychology,* 35 (February 1952), 37-58.

4   Amram Schoenfeld, "The Laugh Industry," *The Saturday Evening Post,* 20 (February 1, 1930), 12.

5   *Ibid.*

6   See, for example, Howard J. Ehrlich and James W. Rinehart, "A Brief Methodology of Stereotype Research," *Social Forces,* 43 (May 1965), 654-675; Lawrence S. Linn, "Verbal Attitudes and Overt Behavior: A Study of Racial Discrimination," *Social Forces,* 44 (March 1965), 353-364; Bernard Berelson and Patricia J. Salter, "Marjority and Minority Americans: An Analysis of Magazine Fiction," *Public Opinion Quarterly,* 10 (Summer 1946), 168-190; Keith K. Cox, "Changes in Stereotyping of Negroes and Whites in Magazine Advertisements," *Public Opinion Quarterly,* 33 (Winter 1969), 603-606; and Thomas R. Cripps, "The Death of Rastus: Negroes in American Films since 1945," in Norval D. Glenn and Charles M. Bonjean, eds., *Blacks in the United States* (San Francisco: Chandler, 1969), p. 261-269.

7   Berelson and Salter, *op. cit.*

8   Richard W. Budd, Robert K. Thorp, and Lewis Donohew, *Content Analysis of Communications* (New York: Macmillan, 1967); Robert C. North, Ole R. Holsti, M. George Zaninovich, and Dina A. Zinnes, *Content Analysis: A Handbook with Applications for Study of International Crisis* (Evanston: Northwestern University Press, 1963).

DANIEL H. MacMEEKIN: RED, WHITE, AND GRAY: EQUAL PROTECTION AND THE AMERICAN INDIAN

An American Indian who rapes a non-Indian woman on an Indian reservation may be executed, while the maximum punishment for an Indian who rapes an Indian woman on the reservation is life imprisonment. In *Gray v. United States,*[1] defendants, American Indians who had raped a Caucasian woman on the Navajo Reservation in Arizona, challenged this statutory scheme, but the Ninth Circuit upheld its constitutionality.

The defendants had been brought to trial under the provisions of title 18, section 1153, of the *United States Code:*

> Any Indian who commits ... rape ... within the Indian country, shall be subject to the same laws and penalties as all other persons ... within the exclusive jurisdiction of the United States.
>
> ... [A]ny Indian who commits the [offense] of rape ... upon any female Indian within the Indian country *shall be imprisoned at the discretion of the court.*[2]

An Indian who rapes a non-Indian is subject, in accordance with the first paragraph of section 1153, to the provisions of title 18, section 2031: "Whoever, within the special maritime and territorial jurisdiction of the United States, commits rape shall suffer death, or imprisonment for any term of years or for life."[3] Under the arrangement established by these sections the availability of capital punishment is dependent upon three factors: the race of the rapist, the race of his victim, and the location of the crime. Capital punishment may be imposed in every case subject to federal prosecution except in the instance where an Indian has raped a female Indian in Indian country.

Defendants challenged the constitutionality of section 1153 on the ground that "the punishment prescribed was based on race and therefore denied the defendants due process of law."[4] The court answered this contention by stating:

> It has long been acknowledged that Congress, in the exercise of its constitutional power, has recognized and established for the Indian people a peculiar and protected status as wards of the Federal government....
>
> Congress has seen fit to diminish the penalty to be imposed upon an Indian who is convicted of rape upon another Indian in Indian Country.... Appellants here seek to challenge as un-

Source: Reprinted by permission from *Stanford Law Review* 21 (May 1969), 1236-1248. Copyright 1969 by the Board of Trustees of the Leland Stanford Junior University.

constitutional this statute ... which is of benefit to them. We cannot say that such a statute denies its beneficiaries due process of law.[5]

I. AN INTRODUCTION TO FEDERAL INDIAN LAW

A. Assimilation and Separation

American Indians[6] are governed, in part, by a body of law distinct from that applicable to the rest of the nation.[7] This body of law, a conglomeration of constitutional provision, treaty, public law, judicial decision, and administrative regulation,[8] is built upon two conflicting themes concerning the proper role of the Indian in American society. These two themes are based on what may be characterized as the assimilative premise and the separative premise. The assimilative premise maintains that the Indian should abandon his cultural identity and become part of the mainstream of American life. It carries the connotation of "civilizing" the Indian. The separative premise holds that the American Indian should be permitted to preserve his cultural identity and should not be forced to merge with the broader American community. Obviously, the motivations underlying this latter premise may range from genuine concern and respect for the distinctive Indian cultures to desire to keep an "inferior" culture isolated. The assimilative premise and the separative premise are not mutually exclusive; the tension between them may be resolved by statutory compromise.[9] However, each of the premises has been dominant at various times and has left its legislative imprint.

American Indian law developed in the context of the westward movement of white settlers onto Indian lands and is thus closely intertwined with the means used by whites to displace Indians. A cynic might suggest that federal Indian law was based on the separative premise when it was possible to move the Indians to other territory and on the assimilative premise when the land scarcity required that the Indian and his lands be brought into the totally alien private-property system of the white man, where the Indian could easily be dispossessed by such devices as inflated tax appraisals and long-term leases returning minimal rents.[10]

The first major legislation dealing with Indian lands was the Indian Removal Act of 1830.[11] This law, an application of the separative premise, authorized the President to negotiate treaties with the eastern tribes, exchanging their lands for land west of the Mississippi River and thus opening eastern territory for white settlement. Although the land exchange was to be arranged by treaty, the Cherokees and Seminoles refused to negotiate and the Army effected their removal.[12]

Shortly after the passage of the Indian Removal Act, the Supreme Court was asked to determine the extent to which Indians were subject to federal and state law; guidelines for the resolution of these problems were set forth by Chief Justice Marshall in the Cherokee Indian cases of 1831 and 1832.[13] In *Cherokee Nation v. Georgia*[14] the Court faced the question whether it had jurisdiction over an action to enjoin the state of Georgia from enforcing its laws within the Cherokee territory. The Cherokee Nation had attempted to invoke the Court's original jurisdiction over controversies "between a State . . . and foreign States."[15]   Chief Justice Marshall's opinion rejected the contention that the Cherokee Nation was a foreign state and instead characterized it as a "domestic dependent nation."[16] After deciding that the Court did not have jurisdiction over the Cherokee bill in equity, Marshall proceeded to characterize the precise nature of the relationship between the United States and the Indian tribes: "[The Indians] are in a state of pupilage. Their relation to the United States resembles that of a ward to his guardian."[17] From this dictum developed the wardship theory of Indian law.

In *Worcester v. Georgia,*[18] the second of the Cherokee Indian cases, the Court was called upon to decide whether the federal or state governments had paramount sovereignty over the Indian tribes. Worcester, a missionary residing with the boundaries of Cherokee territory in Georgia, was tried and convicted in the courts of that state for violating a statute that required all white persons to obtain a state license before taking up residence within the Cherokee Nation. Worcester contended that the Georgia law contravened the Constitution, treaties between the federal government and the Cherokee Nation, and statutes enacted by Congress pursuant to those treaties. The Supreme Court agreed. Chief Justice Marshall again wrote for the Court:

> The Cherokee nation, then, is a distinct community, occupy-
> ing its own territory . . . in which the laws of Georgia can have no
> force, and which the citizens of Georgia have no right to enter,
> but with the assent of the Cherokees themselves, or in conformity
> with treaties and with the acts of Congress. The whole intercourse
> between the United States and this nation is, by our constitution
> and laws, vested in the government of the United States.[19]

By the 1880's, white settlers were pressing hard against the boundaries of western Indian reservations. That fact, combined with the rationale provided by social Darwinism,[20] resulted in the General Allotment Act of 1887,[21] also known as the Dawes Act. This Act authorized the President, at his decretion, to allot individual parcels of reservation land to the inhabitants of that reservation and to declare the remaining undivided land surplus and open to white homesteaders.[22] The Act was assimilative in that it assumed that the Indian, with his own parcel of land, would aspire to the ideal of a successful family farm as did the white homesteader.[23]

The General Allotment Act also provided that citizenship be granted to Indians who moved away from their tribal lands and "adopted the habits of civilized life"[24] and to allottees when they received their parcels. Citizenship had been conferred on some Indians by treaty and statute,[25] but there were still a large number of Indians, most of them living on reservations, who were not citizens. This was remedied by the Indian Citizenship Act of 1924,[26] which, reflecting the assimilative premise dominant at that time, conferred citizenship on all Indians within the United States.

During the Roosevelt administration the separative premise again became dominant, as demonstrated by the passage of the Indian Re-organization Act of 1934,[27] which terminated the allotment process and attempted to increase and strengthen the Indian land base. By 1953, however, the pendulum had started to swing back toward the assimilative premise. This movement was most obviously manifested by efforts to terminate the special relationship that had developed between the federal government and the Indian tribes.[28]

The present situation represents a compromise between the extremes of assimilation and separation;[29] the individual Indian now has, in theory at least, a choice between alternative relationships to the rest of American society.[30] Attempts are being made both to improve the status of reservation Indians and to ameliorate the transition process for Indians who wish to join the mainstream of American society. There has also been some movement toward greater participation by Indian groups in the national political process.[31]

B. Crimes in Indian Country

Indians were first treated by Congress as semi-independent, self-governing tribes, subject only to the federal government's right as a conquering power to regulate their relations with non-Indians.[32] In early enactments dealing with crimes committed within Indian country, Congress specifically exempted those actions in which both the perpetrator and the victim were Indians.[33] This situation remained until 1885, when Congress enacted the Major Crimes Act,[34] the forerunner of the statutory provision involved in *Gray*. The Act was passed in response to public outcry over the Supreme Court decision in *Ex Parte Crow Dog*.[35] In that case, involving a particularly sensational murder, the Court had affirmed the nonapplicability of federal criminal law to crimes committed by one Indian upon another within Indian country. The Major Crimes Act extended the jurisdiction of the federal courts to include the following crimes when committed by Indians in Indian country: murder, manslaughter, rape, assault with intent to kill, arson, burglary, and larceny.[36] The Supreme Court affirmed the constitutionality of the Act in *United States v. Kagama*.[37] The Court's opinion drew heavily on Marshall's dictum in the *Cherokee Nation* case and extended the wardship concept to give Congress virtually plenary power over the Indians.[38]

Jurisdiction over crimes committed on Indian reservations is now divided among the federal, state, and tribal courts.[39] The applicable law in each case depends upon the crime committed, the state in which the reservation is located, the race of the accused, and the race of the victim (if one exists). Certain generally applicable federal laws—such as those concerning smuggling,[40] bank robbery,[41] and counterfeiting[42]—apply to any person on or off a reservation without regard to these distinctions. In six states, state criminal-law jurisdiction exists on reservations as it does elsewhere in the state, regardless of the crime or the race of the accused or his victim.[43]

On reservations in other states, however, the Indian criminal defendant is tried in federal or tribal court. If the offense is punishable under the

Major Crimes Act[44] he is subject to federal jurisdiction regardless of the victim's race. For other offenses by an Indian the appropriate jurisdiction depends upon the race of the victim. If the victim is an Indian the accused is tried in tribal court in accordance with tribal law.[45] If the victim is non-Indian the offender is tried in federal court,[46] either for a federal territorial offense or under the Assimilative Crimes Act.[47] A non-Indian committing a crime against an Indian on an Indian reservation will be tried in federal court, either for a territorial offense or under the Assimilative Crimes Act.[48]

C. Indian Rapists

Defendants in the *Gray* case were charged under the current codification of the Major Crimes Act, section 1153 of the *United States Code.* As noted above,[49] this section provides that when an Indian rapes an Indian woman he will be imprisoned "at the descretion of the court." Capital punishment is authorized when an Indian rapes an non-Indian woman. Rape and assault with intent to commit rape are the only "major" crimes to which this type of differential sanction is applicable. The Major Crimes Act, in its original form, did not distinguish between rape and the other crimes within its purview. The Act merely made the general provisions governing certain territorial offenses (the "major" crimes) applicable to those offenses when committed by Indians within Indian country. In each case, punishment was to be the same for an offending Indian as for any other offender within the federal jurisdiction.

The law was first changed in 1897 by the passage of "[a]n Act To reduce the cases in which the penalty of death may be inflicted."[50] Section 5 of this Act, the only section applying exclusively to Indians, provided that "any Indian who shall commit the offense of rape within the limits of any Indian reservation shall be punished by imprisonment at the discretion of the court."[51] The Act left unaltered the identical treatment of Indian and non-Indian perpetrators of other major crimes.

The statute was revised to essentially its present form by congressional amendment in 1909.[52] The 1897 amendment to the Major Crimes Act had exempted the reservation Indian rapist from the possibility of the death penalty without regard for the race of his victim. The 1909 amendment limited this exclusion to those cases in which the victim of the Indian rapist was an Indian woman.

II. THE CONSTITUTIONAL QUESTION

The defendants in *Gray* argued that the statutory authorization for different maximum penalties based upon the race of a rapist's victim was an arbitrary exercise of federal legislative power. Accordingly, they challenged the statute as a violation of the due process requirements of the Federal Constitution. Although discrimination on the basis of arbitrary criminal-law classifications is usually considered to be a denial of equal protection of the laws,[53] the equal protection clause of the fourteenth amendment applies only to state action;[54] challenges to discriminatory federal action must be made under the due process clause of the fifth amendment.[55]

The question raised by the defense in the *Gray* case is whether the classifications made by section 1153 are so arbitrary as to violate the requirements of due process and equal protection. Those classifications are a reflection of the tension between the separative premise and the assimilative premise. Given the history of the relationship between Indians and non-Indians, it is difficult to fault the invocation of either the assimilative or separative premise as legitimate legislative ends. If Indians are to be integrated into American society there is no need to give statutory recognition to a distinctive Indian culture; but if the Indian is to be allowed to maintain his cultural identity, the law of the United States must necessarily take cognizance of that identity and define it by the two most convenient criteria: geography (the Indian country) and race.

As long as the option of preserving cultural identity is regarded as a legitimate policy objective, and there is no apparent reason why it should not be, the legal regimen must take the cultural identity into account. Thus, at the present time, various statutes do appreciate Indian cultural identity and do use the racial criterion for determining membership in the cultural subgroup.[56] But, although race may properly be used as a means of identifying Indians *qua* cultural members, not every statutory distinction between Indians and others is necessarily legitimate.

A due process-equal protection analysis of section 1153 is complicated by a lack of clear standards for judicial review of separatist legislation. Ordinarily, the federal courts will not overturn legislative classifications that are reasonably related to a legitimate legislative end.[57] However, racial classifications are permissible, if at all, only when necessary to achieve some "overriding statutory purpose."[58] If the word *Indian* as used in section 1153 is racially descriptive, the latter test of validity should apply. On the other hand, perhaps only a "reasonable nexus" between the classification and the statutory purpose would be necessary if *Indian* is used merely to describe a culture that may properly deserve special considerations. This difference follows from the fact that the test for racially classificatory statutes has developed with regard to patently invidious legislation affecting Negroes, and the courts have rejected the separative premise in this context. Hence, an "overriding" purpose is required to support racial categorization. Once some degree of separatism becomes legitimate, however, the constitutional standards must necessarily become more permissive. Whether or not separatism is legitimate in any particular case should depend on whether the statute serves to distinguish different, and preservable, cultural values. The validity of the classification *Indian* may then depend on whether it represents a racial discrimination or a cultural recognition. Assuming that an inquiry into congressional motive is inappropriate in this regard,[59] the operative effect of section 1153 becomes crucial.

As the *Gray* court observed, section 1153 does not seem to discriminate invidiously against Indians, but to operate in their favor,[60]

because only Indians, among all persons subject to federal criminal jurisdiction, can benefit from the death-penalty exclusion.[61] In fact this benefit
is only conferred on those Indians who happen to rape Indian women.
Moreover, while the Indian male with exclusively Indian tastes may receive
favorable treatment under the law, the Indian female may be at a marked
disadvantage. Anyone who rapes a non-Indian female always faces the
possibility of capital punishment, but an Indian who rapes an Indian
cannot be executed. If the execution sanction has any deterrent value when
applicable to rapists, then Indian women are not protected as much as are
non-Indians.

If section 1153 is to be supported by its reasonable relation to the
legitimate legislative ends of the criminal law, it must be rational to assume
that non-Indians, more than Indians, must be deterred from raping Indians
and that Indians must be deterred from raping non-Indians more than from
raping Indians. This disparity of deterrence cannot be justified in either
case on the ground that the one crime is more likely to occur than the
other; so the distinctions are legitimate, if at all, only if it is permissible for
society to treat intracultural rape as a less serious crime than intercultural
rape. Even assuming that such treatment of Negroes and whites would be
an unacceptable manifestation of the separative premise,[62] a similar
assumption may not be indulged when some separation is traditionally
accepted. Nevertheless, the history of the separative premise in Indian law
demonstrates that it is not always invoked for commendable reasons. The
likelihood of invidious discrimination is so great that there should be close
judicial scrutiny of any separatist statute. There is no alternative to
examining the actual congressional purpose, if not the motive,[63] to determine whether it may be considered, at minimum, benign.

When the statute was first enacted in the Major Crimes Act of 1885,
the dominant premise was that of assimilation. Up to that time the major
crimes had been treated in varying ways among the various Indian cultures.[64] The Major Crimes Act ignored cultural differences and attempted
to standardize the treatment of all offenders within the federal jurisdiction.

The 1897 amendment,[65] although also passed at a time when the
assimilative premise was dominant, was an attempt to adjust the law to
conform to differences in cultural values between the Indian and the non-
Indian societies. The amendment was part of an Act that was designed to
overcome jury reluctance to convict for federal territorial offenses when
conviction would result in a mandatory death sentence.[66] The new Act
permitted juries to return a guilty verdict with the qualification "without
capital punishment."[67] Section 5 of the Act, the only section applying
exclusively to Indians, eliminated the death penalty as a possible punishment for the Indian rapist, substituting "imprisonment at the descretion of
the court." This section was added to the House bill by the Senate
Judiciary Committee.[68] Senator Hoar, explaining the Judiciary Committee
amendment on the Senate floor, indicated that the reason for it was the
prevalence of cases in which the Indian "boys ... did not seem to understand that they had committed any very heinous offense, and admitted the
offense readily without any attempt to conceal it whatever."[69]

Implicit in Senator Hoar's statement is the assumption that rape was considered to be a less serious offense within the Indian culture than in the dominant white society. In accordance with the retributive theory of justice, the Indian rapist would be less culpable then his non-Indian counterpart and, consequently, less deserving of punishment. Since the culpability of the rapist was not dependent upon the race of his victim, there was no reason to distinguish among rape offenses on that basis.

In 1909 Congress limited the death-penalty exclusion to those Indians who rape Indian women within the limits of an Indian reservation.[70] The 1909 change was an incidental part of a major effort to codify the existing federal penal laws. During the floor debate in the House of Representatives,[71] Representative Adamson of Georgia inquired why Indians should be singled out for the special benefit conferred by the 1897 amendment. The answer given by Representative Norris of Nebraska differed somewhat from the 1897 statement by Senator Hoar; Representative Norris said: "[T]he morals of Indian women are not alway as high as those of white women, and consequently the punishment should be lighter for an offense against her."[72] At this point it was noted that the 1897 amendment also applied to an Indian who raped a white woman within the bounds of the reservation. Without further debate, an amendment was adopted limiting the death-penalty exclusion to those Indians who raped Indian women. In addition to concern for the offender's culpability, then, the deterrent effect of capital punishment was introduced, along with the notion that low morals of the Indian woman give less reason to protect her than the non-Indian woman. However, this lesser degree of protection was enacted only for the Indian woman who had been raped by an Indian male. Thus it is difficult to conceal a suspicion that thoughts about the relative evil of intercultural rape also played a part in the legislative determination.

From these fragments of legislative history, it is barely possible to construct a statutory purpose. The original statute was clearly meant to bring the Indian under the law of the white man. The later amendments attempted to modify the original enactment in order to recognize value differences between the majority and minority cultures and, possibly, in the case of the 1909 amendment, to indulge the feelings of certain Congressmen concerning cross-cultural copulation. The first amendment clearly tried to make allowance for Indian mores. The second amendment, charitably construed, more narrowly defined the degree to which mores could affect the federal law of rape.

If the reason for limiting the death-penalty exclusion to Indians who rape Indian women is that the morals of Indian women are low, it follows that the non-Indian who rapes an Indian woman should also be able to avail himself of the exclusion. If execution is thought inappropriate because of the lesser culpability of the Indian rapist, the race of his victim should not be relevant. Although this two-edged underinclusiveness might be insufficient to invalidate another type of statute,[73] it is totally inconsistent with the benignity of purpose that should be required to support separative legislation.

The distinction established by the 1909 amendment, the critical distinction in *Gray*, is necessary neither to the maintenance of the separate values of the Indian cultures nor to the assimilation of Indians by the dominant culture, but serves only to make intercultural rape a more serious crime than intracultural rape.

The *Gray* court met a due process challenge by treating it as an attack on Congress' well-established power to regulate the Indians. In so doing, the court ignored the principle that even "plenary" legislative power is subject to constitutional limitations. The field of Indian law is complex, and the acceptable legal relations between the various Indian subcultures and the dominant culture are still nebulously defined. The decision in *Gray v. United States* successfully avoided examining this complexity and nebulosity. An indefensible legislative scheme persists.

NOTES

1   394 F.2d 96 (9th Cir. 1968). The opinion of May 2, 1968, issued on denial of rehearing, replaced an earlier unpublished opinion of September 15, 1967.
2   18 U.S.C.A. § 1153 (Supp. 1968) (emphasis added). "Indian country" is defined as "(a) all land within the limits of any Indian reservation under the jurisdiction of the United States Government, notwithstanding the issuance of any patent, and, including rights-of-way running through the reservation, (b) all dependent Indian communities within the borders of the United States whether within the original or subsequently acquired territory thereof, and whether within or without the limits of a state, and (c) all Indian allotments, the Indian titles to which have not been extinguished, including rights-of-way running through the same," 18 U.S.C. § 1151 (1964).
3   18 U.S.C. § 2031 (1964). The special maritime and territorial jurisdiction of the United States is defined in *id.* § 7.
4   394 F.2d at 97-98.
5   *Id.* at 98-99.
6   On the problems involved in determining who is an Indian see D. Johnston, An analysis of sources of information on the population of the Navaho 3-9 (1966); U.S. Dep't of the Interior, Federal Indian Law 4-12 (1958). *See generally Legal Definition of Race,* 3 Race Rel. L. Rep. 571 (1958).
7   An entire title of the *United States Code* (title 25) owes its *raison d'être* to the Indian. Other laws applying only to Indians are scattered throughout the *Code. E.g.,* 16 U.S.C. § 631c (1964) (permission to engage in seal or sea otter hunting in traditional manner); 18 U.S.C. §§ 1151-65 (1964) (crimes involving Indians or committed in Indian country); 42 U.S.C. §§ 2001-05f (1964) (Indian hospitals and health facilities).
8   F. Cohen, Handbook of Federal Indian Law at v (1941). A list of statutes, treaties, federal-court cases, Department of the Interior rulings, and Attorney General opinions relevant to the legal status of the American Indian is collected at pages 485-637 of this work. The *Handbook* has been periodically brought up to date by the Department of the Interior, but the later editions do not include the list of legal materials. The current edition is U.S. Dep't of the Interior, Federal

Indian Law (1958). The work is again in the process of revision. Pub L. No. 90-284, § 701(a) (2) (Apr. 11, 1968) (36 U.S.L.W. 91).

9 *See* text accompanying note 30 *infra.*

10 *See* H. Fritz, The Movement for Indian Assimilation, 1860-1890, at 16-17, 109-12 (1963); W. Hagan, American Indians 68-69, 139-147 (1961); Haas, *The Legal Aspects of Indian Affairs from 1887 to 1957,* Annals, May 1957, at 12-16.

11 Act of May 28, 1830, ch. 148, 4 Stat. 411.

12 McNickle, *Indian and European: Indian-White Relations from Discovery to 1887,* Annals, May 1957, at 1, 10.

13 For a detailed study of the historical background of these cases see Burke, *The Cherokee Cases: A Study in Law, Politics, and Morality,* 21 Stan. L. Rev. 500 (1969).

14 30 U.S. (5 Pet.) 1 (1831).

15 U.S. Const. art. III, § 2.

16 30 U.S. (5 Pet.) at 17.

17 *Id.*

18 31 U.S. (6 Pet.) 515 (1832).

19 *Id.* at 561. It is apparently bad form to cite this case without noting that President Jackson responded to the decision with the purported challenge: "John Marshall has made his decision; now let him enforce it." *Sic sit.*

20 *See* Haas, *supra* note 10, at 12-13.

21 Act of Feb. 8, 1887, ch. 119, 24 Stat. 388.

22 The proceeds from the sale of the "surplus" land were to be held in trust by the Treasury for the sole use of the tribe that had held the land. *Id.* § 5, at 390. The land was sold at the homestead price of $2.50 per acre. It has been estimated that through the provisions of the General Allotment Act "the Indians were relieved of some ninety million acres, or almost two-thirds of their land base, between the years 1887 and 1930." McNickle, *supra* note 12, at 10.

23 *See* W. Hagan, *supra* note 10, at 140; Haas, *supra* note 10, at 13 n.4.

24 Act of Feb. 8, 1887, ch. 119, § 6, 24 Stat. 390.

25 U.S. Dep't of the Interior, *supra* note 6, at 517-20.

26 Act of June 2, 1924, ch. 233, 43 Stat. 253 (codified in 8 U.S.C. § 1401(a)(2) (1964)).

27 Act of June 18, 1934, ch. 576, 48 Stat. 984. The main provisions of the Act were made applicable to Alaska by the Act of May 1, 1936, ch. 254, 49 Stat. 1250, and to Oklahoma by the Act of June 26, 1936, ch. 831, 49 Stat. 1967.

28 *See, e.g.,* H.R. Con. Res. 108, 83d Cong., 1st Sess., 67 Stat. B132 (1953). *See generally* La Farge, *Termination of Federal Supervision: Disintegration and the American Indians,* Annals, May 1957, at 41; Watkins, *Termination of Federal Supervision: The Removal of Restrictions Over Indian Property and Person,* Annals, May 1957, at 47.

29 *See* Dozier, Simpson & Yinger, *The Integration of Americans of Indian Descent,* Annals, May 1957, at 158; Note, *The Indian: The Forgotten American,* 81 Harv. L. Rev. 1818, 1839 (1968).

30 On the difficulties that the reservation Indian faces in adjusting to life off the reservation see L. Madigan, The American Indian Relocation Program 17 (1956); S. Steiner, The New Indians 175-92 (1968); Fretz, *The Bill of Rights and American Indian Tribal Governments,* 6 Natural

Resources J. 581, 587–88 (1966); Riffenburgh, *Cultural Influences and Crime Among Indian-Americans of the Southwest,* Fed. Probation, Sept. 1964, at 38. *See generally* Dozier, Simpson & Yinger, *supra* note 29. On the difficulties that the reservation Indian faces in maintaining his distinct cultural values on the reservation see Henninger & Esposito, *Indian Schools,* The New Republic, Feb. 15, 1969, at 18.

31 *See* S. Steiner, *supra* note 30, at 231–49; Peterson, *American Indian Political Participation,* Annals, May 1957, at 116, 125–26; *cf.* Vogt, *The Acculturation of American Indians,* Annals, May 1957, at 137, 145–46.

32 United States v. Kagama, 118 U.S. 375–82 (1886); Worcester v. Georgia, 31 U.S. (6 Pet.) 515, 559 (1832).

33 Act of June 30, 1834, ch. 161, § 25, 4 Stat. 733.

34 Act of Mar. 3, 1885, ch. 341, § 9, 23 Stat. 385.

35 109 U.S. 556 (1883). For a description of the events leading to the passage of the Major Crimes Act see Cohen, *Indian Rights and the Federal Courts,* 24 Minn. L. Rev. 145, 152 (1940).

36 Assault with intent to commit rape, assault with a dangerous weapon, robbery, statutory rape, and assault resulting in serious bodily injury are now also included in the enumerated offenses. 18 U.S.C.A. § 1153 (Supp. 1968).

37 118 U.S. 375 (1886).

38 118 U.S. at 382–85; *accord,* United States v. Chavez, 290 U.S. 357 (1933); Perrin v. United States, 232 U.S. 478, 486 (1914); United States v. Pelican, 232 U.S. 442, 451 (1914); United States v. Celestine, 215 U.S. 278, 290 (1909); *In re* Carmen's Petition, 165 F. Supp. 942, 948–49 (N.D. Cal. 1958), *aff'd sub nom.* Dickson v. Carmen, 270 F.2d 809 (9th Cir. 1959), *cert. denied,* 361 U.S. 934 (1960).

39 An Indian committing a crime outside Indian country is subject to the same jurisdiction and law as anyone else.

40 *See* 18 U.S.C. § 545 (1964).

41 *See id.* § 2113.

42 *See id.* §§ 471–509.

43 *Id.* § 1162. This law was passed in the 1950's, when the assimilative premise was dominant and the desire of Congress to terminate the special relationship between the Indians and the federal government was strong. Federal jurisdiction over the Indians was transferred to the state in which there was no significant opposition to the transfer either by the state or by the affected Indian tribes. Several states were precluded from accepting jurisdiction over the Indians by provisions in their constitutions. H. Rep. No. 848, 83d Cong., 1st Sess. (1953).

44 18 U.S.C.A. § 1153 (Supp. 1968).

45 Note, *supra* note 29, at 1834.

46 Exception is made for cases in which the Indian offender has been punished according to the local law of the tribe and for those cases where exclusive jurisdiction over the crime has been vested by treaty in the Indian tribe. 18 U.S.C. § 1152 (1964).

47 Federal territorial offenses are those crimes established by federal statute, *see, e.g.,* 18 U.S.C. §§ 81 (arson), 113 (assault), 661 (theft), 1111 (murder), 1112 (manslaughter), 2031 (rape) (1964), that take place within the special maritime or territorial jurisdiction of the United States. The Assimilative Crimes Act, *id.* § 13, makes punishable, in accordance with the law of the state in which a federal

territory is located, those offenses for which there is no applicable federal law.

48 The same should be true for crimes committed by non-Indians against non-Indians within Indian country, but these offenses fall under state law and are within the exclusive jurisdiction of state courts. *See* New York *ex rel.* Ray v. Martin, 326 U.S. 496 (1946); United States v. McBratney, 104 U.S. 621 (1881).

49 *See* text accompanying note 2 *supra.*

50 Act of Jan. 15, 1897, ch. 29, 29 Stat. 487.

51 *Id.* § 5.

52 Act of Mar. 4, 1909, ch. 321, § 328, 35 Stat. 1151.

53 *See, e.g.,* Skinner v. Oklahoma, 316 U.S. 535 (1942); Strauder v. West Virginia, 100 U.S. 303 (1880).

54 *See, e.g.,* Detroit Bank v. United States, 317 U.S. 329 (1943); Wight v. Davidson, 181 U.S. 371, 384 (1901).

55 The Supreme Court confronted the problem of arbitrary discrimination by the federal government in Bolling v. Sharpe, 347 U.S. 497 (1954), a companion case to Brown v. Board of Education, 347 U.S. 483 (1954). In *Brown* the Court held that "separate but equal" school facilities maintained by the states were a denial "of the equal protection of the laws guaranteed by the Fourteenth Amendment." *Id.* at 495. In *Bolling,* however, the "separate but equal" facilities were maintained by the District of Columbia and thus could not be challenged under the fourteenth amendment. The Court held: "The Fifth Amendment, which is applicable in the District of Columbia, does not contain an equal protection clause as does the Fourteenth Amendment. . . . But . . . discrimination may be so unjustifiable as to be violative of due process. . . . In view of our decision that the Constitution prohibits the states from maintaining racially segregated schools, it would be unthinkable that the same Constitution would impose a lesser duty on the Federal Government." 347 U.S. at 499-500; *accord,* Schneider v. Rusk, 377 U.S. 163 (1964); Bolton v. Harris, 395 F.2d 642 (D.C. Cir. 1968); Miller v. United States, 388 F.2d 973 (9th Cir. 1967); Henderson v. United States, 231 F. Supp. 177 (N.D. Cal. 1964); Dyer v. Kazuhisa Abe, 138 F. Supp. 220 (D. Hawaii 1956).

56 *See* statutes cited in note 7. *supra.*

57 *See, e.g.,* Katzenbach v. Morgan, 384 U.S. 641, 657 (1966); Flemming v. Nestor, 363 U.S. 603, 611 (1960); Boylan v. United States, 310 F.2d 493, 500-01 (9th Cir. 1962); *cf.* Metropolitan Cas. Ins. Co. v. Brownell, 294 U.S. 580, 583 (1935); Missouri, Kan. & Tex. Ry. v. May, 194 U.S. 267, 269 (1904). *See generally* Tussman & tenBroek, *The Equal Protection of of the Laws,* 37 Calif. L. Rev. 341 (1949).

58 Loving v. Virginia, 388 U.S. 1, 11 (1967); McLaughlin v. Florida, 379 U.S. 184, 192 (1964); *see* Korematsu v. United States, 323 U.S. 214, 216 (1944); Hirabayashi v. United States, 320 U.S. 81, 100-01 (1943).

59 The court recently declined to void the draft-card-burning statute on the basis of its alleged unconstitutional purpose and noted that an analysis of motive or purpose was appropriate only as an aid to interpreting legislation and not for invalidating it. The Court also noted that exceptions to this general rule had been made in bill-of-attainder and loss-of-citizenship cases where legislation was invalidated because

of its improper (punitive) purpose. *See* United States v. O'Brien, 391 U.S. 367, 382-84 & n.30 (1968).

60 There is no established constitutional doctrine for applying equal protection guarantees to legislation that discriminates in favor of minorities. For an approach to this problem vis-à-vis "benign" racial quotas in housing see Bittker, *The Case of the Checker-Board Ordinance: An Experiment in Race Relations,* 71 Yale L. J. 1387 (1962); Navasky, *The Benevolent Housing Quota,* 6 How. L.J. 30 (1960); Comment, 70 Yale L.J. 126 (1960). Insofar as the equal protection clause may be thought to mandate substantive equality, the favoring of less-than-equal individuals could be justified on that basis. One would think, however, that such unequal treatment would need to promote equality to be acceptable, rather than just recognize and codify existing differences.

Moreover, there is no reason to believe that the equal protection guarantee was intended only for the protection of minority groups. A statute discriminating in favor of a minority necessarily discriminates against everyone else. However, greater judicial scrutiny may be required when the rights of a minority group are in danger, since a minority cannot so easily avail itself of a remedy through the political processes as can a majority group.

61 The court stated: "Appellants here seek to challenge as unconstitutional this statute, enacted by Congress, which is of benefit to them." 394 F.2d at 98. Some people do not know a good thing when they see it, apparently. The court may have been suggesting that unless the defendants were actually sentenced to death they had no standing to challenge the statute. It would seem that the influence of a possible death penalty on the conduct of the defense and on the sentences actually awarded would suffice to create standing.

62 *Cf.* Loving v. Virginia, 388 U.S. 1 (1967); McLaughlin v. Florida, 379 U.S. 184 (1964).

63 *But cf.* note 59 *supra.*

64 On the traditional methods of handling crime in Indian societies see, for example, E. Hoebel, The Law of Primitive Man 127-76 (1954) (Commanche, Kiowa, and Cheyenne law); C. Kluckholn & D. Leighton, The Navaho 219 (1947); J. Ladd, The Structure of a Moral Code 224, 249-51 (1957) (Navajo law); K. Llewellyn & E. Hoebel, The Cheyenne Way (1941); W. Newell, Crime and Justice Among the Iroquois Nations (1965); J. Richardson, Law and Status Among the Kiowa Indians (American Ethnological Society monograph No. 1, 1940); W. Smith & J. Roberts, Zuni Law: A Field of Values (Peabody Museum Papers, Vol. 43, No. 1, 1954); Riffenburgh, *supra* note 30, at 40-41.

65 Act of Jan. 15, 1897, ch. 29, § 5, 29 Stat. 487.

66 *See* 28 Cong. Rec. 3098-111 (1896).

67 Act of Jan 15, 1897, ch. 29, § 1, 29 Stat. 487.

68 29 Cong. Rec. 461 (1897).

69 28 Cong. Rec. 3316 (1896).

70 Act of Mar. 4, 1909, ch. 321, § 328, 35 Stat. 1151.

71 43 Cong. Rec. 2595-96 (1909).

72 *Id.* at 2596.

73 *See* Tussman & tenBroek, *supra* note 57, at 348-51.

CHAPTER 3

INDIAN EDUCATION

If a single word were required to describe Indian education, the appropriate word would probably be "failure." In the first selection in this chapter, Chadwick's "The Inedible Feast," the dimensions of that failure are explored. A review of available national statistics about the accomplishments and liabilities of education for Native Americans reveals that whatever the indicator used, underenrollment, dropout rates, or scores on achievement tests, the picture is the same: The Indian student is receiving inadequate preparation for participation in either Indian society or the larger society. For example, underenrollment (the proportion of persons of school age who are not in school) for Indian students is over 10 percent; Indian dropout rates average 50 percent, double the national average; and Indian achievement at high school graduation is nearly four years behind the national average.

A search for the tentative "causes" of this general failure revealed that facilities, teachers, and curricula for Indian students were about the same as for non-Indians. The libraries, laboratories, gymnasiums, and kitchen facilities available to Indian students are as good as those used by non-Indian students. Moreover, academic credentials and experience of the teachers of Indian youth are comparable to those of other teachers, and their attitudes towards their jobs and their students are approximately the same. Finally, the curricula of the schools attended by Indians are very similar to those of other schools.

The similarity in available facilities does not carry over into comparable achievement. Adequate laboratories and curricula do not an education make, and the missing ingredient for Indian students seems to be socialization into the norms and values of the white, middle-class culture which permeates the schools. The "opportunity" for education may aptly be described as an "inedible feast" because the Indian student tends to be oriented toward a different set of values. The school system for Indian students is organized along the same lines as other American schools, but the Indian student, because of his unique background and culture, cannot fully participate in nor profit from this educational opportunity. This same general finding has been reported for other minorities, but the cultural conflict experienced by Indian students is probably more intense than for any other group.

Of the factors significantly related to academic failure among Indian students, three stand out: language deficiencies, cultural "deprivation" (conflict), and attitudes about one's self (including one's ability to influence his environment). There are many problems associated with focusing educational programs on these factors. All are complex, long-term characteristics not quickly altered: Language patterns are tied to the home and the community; self-concepts and feelings of powerlessness require extended periods of time to develop; and, given the growth of Red Power movements, it seems probable that cultural conflict will be present for some time to come. In fact, the simplest resolution of the culture-conflict problems seems to be changing the structure of the school rather than instituting expensive "remedial" programs to change the children. Productive changes in the structure of schooling for Indian children might include the teaching of English as a *second* language, the inclusion of Indian parents on school boards, and extensive use of adult education programs and community counseling facilities. All of these involve moving "beyond" the school into the family and the community.

Two of the articles reprinted in this chapter focus on the high rate of Indian students' dropping out of school before graduation. In "The Warrior Dropouts" Rosalie Wax compares Indian youth from the Pine Ridge Reservation with young people from urban ghettoes and argues that the two populations share a number of characteristics such as primary loyalty to peers, parents who desire education for their children, teachers who expect little from them, and the label of being culturally disadvantaged. In addition to these elements, according to Wax, Sioux culture and child-rearing practices develop behavioral patterns of high risk-taking and daring in the boys. These risk-taking characteristics often result in behavior which white teachers and administrators define as delinquent (the boys steal from the kitchens, sneak out of dorms at night, smuggle liquor into the dorms, etc.). Administrators are quick to punish such behavior, and at this point the youth feels rejected by the system and drops out. Wax indicates that many of the Sioux dropouts she interviewed perceived themselves not as dropouts but as "kick-outs" or "pushouts."

In "White Rites Versus Indian Rights" Fisher contends that the widely accepted relationship between educational achievement and occupational success does not apply to certain minority groups, including Indian people. He points out that in Canada, Indian educational opportunities and achievement have increased substantially, but at the same time Indian unemployment has also *increased* rather than decreased. He suggests that the educational system is not responsive to the values and needs of Indian students. Instead, it offers irrelevant values and training, and students' perceptions of this irrelevance lead to the high Indian dropout rate. Fisher's study is unique in that it does not focus upon the individual dropout but upon the school system, which is defined as "a rite of passage or rather series of rites signifying separation from, transition through, and incorporation into culturally recognized statuses and roles." Fisher argues that when the school (rite of passage) is removed from middle-class society with its supporting values and placed in the context of Indian culture with no supporting values or norms, it becomes obvious that the school has failed, not the student. To be a "good" Indian the youth must often be a "bad" student.

Most of the studies of culture conflict and Indian education make at least a passing reference to the concept of "cultural deprivation" or one of its synonyms. Most of the studies of "cultural deprivation" have used blacks or poor whites as subjects. In "Indian Children and the Reading Program" William Philion and Charles Galloway evaluate the "cultural deprivation" perspective as it applies to Indian youngsters and their educational problems. The authors caution against filling the research void about the causes of Indian students' academic problems by too readily seeking theories from other fields or transferring findings based upon the study of other minorities. Concern is specifically registered about the propriety of bringing the concept of cultural deprivation, "born of the Negro ghetto," to the Indian reservation. To test the applicability of the concept, Philion and Galloway evaluated the specific language problems of Indian and white school children in intermediate (4th to 7th) grades on Vancouver Island, British Columbia. Their findings suggest that while some of the language problems of the Indian students were similar to those of "culturally deprived" blacks, many were unique to the Indians.

Reboussin and Goldstein's piece, "Achievement Motivation in Navaho and White Students" is an example of how cultural conflict may produce academic failure. On the basis of previous work reported in the anthropological literature, the authors hypothesized that as a result of the culture conflict they experience, Navaho high school and junior college students would evidence considerably less achievement motivation and drive than a sample of white college students. Much to the surprise of the investigators, the Navaho sample scored higher on an achievement motivation scale than did the white students. In seeking to reconcile the discrepancy between expectations and results, Reboussin and Goldstein suggested that their Indian respondents were not representative of the Navaho population, but instead represented a biased population reflecting a selective factor operating in the particular Indian school they studied. However, after publishing this article they continued to investigate the problem, and finally arrived at a different interpretation of their unexpected findings. In a new footnote prepared especially for this book they withdraw their initial view that unexpected results stemmed from a non-representative sample. Instead, they conclude that the cultural conflict and resulting low motivation was in the mind of the anthropologists, but not the Navaho. Despite previous research findings to the contrary, they assert that achievement motivation *is* a characteristic of Nahavo culture.

The final article reprinted in this chapter, Wax and Wax's "The Enemies of the People," is a vivid illustration of what well-meaning whites may expect when they set up special programs for "improving" the Indians without obtaining input from Indian people at every stage. A Head Start program was established on a reservation by VISTA workers who became so involved in the mechanics of doing paper work and delivering supplies that they neglected to ask the Indian population if they wanted their children to attend, or, more importantly, what the program should include. The ironic aspect of this fiasco was that there were Indians who wanted to be involved, but the VISTA workers perceived them as "politicians" making a power play and consequently refused to let them participate. The results were predictable: Failure. The white man never learns.

BRUCE A. CHADWICK:
THE INEDIBLE FEAST

Education is a beautiful word and a part of our language, whether we speak English, Apache, or Pima. Indian education is a phrase which has a good sound. It is sometimes touted as a cure-all for problems, large and small, but we must keep it in the proper perspective because it means a thousand different things to as many different people.

To the professional educators, it means a career and a job to be done. To the parent and the layman and the general public, it means a system and a method of providing our children with the training and equipment they need to live out their lives in a productive manner. To the dedicated classroom teacher and instructor, it means an opportunity to do something of lasting value as they guide and mold the young people each day. To the Indian people, and I say this in all sincerity, it might very well mean survival or oblivion. We have had Indian education in many forms and many combinations for a long long time now. A hundred years or more. Yet somehow, somewhere down the line, we either failed to do the total job or we took some wrong turns and wound up spinning our wheels.[1]

This statement illustrates the ambivalence of many Indian people toward "Indian education": They perceive education as the key to their future in American society, and at the same time are disappointed and frustrated at the lack of progress it has provided.

The Indian people are not alone in their disappointment. For a number of years Indian education programs have been under strong attack by interested whites. The critics include members of Senate subcommittees, who have marshaled an impressive array of data to support their contentions that Indian education in the United States is a failure. One Senate report states:

> The subcommittee has labored hard to determine the extent of our failure in providing an equal educational opportunity for the American Indian. Senator Wayne Morse and I conducted the public hearing in Portland, Oregon, which revealed that dropout rates for Klamath Indian children had apparently doubled since that tribe had been formally terminated by the Federal Government. The hearing also revealed that many tribes scattered throughout the western part of the State of Washington suffered from school dropout rates of anywhere from 50 to almost 100 percent. These Indian children have been in public schools since the 1930's. . . .
> Perhaps the most shocking finding was that the adolescent suicide attempts on the Fort Hall Reservation in Idaho and the Quinault Reservation in Washington were 10 times or more the national average—in short, of epidemic proportions. In addition, the problem of psychological maladjustment of Indian adolescents was a serious problem on practically every reservation.
> These are only a few of the examples that have come to my attention while serving as a member of this subcommittee. The findings point to both the general neglect and complexity of the problem.[2]

Much of the blame for the failure of Indian education is attributed to schools operated by the BIA. The evidence is especially incriminating in the case of boarding schools. Faulty management, a noninvolvement of Indian parents, and an absence of Indian history and culture in the curriculum all contribute to the disastrous consequences for Indian students of BIA-sponsored "white" education. The destruction of that which is Indian is not necessarily functional for successful involvement in industrial society; it is surely dysfunctional for the cohesiveness of the Indian community and the personality development of Indian children.

One of the most unnecessary and detrimental aspects of Indian education in America has been the systematic devaluation of the student's cultural heritage. In order to sustain himself in American Society, the Indian student needs to learn marketable occupational skills, how to exercise his rights, how to interact successfully with credit managers, employers, or store clerks, and how to obtain necessary social services such as medical or welfare assistance. The inclusion of Indian culture and tradition in the school curriculum would permit the student to develop a meaningful identity along with his occupational and social skills. One consequence of programs designed to foster positive Indian identity is an increase in the options available to Indian people. They would be better equipped to function in either "white" society or the Indian environment, rather than acquiring a trained incapacity to function in either setting.

The absence of courses aimed at the development of Indian identity is only one indication of the failure of Indian education. Its other dimensions include serious underenrollment and underachievement by Indian young people, and an extraordinary dropout rate. These aspects of Indian education will be discussed separately.

Underenrollment

Most of the data compiled concerning Indian education applies only to those Indian children enrolled in school. Few researchers have tackled the problem of determining the extent of nonenrollment of the appropriate-aged Indian children. A recent comprehensive national survey conducted by the Office of Education under the directorship of James Coleman[3] included all public schools and a large number of BIA schools in its sample universe.[4] This study revealed the following rates of school enrollment for Indian children in 1960:

	Percent Enrolled	
Age	*White*	*Indian*
5	45.2	32.2
6	84.1	72.3
7-9	97.8	91.7
10-13	97.7	93.4
14-15	94.6	88.7
16-17	88.6	69.9

Not only was the Indian rate of enrollment considerably lower than the white rate, but Indians had the lowest rate of enrollment of children in school of any minority in the United States! Corroborative evidence appears in a review of studies of various reservations[5] showing enrollment rates ranging from 30 percent among Alaskan Eskimos to 93 percent for the Pima-Papago.

Testimony before the Senate Special Subcommittee on Indian Education translated these percentages into students. Rubin Robinson testified that in 1965 more than 16,000 Indian children between the ages of 8 and 16 were not enrolled in school and that half of these nonenrollments were the direct consequence of lack of facilities.[6]

Several factors may account for the low rates of enrollment among Indian children. As Robinson testified, many Indians are excluded from school because of a serious lack of facilities. In addition, lack of motivation among both parents and potential students probably keeps many Indian youth out of the classroom. Whatever the causes it is apparent from the extent of nonenrollment that programs for Indian education have not provided educational opportunities comparable to those enjoyed by other segments of the population.

Achievement

Probably the most damning evidence against Indian education is the contrast between the academic achievement of Indian children and that of whites. Coleman reports the results of nationwide tests for 1st and 12th grade pupils for fall 1965:[7]

	Test Scores		
	Indian	*White*	*Difference*
1st grade			
Nonverbal	49.2	54.1	4.9
Verbal	45.9	53.2	7.3
12th grade			
Nonverbal	47.1	52.0	4.9
Verbal	43.7	52.1	8.4
Reading	44.3	51.9	7.6
Math	45.9	51.8	5.9
Average of all tests	45.1	52.0	6.9

Indian children in the 1st grade, even at this early stage in their academic career, are behind in verbal and nonverbal achievement as compared to the achievement of white children. By the 12th grade, the gap has widened substantially in most categories. The same trend appears when test scores are translated into grade-level scores. A comparison of all Indian children to white children from the metropolitan Northeastern United States showed that in verbal ability Indian children were 1.7 grades behind at the 6th-grade level, 2.1 grades at the 9th grade, and 3.5 grades at the 12th grade.[8] This means that when the average Indian student completes high school, his verbal ability approximates the verbal ability of an 8th-grade white student! The same pattern holds for other academic skills. At grade 12 the average Indian student is 3.2 grades behind in reading comprehension and 3.9 grade levels behind in mathematics achievement.[9]

Several researchers have noted an interesting "crossover effect." Their data reveal that Indian students perform at or above national standards during early elementary grades but then somewhere around the 4th or 5th grade drop rapidly behind.[10] A variety of influences—including psychological development in adolescence, mediocre teachers, language problems, and the identity crisis—have been singled out as causes of this effect. Saslow and Harrover view the problem within the framework of developmental psychology and hypothesize that the crossover effect occurs at the critical stage when the student is developing an identity or self concept.[11] The identity crisis among Indian students, they argue, is so severe that it contributes disproportionately to underachievement in school.

"Overageness" is another aspect of Indian underachievement. We were unable to find national data concerning overageness for Indian students, but several small-scale studies provide a good indication of the seriousness of this problem. Kelly reports that for Pima and Maricopa Indian children in Arizona the retention rate of the students in the first three grades is almost twice as high as for public school children.[12] In other words, Indian children require four years to complete the first three years of school. As a consequence, 86 percent of 16-, 17-, and 18-year-old Indian students from these tribes are one or more grades behind their white age-peers.

Testimony given before the Senate Special Subcommittee on Indian Education documents further the tragic underachievement of Indian youth.[13] Indian education has failed to prepare Indian students to participate in white society. With an average retardation of nearly four grades by the time of high school graduation, they find opportunities for good employment or for entrance into colleges, universities, vocational schools, or training programs severely limited.

Dropping Out

The final indicator of the success or failure of Indian education is the rate at which Indian students discontinue their education before graduation. According to Coleman the dropout rate for Indian students who start high school is about 50 percent, as compared to 26 percent for white students.[14] More recent data from a survey of schools in 12 western states show that 42 percent of the Indian students who were enrolled in the 8th grade in 1962 had dropped out by 1969. This compares quite unfavorably with the national average of 26 percent. There was great variation among the states: Indian students in Oregon had a 29 percent dropout rate, close to the national average, while those in South Dakota had a fantastic rate of 58 percent, more than twice the national average.[15] Numerous studies of particular reservations have provided corroborating evidence for the patterns apparent in the national and regional statistics.[16] Finally, testimony before the Special Senate Subcommittee in 1968 revealed that the dropout rate for the White Mountain Apache was 68 percent and that for some of the tribes in western Washington it approached 100 percent![17]

Two examples of studies designed to measure dropout rates and to identify factors that lead to dropping out are reprinted in this chapter. In Rosalie Wax's piece, "The Warrior Dropouts," high dropout rates in a school on the Sioux reservation in South Dakota are linked to the institution's intolerance of behavior or misbehavior supported by peer-group norms. Students forced to choose between violating the institution's norms and the expectations of their peers usually resolved the conflict in favor of the peers. The result of that choice often was the imposition of institutional sanctions, and consequently, the student came to feel unwelcome and quit school. Wax emphasizes that many of the youth were not dropouts, but rather "kickouts" or "pushouts." In "White Rites Versus Indian Rights" Fisher takes a unique approach to the dropout phenomenon. Focusing upon the educational institution instead of the student or dropout, he conceptualizes passage through the educational system as a rite characteristic of North American society. It is not lack of intelligence or ability that produces high dropout rates among Indian students, but rather a nonacceptance of an alien rite and of those aliens who have attempted to force them to participate in the rite.

It is obvious that a large percentage of Indian children are not profiting from their educational experience. A fairly substantial number of them (approximately 10 percent) are not even being enrolled in school, and nearly 50 percent drop out before completing high school. The level of achievement of those who do remain in school is several grades behind that of their white classmates despite the fact over three-fourths of the Indian students have been retained in one or more grades. There are some success stories; a few Indian students do excel, and there are some outstanding Indian schools.[18] Nevertheless, the overall picture of Indian education is a grim one.

"CAUSES" OF EDUCATIONAL DEPRIVATION

A number of factors have been identified as "causes" of the failure of Indian education, or at least aspects of the problem which need attention. Among these factors are the facilities available to Indian students, the nature of their curricula, the number and quality of the teachers of Indian children, cultural deprivation, language disabilities, and the nature of the self concepts of Indian students. Each of these factors will be considered.

Facilities

There has been much criticism of the quality of educational facilities used by Indian children, and often it is argued that part of the blame for the present state of Indian education is due to inadequate facilities.[19] The BIA schools have been singled out for special censure in this regard.[20] In fairness, it must be noted that most Indian children attend public schools, not BIA schools. In 1968 there were 152,088 Indian children between the ages of 6 and 18, and according to BIA records, 147,353 (97 percent) of these young people were officially enrolled in some educational institution.[21] Of these students, 59 percent were in public schools, 6 percent were in parochial (mission) schools, and about 35 percent were in BIA schools, including 35,309 students in federal boarding schools and 16,139 students in federally sponsored day schools.[22]

The most recent and comprehensive national study of ethnic differentials in education is the "Coleman report" referred to earlier. It contains comparisons of the facilities of schools attended by Indians (both BIA and public schools) and those available to white students in the same county and to white students in the nation, and as a whole reveals that the quality of facilities available to Indian students is not particularly low. In fact, in a number of categories, facilities available to Indians are superior to those for whites. The Indians are no more likely to have makeshift classrooms than are whites, and they have as many new buildings and as low teacher-pupil ratios. Compared to whites in the same counties, Indian students in secondary schools are slightly less likely to have special facilities such as auditoriums, gymnasiums, and foreign-language laboratories. At the same time, however, they tend to have slightly better elementary school facilities and are on a par with white students with respect to laboratory facilities, shop equipment, library facilities, and availability of current textbooks.[23] In short, the physical facilities for white and Indian students are nearly identical, and the gross differences in the educational achievements of the two populations cannot be explained in terms of differentials in the quality of available educational facilities.

Curriculum

The curricula of Indian schools have also been attacked.[24] Yet the Coleman report suggests that there are only minor differences between Indian students and white students in the kind of course offerings available. White schools are slightly more apt to have offerings in commercial courses, agriculture, and industrial arts (respectively, 96 percent for whites, 90 percent for Indians; 31 percent for whites, 27 percent for Indians; and 77 percent for whites, 73 percent for Indians). But other curriculum areas such as college preparatory, vocational, and general education are virtually identical for the two kinds of schools.[25] Coleman developed a summary measure of "comprehensiveness of curriculums" in which Indian schools scored 87.9 and white schools 88.1, both of which are slightly below the national average of 88.4.[26]

As a consequence of the excellent Indian school curriculums, as well as length of school year, the level of accreditation of such schools compares favorably with white schools in the same counties and with the national average. In comparing accreditations by both state (whites, 64 percent; Indians, 59 percent) and regional associations (whites, 27 percent; Indians, 25 percent), the Indian elementary schools are slightly underaccredited.[27] For secondary schools the differentials are even smaller. Ninety-two percent of the Indian schools and 93 percent of the white schools are state-accredited. Regional associations accredited 77 percent of the white schools and 71 percent of the Indian schools.[28] There are differences, but they are too small to be taken seriously as determinants of massive educational deficiencies.

Teachers

Testimony presented before the Special Senate Subcommittee contained numerous allegations about the poor quality of teachers employed in schools having large enrollments of Indian students. The following is an example directed against public schools in Imperial County, California.

> The parents and members of the Quechan Tribal Council at Fort Yuma, Calif., are very displeased with the Indian education program carried out for our Indian students who attend schools in Imperial County, Calif. Some of the evident reasons are given as follows. The administration of the school does not seem to be interested in whether our children receive an education or not. They seem to be more concerned that our children attend school daily so that the school will not lose out on the Federal moneys that are received by the school because our children are federally connected.
>
> Teachers of the school staff are of very low caliber and their attitudes toward our Indian children seem to be that of discrimination. Our children do not receive the help needed from the teacher when they don't understand some of their school work.[29]

Moreover, it has been suggested that the salaries offered teachers of Indian youth are too low, with the consequence that inferior teachers are attracted, and a high turnover rate is generated.[30] A national survey of elementary teachers, including an unspecified number from BIA schools, revealed that in 1965 the average salary of teachers of Indians ($6100) was higher than the national average ($6000) and higher than for teachers of whites in the same counties ($6000).[31] The same pattern held for secondary schools. Inferior teachers may gravitate to schools having Indian students, but the evidence indicates that the reasons for whatever selection processes may be operating do not include noncompetitive salaries.

The asserted inferiority of teachers of Indian children is difficult to substantiate or disprove. However, data are available showing that teachers of Indian students at both the elementary and secondary levels have academic credentials equal or superior to the national average.[32] As for teachers' attitudes about their present positions, 59 percent of those teaching elementary-aged Indian children would *not* choose to move to another school, as compared to 65 percent of teachers of whites. In secondary schools the difference is somewhate smaller (48 percent versus 51 percent, respectively).[33] In neither case is the difference in reported job satisfaction large enough to account for the higher rates of turnover among teachers of Indians.

Another important criticism directed against teachers of Indian children is that many are prejudiced against Indians. Several studies have shown that some white teachers view Indian students as intellectually inferior, "lazy," "mean," "uncooperative," and "inattentive,"[34] or hold other negative stereotypes about Indian people. The problem with these studies is that they lack "controls," that is, comparative figures are not presented showing the number of teachers who think Indian youths are superior to whites, or how teachers in varying settings feel about their white students. Findings from a national survey suggest that teachers of Indian children tend to rate their students somewhat lower in "ability" than do teachers of white students.[35] While this is not direct evidence that the teachers discriminate against Indian students, it is plain that some of them do maintain negative stereotypes about the academic abilities of Indian children.

Cultural Deprivation

A popular explanation for educational problems of inner-city schools which has developed in recent years is the notion of "cultural deprivation."[36] The idea is that the home life of lower-class children fails to prepare them for successful competing in academic activities. If the family environment does not include reading material, physical objects of various sizes, shapes, and colors, and visible parental models (particularly in verbal behavior), the child is likely to be unprepared for the complex symbol-world of the elementary school.[37] Recently there have been attempts to apply the cultural deprivation rationale to Indian children, and to develop ameliorative programs.[38]

Some experts have asserted that recourse to the cultural-deprivation argument merely provides administrators and teachers with an excuse for the failure of their programs.[39] Wax equates "cultural deprivation" with what he calls "vacuum ideology," rejecting what he views as an implied lack of culture in Indian homes.[40] But the concept of cultural deprivation need not include the notion of a cultural vacuum, but rather merely substantial cultural differences. To assert that the culture of certain Indian families does not prepare the youth to compete in academic tasks does not imply a *lack* of culture. There is an extensive literature which demonstrates quite convincingly that certain childhood experiences produce attitudes and skills which foster academic achievement,[41] and to the extent that such experiences are not part of childhood for the Indian student, he operates at a disadvantage in the white man's schools. The article by Philion and Galloway reprinted in this chapter addresses itself to this problem. After demonstrating that Indian youngsters do bring to the school a serious language handicap, the authors suggest techniques for assessing the nature and extent of language disabilities and for developing remedial programs.

Also, the disparity between the white man's values and those of Indian people may not be as great as some have claimed. The article in this chapter, "Achievement Motivation in Navaho and White Students," is an excellent case in point. Reboussin and Goldstein attempted to measure the conflict between Navaho values of noncompetition and the white cultural value, achievement motivation. They hypothesized that the greater an Indian's level of acculturation, the greater his need-achievement. Much to their surprise, the hypothesis was not supported, and so the authors concluded that their sample was not representative of the entire tribe. However, in personal correspondence included as a footnote, they abandon the "nonrepresentative sample" explanation and argue that, contrary to most anthropological literature, the Navaho do have a highly developed need for achievement. A similar finding is reported in an article by Harriet Kupferer included in Chapter Four, in which it is reported that health practices and educational aspirations among the Cherokee were more a function of social class than of extent of acculturation.

Language

Related to the problem of cultural deprivation is the problem faced by a very large number of Indian youngsters who cannot speak or read English and yet attend schools taught by English-speaking teachers and use texts written in English. The problems such students face were emphasized in testimony before the Senate Special Subcommittee on Indian education.

> We frequently talk of the problems which arise with bilingual children and their difficulty in adopting "second languages." We must realize that English is the second language to most Indian children and it is absolutely essential that they be helped in mastering the use of English in their very early years if they hope to ever gain the full benefits from their educational efforts.[42]

Since many Indian youngsters must learn English as a second language, some educators have argued that it should be taught in school as a second language. Such an approach would require an entirely different philosophy of teaching English, and teachers with special training. But fluency in English is important enough for participation in American society that the additional expense and effort required for such a program would be justified. Even though many Indian children do not learn an Indian language, the English they do learn is substandard and handicaps them in the classroom.[43]

Self-Concept

In their classic *Pygmalion in the Classroom* Rosenthal and Jacobson demonstrated the importance of teacher expectations in shaping the self concepts of students. When teachers' attitudes toward their students (in this case lower-class whites and Mexican-Americans) improved, the students received different cues from the teachers, manifested more positive self-concepts, and their academic work improved greatly.[44] There is much evidence that Indian students feel despair, disillusionment, alienation, frustration, hopelessness, powerlessness, rejection, and estrangement, all elements of negative views of the self.

The Coleman report contained several items bearing on student self-concepts.[45] Forty-four percent of the 12th grade Indian students agreed with the item "I sometimes feel that I just can't learn." The proportion of Indians agreeing with the statement was higher than for any other racial group. By contrast, 37 percent of students of all races combined agreed with the statement. A similar item worded in a positive direction asked students to indicate how bright they felt they were in comparison to other students in the same grade. Most Indian youths rated themselves average. Only 31 percent felt they were above average, compared to 49 percent for the entire nation.[46] The item probably minimizes Indian-white differentials, because Indian students attending Indian schools probably compared themselves to their Indian peers rather than to white students. Yet despite that bias, the responses to these two questions indicate self-conceptions that might produce failure in school. Coleman's analysis of the national data on scholastic achievement has demonstrated that negative self-conceptions are associated with failure in the classroom.[47] However, investigators have cautioned that the relationship between self-concept and achievement is probably a circular one, in which variations in either variable feed back into the other. Thus care ·must be exercised in inferring a causal link between negative self conceptions and low achievement.

Related to the self-concept are one's feelings concerning his ability to control the environment. The Coleman student survey included three items measuring attitudes of ability to control one's fate: "Good luck is more important than hard work for success," "Every time I try to get ahead, something or somebody stops me," and "People like me don't have much of a chance to be successful in life." Indian students answered all three of these items in ways reflecting passivity; in general, they seemed to feel that they could not control their environment. Only one minority (Puerto Rican) manifested greater passivity on these items.[48] Perhaps the most significant finding about negative attitudes concerning one's ability to influence his environment was that for minority students such attitudes were among the most important correlates of academic failure, despite the fact that, unlike the self concept, sense of powerlessness has "no direct logical relation to achievement in school or ability."[49]

The special importance of a sense of control of environment for achievement of minority-group children and perhaps for disadvantaged whites as well suggests a different set of predispositional factors operating to create low or high achievement for children from disadvantaged groups than for children from advantaged groups. For children from advantaged groups, achievement or lack of it appears closely related to their self-concept: what they believe about themselves. For children from disadvantaged groups, achievement or lack of achievement appears closely related to what they believe about their environment: whether they believe the environment will respond to reasonable efforts, or whether they believe it is instead merely random or immovable. In different words, it appears that children from advantaged groups assume that the environment will respond if they are able enough to affect it; children from disadvantaged groups do not make this assumption, but in many cases assume that nothing they will do can affect the environment—it will give benefits or withhold them but not as a consequence of their own action.[50]

We have reviewed six of the factors allegedly linked to the educational deficiencies of Indian students. Examination of evidence from national and regional surveys suggests that three of these factors—available facilities, content of curricula, and quality of teachers—are not important as precursors of educational failure. The important differences, in terms of determining the outcome of Indian education, seem to be the other three factors, namely, language problems, cultural deprivation, and the negative self conceptions of Indian students. The ironic conclusion reached is that the educational feast prepared in good faith by white society is inedible to the Indian student by virtue of his culture. This means that the focus of Indian education must shift from facilities, curricula, and teachers to those factors that result in language deficiencies, culture deprivation and negative concepts of self and environment. Facilities, curricula, and teachers are relevant to these problems; and certainly upgrading facilities, improving curricula, and providing more and better teachers would raise the quality of Indian education. The teaching staff should be strengthened by raising salaries above the national average so as to recruit and retain skilled teachers with positive attitudes toward Indians and their ability to succeed. An effort should be made to provide additional in-service teacher training about the culture, social environment, and psychology of Indian students. The teaching of English as a second language and the development of curricula materials that reflect and build upon the background of Indian youth would be welcome improvements. But while such changes would improve the educational experience of Indian children, they alone would not accomplish the goal of providing these youngsters with an education comparable to that of their white peers.

Inevitably, large-scale improvements in Indian education will derive from programs designed to cope with language deficiencies, reduce cultural deprivation, and alter negative self concepts. It is unfortunate that it is these latter three factors that seem to be the most critical, because they are the factors least capable of immediate alteration. Educational facilities, curricula, and the number and character of teachers are all variables subject to fairly simple administrative control. All that is necessary is for the money to be allocated and administrators to agree to curriculum changes, and these elements can be changed. As mentioned earlier, such alterations may improve language skills, reduce cultural deprivation, and raise self concepts to some extent; but to achieve major improvements in these dimensions, there must be effective programs which extend beyond the school into the community. Many of the changes required involve slow processes and many unknown factors, and hence there is a greater probability of unanticipated consequences in attempting to direct social change. Identities are built slowly, language problems take generations to develop and unravel, and cultural "deprivation" (or more accurately, cultural conflict between the ways of the Indian and of the white man) is likely to continue and perhaps intensify with the emergence of pan-Indianism and Red Power movements.

The difficulties in effecting such changes are not offered as excuses or justification for ignoring the problem. Several tentative steps can be suggested. The first is to include Indian parents on the local school board of schools attended by Indian students and give them a decisive voice in setting policy. Reservation schools serving only Indians could be turned over to the tribe if they have the ability and desire to operate them. Several important consequences should follow this involvement by parents. For one thing, the school administrators would be more attuned to the needs, values, and attitudes of the Indian community; and Indian input into the curricula and schedule would be possible. It is probable that student interest and motivation would increase because of parental interest. Also if parents and other adults were more familiar with the school and its operations, they would be more willing to participate in adult education programs.

A second way to improve the academic performance of Indian students would be to make it possible for Indian people to conduct their own adult education programs. The possibilities are unlimited; offerings could vary from brief workshops in prenatal child care to a two-year program in operating heavy construction equipment. To assure that programs would meet the needs of the particular tribe or reservation, Indian people would have to be involved in all stages of the operation, including the initial planning. The nature and type of adult education offered could be coordinated with reservation development plans, such as the development of a particular industry on the reservation. Some of the anticipated effects of adult education would be a greater awareness of the practical benefits of education, increased interest in educational achievement, and greater facility in English by all members of the family.

Another possible step that might improve Indian education would be the provision of well-trained guidance counselors for the entire community. Ideally, such counselors would be Indians and would provide relatively nonthreatening assistance concerning marital conflict, alcohol or drug problems, legal aid, and vocational guidance and placement. Anticipated benefits of such efforts would include improvements in the socioeconomic context and morale of the Indian community, with a corresponding increase in the development of the positive background experiences and self conceptions necessary for achievement in school.

In summary, our review of the literature regarding Indian education has revealed that the major factors related to academic underachievement are not *within* the school systems themselves, but rather extend to the broader context of family, community, and culture. It is suggested that changes in school facilities and programs may partially compensate for these external factors, but that imaginative efforts must extend beyond the schools if Indian people are to have the opportunity for full participation in American schools—and in American society.

NOTES

1 Statement by Ronnie Lupe, Chairman of the White Mountain Apache. Indian Education Subcommittee Hearings 90th Congress, First and Second Sessions, Part III, March 20, 1968, pp. 1007-1008.
2 Introductory statement by Senator Ralph Yarborough, Chairman, Committee on Labor and Public Welfare, U.S. Senate. Indian Education Subcommittee Hearings, 90th Congress, First and Second Sessions, Part I, p. III.
3 James Coleman et al., *Equality of Education Opportunity* (U.S. Government Printing Office, 1966), p. 450.
4 Correspondence with James McPartland, one of the authors of the Coleman report, revealed that the universe from which the sample of schools was drawn included all public schools and those BIA-operated schools located in counties with a certain percentage of Indian population. We were unable to ascertain the exact percentage of Indian population required or the number of BIA schools excluded because they are located in predominantly white counties. This sampling procedure undoubtedly resulted in an undersampling of BIA schools, but the significance of this bias is reduced as testimony before the Senate Subcommittee on Indian education indicated that public schools serving Indians and BIA schools are fairly comparable in facilities and accomplishments: "Memorandum on Background and Major Problem Areas Prepared by the Staff of the Senate Subcommittee on Indian Education"; Indian Education Subcommittee Hearing, 90th Congress, First and Second Sessions, Part V, p. 1912 and letter from Adrian L. Parmeter, staff director, Senate Subcommittee on Indian Education, to Dr. Karl Menninger; Indian Education Subcommittee Hearing, 90th Congress, First and Second Sessions, Part V, p. 2186.
5 Charles K. Ray, Joan Ryan, and Seymour Parker, "Alaskan Native Secondary School Dropouts: A Research Report" (University of Alaska, College, 1962); Harland Padfield, Peter Hemingway, and Phillip Greenfield, "The Pima-Papago Education Population: A Census and Analysis," *Journal of American Indian Education,* 6, no. 1 (October 1966), 1-24.

6 Prepared Statement of Rubin Robinson, Member, South Dakota Indian Commission, and National President, Working Indians Civil Association. Indian Education Subcommittee Hearing, 90th Congress, First and Second Session, Part IV, p. 1247.

7 Coleman et al., *op. cit.,* p. 20. The data in this table for Indian students were subsequently revised, and the revised statistics are included in this paper. Prepared statement by Nancy Karweit, Indian Education Subcommittee Hearing, 90th Congress, First and Second Sessions, Part I, pp. 55-57.

8 *Ibid.,* p. 274.

9 *Ibid.,* p. 275.

10 Madison L. Coombs et al., "The Indian Child Goes to School" (Washington, D.C.: U.S. Department of the Interior, Bureau of Indian Affairs, 1958); David O. Lloyd, "Comparison of Standardized Test Results of Indians and Non-Indians in an Integrated School System." *Journal of American Indian Education,* 1, no. 1 (June 1961), 8-16; Herbert D. Peters, "Performance of Hopi Children on Four Intelligence Tests." *Journal of American Indian Education,* 2, no. 2 (January 1963), 27-31.

11 Harry L. Saslow and May J. Harrover, Research on Psychosocial Adjustment of Indian Youth, *American Journal of Psychiatry,* 125, (August 1968) 225-231.

12 William Kelly, "A Study of Southern Arizona School-Age Indian Children, 1966, 1967" (Tucson, Arizona: Bureau of Ethnic Research, University of Arizona, 1967), p. 9.

13 Indian Education Subcommittee Hearing, 90th Congress, First and Second Sessions, Parts I, II, III, IV, and V.

14 Coleman et al., *op. cit.,* p. 450.

15 Alphonse D. Sellinger, "The American Indian High School Dropout: The Magnitude of the Problem," Northwest Regional Educational Laboratory, Portland, Oregon, Sept., 1968, p. 137.

16 Brewton, Berry, "The Education of American Indians: A Survey of the Literature," prepared for the Indian Education Subcommittee of the Senate Committee on Labor and Public Welfare, 91st Congress, First Session, pp. 28-30.

17 Statement by Ronnie Lupe, Chairman, White Mountain Apache Tribe, Indian Education Subcommittee, 90th Congress, First and Second Sessions, p. 1009.

18 George A. Dale, "Education for Better Living: A Study of the Pine-Ridge Educational Program" (Washington, D.C.: U.S. Department of the Interior, Bureau of Indian Affairs, 1955); Shailer A. Peterson, "How Well Are Indian Children Educated?" (Washington, D.C.: U.S. Department of the Interior, Bureau of Indian Affairs, 1948).

19 Rubin Robinson, *op. cit.,* p. 1247; Brewton Berry, *op. cit.,* p. 61-62.

20 Edgar S. Cahn, ed., *Our Brother's Keeper: The Indian in White America* (Cleveland: New Community Press, 1969), pp. 27-54.

21 "Statistics Concerning Indian Education," (Washington, D.C.: U.S. Department of the Interior, Bureau of Indian Affairs, 1968), p. 1.

22 *Ibid.,* p. 2.

23 Coleman et al., *op. cit.,* pp. 66-85.

24 Cahn, *op. cit.,* pp. 35-40.

25 Coleman et al., *op. cit.,* pp. 94-100.

26 *Ibid.,* p. 94.
27 *Ibid.,* p. 86.
28 *Ibid.,* p. 87.
29 Statement by Henry Montague, Sr., President, Quechan Tribal Council, Fort Yuma, Calif., Indian Education Subcommittee Hearing, 90th Congress, First and Second Sessions, March 20, 1968, Part III, p. 1013.
30 Cahn, *op. cit.,* p. 30; Berry, *op. cit.,* p. 36; Murray Wax et al., "Formal Education in an American Indian Community," Supplement to *Social Problems,* 2, no. 4 (1964), p. 71.
31 Coleman et al., pp. 149-151.
32 *Ibid.,* pp. 16-17.
33 *Ibid.,* pp. 153-155.
34 Berry, *op. cit.,* pp. 38-39.
35 Coleman et al., *op. cit.,* pp. 153-155.
36 Frank Riessman, *The Culturally Deprived Child* (New York: Harper & Row), 1962; Staten W. Webster, ed. *The Disadvantaged Learner* (San Francisco: Chandler, 1966).
37 Robert J. Havinghurst, "Who Are the Socially Disadvantaged" in Webster, ed., *op. cit.,* pp. 20-29.
38 Wax reviews statements of several school administrators who espouse the culture deprivation rationale. Murray Wax et al., *op cit.,* pp. 67-71.
39 *Ibid.,* pp. 67-69; Berry, *op. cit.,* p. 49.
40 Murray Wax et al., *op. cit.,* pp. 67-70.
41 Robert J. Havinghurst, *op. cit.,* pp. 20-25. Carl Berriter and Siegland Engelman, *Teaching Disadvantaged Children in the Preschool* (Englewood Cliffs, N.J.: Prentice Hall, 1966).
42 Statement by Ronnie Lupe, Chairman of the White Mountain Apache, Indian Education Subcommittee Hearing, 90th Congress, First and Second Sessions, Part III, March 20, 1968, pp. 1007-1008.
43 Berry, *op. cit.,* pp. 55-56.
44 Robert Rosenthall and Lenore Jacobson, *Pygmalion in the Classroom: Teacher Expectations and Pupils Intellectual Development* (New York: Holt, Rinehart and Winston, 1968).
45 Coleman et al., *op. cit.,* pp. 286-290.
46 *Ibid.,* p. 287.
47 *Ibid.,* pp. 332-324.
48 *Ibid.,* pp. 288-289.
49 *Ibid.,* p. 320.
50 *Ibid.,* pp. 320-321.

ROSALIE H. WAX: THE
WARRIOR DROPOUTS

Scattered over the prairie on the Pine Ridge reservation of South Dakota, loosely grouped into bands along the creeks and roads, live thousands of Sioux Indians. Most live in cabins, some in tents, a few in houses; most lack the conventional utilities—running water, electricity, telephone, and gas. None has a street address. They are called "country Indians" and most speak the Lakota language. They are very poor, the most impoverished people on the reservation.

For four years I have been studying the problems of the high school dropouts among these Oglala Sioux. In many ways these Indian youths are very different from slum school dropouts—Negro, Mexican-American, rural white—just as in each group individuals differ widely one from another. Yet no one who has any familarity with their problems can avoid being struck by certain parallels, both between groups and individuals.

In slum schools and Pine Ridge schools scholastic achievement is low, and the dropout rate is high; the children's primary loyalties go to friends and peers, not schools or educators; and all of them are confronted by teachers who see them as inadequately prepared, uncultured offspring of alien and ignorant folk. They are classified as "culturally deprived." All such schools serve as the custodial, constabulary, and reformative arm of one element of society directed against another.

Otherwise well-informed people, including educators themselves, assume on the basis of spurious evidence that dropouts dislike and voluntarily reject school, that they all leave it for much the same reasons, and that they are really much alike. But dropouts leave high school under strikingly different situations and for quite different reasons.

Many explicitly state that they do not wish to leave and are really "pushouts" or "kickouts" rather than "dropouts." As a Sioux youth in our sample put it, "I quit, but I never did *want* to quit!" Perhaps the fact that educators consider all dropouts to be similar tells us more about educators and their schools than about dropouts.

ON THE RESERVATION

The process that alienates many country· Indian boys from the high schools they are obliged to attend begins early in childhood and reflects the basic Sioux social structure. Sioux boys are reared to be physically

Source: Reprinted by permission from *Trans*-action. Copyright © May, 1967 by *Trans*-action Inc., New Brunswick, New Jersey.

reckless and impetuous. One that does not perform an occasional brash act may be accepted as "quiet" or "bashful," but he is not considered a desirable son, brother, or sweetheart. Sioux boys are reared to be proud and feisty and are expected to resent public censure. They have some obligations to relatives; but the major social controls after infancy are exerted by their fellows—their "peer group."

From about the age of seven or eight, they spend almost the entire day without adult supervision, running or riding about with friends of their age and returning home only for food and sleep. Even we (my husband, Dr. Murray L. Wax, and I), who had lived with Indian families from other tribal groups, were startled when we heard a responsible and respected Sioux matron dismiss a lad of six or seven for the entire day with the statement, "Go play with Larry and John." Similarly, at a ceremonial gathering in a strange community with hundreds of people, boys of nine or ten often take off and stay away until late at night as a matter of course. Elders pay little attention. There is much prairie and many creeks for roaming and playing in ways that bother nobody. The only delinquencies we have heard Sioux elders complain about are chasing stock, teasing bulls, or occasionally some petty theft.

Among Sioux males this kind of peer-group raising leads to a highly efficient yet unverbalized system of intra-group discipline and powerful intra-group loyalties and dependencies. During our seven-month stay in a reservation community, we were impressed by how rarely the children quarreled with one another. This behavior was not imposed by elders but by the children themselves.

For example, our office contained some items very attractive to them, especially a typewriter. We were astonished to see how quietly they handled this prize that only one could enjoy at a time. A well-defined status system existed so that a child using the typewriter at once gave way and left the machine if one higher in the hierarchy appeared. A half-dozen of these shifts might take place within an hour; yet, all this occurred without a blow or often even a word.

Sioux boys have intense loyalties and dependencies. They almost never tattle on each other. But when forced to live with strangers, they tend to become inarticulate, psychologically disorganized, or withdrawn.

With most children the peer group reaches the zenith of its power in school. In middle-class neighborhoods, independent children can usually seek and secure support from parents, teachers, or adult society as a whole. But when, as in an urban slum or Indian reservation, the teachers stay aloof from parents, and parents feel that teachers are a breed apart, the peer group may become so powerful that the children literally take over the school. Then group activities are carried on in class—jokes, notes, intrigues, teasing, mock-combat, comic book reading, courtship—all without the teacher's knowledge and often without grossly interfering with the learning process.

Competent and experienced teachers can come to terms with the peer group and manage to teach a fair amount of reading, writing, and arithmetic. But teachers who are incompetent, overwhelmed by large classes, or sometimes merely inexperienced may be faced with groups of children who refuse even to listen.

We marveled at the variety and efficiency of the devices developed by Indian children to frustrate formal learning—unanimous inattention, refusal to go to the board, writing on the board in letters less than an inch high, inarticulate responses, and whispered or pantomime teasing of victims called on to recite. In some seventh and eighth grade classes there was a withdrawal so uncompromising that no voice could be heard for hours except the teacher's, plaintively asking questions or giving instructions.

Most Sioux children insist they like school, and most Sioux parents corroborate this. Once the power and depth of their social life within the school is appreciated, it is not difficult to see why they like it. Indeed, the only unpleasant aspects of school for them are the disciplinary regulations (which they soon learn to tolerate or evade), an occasional "mean" teacher, bullies, or feuds with members of other groups. Significantly, we found that notorious truants had usually been rejected by classmates and also had no older relatives in school to protect them from bullies. But the child who has a few friends or an older brother or sister to stand by him, or who "really likes to play basketball," almost always finds school agreeable.

DAY SCHOOL GRADUATES

By the time he has finished the eighth grade, the country Indian boy has many fine qualities: zest for life, curiosity, pride, physical courage, sensibility to human relationships, experience with the elemental facts of life, and intense group loyalty and integrity. His experiences in day school have done nothing to diminish or tarnish his ideal—the physically reckless and impetuous youth, who is admired by all.

But, on the other hand, the country Indian boy is almost completely lacking in the traits most highly valued by the school authorities: a narrow and absolute respect for "regulations," "government property," routine, discipline, and diligence. He is also deficient in other skills apparently essential to rapid and easy passage through high school and boarding school—especially the abilities to make short-term superficial social adjustments with strangers. Nor can he easily adjust to a system which demands, on the one hand, that he study competitively as an individual, and, on the other, that he live in barrack-type dormitories where this kind of study is impossible.

Finally, his English is inadequate for high school work. Despite eight or more years of formal training in reading and writing, many day school graduates cannot converse fluently in English even among themselves. In contrast, most of the students with whom they will compete in higher schools have spoken English since childhood.

To leave home and the familiar and pleasant day school for boarding life at the distant and formidable high school is a prospect both fascinating and frightening. To many young country Indians the agency town of Pine Ridge is a center of sophistication. It has blocks of Indian Bureau homes with lawns and fences, a barber shop, big grocery stores, churches, gas stations, a drive-in confectionary, and even a restaurant with a juke box. While older siblings or cousins may have reported that at high school "they make you study harder," that "they just make you move every minute," or that the "mixed-bloods" or "children of bureau employees" are "mean" or "snotty," there are the compensatory highlights of movies, basketball games, and the social (white man's) dances.

For the young men there is the chance to play high school basketball, baseball, or football; for the young women there is the increased distance from over-watchful, conservative parents. For both, there is the freedom, taken or not, to hitchhike to White Clay, with its beer joints, bowling hall, and archaic aura of Western wickedness. If, then, a young man's close friends or relatives decide to go to high school, he will usually want to go too rather than remain at home, circumscribed, "living off his folks." Also, every year, more elders coax, tease, bribe, or otherwise pressure the young men into "making a try" because "nowadays only high school graduates get the good jobs."

THE STUDENT BODY: TOWN INDIANS, COUNTRY INDIANS

The student body of the Oglala Community High School is very varied. First, there are the children of the town dwellers, who range from well-paid white and Indian government employees who live in neat government housing developments to desperately poor people who live in tar paper shacks. Second, there is the large number of institutionalized children who have been attending the Oglala Community School as boarders for the greater part of their lives. Some are orphans, others come from isolated sections of the reservation where there are no day schools, others come from different tribal areas.

But these town dwellers and boarders share an advantage—for them entry into high school is little more than a shift from eighth to ninth grade. They possess an intimate knowledge of their classmates and a great deal of local know-how. In marked contrast, the country Indian freshman enters an alien environment. Not only is he ignorant of how to buck the rules, he doesn't even know the rules. Nor does he know anybody to put him wise.

Many country Indians drop out of high school before they have any clear idea what high school is all about. In our sample, 35 percent dropped out before the end of the ninth grade and many of these left during the first semester. Our first interviews with them were tantalizingly contradictory—about half the young men seemed to have found high school so painful they could scarcely talk about it; the other half were also laconic, but insisted that they had liked school. In time, those who had found school unbearable confided that they had left school because they were lonely or because they were abused by more experienced boarders. Only rarely did they mention that they had trouble with their studies.

The following statement, made by a mild and pleasant boy, conveys some idea of the agony of loneliness, embarrassment, and inadequacy that a country Indian newcomer may suffer when he enters high school:

> At day school it was kind of easy for me. But high school was really hard, and I can't figure out even simple questions that they ask me. . . . Besides I'm so quiet [modest and unaggressive] that the boys really took advantage of me. They borrow money from me every Sunday night and they don't even care to pay it back. . . . I can't talk English very good, and I'm really bashful and shy, and I get scared when I talk to white people. I usually just stay quiet in the [day school] classroom, and the teachers will leave me alone. But at boarding school they wanted me to get up and talk or say something. . . . I quit and I never went back. . . . I can't seem to get along with different people, and I'm so shy I can't even make friends. . . . [Translated from Lakota by interviewer.]

Most of the newcomers seem to have a difficult time getting along with the experienced boarders and claim that the latter not only strip them of essentials like soap, paper, and underwear, but also take the treasured gifts of proud and encouraging relatives, wrist watches and transistor radios.

> Some of the kids—especially the boarders—are really mean. All they want to do is steal—and they don't want to study. They'll steal your school work off you and they'll copy it. . . . Sometimes they'll break into our suitcase. Or if we have money in our pockets they'll take off our overalls and search our pockets and get our money. . . . So finally I just came home. If I could be a day scholar I think I'll stay in. But if they want me to board I don't want to go back. I think I'll just quit.

Interviews with the dropouts who asserted that school was "all right"—and that they had not wished to quit—suggest that many had been almost as wretched during their first weeks at high school as the bashful young men who quit because they "couldn't make friends." But they managed to find some friends and, with this peer support and protection, they were able to cope with and (probably) strike back at other boarders. In any case, the painful and degrading aspects of school became endurable. As one lad put it: "Once you *learn* to be a boarder, it's not so bad."

But for these young men, an essential part of having friends was "raising Cain"—that is, engaging in daring and defiant deeds forbidden by the school authorities. The spirit of these escapades is difficult to portray to members of a society where most people no longer seem capable of thinking about the modern equivalents of Tom Sawyer, Huckleberry Finn, or Kim, except as juvenile delinquents. We ourselves, burdened by sober professional interest in dropouts, at first found it hard to recognize that these able and engaging young men were taking pride and joy in doing exactly what the school authorities thought most reprehensible; and they were not confessing, but boasting, although their stunts had propelled them out of school.

For instance, this story from one bright lad of 15 who had run away from high school. Shortly after entering ninth grade he and his friends had appropriated a government car. (The usual pattern in such adventures is to drive off the reservation until the gas gives out.) For this offense (according to the respondent) they were restricted for the rest of the term—they were forbidden to leave the high school campus or attend any of the school recreational events, games, dances, or movies. (In effect, this meant doing nothing but going to class, performing work chores, and sitting in the dormitory.) Even then our respondent seems to have kept up with his class work and did not play hookey except in reading class:

It was after we stole that car Mrs. Bluger [pseudonym for reading teacher] would keep asking who stole the car in class. So I just quit going there. . . . One night we were the only ones up in the older boys' dorm. We said, "Hell with this noise. We're not going to be the only ones here." So we snuck out and went over to the dining hall. I pried this one window open about this far and then it started to crack, so I let it go. . . . We heard someone so we took off. It was show that night I think. [Motion picture was being shown in school auditorium.] . . . . All the rest of the guys was sneaking in and getting something. So I said I was going to get my share too. We had a case of apples and a case of oranges. Then I think it was the night watchman was coming, so we run around and hid behind those steps. He shined the light on us. So I thought right then I was going to keep on going. That was around Christmas time. We walked back to Oglala [about 15 miles] and we were eating this stuff all the way back.

This young man implied that after this escapade he simply did not have the nerve to try to return to the high school. He insisted, however, that he would like to try another high school: "I'd like to finish [high school] and get a good job some place. If I don't I'll probably just be a bum around here or something."

YOUNG MEN WHO STAY IN SCHOOL

Roughly half the young Sioux who leave high school very early claim they left because they were unable to conform to school regulations. What happens to the country boys who remain? Do they "shape-up" and obey the regulations? Do they, even, come to "believe" in them? We found that most of these older and more experienced youths were, if anything, even *more* inclined to boast of triumphs over the rules than the younger fellows who had left. Indeed, all but one assured us that they were adept at hookey, and food and car stealing, and that they had frequent surreptitious beer parties and other outlaw enjoyments. We do not know whether they (especially the star athletes) actually disobey the school regulations as frequently and flagrantly as they claim. But there can be no doubt that most Sioux young men above 12 wish to be regarded as hellions in school. For them, it would be unmanly to have any other attitude.

An eleventh grader in good standing explained his private technique for playing hookey and added proudly: "They never caught me yet." A twelfth grader and first-string basketball player told how he and some other students "stole" a jeep from the high school machine shop and drove it all over town. When asked why, he patiently explained: "To see if we can get away with it. It's for the enjoyment. . . . to see if we can take the car without getting caught." Another senior told our male staff worker: "You can always get out and booze it up."

The impulse to boast of the virile achievements of youth seems to maintain itself into middle and even into old age. Country Indians with college training zestfully told how they and a group of proctors had stolen large amounts of food from the high school kitchen and were never apprehended, or how they and their friends drank three fifths of whiskey in one night and did not pass out.

Clearly, the activities school administrators and teachers denounce as immature and delinquent are regarded as part of youthful daring, excitement, manly honor, and contests of skill and wits by the Sioux young men and many of their elders.

They are also, we suspect, an integral part of the world of competitive sports. "I like to play basketball" was one of the most frequent responses of young men to the question: "What do you like most about school?" Indeed, several ninth and tenth graders stated that the opportunity to play basketball was the main reason they kept going to school. One eighth grader who had run away several times stated: "When I was in the seventh grade I made the B team on the basketball squad. And I made the A team when I was in the eighth grade. So I stayed and finished school without running away anymore."

The unselfconscious devotion and ardor with which many of these young men participate in sports must be witnessed to be appreciated even mildly. They cannot communicate their joy and pride in words, though one 17-year-old member of the team that won the state championship tried, by telling how a team member wearing a war bonnet "led us onto the playing floor and this really gave them a cheer."

Unfortunately, we have seen little evidence that school administrators and teachers recognize the opportunity to use sports as a bridge to school.

By the eleventh and twelfth grades many country Indians have left the reservation or gone into the armed services, and it is not always easy to tell which are actual dropouts. However, we did reach some. Their reasons for dropping out varied. One pled boredom: "I was just sitting there doing anything to pass the time." Another said he didn't know what made him quit: "I just didn't fit in anymore. . . . I just wasn't like the other guys anymore." Another refused to attend a class in which he felt the teacher had insulted Indians. When the principal told him that he must attend this class or be "restricted," he left. Significantly, his best friend dropped out with him, even though he was on the way to becoming a first-class basketball player.

Different as they appear at first, these statements have a common undertone: They are the expressions not of immature delinquents, but of relatively mature young men who find the atmosphere of the high school stultifying and childish.

THE DILEMMA OF SIOUX YOUTH

Any intense cross-cultural study is likely to reveal as many tragic-comic situations as social scientific insights. Thus, on the Pine Ridge reservation, a majority of the young men arrive at adolescence valuing *élan,* bravery, generosity, passion, and luck, and admiring outstanding talent in athletics, singing, and dancing. While capable of wider relations and reciprocities, they function at their social best as members of small groups of peers or relatives. Yet to obtain even modest employment in the greater society, they must graduate from high school. And in order to graduate from high school, they are told that they must develop exactly opposite qualities to those they possess: a respect for humdrum diligence and routine, for "discipline" (in the sense of not smoking in toilets, not cutting classes, and not getting drunk), and for government property. In addition, they are expected to compete scholastically on a highly privatized and individualistic level, while living in large dormitories, surrounded by strangers who make privacy of any type impossible.

If we were dealing with the schools of a generation or two ago, then the situation might be bettered by democratization—involving the Sioux parents in control of the schools. This system of local control was not perfect, but it worked pretty well. Today the problem is more complicated and tricky; educators have become professionalized, and educational systems have become complex bureaucracies, inextricably involved with universities, education associations, foundations, and federal crash programs. Even suburban middle-class parents, some of whom are highly educated and sophisticated, find it difficult to cope with the bureaucratic barriers and mazes of the schools their children attend. It is difficult to see how Sioux parents could accomplish much unless, in some way, their own school system were kept artificially small and isolated and accessible to their understanding and control.

WORKING CLASS YOUTH

How does our study of the Sioux relate to the problems of city dropouts? A specific comparison of the Sioux dropouts with dropouts from the urban working class—Negroes, Puerto Ricans, or whites—would, no doubt, reveal many salient differences in cultural background and world view. Nevertheless, investigations so far undertaken suggest that the attitudes held by these peoples *toward education and the schools* are startlingly similar.

Both Sioux and working class parents wish their children to continue in school because they believe that graduating from high school is a guarantee of employment. Though some teachers would not believe it, many working class dropouts, like the Sioux dropouts, express a generally favorable attitude toward school, stating that teachers are generally fair and that the worst thing about dropping out of school is missing one's friends. Most important, many working class dropouts assert that they were pushed out of school and frequently add that the push was fairly direct. The Sioux boys put the matter more delicately, implying that the school authorities would not really welcome them back.

These similarities should not be seized on as evidence that all dis-privileged children are alike and that they will respond as one to the single, ideal, educational policy. What it does mean is that the schools and their administrators are so monotonously alike that the boy brought up in a minority social or ethnic community can only look at and react to them in the same way. Despite their differences, they are all in much the same boat as they face the great monolith of middle-class society and its one-track education escalator.

An even more important—if often unrecognized—point is that not only does the school pose a dilemma for the working-class or Sioux, Negro, or Puerto Rican boy—he also poses one for the school. In many traditional or ethnic cultures boys are encouraged to be virile adolescents and become "real men." But our schools try to deprive youth of adolescence—and they demand that high school students behave like "mature people"—which, in our culture often seems to mean in a pretty dull, conformist fashion.

Those who submit and succeed in school can often fit into the bureau-cratic requirements of employers, but they are also likely to lack independ-ence of thought and creativity. The dropouts are failures—they have failed to become what the school demands. But the school has failed also—failed to offer what the boys from even the most "deprived" and "under-de-veloped" peoples take as a matter of course—the opportunity to become whole men.

S. M. Miller and Ira E. Harrison, studying working class youth, assert that individuals who do poorly in school are handicapped or disfavored for the remainder of their lives, because "the schools have become the occupa-tional gatekeepers" and "the level of education affects the kind and level of job that can be attained." On the other hand, the investigations of Edgar Z. Friedenberg and Jules Henry suggest that the youths who perform creditably in high school according to the views of the authorities are disfavored in that they emerge from this experience as permanently crip-pled persons or human beings.

In a curious way our researches among the Sioux may be viewed as supporting both of these contentions, for they suggest that some young people leave high school because they are too vital and independent to submit to a dehumanizing situation.

A NOTE ON THE STUDY

In studying the adolescents on Pine Ridge we concentrated on two areas, the high school and a particular day school community with a country Indian population of about 1,000. We interviewed somewhat less than half the young people then enrolled in the high school plus a random sample of 48 young country Indians. Subsequently, we obtained basic socio-economic and educational data from all the young people who had graduated from the day school in 1961, 1962, and 1963. We interviewed 153 young people between the ages of 13 and 21, about 50 of whom were high school dropouts. We used many approaches and several types of questionnaires, but our most illuminating and reliable data were obtained from interviews conducted by Indian college students who were able to associate with the Sioux adolescents and participate in some of their activities.

While "country Sioux" or "country Indian" might loosely be considered a synonym for "full-blood," I have avoided the latter term as connoting a traditional Indian culture which vanished long ago and whose unchanging qualities were a mythology of white observers rather than a social reality of Indian participants. In any case, I use "country Indian" to refer to the people raised and living "out on the reservation (prairie)" who participate in the social and ceremonial activities of their local rural communities, as opposed to those persons, also known as Indians, who live in Pine Ridge town and make a point of avoiding these backwoods activities.

A. D. FISHER: WHITE RITES VERSUS INDIAN RIGHTS

The lyrics of a song in the top ten last summer put the matter unequivocally. "Education's the thing," wails the lead singer of a black group called The Winstons, "if you want to compete. Without it, life just ain't very sweet." Almost everyone in North America, I suspect, would say "Amen" to that. The belief in increasing educational opportunities as the avenue to social progress has become an article of faith, and "going to school" an assurance of secular salvation akin to "good works" and "saving grace" in other times and other religions.

That for many sectors of North American society this belief flies in the face of observable facts should surprise no one. Yet it is a fact that the propitiation of the gods of learning simply isn't working for vast numbers of Americans and Canadians, especially the poor, the black and the Indian. Indeed, for those with whom I am most concerned in this essay, the Indian people of Canada, it can be demonstrated that education has been very nearly a total disaster.

Despite a considerable expansion of the number of schools and in the number of years of schooling available to Canadian Indian children, the unemployment rate among them has increased. Between the years 1959-60 and 1962-63, the welfare costs among Alberta's Indian population jumped from $294,625 to $683,080, and a sizeable portion of the latter figure

Source: Reprinted by permission from *Trans*-action. Copyright © November, 1969 by *Trans*-action Inc., New Brunswick, New Jersey.

went to unemployed but "educated" Indians. The incidence of unemployment among Indians with education is even more graphically illustrated by
comparing the average unemployment of the total Indian population (43
percent) to that of Alberta Indian students who terminated their education
in 1964-65 (64 percent).

While these figures clearly indicate that the Canadian Indian fails to
use whatever education he receives once his schooling is over, other studies
show that he also fails to take advantage of the schooling available to him.
For example, in 1965, a study was made of junior high school dropouts at
the Blackfoot Indian Reserve, Gleichen-Cluny, Alberta. It was determined
that 86 of 168 students, or 51 percent, had dropped out of school in the
years since 1961 and of these dropouts, 95 percent left school before they
had completed grade nine. Something quite obviously happened to these
children between grades five and nine.

Numerous hypotheses have been advanced to explain the phenomenon
of the school dropout by persons of lower socioeconomic class; however
none has been wholly satisfactory. This essay is an attempt to account for
the phenomenon in a more fruitful manner, by redefining the dropout
situation, and by applying this definition to the specific case of dropouts
among Canadian Indians.

It will be useful to list some hypotheses used to explain dropping out,
not because they are the most important or the most misleading, but
because they illustrate the direction of concern among various students of
education. Seymour Rubenfield, in his 1965 study, *Family of Outcasts*,
offers the hypothesis that the dropout as well as the juvenile delinquent
gets that way because of an incomplete socialization that results in a
self-discontent which is then externalized and "lived out" through deviant
behavior, some of which is in relation to the school.

Lucius F. Cervantes' *The Dropout: Causes and Cures* presents the dropout as suffering from the failure of his primary group, his family. The
result of this failure is the inability to achieve success in primary interpersonal relationships, which produces personality disorganization. This
causes an end to interpersonal communication and makes personal satisfaction unattainable. For these reasons the individual leaves school.

Richard Cloward and Lloyd Ohlin, in the immensely influential *Delinquency and Opportunity,* focus on what might be called "objective status
discontent." This implies that the deviant or delinquent individual is alienated from his environment, and the legitimate means to success in that
environment (e.g. "education") because these institutions are, quite objectively, alienating. Because of this alienation, however, the individual turns to
illegitimate means to nurture success. Another author utilizing the theme of
alienation is John F. Bryde, who sees the Indian student of South Dakota as
literally being outside of and between both Indian and white-man cultures. As
such, he is alienated from both the goals of education and his Indian identity,
which leads to his scholastic failure and "dropping out."

Finally, Murray and Rosalie Wax's study of the same Sioux Indian
students that Byrde discussed, indicates that one of the major causes of
dropping out is what can be called "institutional intolerance." The Waxes

argue that the school situation at Pine Ridge, South Dakota, is characterized by a lack of communication between the school functionaries and
those they serve. There is "social distance" between students and teachers
and considerable individual isolation, even within the same school.

THE SCHOOL AS RITUAL

These explanations appear to be suitable for the particular cases they
describe. Almost all of them, however, concentrate upon one variable, the
student or ex-student. They fail to consider the institutional and cultural
variable, the school. It is the latter that I shall focus on in this essay.

In Euro-Canadian society the school is a "primary institution," in the
sense that it is basic and widespread. All Euro-Canadian children are expected to attend school for extensive periods of time and to profit from
the experience. It is, in fact and in theory, the major socialization device of
the industrialized, urbanized segment of the Canadian population. As such
it consumes a tremendous amount of time, substantial amounts of money
and a great deal of energy.

In this paper, then, I define "the school," all formal education from
kindergarten to grade twelve or thirteen, as a rite of passage, or rather a
series of rites signifying separation from, transition through and incorporation into culturally recognized statuses and roles. Within the larger chronological rite there are also numerous other rites and ceremonials indicating
partial transitions and new role relationships.

This redefinition of the school as a rite of passage is likely to provoke
some disagreement. Anthropologists and laymen alike choose to think of
ritual and rites of passage as essentially magico-religious activities, and of
schools as being only partially or minimally engaged in this type of activity. This is not altogether so. Not all ritual must be magico-religious, nor
are schools as institutions, or what goes on in schools, completely free
from magico-religious significance. It is quite difficult to categorize ritual
activity clearly as to religious content. Further, ritual activity ranges from
the purely magical and religious through the pseudo-rational to rational
routine, albeit it is up to the observer to ascertain its rationality. Clearly, in
any case, there are numerous calendrical and other rites and ceremonies in
the public school that signify changes in the student's social life. Thus, the
whole educational structure can be envisioned as a long-term ritual marking
various changes in the social lives of the individuals. It is difficult for an
outside observer to assess their magico-religious or secular content.

Nevertheless, it would be very hard to argue that the majority of
Canadian students, parents and teachers see "education" in a wholly rational light. In a recent study, a noted American educator pointed out that
despite scientific knowledge to the contrary the vast majority of public
school classrooms in the United States operate on the two-thirds theory
(Trans-action, 1967); two-thirds of the time someone is talking, two-thirds
of the time it is the teacher who is talking, two-thirds of the time the
teacher is talking she is lecturing or commenting upon the behavior of

children in the classroom. If this is the case in the United States, then Canadian schools, generally, operate on the three-quarters theory, and schools catering to Indians operate on the seven-eighths theory. The involvement of the school in teaching moral-ethical behavior, the continuing belief in "disciplining the mind" through rigid curricula and repetitive testing, the various rites of prayer and of patriotism, indeed, the whole defensive ethos of the school point to the pseudorational nature of the school.

RITES OF PASSAGE

More succinctly, one can look at "the school" as a series of "ideological rituals," using "ideological" here in Mannheim's sense, as a means to protect and perfect the existing social system, in contrast to the "utopian" striving for revolutionary change. In this sense the public school in North America is indeed an ideological rite of passage. Educators have long thought the institution of the public school as the common ground that allows immigrant and indigenous groups the wherewithal for intelligent self-government, common mores and economic perfection and advancement within the ideological system of North American "democratic" society.

There is little doubt that the characteristic form of North American public education is typical of North American society. It exemplifies and reflects the values of that society, and prepares students for urban, industrialized middle-class society. Finally the whole ritual culminates in a pseudoreligious ceremonial known as "Convocation" or "Commencement" in which it tells the ex-student, "Now do it." Those who "can do it" have been certified for that society. From kindergarten or grade one when the child learns who his "helpers" in the school and neighborhood are, to grade twelve or thirteen when each student is ranked and evaluated on the formalized "external" or Departmental examinations, he passes through a multitude of statuses and plays many roles. The result of the whole process is the development of a particular sort of individual, that is if the process is successful.

But, what would happen if we were to take this ceremonial system out of its context, North American middle-class society, and place it in a wholly or partly alien context such as an Indian reserve? The answer is that unless there were community support for it, it would fail. Let me stress this point. It would be the rite of passage, the rituals recognized and enjoined by middle-class society that would fail; *not the Indian student.*

Since 1944 there has been little doubt among scholars that students of North American Indian ancestry have intelligence adequate for most activities, exclusive of school. Robert Havighurst's well-known 1957 article demonstrates that Indian children perform "... about as well... " as white children on performance tests of intelligence. More recently, in Charles Ray, Joan Ryan, and Seymour Parker's 1962 study of Alaskan secondary-school dropouts, the authors state: "The conclusion to be derived from the data is that intelligence *per se* cannot be considered a major contributing factor to dropouts and that achievement levels are not markedly different." As this essay is focused primarily on dropouts with Eskimo, Aleut, or Tlingit ethnic backgrounds as contrasted with white children, it appears to indicate that the cause of dropout is elsewhere than intelligence. But where are we to find it?

THINKING IN TWO TONGUES

California Achievement Test scores in Alberta and South Dakota among Plains Cree, Blackfoot and Sioux Indians indicate that the young Indian starts out *ahead* of his white peers, but then gradually tails off in achievement. Fourth-grade Indians who had averaged 4.3 on achievement tests while their white counterparts scored only 4.1, had by the eighth grade been surpassed by the white students who achieved an 8.1 average while Indian students had one of 7.7. Test scores consistently decline between grades five and seven. Furthermore, a parallel phenomenon in retardation of grade placement in relationship to age has been indicated in a study of Kwakiutl Indians on Gilford Island, British Columbia. The number of students at the expected grade-level decreased sharply from 4 at grade one to 1 by grade five and 0 by grade six. At the same time, the number of students *below* the expected grade-level increased from 2 at grade one to 4 at grade five. Similar studies done by the Waxes on South Dakota Sioux also reveal that between the fifth and seventh grade the number of students of appropriate grade-age decreases. Thus, where the majority of fifth-grade students are in the 10- to 11-year category, the majority of sixth-grade students are in the 12- to 13-year range. From these patterns of slumping achievement-test scores and increasing age-grade-level retardation, it appears that some sort of difficulty arises in the relationship between "the school" and the pre-pubescent/pubescent Indian. Admittedly, some Indian students drop out later than others but it would appear that in most cases of prolonged schooling it is the enforcement of the School Act that made the difference. The Blackfoot and Blood Indians of southern Alberta, for example, are under considerable compulsion to stay in school. If they do not "fit" the existing academic program, they are enrolled in "pre-employment" courses or in special programs such as "upgrading." It is therefore quite difficult for these students to leave school. The younger student often "solves" this problem by becoming a "trouble-maker" in school (sassing teachers, being truant, refusing to work, etc.) or by becoming "delinquent" outside school (drinking and sexual excapades, fighting and theft). Of these Blackfoot "early dropouts," ages thirteen to sixteen (which is the school-leaving age) 75 percent of the fifteen-year-olds and 70 percent of the sixteen-year-olds were considered "delinquent." Among the older students, ages seventeen, eighteen and nineteen, the amount of delinquent behavior was radically reduced. Apparently, then, when a Blackfoot student passes the school-leaving age, he can choose to stay or to go, and he generally chooses to go.

Another difference leading to local variation in the school-leaving age may be the attitudes of Indians about what is appropriate for them in the school. What the Indian expects to get out of school, what it means to him and what he believes himself to be are really the critical issues. Even though the specific answers to these questions may vary with different tribes, the result of these answers is the same: early dropout and unused education.

Indian expectations of school are conditioned by what the young Indian learns in the environment of his home community. Because what he learns at home often differs widely from what he learns at school, the Indian student is frequently forced to separate the two learning experiences. George Spindler once heard a "successful" Blood Indian say:

> I have to think about some things in my own language and some things in English. Well, for instance, if I think about horses, or about the Sun Dance, or about my brother-in-law, I have to think in my own language. If I think about buying a pickup truck or selling some beef or my son's grades in school I have to think in English.

The languages of Blackfoot and English are kept entirely apart; the former is for thinking about basic cultural elements, while the latter is used for school work. The Indian student grows up in a particular society with its own particular role transitions and in the presence of or absence of appropriate ritual recognition of these changes. Since the expectations about ritual and about role transitions held by any society and recognized as legitimate for that society are peculiar to that society, and to part-societies, at any time the school, as a rite of passage, may become inappropriate to members of a particular society that differs from North American middle-class society. This is what seems to happen to the Indian student.

IDENTITY AND WORK

Young Blood Indians have certain very specific ideas about what they are and what they are going to be. Among a stratified sample of forty young Bloods the most popular choices of a career or vocation were as follows: ranching, automechanic, carpenter, bronc rider, haying and farming. All of these occupations can be learned and practiced right on the Blood Reserve. They chose these occupations for two important reasons: knowledge and experience or, in other words, experiential knowledge that they already held. Among the Blackfoot dropouts and "stay-ins" a very similar pattern emerged. They, too, chose occupations that were familiar to them, even if they pertained little to their academic life. And this pattern emerges elsewhere in only slightly different form.

In Harry Wolcott's "Blackfish Village" Kwakiutl study he mentions in passing the response by students to the essay topic, "What I Would Like to Be Doing Ten Years from Now." Almost all the students thought they would be in and around their village. Two of the older girls guessed they would be married and in the village. Farther north, in Alaska, the Ray, Ryan and Parker study notes that the three primary reasons given for dropping out of secondary school are "needed at home," "marriage" and "wanted to work." Of the secondary reasons, to help at "home," "marriage" and "homesick" were most important. These reasons appear to indicate that the Alaskan dropout was opting out of formal education to return home to what he or she knows. As the authors indicate, "The majority of dropouts saw little relationship between what they were learning in school and jobs that were available to them."

Turning inland from British Columbia and Alaska we note the same phenomenon among the Metis of the Lac La Biche area (Kikino, Owl River, Mission), among the Blackfoot dropouts of Gleichen and Cluny and among the young Blood of southwestern Alberta. In each case the Indian student on the one hand expects to be doing what is now done in the context of his community, and on the other hand sees only a vague, if any, correlation between the demands of formal education in the context of the school and that which he expects to do.

A final point in this regard is made in the Waxes' study of the Pine Ridge Sioux. They state that education and being a good Sioux Indian are two separate processes, if becoming a good Indian is a process at all. They say that the full-bloods think that:

> ... education harms no one, but on the other hand it has almost nothing to do with being a good person. ... [They] do not seem to be aware that their offspring are regarded as unsocialized, amoral or backward by their teachers. That a child could be educated to the point where he would become critical of his kin or attempt to disassociate himself from them is still beyond their comprehension.

In conclusion, these studies show that the expanded educational opportunities for Canadian Indians are not really opportunities at all. For what the school offers is an irrelevant set of values and training. Moreover, the school often comes into direct conflict with certain moral and cultural values of the student. Thus, it is the educational system that fails the student and not the student who fails the system. In trying to be a good and successful Indian, the Indian student must often be a bad and unsuccessful student.

WILLIAM L. E. PHILION, CHARLES G. GALLOWAY: INDIAN CHILDREN AND THE READING PROGRAM

"In an area where facts are few and speculation runs high, it is perhaps inevitable and to the good that people should look far afield for bodies of fact and theory that might be relevant. The price paid for this intellectual speed-trawling, however, is that some far-fetched ideas occasionally capture the imaginations of people who do not understand them well enough to appreciate their fundamental irrelevance" (1, pg. 26). Such has been the case with reference to many of the problems of Indian education. Solutions to questions which range from what the language arts program should include, to whether Indian schools should be integrated, are commonly sought far afield from the area in which the problem exists. If the problems are to be solved, however, much more data than are available at present must be gathered and analyzed in terms of immediate relevance to the problems at hand. This becomes especially true when considering a basic question such as the reading achievement of a certain group of children, for example, the Indian children of a certain specified population.

Going far afield for bodies of fact and theory that might be relevant to the problem of reading difficulty among certain Indian children leads to a consideration of many possible explanations for the difficulty. Among the possibilities available for consideration is Bereiter and Engelmann's suggestion that cultural deprivation be looked at as language deprivation (1). Lest we err, however, in our zeal to do missionary work among the disadvantaged, we must be cautious in bringing this promising but far-fetched idea, born of the Negro ghetto, to the Indian reservation.

Language deprivation among disadvantaged Negro children, referred to by Bereiter and Engelmann, seems to center around two special weaknesses of language usage that are of primary importance for success in school. "One is the tendency to treat sentences as *giant words* that cannot be taken apart and recombined. This leads to an inflexible kind of language that does not make use of the full potentialities of the grammar and syntax, and it makes the learning of new vocabulary and structures more difficult. The second weakness . . . is a failure to master the use of structural words and inflections which are necessary for the expression and manipulation of logical relationships. The problem for culturally deprived children is not so much learning to speak in sentences as learning to speak in sentences that are composed of discrete words" (1, pg. 42).

Before setting about the construction of a language arts program for Indian children in order to take advantage of these interesting findings with

Source: Reprinted with permission of William Philion and Charles G. Galloway and the International Reading Association from *The Journal of Reading* 12 (April 1969), 553-560.

regard to language disadvantage of Negro children, it is necessary first to question whether language disadvantage of Negro children is in fact isomorphic with or even similar to that of certain Indian children. We must ask about the nature and extent of language disadvantage of the population of Indian children in question and then on the basis of the answers we are able to arrive at, try to formulate a language arts program for that specific group of children. Do Indian children show the special weaknesses of language development which seem to be characteristic of lower-class non-Indian children. That is, do they tend to treat sentences as *giant words* and also fail to master the use of structural words and inflections which are necessary for the expression and manipulation of logical relationships? If so, are these the only weaknesses of the language development of certain Indian children?

There are several related ways of going about seeking this kind of information. Two approaches which are reported here have to do with direct observation of children and item analysis of children's responses made to diagnostic test items. Both approaches have the property of being complementary to each other and in addition immediately available to the classroom teacher who, in the final analysis, carries the responsibility for the implementation of all learning programs.

BACKGROUND

The approach being followed in the present attempt to identify specific difficulties in the language development of a specific group of Indian children in the elementary grades and then to plan a language arts program for them involves going far afield for the idea that it might be useful to consider cultural deprivation as language deprivation and then to question how this general idea might be relevant to the particular language and reading difficulties of a certain group of children. The general methods of procedure become that of teacher observations of language patterns of Indian children and item analysis of responses made to diagnostic test items. Information so gathered then serves as clues, giving guidance for the construction of meaningful language arts experiences. Item analysis of responses to tests, such as those in reading, is an absolute must if tests of this sort are to be useful in terms of planning new learning experiences for disadvantaged children. It isn't very helpful simply to know that certain children are reading at a particular level. Knowledge of a grade placement score really provides no information with regard to what the learning experiences should be. This information is available only through careful observation of children's daily behavior and item analysis of the responses children make to specific test items.

The children involved in the present study are residents of a community on Vancouver Island in British Columbia. The area is composed predominantly of loggers and farmers numbering approximately 15,000. The data presented represent reading test scores and observations made by teachers of a group of Indian and non-Indian children from this area. All the children are in the intermediate grades (grades four-seven) of the integrated elementary school. The total school population is approximately 225, of which one third are Indian children.

In September these children were grouped for reading on the basis of their grade placement scores on the Gates Reading Survey, Form One. There were three groups:

Group I . . . . . Grade placement 2.5-4.5
Group II . . . . . Grade placement 4.5-6.0
Group III . . . . . Grade placement 6.0-above

Throughout the school year, September-June, the children were instructed in more or less a conventional reading program as outlined by West, Bowers and Parliament (5). In June, Form Two of the Gates Reading Survey was administered. The scores reflecting achievement levels and increases for various sections of the test were recorded for all Indian and non-Indian children.

Test results from this reading program indicated a difference both for level of achievement and gains made by Indian and non-Indian pupils. These results, reported in terms of achievement level and gains made for vocabulary, comprehension and speed, are presented in Table I.

TABLE 1

Comparison Between Indian and Non-Indian Children of Scores Made from September to June on Speed, Comprehension and Vocabulary Sub-tests of the Gates Reading Survey

Date & Group	Number	Mean	S	t
		READING SPEED		
September				
Indian	28	13.46	4.50	
Non-Indian	36	18.47	5.09	4.13*
June				
Indian	28	17.00	4.29	
Non-Indian	36	20.93	5.49	3.66*
		READING COMPREHENSION		
September				
Indian	28	17.89	4.84	
Non-Indian	36	20.50	4.27	2.25*
June				
Indian	28	18.94	4.41	
Non-Indian	36	25.07	5.52	4.84*
		READING VOCABULARY		
September				
Indian	28	23.18	4.43	
Non-Indian	36	26.00	5.53	2.23*
June				
Indian	28	26.29	5.18	
Non-Indian	36	33.12	5.55	5.64*

*(p < .05)

TABLE 2

Comparisons Between Indian and Non-Indian Children of Increases from
September to June, on Speed, Comprehension and Vocabulary
Sub-tests of the Gates Reading Survey

| Groups | Number | Mean Scores | | Increases | Standard Deviation | t |
		September	*June*			
Speed						
Indian	28	13.46	17.00	3.54	4.93	
Non-Indian	36	18.47	20.93	2.46	4.55	.86
Comprehension						
Indian	28	17.89	18.94	1.05	4.33	
Non-Indian	36	20.50	25.07	4.57	5.60	2.75*
Vocabulary						
Indian	28	23.18	26.29	3.11	5.29	
Non-Indian	36	26.00	33.12	7.12	6.21	2.70*

*(p < .05)

It is immediately apparent that the Indian children do not achieve as well as the non-Indian children in any of the areas of reading. It is also apparent that increases made in vocabulary and comprehension by Indian children are significantly less than those made by non-Indian children (Table 2) during the ten-month school year.

These observations suggest that as time progresses Indian children fall further and further behind non-Indian children in reading achievement. In fact, it is noted that by the end of a ten-month period, achievement for this group of Indian children has not reached the non-Indian's initial (September) level of achievement.

Although increases made in reading speed are not significantly different for the two groups, the Indian children read much slower than the non-Indian children. However, when one examines the relatively poor gains made by the Indian children in vocabulary and comprehension, their normal gain made in reading speed leads one to suspect that perhaps these children are really gaining only in word-naming skill rather than in understanding of word concepts. Whereas the non-Indian children appear to achieve satisfactorily, the Indian children do not. This suggests that the conventional reading program designed essentially for non-Indian children is not adequate for Indian children.

ITEM ANALYSIS AND OBSERVATION: A MODEL

In the past it has been common practice among teachers to gather from tests grade placement information about children and then to use this information as an aid for grouping. For the most part, such a practice has proved to be fairly successful when considering progress of average white children for whom reading programs are essentially designed. However, when one is concerned with progress of less advantaged groups, for example, certain groups of Indian children, it becomes apparent that the design and methodology of the reading program must be modified. It is questionable to generalize a reading program designed for *all* children to a group of *similar* children in any specific classroom; it is even more questionable to generalize such a program to a specific group which shows the wide range of differences displayed in culturally integrated classrooms.

When grade placement scores are used as a major variable in grouping children for reading, the assumption is often made that the important differences among children are those of reading rate (amount of material covered to date, number of books completed, . . .) rather than the kinds of language experiences to which children have been exposed. Test scores used for this purpose have the limitation of not providing information with regard to exactly what the reading program should include for each group, let alone for each individual. It is not sufficient to apply the same program to all children even if at different rates. This view is in agreement with current thinking; for example, Stones (4) believes that extending the range of experience to children who are backward will not automatically remedy existing difficulties. He suggests that a systematic attack on the specific deficiencies underlying failure to learn is needed. That is to say, even a continuous progress approach is inadequate. Individualization must occur. However, before a teacher can individualize a reading program, he must be able to determine the specific strengths and difficulties of each child.

PROCEDURE

Those teachers involved in this study were dissatisfied with the progress in reading being made by most of the Indian children. The teachers felt the reading program was not very meaningful in terms of helping certain Indian children progress at a satisfactory level. Over a period of time these children tended to fall further and further behind the non-Indian children in all areas of reading, especially in vocabulary and comprehension as measured by the Gates Reading Test. Even though the teachers were well aware of the fact most Indian children were not progressing satisfactorily, they found the grade placement scores of little value in offering suggestions for modification of the reading program. What the teachers desired for planning language experiences was a method of making effective use of information at hand, especially of their observations of language patterns and children's responses to test items.

The teachers were instructed in a technique of conducting an item analysis of the children's responses to reading test items. They were also given instruction in making and recording careful observations of language patterns of children.

In conducting an item analysis the teachers recorded all incorrect responses made to all test items. This was done by listing the number of each test item in rows on squared grid paper. Identification numbers assigned to children were listed in columns. The number of the incorrect response, as well as an X for omissions was recorded for each child in a separate square to the right of the item number in the column assigned that child.

With this procedure an examination of the incorrect responses by rows results in a graphic representation of the frequency with which particular items are missed by the group as a whole as well as an indication of the specific kinds of errors the group is making. An examination of the incorrect responses by columns provides information about each child with regard to his specific strengths and weaknesses on that reading sub-test; furthermore, this examination provides specific information which may serve as a basis for grouping according to similar strengths or deficiencies rather than simply grouping on the basis of grade placement scores.

As a result of following the procedure outlined above, the teachers were able to detect specific strengths and deficiencies of each child. At the same time they gained specific information about the total group's performance on each item tested. The simple act of recording the students' responses in such a manner made it immediately apparent that there was no alternative for flexible grouping, and that grouping must be based on the need for specific kinds of experiences.

Their results indicated that for some kinds of reading experiences the class could be treated as one group. For other kinds of specific reading experiences, however, their results suggested the formation of groups of one or more on a temporary basis.

Examination of their data revealed that certain children were having difficulty in the areas of vocabulary and comprehension because of very limited and narrow concept development; for example, the concept *combat*, for most of the Indian children and to a lesser degree of non-Indian children, meant *army* ... the specific army involved in the television program "Combat." Another example of certain children's limited and narrow concept development was evidenced through observation of their language responses to the meaning they attached to the word *core*. For many Indian children this word held no meaning; an applecore was simply the *bones* of an apple. The word *leaf* for many of these children meant only the leaf of a maple tree. The word leaf did not refer to the leaves of other trees in the area, for example, evergreen leaves, not to mention the leaves in a book or magazine. Imagine the meaning for these children of a teachers's direction: "Leaf through your book, please." (The teachers observed that when given this direction the children did turn their pages at the command, suggesting they understood the meaning of leaf in this context. Upon closer observation, however, it was also noticed that many children turned pages only after others started to do so, indicating they were imitating the behavior of others.)

Other sources of difficulty in concept formation for certain children within the specific areas of vocabulary and comprehension were found to involve the following examples:

1 word configuration: *inspiration* chosen as a synonym for *vibration* from a choice of *offense, inspiration, spirit, flying, shaking; adventurous* chosen as a synonym for *tumultuous* from a choice of *fluffy, grand, cloudy, adventurous, disorderly.*

2   words sounds: *growl,* chosen as a synonym for *haul* from a choice of
     push, hold, drag, tear, growl.
3   confusion of synonyms with antonyms: *little* chosen as a synonym for
     big from a choice of *little, large, easy, new, fix.*
4   confusion in the identification of word roots: *embrace* chosen as a
     synonym for *bracelet* from a choice of *jewelry, pair, tool, embrace,
     splint; tale* chosen as a synonym for *talent* from a choice of *trade,
     time, prize, skill, tale.*
5   environmental influences: *arrive* chosen as a synonym for *overcome*
     from a choice of *play, fear, cut, arrive, defeat; hymn* chosen as a
     synonym for *miracle* from a choice of *hymn, wonder, peak, atom,
     shackle; group* chosen as a synonym for *massacre* from a choice of
     group, enlarge, manage, slaughter, section.

The teachers were at a loss to explain conceptual errors such as those
listed in section 5 above in terms of the usual deficiencies in word attack
skills. It was only through careful observation that a logical explanation
could be made for such choices. The explanations seemed to lie in environmental experiences; for example, it was learned through talking with the
children that *arrive* meant *come over,* hence *overcome;* that *hymn* and
miracle were terms heard frequently in church; and, a *group* of people
attended *mass,* hence, *massacre.* There were many additional examples of
how item analysis helped these teachers focus their observation in an
attempt to discover explanations for incorrect responses. It was learned
that for many children the words *cool* and *cold* could be associated only
with winter and hence could not be understood when used as adjectives to
modify nouns such as *clothes* and *lemonade.* Limited environmental experiences were again evidenced in many Indian children's belief that plant life
depends upon soil to the exclusion of other necessitites, light, water and
air. Sailing vessels of all kinds are *boats* and only boats for most of these
children. *Ship* refers to an airplane. In similar fashion, the word *fashion*
exists, for only a small number of these children and then only in the
context of something being *old-fashioned.* Fashion in the sense of style, or
a conventional manner simply has no meaning.

Observations which derived from the process of item analysis led to
observations in other areas of language development. It was observed that
for purposes of getting along socially and of self-expression, language was
more a convenience than a necessity for the young Indian child. It was
quite possible to make one's wants known, to enter actively into play and
other social relationships, and to give vent to one's feelings with little or no
use of language. As Bereiter and Engelmann (1) point out, young deaf
children do this and it appears that Indian children also rely to a considerable extent on nonverbal means for these purposes. Language is apparently dispensable enough in the life of the young Indian child for an
occasional child to get along without it altogether. Frequently was the
report given by these teachers of instances in which a child failed to speak
even a single word in class for periods of time extending to months. Such
children, however, were often indistinguishable from their peers in other
areas of behavior, for example participation in games on the playground.

Furthermore, it was observed that certain Indian children tended to be weak in their ability to make effective use of connecting words such as prepositions and conjuctions. Rather than following through with appropriate responses cued by certain verbal directions, many Indian children seemed to rely on non-verbal cues provided by the teacher for information on what response to make. The important cues for appropriate responding to directions such as "please go around the desk," or "line up in front of the door," seemed to be pointing, looking and other gestures made by the teacher while giving the direction, or the behavior of some child who understood the verbal direction. Upon close observation, it was discovered that nearly all verbal directions were accompanied by a variety of non-verbal cues. With experimenting it soon became apparent that without non-verbal cues many Indian children were not able to follow through with responses appropriate to the requests.

Typically speech of the Indian children seemed to consist not of distinct words, but rather of whole phrases or sounds that function like huge words. Expressions such as: "What are you doing?" sounded like "Wa-ch-dn?"; "Where are you going?" like "Whr-ya-gn?" These *large words* which come to stand for the complete expression are not really uncommon in non-Indian language patterns. They occur frequently in the everyday conversation of most English-speaking groups. In fact, as Bereiter and Engelmann (1) find with certain Negro children, once the listener, and for that matter even the teacher has become accustomed to this type of speech, the teacher may actually begin to hear it as if all the sounds were there, and may get the impression that articles, conjunctions, prepositions, and so forth are being heard when in reality there may only be a pause where the omitted word should be. The teacher may believe the child is using these words when in fact he may be using one sound for all of them or leaving them out entirely.

This pattern of early speech development could be expected to create more of a problem for Indian and other groups with language handicaps than for middle-class white children. Whereas white children have in their repertoire of responses the necessary information to fill in the hurried-phrases, Indian children do not seem to recognize that their *large words* are a kind of substitute for a more explicit and precise phrase. For many of these young Indian children, the *large words* are all there is to an expression. And such inflexibility of words to combine and re-combine, to be transformed from statements to questions, and so on, presents serious difficulties for young Indian children in learning to read.

DISCUSSION

Language becomes a virtual necessity when one moves from the social uses of language to the transmission of knowledge from one person to another and to the performance of certain operations with concepts (1). From what was observed by teachers about verbal communication in many Indian homes, it would appear that the cognitive uses of language are severely restricted, especially in communication between adults and children. Language appears to be used primarily to control behavior, to express feelings and to a degree emotions, and to keep the social machinery of the home running smoothly. These, of course, are important uses of language. Many Indian people seem more skillful in them than better-educated non-Indian people. Especially skillful are Indian people and even very young Indian children in completely non-verbal communication. Indian children learn early to pay particular attention to non-verbal directional cues from parents as well as brothers and sisters in order to gain information about how they should behave. These children display remarkable ability in visual discrimination and in imitating the behavior of others. With no verbal directions at all, even very young Indian children, ages four or five, follow complicated sets of directions.

What appears to be lacking, however, is the Indian child's use of language to explain, to describe, to instruct, to inquire, to compare, to analyze and so forth. And as pointed out by Bereiter and Engelmann (1), who found very similar language difficulties in culturally deficient Negro children, these are the very uses that are not developed in Indian homes to the degree normally observed in middle-class white homes because deliberate verbal teaching does not seem to be a normal or necessary part of the adult Indian role. Hence, neither the skills nor the language peculiar to teaching are developed and maintained. Bernstein (2) discusses similar language difficulties among other disadvantaged children. He refers to this distinction as public and formal language development.

Language deprivation, then, has a double edge. The Indian child is not without language, but he is deprived of that part of language that can only be acquired through verbal teaching—the knowledge, the meanings, the explanations, the ability to question in search of information. Beyond that, the child seems to spend his early childhood in an environment where verbal teaching does not frequently take place and where language with which verbal teaching is carried out is not used; therefore, he may never learn *how* to be taught, and when he is exposed to the typical verbal teaching of the classroom, he may behave much as if he were mentally retarded or devoid of language altogether.

IMPLICATIONS

Essential to the formation of an effective language arts program for these Indian children seems to be a continuing emphasis on concept developments; that is, a continuing effort must be directed towards the expansion of *meaning* for limited and narrow concepts.

Caution and precision must be exercised by the teacher in the verbal models she presents which make use of connecting words and prepositions. Care must be taken to emphasize the small words in sentences which are often not heard clearly by the Indian ear.

Teachers must be aware of the fact that Indian children learn effectively through a process of imitation. This has its advantages as well as its drawbacks. Non-verbal cues which might be imitated may be effective in helping bring about certain desired responses, however, while so doing many opportunities for language development are missed. Indian children come to rely on the non-verbal cues to the exclusion of the verbal exchange necessary for language growth. An advantage of this highly developed ability to imitate may be capitalized upon through providing clear, verbal models of the desired responses to be made by the child; for example, the teacher encouraging the child to speak in clear, complete sentences by providing him a model of the sentence in clear diction and intonation. A further drawback of a highly developed ability to imitate is the danger of Indian children learning to parrot the names of words without understanding their meanings. Consequently, words should appear always in a context meaningful for these children. This drawback, coupled with limited and narrow concepts suggests that perhaps an important part of the language program should involve an emphasis on word games, oral reading and the development of listening skills. As Luria (3) suggests, the aim should be to unlock words from single and restricting situations. Perhaps teachers with these children should read and discuss more stories than they might do with other children with fewer language handicaps.

Although many of the components of the language arts program as designed by these teachers for these children are common to other programs of language development, the specific emphases based upon their observations and test item analysis are applicable only to this group of children. To assume that their results will generalize totally to other groups of children is as dangerous as to group children simply on the basis of grade placement scores.

REFERENCES

1   Bereiter, Carl and Siegfried Engelmann. *Teaching Disadvantaged Children in the Preschool.* Englewood Cliffs, New Jersey: Prentice-Hall, Inc., 1966.

2   Bernstein, B. "Aspects of Language and Learning in the Genesis of the Social Process," *Journal of Child Psychology and Psychiatry,* 1 (1961), 313-324.

3   Luria, A. R. *The Role of Speech in the Regulation of Normal and Abnormal Behavior.* Pergamon, 1959.

4   Stones, E. *An Introduction to Educational Psychology.* London: Methuen and Co. Ltd., 1967.

5   West, W. A., J. L. Bowers, and H. E. Parliament (Eds.) "New Challenges in Reading," *The Canadian Teacher's Guide, 15,* 1, (Autumn 1964).

ROLAND REBOUSSIN, JOEL W. GOLD-STEIN: ACHIEVEMENT MOTIVATION IN NAVAHO AND WHITE STUDENTS[1]

This study compares the scores of Navaho Indians and white university students on an established measure of *n* achievement in order to verify previous statements that achievement motivation is not emphasized in Navaho culture. Kluckhohn and Leighton (1962:300-302), in discussing Navaho values, state that individual success is not such a value. In discussing school grades, they state, "Those at the top of the list may find it embarrassing to be placed publicly ahead of their contemporaries, and the list may seem cruel ridicule to those who have lagged behind" (p. 315). Leighton and Kluckhohn (1947:172) found that children, when asked, "What is the best thing that could happen to you?" responded with the following percentages of ambition and achievement statements:

Less acculturated Navahos (Navaho Mountain)	7%
More acculturated Navahos (Shiprock)	9%
Whites	26%

The standard definition of achievement employed here is that used by McClelland and Atkinson, and their associates. In their system, achievement is "success in competition with some standard of excellence" (McClelland *et al.* 1958:181). The statements above by Kluckhohn and Leighton would lead one to expect low scores for Navahos on a measure of achievement motivation derived from this definition of achievement.

METHOD

The 38 White students in the study were a random sample from two introductory psychology classes at the University of Kansas in the fall of 1962. They were tested in their regular classroom situation.

The Navaho Indians we tested were students at Haskell Institute in Lawrence, Kansas,[2] a federal, tuition-free school for Indians specializing in technical training at the high-school and junior-college levels. There were 39 Navaho subjects, 13 females and 26 males, all from the Southwest. Nearly all of them were from the vicinity of the Four Corners area—Crown Point and Shiprock, New Mexico, and Fort Defiance, Arizona. They were obtained from the total population of 47 Navahos at the school by calling a meeting of all Navahos. This resulted in the attendance of 41 persons. At the outset of the meeting, the study was explained to the students, and it was made clear that participation was voluntary. Anyone who wanted to

Source: Reprinted by permission of the American Anthropological Association from *American Anthropologist*, Vol. 68, No. 3, 1966.

leave could do so immediately. No one left at that point, but two persons left right after the administration of the French test (see below); their scores were not used. This left 39 Navahos remaining in the study.

After the Navahos had been told about the study, they completed the French Test of Insight (French 1958). This is a projective test in which ten simple sentences, rather than pictures, are the stimuli. Sample items and responses are found below under *Results and Discussion.* The test was scored for *n* achievement by an expert scorer using the content analysis method described by McClelland *et al.* (1958). Since this scoring method resulted in many minus scores, all scores for both Navaho and white subjects were transformed for purposes of statistical analysis by adding a constant of 10 to each score. In discussing the scoring of *n* achievement, McClelland *et al.* (1958:184) point out that this scoring method should not be used for other cultures without taking appropriate corrective measures. We used it, however—as did Lowell (1950, cited in McClelland 1953:168)—because we wanted to use the larger American culture, rather than Navaho culture, as the referent in measuring *n* achievement.

After an intervening activity, irrelevant here, an "ethnicity index" schedule was filled out for each Navaho subject by an interviewer of the same sex. This ethnicity index was designed by the authors to assess the degree of acculturation of each subject; it contained 13 items, including places lived, schooling, languages used in the home, parents' occupations, participation in Navaho ceremonials, and life ambition. Items were rated on a scale ranging from -2 to +2. A low score indicates low acculturation. The scores were transformed for purposes of statistical analysis by adding a constant of 5 to each score.

RESULTS AND DISCUSSION

Since the ethnicity index was developed by the authors for this study, some demonstration of its validity is desirable. A psychological anthropologist with long experience of Navaho life scored one item of the index for all subjects.[3] This item gives place of birth and early socialization, and was regarded by him as the best single indicator of acculturation on the index. When the independent scoring of this item was correlated with our scoring of the entire index, a phi coefficient of .52 was obtained. This is equivalent to a chi square value of 9.63 (p < .002, 1 *df*). Thus we are confident that our scoring of the ethnicity index as a whole shows considerable agreement with a measure of validity established by an area expert.

Table 1 shows the means and analysis of variance on the ethnicity measure, by *n* achievement and sex. This analysis was performed to control for the effects of acculturation on *n* achievement. The obtained score range was 0 to 19, and it is clear from the ethnicity protocols that this range of scores reflects a wide range of acculturation among the subjects. The two highest scorers, for example, spoke English at home and had fathers who were, respectively, a chemist and a painter; these students wished to live in areas far removed from home upon graduation. The two lowest scorers, on

TABLE 1

Transformed Ethnicity Scores by n Achievement and Sex

Group	Mean
High n-ach male	5.62
High n-ach female	10.86
Low n-ach male	8.69
Low n-ach female	8.33

Analysis of Variance Summary Table

Source	df	MS'	F
Ach (A)	1	.077	<1
Sex (S)	1	5.961	2.64
A × S	1	7.842	3.48
Within	35	2.257	

the other hand, spoke only Navaho at home and had fathers who were ranchers; these students wished to return home after attending Haskell.

Thus, while it is clear that the Navaho population at Haskell was a selected one, a wide range of acculturation was nevertheless represented. More qualitatively, the interviewers were struck with the acculturation differences in the subjects, whose English language ability, in particular, ranged from that of the typical American teenager on the one hand to near incomprehensibility on the other.

Bartlett's test showed that analysis of variance was not inappropriate for the ethnicity data. Because the Ns are not equal, this and the following analysis of variance used the approximate method for unequal cell frequencies described by Walker and Lev (1953:381-382). It can be seen that neither the main effect nor the interaction is significant. This means that neither n achievement nor sex differences are related to ethnicity scores among our subjects. Since the degree of acculturation is not related to achievement scores, we may proceed to the analysis of n achievement differences between our samples without concern for this variable.

First, however, it may be of interest to cite some examples of the sentences used in the French test and of achievement-related and non-achievement-related responses to them. The following story scored as showing achievement imagery. It was written in response to the sentence "Carol said, 'I'm pretty sure I can do it.' "

She's evasive, not sure but she'll try, she'll keep saying that 'til she changes to "I can do it." She feels accomplishment.

The following two stories show the presence and the absence of achievement imagery in responses to the sentence "Diane never joins clubs or social groups."

TABEL 2

Transformed n *Achievement Scores by Population and Sex*

Group	Mean
Navaho male	9.48
Navaho female	7.92
White male	8.00
White female	4.32

Analysis of Variance Summary Table

Source	df	MS$'$	F
Sex (S)	1	6.86	4.35*
Population (P)	1	6.46	4.10*
S $\times$ P	1	1.13	<1
Within	73	1.58	

*p $<$ .05.

Kind that will isolate herself. May have a horror to do so. Perhaps wants to get ahead rather than to go out. I believe she can be a somebody. [Achievement imagery]

Diane lacks the interest of social affairs. She would be considered a stoical person. [No achievement imagery]

The means and analysis of variance for *n* achievement are presented in Table 2, by population and sex. Bartlett's test showed that analysis of variance was not inappropriate for these data. It can be seen that both of the main effects in Table 2 are significant, while their interaction is not. This indicates for our subjects that males have higher *n* achievement scores than females, that Navahos have higher scores than whites, and that this difference is not different for the two levels of sex and population. That our Navaho students should obtain higher *n* achievement scores than our university students is surprising; it is contrary to the anthropological literature we have cited, and invites speculation.

Our hypothesis was based upon ethnographic and other observations on the larger Navaho society. It becomes evident upon further consideration that our Navaho subjects were probably not representative of this larger Navaho population. They represent rather a highly selected population of Navahos, namely, those younger tribal members who attend Haskell Institute, a school strongly committed to the goal of teaching vocations useful in the general American society. It seem possible that this population of Navahos has a much higher level of *n* achievement than the Navaho population in general, and a level even higher than that of our university student population.

Our university students also represent a selected population with respect to the larger American society. The selective factor would appear to be much greater for Indian students at Haskell Institute, however, than for white students at a state university, probably because proceeding to college is increasingly common in general American society. This would appear to be one reasonable explanation for the Navaho students' high achievement scores.[4]

NOTES

1   This research was completed in part while both authors were supported by Public Health Service fellowships and from the National Institutes of Mental Health. Additional support was provided from a grant by the Kansas City Association of Trusts and Foundations to Dr. James Clifton of the University of Kansas, for whose assistance we are grateful. The assistance of Robert Bechtel with the scoring is also gratefully acknowledged.

2   The authors wish to thank Mr. F. E. Stayton, Superintendent, and Mr. Tony Coffin of Haskell for their permission and cooperation, without which this study would not have been possible.

3   The authors are indebted to Dr. Bert Kaplan for assistance in this matter. Responsibility for any error is borne by us.

4   In the article Reboussin and I conclude that our sample was an especially select one and thus probably not representative of the entire tribe. After further consideration, we no longer hold this to be true. Content analyses of achievement imagery in Navaho folk stories and rankings of the degree of early independence training given their youth (held to be a primary determinant of achievement motivation) agree that the Navaho are an achievement oriented culture (McClelland et al., 1953: 289-297). Their percentage of full time entrepreneurs and emphasis on competitive games, both related conceptually to achievement motivation, are greater than many other cultures (McClelland, *The Achieving Society* [Van Nostrand, 1961], pp. 66 and 491). Reboussin visited the Fort Defiance area of the Navaho reservation during 1967 and found current evidence that high achievement motivation was overtly emphasized. The Navaho termed "ambition" as characteristic of their people in general and they referred to business acumen. McClelland found that a culture's degree of achievement motivation was directly related to its degree of economic development, but only within the limits imposed by the available resources. We believe that the economic underdevelopment of the Navaho is due to previous exploitation. Primarily an agricultural people, their reservation is composed almost entirely of barren and eroded lands (Kluckhohn and Leighton, 1962: 48-51). These data supporting the view that achievement motivation is characteristic of the Navaho in general are in accord with our finding that achievement motivation was unrelated to the degree of acculturation of our research subjects.

REFERENCES CITED

French, Elizabeth (1958), Development of a measure of complex motivation. *In* Motives in fantasy, action, and society. John W. Atkinson, ed. Princeton: D. van Nostrand.

Kluckhohn, Clyde, and Dorothea Leighton (1962), The Navaho. Rev. ed. Garden City, N.Y.: Doubleday.

Leighton, Dorothea, and Clyde Kluckhohn (1947), Children of the people. Cambridge: Harvard University Press.

Lowell, Edgar L. (1950), A methodological study of projectively measured achievement motivation. Unpublished M.A. thesis, Wesleyan University.

McClelland, David C. (1953), The achievement motive. New York: Appleton-Century-Crofts.

McClelland, David C., John W. Atkinson, Russell A. Clark, and Edgar L. Lowell (1958), A scoring manual for the achievement motive. *In* Motives in fantasy, action, and society. John W. Atkinson, ed. Princeton: D. van Nostrand.

Walker, Helen M., and Joseph Lev (1953), Statistical inference. New York: Holt.

MURRAY L. WAX, ROSALIE H. WAX: THE ENEMIES OF THE PEOPLE*

Our title has a fitting ambiguity in relation to our text, because *The Enemy of the People* is the title Henrik Ibsen gave to his dramatic presentation of the assault upon an apostle of enlightenment and rationality by the traditionalist and conservative folk. Ibsen had little sympathy for these rural Norwegians; in his drama they appear as selfish, yet congregately stupid, as contrasted to his scientific protagonist, who was strongest because he stood alone. In a curious way, Ibsen's drama foreshadows the interactions which have been characteristic of the white reformer and the Indian tribal community: on the one hand, scientific rationality, Western medicine, the ethos of the individualistic hero, and the rationalistic conception of social welfare; on the other hand, the traditionalist folk, skeptical of the proposals justified by science, mistrustful of the individual who stands apart from their society, protective of their established interests, and unwilling to alter their conduct even in the face of what appears to be catastrophe. Yet, in contrast to the Norwegian drama, on the Indian reservations it has been the reformer who has had the political and financial power with which to manipulate the folk and institute his programs and, despite his ideological creed of devotion to the general welfare, the question of whether he is friend or enemy to the local Indian community perplexes the sociological observer. If the stark antagonism of reformer and folk com-

Source: Reprinted from Howard S. Becker, Blanche Geer, David Riesman, and Robert S. Weiss, editors, *Institutions and the Person* (Chicago: Aldine Publishing Company, 1968); copyright © 1968 by Howard S. Becker, Blanche Geer, David Riesman, and Robert S. Weiss.

munity made exciting melodrama, the contemporary and actual conflict between the two parties now appears more akin to Kafka and the theatre of the absurd.

The barriers to understanding which Ibsen depicted in rural Norway are greatly increased between Indian and white, so that we, as scholars and social scientists, have been attracted to this instance of what Robert Ezra Park and Everett Cherrington Hughes have labeled as a "frontier"—where peoples meet. Particularly have we taken to heart their injunction that scholars and reformers tend to fall into the bias of focusing their attention on only one of the participants in the frontier interaction. Instead, then, of adding to the countless publications of "the Indian problem," which constitute statements of how Indians are problems to whites, or instead of adding to equally large numbers of publications describing how the invading whites defrauded the Indians of their lands, we have tried to add to the handful of works which analyze how it is that Indians and whites are problems to each other. In this respect we have not always been successful in assuming a judicious impartiality, for, since the traditionalist Indians do constitute the underdog and unsophisticated minority, we tend, as moral beings, to devote major efforts to presenting their view of the programs intended for their reformation or transformation; and we feel this to be the more necessary, inasmuch as ethnohistorians have condemned these Indians as not "authentically traditional," while the reformers have scolded them for "clinging to a romantic past." If, then, we fail in this essay to suppress our moral passion, we can justify ourselves on the grounds that the viewpoint of the reformers has amply been presented in the rehabilitative and sociological literatures, where peoples like the Sioux or Chippewa are labeled as culturally deprived, deculturated, and generally lacking in the institutions and traits of whole men.[1]

In the present essay-duet, we try each to show how it happens that some of the current programs of reform (the "War on Poverty") and some of the current apostles of reform (Volunteers in Service to America or VISTA) fail to be of assistance to a reservation of traditionalist Indians. Rosalie Wax prepared her piece in the style of an ethnographer and, rather than alter her vivid and personal prose, Murray Wax prepared a separate, somewhat more analytic and interpretive commentary. She shows how we, as "meta-reformers," failed in our efforts to bring the VISTA volunteers into contact with the Indians and so failed to restructure their definition of their task; and he argues that the context in which these volunteers operate is such as to minimize their chances for giving constructive assistance. She also describes how the programs for communal improvement which were initiated among reservation communities were ignored and superseded by programs plotted in Washington and fulfilled by a reservation elite; and he then argues that the nature of federal operations is such as to render unlikely any support for a program that emerges from among the poor and that is designed to better their economic lot and increase their political power.

REPORT OF AN ETHNOGRAPHER (R. WAX)

As social scientists and teachers, my husband and I have until very recently believed that the almost impenetrable wall between American Indians and the people and organizations who wish to help them could be crossed or dissolved by proper means of communication.[2] If the Indians who need help could learn how to plug into the right channels, if the white people who man these channels could come to understand Indians, then the stalemate of Indian helplessness, isolation, and bitter poverty might be broken. We realized, of course, that, compared to other people in the U.S., the Indians had very little power and, ourselves being professors, we had good reason to appreciate that knowledge is *not* power. Nevertheless, we reasoned, power is hard to acquire without knowledge and knowledge rests on communication.

It was in the spirit of this belief that we participated in many workshops and conferences—both for Indians and for the teachers of Indian children.[3] It was also in the spirit of this belief that we designed and carried out an intensive study of a reservation school situation where academic achievement was notoriously low.[4] There we observed that in some classrooms the children were learning virtually nothing of a scholastic nature. By the fifth or sixth grade they had become adept at disrupting and inhibiting the process of instruction. They feigned stupidity, refused to listen, sharpened pencils loudly when asked to recite, and wrote on the board in letters so small no one could read them. When asked to read aloud they held their books before their faces and mumbled a few incomprehensible words. (The teacher was not aware that other pupils were teasing the reader, by signs and whispers in their native language.)

The efficiency of social organization of these children excited our admiration. Nonetheless, when we talked to their parents we found that most wanted their children to acquire education and, moreover, believed that they were getting it. Investigating further, we found that the parents rarely entered the school and never saw what went on in the classrooms; whereas the teachers, for their part, never visited the parents or attended any of the local Indian social events, such as fairs, dances, give-aways, or bingo parties. Indian elders were not permitted to use the schools for gatherings or entertainments, lest they dirty the floors and destroy government property. Around each consolidated school was a compound in which the teachers lived and kept to themselves.

It seemed to us that if the teachers genuinely wished to educate the Indian children and if the parents genuinely wished their children to be educated, they might do well to break down this elaborate system of *dharma*, get together, and devise means by which the spirited youngsters could be controlled. Among the more radical of our recommendations (though I now consider it the most sensible) was the suggestion that the Indian communities run their own schools with monies from the federal government. Eccentric and off-beat such schools might be, but they could not teach the children less than now. Among our other or less radical suggestions were that mothers be hired as classroom aides, that parents be invited to social gatherings held at the school, that teachers be given time off to visit parents in their homes, and that Indians sit on the school board.[5]

Having spoken so strongly in favor of involving the Indian parents and communities in the education of their children, we subsequently welcomed the opportunity to observe and report on Head Start Projects among the Indians living in the Dakotas and Minnesota. In these projects, or so it seemed to us, the Office of Economic Opportunity was sponsoring exactly the kind of grassroots activity that would help to dissolve the wall between the Indian parents and the schools. For example, communities needing aid were to request it. If funds were granted, the projects were to be directed and carried on by the people who had asked for assistance—and not, primarily, by outsiders. Should outside professional assistance be required, the professionals were directed to involve the parents. We were particularly eager to see what was happening in the several Indian communities which, a year before, had been visited by a representative of the Community Action Programs, who had urged the people in the various districts to form committees, make plans for community improvement, and submit them to Washington. We had heard that several communities had prepared such plans and had ourselves seen the one submitted by the Standing Man Community. So far as we know, it is the only poverty program introduced by a poem:

> Go in search of the people
> Live with the people
> Learn from them
> Love them
> Serve them
> Make plans together with the people
> Begin with what they know
> Build on what they have.

It further explains that: "Many members [of the community] expressed that they had not realized that poverty existed, as so many of them grew up in conditions which are now described as poverty but was not identified as such prior to this time." and that: "The older people have given their consent to let the young people plan the future of the community. They have said that the younger generation is the one who will have to live with the proposed programs."

The plan included such items as a summer youth program, adult education, and self-help housing. Its budget was extremely modest, and it emphasized that: "the community feels that the programs presented for the Poverty Program Committee can be effective in establishing a foundation for stabilizing the impact of the dominant culture if administered by the people themselves, and thus, maintain the dignity and respect for themselves as Indian people." It requested, in addition, a professional person "who will help and work with the people in the community [and help] develop able trainees from the local people in the community."

So far as we knew, this program had not yet been funded. On the other hand, we were informed that the OEO expected to establish Head

Start projects on this reservation, and, this being so, we were to investigate and report on how this might best be done. Accordingly, on our arrival we began to visit Indian friends and acquaintances in the districts and ask them what they thought about a playschool for 4- and 5-year-olds. Most parents and elders opined that if the hours were not too long and if the teachers were young and happy instead of old and crabby, a school in which the little children could learn and play might be a good thing. Some felt that the children should be taught something about "Indian things," and others, that it would be a good idea if some of the teachers or teachers-helpers spoke the native language. Asking about recent developments, we were told that the newly established program of work for youth (Neighborhood Youth Corps) was a good thing, but that, of course, what the people really needed was work for adult men who had to support families. When we asked about the new and handsome looking Old Peoples Home erected since our last visit, we were told that the old people did not like it and so nobody was living in it now but VISTA workers and some nurses' aides.

After three days, this phase of our investigation was brought to an abrupt close when we discovered, quite by accident, that an elaborate program of Head Start and Child Development Centers was already funded and under way. Curious as to how such a program could exist without any of the people knowing anything about it, we inquired further and were referred to "the VISTA workers." These young people, looking wan and harassed, told us that they had been so busy doing paper work and arranging for the delivery of Head Start supplies, that they had not had the time to leave the Agency Town and get out on the reservation. From them we learned that the existing program had been spearheaded by the (white) Tribal Attorney, with the consent of the Tribal Council. It was now being directed by another white man, who was supervising their work. A highly qualified young white woman with a master's degree in child development had been hired to take charge of instruction. Several of the Head Start schools would be ready to open within a few weeks.

We expressed sincere astonishment at the amount of progress which had been made through the efforts of so few people. Nonetheless, we suggested that the program as it was now being conducted seemed somewhat lacking in community involvement and parental participation. Would it not still be possible to arrange a few meetings at which hours, curriculum, transportation, and other matters might be discussed with the parents? The young people explained that they had suggested this, especially since one of the schools was about to open, and " 'the people out there' must be beginning to wonder what it's all about." But the temporary director had vetoed the idea, because, he said, "As soon as 'the people out there' discover that a program has been funded, they will come to my office in droves trying to get jobs for their relatives."

We pointed out that the contract with OEO specifically called for the involvement of parents in the planning of the program and went on to ask to what extent community leaders had been involved. "We haven't been able to find any," said the young folk rather aggrievedly. When, later in the conversation, we named several of the men who had helped to prepare the original "poverty programs," the young people's faces hardened with distaste. These men, they confided, were selfish politicians who wanted only to help their family and kin but cared little for the reservation as a whole. "They're not going to get a thing from us." Warming to the subject, the young folk informed us that "we have decided" that the Standing Man Community, which had been making the most fuss of all (apparently, we gathered, by asking what had happened to their poverty program of the year before), was to be taught a lesson. It was to be the last district on the reservation to be granted a Child Development Center.

In subsequent discussions we tried to point out to the young VISTA workers that the grand, overall reservation community with which they were trying to interact did not exist. Instead, the reservation always has been and still is divided into people who call each other Fullbloods and Mixedbloods. Most of the Fullbloods live out on the reservation in small local communities, which they themselves call *tiyospaye* and which were predominantly composed of kin. Each of these small communities maintains an internal organization and economy of extraordinary efficiency. They are extremely poor, but they are also extremely tough and tenacious. On the other side are the Mixedbloods, who, for three generations, have served as mediators between the local bands, or *tiyospaye,* and the larger society. First existing as scouts and traders, they later became entrepreneurs; in recent years, many have become liaison men and federal administrators. Their social organization is much more diffuse than that of the Fullbloods, and, while they are seldom wealthy, they are usually better off than the latter. Since the white and Mixedblood members of the bureaucracy insist (and sometimes believe) that there is only one reservation-wide community, they can and do monopolize all the influential and well-paid jobs. This is not to say that they do not need jobs. But the Fullbloods, who rarely get within reach of a good job, are for the most part, bitterly poor. As in many symbiotic relationships neither side trusts the other. The Mixedbloods consider the Fullbloods unreliable and backward, because "they are always favoring their relatives." The Fullbloods mistrust the Mixedbloods because they have no (local) community allegiance and so are "not really Indian."

We did not tell the VISTA workers that the Fullbloods do not always regard the members of the Tribal Council as their "representatives" and that, though able and honorable men sometimes sat on the council, it had been created by the Indian Bureau to operate according to the white man's rules. Nor did we tell them we had small confidence that the Tribal Attorney or the incumbent director of the Community Action Program had any real understanding of the social dynamics of reservation life. The attorney, who is dedicated to helping Indians but has never striven to understand them or to grasp their values, had recently involved the Tribal Council in several elaborate and expensive ventures, like the then uninhabited Old Peoples Home.[6] The director has devoted a lifetime to trying to change the Fullbloods into his conception of good citizens, but he pointedly refrains from attending their social or ceremonial affairs (which would put him on a level of parity with them) and participates instead in the Rotary Club, the Kiwanis, the American Legion, and other organizations whose cultural basis is non-Indian; nor has he learned the native language in which Full-bloods carry on most of their social, economic, and political affairs. We did recommend most strongly to the young people that they get out of the Agency Town and make the acquaintance of the so-called Fullbloods, feel-ing that if they obtained a more complete picture of the situation, they would be able to make their own judgments. One of the VISTA workers accepted my invitation to accompany me on some home visits. But talking to the Fullblood mothers about their children seemed to make little im-pression on her. On the ride back to the Agency Town she expressed concern because we had been doing something contrary to the local pro-gram, namely, consulting the parents beforehand.

Some five months later, we were again given the opportunity to visit Thrashing Buffalo Reservation and report on the now functioning Head Start Program. By this time the VISTA workers had been replaced by a considerable staff of white people and Mixedbloods. These persons talked about "selling the program to the Indian people" and pointed out that a great deal of work would have to be directed toward the Indian people "in order for them to comply with our attempts and efforts, as workers, to help them." They also stressed the "lack of communication" and com-plained about the difficulty of making "an effective penetration into the Indian areas." Meanwhile, the Fullbloods were voting with their feet. Some pointed out to us that the Community Action Program directorate in the Agency Town had, as usual, hogged all the funds that might otherwise have flowed directly from the federal government to the people of the *tiyo-spaye*. When asked what their neighbors thought of the Head Start Pro-grams, they remarked delicately: "Since these programs are not their own programs, they are not too much interested."

At one indoctrination meeting, the few local people who attended were less diffident. They told the CAP representatives that they did not want a nursery school, because 4-year-old children would not grow as they should if taken from their mothers. Besides, without her little children to care for, a mother would feel lost and useless. They regarded with strong disfavor the suggestion that they donate their community building to serve as a Head Start classroom, because (we suspect) they feared that if the school authorities took it over they would never give it back.

A year after its inception, the Thrashing Buffalo Head Start Program was limping along with neither "side" giving an inch. Indeed, the director, an energetic specialist in child development, openly announced that the purpose of the program was to change Indian culture. When members of a *tiyospaye* approached her with the suggestion that some older Indian people be hired to teach some elements of Indian culture, she explained that this is not possible because "nursery age-levels do not permit factual and conceptual learning."

We visited many other Head Start Projects for Indian children, and in most of them we found that the programs had been funded, planned, staffed, and put into operation with virtually no involvement of the children's parents. At several schools the parents had subsequently approached the directors and teachers with complaints and suggestions concerning the operation of the schools. But in every case, the professional staff regarded this parental interest with distress, as if it reflected a failure in either planning or procedure. Parental involvement was defined as the parents' complying with the suggestions of the teachers. Thus, the directors were pleased when the parents made blocks for the children according to the specifications laid down by the teachers, or when the parents, as requested, "volunteered" to accompany the classes on bus trips.

To the directors and teachers we remarked that the complaints and suggestions of the parents could profitably be viewed not as judgments on their professional competence but as opportunities to involve the parents in participation. Meetings might be held in which the various problems and proposals could be discussed and the advice and assistance of the parents might be solicited. If, for example, the parents felt that their children were being "picked on" during free play periods, they might be willing to send more volunteers to watch the children. At this time we did not realize that we were preaching heresy. But two weeks later, when we made the same suggestion at a workshop for teachers of Indian children, we were summarily rebuked by a high school principal, who pointed out that "consulting with parents would detract from the authority of the schools."

THE IRONIES OF FEDERAL PROGRAMS FOR REHABILITATING THE POOR (M. WAX)

The Federal Government

I must begin where my competence from personal research is weakest—with the higher levels of the federal government. Yet I cannot avoid the discussion without attributing more responsibility to local administrators than they actually do have. For it is the acts and appropriations of the Congress and the edicts and operations of the Washington bureaucracy that provide the institutional context for reservation programs. Those who administer such programs locally, or who review their administration in Washington, reflect by their activities and worries their forecasts of how the Congress, the President and his executive assistants, and the federal review agencies (e.g. the Bureau of the Budget), will respond both to exterior events and to the reports concerning these programs. Our discussion here must take cognizance of this orientation.

Politically sociology instructs us that, insofar as politicians are professionals, making their careers of political office, their primary task is re-election. Amateurs and ideologists among congressmen can indulge the luxury of political causes, but those for whom politics is a vocation must regard re-election (or election to higher office) as the symbol of correct political behavior. From such a disenchanted orientation, programs such as the "War on Poverty" represent an opportunity for the congressman to funnel money into his district. Insofar as his district contains a significant plurality of poor people, and insofar as these poor are active participants in the electoral process, the congressman will be pleased to assist in their being given some modest share of federal funds. Programs that involve mothers and infants, or that involve educational goals, are naturals for his support, inasmuch as they promise to appeal not only to the poor themselves but also to the remainder of his constituency.

Yet the disbursal of money to the poor can never be a simple matter in a country such as the United States, whose English tradition embodies the workhouse as a locus of such discomfort and misery that no one would voluntarily seek admittance except those who were utterly destitute and without hope. Contemporary rehabilitative programs are tinctured with the same sadistic ethos, for the misery of the poor is attributed to their own (moral) failings (rather than to social and economic arrangements), so that the programs are typically designed not to alleviate misery but to alter the "work habits" of the poor so as to make them more competitive in the labor market. This ethos is structurally buttressed by the fact that poverty is a matter not simply of absolute economic deprivation but of relative social and political inferiority.[7] Insofar as the U.S. has had an economy of abundance, improvements of the economic situation of a group have been possible without seriously incommoding other groups, but the areas of social status and political power have nonetheless remained more akin to the zero-sum games of the game theorists, where improvements in the position of the poor and lowly can only be accomplished at the expense of their rivals. Really to alter the status of the poor would be to elevate them to a position of equality with their neighbors, and so drastic an alteration of the status system would constitute a real threat to these latter. Particularly if the poor are ethnically distinct or socially visible, as Negroes, Indians, or Puerto Ricans, the raising of their social and political status is bound to arouse such hostilities as to endanger any federal program which is associated with the process.

Thus, those who frame policy for the War on Poverty are caught in a situation of conflicting imperatives. Many of them are familiar with the findings of community development research which emphasize that significant social change must involve the initiative of the community itself. Yet if a program is to avoid the arousing of political opposition from the neighbors of the impoverished, it must restrict itself to such morally worthy tasks as rehabilitation and education, while inhibiting any challenges to the sociopolitical establishment. Further, the program must meet the stern and miserly rules of the Bureau of the Budget, so that its funds must be guarded and audited and not utilized for such happy purposes as a community "feed" or a ceremonial gathering. Moreover, given the numbers of the poor and the small sums of federal money that are being appropriated, there is a genuine need to economize to the point of miserliness, if anything is to be accomplished besides the undisciplined distribution of funds in an impoverished area. The resultant of these pressures and meager resources is that by the time the programs reach the reservation they are so packaged, and entangled with such conditions, that they can only be accepted if the local community established within itself a miniature version of the federal bureaucracy.

The Reservation

Indian reservations encompass such a strange heterogeneity of peoples that it is difficult to do justice to the social dramas that are staged within them.[8] The aggregate of human beings who are called (or who call themselves) "Indians" includes persons of different religious faiths, levels of literacy, wealth, and occupation, not to mention differing involvement with the cultural traditions and folk responsibilities of the particular tribe. The reservation is not a unity but is split into cliques and parties and loose alliances of persons of common background, or co-residence, or similar interests. Yet one configuration tends to endure, that in which the reservation is an administrative unit organized about a zone of poverty (and powerlessness) within a larger society of relative abundance. Thus, to outsiders and high-level planners, "the reservation" appears as a homogeneous and unified body of impoverished and ignorant folk whose destinies are being guided by representatives of the various "helping professions" who have their roots in the greater society: teachers, nurses, welfare workers, vocational counselors, ministers, and the like.

The impoverished who form the base of the reservation status system do include the persons most directly linked to the Little Traditions of the Indian folk; when their social existence has not been disorganized by the various onslaughts of the greater society, they tend to live in small bands of kith and kin. These bands are tenacious in their structure, having been forged over generations of jointly confronting a hostile, uncertain, and alien world; for the traditional Indians, life revolves about interaction within these bands. Like many other little communities of folk peoples, the bands are marked by institutionalized systems of sharing and leveling: those persons who enjoy a windfall are expected to share their prosperity throughout the band.[9] Those who participate in the system of sharing are members of the band; those who abstain and refuse are not, no matter how otherwise distinguished their claims to Indian heritage. To outside reformers, imbued with the individualistic ethos of Protestantism, this institutionalized sharing has long been viewed as the supreme vice of Indian communities (and it is one of the ironies of field research to hear Christian missionaries denounce the practices of sharing). The leveling principle also affects the system of leadership, as these bands have a long tradition of voluntary membership and participation. Most Indian tribes lacked the coercive political system of the nation state and could institute communal action only on the basis of concensus. Those individuals who were thus propelled forward as "chiefs" were not the possessors of an arbitrary power but had been chosen, whether they liked it or not, as spokesmen of the group. Traditional communities did not act on the basis of the orders of "chiefs," nor did they follow the directives of committees; instead they discussed continually until a consensus emerged, after which they propelled into acting as their representatives those they thought most suited for the onerous tasks.

Accordingly, the tribal government, which supposedly expresses the voice of the Indian people of a reservation, is an alien and extraneous body to the traditional system of band organization.[10] Neither the reservation as a territorially based political body nor the tribe as an all-encompassing association with centralized authority fit traditional patterns. A fit with traditional patterns conceivably might have emerged within the new conditions of reservation life, but the fact that the tribal government is and must act as a coercive political body renders it incompatible with traditional attitudes and serves to make its activities continually abrasive. Outside liberals and reformers tend to regard the reservation as a single community and its tribal government as the agency whereby that community organizes itself to take collective action, but this is a gross and convenient exaggeration. To the unemployed and Little Traditional Indians of the reservation, their government appears primarily as a configuration of patronage, whose positions are to be awarded to their friends or, alternatively, to be bestowed on those individuals who can belabor and pressure the Bureau of Indian Affairs and kindred agencies. In these regards, their government may not be too different from the government of many municipalities and counties within the U.S. but, since reformers tend to view it as the instrument whereby "the reservation community" can reorganize itself to adapt to the greater society, it is necessary to provide these debunking comments.

Yet, anomalous as is the situation of the tribal government, we would not wish to dismiss its role. Over time, the traditional bands within the reservation have been acquiring the savvy to utilize the apparatus of their government, and the representatives on the tribal council are frequently sensitive to the wishes of their constituents and able to bring them forcefully to the attention of pertinent officials and agencies. Able and decent men do get elected to high tribal office, and their caliber is sometimes strikingly superior to that of municipal and county officers elsewhere in the U.S. But these men are caught in a bind. The regulations and requirements of the outside agencies with which they must deal coerce them into non-Indian modes of conduct and so undermine the confidence and support of the Indian populace.

The Program on the Reservation

The impoverished Indians do not see themselves as "poor" nor as requiring rehabilitation, but rather as having less cash than they would prefer and as having little access to jobs. When they cast about to attribute responsibility for their condition or their difficulties, they lay the blame, not to their lack of the Protestant virtues of thrift, diligence, and individualistic initiative, but to the invading whites who swindled their land and then welched on their treaty obligations. When these Indians learn of a new federal program bringing monies to the reservation, they interpret it as being a response to their needs, an overdue sharing by the rich and powerful whites. Knowing that other bands will be competing for a share of the booty, they begin at once to maneuver to secure their share. In a profound sense, these bands may be correct in their interpretation of the federal program, for it is more than likely that their congressman authorized the program so as to bring money to his electorate in such a fashion as to redound to his credit.

Regardless of the schemings and plannings of the traditionalist bands, the juiciest plums of the federal program fall into the laps of the Mixed-blood elite of the reservation and their non-Indian allies. Partially in response to the push of the reservation elite, the new federal program tends to be sealed off from the impoverished and ignorant folk; it is beyond their knowledge and control. In the area of personnel employment, the emphasis upon federal rules of procedure plays into the hands of the elite, since the natural thing is to give weight to formal education and to experience within formally organized institutions; as a consequence, the older, wiser, and more respected members of band communities are so disqualified from responsible positions of executive employment that no one even raises the question of their possible competence. Likewise, the emphasis upon federal procedures. of accounting and organization serves to disqualify bands or associations of the impoverished and uneducated from presenting their programs for community development in competition either with the tribal government or with any other organization that has gained the support and assistance of professional experts.

Within this context we can place the Helpers and Developers who have been hired and recruited for these programs. To begin with, we have the Mixedblood group who are native to the reservation and whose ancestors have long had the role of being intermediaries between the traditional Indian society and the invading Whites. (In Siouan, the very word used to denominate the Mixedblood has the primary denotation of "interpreter," and this, to be sure, was the role that their male ancestors, usually French, came to occupy when they intermarried and established their trading posts among the Indians.) Today, this population of Mixedbloods includes persons with considerable education and training and a cultural predisposition for occupying the middleman's role in the administration of Indian affairs. In the federal programs under consideration they are joined by a corps of people of various sorts. The directors of Head Start and Child Development Centers will be persons with graduate degrees in education or child development, and the heads of parallel programs in public health will have comparable levels of training in nursing or the like; these professionals will be more than likely to be itinerants. Meanwhile, the secondary level of staff will have been recruited from the towns near the reservation from among persons with more modest trainings as educators, nurses, social workers: mostly youthful, footloose, and with much curiosity and enthusiasm. All of these persons are likely to be financially well off, as compared to the Indian bands, although none of them are likely to have much wealth, except perhaps for the parents of some of the VISTA volunteers.

Most of these Helpers and Developers rationalize their roles within the program on the grounds of moral service to the Indian people. The outsiders, and particularly the VISTA volunteers, may also cherish the romantic notion of assuaging the white man's guilt for having appropriated the lands of the Indians. On the other hand, the secondary staff from the nearby towns will rather regard themselves as providing moral uplift to a recalcitrant folk. Implicit in all these rationalizations is the image of a service whose content is set by the professional staff. Everett C. Hughes has contrasted the classical role of the free professional with that of the professional within the three-layered institution composed of board, professionals, and clients.[11] In both cases, conflicts will develop between professionals and clients concerning the nature of the service to be performed and the judgment as to the quality and competence of the service. Since the ideal type of relationship of free professional and client is voluntary on both sides, the dissatisfied client can always terminate the relationship; however, in the three-layered model, both parties have usually less freedom and less power. The federal programs on the Indian reservation assume the latter format, for the professionals are bound by the dimensions of the program and the rules of the federal bureaucracy, while the Fullbloods confront programs concerning which they have little knowledge or control. The Helpers and Developers may think of themselves as there to be of service to the Indians, but definitely they are not servants of the Indian communities, and their actual roles reveal the traditional ambiguity of the English word, "service."[12]

To the extent that the programs do operate, they do so by a species of bribery (as candy to infants). If preschool children attend Child Development Centers, they are given nourishing meals, and if adolescents join the Job Corps they enjoy the same and other benefactions. In return, the Helpers have acquired the bodies of the Indians, and they hope to win their souls. In this sense there is a struggle concerning the programs, as the Indian bands try to loot the programs for consumables, while the directors try to exploit their mandate to reform the Indian poeple. The sequences of events that result sometimes have the hysterical quality of a Buster Keaton silent film, where the observer can perceive the continued blind misunderstandings and actions at cross-purposes by both parties. Soon, a situation is achieved where programs are threatened with utter collapse. In compensation, the programs must be overstaffed, since the Indian clientele cannot be relied upon to maintain the spirit of the undertaking. So, as new professionals arrive on the reservation, they are deluged with responsibility for faltering programs. The reservation may be jammed with unemployed Indians, of whom some are persons of considerable talent and sophistication (albeit lacking in formal learning), but the demands upon the time of Helpers become overwhelming. Dropped into an atmosphere of crisis, the new member of a professional team such as VISTA has no time to become acquainted with the local Indian folk and, indeed, the more sincere and the more dedicated he is to serving the Indians, the less time and opportunity he will have to associate naturally with them. So, by a paradoxical involution, the only staff members who learn to know individual Indians well are those who are less than conscientious—the cynical and the time-servers and those who covertly regard the program as a federal boondoggle; as they loiter in taverns, chase Indian women, or poach game on Indian lands, they learn much about some aspects of Indian life, but not in any fashion that is publicly mentionable.

CONCLUSIONS (M. AND R. WAX)

A major assumption of certain professional and semi-professional Helpers is that the giving of assistance is an entirely one-sided process. It is the Helpers who determine who needs help and what type of help is needed, it is they who then plot the strategy of administering help or, as one school principal put it: "Our problem is how does one motivate . . . students and people toward a better life and higher standards when they themselves don't want it." In the U.S. past, this policy and definition of role seems to have been acceptable to the children of poor immigrants. But it is not working today with the Negro people, and it has never worked with the traditionalist Indians, for the latter have continued to define help as a process that begins with the person or people who need help. One may give a gift to an Indian whom one admires or wishes to ingratiate. But one does not offer to help him without first making sure that without giving offense he is free to refuse.

All of the above points have, of course, been made many times. The one genuinely new phenomenon in the ethnographic narration presented initially is the presence of ourselves as social scientists, trying and failing to get even the youngest and most uncommitted of the Helpers to inquire as to the point of view of the people who were supposed to be helped. As social scientists we were, of course, well-aware that much professional training unfits the individual to take any but the view of the bureaucracy which he serves. But we were shocked and dismayed that untrained and idealistic young people, who clearly wished to help the unfortunate, could be so easily and efficiently encapsulated within the self-protecting philosophy of the professional Helpers.

Part of this dismay sprang from our realization of the power of Helpers' philosophy and a corresponding insight into the degree of alienation and withdrawal from reality which it imposes on its adherents. Another part of the dismay involved our professional integrity. Was there any value, we asked ourselves, in observing and describing the various views of the peoples who contribute to a frontier situation when the reluctance to consider any view but one's own is so extreme?

To this question there is one comforting answer. Long ago we held attitudes very like those which we now ascribe to the professional helpers. But having been reared in an academic tradition which emphasized the value of understanding the views of all participants to a situation we gradually (and not without many hard knocks) began to understand why the helpers were so helpless. If this can happen to us it could perhaps happen to others. In this expectation we have prepared the foregoing discussion hoping that it might prove enlightening to at least some of the eight or nine different groups, organizations, and *tiyospayes,* involved in the complicated endeavor of giving assistance to the Indians and other poor.

NOTES

*The argument of this essay grows from our experiences and from those of various associates and friends who have conducted field research among communities of American Indians. For purposes of dramatic simplicity and emphasis, these materials have been synthesized by R. Wax in the section titled "Report of An Ethnographer" so as to yield a fictional narrative of two researchers and one reservation, "Thrashing Buffalo." However, to give one example, the benevolently paternal attorney depicted in the narrative has his counterparts elsewhere among professional workers who have an insider's access to federal programs and who devote themselves to mediating those programs to Indian reservations.

Our field work among Indians and that of our associates has had a variety of sponsorship and support. Much of the writing of this essay occurred when we were engaged in a project sponsored by the University of Kansas and conducted under contract with the U.S. Office of Education. Our field research has been supported by the U.S. Office of Economic Opportunity, and in previous years the sponsor of our projects was Emory University. Needless to say, only we are responsible for the opinions expressed in this essay.

1 See Everett C. Hughes. "Comment on 'Sociological Analysis and Poverty' by J. L. Roach," *American Journal of Sociology* (1965), 71: 75-76; Georg Simmel, "The Poor" (translated by Claire Jacobson), *Social Problems* (Fall 1965), 13(2): 140-48; Murray and Rosalie Wax, "Cultural Deprivation as an Educational Ideology," *Journal of American Indian Education* (Jan. 1964), 3(2): 15-18; Richard A. Kurtz, "The Public Use of Sociological Concepts: Culture and Social," *American Sociologist* (August 1966), 1: 187-89; John R. Seeley, "Progress from Poverty," *Liberation* (August 1966), pp. 9-14.

2 See Rosalie H. Wax and Robert K. Thomas, "American Indians and White People, " *Phlyon* (Winter 1961), 22(4):305-17.

3 We have participated over a number of years in the Workshop on American Indian Affairs, which is sponsored by American Indian Development, Inc. (Executive Director, D'Arcy McNickle), and held each summer on the campus of the University of Colorado. Annual reports of these workshops are available from sponsoring organization. In 1961 R. Wax conducted a mail survey of the workshop students of previous years and wrote a brief history and report.

4 This research has been reported in several publications: Murray L. Wax, Rosalie H. Wax, and Robert V. Dumont, Jr., *Formal Education in an American Indian Community*, Society for the Study of Social Problems, Monograph No. 1, 1964; Rosalie and Murray Wax, "American Indian Education for What? *Midcontinent American Studies Journal* (Fall 1965), 6(2); 164-70. Rosalie H. Wax, "The Warrior Dropout," *Trans-Action* (May 1967), 4: 40-46.

5 Wax, Wax, and Dumont, *op. cit.,* chap. vii.

6 Such ventures are the topic of considerable self-congratulation at ceremonial, political occasions, and it is true that they have the important effect that, during their construction, employment and monies are brought into the reservation area. On the other hand, honesty requires that we note their defects. Since these projects are heavily underwritten by the federal government and do promise opportunity to do good, it is difficult for the tribal government to assess them ration-

ally and critically. Thus, this government is propelled into ventures which require a significant share of its income both for maintenance and for servicing the debt. Meantime, the more traditional Indians, who exist on a narrow margin of subsistence, are not inclined to devote tribal monies or energies to projects in which they have no real emotional investment.

To be more specific, almost all persons on the reservation, and of whatever background, would be inclined to favor projects to assist the aged Indians who are impoverished. But it is doubtful if these aged would have defined their needs in terms of institutional housing ("a home") and it is equally doubtful whether they or their kin were polled on the matter.

7 See the essays cited in note 1 above.

8 This heterogeneity has often been overlooked, by both ethnographers and planners. One of the few to emphasize it has been Edward Spicer in his historical account of Indians in the southwestern United States and Mexico, *Cycles of Conquest* (Tucson: University of Arizona Press, 1962), Chap. 19.

9 One of the finest presentations of the operation of leveling mechanisms is by K. O. L. Burridge in *Mambu: A Melanesian Millenium* (London: Methuen, 1960).

10 See the vivid analyses of American Indian politics by Robert K. Thomas, "Colonialism: Classic and Internal," and "Powerless Politics," in *New University Thought* (Winter 1966/67), 4(4): 47-44; 44-53.

11 Everett C. Hughes, *Men and Their Work* (Glencoe, Ill.: The Free Press, 1958). See also the discussions of physicians, clinics, and hospitals in the essays of such of his students as Oswald Hall, Anselm L. Strauss, Howard S. Becker, and Eliot Freidson. A striking parallel to the Indian situation is Herbert J. Gans' chapter on "The Caretakers" in his *The Urban Villagers* (New York: The Free Press of Glencoe, 1962).

12 See the following discussion of the "professional reformer," which is excerpted from an editorial in *Ramparts,* (January 1967), 5(7): 8, and which refers to an article in *The New Republic* written by Daniel Moynihan:

Mr. Moynihan believes that the day has passed for popular movements, the civil rights movement and antipoverty movements among them, to force effective national reforms. Now the injured and oppressed of society should hand over their causes to the more sophisticated "professional reformer."

Such a "professional reformer,"(and presumably Mr. Moynihan would, if pressed, include himself in the select group), would be quick to see, for instance, the opportunities that the Selective Service System affords for social change, he suggested.

One of the most effective ways for Negroes to make it in this society Mr. Moynihan said, is the Army way. The sight of Negroes fighting in Vietnam, he said, "may be the single most important psychological event in race relations in the 1960's," since "acquiring a reputation for military valor is one of the oldest known routes to social equality."

Mr. Moynihan is enough of a serious intellectual to openly admit the logical extension of his position: "Expectations of what can be done in America are receding. Very possibly our best hope is seriously to use the Armed Forces as a socializing experience for the poor."

Perhaps the best counter to the thesis of Moynihan (as given above) was by John Seeley, "Poverty is a lack of power to command events." *op. cit.,* p. 9.

CHAPTER 4

ACCULTURATION
AND IDENTITY

The term *acculturation* refers to the processes of cultural change resulting from intercultural contact. The concept was widely used before a formal definition was attempted. The most influential attempt at definition was a 1935 memorandum by Redfield, Linton, and Herskovits, which stated: "Acculturation comprehends those phenomena which result when groups of individuals having different cultures come into continuous first-hand contact, with subsequent changes in the original culture patterns of either or both groups."[1] A few years later Linton noted that "to the average worker in the social sciences it [acculturation] seems to convey little more than a sense of a heterogeneous, unanalyzed collection of processes any or all of which may be set in train by contacts between representatives of different societies and cultures,"[2] and as late as 1968 an essay in the *International Encyclopedia of the Social Sciences* stated that "the term 'acculturation' and its derivatives remain somewhat ambiguous... inconsistency is often apparent in the writings of American anthropologists with regard to whether the term is applied to results or to processes of change."[3]

Despite the ambiguity about the breadth of acculturation studies as an anthropological specialty and about its relationship to related concepts, a number of excellent summaries of acculturation theory and research are readily available.[4] The interested reader is referred to them for general discussions of acculturation as a concept and for extensive case studies of acculturation among American Indians. In addition, many of the studies reprinted elsewhere in this book might be considered studies of acculturation. The chapter on education (Chapter 3) is an obvious example. And since some of the processes categorized by anthropologists as acculturation are the same ones defined by sociologists as elements of urbanization,[5] the chapter on the urban Indian (Chapter 6) also is relevant.

Spicer has concluded that in the 1960s "the main line of development of acculturation studies continued to be descriptive,"[6] and the papers in this chapter reflect that emphasis. At the same time, however, at least six dominant "foci of interest" have emerged in the literature on acculturation, including nativistic movements, cultural fusion, personality and acculturation, biculturalism, social scale and cultural change, and techniques in directed change.[7] Of these, the category "personality and acculturation" has been most represented in recent anthropological research on Indian people, although there have also been several studies of biculturalism and a good deal of work relevant to the relationship between social scale (the extent of the "area" of social interaction of a population) and cultural change. The pieces included in the present chapter all can be located within these three foci of interest. The article by Wax and Wax reprinted in the chapter on Indian education is relevant to the sixth category, "techniques in directed change."

The historical context within which studies of Indian people have taken place has dictated a major concern with cultural loss, cultural disintegration, and cultural assimilation. As with acculturative studies of other colonial peoples, studies of acculturative processes accompanying culture contact between whites and Indians have tended to be ethnocentric, that is, anthropologists have carefully charted the influence of white culture on Indian people, but have largely ignored the impact of Indian culture on white America.[8] Among the few researchers who have studied the acculturation process from the latter perspective is Irving Hallowell.[9] He notes that although acculturation has been conceptualized as a two-way process, "in practice, American anthropologists have investigated it as a one-way process."[10] It is difficult to explain why this should be so, since acculturation has been conceptualized as not only a "culture-receiving process" but also a "culture-producing process," and the "cultural creativity" is much easier to document in advanced than in preliterate societies.

One important component of the "backwash of the frontier," Hallowell's phrase for Indian influence on American culture, was the "white" borrowing of the maize-complex. Among the other elements of modern American culture which include patterns borrowed from the Indians are our speech, economic life, clothing, sports and recreation, religious groups, curative practices, music, literature, personality, and anthropology.[11] Perhaps the most important of these, and certainly the most studied, has been the influence of the Indian on American literature and art, an influence analyzed brilliantly by Fiedler,[12] and earlier by Pearce and Wilson.[13] Finally, we should note Hallowell's suggestion that the Indian may have contributed a "characterological 'gift' " to the personality of some white Americans: "If there ever comes a time when we are able to grapple with such a complex question as the historical development of an American national character, the psychological effects of frontier contacts with the Indians need to be more fully explored and evaluated."[14]

The first selection in this chapter is Hallowell's "American Indians, White and Black: The Phenomenon of Transculturization." Hallowell observes that "Indianization," the adoption of Indian culture by members of other cultures, is one of the many aspects of the impact of Indian culture on other cultures that has received little attention from scholars. He provides historical and and literary examples of the process as experienced by whites and blacks, and then identifies it as a category of a more general phenomenon which he labels "transculturalization," and distinguishes from acculturation in that it involves changes in individual persons rather than changes in sociocultural systems. There are varying degrees of transculturalization, ranging from permanent identification with a second culture to relatively superficial and temporary adjustment. Some whites were Indianized as a consequence of their being captured, often at an early age, but others accepted Indianization voluntarily, as adults. Hallowell notes the apparent ease with which whites became Indianized, and contrasts it with the difficulties experienced by Indians who tried to accept white culture. Among the institutional factors affecting the different permeability of the two cultures was the institutionalized pattern of adoption among the Indians, part of a basic receptiveness of Indian society to transculturites that was not paralleled in the relatively closed white society. Numerous legitimate and socially esteemed roles were available to the white (or black) transculturite; in contrast, there were few roles available to the Indian in white society. Hallowell concludes by stressing that the receptivity of a culture to alien individuals depends upon the nature of its social values and institutions rather than the good- or ill-will of its citizens.

Redfield, Linton, and Herskovits identified "assimilation" as a process "which is at times a phase of acculturation."[15] Spicer notes that "persistent usage gives it the meaning of cultural assimilation."[16] In the second paper reprinted in this chapter, Roy adopts a somewhat differing theoretical framework. Following the work of Harold Jacoby, he identifies acculturation as the first of three stages of the assimilation of Indian people. The subsequent stages are social integration (participation in white formal organizations) and amalgamation ("biological miscengenation"). Analysis of data from interviews with a random sample of 40 families living on the Spokane Reservation indicated that Indians have *not* been sufficiently acculturated to compete on an equal basis with urban whites. Nevertheless, considerable social integration and amalgamation have taken place. Accordingly, it can be concluded that the designated stages of assimilation need not proceed in the order given, but, in fact, may be interchangeable.

The third selection in this chapter derives from a study of the Spokane Indians conducted a few years after Roy's analysis, and which obtained data from urban Indians as well as those on the reservation. In "Urban Residence, Assimilation and Identity of the Spokane Indian" Lynn White and Bruce Chadwick assess the relative utility of several measures of acculturation, social integration, and amalgamation as predictors of the extent to which Indian people identify themselves as whites. They report that 31 percent of their sample (48 residents of the Spokane Reservation and 39 Spokane Indians living in the city) identified themselves as whites. Evaluation of the relative importance of eight correlates of "white identification" revealed that the most important correlates were the perception that one "fit in" with white people and the degree of one's spouse's white ancestry. Thus, when total assimilation (identification of oneself as white despite one's tribal membership) is the dependent variable, it appears that some of the traditional correlates of assimilation such as education or steady employment are much less important than one's perception that he is accepted as an equal by his white peers, or one's marriage to a white.

The paper by Bushnell describes the consequences of a dramatic increase in extent of involvement with representatives of "outside" society by the Hupa, a California tribe previously severely isolated. Due to their remote location and other fortuitous circumstances, the Hupa were allowed to remain on their ancestral lands, and until World War II maintained many of the essentials of their traditional culture. Between 1940 and 1950, World War II, the coming of the logging industry, and the arrival of electric power at the reservation combined to create economic prosperity and almost instant updating of their culture. But the increase in social scale (i.e., the decrease in isolation) was accompanied by the inevitable disorganization of the traditional patterns. Now much of the original culture has been lost, and concerned members of the community are encouraging increased involvement in traditional activities and at the same time resisting the attribution to themselves of elements of the cultures of other Indians which had no place in the Hupa tradition. Despite what Bushnell describes as "a thoroughgoing Americanization and modernization of most aspects of the reservation culture," many elements of traditional religious belief and ceremonial life have endured. The combination of a viable core of elements of Indian identity with the thorough modernization of reservation culture leads Bushnell to the conclusion that "American Indians" is an inappropriate appellation for these people. Their acculturation has progressed to the point that they should be designated as "Indian-Americans," and the former term should be reserved for peoples whose culture is less "American" and more distinctive.

The selections by Parker and Downs illustrate different approaches to the problematic relationship between acculturation and personality. Because the. internalization of values and goals of white society may run ahead of the acquisition of the skills and opportunities necessary for the attainment of those goals, a consequence of acculturation among Eskimo youth is an increased ambivalence about their own and other ethnic groups. And because a "receiving society" always selects only fragments of the culture "offered" by a "donor society," the Piñon Navahos have adopted an image of white Americans that is more distortion and myth than accurate representation of white values, and the incorporation of this image into Navaho identity has enhanced sex differences in rate of acculturation among them because the cowboy image has no viable feminine counterpart compatible with reservation life.

Parker's "Ethnic Identity and Acculturation in two Eskimo Villages" represents the application of projective techniques—the Rorschach test is a well-known example of such techniques, and has itself been used in the study of the acculturation of Indian people[17] —in the assessment of ethnic identification among teen-aged Eskimos. The research sites were Eskimo villages representing two stages of acculturation. Subjects were asked to look at a set of pictures presented by an anthropologist and to tell a story about each picture. The recorded stories were coded for expressions of hostility, interethnic social distance, degree of attraction to symbols of Western society, affect toward white adult figures, and other variables. Intervillage contrasts on these variables revealed, as expected, that Eskimo young people who were most attracted to symbols of Western culture (i.e., the more acculturated) manifested high levels of generalized hostility and ambivalence toward white society *and* toward their own culture. Parker invokes Robert Merton's theory of anomie and deviant behavior as an interpretive device; the disjuncture between goals and means for their attainment in the village, representing the later (internalizing) stage of acculturation, seems to lead to negative ethnic attitudes, generalized hostility, and even, Parker suggests, juvenile delinquency.

In "The Cowboy and the Lady" James Downs maintains that the apparent sex differentials in rate of acculturation among Navahos stem from the fact that males have a white model, the cowboy, that is not incongruent with their life situation, while none of the feminine models presented to the Navaho girl by the white world are appropriate, or even possible, as long as she remains on the reservation. The acceptance of the cowboy model by the males is itself ironic, since it represents to some degree a misperception of the values and practices of white society. The cowboy is not a major figure in present-day American society, yet it is the figure found compatible by the Navaho. Thus Downs illustrates the unanticipated consequences of culture contact: the donor society often has little control over which aspects of its culture a receiving society will accept. Having accepted the cowboy image, the Piñon Navaho has his stereotypes confirmed by the television westerns which have represented a substantial segment of his contact with white society.

The final articles in this chapter are attempts to demonstrate the inadequacy of lineal models of acculturation frequently used by students of Indian acculturation. Kupferer questions the assumed homogeneity of "white" culture, noting that the existence of social-class differences among whites provides alternative ends for acculturation. One is never acculturated into the general white culture, whatever that is, but rather into specific subcultural patterns. In other words, some highly acculturated Indians may not conform to the norms of the white middle class because they have been acculturated into the subculture of the white lower-lower class. The extent of acculturation, that is, the degree to which the Indian person's behavior differs from traditional ways, may be greater in the latter case than for persons acculturated to middle-class behavior, yet the anthropologist might classify the acculturated lower-lower class Indians as *less* acculturated than more middle-class Indians, simply because their new behavior patterns happened to deviate from the middle-class "white" standard.

Kupferer collected data on health, medical practices, and education among the Cherokee in North Carolina. Her findings reveal that the Cherokee families do not fall into the clusters expected on the basis of the lineal model of acculturation. The specific lineal model tested is Thomas' tentative identification of four acculturative types of North Carolina Cherokee, namely "conservative," "generalized," "rural-white," and "middle-class" Indians. But the differences observed by Kupferer do not correspond to these types; in fact, sometimes only two or three types appear, rather than the four anticipated, and the characteristics of the types that do appear are not those predicted by the acculturative model. At least two distinct processes of change have produced the types of Cherokee observed, with acculturation accounting for change on the conservative-nonconservative dimension and behavioral differentials among the nonconservatives accounted for by socioeconomic factors.

In the final piece, McFee proposes that the continuum model with assumed "replacement" may not fit the processes of individual acculturation. In fact, individuals may learn new ways without abandoning the old. Comparisons of Blackfoot males' scores on "percentage of Indian-orientation" and "percentage of white-orientation" revealed a number of cases who were "well versed in both cultures." Such persons might be coded as manifesting 90 percent white orientation and 60 percent Indian orientation, hence, McFee's title, "The 150% Man." Frequently they occupy important roles as mediators between white and Indian societies; they live with Indians and maintain Indian identity, yet are well educated and capable of competing successfully in the white community. McFee suggests that the retention of Indian ways, as opposed to their replacement, depends upon the extent to which they are seen as having continuing utility for the individual. In the perspective of this article, the traditional problems of the "marginal man" can be seen as advantages rather than liabilities. Rather than being "lost between two cultures," those persons with bicultural capabilities can be seen as having unique combinations of skills which may serve the advantage of both Indian and white society.

NOTES

1 Robert Redfield, Ralph Linton, and Melville J. Herskovits, "Memorandum for the Study of Acculturation," *American Anthropologist*, 38 (January-March 1936), 149.
2 Ralph Linton, ed., *Acculturation in Seven Indian Tribes* (New York: Appleton-Century-Crofts, 1940), p. 464.
3 Edward H. Spicer, "Acculturation," in David L. Sills, ed., *Inter-*

national Encyclopedia of the Social Sciences (New York: Macmillan and the Free Press, 1968), vol. 1, p. 21.

4 Spicer, *op. cit.*, pp. 21-27; Edward H. Spicer, "Types of Contact
and Processes of Change," in Edward H. Spicer, ed., *Perspectives
in American Indian Culture Change* (Chicago: University of
Chicago Press, 1961), pp. 517-544; George D. Spindler, *Sociocul-
tural and Psychological Processes in Menomini Acculturation*,
University of California Publications in Culture and Society, vol.
5 (Berkeley: University of California Press, 1955); Ralph Beals,
"Acculturation," in A. L. Kroeber, ed., *Anthropology Today*
(Chicago: University of Chicago Press, 1953), pp. 621-641; Sol
Tax, ed., *Acculturation in the Americas* (Chicago: University of
Chicago Press, 1952); Ralph Linton, ed., *Acculturation in Seven
American Indian Tribes*.

5 Ralph L. Beals, "Urbanism, Urbanization and Acculturation,"
American Anthropologist, 53 (January-March 1951), 1-10.

6 Spicer, "Acculturation," p. 23.

7 *Ibid.*

8 *Ibid.*

9 A. Irving Hallowell, "The Impact of the American Indian on
American Culture," *American Anthropologist*, 59 (April 1957),
201–217; and A. Irving Hallowell, "The Backwash of the Frontier: The Impact of the Indian on American Culture," in Walker
D. Wyman and Clifton B. Kroeber, eds., *The Frontier in Perspective* (Madison: University of Wisconsin Press, 1957), pp. 229-258.

10 *Ibid.*, p. 204.

11 Hallowell, "The Backwash of the Frontier."

12 Leslie A. Fiedler, *The Return of the Vanishing American* (New
York: Stein & Day, 1968).

13 Roy Harvey Pearce, *The Savages of America* (Baltimore: The
Johns Hopkins Press, 1953); Edmund Wilson, *Apologies to the
Iroquois* (New York: Farrar, Strauss & Giroux, 1960).

14 Hallowell, "The Impact of the American Indian on American
Culture," p. 211.

15 Redfield et al., *op. cit.*

16 Spicer, "Acculturation," p. 21.

17 Louise Spindler and George Spindler, "Male and Female Adaptations in Culture Change," *American Anthropologist*, 60 (April
1958), 217-233.

A. IRVING HALLOWELL: AMERICAN INDIANS, WHITE AND BLACK: THE PHENOMENON OF TRANSCULTURALIZATION

My first acquaintance with Indians "at home" was in the twenties when, as a graduate student under the tutelage of Frank G. Speck, I began visiting the St. Francis Abenaki at Odanak, Quebec, Canada. In this little Indian community an Algonkian language could still be heard, but the dominant speech was French-Canadian, and many persons could also speak English. There were a few old-timers left who occasionally hunted and trapped, although there was little ostensible evidence of an aboriginal mode of life. The Abenaki had been Christianized for generations, the majority of them being devout Roman Catholics. Across the railroad track was a typical French-Canadian village. In short, the St. Francis Abenaki were a highly acculturated group of Indians.[1] I did not go there to study acculturation, however, for this was a decade before studies of acculturation had been "legitimatized" in American anthropological research. My purpose was to secure information about the vanished culture of their aboriginal past. Being very green in cultural anthropology, and knowing even less about Indian-white relations in American history, I was surprised to learn about their famous white chief, Joseph-Louis Gill, who had served in this capacity during fifty years of the eighteenth century. I had never given any thought to the circumstances under which a white man could become an Indian chief. Indeed, nothing had led me even to conjecture that the impact of European culture on Indian culture would produce white Indian chiefs.

Joseph-Louis Gill was white only in a biological sense. In the early eighteenth century the Abenaki had captured two English children, a boy and a girl, in one of their raids across the border. These children had been adopted into Indian families and raised in Indian fashion and also as Catholics like their adoptive parents. Later, these captives married each other and remained with the Abenaki for the rest of their lives. Joseph-Louis, born in 1719, was the eldest son of his "captivated" father and mother who raised a family of seven children. His first wife was an Indian who was killed by Rogers' Rangers; his second wife was French. He became chief in 1747. (See Maurault 1866 and Huden 1956).

Here, then, in the history of the Abenaki we have epitomized all of the complex relations of whites and Indians that arose in the frontier areas: the intrusion of Europeans, trade, warfare, white captives, Christianization of the Indians, interracial marriages. Although changes were initiated in the mode of life of this Indian group, there were resistant tendencies toward

Source: Reprinted by permission from *Current Anthropology* 4 (December 1963), 519-531.

linguistic and cultural conservatism. Fitting into the old pattern was the "Indianization," the cultural assimilation, of captured individuals.

Problems of historical research derived from the consequences of such complex events on American frontiers have long engaged the attention of historians, linguists, anthropologists, and others. Many American writers, too, have been fascinated by this historical material. Cooper's romances of the frontier, the historical novel and the dime novel, the western, have been immensely popular since the beginning of the nineteenth century. Interestingly enough, it has been mainly the American novelist, rather than the scholar, whose interest has been caught by the phenomenon of "Indianization." Possibly it was due to the immense popularity of actual accounts of captivities in the eighteenth century that early writers took up the theme.

"Indianize," in the sense of "to adopt the ways of Indians," is an Americanism dating back to the late seventeenth century. Cotton Mather asked: "How much do our people Indianize?" While the word has sometimes been used in a collective sense, in its later usage it seems to have been employed primarily with reference to individuals who adopted the ways of Indians (Mathews 1951). In his article entitled "White Indians," in which eight cases of captured children who became Indianized are analyzed in detail, Ackerknecht (1944) uses the term only for individuals. I am using Indianization in this old American sense.

Probably the earliest introduction of the Indianization theme in American literature occurs in the poem published in 1790, *Ouâbi,* or *The virtues of nature,* by Mrs. Sarah Wentworth Morton writing under the pen name Philena. Celario, a white man, falls in love with Azakia, an Illinois girl who is already married. He becomes identified with her people, leads a war party and rescues her husband, Ouâbi. He finally is able to marry Azakia when Ouâbi recognizes their love and his debt to Celario for saving his life. Mrs. Morton most have felt the novelty of her theme because she says in the Introduction:

> I am aware it may be considered improbable, that an amiable and polished European should attach himself to the persons and manners of an uncivilized people; but there is now a living instance of a like propensity. A gentleman of fortune, born in America, and educated in all the refinements and luxuries of Great Britain, has lately attached himself to a female savage, in whom he finds every charm I have given my Azakia, and in consequence of his inclination, has relinquished his own country and connections, incorporated himself into the society, and adopted the manners of the virtuous, though uncultivated Indian.

(For further information see Bissell 1925:207 ff.).

In two early American novels white girls marry Indians. In *Hobomok: a tale of early times* (1824), by Lydia Maria Child, the young chief, for whom the novel is named, marries Mary Conant after his fiancé is thought to be dead. They have a child. The lover returns, and Hobomok, a noble savage, magnanimously disappears in the forest leaving Mary a newly killed deer. In *Hope Leslie* (1827), by Catherine M. Sedgwick, Faith Leslie is abducted by the Indians, marries a brave, and chooses to remain with him. N. M. Hentz attempted to draw the character of a white girl brought up among the Indians in *Tadeukund, the last king of the Lenape* (1825).[2]

It was Cooper, however, who was the first American writer to dramatize the Indianization theme in any psychological depth, to come to grips with the actual consequences of intimate identification of whites with Indians. In *The wept of Wish-ton-Wish* (1829), Ruth Heathcote was captured as a child of seven or eight and lived a decade with the Indians as Narramattah (Driven Snow), before she returned to her Puritan family with her Indian husband to face tragedy. Confronting her white relatives after so many years, Cooper writes (p. 348):

> In air, expression, and attitude, (she) resembled one who had a fancied existence in the delusion of some exciting dream. Her ear remembered sounds which had so often been repeated in her infancy, and her memory recalled indistinct recollections of most of the objects and usages that were so suddenly replaced before her eyes, but the former now conveyed their meaning to a mind that had gained its strength under a very different system of theology, and the latter came too late to supplant usages that were rooted in her affections by the aid of all those wild and seductive habits that are known to become nearly unconquerable in those who have long been subject to their influence.

Leatherstocking, of course, was a semi-Indianized white man. Carl Van Doren (1917) has declared him "the most memorable character American fiction has given to the World." His early life was spent among the Delaware, and long before they called him "Deerslayer" he had sucessively borne three other Indian nicknames. He acquired "knowledge of most of our Indian dialects," and absorbed Indian values. When contemplating torture by the Hurons, he says he will strive "not to disgrace the people among whom I got my training." (Quotations from *The Deerslayer).*

In nineteenth century fiction we also find the renegade theme—the white man who, becoming Indianized and finding "savagism" good, symbolized the rejection of progress, civilization, and Christianity, and was easily cast as a villain. *Shoshone Valley* (1830), by Timothy Flint; *The renegade* (1848), by Emerson Bennett; *Old Hicks the guide* (1848), by Charles Webber, are all early novels of this type. Among the later dime novels, for example, *The jaguar queen, or the outlaws of the Sierra Madre* (1872) by Frederick Whittaker, characters like the latter's Count Montriche, who became an Apache chief and a renegade, often appeared. (See Pearce 1953:244-25 and Smith 1950:114-15).

Despite the radical changes in intellectual climate from the eighteenth century, when the colonists were confronted with the disturbing realities of capture and many accounts of captivity experiences were published, up until the present day—a period of two hundred years—Indian captivity, the renegade, and Indianization have never lost their fascination for the American public. These themes have as much vitality in popular fiction as they ever had. In the early years of this century *The Squaw Man* (Royle 1905) was a very popular sentimental play. In it an Englishman marries an Indian girl who has saved his life. When she discovers that he has inherited an earldom she leaves him and their children and commits suicide. First staged in 1905, this play is historically noteworthy since it later became the first full-length motion picture, directed by Cecil B. DeMille (Blum 1953).

Currently, more than an occasional story is woven about the white man, woman, or child who, whether "captivated" or not, has been Indianized to some degree and is sometimes a renegade. Without any systematic search, I have picked up over a dozen of these in paperbacks that have appeared within the past decade or so. The leading character in *Arrow in the hill* (Jefferson Cooper 1955) was raised from childhood by the Mohawk; the villain is a renegade Englishman disguised as a Huron who leads war parties and spies for the French. *Thunder on the river* (Laird 1950) deals with divided loyalties in an adopted captive who marries an Indian girl. In *Green centuries* (Jordon 1953) a white captive boy becomes completely identified with the Cherokee. Conrad Richter's *The light in the forest* (1954), later transferred to the screen, is concerned with a captive boy who is formally adopted by the Delaware but develops a conflict in values and leaves them. An English lord appears as a "white Indian" in *King's rebel* (Horan 1955). *The Kentuckians* (Giles 1955) contains a villain who is a white man who hates the settlers and identifies himself with the Indians. The hero of *Roanoke renegade* (Tracy 1955) finally chooses to make his life among the Indians. In *White Warrior* (Patten 1956), a story told in the first person, the narrator is captured by the Arapaho at the age of nine when his mother and father are killed. He is formally adopted by an Indian family in place of a lost son. The manner in which his foster parents train him to be an Arapaho, the affection with which they treat him, the way he gradually identifies himself more and more fully with the Indians is convincingly portrayed. *The Searchers* (Le May 1956), made into a moving picture, is concerned with a six-year search for Debbie, a white child captured by the Comanche at the age of ten. When the hero finds her it is a nightmare for him. "Behind the surface of this long-loved face was a Comanche squaw." Her Comanche speech was fluent, but her English almost forgotten. She did not wish to leave "her people." The author says it was as if they had taken out her brains and put in an Indian brain instead. "You—you are Long Knives," she said, "We hate you—fight you— always, till we die." Another Indianized white girl is one of the main characters in *Pemmican* (Fisher 1957).[3] *The double man* (Pryor 1957) and *Cherokee* (Tracy 1957) both portray divided loyalties. Tsani, the hero of the former, becomes war chief of the Cherokee at eighteen. But he is not an Indian; his parents were English, ambushed and killed when he was an infant. *Comanche captives* (1960) by Will Cook, is a highly realistic account of the pressure brought upon the army to redeem captured whites. The plot turns on the lack of understanding by relatives and others of the psychological depth of the emotional ties Indianization may bring about and the consequences of a blind demand for captives' redemption. One boy had become completely identified with the Comanche and fought against his rescuers, saying over and over again, "I am a Comanche!" When his white mother "cooked a meal for the boy, a homecoming meal that had been long planned and was the best she had, . . . he picked up the laden tin plate and threw it in her face." His father "did not know whether to hit the boy or forgive him; he touched him and the boy seized his arm and bit it deeply. . . ."[4]

Although Indianization has been a distinctive feature of American historical experience and the Indianization theme still strongly appeals to readers of light fiction, why is it, then, that (like so many other aspects of the impact of the Indian upon us) it has remained a neglected topic of scholarly research? Dr. Wilcomb Washburn has pondered the same question and thinks it has been too simply passed over. In a paper contributed to the American Indian Ethnohistoric Conference in 1956 and published in 1957 (4:51-52), he observes:

> Most of us know that an extraordinary number of whites preferred Indian society, while almost no Indians preferred white society. Why did the Spanish report in 1612 that forty or fifty of the Virginia settlers had married Indian women, that English women were intermingling with the natives, and that a zealous minister had been wounded for reprehending it? Why were there, at this time in Virginia, such severe penalties for running away to join the Indians? Why, indeed, did so many whites *want* to run away to join the Indians? Some have dismissed the evidence as showing merely that white civilization is so fragile and sophisticated that men tend to revert to the primitive when given the opportunity.

The problem is further complicated if American Negroes as well as whites are taken into account. Negro slaves in the South ran away and took refuge with the Seminole, Cherokee, Creek, Choctaw and Chickasaw, the so-called "Five Civilized Tribes" (Hodge 1907, 1910. *Handbook of American Indians* 2:600). While in the colonial period of our history some Indians shared the status of slaves with Negroes (Crane 1956:113-14),[5] basically the relations of the Indians with whites was structured in a totally different way from white-Negro relations. Despite the vicissitudes of contact, the indigenous Indians managed to maintain a high degree of cultural autonomy in organized communities. This was particularly true in the case of the Five Civilized Tribes in the South. On the other hand, whatever their retention of Africanisms may have been, groups of Negroes never constituted autonomous socio-cultural units in the United States. Forcibly detached from various tribal groups in their homeland and transported to the New World, it was solely in their individual roles as slaves that they became an integral part of socio-economic systems in the United States. Primarily they were slaves of the whites but in some cases they subsequently became slaves of the Indians when several Southern Indian nations acquired the institution of slavery from their white neighbors. Under these circumstances Negroes were assimilated to the same role in an Indian culture that they had played in white society. However, there appears to have been a notable difference, for Negro slaves continued to run away from their white masters and offer themselves as slaves to the Indians. Negro freedmen, too, often chose to cast their lot with the Indians. Furthermore, the Indians intermarried with both slaves and freedmen. Thus like some whites there were Negroes who became completely Indianized.[6]

Outside the South, the Indianization of Negroes occasionally occurred but it did not involve slavery. To mention a few examples: in the West the famous Negro, Jim Beckwourth, was a Crow Chief. An active participant in the Sioux massacre of 1862 was an Indianized Negro named Godfrey.[7] When Henry R. Schoolcraft made his journey through the Great Lakes country, to the source of the Mississippi River, he discovered a Negro living in an Ojibwa village of sixty people near the mouth of the St. Louis River. This Negro, a freedman, had been in the service of the Hudson's Bay Company for many years and had married an Ojibwa woman by whom he had had four children (Schoolcraft 1953:139). Swanton early in this century noted the fact that the richest man among the Skidegate Haida on the Northwest Coast was a Negro (See "Negro and Indian," Hodge, 1907, 1910. *Handbook of American Indians* 2:53) Dr. Ruben Reina tells me that today there is a Caribbean Negro from Belize (Honduras) who married an Indian woman from San Jose in Peten and has been living in her village for the past quarter of a century. She is a midwife and he is recognized as having an expert knowledge of the forest and "good power." They have raised a family of six children.

So far as I am aware, the experience of Negroes in Indian cultures has been almost completely neglected in fiction. The only examples I know of are Tarquinious, a minor character in *Alabama Empire* (1957) by Wellbourn Kelley, and Spence in Dale Van Every's *The Voyagers* (1957).[8] The period of the former novel is the late eighteenth century and the famous Creek chief Alexander McGillivray, who was himself mixed Indian and white, is a major figure in it. Tarquinious speaks Creek fluently. Perhaps racial attitudes in the United States have made the Indianization of Negroes a less romantic theme for the general reader. The same racial attitudes have made it a sensitive subject from the point of the Indians who in many parts of the country have struggled to achieve the social status of whites.

A further question now arises. The term Indianization has a provincial ring. Is it a phenomenon unique to American history, or is it only a particular manifestation of a far wider phenomenon? I believe the latter to be the case.

First of all, is it simply one aspect of acculturation? What American anthropologists have called *acculturation*, British anthropologists, *culture contact*, and the Cuban scholar Ortiz, *transculturation* (1947:98ff. and Introduction), refer primarily to the effects of contact upon the subsequent cultural attributes of organized *groups*. While individuals belonging to these groups are, of course, involved and play a variety of mediating roles in the process, the characteristic focus in acculturation studies is upon the changes induced in the mode of life of either, or both, groups. From the beginning, acculturation has been recognized as one aspect of the study of cultural dynamics. The pioneer memorandum of Redfield, Linton and Herskovits in 1936 (38:149-52) and the Social Science Research Council, Summer Seminar on Acculturation, which reviewed this field of study in 1953 (56:973-1002) delineated the fundamental problem in much the same terms. The Summer Seminar defined acculturation as "culture change that is initiated by the conjunction of two or more autonomous cultural systems" (56:974).

While sometimes occurring in the same historical context as acculturation, Indianization can be categorically distinguished from it and requires
conceptual and terminological differentiation. It is a phenomenon that involves the fate of *persons* rather than changes in socio-cultural systems. The
fact that the identification of these persons with the group to which they
formerly belonged has been broken, or modified, distinguishes them as a
class from persons undergoing readjustment who remain functioning members of an organized group undergoing acculturation. Since I have not
found a generic term already in use that characterizes this phenomenon, I
have had to coin one. *Transculturalization* seems appropriate. It is the process
whereby *individuals* under a variety of circumstances are temporarily or
permanently detached from one group, enter the web of social relations
that constitute another society, and come under the influence of its customs, ideas, and values to a greater or lesser degree. A correlative term,
transculturite, can then be used to designate those individuals who have
undergone transculturalization.

In transculturalization, at one polar extreme are individuals who become
permanently identified with the second culture. In such cases there is more
than a cultural readaptation—typically, there is a psychological transformation. At the other extreme, readjustment may be relatively superficial and
have little psychological depth. Manners and speech may be affected, but
not basic attitudes and values. In between, we have cases where historical
circumstances combined with unusual personality characteristics have motivated some individuals to play a dual role effectively. For example, on the
American frontier we have the unusual double identification of Sir William
Johnson. His most recent biographer, James T. Flexner (1959:38), refers
to:

> ... Johnson's "singular disposition" which included a quality
> much rarer than the appreciation and practice of Indian skills—
> throughout American history thousands of white men joyfully ex-
> changed breeches for breechcloth. His unique gift was his ability
> to feel simultaneous loyalty to both Indian and white institu-
> tions. . . .[9]

The degree of transculturalization depends, of course, on a number of
different variables: the age at which the process begins; the previous attitude toward the people of the second culture; length of residence; motivational factors; the nature of the roles played, and so on. Indianization is
thus a specific example of the wider human phenomenon of transculturalization. The same process has occurred in other parts of the world.

In the Pacific, for instance, some of the first missionaries sent out by
the London Missionary Society in the late eighteenth century became transculturites (Wright and Fry 1936: chapter 1). They were among the earliest
"squaw men" of the South Seas. There were also other white men who
married native women but became more than squaw men in the narrow
sense. Churchill of the "Bounty" became a Tahitian chief; John Young and
Isaac Davis, British seamen captured in Hawaii, married into the native
aristocracy and achieved chiefly rank (Furnas 1947:121, 215). William Mariner, a boy under sixteen when his life was spared in Tonga in 1806,

became Chief Toki Ukamea and a landowner. His sojourn as a transculturite was temporary, however. He did not marry a native girl, but after four years returned to England where he married and raised a family of eleven children. These few selected cases illustrate the varying degrees of transculturalization which took place in the Pacific and the differing conditions under which it occurred. To appreciate the importance of the transculturites in the Pacific Islands in the late eighteenth and the nineteenth centuries we must realize that even the many recorded cases are only an insignificant sample; their numbers reached the proportions of a migration. Ernest S. Dodge says, "No one knows how many runaway sailors settled in the various Polynesian islands and became absorbed in the native population, but there were literally thousands" (1963:106).

While the expansion of European peoples since the fifteenth century has tremendously accelerated contacts between all varieties of the culture of Europe and all other cultures of the modern world, neither acculturation nor transculturalization has been limited to this period. The historical setting for acculturation is provided whenever peoples of different socio-cultural systems come into contact, and transculturalization is possible whenever conditions arise which permit an individual to become detached from one cultural group and temporarily or permanently to become affiliated with another. In principle this also applies at the sub-cultural level, for example, between nations or between religious or caste groups. At this level we have many instances of transculturalization. I will only give one of them here.

A distinctive feature of the Ottoman state, perfected by Murad I (1359-89) and continued by successive Sultans for three centuries, was the systematic transculturalization of Christian children drawn from dependent provinces. The aim of this high policy, based upon a form of human tribute, was to insure the active cooperation of the vast Christian population over which the Turks were politically dominant. Thousands of boys were taken regularly from their native villages and trained for the Sultan's service. Every three or four years agents were sent to subject villages where lists of all youths of adolescent age were obtained from the priests. These boys were personally examined, and the handsomest and strongest selected. They were removed from their villages, and indoctrinated with Moslem values by being rigorously trained in special schools or in Turkish families of the highest status, even in the Sultan's seraglio itself. "Their early duties as pages were connected with all branches of the palace service, four favored ones being designated to keep watch with dagger and torches in the Sultan's chamber." Particularly interesting is the fact that for all these transculturites "possibilities of advancement, based on merit, were almost unlimited. Here was a democratic practice of promotion where it would be least expected . . . a simple page might become grand vizier through sheer ability. . . ." Indeed, transculturalization was so effective that many of the former Christian boys became fanatical members of the Turkish elite corps, the *Yeni Cheri* (New Troops) or Janissaries as they became known in the West. (Rouillard 1941:13-14, 173, 210, 225).[10]

Although the conditions under which transculturalization has occurred have not yet been studied systematically on a wide comparative scale, the American material on Indianization provides clues to the kind of analysis that is needed and possibly to the kind of generalizations that may emerge. In America, two specific conditions initiating the detachment of an individual from his primary cultural affiliation can be distinguished: involuntary detachments and voluntary ones.

We know, of course, that involuntary detachment—capture—did not necessarily lead to transculturalization. But in the case of children it seems to have been the major condition that led to the most complete transculturalization, even without any systematic indoctrination such as that adopted by the Ottoman Turks. What aroused the astonishment of the early American colonists was the fact that captives often refused to be redeemed. One of the earliest and best known of such cases was Eunice Williams, the daughter of a Deerfield pastor, who was "captivated" in 1704 when she was seven. In an Indian raid her mother was killed and her father and brother shared the fate of Eunice. The latter were redeemed a year later, but Eunice, formally adopted by a Caughnawaga woman, refused to leave her foster parents. She had forgotten how to speak English by the time she was seventeen; she married an Indian and lived to be ninety years old. Although we shall never know how many captive children remained with the Indians, Barbeau (1950:529) refers to the fact that:

> In his investigations among the Wyandots of Oklahoma, in 1911, 1912, [he] heard that the familiar names among them of Dawson, Walker, Brown, McKee, Boone, Johnson, Young, Armstrong, Clarke, etc., had originated among them through captive children of Virginia. After they had grown up, they were given the choice of returning to their white parents or of staying with their adopted kinsmen. And they preferred to stay.

On the other hand, it would be hard to imagine the captured Mrs. Mary Rowlandson becoming Indianized under any circumstances. She was too firmly entrenched in Puritan beliefs. Her seventeenth-century editor concluded, "None can imagine what it is to be captivated, and enslaved to such atheistical, proud, wild, cruel, barbarous, brutish (in a word) diabolical creatures as these, the worst of the heathen" (quoted by Pearce 1952:205).

Even more astonishing to many "civilized" Americans and Europeans were the cases where individuals Indianized by choice. It was particularly shocking to the Puritans, convinced as they were that the Indians were indeed Satan's children, that the religion of the aborigines was literally Devil worship, and that "wherever the Indian opposed the Puritan there Satan opposed God" (Pearce 1952:204).[11] To the Puritan mind it was only right in the cosmic scheme of things that the Indian should become civilized and Christianized or perish. No wonder, then, that to Indianize voluntarily was tantamount to a crime. Yet there were such cases among the Puritans. In 1677, two years following the capture of Mary Rowlandson, William Hubbard denounced a man who, during King Philip's War, "renounced his religion, nation, and natural parents, all at once fighting against them." This man had gone off with an Indian woman. Captured later he was subjected to examination and condemned to die. (Pearce 1952:209).

In the less constricted cultural outlook of the eighteenth century cases of voluntary Indianization apparently became more common, although they were still considered a puzzling phenomenon.[12] Particularly perplexing was the fact that transculturalization seemed to operate in only one direction. We find the repeated comment that whites who had been brought up among the Indians, or lived with them, chose to remain, whereas the reverse was true in the case of Indians who had sampled a "civilized" existence. Crevecoeur (1957:208-9) in his famous *Letters from an American farmer* wrote:

> By what power does it come to pass, that children who have been adopted when young among these people, can never be prevailed on to readopt European manners? Many an anxious parent I have seen after the last war, who at the return of peace, went to the Indian villages where they knew their children had been carried in captivity; when to their inexpressible sorrow, they found them so perfectly Indianised, that many knew them no longer, and those whose more advanced ages permitted them to recollect their fathers and mothers, absolutely refused to follow them, and ran to their adopted parents for protection against the effusions of love their unhappy real parents lavished on them! Incredible as this may appear, I have heard it asserted in a thousand instances, among persons of credit. . . . It cannot be, therefore, so bad as we generally conceive it to be; there must be in (the Indians') social bond something singularly captivating, and far superior to anything to be boasted of among us; for thousands of Europeans are Indians, and we have no examples of even one of those Aborigines having from choice become Europeans![13]

To appreciate fully the phenomenon of Indianization in America it needs to be set within the historical context of an expanding frontier and basic contemporary American values and attitudes, on the one hand, and of the values and characteristic institutions of the Indians with whom social interaction was taking place, on the other. For one thing, the implicit, if not always explicit, moral evaluation of Indianization on the part of the whites directly reflected the increasing consciousness of the eighteenth-century European of the meaning of "civilization" which arose along with the term itself (cf. Smith 1950:218 ff. and Cohen 1947:231). The values inherent in "white" culture were necessarily "higher" than those which prevailed in any aboriginal culture because they embodied the consequences of a progressive improvement in the life of mankind which "led up to" the contemporary "civilization" of the European peoples (Pearce 1953:155-59). In the New World this was all a contemporary reality. "Looking at the Indian in his relation to the whole of their society, Americans could see manifest the law of civilized progress" (Ibid.:155). More than this, the graded steps of progress did not have to be abstractly conceived; they were geographically visible. In his later years, Jefferson wrote in a letter to a friend (quoted in Smith 1950:219):

> Let a philosophic observer commence a journey from the savages of the Rocky Mountains, eastwardly towards our seacoast.

These he would observe in the earliest stage of association living under no law but that of nature, subsisting and covering themselves with the flesh and skin of wild beasts. He would next find those on our frontiers in the pastoral state, raising domestic animals to supply the defects of hunting. Then succeed our own semi-barbarous citizens, the pioneers of the advance of civilization, and so in his progress he would meet the gradual shades of improving man until he would reach his, as yet, most improved state in our seaport towns. This, in fact, is equivalent to a survey, in time, of the progress of man from the infancy of creation to the present day.

"The theory of the progressive stages of history," says Pearce, "and of the relationship of character to circumstance explained the savage's essential inferiority, the final inferiority of even his savage virtues" (1953:95). Thus, regardless of individual needs or motives, and despite the romantic treatment of the Indian in literature, for a white person to become Indianized was necessarily a retrograde step. If the frontier farmer was "a rebellious fugitive from society" (Smith 1950:218), the squaw man was doubly indictable. Wissler (1938:185-86) writing of early twentieth-century squaw men on western reservations, says:

> Almost without exception . . . if I called at the home of a white man with an Indian wife, my host sooner or later offered apologies. . . . The squaw man was aware of the contempt in which he was held by those of his kind married to white women. One only needed to sense the "emotional slant" of the term as used in speech to understand the social position of these white derelicts. . . .

The special opprobrium attached to the white renegade—those who not only became identified with Indians, but actively *opposed* "civilized" white men in trade, politics or war—is easily understood. Such individuals had plunged into the deepest pit of social degradation.

An evaluation somewhat similar to that accorded transculturites was also applied to frontier communities in the late nineteenth and early twentieth centuries by scholars who fully recognized the direct impact of Indian culture on these marginal segments of American civilization, and sought to fit the events into a unilinear sequence of cultural development. Frederick Jackson Turner conceptualized the frontier experience as "the meeting point between savagery and civilization . . . [It] strips off the garments of civilization and arrays [the frontiersman] in the hunting shirt and the moccasin" (1920:2-3). It is a cultural step downward which, although necessary for survival, must always be transcended.[14] A. G. Keller (1915: 276-77) in his *Societal evolution* took a similar position.

> [The frontier group, or colony,] is a reversion. But that means no more than that it is an adaptation to a set of conditions out of whose range old societies have passed. Reversion is as much adaptation as is progression. . . .[The frontier society sacrifices much] of the civilization which it had, in favor of forms of adaptation which. . . are successful as they resemble those of the na-

tives. Acculturation takes place, strange to say, from the *lower* toward the *higher* race; thus the colonists in New England. . . . "Indianized."[15]

Both Turner and Keller were writing at a time when anthropologists were beginning to question and reject unilinear theories of cultural evolution, but more than a decade before intensive studies of acculturation were undertaken. With the abandonment of the theory of regular progressive stages in the cultural history of all peoples, we are now free to examine processes of acculturation and transculturalization more objectively and without moral prejudice. We do not have to ask whether transculturalization is a "reversion" to a more "primitive" level, or an "escape" from "civilization." Like other non-literate peoples of the world, the aborigines of America lived in societies which were as regularly patterned in terms of their own value systems as the culture of the European intruders. Whether there was "in their social bond something singularly captivating, and far superior to anything boasted of among us" that lured and held so many whites, is a psychological question to which we cannot give a final answer.[16] There are other and related questions, however, which a reexamination of cases of transculturalized whites and Negroes suggest. They are not primarily what their motives were, nor a moral evaluation of their choices, but rather: What cultural factors were present in Indian societies that made it possible for alien individuals—so often enemies—to become functioning members of them? Why were the Indians motivated to accept them? What social mechanisms and values in Indian societies mediated the acceptance and assimilation of these strangers? What roles did whites and Negroes play in Indian cultures? Conversely, what values and attitudes prevailed in American culture that limited the roles which it was possible for Indians to play among us?

From the very beginning white intruders in North America repeatedly commented upon the hospitality of the Indians. Many years ago, James Mooney pointed out, "The narratives of many pioneer explorers and settlers, from DeSoto and Coronado, Amidas and Barlow, John Smith and the Pilgrims, down to the most recent period, are full of instances of wholesale hospitality toward white strangers, sometimes at considerable cost to the hosts" (Hodge, 1907, 1910 *Handbook* 1:571). In the seventeenth century some of the Jesuits were very much surprised by the hospitality with which they were received. Father Le Jeune, for example, wrote (Thwaites 8:94-95):

> As soon as I was perceived in the village someone cried out . . . and at once everyone came out to salute and welcome me. . . . I lodged with a man who was one of the richest of the Hurons. You can lodge where you please; for this Nation above all others is exceedingly hospitable towards all sort of persons, even toward strangers; and you may remain as long as you please, being always well treated according to the fashion of the country.

Among the Indians, moreover, there was the well-known custom, antedating white contact, of adopting persons captured in war. There were special rites involved. Indians formally adopted in this manner could not return to their own tribal group. This custom, then, must have led to the transculturalization of Indians by Indians. The same practice was carried on in the period of white contact, but there was a modification. The Indians found they could profit materially in many cases. Whether adopted or not, white captives could return to their own society if they were ransomed. (*Handbook* 1: "Captives"; 2: "Slavery.")

In some tribes adoption was specifically motivated by the desire to replace a dead child or other relative. This involved the building up of all the affective ties of Indian family life, the social integration of the individual into the kinship system, and his orientation to all the values and social sanctions of the group. Functionally, it was equivalent to the normal processes of socialization in all societies, on which the psychological structuralization and personal adjustment of the human individual depends. No wonder, then, that many white children who had been subjected to this process found it impossible to leave the Indians. The result is predictable. Not that in every case the old white personality quickly faded into the new Indian one. Writers like Conrad Richter in *The light in the forest* and Lewis B. Patten in *White warrior* (rather than social psychologists or anthropologists) have attempted to depict for us the conflicts that may also arise.

In contrast to the institutionalized pattern of adoption in Indian cultures, consider the picture presented in the society of the white European settlers. There was no comparable institution of adoption. The few Indians who became associated with the whites must have found themselves confronted with a social situation in which intimate personal contacts were narrowly restricted. They might be offered a formal education, but not acceptance as fully fledged members of a family group. The social isolation of the Indian boy in Cooper's *The wept of Wish-ton-Wish,* living among whites in a household rigidly molded by Puritan values, is a fictional example which is close to the reality. It was not that the Indian could not be raised "up" to the level of civilization but rather, the lack of an equivalent desire on the part of whites to welcome and assimilate the Indian, and the absence of any established cultural means that would mediate the transition from one culture to the other in a manner that was psychologically sound. Swanton quotes from a report written by some New England missionaries which documents this (1926:502):[17]

> An Indian youth has been taken from his friends and conducted to a new people, whose modes of thinking and living, whose pleasures and pursuits are totally dissimilar to those of his own nation. His new friends profess love to him, and a desire for his improvement in human and divine knowledge, and for his eternal salvation; but at the same time endeavour to make him sensible of his inferiority to themselves. To treat him as an equal would mortify their own pride, and degrade themselves in the view of their neighbors. He is put to school; but his fellow students look on him as being of an inferior species. He acquires some knowledge, and is taught some ornamental, and perhaps useful accomplishments; but the degrading memorials of his inferiority,

which are continually before his eyes, remind him of the manners and habits of his own country, where he was once free and equal to his associates. He sighs to return to his friends; but these he meets with the most bitter mortification. He is neither a white man nor an Indian; as he had no character with us, he has none with them.

There is a further point to be made. The Indian institution of adoption entailed the fullest kind of socialization of the white child. It prepared him for *all* the various roles which were open to him in Indian society. I have already mentioned several cases of whites and Negroes becoming Indian chiefs; in their review of cases of Indianization both Ackerknecht and Swanton cite a number of other instances. Old White Boy, who was captured in 1760 when he was about four years old, could never remember his name. "Not only he himself but all his sons . . . became famous Seneca chiefs. When his youngest son was elected chief, he feared that the jealousy of the Indians might be aroused by his continued success and therefore he wanted to leave; but they begged him to stay, so he did" (Ackerknecht 1944:17). Of the thirty cases of captivity, fifteen male and fifteen female, examined by Swanton (1926:501), three or four of the men became chiefs and a similar number of the women became chiefs' wives.[18] The fact that white or Negro men could become chiefs in Indian societies is one indication of the complete receptiveness of these cultures to transculturites. This basic receptiveness was mediated to a large degree by the nature of their social organization and kinship structures. It explains why it was that *adult* whites and Negroes could by choice, and with relative ease, become assimilated to an Indian manner of life. Squaw men, for example, did not all become transculturalized in equal degree; nevertheless marriage with an Indian woman, residence with her people, and the acquisition of an Indian tongue mediated the social roles of these individuals in such a manner that they inevitably were drawn into the web of interrelations of the society. Indeed, the use of kinship terms alone prescribed patterns of conduct as well as rights and obligations in daily social interaction that were inescapable. This is undoubtedly the reason for the often heard complaint of squaw men that "when you marry an Indian girl you marry a whole damn tribe!"

On the other hand, what roles were open to an Indian in white society? Even if educated, the presumption was that he would return to his people as a missionary. Samson Occam (1723-92), "the pious Mohegan," is a case in point. He became transculturalized, achieving great fame as a preacher in America and England. Clad in a black suit and knee breaches, an *Indian* clergyman "with the garb, mannerisms, and habits of thought of the Puritan divine," Occam was a novelty in England (C. T. Foreman 1943:87). Most of Occam's life, however, was spent in missionary work among Indians in this country. He *spoke* from many pulpits, but he received no call to *occupy* a pulpit in America. Despite his education, his personal talents, the money he had helped raise for Dartmouth College, and the evident success with which he had adopted the way of life of his Christian contemporaries, the missionary role was the only one open to him.[19]

In the case of the Negroes, certain other conditions were added to their transculturalization. Once the southern Indians had borrowed the institution of slavery from Europeans, they *wanted* Negro slaves. The system being less rigid than among whites, it is intelligible why some Negroes ran away to join the Indians. It might be thought that having an African background in the first place, they were seeking to escape the more rigorous demands of "civilization," but this is more ironic than illuminating. Under the circumstances, they were inexorably caught in a role from which there was no immediate escape; they simply chose to play it under better conditions. The Seminoles, for example, "held their vassals in a form of benevolent bondage, exacting only their fealty and a small amount of corn, stock or peltries" (G. Foreman 1932:315). Speck writes of the Creeks in general (1908:107):

> It is said among the descendants of these slaves today that the Indians were easy masters, and that the servitude to the Negro was more like a form of hired service, where they were supported and protected by the Indians to whom in return they tendered their aid in agriculture and household labor. [Adding from Colonel Benjamin Hawkin's observations in 1798-99] Where the Negroes were there was more industry and the farms were better.... During the Seminole War, Negro slaves and their mixed offspring played an important part in the ranks of the Indians. Even Osceola, the Seminole leader, is believed to have had Negro blood in his veins.

Furthermore, those who were transculturalized and remained with the southern Indians until after the Civil War were able to transcend their earlier formal status as slaves. Foster says (1935:65-66):

> Seminole Negroes continued to live among their Seminole relatives, friends and former masters. The Indians adopted their former slaves and also the Negro freedmen among them, making them citizens of their country. They were given equal rights to land and annuities. Those now living ['1929-30] who remember these times have informed the author that they scarcely knew the difference between being free and being in slavery. They maintain that the Seminole Negroes continued to live an "Indian life," and that many of the older ones were "Indian" in their religion as well as in their social and economic practices. Instances have been cited ... of three Seminole Negroes who were religious leaders among the Seminoles. The Seminoles and the Negroes continued to intermarry, as they had done in former years. The Negroes continued also to form a part of the Seminole Council. There were even Seminole Negroes connected with the "Crazy Snake Rebellion."

Whatever choices were involved in the course of their personal readjustment as transculturites, there is no reason to suppose that these Negroes weighed in any abstract fashion the values of "savagery" versus "civilization."

Turning to the South Pacific, even a superficial examination of a few cases of transculturalization illuminates the motivations of chiefs as well as the institutional basis of the process. The Tonga chief, Finau II, found Mariner and other white seamen of particular use in enhancing his political ambitions through the conquest of additional islands. Furnas (1947:215) says that in the forties of the last century,

> Wilkes found well-fed beachcombers, on several islands in the Gilberts, treated with respect and long married to young women of standing; they usually wanted to go home, but had little to complain of. In the early days many Fijian chiefs had such tame white men, regarding them as mannerless but useful; to have one was part of a chief's prestige.

CONCLUSION

From this brief survey of Indianization in America, it is obvious that not all socio-cultural systems are equally receptive to the assimilation of alien individuals, and that the degree of receptivity of a culture depends not primarily on individual good or ill-will, but on *social* values and attitudes, and on institutions to mediate the induction of alien individuals into it. In studies of diffusion and acculturation it has always been assumed that selective factors were at work which were a function of the organization or patterning of the culture. The same seems to be true of the reception of transculturites. In some societies, such as these Indian ones highly receptive to transculturites, it is difficult for an alien individual to remain peripheral except as a guest, or visitor, or trader. To live *in* them he must in a sense be "reborn" into them. On the other hand, aware of their "advanced" European heritage, the small communities of Europeans in America erected a defensive wall of heightened consciousness of superiority against the surrounding Indians. To condescend to "raise up" the Indians was the greatest magnanimity. In the case of the Puritans' religious communities, their fierce opposition to Indianization was only an extension of their antagonism to all of different belief—witness their persecution of the Quakers. Their somberness and rigidity of outlook was also the antithesis of that of the Indians who, for the most part, must have been repelled by it. An Indian transculturite in such circumstances, even if he had loyal friends among them, remained an alien. At a level of social organization transcending the tribal or family group, such as a political community where an alien can become a citizen with legal rights, his assimilation in the society may be extensive or limited, depending on the nature of these legal rights, on circumstances, and on the individual. The trader may be permitted a limited role; special groups may be permitted to live in restricted areas, but not be members of the community. If all such factors were known in particular cases, they might explain the varying degrees of assimilation it is possible for alien individuals to achieve in different cultures, and to rate cultures on a scale of receptivity.

The role of transculturites in the promotion of culture change in the group with which they become affiliated is another question that might be investigated. So far as America is concerned, it is clear that, in the nature of the case, abducted children who became transculturalized did not play such a role. Old White Boy, for instance, became converted to Christianity in the same acculturation process that led to the Christianization of his fellow Seneca. In the South Seas, on the other hand, although I have not examined these cases in detail, my impression is that some of the captured seamen did play a role in acculturation. Hypothetically, the role of trans-culturites as agents in the acculturation process may be a function of the degree to which they explicitly reject the culture of their natal group and become identified with the central values of their adopted culture. The Baptist missionary, Isaac McCoy, writing in the nineteenth century, thought the squaw men were obstacles to "organizing an Indian territory and of rendering the Indians secure in their posessions. [These white men] who identify themselves with the Indians as much as possible . . . [and] who have preferred savage to civilized society do not desire the improvement of the former" (1840:529). Psychological and cultural identification, however, does not exclude the influence of transculturites on culture change. Many years ago Speck (1908:109) was convinced that " . . . in mythology the culture of the Creeks and other southeastern tribes has been subjected to modification by the Negroes [who] being more amenable to white in-fluence than the Indians . . . have been the entering wedge in the past cen-tury for many new ideas and new interpretation of old ones."[20]

Swanton (1926:512) in his examination of thirty cases of white cap-tives concluded his essay by saying: "The number should be very much increased, [and] similar studies of white captives among other peoples of the world should be made, and the whole checked by reciprocal cases of captives from the various primitive races held by white."

This task still remains to be done. Our perspective might be further expanded by including a careful examination of the consequences of the policy adopted by the Ottoman Turks, or other comparable cases, and by collecting and analyzing cases of voluntary transculturalization of various kinds. The comparative investigation of transculturalization as a human phenomenon, the conditions under which such cases have occurred, the motivation of the individuals concerned and the relation of differential cultural values and patterns to their readjustment would greatly enrich our knowledge of crucial psychological and cultural factors underlying the func-tioning of group identification and alienation, as well as culture change.

NOTES

1 For information on the history and ethnography of this group see Leger (1929), Maurault (1866), and Fried (1955). Gordon M. Day, in a recent article on the relations of the St. Francis Abenaki to Dartmouth College (1959), writes:

"These were the Abenakis whom the Jesuits extolled for their native mild-ness, their exemplary piety, and whom Canadian historians lauded for their loyal-ty and military qualities in the service of New France. These were the model converts whose conversion consoled the Fathers for the destruction of the Huron Nation by the Iroquois and the debauching of the Algonquins of Three Rivers by the fur traders."
From this village, too,

"came the war parties which raided the New England frontier and warriors who ambushed Braddock; from it came Hannah Dustin's captors and the attackers of Fort Number Four, now Charlestown, New Hampshire. This is the village where John Stark was captive and which was burned by Rogers' Rangers. And oddly enough, this is the village which provided one of Eleazar Wheelock's strongest motives for locating his Indian school at Hanover. . . ."

The purpose of the school was to train Indians and missionaries to the Indians. After Wheelock lost his Six Nations pupils and the cooperation of Sir William Johnson, most of the Indian recruits over the next 80 years came from St. Francis, thus reinforcing the Protestant tradition in the Canadian village. "At the present time," says Day, "about 130 Indians live at Saint Francis, but the band numbers over 500 registered members. There is in addition a sizable number of persons of Saint Francis descent who have given up formal connections with the band and live in other parts of Quebec, in Ontario, and in the Northeastern States, often not known as Indians by their neighbors. In all this number there remain only about fifty persons who can speak the native language fluently. The native speakers are mostly over 65 years of age, and with few exceptions the children are not learning the language."

2 Long before these American novels appeared, Smollett in *Humphrey Clinker* (1771) had introduced an episode in which the Scot, Lismahago, fighting on the early American frontier, had been captured and adopted by an Indian sachem to replace his lost son. Lismahago marries the betrothed of the latter and has a son by her. He becomes a sachem and is "acknowledged first warrior of the Badger tribe (clan)." Then his wife dies, he exchanged for an Indian and returns to Britain after the war. Still earlier, in France, Voltaire had published *L'Ingénu* (1767), a witty little tale about an Indianized French boy who had been raised by a Huron foster mother after his parents had been killed in the New World. Returning to France as a young man he declares himself a Huron, but is identified by his uncle and aunt as their nephew. For the purposes of the story, which is a vehicle for satirizing French attitudes, customs and institutions, what are purportedly Indian attitudes are given The Simple Soul. But these are superficial and have no psychological depth. While this story is historically important so far as the Indianization theme is concerned, it does not come to grips with the actual consequences of early association with Indians on the part of white children. For the literary background of Voltaire's story see, Eugene E. Rovillain, "L'Ingénu de Voltaire: quelques influences." *Pub. Modern Language Association of America* (1929 44:537-45).

3 In his *Foreword* the author, Vardis Fisher, writes:
   If any reader thinks it unlikely that a white girl could have been on the scene as an Indian, I would refer him to John Henry Moberly, an HB (Hudson Bay) factor of a little later time, who says in his *Journal:*
   "Quite a number of women among the Indians who came to the trading posts in those days had no sign of a drop of Indian blood. Their hair was light, they had blue eyes and good figures and, except for sunburn, were as fair as any white woman. For this there was an explanation: when the Indians raided an immigrant train on the American side they killed all grown people and boys but preserved the female children, who grew up perfect Indians in their ways. Rarely could they be persuaded to leave their Indian friends."

4 I have omitted reference to short stories in which the Indianization theme can also be found. In this genre Dorothy M. Johnson's *Indian*

Country (1953) is an outstanding contemporary example. It contains three distinguished stories dealing with captivity and Indianization which first appeared in *Argosy* and *Colliers* prior to the date of publication in book form. "Flame on the Frontier," for example, is concerned with two sisters who are captured. One of them marries an Indian and refuses redemption. The other goes back and marries a white man by whom she has two children. One of her Indian suitors never forgets her and after an interval of ten years makes a long journey to see how she is. Her husband says, "What's that bloody Injun doing here? ... If I ever set eyes on that savage again, I'll kill him. You know that, don't you, you damn squaw."

5 In Charleston there were markets in which both types of slaves were sold. In 1708, when the total population of South Carolina was 9,580, the slave population was more than 44 percent of this figure; the Negro slaves numbered 2,900, the Indian slaves, 1,400. At this time there was a market for Indian slaves in New England. Crane says, "In the early eighteenth century the Boston News Letter printed frequent advertisements of runaway Carolina Indians."

6 Johnson (1929) calls attention to the fact that in 1832, when the first census of the Creek nation was taken, the commissioners were confronted with questions concerning the status and rights of individuals with Negro blood for which they sought authoritative decisions. They reported (1) cases in which an Indian has "living with him as his wife a Negro slave, the property either of himself or of another," and (2) the existence of "free black families that seem to be in every way identified with these people and the only difference is color." The decision in such cases was:

(1) An Indian, whether full or half blood, who has a female slave living with him as his wife, is the head of a family and entitled to a reservation; (2) free blacks who have been admitted members of the Creek nation, and are recognized as such by the tribe, if they have families are entitled to reservations of land under the second section of the Creek treaty.

Herskovits says (1930:279):

"Although the Indian element is not readily discernible in the analysis of traits within the genealogical classes, there is no reason to doubt the statement of 29% of the persons measured who claim to have partial Indian ancestry, partly because of known historical contacts between the Negroes and the Indians, and particularly because the statements as to the amounts of Negro-White ancestry check so satisfactorily with the results of anthropometric measurements."

7 See Bonner 1931; Heard 1863: Chapter 13. Godfrey's father was French Canadian and his mother was a Negro. At the time of the Sioux uprising he was 27 years old. He had been married 4 years to a Sioux woman, daughter of Wakpadoota. Godfrey's father-in-law was later executed but his own part in the massacre was never fully clarified. Although the commissioners found him guilty of murder, they recommended that the penalty be commuted to ten years imprisonment.

8 In a more recent historical novel, *Trask,* (Berry 1960), the scene of which is laid in Oregon Territory in the forties of the last century, Don Berry has introduced a character who is a descendant of a Negro. The latter, a blacksmith, was a castaway from a wrecked ship, who married a Killamook (Tillamook) woman. Kilchis (his son or grand-

son?) who was tyee of the Killamook at the time of the story is a major character. He "stood several inches over six feet" and his face was like "an ebony mask." Trask says to his Indian companion: "That man's a nigger! He's no more Indian than I am." The reply is: "He is a Killamook. What color doesn't matter. He was born a Killamook and lives and will die a Killamook."

9   Reconstructing Johnson's participation in an Indian dance in his younger days, Flexner writes (p. 54):

> "Round and round Johnson went, yelling as he drove an imaginary hatchet into an imaginary skull, and gradually his mind was washed clean of every European thing. No longer was he an ambassador on a ticklish mission from another world: he was one of his fellow dancers, one flesh, one heart, one brain. And when he too sank to the ground in exhaustion, his war-painted body was hardly distinguishable from the bodies that lay around him. But when he awoke the next morning, his mind awoke with him, and he returned to his scheming for English ends."

And speaking of George Croghan he says: "He became second only to Johnson as the most powerful white Indian on the continent." (p. 126)

10 In the seventeenth century changes were occurring which, according to the French observer Deshayes, were weakening the Ottoman Empire. Turkish children in larger numbers were being substituted for transculturalized Christian boys and the merit system was being corrupted by graft. In the opinion of this observer "native Turks can never have the singleness of interest and loyalty to the Sultan that the trained renegades had" (1624:247-48).

11 Dorson points out, "If the English accepted a personal Devil and his human consorts, they could not very well deny practice in the black art to the red heathen, especially ones so gifted in necromancy" (1950:5).

12 Crevecoeur, referring to the period of the Revolution when loyalty to the English or to the "Rebel" government came up, wrote (1925:23):

> "Many of those who found themselves stripped of their property took refuge among the Indians. Where else could they go? Many others, tired of that perpetual tumult in which the whole settlement was involved, voluntarily took the same course; and I am told that great numbers from the extended frontiers of the middle provinces have taken the same steps,—some reduced to despair, some fearing the incursions with which they were threatened. What a strange idea this joining with the savages seems to convey to the imagination; this uniting with a people which Nature has distinguished by so many national marks! Yet this is what the Europeans have often done through choice and inclination, whereas we never hear of any Indians becoming civilized Europeans. This uncommon emigration, however, has thrown among them a greater number of whites than ever has been known before."

13 The same point of contrast is made by Peter Kalm (Kerkkonen 1959:184) and by Colden (1922:203-4). Voluntary Indianization is referred to by Lawson (1860:302). In his chapter on "The American Captives" Henry Beston observes (1942:47),

> "The Indian path had its own gods; it was strong medicine. Those who had followed us, and were later returned to their own white inheritance, often heard the shaking of the Indian rattle and the voices of Indian ghosts. I remember the man from Wells who all his life sat on the floor like an Indian and maintained that they were 'better people than the whites.' "

14 Mood (1943) points out that the theory of social evolution was the "fundamental unifying concept" of Turner's early writings.

15 Keller, *op. cit.*, 276-77. This author's use of the term *acculturation* in 1915 is worth noting. *Indianized* is used correlatively for the general influence exerted.

16 When Crevecoeur referring to the Indians says:

"Without temples, without priest, without kings, and without laws, they are in many instances superior to us. And the proofs of what I advance are, that they live without care, sleep without inquietude, take life as it comes, bearing all its asperities with unparalleled patience, and die without any kind of apprehension for what they have done, or for what they expect to meet with hereafter,"

and then asks: "What system of philosophy can give us so many necessary qualifications for happiness?" (1957:210), he reflects the literary tradition of the Noble Savage, rather than any precise, ethnographic knowledge of Indian life. Fairchild (1928:103-4) has pointed out that later Crévecoeur reversed his earlier attitude towards the Indians expressed in the *Letters*. The evidence is to be found in *Voyage dans La Haute Pennsylvanie* . . . published in 1801, but never translated into English. In this book the author says he has been an eye-witness of such brutalities as devastating war parties, tortures, and scenes of drunkenness among the Indians.

17 In her short story "Back to the Blanket," Alice Marriott dramatizes the situation (1945:247, 250). Leah, a Kiowa child had been sent east to school at nine. Leah though it would be easy to go home, "go to the mission, work to uplift her people. Then she would marry some good young man, not an Indian, a missionary, and go away and do good all her life." But when she got home it was not so easy. "Here was her own sister calling her Indian." And when the local missionaries called and wanted her to go live with them she refused.

"What good would it do to live at the mission? There was no warmness for her to Mr. and Mrs. Gaines. There was respect, that was all. Here there was warmness towards the people around her and towards her, anyway. Yes, and there was the beginnings of respect."

18 Simon Girty, the famous "white savage" renegade of the Revolutionary period told Oliver Spencer, a white captive, that although he would never see home, if he turned out to be a good hunter and a brave warrior, he might someday be a chief (Boyd 1928:211-12).

19 There are, of course, a few individual exceptions. As early as 1504 a Brazilian Indian was taken to France by Captain de Gonneville and became completely transculturalized. He was converted to the Catholic faith, married the captain's daughter, founded a family which long flourished in France (Lee 1929:242). Since many Elizabethan voyagers had made it a practice to bring a few American Indians back to England, it was thought by some that the number should be increased, with the aim of making such individuals "into civilizing instruments among their own people." This idea came to a head in 1620 when

"a serious proposal was ventilated to extend the practice by importing into England a large number of Indian lads to be educated on English lines. It never reached fruitation, however, the chief argument against it being that the Indian who had lived in England awhile tended to assimilate the vices rather than the virtues of civilized life (Lee 1929:242; see also C. T. Foreman 1943:28)."

The most famous Indian to undergo transculturalization in the seventeenth century was the world-renowned Pocahontas. And her son, Thomas Rolfe, returning to America, became the progenitor of distinguished descendants. Yet all these cases were exceptional and incomparable in numbers with the whites and Negroes on the other side of the Atlantic who became Indianized.

20 Some Americans, debating "the Indian question" in the second half of
the nineteenth century, thought the problem could be solved by a very
strict segregation of the Indians on Reservations. In the opinion of one
writer, F. A. Walker, whose statements undoubtedly reflect more widely held views, the abiding presence of Indians in our midst was complicated by the evil influence of white transculturites who, backsliders
as they were from civilization and sunk to the lower level of Indian
culture (conceived as practically anarchical), were likely to corrupt the
latter rather than to improve it (1813:385).

"White men will still be found" he says, "so low in natural instincts, or so
alienated by misfortunes and wrongs, as to be willing to abandon civilization and
hide themselves in a condition of life where no artificial wants are known, and in
communities where public sentiment makes no demand upon any member for
aught in the way of achievement or self-advancement. Here such men, even now
to be found among the more remote and hostile tribes, will, unless the savage
customs of adoption are severely discountenanced by law, find their revenge
upon humanity, or escape the tyranny of social observance and requirement.
Half-breeds bearing the names of French, English, and American employees of
fur and trading companies, or of refugees from criminal justice, 'in the settlements,' are to be found in almost every tribe and band, however distant. Many
of them grown to man's estate, are among the most daring, adventurous, and
influential members of the warlike tribes, seldom wholly free from suspicion on
account of their relation on one side to the whites, yet by the versatility of their
talents and the recklessness of their courage, commanding the respect and the
fear of the pure-bloods, and, however incapable of leading the savages in better
courses, powerful in a high degree for mischief."

REFERENCES CITED

Ackerknecht, Erwin H. (1944), White Indians. *Bulletin of the History of
Medicine* 15:18-35.
Barbeau, Marius (1950), Indian captivities. *Proceedings of the American
Philosophical Society* 94:522-48.
Bennett, Emerson (1848), *The renegade*. Cincinatti.
Berry, Don (1960), *Trask*. New York: The Viking Press.
Beston, Henry (1942), *The St. Laurence*. New York: Farrar and Rinehart.
Bird, Robert Montgomery (1939), *Nick of the woods*. American Fiction
Series, ed. by Cecil B. Williams. New York: American Book Co. (First
edition 1837).
Bissell, Benjamin (1925), *The American Indian in English literature of the
eighteenth century*. New Haven: Yale University Press.
Blum, Daniel (1953), *A Pictorial History of the Silent Screen*. New York:
Putnam, pp. 53, 54, 172.
Bonner, T. D., ed. (1931), *The life and adventures of James P. Beck-
wourth*. New York: Alfred A. Knopf, Inc.
Boyd, Thomas (1928), *Simon Girty: The white savage*. New York: Minton,
Balch & Co.
Child, Lydia Maria (1824), *Hobomok: A tale of early times*. Boston.
Cohen, Morris R. (1947), *The Meaning of Human History*. La Salle: Open
Court.
Colden, Cadwallader (1922), *History of the Five Nations*. New York (First
ed. London 1747).
Cook, Will (1960), *Comanche captives*. New York: Bantam Books, Inc.
(Serialized in *The Saturday Evening Post* 1959).

Cooper, James Fenimore (1883), *The wept of Wish-ton-Wish.* New York: Appleton (First ed. 1829).

—— (1952), *The Deerslayer.* New York: Dodd, Mead & Company (First ed. 1841).

Cooper, Jefferson (1955), *Arrow in the hill.* New York: Dodd, Mead & Company, and Pocket Books, Inc.

Crane, Verner U. (1956), *The Southern Frontier, 1670-1732.* Ann Arbor: University of Michigan Press (First ed. 1929).

Crévecoeur, J. Hector St. John de (1957), *Letters from an American farmer.* New York: Dutton (First ed. 1782).

—— (1925), *Sketches of eighteenth century America: More letters from an American farmer.* Ed. by H. L. Bourdin, R. H. Gabriel and Stanley T. Williams. New Haven: Yale University Press.

Day, Gordon M. (1959), Dartmouth and St. Francis. *Dartmouth Alumni Magazine,* November, 1959.

Deshayes, Louis (Baron de Courmenin) (1624), *Le voyage de Levant fait par le commandement du roi, L'année 1621.* Paris (Republished 1629, 1632, 1645, 1664).

Dodge, Ernest S. (1963), Early American contacts in Polynesia and Fijji. *Proceedings of the American Philosophical Society* 107:102-6.

Dorson, Richard M. (1950), *America begins.* New York: Pantheon.

Fairchild, Hoxie Neal (1928), *The noble savage.* New York: Columbia University Press.

Fisher, Vardis (1956), *Pemmican.* New York: Doubleday & Co., Inc. (Pocket Books, Inc., 1957).

Flexner, James Thomas (1959), *Mohawk baronet: Sir William Johnson of New York.* New York: Harper and Brothers.

Flint, Timothy (1830), *Shoshone Valley.* 2 vols. Cincinnati.

Foreman, Carolyn Thomas (1943), *Indians abroad, 1493-1938.* Norman: University of Oklahoma Press.

Foreman, Grant (1932), *Indian removal.* Norman: University of Oklahoma Press.

Foster, Laurence (1935), *Negro-Indian relationships in the Southeast.* Ph. D. dissertation, University of Pennsylvania. Philadelphia: privately printed.

Fried, Jacob, ed. (1955), *A survey of the aboriginal populations of Quebec and Labrador.* Eastern Canadian Anthropological Series, number 1. Montreal: McGill University.

Furnas, J. C. (1947), *Anatomy of paradise.* New York: William Sloane Associates.

Giles, Janice Holt (1954), *The Kentuckians.* New York: Houghton Mifflin Company (Bantam Books, Inc., 1955).

Gordon, Caroline (1941), *Green centuries.* New York: Charles Scribner's Sons (Bantam Books, Inc., 1953).

Hallowell, A. Irving (1957), "The backwash of the frontier: The impact of the Indian on American culture," in *The frontier in perspective.* Ed. by Walker D. Wyman and Clifton B. Kroeber. Madison: University of Wisconsin Press (Reprinted in *Annual Report of the Board of Regents of the Smithsonian Institution,* 1958. Washington: Government Printing Office, 1959).

—— The impact of the American Indian on American culture. *American Anthropologist* 59:201-17.

Heard, Isaac V. D. (1863), *History of the Sioux War and massacres of 1862 and 1863.* New York: Harper and Brothers.

Hentz, N. M. (1825), *Tadeuskund, the last king of the Lenape.* Boston.

Herskovits, Melville J. (1930), *The anthropometry of the American Negro.* New York: Columbia University Press.

Hodge, F. W., ed. (1907, 1910), *Handbook of American Indians.* Parts I and II. Bureau of American Ethnology, Bulleton 30. Washington: Government Printing Office.

Horan, James D. (1953), *King's rebel.* New York: Crown Publishers (Bantam Books, Inc., 1955).

Huden, John C. The white chief of the St. Francis Abenaki—Some aspects of border warfare: 1690-1790. *Vermont History* 24:199-210.

Johnson, Dorothy M. (1953), *Indian country.* New York: Ballantine Books.

Johnson, J. Hugh (1929), Documentary evidence of the relations of Negroes and Indians. *Journal of Negro History* 14:21-43.

Keller, A. G. (1915), *Societal evolution: A study of the evolutionary basis of the science of society.* New York: Macmillan.

Kelley, Wellbourn (1957), *Alabama empire.* New York: Rinehart & Company, Inc. (Bantam Books, Inc., 1958).

Kerkkonon, Martti (1959), *Peter Kalm's North American Journey, its ideological background and results.* Helsinki: The Finnish Historical Society.

Laird, Charlton (1949), *Thunder on the river.* New York: Little, Brown & Company (Bantam Books, Inc., 1950).

Lawson, John (1860), *The history of Carolina.* Raleigh (First ed. London, 1714).

Lee, Sir Sidney (1920), *Elizabethan and other essays.* Ed. by F. S. Boas. Oxford: Clarendon Press.

Le May, Alan (1954), *The searchers.* New York: Harper and Brothers. (First serialized as *The avenging Texans* in *The Saturday Evening Post,* 1954; Popular Library, 1956).

Leger, Sister Mary Celeste (1929), *The Catholic Indian missions in Maine (1611-1820).* The Catholic University of America Studies in American Church History 8.

McCoy, Isaac (1840), *History of the Baptist Indian missions.* Washington and New York.

Marriner, William (1817), *An account of the natives of the Tonga Islands, by John Martin, M. D.* London: privately printed.

Marriott, Alice (1945), *The ten grandmothers.* Norman: University of Oklahoma Press.

Mathews, Mitford M., ed. (1951), *A dictionary of Americanisms on historical principles.* 2 vols. Chicago: University of Chicago Press.

Maurault, L'Abbe J. A. (1866), *Histoire des Abenakis depuis 1605 jusqu'a nos jours.* Sorel, Province of Quebec.

Mood, Fulmer (1943), The development of Frederick Jackson Turner as a historical thinker. *Publication of the Colonial Society of Massachusetts* 34:304-7.

Morton, Sarah Wentworth (1790), *Ouâbi, or The virtues of nature.* Boston.

Ortiz, Fernando (1947), *Cuban counterpoint: Tobacco and sugar.* Introduction by B. Malinowski. New York: Alfred A. Knopf, Inc.

Patten, Lewis B. (1956), *White warrior.* New York: Fawcett Publications.

Pearce, Roy Harvey (1947), The significance of the captivity narrative. *American Literature* 19:1-20.

——— (1952), The "ruines of mankind": The Indian and the Puritan minds. *Journal of the History of Ideas* 13:200-17.

——— (1953), *The savages of America: A study of the Indian and the idea of civilization.* Baltimore: Johns Hopkins University Press.

Pryor, Elinor (1957), *The double man.* New York: W. W. Norton & Company, Inc.

Redfield, Robert, Ralph Linton and Melville J. Herskovits (1936), Memorandum on the study of acculturation. *American Anthropoligist* 38:149-52.

Richter, Conrad (1953), *The light in the forest.* New York: Alfred A. Knopf, Inc. (First serialized in *The Saturday Evening Post* 1953; Bantam Books, Inc., 1954).

Rouillard, Clarence Dana (1941), The Turk in French history, thought, and literature (1520-1660). *Etudes de Literature E'strangère et Comparée.* Paris: Boivin.

Rovillain, Eugene E. (1929), *L'ingénu* de Voltaire: quelques influences. *Publications of the Modern Language Association* 44:37-45.

Royle, E. M. *The Squaw Man.* Play, first produced in 1905; in 1908 produced in England as *The White Man.* James D. Hart. 1944. *The Oxford Companion to American Literature.* New York; London; Toronto.

Schoolcraft, Henry R. (1953), *Narrative journal of travels through the northwestern regions of the United States extending from Detroit through the great chain of American lakes to the sources of the Mississippi River in the year 1820.* Ed. by Mentor L. Williams. East Lansing: Michigan State College Press.

Sedgwick, Catherine M. (1827), *Hope Leslie, or Early times in Massachusetts.* 2 vols. New York.

Smith, Henry Nash (1950), *Virgin land: The American West as symbol and myth.* Cambridge: Harvard University Press.

Smollett, Tobias G. (1929), *Humphrey Clinker.* New York: Modern Library Edition (First ed. 1771).

Social Science Research Council Seminar in Acculturation (1953), Acculturation: An exploratory formulation. *American Anthropologist* 56:973-1002.

Speck, Frank G. (1908), The Negroes and the Creek nation. *Southern Workman* 37:106-10.

Swanton, John R. (1926), Notes on the mental assimilation of races. *Journal of the Washington Academy of Sciences* 16:493-502.

Thwaites, Ruben Gold, ed. (1896-1901), *The Jesuit Relations and allied documents.* Cleveland.

Tracy, Don (1951), *Cherokee.* New York: Dial Press (Pocket Books, Inc. 1958).

——— (1954), *Roanoke renegade.* New York: Dial Press.

Turner, Frederick Jackson (1920), *The frontier in American history.* New York: Holt.

Van Doren, Carl (1917), "Fiction: Brown, Cooper," in *Cambridge History of American Literature,* Vol. 3, Chapt. 6. Cambridge: Cambridge University Press.

Van Every, Dale (1957), *The voyagers.* New York: Henry Holt and Company (Bantam Books, Inc., 1959).

Voltaire, F. M. A. (1926), "The simple soul [*L'ingénu*]," in *Zadig and other romances of Voltaire.* Translated by H. I. Woolf and Wilfred S. Jackson. New York: Dodd, Mead & Company (First ed. of *L'ingénu,* 1769).

Walker, F. A. (1873), The Indian question. *North American Review* 116:329-88.

Washburn, Wilcomb E. A moral history of Indian-white relations: Needs and opportunities for study. *Ethnohistory* 4:47-61.

Webber, Charles (1848), *Old Hicks the guide.* New York.

Whittaker, Frederick (1872), *The jaguar queen, or The outlaws of the Sierra Madre.* Beadle's New Dime Novels, number 389.

Wissler, Clark (1938), The enigma of the squaw man. *Natural History* 41:185-89.

Wright, Louis B. and Mary Isabel Fry. (1936), *Puritans in the South Seas.* New York: Holt.

PRODIPTO ROY: THE MEASUREMENT OF ASSIMILATION: THE SPOKANE INDIANS[1]

ABSTRACT

The model for the measurement of assimilation is broken down into three social processes—acculturation, social integration, and amalgamation. Comparison is made between a random sample of Spokane Indians and a sample of whites residing in the same community. Acculturation measured in terms of socioeconomic-status variables—education, level of living, and occupation—showed that Indians have much lower status than whites. Social integration measures showed integration in the formal institutional systems which are set up primarily for Indians and cleavage in the voluntary organizations. Amalgamation—the percentage white ancestry among Indians—was inversely related to age and directly to education, level of living, and income.

American anthropological and sociological literature is replete with studies of assimilation and acculturation, possibly because American society is composed of immigrants, with the natives contained in cultural islands. Sociological literature is mainly concerned with European immigrants to the New World, while anthropological literature generally deals with the impact of "white" culture upon American Indians or upon an African or Asian culture. Cultural contact in this modern world is rapidly increasing. As a result, such groups as students in foreign universities,[2] technical economic missions,[3] political and military stations, etc., provide excellent opportunities for experiments. Therefore, the need for empirical models to study the process becomes all the more imperative.

Source: Reprinted by permission from *The American Journal of Sociology* 67 (March 1962), 541-551. Copyright 1962 by the University of Chicago.

The process of assimilation has eluded empirical definition. Whetten and Green conclude that the concept is an imprecise and unwieldy formulation which cannot be made to fit a particular observation.[4] Subsequent research using it has done little to provide any commonly accepted empirical referents. This paper attempts to demonstrate that assimilation can be empirically measured and is too important a sociological concept to remain an imprecise and unwieldy tool of analysis.

One source of ambiguity is that the words "acculturation" and "assimilation" are used interchangeably. Anthropologists tend to use the generalized term "acculturation" in approximately the same way that sociologists use the term "assimilation." The classic conceptualizing of assimilation by Park and Burgess in 1924 seems to persist in textbooks published thirty years later.[5] The formulation is so broad that it permits research on many detailed facets: for example, Whetten and Green studied certain culture traits and social organizations, whereas Dornbush studied a formal code of ethics and informal rules.[6] Sociologists have made no systematic effort in published symposiums or seminars to arrive at any common agreement on the empirical concept of assimilation.

By contrast, anthropologists have done much toward coming to grips with the term "acculturation." Ralph Beals's chapter in Kroeber's symposium, Siegel's monograph, the 1953 Social Science Research Council seminar, and Paul Radin's work[7] are all evidence of the long-term interest and efforts to systematize this concept. Nevertheless, field research on acculturation can deal with almost any facet of diffusion of culture traits from the entire inventory of either the donor or the recipient culture. Mead's study of the Antlers, Eaton's study of the Hutterites, or Humphrey's study of the Detroit Mexican family—all describe the adoption of material or non-material traits.[8]

In short, these studies illustrate that field research on acculturation and assimilation is conducted on a wide range of traits but is generally done at a descriptive level, leaving the empirical referents fairly ambiguous.

THEORETICAL FRAMEWORK

Owing to the existing ambiguity, an operational formulation amenable to empirical research was found essential for the present study. The author used Harold S. Jacoby's conceptualization, which breaks down "assimilation" into three related but distinguishable facets:

> When an immigrant group . . . enters a territory occupied by another, and usually larger, body of people, the two groups are separated from one another in three different ways. *First,* they are culturally separate. Each has its own language, manners, beliefs, food preferences, and clothing styles. *Secondly,* they tend to be separate in their more durable social relationships . . . separate families, separate friendship groups, separate religious groups, separate clubs and organizations. And *thirdly,* the family lines will be biologically separate. Where families exist, ancestral lines will remain wholly within one or the other population.[9]

In short, assimilation can be broken down into three processes: (1) acculturation, (2) social integration, and (3) amalgamation. The assumption made in this study is that the smaller American Indian society will be assimilated into the larger white American society with practically no perceptible impact on the culture of the latter.

Acculturation

This process can be defined simply as the adoption of white culture traits by the Spokane Indians. A more complete analysis, including an ethnographic description of the culture of the Spokanes prior to white contact and the historical contact continuum, provides historical depth to the study of the problem.[10]

The research problem posed here was the selection of traits to be used from the total cultural inventory. Since it was assumed that acculturation would involve a flow of traits from the whites to the Indians, only white cultural traits were used in the measurement. A minimum of traits was selected to meet the requirements of this study. If Indians are being assimilated into white society, to what extent have they acquired traits that will give them social prestige among whites? Hence, it was decided to use items that have been demonstrated to measure socioeconomic status among rural people.

Three aspects of socioeconomic status—education, level of living, and occupation—were treated separately. Each was measured independently, and the Indian population was compared with the rest of Stevens County, Washington.

Social Integration

The acquisition of traits that give social prestige does not automatically insure social acceptance or social integration. The process of social segregation is further hindered when the two groups involved are politically separated and one lives on a reservation.

This physical separation, it was felt, artificially hampered the measurement of social integration. The Indians could not operate in all the *same* social groups as the surrounding whites, simply because they lived in a separate geographic area. Hence, the participation in all non-Indian formal organizations available in the county was the best measure of social integration that was available. (It should be added that there are whites living on the reservation who participate in the organizations on the reservation. Therefore, these organizations can in no sense be considered segregated.) A list of formal organizations was made up to determine the degree of participation in these organizations.

Amalgamation (Miscegenation)

Even after acculturation and social integration have taken place, family lines may be kept separate; hence, a third facet of assimilation—amalgamation—can be measured independently.

Evon Z. Vogt suggests that amalgamation would be one fairly good index of assimilation. He states that "biological miscegenation leads to

profoundly different self-conceptions and evaluations; to the kinds of reference groups that seem to provide a kind of natural 'ladder of acculturation'
in many areas of Mexico that is so conspicuously lacking in the United
States."[11]

The generalized white American attitude toward the American Indian
has been a tangled skein of logical contradictions. At first the Indian was
regarded as a menace. After the breaking of Indian military power and the
formation of reservations, the Indian came to be idealized as the "Noble
Red Man." The original half-breed was an object of contempt. Yet later a
"trace" of Indian ancestry was readily and proudly admitted.

On some reservations there is every shade of Indian-white mixture.
This miscegenation, as Vogt suggests, probably leads to profoundly different self-conceptions and evaluations, which in turn manifest themselves
in different behavior patterns. It was therefore hypothesized in this study
that various degrees of Indian ancestry would be related to other measures
of assimilation.

Assumptions

1. The model presented in Figure 1 seems to imply a chronological
order in these three subordinate processes which can be diagrammatically
visualized on both a time scheme and a three-step submergence into the
host culture. The time sequence implies that the acquisition of cultural
traits, in this case by Indians from whites, or acculturation, is a necessary
but not a sufficient condition for social integration. It is further implied
that acculturation and social integration are necessary but not sufficient
conditions for amalgamation.

2. The model assumes that the smaller society will be assimilated into
the larger dominant society with no perceptible impact on the traits of the
latter. This is only one of the many possible social situations which are
preconditions of assimilation. It is possible, for example, that two societies
being studied may be of roughly equal size, like the French and British in
Canada; or that the smaller society is the "donor" like the British in India.

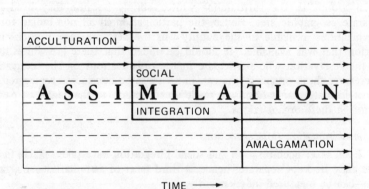

TIME ⟶

Figure 1

How well this model will fit into other preconditions will be determined by subsequent research.

3. In this model, the process of acculturation has been subsumed under the process of assimilation. In this respect it differs from the Redfield, Linton, and Herskovits formulation, that "acculturation is to be distinguished from assimilation, which is at times a phase of acculturation."[12] The anthropological formulation is more useful when universal patterns are examined over a long period. That is, in the diffusion of culture traits over the world one culture may be assimilated into another culture, and both may have ceased to exist, while their culture traits have spread and influenced many other cultures.

4. The theoretical formulation presented here is concerned mainly with the assimilation of a whole group, not of an individual.

METHOD

This study was conducted in the spring of 1958 as part of an appraisal of the socioeconomic levels of living and the needs of a county selected for rural development.[13] The population of Stevens County, Washington, is predominantly rural; the only urban center has a population of 4,000. The study compared a sample of whites and Indians living in the county. The white sample consisted of a two-stage area probability sample which dealt with the town and open country separately.[14]

The Indian sample consisted of a random selection of forty families from a list of 110 families obtained from the tribal roll at the Spokane Indian Agency. About an equal number of Indian families who were on the tribal roll but did not live on the Spokane reservation were therefore excluded from the universe from which the sample was drawn. Probably, families that had left the reservation are much better assimilated into white society than Indians living on the reservation. Some were living in the city of Spokane, some in other cities throughout the United States. Thus, it did not seem feasible to interview any systematic sample for this study. Theoretically, while the exclusion of off-reservation Indians from the sample impairs the content of the study of Spokane Indian assimilation, it does not seriously impair the method of measuring assimilation.

Statistical Techniques

The general thesis being empirically tested for this study may be stated thus: Do the norms of the Indian population differ from the white population norms in certain measurable ways? The test most applicable for this thesis was the chi-square test for goodness of fit. Since the white population was used as the cultural norm into which the Indians will be assimilated, the measurements of the white population were used as the theoretical distributions, and the deviations observed in the Indian population were statistically tested for significance.[15] Pearsonian correlation was used to show the association between the variables for the Indian data.

DEGREE OF ACCULTURATION

Education

The simplest, most common measure of education is the total years of formal education completed. A comparison of adult Indians living on the reservation with adult whites living in the rest of Stevens County showed that the whites had more formal education. Indian men had completed a median of 8.50 years of school compared with the white norm for Stevens County, 10.18 years. Indian women had completed 9.18 years of schooling compared with the white norm of 10.83 years. Expressed as percentage, Indian men had about 83.5 per cent as much education and Indian women had about 84.8 per cent as much education as the whites.[16] When standardized for age, the data indicate that the divergence in the years of education was far greater for older than for younger people. That is, younger Indians are coming much closer to achieving the same degree of education as their white counterparts.

Level of Living

The second measure of acculturation used in this study was level of living. Thirty-two items were grouped into what seemed like four logically coherent clusters related to (a) size, structure, and appearance of house, (b) piped water and related conveniences, (c) electrical appliances, and (d) magazines, newspapers, insurance, and possession of an automobile. The whites possessed thirty out of thirty-two items more often than the Indians; the differences in proportions were statistically significant for twenty-six items. Indian families possessed only two items more often than the whites—a television set and an automobile manufactured in 1953 or later. Neither of these differences was statistically significant.

There is evidence that the equal weighting of items in the construction of the level-of-living scale provides approximately the same results as the differential weighting of items.[17] Hence, in Table 1 a simple average of the percentages of households possessing each of thirty items is shown.[18] The degree of acculturation achieved by the Indians is the ratio of 35.88 to 63.26, which expressed as a percentage is 56.72.

These results indicate that with respect to the items that constitute a high level of living in white society, Indians have only acquired these items about half as often as whites: As a group they have only acquired about half the material goods that would give them an equal level of living in the adjacent white society.

Occupation

The literature on stratification emphasizes occupation as one of the most stable measures of socioeconomic status. One question was asked to determine the present occupation of the heads of household. Indians had a higher proportion of retired and unemployed heads of households, 37.5 per cent compared with 21.4 per cent for whites. Whites had a higher proportion of professionals, managers, and proprietors, and also farmers.

The stability of the occupational structure was measured by the number of years the respondents had been employed at their present jobs. More

TABLE 1

Socioeconomic Status Variables Comparing Indians and Whites

Variable	Indians	Whites	x^2	Degrees of Freedom	Probability
Education:					
Median years of school:					
Husband	8.50	10.18	22.022	2	.001
Wife	9.18	10.83	8.721	2	.02
Level of living:					
Average per cent of 30 items					
possessed	35.88	63.26	–	–	.001*
Occupation:					
Per cent retired and unem-					
ployed	37.5	21.4			
Per cent professionals, man-				12.470	6	.05-.10
agers, or proprietors	5.0	17.2			
Median years on present job	1.92	11.42	26.504	3	.001
Average number of months					
employed	7.88	10.05	7.252	2	.05
Median income	$1,406	$3,695	–	–	.001*
Number of respondents	40	620	–	–	–

*The *t*-test was used.

than half the employed Indians but only 16 per cent of the white household heads had worked on their present jobs for two years or less. In the middle ranges of job stability—from three to nine years and from ten to nineteen years—the whites showed much greater job stability. The median number of years that the Indians had been employed on their present job was 1.92 compared with 11.42 for the white population.

Another question asked how many months the husband had been employed in 1957. About 76 percent of the white men had been fully employed for twelve months compared with about 58 per cent of the Indians. The average number of months employed was 7.88 for the Indians and 10.05 for the whites.

The three indexes of employment indicate that the Indians tend to work in lower-prestige occupations and that they have considerably more instability in their employment, both in terms of number of months worked during the year and the number of years they had worked on their present job.

Perhaps one acceptable single measure of the relative occupational prestige and stability of employment is family income from earnings. Salary or wages reflect occupational prestige, the period of employment during the year, and rewards for seniority. The median family income for the previous year for Indians was 1,406 compared with 3,695 for the white families. This suggests that the Indians are about 38 per cent acculturated with respect to occupation.

SOCIAL INTEGRATION

Social integration, according to the theoretical frame of reference, is the second phase of the process of assimilation. In its broadest sense, social integration implies common participation in all social groups, from the most informal and transitory friendship groups to the most formal social institutions. The schedule provided a list of organizations with a space for further additions: Table 2 compares the percentage of Indian and white respondents who checked membership in these organizations.

In general, the Indians, both men and women, had a lower proportion of membership in nearly all the organizations listed than whites. The major exceptions were church membership and public offices. Indians held public offices more often partly because reservations are self-governing units and need a relatively higher proportion of officials.

To summarize social integration as measured by the participation in formal organizations and election to public office, a social-participation index was constructed. This index assigned one point for membership, one point for attendance at one-quarter of the meetings, and one point for being an officer of an organization, plus five points for being elected to a

TABLE 2

Social Participation of Whites and Indians
(Percentage of Members)

Social Groups	Men		Women	
	Indians	Whites	Indians	Whites
Voluntary organizations:				
Grange	5.0	20.4*	5.0	15.1*
Pomona grange	0	4.1	0	3.6
Farm bureau	0	0.1	0	0.3
SCS district	2.5	0.8	0	0.1
Co-op	0	7.5*	0	2.6
Commodity organizations	0	2.5	2.5	1.0
Service clubs	0	8.2	0	7.5
Chamber of commerce	0	8.4*	0	1.4
Lodges	0	17.6**	0	12.1*
Veterans organization	2.5	11.8	0	3.2
PTA	5.0	9.2	2.5	18.8**
Labor unions	5.0	7.8	0	0.3
4-H leaders	5.0	0.9	2.5	1.9
Home economics club	0	0	5.0	21.2*
Sports club	5.0	2.5	2.5	2.0
Institutions:				
Church membership or participation	50.0	36.0	62.5	57.4
Per cent holding public offices in past five years	34.4	12.2**	14.7	3.2*
Number of respondents	40	577	40	577

*Difference significant at 5 per cent level.
**Difference significant at 1 per cent level.

public office. The median social-participation index for Indian men was 1.42; for white men, 1.93. The median social-participation index for Indian women was 2.36; for white women, 2.36. The differences observed were statistically significant for both men and women. If the norm for participation in formal organizations and public offices is that of the white men and women and the median is the best measure of central tendency, Indian men were socially integrated to a lesser extent (74 percent) than Indian women (89 per cent).

These percentages suggest a spuriously high degree of social integration. The data show cleavage in some organizations and integration in others. The most institutionalized social groups—government and the church—showed that Indians participated more than whites but the voluntary formal organizations, particularly the fraternal ones, showed very little social integration.

The data gathered in this study were not specifically designed to measure social integration and have been somewhat strained to fit the theoretical model. First, the physical separation of Indians on a reservation limits common social participation. Second, the exclusion of the off-reservation Indians probably eliminated Indians who have a higher degree of social integration. Third, the Tribal Council, although patterned after democratic forms, is a carry-over of the pre-1800 government institution of the Spokane culture and it is the only segregated social group on the reservation. For these reasons the correlation analysis shown later manifests little association of the social-participation index with other variables. Some new and different methods need to be devised to measure the dimension of social integration.

AMALGAMATION

Ever since the practice of keeping a tribal roll was initiated, it has been required to record the amount of Indian ancestry for each member on the roll. For the sample of Indians interviewed these data were recorded. The average percentage of Indian ancestry for the men was 55 per cent; for the women, 59 per cent. These figures are concise measures of the degree of amalgamation.

Another way of looking at these data is to examine the marriages of the twenty-eight couples in the sample. Twenty of the twenty-eight couples involved amalgamation—part Indians with part Indians, part Indians with whites, or part Indians with full-blood Indians. Only eight of the twenty-eight marriages were between Indian full-bloods. Hence, using the criterion of participation in mixed marriages, one could say that over 70 per cent of the families of the Spokane reservation manifested some form of amalgamation and about 30 per cent did not. People with a high percentage of Indian ancestry tended to select mates with a high percentage of Indian ancestry and vice versa. This relationship is manifested in a Pearsonian correlation coefficient of .777 of the percentage of Indian ancestry between husband and wife.

If all persons of unmixed Indian ancestry were married to persons of

TABLE 3

Intercorrelations Between All Variables Used to Measure Assimilation*

	X_0 Husband (Age)	X_1 Wife (Age)	X_2 Education (Husband)	X_3 Education (Wife)	X_4 Level of Living	X_5 Soc. Part. Index (Husband)	X_6 Soc. Part. Index (Wife)	X_7 Income	X_8 Per Cent Indian (Husband)	X_9 Per Cent Indian (Wife)
X_0 Husband (age)										
X_1 Wife (age)	.952									
X_2 Education (husband)	−.738	−.675								
X_3 Education (wife)	−.702	−.688	.797							
X_4 Level of living	−.394	−.340	.541	.639						
X_5 Soc. part. index (husband)	.027	.147	.216	.129	.369					
X_6 Soc. part. index (wife)	−.025	.068	.153	.285	.188	.078				
X_7 Income	−.407	−.400	.371	.436	.561	.108	.201			
X_8 Per cent Indian (husband)	.345	.369	−.383	−.424	−.415	.073	.046	−.437		
X_9 Per cent Indian (wife)	.297	.343	−.303	−.386	−.530	−.043	.023	−.494	.777	

*$r = .304$ for $P < .05$, $r = .393$ for $P < .01$.

unmixed white ancestry, their children might be regarded as having 50 per cent Indian ancestry.

The above data indicating the averages of 55 per cent Indian ancestry among the men and 59 per cent among the women would imply that between 80 and 90 per cent of the Indians on the reservation had participated in some form of amalgamation.

INTERCORRELATION OF VARIABLES

The data show some assimilation in all the subordinated processes of the theoretical model used in this analysis—acculturation, social integration, and amalgamation. The results seem to refute the time presupposition that acculturation was a necessary but not a sufficient condition for social integration, and that acculturation and social integration are necessary but not sufficient conditions for amalgamation.

A closer examination of these data, however, indicates that within the group the individuals who have a high degree of acculturation are socially integrated and have intermarried. The best way to elucidate these associations statistically was to compute intercorrelation coefficients between all variables used.[19] Table 3 presents the Pearsonian intercorrelations between all variables used to measure assimilation in this study. Since only forty observations were available, regression seemed to be the most efficient method of analysis.

To observe the linear associations with changes over time, the correlations with age were examined. The Indians born at different times were "socially determined" in different ways of reflecting changes in their social milieu. Hence, Indians of different ages reflect changes in the group norms of their culture during the past half-century.

All the socioeconomic measures of acculturation were inversely related to age. The four correlation coefficients of education with age were about −.7. The correlation coefficients of level of living and income with age were about −.4.

Social participation did not seem to be related to age; the correlation coefficients were low and not statistically significant.

The percentage of Indian ancestry was directly related to age: The correlation coefficient for the men was .429; for the women, .349; both were statistically significant. If extrapolation of this as a linear relationship into the future is valid, ultimately the Spokane Indians will merge into the white population.

In short, the results of the simple correlations indicate that the younger Spokane Indians are progressively better educated, have a higher level of living and more income, and have fewer Indian ancestors.[20]

The *socioeconomic status* variables used to measure acculturation were not related to social participation except in one of eight correlations. (A positive correlation was found between social-participation index of husband and level of living.) The socioeconomic status variables were consistently inversely correlated with the degree of Indian ancestry. These correlations fairly conclusively show that the amalgamated Indians, that is, the Indians with more white ancestry, have a higher socioeconomic status.

The two *social-participation* indexes did not seem to be correlated with any of the other variables (the one exception is noted above). This lack of association suggests that the cumulative social-participation index as computed in this study needs revision or alteration to be a satisfactory measure of social integration. In its present form it does not seem to be a true measure of social integration and therefore does not test the relation of this variable with other measures of assimilation.

In the theoretical framework Evon Vogt suggested that the different *degrees of Indian ancestry* would result in profoundly different self-conceptions which would affect behavior patterns. The correlation coefficients showed negative associations with all the socioeconomic status variables. As percentage of white ancestry increased so did the years of schooling completed, the level of living, and income. These correlations suggest that the prototype of the Indian has changed from the old "pure-blooded" Spokane Indian with little education to the partially amalgamated young Spokane Indian with more education, higher level of living, and more income.[21]

CONCLUSIONS

1. Using single measures of socioeconomic status to indicate the degree of acculturation, it can be said that (a) Indians have about 84 per cent as much education as whites, (b) Indians have about 56 per cent as high a level of living as whites, and (c) occupationally, Indians earn about 38 per cent as much income as the whites. These simple measures are gross averages, around which the data show considerable variation. From these data, however, it may be concluded that the Indians have *not* acquired the traits that would give them an equal position in their surrounding white society.

2. Some degree of social integration has taken place, particularly in formal institutionalized social structures such as the church, the school, and government. In view of the fact that these institutions are set up separately for the Indians, it is no surprise that the participation in the remaining social systems also showed a separation of Indians from their counterparts in white society. The physical separation of Indians on the reservations will continue to impede social integration.

3. The third measure of assimilation—amalgamation—indicated that the Spokane Indians had an average of about 43 per cent white ancestry. This simple average, however, has considerable variation which can be explained in several ways: (a) socioeconomic status variables—education, level of living, and income—were inversely related to the per cent of Indian ancestry, (b) a correlation was found between age and per cent of Indian ancestry, indicating that the process of amalgamation has been continuing during the past generation, (c) the pattern of amalgamation indicated a close correlation between the amount of Indian ancestry in the husband and the wife.

4. The intercorrelation between all the measures of assimilation showed that Indian adults have been progressively achieving higher socio-

economic status, more education, higher level of living and income, and are being amalgamated into white society. Most of these changes have taken place in the past fifty years.

NOTES

1 Scientific Paper 2083A, Washington Agricultural Experiment Stations, Pullman, Research for this paper was conducted under Project 1415. The author wishes to acknowledge the suggestions, criticisms, and interviewing help of I. Roger Yoshino, associate professor of sociology, University of Arizona, Tucson. A more complete report of this research with an ethnography and a description of the historical contacts is included in a forthcoming bulletin, *The Assimilation of the Spokane Indians,* by Prodipto Roy and Della M. Walker ("Washington Agricultural Experiment Stations," Bull. 628 [Pullman, Wash.: Washington Agricultural Experiment Stations, May 1961]).

2 See William H. Sewell and Oluf H. Davidsen, *Scandinavian Students on an American Campus* (Minneapolis: University of Minnesota, 1961); Richard D. Lambert and Marvin Bressler, *Indian Students on an American Campus* (Minneapolis: University of Minnesota, 1956); John Useem and Ruth H. Useem, *The Western Educated Man in India* (New York: Dryden Press, 1955).

3 William J. Lederer and Eugene Burdick, *The Ugly American* (New York: W. W. Norton & Co., 1958); Gerard J. Mangone, "New Americans in Old Societies," *Antioch Review,* Vol. XVIII (Winter 1958).

4 Nathan L Whetten and Arnold W. Green, "Field Research and the Concept of Assimilation," *Rural Sociology,* VII (September 1942), 260.

5 Robert E. Park and Ernest Burgess, *Introduction to the Science of Sociology* (Chicago: University of Chicago Press, 1924), p. 735; Edward C. McDonagh and Eugene S. Richards, *Ethnic Relations in the United States* (New York: Appleton-Century-Crofts, Inc., 1953), p. 205; Kimball Young and Raymond M. Mack; *Sociology and Social Life* (New York: American Book Co., 1959), p. 149; see also George A. Lundberg *et al., Sociology* (New York: Harper & Bros., 1958), p. 248.

6 Sanford M. Dornbush, "The Military Academy as an Assimilating Institution," *Social Forces,* XXXIII (May 1955), 316-21.

7 See "Acculturation" in *Anthropology Today,* ed. A. L. Kroeber (Chicago: University of Chicago Press, 1953), p. 627; Bernard J. Siegel (ed.), *Acculturation* (Stanford, Calif.: Stanford University Press, 1955); SSRC Summer Seminar on Acculturation, 1953, "Acculturation: An Exploratory Formulation," *American Anthropologist,* LVI (December 1954), 973-95; Ralph Linton (ed.), *Acculturation in Seven American Indian Tribes* (New York: Appleton-Century-Crofts, 1940).

8 Margaret Mead, *The Changing Culture of an Indian Tribe* (New York: Columbia University Press, 1932); Joseph W. Eaton, "Controlled Acculturation: A Survival Technique of the Hutterites," *American Sociological Review,* XVII (June 1952), 331-40; and Norman D. Humphrey, "The Changing Structure of the Detroit Mexican Family: An Index of Acculturation," *American Sociological Review,* IX (December 1944), 622-26.

9 Harold S. Jacoby, *A Half-Century Appraisal of East Indians in the*

United States (Stockton, Calif.: Sixth Annual College of the Pacific Faculty Research Lecture, May 1956), p. 2.

10 See Roy and Walker, *op. cit.*

11 "The Acculturation of American Indians," in *American Indians and American Life, the Annals,* CCCXI (May 1957), 144–45.

12 See Ralph Beals, "Acculturation," *op. cit.,*

13 *Human Resources in Stevens County—an Appraisal* (Pullman, Wash.: Agricultural Extension Service, Washington State University, September 1959).

14 See W. L. Slocum and Carol L. Stone, "A Design for Area Probability Sampling," *Rural Sociology,* XXIV (June 1959), 176–77.

15 The chi-square goodness-of-fit test assumes a known theoretical distribution. In this study a 10 per cent sample of the white population is used as the theoretical distribution which is subject to sampling error. Notwithstanding, the chi-square goodness-of-fit test was considered superior to the chi-square independence test. The chi-square independence tests were computed and yielded results with the same inferences.

16 Since the use of medians to compute percentages is a violation of mathematical procedures, these and subsequent comparative percentages have lost their mathematical integrity. They are used here merely as numerical indexes for the purpose of comparison and are not used in other computations.

17 See Belcher and Sharp, *A Short Scale for Measuring Farm Families Level of Living: A Modification of Sewell's Socio-economic Scale* (Oklahoma Agricultural Experiment Stations, Technical Bull. No. T–46 [Stillwater: Oklahoma Agricultural Experiment Stations, September, 1952]); and Mary J. Harris, *Review of Methods of Scale and Item Analysis and Their Application to a Level of Living Scale in North Carolina* (North Carolina Agricultural Experiment Stations Progress Report, R.S. 13 [Raleigh: North Carolina Agricultural Experiment Stations, 1951]).

18 If each household was scored for each of the thirty-two items possessed and a level of living index computed for each household, the average index for the whites would provide a norm against which the Indians could be compared. Mathematically, the same end could be achieved by simply averaging the percentages of households possessing each item.

19 All the variables are measured in interval scales except social participation and level of living. Therefore, the Pearsonian regression was used as the best test of association. There were missing data due to absence-by-death of a husband or wife and to refusals to give answers on the income variable. Interpolations were made in the following manner: (1) percentage of Indian ancestry for missing parents was determined from the other parent and children; (2) age of husband was closely related to age of wife ($r=.937$) and the mean difference was 4.7 years; hence missing husband's age equalled wife's age +4.7; (3) years of school for husband and wife were closely intercorrelated ($r=.627$) and the mean difference in favor of the wife was 0.5 years; hence husband's years of school equals wife's schooling -0.5 years; (4) the intercorrelation for the social participation indexes was low ($r=.124$) and therefore the best measure of central tendency, the median, was interpolated for each missing statistic; (5) there were six missing statis-

tics on the income data. The author had partial information of five out of six families and the median was used for the sixth family.

20 The multiple correlation coefficients and the coefficients of determination for the relations between age of the husband and wife with the other eight variables are:

$$R1.23456789=.832; R^2=.693$$
$$R0.23456789=.809; R^2=.655.$$

The coefficients of determination mean that about 65–70 per cent of the variance of changes in time can be explained by linear relationships with the variables used to measure assimilation. This would suggest that most of the assimilation process as measured by variables used in this study had taken place during the past 50 years.

21 In a factor analysis of the intercorrelations, the highest factor loading for the first common factor was percentage of Indian ancestry. This factor explained 49 percent of the total variation and the next two factors explained 19 per cent and 13 per cent, respectively. The factor analysis suggests that three dimensions were being measured which could be named—amalgamation, social integration, and acculturation— and thereby supported the theoretical framework of analysis (see *Assimilation of the Spokane Indians, op. cit.*, pp. 47-48).

LYNN C. WHITE, BRUCE A. CHADWICK: URBAN RESIDENCE, ASSIMILATION AND IDENTITY OF THE SPOKANE INDIAN[1]

Typically, studies of the assimilation of American Indians into white society have used as indicators of assimilation Indian participation in white institutions, such as educational attainment, employment, arrest rates, or residential location. The present study is concerned with a more psychological variable, namely the individual's self-identification as an Indian or a white. The relationship between self conception and several factors previously identified as correlates of assimilation are tested, using data obtained from members of the Spokane tribe in 1967.

Assimilation will be defined as the process in which members of one group are absorbed into another, usually larger, group to the point that members of the assimilating group consider themselves full-fledged members of the larger group, and are so defined by other members of that group. Assimilation may be divided into phases or stages. Three of these, acculturation, social integration and amalgamation (miscegenation), have been described by Roy.[2] With reference to Indian-white relations, acculturation may be defined as the process whereby Indians (or whites) adopt white (or Indian) culture traits. The second stage, social integration, refers to increased interaction between Indians and whites, and the third stage, amalgamation, includes biological mixing between the two groups, generally through intermarriage. The final phase occurs when an Indian comes to identify himself as a member of the white society.

The use of the term *stage* implies that there is a progressive relationship among the stages, that is, acculturation occurring before integration, and integration preceding amalgamation. In considering the groups in their entirety, the implication of progression from stage to stage may well be justified. Thus, it is probable that fairly extensive integration will have to have occurred before the probabilities of amalgamation are very high. However, when the focus of attention is the individual Indian (or white) rather than the group as a whole, the implied progression from acculturation to total assimilation is much more problematic. In fact, indicators appropriate to the acculturation or integration phases may be better predictors of a person's self-perceptions than indicators of the extent of "amalgamation" represented in his history. Accordingly, in the present study we have relaxed the assumption of sequence in the stages of assimilation, and instead have tried to assess the extent to which variables appropriate to each of the initial three stages are linked to an Indian's perception that he is white. As a beginning, the presumed relationship between selected indicators of the stages of assimilation and identification with the dominant group will be reviewed briefly.

ACCULTURATION

Several investigators have identified educational achievement as an indicator of acculturation.[3] It is argued that the more education (including vocational training) an Indian obtains, the greater his ability to function satisfactorily in the dominant society and the greater his identification with the values and practices of this society. The basic notion is that attendance at white-controlled schools teaches Indians to think and act as whites. Thus, our first hypothesis is that *the extent to which an Indian identifies himself as white is directly related to his educational achievement.* (Hypothesis 1)

Occupational success has also been used as an indicator of assimilation into white society.[4] Some support for this idea is provided by research concerning successful "adjustment" or assimilation in the city. Graves used rates of arrest for alcohol-related behavior as a measure of the personal adjustment of Navaho migrants to an urban environment.[5] He found that Indians with the greatest opportunity for acquiring skills for holding down good jobs were much less likely to be arrested than those who did not have such opportunities. More importantly, Navaho migrants who were successful in achieving economic well-being displayed the lowest rates for drunkenness. In fact, the Navaho migrant's economic position within the city was such a good predictor of arrest rates for drunkenness that Graves stated that "if we were to look at no other variables than a migrant's economic position in the city, we would still have achieved a major understanding of his drunkenness and arrest problems."[6] Other factors, such as marital status or perceptions of the opportunity structure within the city as compared with that of the reservation, were also identified as important predictors of adjustment.

The importance of employment in making it possible for Indian people to survive in the urban environment also has been stressed by Weppner, who concluded that vocational training prior to urban relocation was positively correlated with the Indians' remaining in the city.[7] The hypothesized relationship may be stated: *The extent to which an Indian identifies himself as a white is directly related to the steadiness and status of his employment.* (Hypothesis 2)

Roy argues that "level of living" as indicated by adequacy of housing or ownership of material objects is an important indication of acculturation.[8] The basic idea is that certain cultural and material possessions are indicators of social prestige in American society, and if the Indians are to be assimilated into that society, they must acquire the traits or possessions that will assure them an acceptable status. Without such possessions, the psychological costs of becoming a part of the white system are too severe, and it is to the Indian's advantage to remain in a system where prestige derives from some other source than economic achievement. Therefore it was hypothesized that *the extent to which an Indian identifies himself as a white is directly related to his standard of living.* (Hypothesis 3)

SOCIAL INTEGRATION

Social integration implies common participation of Indians and whites in social groups of all kinds. Social integration presupposes propinquity, and hence an important factor facilitating the social integration of Indians and whites is the extensive and continuing migration of Indian people from the reservation to the city. In 1950 only 16 percent of the Indians lived in urban centers; by 1960 this percentage had almost doubled, and it appears likely that the 1970 census will reveal that at least 50 percent of the Indians in the United States reside in urban areas.[9] Theoretically the migration to urban areas will increase the level of social interaction between Indians and whites, and build Indian identification with whites. On the other hand, researchers who have investigated Indian adjustment to urban living have reported the maintenance of a very strong sense of Indian identity. For example, Ablon reports:

> Almost every Indian I encountered in the course of my research [in the San Francisco Bay area] was impressed with an unmistakable stamp of identity of which he always seems to be acutely aware. The personal dimension of identity frequently is manifest in manner as well as by constant references to the fact of one's Indianness or to stories about the home reservation.[10]

Similar vitality of Indian identity among urban Indians is reported by Anderson and Harvey, who discovered an active "rejection" of white culture among Navahos who relocated either to border towns (small towns close to reservations) or to cities.[11] They suggest that increased social integration (living in an urban environment) leads Navahos to attach greater importance to traditional values. Despite these studies suggesting possible null or even negative relationships between integration and identity, the hypothesis was stated in harmony with the usual integration-assimilation linkage: *The extent to which an Indian identifies himself as a white is directly related to his social integration with white people and institutions.* (Hypothesis 4)

AMALGAMATION

In a discussion of factors related to the acculturation of American Indians, Vogt has argued that "persisting Anglo-American 'racial' attitudes" have limited intermarriage between Indians and whites and thereby prevented complete assimilation.[12] Vogt considers miscegenation an important part of assimilation not only because it reduces biological differences but also because it leads to profoundly different self-conceptions and identity. The idea is stated formally in this hypothesis: *The extent to which an Indian identifies himself as a white is directly related to the extent of his white ancestry.* (Hypothesis 5)

METHODS

A random sample of 100 adults aged 20 to 45 was drawn from the roles of the Spokane tribe. To insure an adequate number of urban Indians in the sample, the sample was drawn in two stages, each of which produced a subsample of 50. The sampling universe for one of the subsamples contained only persons residing on or near the reservation, and the other included members of the tribe living in Spokane, Washington. Interviews were conducted during the summer of 1967, and were completed with all but two of the reservation sample. Persons in the urban sample were more difficult to locate, and only 39 of the 50 potential respondents were interviewed. The refusal rate was surprisingly low; the main reason for incompleted interviews was that several urban Indians could not be located.

The dependent variable was the respondent's perception of himself as being either an Indian or white (white identification). The instrument included the question, "In the way you think and act, do you feel that you are more of an Indian or a white?" Possible responses covered a five-point scale ranging from "definitely more Indian" to "definitely more white."

The present analysis is limited to the relationships between eight independent variables and "white identification." Three of these eight are indicators of acculturation linked to the first three hypotheses listed above. The first, education, represents the years of schooling completed, including vocational training. The second, "regularity of work," was a numerical measure of the number of weeks the respondent was employed during the twelve months preceding the interview. Finally, "adequacy of housing" was used as an indicator of standard of living, with each residence being evaluated on a seven-point scale with respect to the nature of the house itself as well as the neighborhood in which it was situated.

Two independent variables were indicators of extent of social integration. One of these was the respondent's perception about how well he "fit in" with whites and with Indians; the other was a four-point scale representing degree of urban residence (categories were reservation, non-reservation rural, nonreservation small community, and urban; almost all respondents fell into either the reservation or the urban categories). The information about "fitting in" in activities with members of either race came from two questions: "We would first like to know how you feel that you fit in with most Indians" and "We would also like to know how you feel that you fit in with most whites." Responses were coded on a four-point scale ranging from "definitely better with Indians" to "definitely better with whites."

Two independent variables were indicators of amalgamation. These were degree of Indian ancestry of the respondent and his spouse as obtained from tribal records. To be conceptually consistent with the dependent variable, these variables were labeled "white ancestry" and "white ancestry of spouse." The respondent's age was included as a final independent variable.

As a first step in the analysis, zero-order correlation coefficients were computed for the association between white identification and each of the independent variables. Following the examination of the bivariate relationships, a stepwise multiple-regression analysis was conducted. This type of analysis permits each of the independent variables to compete with the others in respect to their power in "explaining" the dependent variable. One product of the multiple-regression analysis is an accumulative measure of the variance of the dependent variable that can be accounted for by different combinations of the independent variables.

FINDINGS

Fifty-five percent of the Indians interviewed in this sample clearly identified themselves as being Indian. Another 31 percent identified themselves as being white, and 14 percent were ambivalent about their racial identity.

Table 1 presents the zero-order correlations between white identification and the eight independent variables. Of the five variables showing significant correlations, two were indicators of social integration, two were measures of amalgamation, and the final one was an index of acculturation. Three of the five hypotheses received preliminary support. Only the hypothesized relationships between white identification and education (Hypothesis 1) or regularity of work (Hypothesis 2) were not supported.

The perception that one "fit in" with whites, a measure of social

TABLE 1
Correlation Between "White Identification" and
Eight Independent Variables

Variable	r	r^2
"Fits in" (Hypothesis 4)	.716[a]	.513
White ancestry of spouse (Hypothesis 5)	.576[a]	.332
Urban residence (Hypothesis 4)	.516[a]	.266
Adequate housing (Hypothesis 3)	.475[a]	.226
White ancestry (Hypothesis 5)	.391[a]	.153
Regularity of work (Hypothesis 2)	.153	–
Education (Hypothesis 1)	.082	–
Age	.053	–

[a]Significant at .001 level.

integration (Hypothesis 4), emerged as the strongest correlate of white identification. It should be noted that the strength of the coefficient ($r = .716$) may be inflated by the existence of common elements in the two variables. Feelings of "fitting in" with whites and white identification are not entirely independent of one another on the conceptual level.

The high correlation ($r = .576$) between white identification and white ancestry of spouse (amalgamation: Hypothesis 5) came as a surprise, because it was expected that the respondent's own ancestry would be more significant. To explore the nature of this finding, the data were examined separately for males and females, under the rationale that in a primarily male-oriented (white) society where the family's status depends to a very considerable extent on the husband's characteristics (education, occupation, income), the wife should tend to identify with the racial group of her husband much more strongly than he would identify with her racial group. Thus, white ancestry of spouse would be expected to have a stronger relationship to white identification for females than for males. This idea was tested by controlling for sex and computing the two correlations between ancestry of spouse and white identification. The expected sexual differential did appear. For husbands the coefficient was somewhat lower than for the whole group ($r = .534$), and for the wives it was much higher ($r = .703$). The expectation was that people would tend to have developed a fairly stable racial identity before marriage and that they were likely to marry someone who matched their identity. The above findings suggest (1) that the racial identity of one's spouse is a significant factor in determining extent of white identification, and (2) that it is a more potent factor for wives than for husbands.

Urban residence, another measure of social integration (Hypothesis 4), manifested the third-strongest correlation to the dependent variable. Indian people who lived in Spokane tended to identify themselves as being white, while those who lived on the reservation tend to identify themselves as Indians. This relationship is stated as if residence determines identity, but it might just as logically be stated in the reverse form. In fact, one of the important research problems that deserves further work is to distinguish the effects of Indian-white identification prior to migration to the city from the acculturative effects and change in identity that accompany the urban experience.

The fourth variable to show a significant correlation with white identification was adequacy of housing (acculturation: Hypothesis 3). This finding also supports the hypothesis that the more nearly the respondent's level of living approximates that of the members of the dominant society the greater the assimilation into the identification with that society. However, caution is advised in interpreting these findings because adequacy of housing may be a function of place of residence; the range of "adequacy" available is likely to be more circumscribed on the reservation than in the city. To assess the possible overlap between urban residence and adequacy of housing, the correlations among the independent variables were examined. The figures in Table 2 reveal that the correlation between adequacy of housing and urban residence is significant ($r = .362$) but is not as strong as the correlation between the former and white identification ($r = .475$). Thus, adequacy of housing (acculturation) may be seen as making an independent contribution to the variance in white identification.

The other variable significantly related to white identification was white ancestry (amalgamation: Hypothesis 5). Because the amount of Indian ancestry is a very real biological fact, often accompanied by obvious physical characteristics, it was expected that the correlation coefficient would be much higher than it was ($r = .391$). Moreover, there is a rather striking difference between this correlation and that between white ancestry of spouse and white identification ($r = .539$). It may be that the modest correlation between white ancestry and white identification is influenced by reservation-urban residence: On the reservation, Indians may

TABLE 2

Intercorrelations Among Five Independent Variables That Were Significantly Related to "White Self-Identification"

	Acculturation	Social Integration		Amalgamation	
	Adequacy of Housing	"Fits in"	Urban Residence	White Ancestry	White Ancestry of Spouse
Acculturation					
Adequacy of housing	1.00	.445[a]	.362[a]	.360[a]	.279[a]
Social integration					
Fits in		1.00	.528[a]	.363[a]	.458[a]
Urban residence			1.00	.146	.373[a]
Amalgamation					
White ancestry				1.00	.525[a]
White ancestry of					
spouse					1.00

[a] Significant at the .001 level.

be generally accepted by their fellow Indians and their few white neighbors according to nonbiological criteria, and thus perceive no relationship between biological identity and sociological identity, but in the urban setting this may not be so. This idea was tested by controlling for residence and computing the two correlation coefficients between white ancestry and white identification, one for reservation Indians only and one for urban Indians. As expected, among the reservation group there was no relationship ($r = .010$), but for the urban group there was a substantial correlation between white ancestry and white identification ($r = .549$). Thus, it seems that Indian people living on the reservation tend to identify themselves by criteria other than biological ones, while in the urban setting white ancestry plays a fairly important part in determining white identification.

Finally, it should be noted that education and regularity of work, two acculturative factors found to be important in previous studies, were not significantly related to white identification. Also, the notion that the young are more assimilated into white society than the old was not supported;[12] instead, there was no relationship between age and white identification.

Concern was expressed earlier about the potential overlap of two independent variables, urban residence and adequacy of housing. In fact, the magnitude of the intercorrelations among the five variables identified in Table 1 as important correlates of white identification suggests that there is serious overlap among them all. Nine of the ten possible combinations of the five variables manifested statistical significance (see Table 2).

Stepwise multiple-regression analysis is a technique which attempts to control for overlap between independent variables. The basic strategy is for the independent variables to enter the regression equation one at a time, while the dependent variable is "partialled" on the variable(s) already in the equation.[13] In effect, this permits the independent variables to compete with each other to determine which have the strongest relationships with the dependent variable, and by controlling for overlap provides a cumulative measure of how much variation of the dependent variable can be explained by sequential combinations of the independent variables.

The results of the analysis are presented in Table 3. The first variable to enter the equation (i.e., the single most important predictor of white identification) was feelings of fitting into white society. It will be recalled that this variable had the highest zero-order correlation with urban residence, and so its dominant position in the multiple-regression analysis was no surprise. The next three variables to enter the multiple regression equation also entered approximately in the order of the size of their zero-order correlations with white identification. However, the last two variables to emerge as significant predictors, namely education and age, were not expected on the basis of their bivariate correlations with white identification. Apparently when one controls for the extent to which one "fits in" with whites, white ancestry of spouse, adequacy of housing and urban residence, education does make a contribution to the variation in scores for white identification. To assess this effect more completely the correlations between education and white identification were calculated for those living on the reservation and those living in the city separately. Among the Indians

TABLE 3

Summary of Stepwise Multiple-Regression Analysis of Eight Independent Variables on White Identification

Step Number	Variable Entered	Multiple R	Multiple R^2	Increase in R^2
1	"Fits in" (Hyp. 4)	.716	.513	
2	White ancestry of spouse (Hyp. 5)	.769	.591	.078
3	Adequacy of housing (Hyp. 3)	.783	.614	.023
4	Urban residence (Hyp. 4)	.789	.622	.008
5	Education (Hyp. 1)	.793	.624	.007
6	Age	(−).797	.635	.006
Total Multiple R and R^2		.797	.635	
Multiple R^2 corrected for "shrinkage"			.612	

who were city dwellers, education *did* make a difference in predicting white identification; the more highly educated Indians tended to identify themselves as whites. But among Indians living on the reservation there was a positive relationship between education and *Indian* identification. Thus, there is nothing about years of schooling per se that makes the Indian more assimilated. In fact, if the education takes place on the reservation, the strength of the individual's identification with Indian people is likely to be enhanced. Another interesting factor to emerge was age. There was essentially no relationship between age and assimilation as measured by white identification. However, *after* the effects of other variables were taken into account, age did have some slight predictive value. To overstate the relationship somewhat, younger people who had a spouse more nearly white than themselves, a relatively nice house, a home in the city and a better than average education were more likely to consider themselves whites than were older people with the same characteristics.

As Table 3 shows, the multiple R for the six independent variables acting simultaneously upon the dependent variable, white identification, was .797 and following correction for shrinkage R^2 was .612.[14] These findings may be interpreted to mean that about two-thirds of the variance for white identification can be accounted for by the variation in the six independent variables listed in Table 3.

Because of the possibility of a conceptual tautology between white identification and feelings of "fitting in," a multiple-regression analysis was conducted with this variable excluded. Results paralleled those of the initial analysis; the remaining variables entered the regression equation in exactly the same order. The most serious consequence of omitting the variable "fits in" was a reduction of explained variance from 61 percent to 50 percent.

In summary, factors found to be significantly related to Indian peoples' identification of themselves as being white included measures of acculturation, social integration, and amalgamation. A measure of social integration with whites emerged as the most powerful predictor of such a self conception, followed by social amalgamation (white ancestry of spouse). Thus it appears that complete assimilation occurs most easily when Indian people are accepted as equals by whites, and are *aware* of that acceptance. Accordingly, if assimilation is the goal, then free interaction, including the possibility of intermarriage, between the two groups is to be encouraged. Also, it appears from this study that some factors which have long been thought crucial in the assimilation process (such as education or successful employment) are not the most powerful predictors of assimilation. Rather, it seems that Indian-white interaction *on an equal basis,* either on the reservation or in the city, is a more critical factor.

NOTES

1   Appreciation is extended to Howard M. Bahr for his assistance in developing this paper.

2   Prodipto Roy, "Assimilation of the Spokane Indians," Bulletin 628, Washington Agricultural Experiment Station, Institute of Agricultural Sciences, Washington State University, May 1961.

3   Joan Ablon, "American Indian Relocation: Problems of Dependency and Management in the City," *Phylon,* 26 (1965), 362-371; Bernard E. Anderson and Donald F. Harvey, "American Indian Labor Mobility: A Problem of Cross Cultural Adjustment," mimeographed (Flagstaff, Arizona, 1970); Robert S. Weppner, "The Economic Absorption of Navajo Indian Migrants in Denver, Colorado," Navajo Urban Relocation Research. Report No. 8 (revised), mimeographed (November 1965); Harriet J. Kupferer, "Health Practices and Educational Aspirations as Indicators of Acculturation and Social Class among Eastern Cherokee," *Social Forces,* 41 (December 1962), 154-162; John A. Price, "Migration and Adaptation of American Indians to Los Angeles," *Human Organization,* 27 (Summer 1968), 168-175; Roy, *op. cit.,* p. 28.

4   Theodore E. Graves, "The Personal Adjustment of Navajo Indian Migrants to Denver, Colorado," *American Anthropologist,* pp. 35-54; and Roy, *op. cit.,* p. 33.

5   Graves, *op. cit.,* pp. 35-54.

6   *Ibid.,* p. 45.

7   Weppner, *op. cit.,* p. 4.

8   Roy, *op. cit.,* pp. 30-33.

9   U.S. Bureau of the Census, U.S. Census of Population: 1960. Subject Reports, Nonwhite Population by Race, Final Report PC(2)-IC. (Washington, D.C.: U.S. Government Printing Office, 1963), p. 2.

10   Joan Ablon, "Relocated American Indians in the San Francisco Bay Area: Social Interaction and Indian Identity." *Human Organization,* 23 (Winter 1964), 302.

11   Anderson and Harvey, *op. cit.*

12   Roy, *op. cit.,* p. 42, 49-50.

13   "This program computes a sequence of multiple linear regression equations in a stepwise manner. At each step one variable is added to (or taken from) the regression equation. The variable added is the one which makes the greatest reduction in the error sum of squares. Equivalently it is the variable which has highest partial correlation with the dependent variable partialled on the variables which have already been added and equivalently it is the variable which, if it were added,

would have the highest F value. . . . Variables are automatically re-moved when their F values become too low." W. J. Dixon, ed., *BMD: Biomedical Computer Programs* (Los Angeles: Health Sciences Computing Facility, Department of Medicine and Public Health, School of Medicine, University of California at Los Angeles), p. 233.

14 When Multiple R is used there is a tendency for a slightly inflated R due to the smaller number of degrees of freedom because of additional calculations. This bias towards an inflated R increases as the number of variables in the equation (n) approaches the number of cases (N). In this study, since the N's are relatively small, the bias toward an inflated R may be substantial and a correction for shrinkage is employed. Quinn McNemar, *Psychological Statistics* (New York: Wiley, 1962), p. 184.

JOHN H. BUSHNELL: FROM AMERICAN INDIAN TO INDIAN AMERICAN: THE CHANGING IDENTITY OF THE HUPA[1]

ABSTRACT

An examination of the cultural history of the Hupa over the last hundred years indicates that the traditional designation "American Indian" is most relevant when applied to the life style developed as an accommodation to reservation living. Rapid modernization following World War II and a changing status vis-à-vis the larger society have placed the contemporary Hupa in a position that may be appropriately characterized by the transposed term "Indian American." In this the Hupa parallel other minority groups in the United States inasmuch as they possess a culture that is largely American in content yet retains a unique sense of ethnic identity. The viability of the Indian component of this identity is discussed in the context of cultural survivals and current interests and concerns within the tribe.

On the Hoppa Valley Reservation surviving aspects of the aboriginal culture are found primarily in attenuated or covert form and the present-day community is for the most part indistinguishable from other rural settlements in northwestern California. Thus the tribal members are un-equivocally members of the predominant American culture. Notwithstanding the overwhelming preponderance of white content in their contemporary Reservation culture, however, the Hupa retain a sense of their own distinctive identity, based on their Indian heritage and ancestry. In this

Source: Reprinted by permission of the American Anthropological Association from *American Anthropologist*, Vol. 70, No. 6, 1968.

they parallel other ethnic minorities in the United States that have moved into the cultural mainstream but continue to identify with a way of life that in reality is once removed in time or space and is largely ceremonial, symbolic, and emotional in its manifestations.

Therefore, I feel it is better to restrict the application of the term "American Indian" to the Hupa as they lived within the framework of the traditional reservation milieu and to designate the contemporary Hupa as "Indian American." This latter term would appear to reflect accurately the culmination of fundamental and far-reaching changes that have transformed Hupa society and culture, particularly since the onset of what may be called the modern period beginning with World War II. In supporting this viewpoint, I will first focus upon the major events and forces that have produced the present-day Hupa with their Indian-American status and self-image. A brief review of the aboriginal culture and a recounting of the life style developed as an accommodation to the imposition of the reservation system will be followed by a description of the transition to the contemporary culture and consideration of a number of the factors that can be seen as functioning in support of the Indian component of this Indian-American identity.[2]

I

Throughout their known history the Hupa have inhabited a broad, scenic mountain valley lying along the Trinity River not far from its confluence with the Klamath. According to Hupa mythology, their first ancestors came spontaneously into being in this same valley. In aboriginal times their permanent villages were situated on the banks of the Trinity, each settlement consisting of a cluster of a dozen or so semisubterranean plank houses. The women and children of the family lived in one house type while the men and older boys from several families shared a sweathouse for lounging and sleeping.[3]

The Hupa lived under unusually favorable conditions. The winters could be cold but never severe; in the summer they moved into temporary shelters at the river's edge to avoid the hotter weather. Virtually all of the material needs of the tribe were met by resources immediately at hand. Clothing was fashioned from buckskin or the hides of smaller animals and decorated largely with local items such as feathers, quills, seeds, and bark fibers, although shells from the coast were a prized addition especially for ceremonial dress. The substances required to weave the baskets for which the northwest California Indians were justly famous were native to the area. Deer, elk, acorns, bulbs, berries, and nuts were taken from the pine and oak forests of the surrounding mountains, while the Trinity provided an abundance of salmon, steelhead, sturgeon, and eel to be eaten fresh and to be dried for storage. Food reserves might run short in the wintertime but this was the exception rather than the rule. The fact that the Hupa had no need to migrate to summer camps in order to insure a year-round food supply as did some California tribes reinforces the picture of close and permanent ties with their home territory.

Given the bounty of river and woodland, contact with neighboring Indians was based more on ceremonial and social relationships than economic exigency. However, dugout canoes made of redwood were obtained from the Yurok who lived downstream on the Klamath and who also supplied the Hupa with seaweed, a source of salt, and dentalium shells, which served a very important function as a medium of exchange. The Hupa were also friendly with the Karok upstream on the Klamath although they had nothing in particular to trade with them. There was some intermarriage among the members of these three groups. They also made a practice of attending one another's dances both as observers and as rival performers. (This trio of tribes has been of considerable interest to anthropologists because they have a common culture but speak three distinct languages.)

The relative ease with which the necessities of life could be procured made time available for cultural elaboration in nonessential areas. Daily living was interwoven with ritual formula and prayer. The Hupa world was populated with spirits and guarded over by a small pantheon of deities. Healing was in the hands of medicine-makers and shamans, the latter specializing in either diagnosis or curing by sucking. Herbal remedies were not limited to the alleviation of physical ills but could be formulated to ward off evil and promote good fortune in such a variety of undertakings as hunting, gambling, basket weaving, love-making, and childbirth.

As would be anticipated in this southern extension of the Northwest Coast complex, two dominant and interrelated themes in Hupa life centered upon wealth and the litigation that a money system facilitated. Dentalium shells, graded by length, served as currency while other objects largely lacking in intrinsic value such as long obsidian blades, dance regalia, and red-headed woodpecker scalps were also regarded as items of wealth. The private ownership concept was extended beyond personal possessions to include the rights to hunting, fishing, and gathering sites.

The monetary scheme provided not only a medium of exchange in daily living but also a major criterion for ascribing social status. Thus one's position in the community was determined largely by the bride-price one's mother had commanded at the time of her marriage with the result that an individual born of a woman for whom nothing had been paid was automatically an outcast or slave at the bottom of the social hierarchy.

Just as the social structure of the tribe was closely tied to the emphasis on wealth, so was its political and ceremonial organization. The richest man in each settlement was looked upon as the leader, the Hupa having no tradition of hereditary chiefs. Leaders with their superior economic resources were expected to augment the food supplies of less well-to-do neighbors during an occasional winter period of scarcity. They were also responsible for the resolution of intra-village feuds and with their monetary assets met the challenge of damage suits from other Hupa settlements. Lawsuits and feuds over insults, bodily injuries, deaths, charges of witchcraft, or property damage could involve not only families or villages but even tribes as adversaries, with protracted negotiations frequently required before payments were agreed upon and the matter closed.

For ceremonial purposes the tribe was split into a northern and a southern division with the leading man of wealth in each section jointly sponsoring the White Deerskin Dance, a world-renewal ritual requiring a preliminary payment to all families bereaved by a death during the year and the accumulation and preparation of sufficient foodstuffs to feed all who attended.

Excepting major ceremonies, the tribe rarely functioned as a single entity. The villages tended to be separatistic in attitude and competed against each other through the medium of games and gambling as well as litigation. Inasmuch as internal jealousy and rivalry seem to have constituted a more or less chronic state of affairs, it is not surprising that village and, especially, tribal affiliation assumed less significance in the life of the Hupa than the family unit, which was the primary locus of loyalty and trust.

II

Compared to the fate of other California tribes whose numbers were decimated by bullets and disease to the point where they ceased to function as societal entities, the Hupa were relatively fortunate in their relationship to the whites.[4] Their remote mountain location shielded them from significant contact until the time of the gold rush. They were temporarily inundated by gold-seekers in 1850, but the sandbars in the Hoopa Valley were quickly exhausted and the number of outsiders dwindled to a few whites who settled and began to farm.

There were occasional conflicts in the immediate post-contact years. Minor incidents would lead to Hupa attacks on pack trains; the whites would burn a Hupa village. The Indian practice of exacting blood revenge upon the outsider most conveniently at hand was particularly disquieting to the whites. To maintain order a military post, Fort Gaston, was established in the center of the valley in 1855 and remained the sole authority in the region for the next decade.[5] Although intermittent hostilities continued for a time, Indian losses from clashes with the Army were relatively slight, e.g., 20 casualties between 1855 and 1860. In 1864 the central territory of the Hupa was designated as a reservation by federal edict and local whites were reimbursed for the lands they were subsequently forced to relinquish. Soldiers continued to be stationed at the fort while agents appointed by the Commissioner of Indian Affairs were charged with administration of the reservation. Hupa living up-river on the Trinity beyond the 12-mile square of the new reservation at first resisted relocation and a series of skirmishes ensued until the recalcitrants were forcibly brought under government control. Some ten years later for reasons that are not clear, the agency administration collapsed and plans were made to abandon the reservation altogether and to remove the tribe to the Round Valley Reservation to the south. Cattle and horses owned by the Hupa had already been driven to Round Valley when plans were reversed and the Army was ordered to assume full charge of the Hoopa Reservation. The military force remained in command until 1892 when the soldiers were withdrawn completely and responsibility reverted once again to the Bureau of Indian Affairs.

The aboriginal settlement pattern persisted for two or three decades following the early contact period although at least one Hupa village had been abandoned soon after the whites arrived because of its proximity to the area taken over by the fort and the agency. The allotment system authorized in 1887 largely disrupted the custom of living in clusters by the river. Families dispersed throughout the valley as they were assigned land for house sites and farming where they built simple homes of mill-cut lumber more or less patterned after the general style then current for rural America.

By and large, the Hupa readily adapted to the clothing, guns, iron tools, horses, and money system of the white men as well as to the basic foodstuffs stocked at the local trading post. However, flour, meat, coffee, and sugar did not supplant but rather came to complement the venison, salmon, and acorn soup of the native diet.

With a shift in federal policy from simply isolating the Indian to "uplifting" and "civilizing" him, a boarding school for the Hupa and neighboring tribes was established on the reservation in 1893. All pupils were required to reside at the school with home visits limited to once or twice a month. The children adhered to a quasi-military regimen that included drilling, calisthenics, unquestioned obedience, and severe punishment for infractions. They were also obliged to perform heavy chores vital to the maintenance of the residents and the operation of the physical plant. Instruction was in English and conversing in an Indian language was strictly forbidden. In addition to the three R's and occasional activities such as singing, games, and holiday programs there was vocational training for the boys in agricultural techniques and in trades such as blacksmithing and carpentry, and practice in domestic skills for the girls. Runaways were a chronic problem reflecting the resistance of many of the Hupa children and often their parents to the imposition of this institution, which for them was an alien and cruel system. Nevertheless, it is probable that the school with its forcible inculcation of white culture was one of the more effective instruments in the campaign to eradicate as many aspects of the aboriginal life style as possible.

Protestant missionaries were active in the valley as early as 1873. Although they had the support of the local Indian agent, their proselytizing seems to have made few inroads in subsequent years. Thus by the turn of the century the reservation contained two churches (Presbyterian, Episcopalian), three missionaries (one male, two female), and 14 converts.

At about this time officials complained of the frequent firing of guns to frighten away the Indian devils, of the distressing practice of curing by sucking, of the persistence of gambling games, and of the difficulty of rooting out native marriage customs, the court of Indian offenses notwithstanding.

For the first third of the twentieth century the cultural status of the Hupa remained in most essentials much the same as in the late 1800s.

Many Indian families continued to support themselves by combining hunting, fishing, and gathering with limited farming and stock raising on their land allocations. A small number obtained some income by hauling freight with team and wagon for traders or the government. Although there were occasionally opportunities to work in a local sawmill or in a logging or tanbark operation, the only jobs likely to be available were those attached to the school, agency, hospital, or forestry and road crews. A few of the more elderly people preferred to live on in the old semisubterranean houses with the assistance of government rations.

A number of whites were now living on the reservation. These were either "squaw men" who had married into the tribe or outsiders who had purchased land from Indians holding deeds to their property. Over the decades since the establishment of Fort Gaston, the Hupa had acquired from both soldiers and settlers a substantial infusion of white "blood" so that their physical appearance ranged from the characteristic broad-faced Indian with a stocky body build to individuals who would appear to be totally Caucasoid in their ancestry.

The potential for change increased progressively during the 1920s and 1930s but actual alterations in reservation life were slow in coming. The granting of citizenship to Indians in 1924, while undoubtedly of symbolic significance, seems to have had virtually no effect upon the day-to-day concerns or the overall outlook of the Hupa at that time. The tribe voted not to participate under the Indian Reorganization Act of 1934. Changing federal policy was reflected in the conversion of the Indian boarding school to a public elementary day school during the 1930s and the eventual addition of a four-year high school. While the Hoopa school was no longer deliberately employed as an instrument for de-Indianization, it served increasingly as an agent for noncoercive acculturation.

The isolation of the reservation continued for a considerable time despite the advent of the automobile. Few of the Indians could afford a car, the roads were poor, and the river had to be crossed by ferry. The paving of the one road that ran through the valley and the addition of a bridge in the mid 1930s facilitated travel but most Hupa made the 50-odd mile trip to Eureka only once or twice a year when they could arrange a ride or afford the bus that arrived daily with the mail.

Rudiments of modern facilities—electric generator, telephone, piped-in spring water—were to be found only in the immediate area of the agency buildings and were generally restricted to official use. Most Hupa families relied upon kerosene for light, wood for fuel, a spring or hand pump for water, and word-of-mouth for communicating with each other.

Those aspects of the aboriginal culture that had survived the nineteenth century, e.g., the use of native foods, the basket weaving, the ceremonies and games, the curing rituals, and many of the supernatural beliefs, continued as important though often diminished facets in the lives of many of the people. Thus the native language was beginning to lose ground as the younger generation spoke Hupa with their elders but usually conversed in English among themselves.

The interval between 1865 and World War II, which has just been summarized, can be described as the traditional reservation period in the history of the Hupa Indians. These were the decades during which the Hupa, as wards of the government, were denied any institutions or channels that would give them an effective voice in directing their own affairs. The reservation was a self-contained unit with its own hospital, its Indian police, and its welfare system. All complaints and all matters requiring official action or approval came before the Indian agent whose authority was frequently experienced as highly dictatorial. The alleged exploitations and felt injustices attributed to bygone agents can still be recounted at length by older Hupa Indians.

During this long period when, as some of the more militant members of the tribe put it, "We were in the Department of the Interior along with the buffalo," they were consistently regarded by whites as a special breed that was to be segregated first and later to be "civilized" for eventual assimilation. In the very act of attempting to eradicate the more tenacious survivals of aboriginal culture (it will be recalled that as late as 1923 the BIA forbade the practice of Indian religions), the dominant society, more often than not, was underscoring and denigrating the distinctions that differentiate the Indian from the white. It was within this context with its stress upon anomaly and separateness that the term "American Indian," or simply "Indian," was appropriate. The adjective "American" had become, of course, the noun by which whites identified themselves and its use as a modifier preceding the word "Indian" was little more than a convention designed to separate the natives of India from those of this continent rather than to suggest commonalities between the original American and his conqueror.

III

Although drawing the line between the closing of one epoch and the opening of the next is often of necessity a somewhat arbitrary matter, World War II can be said to mark the beginning of the modern reservation period even though the war itself did not at first effect significant changes in the life of the Hupa. Sixty-three members of the tribe served in the armed forces during the war, most of them subsequently returning to the valley. A study of the acculturative role of these ex-GI's by the writer in 1948 revealed that the war experiences had not notably altered either attitudes, values, or plans for the future (Bushnell 1950). Once having spent their mustering-out pay and drawn their "52-20" (virtually no use was made of the long-range benefits of the GI Bill of Rights), these veterans expected to resume the life style they had known before, i.e., hunting and fishing year-round, living on tax-free land, perhaps farming and, if the need arose, working at whatever job might be available with the knowledge that the agency had usually supplied work when other sources of livelihood failed. In actuality, the reservation they had known was considerably modified during the post-war years by the introduction into its midst of a booming lumber industry that created an abundance of relatively well-paid jobs in the mills and in the woods. Most of the timber was being cut from forests owned by the tribe and the Hupa became the beneficiaries of stumpage fees with per capita payments to each man, woman, and child on the tribal roll amounting to several hundred dollars twice a year. New businesses—another general store, a restaurant, a garage and gas station—began to appear. Several hundred whites moved into the valley, living in trailers, cabins, or tents and working in the sawmills or logging operations.

Per capita funds and the shift to a wage economy, which provided employment for all Indian males willing and able to work, brought an end to virtually all farming. The new affluence was perhaps most immediately evident in the proliferation of automobiles on the reservation. Trips to Eureka or Redding became commonplace, and the younger generation, in particular, would joy-ride up and down the valley, sometimes going outside to buy a case of beer or to drink at a bar that would serve Indians. More and more dependence was placed upon purchased foodstuffs. Salmon and steelhead were still taken from the Trinity during the spring and fall runs, but most hunting and gathering activities declined to a point where they no longer contributed significantly to the food supply.

By 1950, after many years of delay, power lines finally reached the reservation, a development that, in combination with their growing prosperity, enabled the Hupa to bring the material side of their culture up-to-date, one might say, almost instantaneously. Television, refrigerators, deep freezers, washers, dryers, and other electrical applicances became standard household equipment for all but the most marginal families.

A decade later telephone wires were strung through the valley. A barber shop, a beauty shop, a TV repair service, a laundromat, a gift shop, a clothing store, a supermarket, two new gas stations, a drive-in, a motel, another restaurant, a trailer park, even a landing strip for small planes were added to the expanding number of goods and services available to the community. An enlarged and consolidated school district was formed and a modern complex of buildings constructed for what had become an integrated student population.

A small but increasing number of Hupa, together with a larger proportion of whites, were directly involved in this mushrooming activity. They owned some of the small businesses, rented cabins and trailer space, helped organize a miniature Chamber of Commerce, and served on the school board. During this period there was a pronounced increase in the number of intermarriages between Hupa and whites, the latter outnumbering the Indian population by the mid-1950s.

The existence of the persisting aboriginal traits became more precarious. Only the older people spoke Hupa as a first tongue and the younger generation was likely to know at best only a few native words, often the profane ones. The tribal folktales were rarely recounted by parents to children. The two native plank houses preserved on one of the dance grounds were buried by one flood in the mid-1950s and swept away by a second flood during the winter of 1964/65. The major ceremonial, the White Deerskin Dance, was held at seven or eight-year intervals rather than biennially as had been the custom. The number of skilled basket weavers declined to one or two women who worked at the craft only sporadically. Although a few canoes and hand-woven gill nets were still in use, it had become common practice to catch salmon in a nylon net of modern manufacture, strung across the river channel with the aid of an inflatable life raft or a fiberglass boat.

Thus it seems clear that, notwithstanding the survival of certain indigenous elements, the decades since World War II have witnessed a thoroughgoing Americanization and modernization of most aspects of the reservation culture. Inasmuch as the Hupa, judged by both cultural and behavioral criteria, are far more American than Indian, it seems appropriate at this point to reverse the customary designation "American Indian" to the more definitive "Indian American." As such, they share a status similar to that of other hyphenated minority groups, e.g., Italian Americans or Japanese Americans, in that they possess a culture that is largely American in content yet retain a unique sense of ethnic identity.[6] The term gains further validity from the fact that, beyond the Indian-white ratio of culture content per se, the image of the Hupa has been changing both in their own eyes and in those of their white neighbors. Closely related to the modification of this image is the transition from a dependent to an increasingly independent legal and quasi-legal status as reflected in the extension to the tribe of nearly all the rights and duties applying to other citizens.

The Hupa were subject to the draft during World War II and subsequent conflicts. They have the right to vote and the obligation to pay taxes (trust lands excepted). State law and county ordinances now include the reservation under their jurisdiction and the county sheriff and his deputies have supplanted the Indian police. It is no longer illegal for an Indian to possess or drink liquor although the Hoopa Tribal Council has yet to approve the sale of alcohol on the reservation. The government hospital was closed a number of years ago and a community clinic and hospital established in conjunction with a voluntary prepaid medical plan. The federal Public Health Service retains its operations in the field of sanitation (which had been transferred from the Bureau of Indian Affairs in 1955) but other public health and social welfare services are administered through county agencies and personnel.

Thus, the larger society by law and administrative edict has reached the point of according virtual equality to the Hupa Indian. The wardship system is gone and the nineteenth-century concept of fundamental and disabling differences in race and culture has been supplanted by two contemporary ideas: first, that racial distinctions are not a valid basis for exclusion; and, second, that cultural differences are worthy of preservation. Although the Hupa have at times in their history experienced the humiliation and bitterness of a subjugated people, they seem never to have been exposed to the devastating bigotry and discrimination that have characterized Indian-white relationships in many areas of the country. In some measure this may have contributed to the present picture of an interaction between Hupa and non-Indian residents of the reservation that is relatively free of friction, slights, or chauvinism based on race. As for the matter of cultural worth, the self-esteem of the Hupa has been bolstered in recent decades not only by the growth at the national level of a concern for the status and problems of the Indian qua Indian but also by the periodic visits to the reservation of ethnologists, linguists, musicologists, and other scholars and students.

IV

Notwithstanding the near-total sweep of the modern culture supported as it is by the economic system, the mass media, and the accelerating technological revolution, the Indian component of the Hupa identity exhibits considerable viability. This phenomenon seems to be related to several factors among which may be noted the protective and unifying aspects of the reservation system, the beginning of what appears to be a small Hupa renaissance, and the tenacity of certain covert aboriginal features, particularly in the realm of belief, that survive in the face of rapid and continuing culture change.

The territorial integrity provided by the reservation has enabled the Hupa to remain on the land of their ancestors with its ancient village sites, burial grounds, and dance fields. The support for the tribal image deriving from this geographic continuity is reinforced by the off-season hunting privileges and the right to use fish nets granted to the local Indians and denied to whites living in the same valley. The ubiquitous problems growing out of the reservation system—a stalemate over reallotment, the question of termination, land claims against the federal government, the threat of inundation of the reservation if and when a proposed dam is constructed on the Trinity, chronic issues before the Tribal Council and its subsidiary committees, the sending of delegations to Sacramento and to Washington—constantly serve to underscore the Indian side of their Indian American status.

Faced with the possible extinction of most of the remaining aboriginal traditions within a generation or two, a number of community leaders have reacted with a sense of urgency and are attempting either as individuals or in small groups to perpetuate or revive some of the more cherished and valued aspects of the old way of life. While these efforts tend to be sporadic and, more often than not, to fall short of the goal, they reflect a deeply felt pride that communicates to other members of the tribe. In recent years the ceremonial dances have been largely the result of the work of a handful of such people who, for example, built a new sweathouse in 1965 prior to the annual Brush dance as a replacement for the one lost in the flood. The dances are attended by the tribe almost in its entirety and it is significant that numbers of the younger Hupa have been joining with the older generation in the dance pit. Efforts to engage the neighboring Yurok or Karok in the traditional shinny contest have not always been successful in the last few years but the concept of continuing the competition remains alive. For a time there was a course in native basket weaving for high school girls and the ceremonial leader of the Hupa has given several demonstrations on tribal crafts and lore to elementary school classes. A number of women have experimented with the utilization of aboriginal techniques and/or decorative motifs for such items as pottery, pendants, basketry, earrings, and woven mats. Several individuals have indicated an interest in recording some aspect of their cultural heritage: one person would like to write an autobiography; another, a tribal history; a third, a volume of Hupa tales. There is talk of the need for a local museum, of the possibility of placing the reservation in the status of an historical monument, and controversy over the propriety of filming the dances and recording the sacred songs.

Although renaissance as a term probably overstates the actual situation, there is unquestionably a growing involvement in the Hupa tradition, particularly so if a comparison is drawn with the immediate post-World War II years when a depressed community with its own "lost generation" of youth presented a picture of rapid demise for its Indian culture coupled with a prospective termination of the reservation, which had been announced as imminent. Today the demand for basket hats among the Hupa is such that the limited output of the very few women who still weave is committed to meeting a backlog of requests from their own people. The Hupa regalia and other native artifacts are treasured by their owners who bring them out on the occasions when dances are held. Families who have resisted the temptation over the years to sell such items either to other tribal members or to outsiders are counted as fortunate. The basket cradle is sufficiently well adapted to the needs of both mother and infant so that it is used not only by the Hupa but also by a number of white families living on the reservation. Although acorns are gathered only sporadically and prepared with aid of a coffee grinder or blender rather than a mortar and pestle, acorn soup retains a special significance both as a direct link to the past and as a ceremonial food in surviving ritual. Even the younger generation is prone to agree with the elders that acorn soup tastes best when made by the stone-boiling method.

The growing concern for the fate of the Hupa heritage can be characterized as a largely endogenous development that has proceeded with little, if any, reference to a generalized pan-Indian movement. The Hupa tend to be possessive about their native traditions and insistent that they be kept unadulterated, i.e., not mixed with imports from other tribes, for example, the Plains Indian war bonnet or the use of the term chief. One or two families have presented Hupa dances in costume at Indian shows held away from the reservation and have met with varying degrees of disfavor on the part of tribal members not only because of the commercial exploitation involved and the use of such props as a tipi and a fake campfire but also because a public display of authentic aboriginal ceremonies and objects out of context is seen as a defilement of the sacred.

Some of the deepest feelings associated with the Hupa sense of Indianness are related to beliefs that have roots in the pre-White past. For those who have grown up on the reservation it can probably be fairly said that nearly everyone from the least to the most acculturated gives credence (not always openly acknowledged) to the power of native prayer, to the presence of Indian spirits, to the concept of good and bad "medicine," or to the inevitability with which retribution will follow violation of a religious proscription. Thus no one would go behind the line of performers at the Deerskin Dance and take the chance of "spoiling the world." Field work following the two most recent floodings of the reservation revealed a prevailing set of attitudes centering around a conviction that the high waters and the havoc wrought were the consequence of personal or ritual transgressions and desecration of the dance grounds (Bushnell 1967). This persisting substratum of belief in the continuing sanctity and efficacy of Indian paraphernalia, religious ritual, and ceremonial sites can be seen as one of the more significant forces serving to perpetuate an enduring core of Indian identity in the midst of a twentieth-century America.

NOTES

1   An abbreviated version of this paper was presented at the twenty-sixth meeting of The Society for Applied Anthropology, Washington, D.C., May 6, 1967. The author wishes to express his appreication to the Department of Anthropology at the University of California, the National Academy of Sciences—National Research Council, and the Wenner-Gren Foundation for Anthropological Research for grants supporting field work on the Hoopa Reservation in 1948, 1956, and 1965 respectively.

2   At the reading of this paper Margaret Mead noted that an attempt had been made to popularize the term "Indian American" during World War II. The intent seems to have been comparable to present efforts to upgrade the image and status of the Negro in the United States by adopting the term "Negro American." However, in the present paper the rationale for the transposition of the designation American Indian to Indian American lies in the fact that the terminology does, in fact, reflect the changing cultural and social reality of the Hupa tribe.

3   The major reference on the aboriginal Hupa is Goddard (1903). See also Kroeber (1925), Wallace (1947a, 1947b), and Goldschmidt (1951).

4   This summary of the contact and reservation period is based upon Goddard (1903: 8-11), Cook (1943), Anderson (1956), Department of the Interior (1903), Barnett (1940), Goldschmidt and Driver (1940), and informant accounts.

5   Anderson (1956: 98) takes exception to Goddard (and therefore also to Kroeber who followed Goddard on this point) and places the founding of Fort Gaston in the year 1858.

6   In discussing this paper at the Applied Anthropology meetings, Alexander Lesser correctly observed that while for most minorities in the United States there exists a motherland that serves as a source of sustenance for the perpetuation of ethnic identity in the face of increasing assimilation, the Indian American has no such fountainhead to draw upon as his culture disappears.

REFERENCES CITED

Anderson, G. E. (1956), The Hoopa Valley Indian Reservation in north-western California: a study of its origins. Unpublished M.A. thesis. Berkeley, University of California.

Barnett, H. G. (1940), Culture processes. American Anthropologist 42: 21-48.

Bushnell, J. H. (1950), Hupa veterans: a key to acculturation barriers. Paper presented to American Anthropological Association, Western States branch meeting, Berkeley.

———(1967), Hupa reaction to the Trinity River floods; post-hoc recourse to aboriginal belief. Paper prepared for annual meeting, American Anthropological Association, Washington, D.C.

Cook, S. F. (1943), The conflict between the California Indian and white civilization. Ibero-Americana 22 (21-24).

Department of the Interior (1903), Report of the Commissioner of Indian Affiars, 1901-02. Washington, D.C.

Goddard, P. E. (1903), Life and culture of the Hupa. University of California Publications in American Archaeology and Ethnology 1: 1-88.

Goldschmidt, W. R. (1951), Ethics and the structure of society: an ethnological contribution to the sociology of knowledge. American Anthropologist 53: 506-524.

Goldschmidt, W. R., and H. E. Driver (1940), The Hupa white deerskin dance. University of California Publications in American Archaeology and Ethnology 35: 103-142.

Kroeber, A. L. (1925), Handbook of the Indians of California. Bureau of American Ethnology, Bulletin 78: 128-137.

Wallace, W. J. (1947a), Hupa child-training—a study in primitive education. Educational Administration and Supervision 33: 13-25.

———(1947b), Personality variation in a primitive society. Journal of Personality 15: 321-328.

SEYMOUR PARKER: ETHNIC IDENTITY AND ACCULTURATION IN TWO ESKIMO VILLAGES[1]

The major purpose of this paper is to examine some attitudes concerning ethnic identity in two Eskimo populations in Alaska. These attitudes and their interrelationships will be viewed within the context of two villages representing different stages on the acculturation continuum. The term "ethnic identity," as used here, refers to the evaluation of one's

Source: Reprinted by permission of the American Anthropological Association from *American Anthropologist,* Vol. 66, No. 2, 1964.

membership identification with his own and other ethnic groups. It includes the degree of attraction to or repulsion from these groups. Hopefully, the findings will contribute to an understanding of the relationship between institutional and psychological change and will provide insight into the behavior of ethnic groups which are acculturating to Western society. This in turn has bearing upon the question of the type of individuals in such groups who are most receptive to Western influences and innovations. A subsidiary aim of this paper is to comment on the use of imaginative projective stories to obtain meaningful data on selected attitudes during a short field-work period (see Goldschmidt and Edgerton 1961). When the stories are viewed against the background of the social roles of young people in the two villages, it will be possible to learn more about the articulation of projective test data with motivational elements in an ongoing social situation.

Some investigators (Rainey 1947:280; Spencer 1959:280; Chance 1960) report that the groups they have studied maintain a clear (and comfortable) identity as Eskimos, while others (Hughes 1958; Leighton 1959:117; Stefansson 1958:80) have been impressed with the considerable confusion and ambiguity in this area. Since no single set of attitudes concerning ethnic group membership accompanies all degrees of culture contact and acculturation in different villages, it is not possible to generalize about acculturation of *the* Alaskan Eskimo. Hallowell's (1950) work on the Ojibwa indicates that attitudes among sub-groups of a society will vary considerably with their position on the acculturation continuum. Such attitudes can best be viewed as a function of the web of social roles existing in the respective groups (James 1961).

Although descriptions and classifications of the stages of acculturation in the anthropological literature are both profuse and varied, the occurrence of two nodal points is emphasized consistently (Caudill 1952; Vogt 1951:88-89; Hughes 1958). At the first stage delineated beyond the relatively unacculturated phase, aspects of the material culture and attitudes of Western society are utilized in an *imitative* manner. These do not affect the basic self-identity of the individuals concerned and are not significantly related to their lives. Vogt (1951:88-89) exemplifies this by the Navaho Indian who wears a wrist watch and consults it frequently, but who is not basically concerned with punctuality or with carefully allocating time for future activities. At the second stage in the acculturation process, individuals actually begin to *internalize* Western values and patterns of behavior associated with the use of technological elements; these values cease to be 'epiphenomena and become part of the motivational system and self-identity. Hughes (1958) suggests that "individuals do not merely imitate the cultural forms of the host group; rather, they identify with it, or with that segment which is most congenial to their own personality and cultural values." At this stage problems of ethnic identity frequently become prominent. The villages chosen for study represent, respectively, these two stages of acculturation.

It has been noted in studies of acculturation among non-Western peoples and minority groups in our own society that individuals who wish to "move toward" Western cultural values and practices also frequently have negative feelings about their own group (Leighton 1959; Boggs 1960; Barnett 1941). Since they regard their ethnic (or minority) group membership as an impediment to further mobility, their attempts to disassociate themselves psychologically from their own group are understandable. Such individuals are also likely to have a high level of hostility (De Vos 1961:606; Doob 1957; Vogt 1951:106) directed toward the dominant White group, to which they are oriented and wish to emulate (Frazier 1962:176; Lewin 1941:189, ff). Doob (1957) reports that African youth who have considerable contact with Westerners tend to be more frustrated and aggressive than others, and to be relatively more hostile toward Western society. This hostility may stem from their internalization of some of the prevailing negative ethnic stereotypes, or from feeling seriously disadvantaged in the competition with Westerners for material goods and social status. In order to understand further the dynamics of ethnic identification in the populations studied, the findings of this study will be viewed against the background of some of the social-role conflicts existing in the two villages.

METHODS

The data presented in this paper were gathered in the course of a more inclusive study of the relationship between cultural values and receptivity to Western schooling in two Eskimo and one Tlingit Indian village.[2] This study, sponsored by the Department of Education of the University of Alaska, involved a one-month stay in each of the two Eskimo villages. During this short period, I employed such anthropological field methods as interviewing key informants and participant-observation; in addition, I utilized five pictures designed to elicit stories relevant to ethnic identity. Stories obtained in response to two of these pictures will be analyzed in this paper. The pictures ... were each drawn on 9 × 12-inch card and portrayed situations, people, and objects from Western and Eskimo society. Card 1 depicts an Eskimo village in which an airplane pilot is speaking with two adolescent Eskimo boys wearing Western-type clothing. A short distance away, a child and three adult Eskimos in traditional costume are watching them. Card 2 pictures two Eskimo adolescents walking on the street of a Western Community; nearby are a well-dressed "White" couple who seem to be looking at the young people.

Stories were obtained from a total of 60 Eskimos, aged 13 to 20, in the two villages. Thirty-three of these were from the village of Alakanuk and were divided approximately equally between both sexes. They had a mean age of 15 years and an average school grade attainment of 5.2. The 27 subjects from Kotzebue had a similar sex composition, a mean age of 15.8 years, and an average school grade attainment of 8.8.

The cards were presented to the subject only after an informal interview about aspects of life in the village. This procedure facilitated a more relaxed relationship and partially accounted for the low number (three) of incomplete sets of stories. Each subject was instructed to look at the card for as long as necessary and then to "tell what is going on now, what happened before, and how it is going to end." The stories were fully recorded with no interruptions or prompting. All of the interviews were obtained through referrals from individuals who themselves had been previously interviewed. I am not aware of any circumstances that would have introduced a bias in selecting the samples.

Scoring categories were devised and defined as precisely as possible. A research assistant and I then scored some sample stories independently until we obtained a high degree of reliability. My assistant scored the stories after all data identifying the particular village were removed from the protocols.

In this paper, the following sequence of presentation will be observed. The two villages representing, respectively, an early (imitative) and a later (internalizing) stage of acculturation will be described briefly in order to provide the social context and some social-role problems of adolescents in each situation. The data relating to ethnic identity among the sample of young people in the two villages will then be described and analyzed.

THE VILLAGE OF ALAKANUK

Alakanuk is located on a fork of the lower Yukon, approximately 15 miles from the Bering Sea. The village is made up of about 60 mud-packed wooden one- (or occasionally two-) room dwellings, a small trading post, a salmon cannery that operates during the summer months, and a post office. According to a recent Bureau of Indian Affairs census, Alakanuk has a population of 278, most of whom are "full-blooded" Yupik-speaking Eskimos. There are only nine residents of "mixed blood" and two permanent white residents (the Roman Catholic priest, who has lived in Alakanuk for more than 20 years, and a retired postmaster); in addition, a white school teacher and his family have recently moved there.

The community is relatively isolated from sizeable Eskimo and white population centers in Alaska, and the surrounding region has very few large-scale cannery operations, mines, or military installations. Air and river transportation to the village is poor. Except for the Catholic church that was established in the area around 1900, there have been almost no local missionary activities.

Young people in Alakanuk identify their essential economic roles as hunters, fishermen, or housewives. These traditional Eskimo pursuits are given social approval and carry prestige with the villagers. There are almost no alternative occupations in the local area, nor are there strong aspirations to enter into Western vocational roles. In the 1960 Bureau of Indian Affairs census, only four Eskimo residents (the storekeeper, the postmaster and agent for the airlines, the cannery foreman, and the school janitor) listed occupations other than "hunting and fishing." The dominant reference group for young people in Alakanuk are members of their own society who excel in these tasks, rather than representatives of Western

society. The significant socialization experiences of childhood and adolescence are geared to provide both the technical skills and the motivation
to perform these economic roles efficiently. Consequently, there is little
discontinuity between early technical and motivational preparation for
economic tasks and the role requirements later in life. Usually the actual
(and/or anticipated) economic role of the adolescent is clear, receives
approval of significant others, and is well within the young person's
competence. Despite an increasing interest in schooling and skilled jobs, the
majority of young people plan to live in Alakanuk when their education is
completed. The operation of the small salmon cannery for six to eight
weeks of the summer fits neatly into the pattern of traditional economic
activities during this season (i.e., salmon fishing and processing fish for
storage). Aside from this limited source of wage labor, the cycle of
subsistence activities is not radically different than in the past.

Although the consumption of "store-bought" Western commodities is
increasing, there is no strong desire for a qualitatively different economic
existence, nor is there a basic dissatisfaction with the prevailing mode. In
spite of their meager subsistence, many of the villagers contrast the relative
plenty of the present with their traditionally marginal existence. Few of
the Eskimos have worked in any of the larger Western communities in
Alaska. Visits to such centers as Anchorage are mainly confined to the
two-week National Guard training period for some of the men, and to stays
in the government hospital. This limited contact with urban centers or with
Western mass media of communication has prevented a rapid expansion of
desires for material commodities or for larger socio-economic goals.

The first school in the village was opened by the Bureau of Indian
Affairs in 1960. The average educational attainment of villagers aged
40-and-over and 20-30 is 1.9 and 3.1 grades, respectively. Although the
grade attainment is somewhat higher for those aged 19 and younger, only
four individuals in this group have reached the high-school level. English is
seldom spoken in any of the homes or used in ordinary social interaction.
The major motivation for education among the young villagers is to acquire
some basic skills to facilitate transactions with Western society (i.e., reading
and ordering from store catalogs, communication with government agencies
regarding pensions, relief, taxes, etc.). They also feel that such skills might
enable them to obtain occasional temporary jobs in one of the towns to
supplement their incomes. Their low school-grade attainment reflects the
fact that opportunities to utilize educational skills for vocational employment in the local area are meager and that prestige is still associated with
hunting and fishing.

THE VILLAGE OF KOTZEBUE

Kotzebue is located 26 miles above the Arctic Circle, on the northern
part of a peninsula bounded by Kotzebue Sound on the west and north,
and by Hotham Inlet on the east. Since the early nineteenth century it has
been an important trade and recreation center for neighboring inland

Eskimo settlements, whalers, and prospectors in search of gold. The community has grown rapidly since World War II, due to the influx of government installations and private business. Most of the houses in the village contain such items as Western furniture, oil stoves, and radios. There are 1,290 residents (1960), of whom about 250 are white; a large portion of the Eskimo population is of "mixed" Eskimo-Caucasian extraction.

Economic life in Kotzebue involves wage employment for part of the year and the traditional Eskimo pursuits of hunting and fishing for the other. Although more than half their real income is obtained from the natural resources of the area, the villagers do not regard themselves primarily as hunters and fishermen. In the 1960 Bureau of Indian Affairs census, over 90 percent of the adult males listed "laborer" or various semi-skilled and skilled occupations. Most of the locally-available jobs (mainly on construction projects) pay high wages although they are un-skilled and notoriously unstable and seasonal. In the construction work and the permanent enterprises in Kotzebue (e.g., the Public Health hospital, the Wien Airlines, and the local barge company), the more skilled and super-visory positions are almost always held by whites. It has been a long-standing practice for many villagers to migrate for part of the year to work in one of the large population centers in Alaska. Summer employment in fish canneries in the southwestern part of the state is still frequent, but work on the railroads and in the mines of Nome and Fairbanks has declined.

The increase of cash income, as well as the extensive contact with a white population and Western mass media of communication, has engendered a growing dissatisfaction with hunting and fishing, especially among the younger generation. They feel that these traditional economic tasks are too demanding as full-time pursuits, yield an insufficient income, and bear but little relationship to the assignment of prestige or leadership positions in the community. The "important" people are likely to be whites whose economic and educational achievements are usually beyond the reach of most Eskimo youth. Young Eskimos in Kotzebue no longer desire "things" from Western society; they now aspire to many of its material *and* social values.

Kotzebue has had a Bureau of Indian Affairs elementary school for many years, and the Friends Church has operated a high school in the community since 1960. The average educational attainment of those villagers aged 40-and-over is slightly more than grade 5; the corresponding grade levels for those aged 20-29 and 15-19 are 6.7 and 8.2, respectively. English is spoken with varying degrees of facility by almost all the villagers. Although many young people begin high school, a large percentage drop out before graduation.

In addition to an increasing discontent with the traditional Eskimo way of life, most of the youth in Kotzebue are confused about the kinds of occupations they would like, and where (and how) to live. Their reference values and role models derive mainly from Western society but are essentially unclear and shifting. There are generational differences about acceptable goals for young people, as well as conflicting evaluations of

Western and traditional Eskimo society. Traditionally-valued Eskimo activities can neither fulfill their growing desires for material items, nor provide the prestige and status they seek. Their lack of education, vocational skills, and general knowledge of white society provokes anxiety about competing in the white world; yet they are increasingly impelled to do so.

In addition to the conflict over economic role alternatives for the youth of Kotzebue, there is the concomitant development of ambivalence in ethnic identity. As their reference values stem increasingly from Western society, the young people are beginning to feel ashamed of their Eskimo background. This ambivalence is sharpened by the relative absence of Eskimo prestige models and by their frequent encounters with the negative ethnic stereotypes held by some of the white transients (laborers and servicemen) in the community. Although they are beginning to incorporate these negative evaluations as part of their self-image, they also resent members of the dominant group who evoke them. Under such conditions, it is understandable that many young people have a devalued image of their "Eskimo-ness" (and the associated way of life), which they perceive as a barrier to achieving goals in Western society. At the same time, they have serious doubts about their ability to compete with Whites for desired jobs and status. This perception of whites (and white society) as a source of their frustration generates hostility toward them.

In present-day Kotzebue, the traditional Eskimo value of "familism" (i.e., family cohesion and mutual aid patterns) poses another instance of role conflict for many young people. On one hand, they are increasingly exposed to the value of individualistic success, which stresses the acqui- sition of an education and a job in which they can apply and develop their skills. However, since this requires an extended absence from home and the diversion of available funds for education and vocational training, it con- flicts sharply with their self-image as a "good" son or daughter. This latter role requires staying with, and helping, family members who are in need. Thus, young people find themselves on the horns of a dilemma, regardless of their choice. This problem manifests itself in the high rate of school drop-outs in Kotzebue, and in the reluctance to accept vocational oppor- tunities involving long and distant separations from their families.

FINDINGS

This section consists of an analysis of attitudes related to ethnic identity in stories produced by adolescent subjects in Alakanuk and Kotzebue. The categories used to score these attitudes are described in the text and in the relevant tables. The data derived from the stories elicited by Card 1 (Eskimo-village setting; see Methods) are presented first.

Table I shows the relative degree of generalized hostility in the two village samples. There was significantly[3] more hostility expressed by subjects in Kotzebue.

The following two tables are concerned with the direction of this

TABLE I

Hostility

(Card #1)

| | Expression of Hostility* | | |
Village	1. Absent	2. Present	Total
Alakanuk	76% (25)	24% (8)	100% (33)
Kotzebue	37% (10)	63% (17)	100% (27)

p = <.01>.001

*Any definite expression of interpersonal negative affect (anger, suspicion, annoyance, etc.) on the part of one of the characters in the story.

TABLE II

Inter-Ethnic Social Distance

(Card #1)

| | Inter-Ethnic Social Distance | | | |
Village	1. Absent	2. Present— small degree*	3. Present— large degree**	Total
Alakanuk	73% (24)	15% (5)	12% (4)	100% (33)
Kotzebue	33% (9)	22% (6)	44% (12)	100% (27)

p = <.01>.001

*Feelings of suspicion, discomfort, or estrangement between the pilot (i.e., Caucasian) and any of the Eskimo figures.

**Overt expression of hostility or aggression between the pilot and any of the Eskimo figures.

hostility. Table II indicates the degree of "inter-ethnic social distance" expressed in the stories. As used here, this concept includes not only definite expressions of overt hostility, but also feelings of estrangement, discomfort, or suspicion between any of the Eskimo characters and the White pilot. There was significantly more inter-ethnic social distance manifested in the stories from Kotzebue than in those from Alakanuk.

Next, let us consider "intra-ethnic social distance" (Table III), which was determined in the stories by: (a) explicit expressions of contrasting attitudes toward the same object by members of the two different Eskimo groups (e.g., the boys "are interested in the pilot and want to know all about what he is doing," while "these others are saying that they wish the pilot would go away and not come back anymore"); and (b) an expression of overt hostility by members of one Eskimo group toward members of the other. Table III indicates that there was considerably more intra-ethnic social distance in the Kotzebue sample. When the two response categories (i.e., Table III, columns 2 and 3) were combined, the differences between the villages reached the .001 level of probability.

Subjects from Kotzebue manifested more generalized hostility, more inter-ethnic, and more intra-ethnic social distance than subjects from Alakanuk. In Table IV we consider differences between stories from the

TABLE III

*Intra-Ethnic Social Distance**
(Card #1)

	Intra-Ethnic Social Distance			
Village	1. Absent	2. Explicit differences	3. Expressions of hostility	Total
Alakanuk	91% (30)	3% (1)	6% (2)	100% (33)
Kotzebue	41% (11)	22% (6)	37% (10)	100% (27)

*The numbers in the individual cells were too small to use the chi-square test of significance.

TABLE IV

Degree of Attraction to Symbols of Western Society
(Card #1)

	Degree of Attraction				
Village	1. Absent	2. Interest in or curiosity about	3. Desire to be like or to partake in	4. Consummation of desire to be like or partake in	Total
Alakanuk	48% (15)	21% (7)	27% (9)	6% (2)	100% (33)
Kotzebue	26% (7)	18% (5)	18% (5)	37% (10)	100% (27)

$p = <.05>.02$

two villages in regard to the degree of attraction to symbols of Western society. Four degrees of such attraction were established: (a) no expression of interest in, curiosity about, or desire to emulate the pilot or any other aspect of Western society; (b) an expression of interest or curiosity on the part of any of the Eskimo figures about an aspect of Western society (e.g., the pilot, the mechanism of the plane, the nature of life in Western communities); (c) an expression by one of the Eskimo characters of a desire to be like, or partake in, any of the aspects of Western society; and (d) an expression of an Eskimo figure's actual consummation of a desire to be like, to possess, or to partake in any of the aspects of Western society (e.g., the subject becomes a pilot, possesses an airplane, goes to live in a large urban center). The degree of attraction was significantly higher in stories from Kotzebue than in those from Alakanuk (see Table IV).

Although the mean age of subjects from each village was fairly similar, the mean school grade attainment in Kotzebue was considerably higher (8.8 versus 5.2). In order to determine to what extent the differences in attitudes reported above could be explained by education alone, the responses of subjects of "low" and "high" school grade achievement in each village[4] were compared. None of the differences between the education groups in either village was statistically significant for generalized hostility, inter-ethnic, or intra-ethnic social distance; however, there was a consistent tendency for the "high" education group in Kotzebue to exhibit the above attitudes more frequently. The difference between the two educational groups concerning the degree of attraction to Western society was not significant in Alakanuk, but extremely so (p = < .01 > .001) in Kotzebue. While education in itself does not seem to be a crucial factor in determining attitudes of ethnic identity, it appears to exert some influence at the higher grades, This idea supports Doob's (1957) finding in his study of acculturation of African youth.

It was shown previously that the different attitudes comprising ethnic identity (Tables I-IV) exist as a cluster at the community level. To investigate whether such clusters may also characterize individuals, the association among these attitudes within individuals, regardless of village affiliation, must be determined. Table V shows the relationship between the degree of attraction to symbols of Western society and intra-ethnic social distance. Those who were most attracted to Western society also evidence the most social distance from members of their own group. This finding is consistent with previously-mentioned studies indicating that minority group members who are most desirous of "moving toward" the dominant group often try to disassociate themselves from their own group. In this context, their negative attitudes toward their group may be "functional" but are, at the same time, maladjustive. This reasoning also elucidates the finding (Table I) that subjects from Kotzebue exhibited more generalized hostility in their stories than those from Alakanuk.

We now turn to the stories produced in response to Card 2 (Western-community setting; see Methods). In analyzing these stories for inter-ethnic attitudes, all respondents who regarded the adolescent and adult figures on the card as the same ethnic group[5] were eliminated. As shown in Table VI, the affect characterizing the relationship between the (Western) adult figures and the (Eskimo) adolescents was "primarily negative" in the Kotzebue sample and "neutral" in that of Alakanuk; however, even in the Alakanuk stories, the negative affect was more prominent than the positive. These findings confirm those in Table II (Card 1), dealing with inter-ethnic social distance. It is noteworthy that the adolescent characters in Card 2

TABLE V

Relation Between Degree of Attraction to Symbols of Western Society and Intra-Ethnic Social Distance

Degree of Attraction to Symbols of Western Society	Intra-Ethnic Social Distance		Total
	1. Absent	2. Present*	
Low degree of attraction**	86% (30)	14% (5)	100% (35)
High degree of attraction***	44% (11)	56% (14)	100% (25)

p = <.01>.001

*An explicit difference between Eskimo groups, or an expression of hostility between them (i.e., categories 2 and 3 in Table III).

**Either no evidence of attraction, or merely an interest in or curiosity about such symbols (i.e., categories 1 and 2 in Table IV).

***A stated desire, or a consummation of a wish, to partake in Western society (i.e., categories 3 and 4 in Table IV).

TABLE VI

Relationship Between Eskimo Adolescents and White Adults
(Card #2)

| Village | Relationship Between Adolescents and Adults | | | |
	1. Primarily positive*	2. Neutral**	3. Primarily negative***	Total
Alakanuk	14% (4)	62% (18)	24% (7)	100% (29)
Kotzebue	9% (2)	17% (4)	74% (17)	100% (23)

When categories 1 and 2 were combined and compared to category 3, p = $<$.001.

degree of positive affect or attraction, such as sympathy, desire to help, emulate, etc.

**No affect could be imputed to the relationship between adolescents and adults.

***Any degree of negative affect, ranging from feelings of loneliness, estrangement, and disapproval, to outright hostility. In almost all instances, the negative affect was definitely associated with the adolescent-adult relationship. In a few cases, where generalized negative affect was expressed, it was assumed that this relationship was implied.

TABLE VII

Relationship Between Eskimo Adolescents and White Adults and
Degree of Attraction to Symbols of Western Society

| Degree of Attraction to Symbols of Western Society** (Card #1) | Relationship Between Adolescents and Adults* (Card #2) | | | |
	1. Primarily positive	2. Neutral	3. Primarily negative	Total
Low degree of attraction	7% (2)	55% (16)	38% (11)	100% (29)
High degree of attraction	17% (4)	22% (5)	61% (14)	100% (23)

When categories 1 and 2 were combined and compared to category 3, p $<$.10$>$.05.
*For definitions of the three scoring categories, see footnotes to Table VI.
**For definitions of the two scoring categories, see footnotes to Table V.

(particularly in stories from Kotzebue), in an *urban setting,* showed a high degree of negative affect toward the white adult figures. On the other hand, the relatively high level of inter-ethnic social distance in the stories from Kotzebue, stimulated by the *Eskimo village setting* of Card 1 (Table II), was due almost exclusively to the feelings of the (traditionally-dressed) adult Eskimo figures; the adolescent characters were primarily responsible for the high degree of attraction to aspects of Western society. Thus, the adolescent characters in the Kotzebue stories exhibited different attitudes toward whites, depending on whether the environmental setting was Eskimo or Western. The latter setting may have provoked anxiety about rejection by whites and discomfort associated with the anticipation of "making one's own way" in a competitive white society. This notion is indirectly supported by the analysis of (Card 1) stories from Kotzebue: the very stories that showed high attraction to the symbols of Western society also evidence a high degree of inter-ethnic social distance. It appears that subjects isolated the contrasting aspects of their ambivalent attitudes toward Western society and projected them into the different Eskimo figures. The data in Table VII offer an alternative and more direct way of exploring this possibility. It was hypothesized that those who manifested a high degree of attraction to Western society (Card 1, Table IV) would characterize the relationship between the adolescents and adults with more negative affect (Card 2, Table VI). This hypothesis was confirmed in Table VII. Those with a low degree of attraction to Western society tended to view this relationship primarily in neutral terms, while the highly-attracted group exhibited predominantly negative affect. When the "primarily positive" and "neutral" categories were combined and compared to the "primarily negative" category, the differences between the high- and low-attraction groups were statistically significant.

CONCLUSIONS

Before presenting the conclusions that emerge from the major findings of this paper, I will comment on the usefulness of the "picture technique" and on the nature of data derived from such projective devices. The use of imaginative stories for studying attitudes during a short field period had several advantages. The element of disguise introduced by this technique enabled the subjects to communicate emotionally-charged material with minimal self-consciousness and inhibition. Also, since it was easier to keep the stimulus condition constant in this situation than in the usual un-structured interview,[6] the responses of different subjects could be compared with confidence and manipulated statistically. Another advantage of this procedure was its ability to delineate the relationship between variations in the attitudes expressed and the different social situations portrayed in the pictures. It has been noted that attitudes toward whites differed, depending upon whether the setting in the picture was an Eskimo village or a Western urban community.

As social scientists engage increasingly in applied studies, the problem of time becomes an important one. In my opinion, the picture technique is a valuable supplement to the more usual anthropological methods, *mainly* when there is a short period of field investigation. A more lengthy anthropological field study, combined with a precise method of content analysis of field notes, would allow equally valid statistical handling of the data and might also provide a richer yield of information.

The analysis of the stories also permits speculation about the relationship between projective data and social processes in the community. Attitudes expressed in the stories toward symbols of Western society were linked to the community context of the pictures. Those who expressed favorable attitudes toward these symbols in one situation also verbalized the most negative affect toward them in another. If this is conceived in terms of "trait" psychology, it implies that these individuals simultaneously have contradictory attitudes toward the same object. However, if personality is conceived as social behavior rather than as a number of entities within a person, these attitudes can then be viewed as a resultant of the different motivational forces activated by the perception and definition of the social situations portrayed in the pictures.[7] As noted earlier, the young people in Kotzebue experienced feelings of insecurity, ambivalence, and inferiority, provoked by their desire to take part in the Western world. These reactions were "triggered off" by Card 2 and gave rise to negative ethnic evaluations. Attitudes (and personality traits) are situationally bound (Kaplan 1961:243-244) and should be interpreted in this manner.

Although the stories evoked by the two situations were markedly different, these projective data per se did not indicate the underlying reasons. To do this, it was necessary to determine the subjects' social roles and the institutional setting in which they were played. Such information is particularly important in studies of non-Western people, where assumptions about the meaning of projective data and normative situational definitions can so easily be ethnocentrically biased.

The major findings of this study are relevant to the problem concerning the type of people in underdeveloped areas who are most likely to be attracted to Western technological and social innovations. Many studies have found that such individuals are also likely to have a high level of generalized hostility. While confirming this, the present paper also indicates the directions of this hostility and some of its underlying causes. No evidence has been presented about whether or not the *original* impetus to accept Western goals is motivated by hostility and by disturbed relationships within one's own ethnic group. However, whatever the original motivation, the minority group member attracted to Western society is more likely to *develop* negative attitudes, toward his own and the dominant ethnic group, when he perceives barriers to his newly acquired aspirations. A devalued ethnic self-image and hostility toward Western society emerge from a situation where individuals set new goals, which they then perceive cannot be reached. It is this process, rather than acculturation per se, or "cultural confusion," that produces ambivalence toward Western society and toward one's own ethnic group. In such situations, people are often equally prone to accept all values and goals of Western society indiscriminately, or to reject them violently (i.e., as in some nativistic movements).

Although the stages of acculturation can be described in terms of institutional changes, there are also related changes in individual attitudes. At the early (imitative) stage of acculturation that existed in Alakanuk, no essential shifts in reference values or in aspirations were occurring. Consequently, there were no significant alterations in the criteria for evaluating one's ethnic group membership. In Kotzebue, however, such changes were well advanced and led to serious role conflicts and discontinuities among adolescents and young adults. Viewed from another vantage point, there was a considerable disjunction between the goals of such individuals and the means available for reaching them, a situation fulfilling the conditions outlined by Merton (1949:125-129) for the development of "anomie" and deviant behavior. It is interesting that juvenile delinquency is a growing problem in Kotzebue, but it is almost non-existent in Alakanuk.

What are the implications of these findings for programs of social and technological change among non-Western groups? If the negative ethnic attitudes discussed in this paper result from a disjunction between goals and the means available for achieving them, more attention should be given in developmental programs to the congruence among the various facets of social change. Serious social problems may result if innovations in the educational system inculcate widespread aspirations which have but a small chance of being fulfilled in the existing economic structure. The fault may lie not in the nature of the educational innovations themselves, but in an uneven relationship between them and other areas of social life. It is likely that *differences* in the rates of change of elements in the social system are more crucial in social and personal disorganization than are the absolute rates of change.[8]

NOTES

1 I wish to express my thanks to Dr. Margaret Lantis of the U.S. Public Health Service, and to Miss Judith Fine of Jefferson Medical College, Philadelphia, Pa., for their very helpful suggestions in preparing this paper.
2 A monograph on this subject has been prepared for publication.
3 All measures of statistical significance reported in this study were computed by the chi-square method. Differences that reached the .05 level of probability were considered significant.
4 For Alakanuk: "low" was no schooling through grade 7; "high" was grade 8 and above.
  For Kotzebue: "low" was no schooling through grade 9; "high" was grade 10 and above.
5 In cases where these identifications were not spontaneously made in the story, the subjects were questioned about the ethnic identity of the figures.
6 This quality of minimal formal structuring of the interview situation in the usual anthropological field methods has important advantages of its own.
7 The "situation" also includes the perception of the investigator and the entire context in which the "test" is administered.
8 In this connection, see Norman Chance's (1960) discussion of change in an arctic village.

REFERENCES CITED

Barnett, Homer G. (1941); Personal conflicts and cultural changes. Social Forces 20:160-171.
Boggs, Stephan (1960); Culture change and the personality of Ojibwa children. American Anthropologist 60:47-58.
Caudill, William (1952); Japanese-American personality and acculturation. Genetic Psychology Monographs 45:3-102.
Chance, Norman A. (1960); Culture change and integration: an Eskimo example. American Anthropologist 62:1028-1044.
De Vos, George (1961); Symbolic analysis in the cross-cultural study of personality. *In* Studying personality cross-culturally, Bert Kaplan, ed. (Illinois: Row Peterson and Co.).
Doob, L. W. (1957); An introduction to the psychology of acculturation. Journal of Social Psychology 45:143-160.

also responded to the urgings of traders and the lures of economic gain and changed their weaving styles and techniques to meet market demands. Weaving itself with its necessary attendant sheepherding is only something over two hundred years old among the Navajo.

Moreover, during the course of this study it became increasingly clear that Navajo women in the Piñon area, despite their observed conservatism, were not resistive to new ideas. The post office does a large business in handling mail orders for clothing purchased by women. Women, as well as men, eagerly look forward to the introduction of the electric light, envy the white world running water, thoroughly enjoy a trip to the nearest town with its wider selection of goods in the stores and cheaper prices, and whenever possible take their washing to the community washing machine which has recently been installed in the Piñon tribal chapter house. In this latter case, women will often go to considerable time, expense and trouble to be able to use a washing machine sometimes five or ten miles away from home. Moreover, they are willing and eager to take their children to hospitals and clinics (although at the same time the most frequent initiators of ceremonial curing activities) and to have their children delivered in hospitals. Nevertheless they have developed these behaviors within a traditional context.

Spindler has suggested in the Menomini case that the contact situation was one in which women could continue their traditional patterns without experiencing pressure to change from the white world. My argument will not contest but rather elaborate and expand on hers in this area. The problem is to explain why, in view of the facts outlined, the marked difference between men and women exists.

In the matter of adopting new clothing styles, work skills, etc., the problem is relatively simple in a general sense. Efficient tools, metal versus stone for instance, seem always to be adopted. Clothing which is easy to obtain and which eases tensions due to differing views of modesty has been adopted by many non-western peoples. Agriculture or husbandry as more dependable alternatives to hunting and gathering have been adopted by most of the peoples of the world. In each case, however, the adopting society has required some sort of model on which new behavior could be based. In most cases the model has not been followed perfectly either because it was not presented in its entirety or has been imperfectly perceived or, and in the case under consideration this seems most germane, the conditions of life of the "receiving" culture precluded the total adoption of the observed model no matter how completely it was revealed or accurately it was perceived. An alternative is that the "donor" society does not present models meaningful in the specific situation.

In the Navajo case, partial models, that is, discrete bits of behavior such as using cloth purchased from traders to make dresses rather than weave wool cloth at home, the use of a sewing machine, the techniques of dipping sheep or driving a truck or using a wood stove could be learned piecemeal and incorporated into Navajo life without trouble. On the other hand, an entirely new model based on Anglo-American behavior could not be followed for a number of reasons. The first and perhaps most important of these in terms of Piñon Navajo as a whole is physical isolation. Many Navajo even today have had little opportunity to observe the possible models in American life. Many have spent most of their lives on the reservation, coming in contact with whites only as they appeared as Bureau of Indian Affairs employees, traders, missionaries, or occasional travelers. In many more cases, even Indians with off-reservation experience have had little opportunity to observe or participate in general American life, being, as they were, students in BIA schools, members of all-Indian work gangs or members of the armed forces. From each of these sources particular behavior patterns and material culture items have been introduced into Navajo life. In addition, the institution of the Navajo trader has continuously fed new items of material culture into Navajo life and established new social relationships. Similarly, the new completely "Navajo political organization" (Shepardson n.d.) was introduced from the outside but developed largely in response to Navajo attempts to deal with new problems. In general, each of these sources has provided models of behavior for a few individuals, but American society or culture has, until recently, not provided any overall model from which the Navajo could learn new behaviors and in which new aspirations suitable to changing conditions can be derived. Thus, until recently the Navajo has displayed extreme conservatism as he attempted to adjust the old model to meet new conditions, a device which worked well for a number of years but which in the past two decades, particularly since the enforced reduction of livestock, has not served him well.

The old model, that is the model which has served as a guide for Navajo behavior since and to a large part before 1868, is one based on sheep husbandry which we can call the sheepherder model.

The ideal sheepherder lived out his life dependent on the increase of his flocks which provided him with meat and wool which could be converted into material goods through trade in the raw or as rugs. Both men and women were involved in sheepherding with both actual well being and social status being largely determined by the number and condition of one's sheep herds. In addition, horses, essential to maintaining life on the reservation, took on a value in the system of social symbolism. Cattle, although the Navajo appear to have kept them as long as they have kept sheep (Hill 1940:414) played much less of a role in Navajo life either actually or symbolically, and were generally owned by only the rich. As long as environmental and economic conditions were in the least favorable, the Navajo could depend on sheep and through them retain his social separateness, obtaining those material items he had learned to use and desire through the institution of the trading post. The nature of the trading post restricted the amount of direct contact with the white world for the individual Navajo. Often the only white man with whom a Navajo had had any contact was the Navajo-speaking trader who might himself have been born on the reservation and be as foreign to general Anglo-American culture and society as was his Indian customer. Thus isolated, the Navajo could aspire and achieve within a Navajo context with minimal reference to the outside world. In a general sense it is to this situation which the older Navajo refer when they speak with vigorous nostalgia of the "old times." If we could personify the sheepherder Navajo he would be a man who wears moccasins or perhaps work shoes, wears an ordinary denim shirt and Levi's under which he wears a breech clout. When he is cold he may wear a cast-off white man's dress coat but probably prefers a blanket. His ears are pierced and he wears turquoise earrings in them, at least on special occasions. His hair is long and clubbed in the back with a binding of wool. He carries a buckskin sack of corn meal and other charms against witch-craft. He binds his hair with a turban-like cloth. If he wears a hat it is purchased at the store and worn full-crowned just as it came from the box. At a squaw dance or other ceremonial or social occasion he wears a plush shirt with the tail out, an ornate silver and turquoise belt, a necklace of silver and turquoise and another of coral and perhaps another of raw turquoise. His life is centered in his sheep herd and the daily and yearly cycle of sheep husbandry. He trades almost exclusively at a single trading store and is usually deeply in debt, which debt he may pay off when he sells his wool in the spring.

Within Navajo context he is independent and self-supporting and takes pride in being so. At the same time he has a dependent attitude toward the Bureau of Indian Affairs inasmuch as he expects the Bureau or some other facility to act to meet emergencies or redress grievances, make improve-ments in water supply, etc. Within Navajo context he may be extremely active politically, but if so, he is generally opposed to what he sees as white domination and is distrustful of the Bureau, the Tribe as a political body, and the white world in general.

Although this is composite, the details are drawn from observation and not a few such men are to be found in the Piñon area. If they have been able to maintain wealth, at least in the reduced degree possible under today's conditions, they are generally admired by all elements of the community. If they have not, they are pitied and have little political or social influence although they may be admired for what they once were. There are in the Piñon area at least a few younger men who still strive to emulate this model and even smaller numbers of boys who are being trained to aspire toward these traditional goals.

The sheepherder's wife, the traditional female, is a suitable mate for the man described above. She is not only content with, but often strongly attached to, a hogan. She wears the traditional Navajo plush blouse and sateen or plush skirt. Although she may use a sewing machine and buy material at the traders, she knows only a single dress pattern and experi-ments not at all. She prides herself on her ability to weave, cook fried bread and mutton. She is a good sheep herder, a skillful horsewoman, and desires a number of children. Like her husband, her hair is long and bound with wool. She wears all the silver, turquoise and coral she can afford, and pawns it when cash is needed. She is independent of her mate and firmly attached to her matrilineage and the matrilineal household. Although she has accepted many new ideas, as mentioned above, she does not appear to aspire toward goals any different, except in a rather limited material sense, from those of her mother. This is equally true if she is an old woman or a high school girl.

Although the Navajo girl may come home from school with fingernail polish, a permanent wave, and fashionable and attractively-fitted capri pants, she will soon revert to the more traditional type of clothing. Weaving lessons, which were ignored during her school years, will often be taken up again. Her English becomes less and less intelligible in an incredibly short time. Her wardrobe of "white" clothes made during her stay in school will be stored away or given to younger sisters. As long as she is unmarried she will in all likelihood wear a blouse and dungaree trousers, but once married she will quickly shift into a modified form of traditional dress. Her interests in the sheep herd will increase, and at sheep dipping time, to herd and dip sheep, she, like all the other women, will dress in her finest clothes and wear all her jewelry. She may seek employment as a dormitory mistress at the local boarding school, but such jobs are hard to hold because of the demands of her family. Should she not fall into the traditional pattern, she has almost no alternative but to leave the community to find work in some white town or at some distant agency facility. Particularly in the former instance she runs the risk of becoming involved with white men, Mexicans, or non-Navajo Indians, and in many cases succumbs to the demands of the family to give up such relationships and return to the homestead and "help out" while seeking a more acceptable Navajo husband.

With almost no exceptions this describes the conditions and behavior of the Navajo woman of the Pinon area. Despite any specific desires she may have acquired or any general knowledge of the non-Navajo world, if she remains in the community she falls into some modification of the traditional Navajo pattern. However, in seeking a mate she does not turn to her relatively few age mates who have maintained the traditional goals of Navajo life. With eminent practicality she looks for a young man who has a job on- or off-reservation, even though this may mean that they will be separated over long periods while he goes off-reservation to work and she remains behind at the family homestead.

Having married such a young man, however, she often finds herself, against the plans of her new husband, siding with her mother and sisters, or even with female in-laws, should the couple be living with his, rather than her mother. These conflicts, which in many cases create serious rifts in the extended family, are caused by the desire of the younger men to eliminate the sheep herd and buy cattle or at least to divert funds and effort from sheep to cattle husbandry. In many cases this shift into cattle husbandry is carried out against the active opposition of the women of the family. Sometimes men will buy calves and have them cared for by a friend until such time as the womenfolk are away. He will then bring his cattle to the family's traditional range and present the women with a *fait accompli*. In other cases he will buy the cattle for his wife who cannot in good conscience turn down a gift so valuable as a cow or calf.

The behavior of a woman toward cattle is markedly different from a man's and enormously different from her attitude toward sheep. Cattle are clearly the affair of men in which women seldom participate. While vaccination or sheep dipping are occasions for the display of clothing and wealth and clearly viewed as important social events by women, the time set aside for the community cattle branding is ignored by them and is strictly a male function. Men, cattle owners or not, spend the day watching and helping at the corrals while their wives remain home or spend the day shopping at the trader's store. The only females interested are those of high school age who almost invariably wear the bell bottom style trousers known as "rodeo pants" on this or any other "dress up" occasion.

The Navajo, as it has frequently been pointed out, view the world as dangerous and feel little compunction about displaying fear. Cattle, particularly bulls, are viewed as extremely dangerous. Whenever cattle appear near the homestead, the women evidence great fear and call upon the men to drive them away. The appearance of a bull immediately sends all the women and children into hiding, there to remain until the men of the family go out and drive off the animal. The fear exhibited is far out of proportion to the danger involved and seems in part simulated to express yet another objection to the shift in emphasis from sheep to cattle.

These conflicts point to the dilemma of the Navajo woman, particularly the younger woman who has received an off-reservation education, and brings us to the question of models. What is the new model for Navajo men? And, if a new model has been found by the men, do not the women also have a new model from white society on which to base their future behavior?

The typical younger Navajo is much more difficult to describe than is the traditional male because he has had more experience outside the reservation and therefore more opportunity to adopt varying patterns of behavior. It must be understood that if he, as an individual, has rejected the old model entirely and aspires to some completely white model, he has no recourse save to leave the community—or take on the deviant role of the grandiose and usually drunken dreamer of great dreams. However, the majority of young men fall into neither of these categories and can be described in a general way. He may have any number of specific ambitions from teaching mathematics to becoming an auto mechanic. However, he is most often inadequately educated and seldom can realize ambitions requireing college or other advanced training. In addition, to be an auto mechanic generally requires that he leave the reservation and compete with whites. In this competition, handicapped by a vague but real fear of white people, loneliness, distaste for city noise, racial discrimination in unions, social life, and housing, speaking his own brand of English and not blessed with the American competitive spirit, he often gives up and returns home.

Once home this typical younger Navajo participates in the family herding activities but seeks unskilled or semi-skilled work on the railroads, in migrant agricultural work, or on tribal or Bureau projects. In most cases he expresses a desire to remain on or near the reservation and his family, to participate in Navajo society and political life, and to work out a destiny in the familiar surroundings of the reservation. However he rejects the traditional means, sheepherding, and often uses this word as a term of contempt. He takes wage work hoping to save enough money to buy some cattle and start a herd. He plans with other male relatives to dig a well or otherwise improve the family's traditional grazing grounds as a cattle ranch.

He complains about the demands which a sheep herd makes on a man and quite realistically points out that with the present grazing restrictions it is impossible to make an adequate living raising sheep. Instead of moccasins he wears colorful low-heeled western boots, tight Levi trousers, a wide tooled-leather belt with a fancy western buckle. His dress-up shirt is a colorful tailored western style with numerous pearl buttons. His hair is usually short, although a few young men still retain the long clubbed hair. His hat is straw, molded felt, or even plastic, with the wide brim shaped in what is known as the batwing style. He is, in short, the living embodiment of that well-known figure—the drugstore cowboy.

Since his earliest days he has practiced with a lasso and has graduated from chickens, dogs, and younger brothers to sheep and goats, and finally to horses and cattle. He may become one of the limited number of hoop dancers who travel from rodeo to rodeo in the summer accompanied by an admiring coterie (very much like a boxer in the white world), but he more than likely seeks recognition in rodeo competition. In fact, to him "cowboy" means a person who competes in rodeos and not a man who works with cattle. Success in rodeo competition gives a young man considerable status which he carries long after he has retired from competition, and considerable advantage in securing an attractive and educated young wife.

Rodeo might quite accurately be described as a near mania among the young. Communities throughout the reservation have formed rodeo associations as collective enterprises, built arenas and stock pens, and stage regular summer rodeo. The Navajo Cowboy Association conducts an annual competition for cumulative points and awards a saddle to the Navajo champion cowboy of the year. So popular is rodeo that the traditional summer recreation of rabbit hunting on horseback, an exciting and dangerous game, is gradually disappearing in the Piñon area because most of the younger men are attending a rodeo somewhere every weekend. Even if he does not compete, a young man will attend to watch the events, drink, assist with the stock, and generally associate with the rodeo and rodeo performers.

The rodeo in its broadest sense is not exclusively a young man's game. In the Piñon area the rodeo association is the nexus of political activity, and no one who has aspirations to political power can afford not to belong to the association and participate in some way in its activities. It is interesting and very possibly significant that, in the Piñon area, at least, the association was formed at the suggestion of one of the areas' most respected leaders, who is cast in the traditional mold and generally hostile toward the tribal government and the Bureau of Indian Affairs. Despite these conservative aspects of his person he is also the prime innovator, having been among the first bootleggers, the first to introduce the practice of selling candy and soft drinks at squaw dances, in addition to his role in starting the rodeo association. He and most of the population view this as a strictly Navajo activity which has nothing to do with, and was not carried out in response to, either the government, the tribe, or missionaries. Uniquely, this is one of few Navajo institutions, outside of the trader's store, which requires regular contact and association with white men. As the performers have become more expert and spectators more sophisticated, it has been necessary to stop using stock collected in the community and contract with regular rodeo stock suppliers for bucking horses and bulls for the bull-riding contests. In addition the Indian rodeo performers seek recognition from white performers, and to gain it subscribe to regular Rodeo Cowboy Association rules and employ authorized white judges. Moreover, at Pollacca, the Navajo and Hopi display a rare example of cooperation in planning and staging an annual rodeo.

In Piñon the association is a meeting place on a basis of equality of both the informal political leaders of the area and representatives of tribal government. These latter are in the person of the district chapter delegate, the local representatives and chairman of the quasi-political grazing committee, and the tribal brand inspector, all of whom take an active role in the planning and conduct of the rodeo and have considerable power in their various spheres. Tribal funds to build arena and corrals needed for the affair are obtained through the agency of the delegate.

The rodeo itself is symbolic of the changing patterns of Navajo life. After the competition a night performance is held in front of the trader's store, illuminated by floodlights which he supplies. The store is kept open until the performance is over and the trader has contributed a saddle and various other prizes for the contestants. The performance includes a number of long speeches by the delegate and other tribal officers, the chairman of the grazing committee, local members of the school committee, etc. Entertainment is provided by a number of male and a few female hoop dancers (a teenage girl hoop dancer wears an adaption of the male costume which displays the entire length of her leg—an extremely daring performer indeed) dancing what the Navajo called "dances we borrowed from the Pueblos." A few traditional chants are usually sung by men and women who travel from rodeo to rodeo throughout the summer. Usually a number of Navajo composers are on hand to sing modern songs done in Indian style to the accompaniment of a hand drum. Such songs are often warnings against indulgence in alcohol (Wine Will Make a Fool of You) or rather-uninspired love songs (Are You Mine, Really Mine, Are You Mine?). As a capstone one is treated to the performance of a young Navajo boy with an electric guitar singing his own songs or popular songs with particularly Navajo interjections (usually joking about drinking and being arrested) in a combined "Western and Country" and "Rock and Roll" style known in the music trade as "rockabilly." At the conclusion of the night performance the younger element of the community go to a dance at the chapter house. The music is most often supplied by a group of Hopi boys who have formed a locally popular band known as the Hopi Clans, and the dances are the same as those performed in dance halls throughout the United States.

Throughout the entire rodeo performance, the figure of the cowboy is dominant. With the exception of the most traditional old men, males strive to dress, as nearly as their finances will permit, to the cowboy ideal. Riding to the rodeo on a horse is important for younger men who will pass up a ride in a truck or car to come mounted. Not only men carry out the cowboy theme. Adolescent girls, home from boarding school for the summer, adopt if they can afford it a style of trousers with bell bottoms generally described as rodeo pants. Pre-pubertal girls, girls who have not gone to school, and married women, retain the traditional dress and are clearly spectators, rather than participants, during the entire rodeo.

The rodeo serves as a focus of action for a new Navajo ideal—the cowboy—and the cowboy serves as a platform from which new and non-traditional aspirations can be formed. Although a young man may wish to become a mathematics teacher, a tribal policeman and tractor driver, or leave the reservation entirely to take up a new life in the city, he views himself as basically a cowboy who can rope, ride, and participate in rodeo, a man who knows something of cattle and cattle lore, who dreams of owning cattle and becoming a rancher or cattleman. Significantly, at a number of functions held at the Oakland California Inter-Tribal Friendship House, a center for re-located Indians, dressing up called for most of the Navajo men and boys who were newly off the reservation to wear cowboy clothes including western boots. Only the young boys who had spent several years in the city wore the same "uniforms" as do white youths.

The cattleman posture is adopted by adult males in Piñon almost in a direct ratio to the degree of "acculturation." Thus the tribal brand inspector, involved in the daily business of recording sales of livestock, supervising branding and castration of horses and steers, cooperating with the grazing committee, directing range development work, etc., wears Levi trousers, western boots, colorful shirt, and ten gallon hat as a matter of course. So does the tribal council delegate, although his livestock holdings are largely in sheep and his income is in large part derived from his political position and from renting a small building to a white trader. The members of the grazing committee, with one exception, affect cowboy as opposed to sheepherder clothing, and all are active in rodeo affairs. The exception is the representative of the most remote and traditional area within the Piñon grazing zone.

This rather detailed recounting of the rodeo and the expressions of the cowboy theme in Piñon has been presented in order to support the argument that Navajo men in this area have in large part accepted a new ideal pattern against which they can measure their own behavior. This figure does not develop out of the Navajo past, but is a result of continued exposure to ideas and behavior of an alien culture and society, that of the Anglo-American. Piñon is interesting in this point because, situated as it is well away from the boundaries of the reservation, the population as a whole does not experience day-to-day first-hand contact with any white community. Regular contact with the trader and sporadic contact with various employees of the Public Health Service and the Bureau of Indian Affairs constitute almost the only exposure to white men *in situ* as it were. However, it should be kept in mind that although these whites are storekeepers, doctors, sanitarians, teachers, or extension agents by profession, they, as often as not, affect one or more features of the cowboy figure, the large hat, a colorful shirt, Levis, or boots.

Prior to World War II, Piñon's associations with the white world were far more limited than they are today. Automobiles were unknown in the area. Williams, the nearest town, was a two-day ride on horseback, four days in a wagon. Piñon remained a classical Navajo reservation community, revolving around the trading store, with occasional and often hostile relationships with the Bureau of Indian Affairs. Since the war roads have increased, radios are widespread, weekly movies are shown in the chapter house, regular trips are made to Gallup, Flagstaff, Williams, and Holbrook; the Gallup Indian Days Celebration and the Flagstaff Powwow are important holidays in the Piñon area, as is the tribal fair at Window Rock. Most of the younger children spend much of the year in off-reservation boarding schools scattered from California to northern Utah. Entire families travel in Colorado, California, Utah, and Idaho to work as migrant labor. In short, Piñon has during the past two decades been subject to a bombardment of new ideas and patterns of behavior as well as actual changes in the environment in the form of roads, wells, catchment dams, telephones, and so forth.

Most important of all, the impact of the stock reduction programs of the late thirties and early forties created a situation in which a young man could no longer aspire toward the old goals of Navajo life. It became illegal and impossible to amass large herds of a thousand or more sheep and several dozen horses. Men who had been rich in Navajo terms and who could have been expected to leave their children substantial numbers of sheep were made destitute, from the Navajo point of view. The legal herd limit of seventy-four makes it impossible to earn even a minimal income from husbandry, and although many families violate this limit, none are able to maintain themselves entirely from the sheep herd, although it continues to play an important, and at the moment, irreplaceable role in the economy of the area.[2] While old men lament the old days and demand that somehow the tribe or the government bring them back, the men who have grown to maturity in these two past decades realize, albeit reluctantly, that such a thing is impossible. At the same time they have been unwilling and unable for educational, social, financial, and cultural reasons to abandon their homes and, as the Bureau of Indian Affairs so clearly would like them to do, go into the cities to find work in the white world. Instead they have chosen from the white world a new image which fits easily into the environmental and cultural background of Navajo life. The model they have chosen presents an interesting example of the picture white culture and society presents to outsiders, of which we are often quite unaware.

The Navajo live in the southern part of what we might call facetiously the "cowboy culture area" of the United States. This area begins in Texas and Oklahoma and includes all of the west, save perhaps the coastal areas of Washington, Oregon, and northern California. This area is, or course, the great grazing and range cattle zone of American animal husbandry. However, the number of people involved in these activities is relatively few. Taken as a whole, ranching does not dominate the western and southwestern portion of the nation as it once did. Moreover, as elsewhere, most of the population is urban or suburban in residence and non-agricultural in employment. However, the figure of the cowboy, not as he exists on ranches today with a jeep, helicopter, horse trailer, and butane-heated branding iron, but as he has been immortalized in American mythology, is of overriding cultural importance. The cowboy costume is found in sportswear, police uniforms, and waitress dresses. The theme appears in murals, post offices, city halls, and motels. Ranch language and ranch equipment find themselves worked into business names and the décor of doctors' offices, department stores, and curio shops. Dude ranches abound as vacation retreats. Entire towns consciously carry out the cowboy theme. Rodeo and quarterhorse racing closely associated with ranching are top drawing spectator sports. Many towns boast a local roping club in which businessmen and high school boys pay dues for the privilege of roping calves kept for the purpose in an arena built by the club. The sheriff's mounted posse composed almost entirely of townsmen is an important, if not indispensable, part of the political organization of every county. These posses, often composed of the area's most influential men, ride in parades dressed in theatrically styled cowboy uniforms and from time to time act as police auxiliaries in searching for lost vacationers or downed aircraft.

Few towns of any size do not have a Frontier Days celebration complete with rodeo or race meet.[3] It is within this area that stylists have developed western-style suits and dresses for every occasion, formal or informal. Businessmen often appear in offices or stores in "frontier pants" and western-style shirts. The "bolo" tie has in some communities completely replaced the four-in-hand or bow tie for all occasions save full dress. Riding clubs are to be found in most communities, and annual trail rides of several days duration are often considered as the male social event of the year during which the political and economic leaders of the area congregate for a round of riding and relaxation. Owning horses for pleasure riding is widespread. Horse shows invariably include classes for trail horses, stock horses, and not infrequently for cutting horses. Cutting horse competitions have become popular spectator sports with top horses bringing prices in five figures. It is to be emphasized that most of the people participating in this cowboy culture pattern are not cowboys, nor are they in any way involved in the cattle business. In areas where it is possible, involvement in the cattle business, even to the minor extent of owning only a head or two of cattle pastured on the ranch of a friend, is a prestige activity. For many it may be a financial loss, but it provides an excuse to spend at least a few days a year assisting the ranch owner in range work. A common response to business success throughout the west, whether success be in law, medicine, or the sale of used automobiles, is to buy and attempt to operate a cattle ranch, which often includes donning flamboyant western clothes which help to secure identification as a cattleman.

It is this which the Piñon Navajo sees when he is off-reservation, and in many ways he receives this impression in heavier doses than do the white residents of the community. As often as not he comes to town when some western-oriented celebration is in progress. He is impressed by the fact that the tractor drivers, Bureau of Indian Affairs employees, and store clerks all wear western hats, and affect cowboy clothes. He cannot help but conclude that this role is one which is honored and respected in the white world. He is already well aware that in those areas adjoining the reservation the traditional role of the Indian is anything but respected. Moreover he knows that at least some Indians have become successful rodeo cowboys subject to the rewards both economic and psychological of participating in this sport. He also finds it easier to take on wage work if he has a cattle herd which requires far less attention from day to day than does a flock of sheep. In addition the idealized life of the cowboy is not too much of an alteration from traditional Navajo life. The life of the range and trail drive and cow camp is much closer to the life of the Navajo homestead than is any other role in modern American life. It requires that a man be a horseman and a roper, have a knowledge of animal ways, and a number of outdoor skills which the Navajo already possesses.

Perhaps the most important factors are the new conditions under which the young Navajo grows up. In the very recent past the children of Piñon were introduced to the techniques, attitudes, and values of a traditional socialization process within the context of the extended family homestead (cf. Downs n.d.; Kluckhohn and Leighton 1947). By the time they reached puberty they were confirmed in the traditional sheepherder ideal and in addition possessed all the skills necessary to make their way in the traditional scheme of things. Today the vast majority of the children receive only the earliest phases of this indoctrination before their fifth, sixth, or seventh year, when they are removed from the family homestead to attend full-time boarding schools. In the Piñon area only a few children attend school on a day basis and many cannot be accommodated at Piñon but must attend schools in other parts of the reservation or even off-reservation. Young men and women reaching high school age will have spent from five to twelve years away from home influences except during the summers; however, they will not have participated fully in off-reservation life.

Most Indian Service schools are mono-racial and tend by accident or design to isolate the students from too much direct contact with the white world. Excursions to nearby towns are limited and usually permitted only in groups. Associations with non-Indians are short and highly formalized-exchange plans or inter-school visits. The efforts of the teachers to "unteach" Indian patterns of language, dress, and behavior make the constantly reiterated point that the rest of the world looks down on the traditional Indian while the student's natural resentment of punishment for speaking Navajo or criticism of their dress, hair arrangement, or eating habits develops a core of resistance to any real internalization of the new behavior patterns. Moreover much of what is taught in school is so obviously impossible in the context of their reservation homes that students soon compartmentalize their behavior into "white" and "Navajo" segments.

At the same time the children and young people have access to television and regular motion pictures and have before them a monotonously repeated pattern in the form of the mass-myth cowboy.[4] They are quick to realize that the cowboy is a person of value in white society and are eager to imitate him. Their experiences with the white world tend only to confirm the idea that the cowboy is a figure of prestige and one to which they can aspire. This gives us some idea of how and why the modern Navajo youth has taken a model from the white world, but it does not, at first glance, explain why the Navajo girl remains far more conservative than her brother.

The American myth figure, the cowboy, whether he appears in literature, motion pictures, or television, is a single man, most frequently without antecedents or relatives. Alone or with a "side-kick" he drifts through a series of adventures among, but not as a part of, the society. Not infrequently a western story ends with the cowboy hero riding away, alone, from the group with which he has temporarily interacted. Although certain alterations have been permitted in recent years, the cowboy's relationships with women are seldom permanent. If the cowboy hero does "get the girl," he ceases to be a cowboy. He settles down, a phrase which in the western genre describes his giving up of the roaming, lonely life of the cowboy hero errant.

In effect the western myth provides a model for male behavior, but does not provide a model for female behavior. The cowboy has no wife. Thus the young Navajo girl, exposed to much the same influences as her male contemporary, is not exposed to a total figure which she can emulate and use as a model for her future behavior on the reservation. That she is influenced by the cowboy myth is revealed in her selection of "non-Navajo" clothing and her attitude toward the rodeo and cattle as contrasted to her mother. She does have thrust before her a number of female models unrelated to the cowboy. The teacher, the nurse, the well-groomed and comfortable housewife of the woman's magazines all play a part in suggesting modes of life alternative to that of the traditional existence. However, reservation life, while it permits parallels and analogies to the cowboy model, cannot support the picture of the average American homemaker. The starched and relatively expensive advertised clothes are out of place and unobtainable. The polished floors and picture windows which generated her envious school-dreams are so removed from the hogan or log cabin as to become unreal. The many convenient appliances are too expensive and would not run without electricity. The clean and smiling children require more water than the Navajo family can afford the time to haul. Parent Teacher Association meetings, of which she may have read, are the product of tax-supported schools with the parent in the ultimate role of employer. On the reservation the government-appointed teacher is viewed more as an authority figure than a public servant. To take an active part in politics would require that a young woman violate the codes of expected behavior and embarrass not only herself but her entire family.

In short, the economic, social, and cultural factors of reservation life make it impossible for a young woman to realize more than a minor part of her aspirations. The role of an average American housewife and mother, no matter how appealing it may have been, simply cannot be played out in the reservation atmosphere. While the Navajo boy can imitate the cowboy and stand with a foot in both the Navajo and the white world, observe the more important of the old traditions and still aspire in terms of a new future, the girl simply cannot. The alternatives are to leave the community, and the comforting presence of the family and the home country, or to avoid frustration by conforming to traditional Navajo standards for women. The latter course is easier and most frequently followed with only minor variations of a material nature. In this role, a girl finds herself with a set of expected behaviors which she understands and which her mother and grandmother approve. Having set her foot on this road she is less demanding than the girl who refuses to give up her borrowed dream, and because of this is more desirable as a wife.

Thus a future husband can continue in his borrowed role, comfortable in the knowledge that his wife is more or less satisfied, willing to live with her (or his) parents, content with the pattern of constant debt at the trader's, amenable to his periodic drinking sprees, less concerned with his casual infidelities. However, in return for this comfort he must pay with a stiffening resistance to any plans of his which would materially disturb the relationships which determine the traditional role of women. The young man who marries a girl who is not reconciled to reservation life is faced with even greater turmoil inasmuch as his wife is not infrequently in conflict with her own parents and her behavior is less than acceptable to his family. The tensions created as she tries to maintain her children according to white standards, or to keep herself and her house cleaner than expected by Navajo standards, almost inevitably force him to set up a new home away from the family and its all-important cooperation, leave the reservation and the plans he can make in view of his relationship to reservation land, or terminate his marriage.

This situation has been presented in some detail to point up three major considerations:

1 The difficulty of determining what aspects of one culture the bearers of another will accept. This is influenced not only by the conditions within the receiving society, which have been emphasized so much, but by the way the receiving society perceives the donor society. In this instance few Americans and fewer anthropologists would view the cowboy figure as either central or important in our society, yet this has obviously been the aspect of the white world to which the Navajo has been both willing and able to respond.

2 Differences between sexes in the area of change may not always be related to any fundamental factors but to the nature of the contact and the nature of the model from the donor society which each sex selects. In this case neither the communication media nor educational programs have presented to Navajo women an alternative behavior pattern which can be imitated within the reservation context.

3 The nature of inter-cultural contacts has seldom included such factors as the effect and/or extent of use of mass media such as motion pictures, television, and radio. In many instances, the Piñon example being a case in point, the white world makes far more impression through these means than through any type of face-to-face contact.

This paper in substantially the same form was delivered at the fifth annual meetings of the Kroeber Anthropological Society in Berkeley in May, 1961. Since that time I have had two opportunities to return to Piñon[5] and have been able to add certain data which were not available when the paper was presented. This material is in large part that dealing with the rodeo and the rodeo association. Also, since this was presented, Louise Spindler has published her work on the acculturation of Menomini women which approaches this same question from a different direction.

NOTES

1 "Traditional" is the current circumlocution of more objectionable terms such as backward, primitive, or old-fashioned. It is used by both the Bureau of Indian Affairs and the Navajo Tribe, which among other things selects a traditional and a modern princess to reign over the annual tribal fair. It is, however, not used by the average Navajo.

2 Although no individual or family can exist entirely on income from the sheep herd, most Navajo in the Piñon area must depend on the herd for food and employment during periods when they cannot find work elsewhere.

3 A curious and illustrative example is the Tournament of Roses, celebrated in Pasadena, California, each New Years Day. This event originated from a New Years Day observance of the local hunt club modeled after the British fox-hunting clubs. However, by the 1930's all vestiges of this origin were erased, marshalls were costumed in Spanish caballero costumes, and the frontier theme emphasized by the inclusion in the parade of many western mounted units.

4 As is usual throughout the rural west, "cowboy" pictures and "cowboy" literature are the most popular mass entertainment. The television stations program western series in large number. The opportunity to view these epics on school-owned television sets is not lost by the young Navajo who knows the names and characteristics of all the current western heroes. They play cowboys and Indians endlessly, the only difference between their activities and those of contemporary white boys being the willingness and enthusiasm with which the role of "Indian," with its inevitable death scene, is accepted.

5 The research on which this paper is based was supported by a National Institute of Mental Health training fellowship and a post-doctoral research grant from the same organization. The research was carried out during 1960 and 1961. Statements are based on observations made during approximately nine months residence in Piñon in intimate contact with a Navajo extended family which permitted us to occupy a hogan and admitted us to participation in the economic, recreational, and ceremonial activities of the group. In addition, contact was maintained with relocated Navajo in the San Francisco Bay area, some of whom were members of the host family in Piñon. Finally, the literacy of some of our informants contributed something over one hundred letters which have served as extremely useful sources of information.

BIBLIOGRAPHY

DeVoto, Bernard (1947), Across the wide Missouri (Boston: Houghton-Mifflin).

Downs, James F. (n.d.); Animal husbandry in Navajo society and culture (in press).

Hill, W. W. (1940), Some Navajo culture changes during two centuries. In *Essays in historical anthropology of North America*, Smithsonian Institution Miscellaneous Collection 100:395-416. Washington, D.C.

Kluckhohn, Clyde, and Dorothea Leighton (1947), *The Navajo* (Cambridge, Harvard University Press).

Linton, Ralph (1936), *A study of Man* (New York).

Shepardson, Mary (n.d.), Developing political process among the Navajo Indians. Ph.D. dissertation, University of California, Berkeley, 1960.

Spindler, Louise S. (1962), Menomini women and culture change. American Anthropological Association Memoir 91, LXIV(1), Part 2 Menasha.

HARRIET J. KUPFERER: HEALTH PRACTICES AND EDUCATIONAL ASPIRATIONS AS INDI-CATORS OF ACCULTURATION AND SOCIAL CLASS AMONG THE EASTERN CHEROKEE*

ABSTRACT

Research among the Eastern Band of Cherokee Indians would indicate that visible differences among the people in matters of health and education are not only a result of acculturation. Social class behavior seems to figure prominently as a factor in disparate behavior manifested by nonconservative Cherokees.

Implicit in most models of American Indian acculturation seems to be the assumption that "white" culture is homogeneous, therefore, as native people alter their premises, attitudes, and behavior they too become like the homogeneous "whites." Given the volumes of research which attend to social stratification and class differences in the dominant white society, it is evident that gradients of acculturation are inadequate as conceptual models or as descriptive typologies. Yet lineal schemes have appeared frequently in recent studies of acculturation among North American Indians.[1] Lineal models vary in terminology, but they all plot types of Indians on a continuum which has at its polar points such designations as "native oriented" or "native modified" and "white oriented or American modified." George Spindler also emphasizes lineality although he separates the most acculturated Menominee into an elite acculturated and a lower status acculturated.[2]

More recently Robert K. Thomas[3] posited a tentative continuum of North Carolina Cherokee Indian acculturation in which he identified four groups: Conservative Indians, Generalized Indians, Rural White Indians,

Source: Reprinted by permission from *Social Forces* 41 (December 1962), 154-162.

and Middle Class Indians. These categories were established on the basis of differing world views and integrative values. The Conservative views himself as a different order of man from the rest of men. Overtly, he is still the stoic Red man. To the extent that there are Indian traits present for example, native speech and medicine, he is characterized by their use. The Generalized Indian considers himself *both* an Indian and an American. He demonstrates inconsistency in statements of values, shifting between western values and conservative values. He interacts more readily with whites than does the Conservative. Rural White Indians, says Thomas, are very much like southern rural whites both in behavior and, incidentally, in physical appearance. Some are sensitive and defensive about their status as Indians; others become aggressively "Indians" in response to a derogatory attitude shown to them by Conservatives. Indians in the Middle Class stem from both the Rural White group and the Generalized Indians. They have arrived financially and are committed to progress and achievement.

Although Thomas' nomenclature differs from that used by other scholars, the model is essentially the same. It suggests that internal differences within an Indian tribe can be viewed in terms of a gradient running from groups who are traditionally oriented to those which are white oriented. While the recognition of the complexity of the larger society does not demand a rejection of the lineal model it does require that the model be enlarged to accommodate both social differentiation and acculturation.[4] Thomas tacitly recognizes vertical change among the Cherokee in his use of Middle Class as a position at the terminal end of the acculturation continuum. However, this still leaves unexplained the presence of people, who, while they are not Conservative, are by no means Middle Class. Therefore, it is the intent of this paper to examine the extent and nature of culture change in the Eastern Band of Cherokee and to demonstrate that a lineal acculturation model is inadequate to describe the differences extant among the people.

The field data were gathered during 1958-1960 among the Cherokee. Observations were focused on three socio-cultural variables which we hypothesized would reveal not only differences in acculturation but also differences in social class. These variables[5] were: (1) health and medical practices; (2) attitudes and behavior toward education; and (3) adherence to dominant value systems. In this paper the data relevant to health and education will be presented.

THE CONTEMPORARY CHEROKEE COMMUNITY

The North Carolina Cherokee occupy a reservation of approximately 56,572 acres in the western portion of the state. The region is mountainous: therefore, most of the land is in second or third growth timber. Roughly 4,000 acres are suitable for farming.

In 1960 there were 4,494 people who were considered eligible for tribal membership.[6] Of this group approximately thirty percent have three-quarters or more Indian inheritance, or as the Indians say, are "full blood" or nearly "full blood." Tribal members who are less than one-half in Indian inheritance and who appear nearly white are called "white Indians" both by members of the tribe and by the surrounding white population. So to the Cherokee themselves there are but two groups present, Indians and white Indians.

The main sources of earned income derive from the tourist industry, two small white-owned factories on the reservation, and miscellaneous wage labor. Tourist trade is a vital element in the Indian economy. In addition to profit accruing to business proprietors (motel owners, craft shop proprietors, and restaurant owners) money passes to other people who are waitresses, and sales personnel or who are employed in ancillary capacities. The persistence of home crafts is in part a function of tourist trade. Gross incomes of Indian owned and operated businesses varied in 1959 from $307,131 (an individually owned motel, restaurant, and craft shop) to less than $1,000 grossed by the owner-operator of a one-vehicle taxi business. The two factories provided a weekly payroll of $8,000 during this period. In addition to earned income, public assistance programs and Federal Indian welfare funds supplement the local economy. Expenditures from the Indian welfare program totaled $114,405 for the fiscal year, 1959.

Cherokee Health Practices

Three aspects of Cherokee life associated with the broad field of health were examined: (a) sanitation and home hygienic measures; (b) behavior evidenced in the public health clinics; and (c) actions induced by illness.

(a) Sanitation and Home Hygienic Measures. We found it possible to separate types of Indian housing and sanitary practices into four categories which, within the context of the Cherokee community, range from poor to good.[7] The first includes homes where sanitary observances are all but absent. The second is composed of homes whose occupants make an effort to maintain some semblance of hygiene. Families in categories three and four have practices which by our standards are adequate. In the fourth, families are indistinguishable from middle class American families at large. The fundamental differences between the third and fourth categories are a matter of extras present in the environment of the latter, e.g. fully equipped kitchens, modern baths, and other appurtenances.

The homes in the first category are small, the number of rooms is seldom more than three. The yards are littered with debris: rusted cans, broken bottles and garbage are scattered over the yard. Chickens, ducks, dogs, and cats dispute over the edible refuse and spread their excrement in the vicinity of the home. The interiors of these houses are similar. There are no plumbing facilities. Two or more double beds are present in all the rooms. Soiled blankets are commonly wadded upon the beds or spread in a casual manner over stained mattresses. The number of occupants to a bed is contingent upon the size of the family but since the dwellings are always crowded, three or four children usually sleep together. Associated with this category of residence is a general cavalier behavior with regard to basic sanitary precautions. For example, during a visit to a home of this type, a baby was given a bottle (supplement to breast feeding) which was picked from the floor and filled. The baby drank part of it. Then it was passed on to the "yard baby" who drained it. In looking for some ideas of relationship between endemic conditions and prevailing practices I discussed worms with the mother. She said that two of her children had "killed" (passed) nearly a hundred of them. I asked the cause of worms. She replied that she didn't know what caused them, "Kids just get 'em." The young children of the family were covered with sores and scabs, especially on their heads. The mother said that these were gnat bites. A final excerpt from notes of a visit made in 1959 summarizes these generalizations about sanitation and hygienic practices. "I visited with Dorothy on her porch. The house was a two room cabin with four double beds. All of them were unmade; soiled blankets were heaped upon them ... the kitchen table had dishes on it which appeared to have been unwashed for some time. With the dishes was an open jar of beans. Later I glanced up to see a chicken on the table foraging among the unwashed dishes."

In the second category the houses are also small in proportion to the number of occupants but they are not as crowded as those in the first. Some efforts are made toward maintaining a semblance of neatness. The yards are often raked and swept; there is a noticeable decrease in the visible litter. The interior of these dwellings is somewhat more orderly and varied than those which are characteristic of the first group. Floors are frequently covered with linoleum, and several homes have refrigerators. People in this category frequently mention cleanliness and good health habits although occasionally nonchalant behavior prevails in this regard. Their remarks about cleanliness are often unsolicited. An elderly informant with whom I often took meals observed:

> I always use soap and scald the dishes because it keeps the germs away. That's what I learned when I cooked at Berry's camp and at that camp if one dish got cracked, we had to put it away because a germ could get in it ... after he went away we used the cracked ones. [I noticed that some of the dishes still had food clinging to them after she put them away.] I've always been clean and I taught my daughters to be clean.

The third category of homes is typified by neat exteriors. The interiors are also tidy but not elaborate. Electric appliances are commonplace. By and large people living in these homes follow standardized ways of behaving with respect to hygienic practices.

In category four there is variation in the quality of the dwellings and furnishings. These people share with those in category three a mutual concern for and adherence to typical health habits. This emphasis is not stressed verbally unless the conversation turns to "full bloods." Should this occur, remarks are directed toward the careless habits of "full bloods." "I can't understand those Indians who work all day; come in, eat supper and go to bed. They'd feel so much better if they bathed." Comments such as this are made without regard for the fact that many of the people to whom they refer have no running water and nothing in which to bathe.

Although four categories of housing and associated practices are discernible, these do not correspond neatly with Thomas' four acculturative groups. There are Conservatives, Rural Whites and Generalized Indians in category one; Conservatives, Rural Whites and Generalized Indians in the second category; Rural Whites, Generalized Indians and a few Middle Class in category three; and category four includes Middle Class plus a few Rural Whites and Generalized Indians. Table 1 demonstrates the distribution of 73 informant families according to their environments.

TABLE 1

*Distribution of Selected Cherokee Families by
Types of Sanitary-Hygienic Environment*

Types of Sanitary-Hygienic Environment	Selected Families, According to Thomas' "Acculturation Types"							
	Conservative		Generalized		Rural White		Middle Class	
	No.	Percent	No.	Percent	No.	Percent	No.	Percent
Category 1–Low	13	56.5	1	6.0	4	28.6	0	0.0
Category 2–Minimal	9	39.1	7	41.2	4	28.6	0	0.0
Category 3–Adequate	1	4.4	6	35.2	5	35.7	4[a]	21.1
Category 4–Very adequate	0	0.0	3	17.6	1	7.1	15	78.9
Totals	23	100%	17	100%	14	100%	19	100%

[a]Three of the four are homes of single men.

The data presented in this table are valid solely in terms of the cases selected for observation. They illustrate that there is only a rough fit between Thomas' groups and their sanitary and hygienic practices. It is also apparent that factors other than acculturation are present which affect the types of environment typical of Cherokee Indians.

(b) Public Health Clinic Behavior. Associated with the maintenance of healthful surroundings is the actual day-to-day attention given to disease prevention. This includes, in addition to ordinary precautions which have already been discussed, the utilization of public health clinics and periodic physical examinations for children and adults. All Cherokee with the exception of Thomas' Middle Class Indians use the Public Health clinic service. Since all Cherokee families exclusive of the Middle Class are drawn into such clinics as the Diabetic clinic, Well Baby clinic, and the pre-school clinic, we cannot distinguish between groups on the basis of clinic participation. Differences do occur, however, in behavior during clinic visitations and in attitudes toward inoculations, and make it possible to identify two distinct categories. These are clearly marked by the demeanor or pose assumed in the clinic, both in the waiting room and in the dispensary. While waiting to be called, those of the first category sit quietly outside. Their children, both babies and toddlers, also sit with solemn expressions. If they speak, it is very softly and often in Cherokee. People in the second laugh and visit noisily with one another while awaiting their turn. Their children wander about, talk to others in the waiting room, or thumb through the children's books which are provided.

Both the adults and children in the first category are inarticulate and acquiescent. Although the public health nurse greets everyone in a jocular manner, these people reply to the greeting almost inaudibly. Their main purpose in bringing a child into the well baby clinic is for inoculations which they realize all children must have. They seldom initiate a discussion of other health matters. Commonly these people fail to complete a series of inoculations. They appear for an initial injection but often do not reappear for others within the stipulated time period. For example, a couple brought a child into the clinic. After the small baby was inoculated, the mother murmured, "I got another one in the car; maybe it might need something." The record was checked, and it was found that one inoculation had been administered two years earlier. Reasons are seldom provided for neglecting to follow through. People in this category are Conservatives. Some of them attend clinics irregularly, others are more regular. All of them are passive participants. Communication emanates from the medical staff and is largely one way. The Indians speak when spoken to.

Members in the second category contrast sharply to those in the first. They joke with the nurse and pass on local news. They tell children old enough to understand that "it won't hurt." If a child should cry, he is frequently told not to cry. Discussions of the injections are common, and advice is sought on other matters pertaining to the children and occasionally themselves. Persons in this category are Rural Whites and Generalized Indians. They are clearly differentiated from those in the first by their *active* interest and participation in clinic and health matters. Conversely, the Conservatives are reticent and compliant in the presence of the professional staff. Their demeanor suggests vagueness and a lack of comprehension of the principles of immunization. These categories are clearly distinct, separating Conservatives from all others by actions displayed in the clinic.

(c) Behavior Prompted by Illness. Illness disturbs family equilibrium. If the condition persists, it demands a decision to act. The choices made by the Cherokee from the alternatives open to them for coping with illness make it possible to place them into three categories: those who rely on Indian doctors, usually in combination with some modern medicine; those who rely almost exclusively on the Public Health Hospital and staff; and those who seek private medical care to the exclusion of the provided services.

Indians who continue to depend on Indian doctors are Conservatives, but they seldom do so to the complete exclusion of modern medicine. Some of the older people, however, attempt to confine themselves to the native practitioner. These elderly Indians believe that the hospital is a place where people die. One aged woman said firmly, "I'd never go to the hospital; I'd never go to anybody but an Indian doctor . . . I want to die in my own bed." When these older Indians do go to the hospital, it is at the insistence of another member of the family. Admittedly, those people who actively resist modern medical aid are few. The most common practice is that of employing a combination of the two forms of treatment. Occasionally this combination occurs simultaneously, or nearly so. If the patient is not hospitalized he will seek treatment for the condition both from a Public Health physician and from a native doctor. This pattern of combining professional and nonprofessional care is not as common as using either the one type or the other as different occasions demand. It is difficult to discover what dictates the choice of therapy. However, the data suggest that a knowledge of the nature of the ailment is a factor, particularly in the case of children's illnesses. If the ailment is not diagnosed, the child is most frequently taken into the hospital for a "shot." If on the other hand, the trouble is an earache, a cold or a fever, an Indian doctor is called in. The general consensus seems to be that Indian doctors know more about babies than white doctors.

The second category is composed mainly of the Rural Whites and the Generalized Indians who use to the fullest extent the facilities offered by the Public Health Service; occasionally a Middle Class Indian uses the service, usually for emergency treatment. Unless they are referred to other physicians or specialists, the people of category two seldom leave the reservation for medical treatment. While none admit using Indian doctors, some may employ herbs which they regard as effective. Some have patronized Indian doctors in the past. One older Rural White informant said. "Anybody would be a fool to go to one of them." His wife reminded him that he had gone to one years ago. He replied:

Aw, hell, I was so damn drunk I didn't know what I was doing . . . it would have gotten better anyway. I fell off a damn mule and my leg swelled up and kept bothering me. So I got a jug of whiskey and went over to her place [Indian doctor] and said I wanted my leg doctored. She went over to the stove and warmed her hands and rubbed them on my knee. Then she took a scratcher with snake rattles on it—snake teeth too I reckon—and scratched my leg 'til the damn thing bled. She told me it would get better in four days . . . got well after a while, but not in four days . . . damn foolishness!

The final category is comprised of people who use private health services almost exclusively. It is made up primarily of the Cherokee Middle Class, but there are a few Rural Whites and Generalized Indians in it. Their reasons for relying on private medical care are varied and complex. It is alleged by many people that the Public Health doctors are poorly qualified. "Public Health officials can't make a go of it in private practice." "They are more concerned with their salaries than they are with the people." Although there may be some truth in the charges, comments suggest that a matter of status is equally operative in the choice of therapy. This is borne out by such remarks as, "I can afford my own doctor bills," and "I'm no charity patient."

Indians in the third category are much more sophisticated in health affairs than are those in the second. Although they treat themselves at home, they seldom permit a chronic condition or unusual symptom to continue unattended. In general there is no distinctive difference between Indians of the third category and white people who possess similar educational and economic background. Their health practices accord with general middle-class behavior.

Distribution of Selected Cherokee Families
by Type of Medical Care

	Selected Families, According to Thomas' "Acculturation Types"							
	Conservative		Generalized		Rural White		Middle Class	
Type of Medical Care	No.	Percent	No.	Percent	No.	Percent	No.	Percent
Indian "doctors"	22	91.7	1[a]	5.9	1[a]	7.1	0	0.0
Public health	2	8.3	13	76.5	10	71.5	1	5.3
Private practice	0	0.0	3	17.6	3	21.4	18	94.7
Totals	24	100%	17	100%	14	100%	19	100%

[a] There is no conclusive evidence that these informants utilize Indian doctors, but conversations hint at the possibility.

Table 2 illustrates the distribution of 74 informant families by their choice of medical practitioners.

In examining data pertaining to health, we find that only in the matter of housing and environment does overt behavior reveal a four-fold classification of individuals. The four categories do not, however correspond with Thomas' acculturation gradient. The clinic situation reveals only a two way division, Conservatives and nonconservatives. The choice of therapy made by the people permits us to identify three categories: those who in some way or other use indigenous curers; people who rely on public health services; and Indians who are patients of private physicians. These findings are suggestive in that they resemble class behavior as well as differing cultural behavior.

Education Attitudes and Aspirations

Evidence secured on attitudes toward education and parental aspirations for the education of their children support the postulate that both social stratification and acculturation are characteristic of the Cherokee.

Based upon their aspirations, the Cherokee were placed into three categories: (1) those who aspire to a high school education for their children; (2) those who regard some further training, usually vocational, as necessary; and (3) those who anticipate collegiate education for their children.

Among people who envisage high school education as necessary preparation for young people, verbalization on the importance of this achievement is a recurrent phenomenon. By and large, the reasons given for this desideratum are similar. A common one is the desire to have children better educated than their parents. One informant who is raising the illegitimate son of one of her daughters told me that she wants "him to be something when he grows up, not a dummy like me. I most forgot everything I ever learned—arithmetic, it's like when you lie down to go to sleep, you put everything away." Her formal education was restricted to three or four years at the boarding school in the years around 1900.

Another reason proposed for finishing school, closely related to the first, reflects concern for employment opportunities. There is agreement that nowadays, a high school education is imperative if one is to get any kind of a job. The fact has been underscored by the presence of the small industry on the reservation. Many applicants have been refused employment because of insufficient education. Some people are implementing the goal by seeing that their children attend school regularly. On the other hand, others are much less assertive about school attendance. The records of their children indicate that they do not press their children to attend regularly. Other evidence supports this lack of coercion; for example, the variation found among children within the same family in the number of grades completed. Often the fact that a child does not want to go to school some morning is sufficient reason for his absence. I asked an informant one day why her son was not in school. She replied, "He got ready to go this morning; he put on clean socks but he didn't go." Another said in response to the same question, "She just didn't want to go today."

Some Rural Whites, Generalized Indians and Conservatives are found in Category 1. They all share the same levels of aspiration, but the steps they take to insure achievement vary. Generalized Indians and Rural Whites are usually more forceful in insisting upon regular attendance, and they attempt although not always successfully to keep children enrolled until they graduate from high school. Customarily, Conservatives do not pressure their children to comply with their wishes. However, there are a few who, although traditional in many ways (choice of medical treatment and Cherokee speech), are determined to see that their children receive more education than they did. At this writing they are taking measures to satisfy this ambition, but these children are young. Whether the adults will continue to influence them as they mature is a moot point.

The second category, noncollegiate post-high school training is a common goal for many of the people and one well within the reach of most of them, as the Federal government maintains free vocational schools for Indians. The major cost is transportation. Cherokees who take advantage of these schools go either to Haskell Institute in Kansas, or to Chilocco, Oklahoma. The reasons parents give for encouraging their children to continue almost always refer to better economic opportunities.

People who comprise Category 2 are Generalized Indians, Rural Whites, and a few Conservatives. Most, although not all, of the Conservatives who are in this aggregate are there by virtue of the fact that some of their children are presently enrolled in Haskell or Chilocco. But we suspect, with good reason, that this is due, at least in part, to outside influences and personal choices of the children, rather than as a direct consequence of parental pushing.

There is some merging between ambitions for vocational training and for college education among a few of these people. Some do not make a clear distinction between the two alternatives because they do not understand the difference between the two kinds of institutions. For others, the economic differential between the two kinds of advanced training is the reason for the lack of definitive goal.

A small number of Cherokees regard college education as a normal expectation for their children. Some children in Category 3 are currently in college; others who are not yet there are reminded of this goal in many ways. Economic position is, of course, important for realizing this ambition, but it is not the sole reason. There are several families for whom the expense of maintaining even one child in college represents a financial strain, yet they plan on sending their children. There are other motives present among all of these people which are lacking in Indians of Category 2. One sentiment, often disguised, holds that a college education will prove that Indians can amount to something. Other comments conceal recognition of the prestige which a college degree confers irrespective of race. A statement from a young informant typifies this attitude. His parents have a very well established business in which he works during the summer and which he plans to join after he finishes college. I asked him why he was continuing in school. "Oh, I don't know," he said. "Just to say I did it, I guess . . . it would be nice for the children to say they had a daddy who went to college . . . I'll never use it [college education] , I guess."

Some people in this category who have achieved a stable socio-economic position desire higher education for their offspring, not so much because they are striving for prestige, but because they have accepted college as an expected norm for their social position. There are others whose socio-economic status is not typically that of the Middle Class, but whose goals are similar. These families are currently mobile. None of the reasons given for a college education are mutually exclusive. And, of course, employment possibilities are woven through all the motives. Most of the people in this category correspond to Thomas' Middle Class. However, there are a few Generalized Indians and Rural Whites who although not having the economic base of the Middle Class have the educational orientation. Strangely enough, there is among our cases at least one who is in many respects a Conservative.

The analysis of educational aspirations has yielded three distinct clusters among the Cherokee. The members of these categories fit the Thomas model in only a crude way. The category with the lowest level of aspiration includes a large number of Conservatives, Rural Whites, and

TABLE 3

Distribution of Selected Cherokee Families
by Educational Aspirations

Educational Aspirations	Selected Families, According to Thomas' "Acculturation Types"							
	Conservative		Generalized		Rural White		Middle Class	
	No.	Percent	No.	Percent	No.	Percent	No.	Percent
High school oriented	7	63.6	3	27.2	3	33.3	0	0.0
Post high school vocational training	3	27.2	5	45.6	3	33.3	1	10.0
College oriented	1	9.2	3	27.2	3	33.3	9	90.0
Totals	11	100%	11	100%	9	99.9%	10	100%

Generalized Indians. The second with the intermediate goal is made up of Generalized Indians, Rural Whites, a few Conservatives and one or two Middle Class people. The largest single group in the college-oriented category is the Middle Class. Table 3 demonstrates the frequency distribution of Cherokee informants according to their educational aspirations.

The differences among the Cherokee with respect to education are, we suggest, both the result of acculturation and moreover, the result of internal processes among the nonconservatives. These internal differences hint at social class distinctions as do data pertaining to health practices.

CONCLUSION

We have suggested that the findings of this research on overt behavior and attitudes with respect to the matters of health and education reveal more than just differences in degrees of acculturation. For if acculturation were the sole process, we would expect to find four more or less distinctive and discrete clusters of behavior attendant upon the two variables. Furthermore, we should be able to recognize each of the four groups of Cherokee (Conservatives, Generalized Indians, Rural Whites and Middle Class) by their characteristic comportment. But this is not the case. Only in the analysis of environment and sanitation was it possible to construct four categories. But these do not accord with the acculturative types. For example, some 52.8 percent of the Generalized Indian Informants fall in categories three and four (acceptable in sanitary observances) which is higher than would be expected, and 57.1 percent of the Rural Whites fall within categories one and two (least acceptable) which is lower than would be anticipated if a good fit existed between sanitary and hygienic practices and the Thomas acculturation continuum. One is led to believe that much of the difference in the environments of the Generalized Indian, the Rural Whites and the Middle Class Indian is due to socio-economic circumstances rather than to differences in acculturation. Similarly, the data pursuant to choice of therapy suggests that choices made by nonconservatives are contingent upon differences in status and styles of life rather than upon differences in acculturation. The Generalized Indian and the Rural White who use the Public Health facilities and staff frequently do so because they cannot afford private medical care.

The findings on educational aspirations have also disclosed differences among the Cherokee, but the differences do not correspond with Thomas' four types of Indians. Distinctions among nonconservatives are not a by-product of acculturation but stem from disparities in social class behavior. The findings here are similar to the conclusions of a number of studies which examine education as an aspect of class behavior.[8]

Consequently, we suggest that two processes of change figure in the current constellation of Cherokee types. The presence of conservatives and nonconservatives is explained by acculturation, which is an on-going process. The manifest differences among the nonconservatives derive from incipient social class structure with accompanying definitive behavior.

NOTES

*The research for this study was supported by a grant from the National Institute of Mental Health of the Department of Health, Education and Welfare. Drafts of this paper were read by John J. Honigmann, M. Elaine Burgess, and Richard Lieban. The writer is grateful to them for their cogent comments.

1 See for example: Irving Hallowell, "Ojibwa Personality and Acculturation," in Sol Tax, editor, *Acculturation in The Americas,* Proceedings and Selected Papers of the XXIXth Congress of Americanists (Chicago: University of Chicago Press, 1952); Fred Voget, "Crow Sociocultural Groups," *ibid;* Fred Voget, "A Shoshone Innovator," *American Anthropologist,* 52 (January-March 1950), pp. 53-63; Edward M. Bruner, "Primary Group Experience and The Process of Acculturation," *American Anthropologist,* 58 (July-September 1956), pp. 605-623.

2 George Spindler, *Sociocultural and Psychological Processes in Menomini Acculturation,* University, of California Publications in Culture and Society, 5 (Berkeley: University of California Press, 1955).

3 Robert K. Thomas, "Eastern Cherokee Acculturation," Mss. Cross-cultural Laboratory, Chapel Hill, University of North Carolina, 1958. The writer is indebted to Mr. Thomas for his acute observations on the Eastern Cherokee and for the stimulation which his work has provided.

4 Two recent studies recognize the presence of class as a factor in understanding Indian behavior. Bernard J. James, "Social-Psychological Dimensions of Ojibwa Acculturation," *American Anthropologist* 63 (August 1961) pp. 721-745. James describes an Ojibwa community as economically lower class. The community has become deculturated, and the minimal appropriation of new culture traits has produced a poor-white type of subculture. Research on the Alberta Metis suggests that the current plight of the Metis is not from a lack of acculturation but from acculturation into the lower classes of Euro-Candian society. Gordon K. Hirabayashi and Cyril L. French, "Poverty, Poor Acculturation and Apathy: Factors in The Social Status of Some Alberta Metis," A paper read at the Canadian Political Science Association, Montreal, Canada, June 1961.

5 These criteria have been used as indices in establishing class boundaries or determining class behavior. See for example: Bernice Goldstein and Robert L. Eichorn, "The Changing Protestant Ethic: Rural Patterns in Health, Work and Leisure," *American Sociological Review,* 26 (August 1961) pp. 557-565; August B. Hollingshead and Frederick C. Redlick, *Social Class and Mental Illness* (New York: John P. Wiley and Sons, 1958); Lloyd D. Warner, et al., *Social Class in America* (Chicago: Science Research Associates, 1947). Health has also been employed as a marker of acculturation. For example see Peter Kunstadter, "Culture Change, Social Structure and Use of Medical Care by Residents of The Mescalero Apache Reservation," paper read at the American Anthropological Association, Minneapolis, Minnesota, November 1960. For a more complete description of the application of these variables see: Harriet J. Kupferer, *The "Principal People," 1960: A Study of Cultural and Social Groups of The Eastern Cherokee.* Unpublished PhD. Dissertation (Chapel Hill: University of North Carolina, 1961).

6 Among the requirements for tribal membership are: at least 1/32 Indian inheritance, parents who were included on the Baker Roll, and residence on the reservation.

7 In January 1955, The Jackson-Macon-Swain District Health Department conducted a health and sanitation survey on the Big Cove Community of the Cherokee Indian Reservation in which it is reported that aside from "a half dozen or so of the more affluent homes, the houses—no matter the number of rooms noted—are of substandard construction and badly maintained. . . . Many of these houses are unfit for human habitation." Memorandum to Health Officer for Sanitarian, District Health Department Files, January 1955.

8 For example see Joseph A. Kahl, "Educational and Occupational Aspirations of Commonman Boys," *Harvard Educational Review,* XXIII (Summer 1953), 188; Byron S. Hollinshead, *Who Should Go To College* (New York: Columbia University Press, 1952) in Joseph A. Kahl, *The American Class Structure* (New York: Rinehart and Co., 1957) pp. 280-293.

MALCOLM McFEE: THE 150% MAN, A PRODUCT OF BLACK-FEET ACCULTURATION[1]

ABSTRACT

Some work with the "levels of acculturation" concept seems to assume a continuum of change and often entails an unintended correlate of cultural loss and replacement. An assessment of individuals among the Blackfeet using two scales, one a measure of Indian orientation and the other of White orientation, reveals that this view may be incorrect. New ways can be learned without abandoning the old. The bicultural reservation community provides a variety of roles and situations for selective use of both. It is suggested that a matrix model would be more meaningful than the continuum model for the assessment of individual acculturation, and that more attention should be paid to situational factors.

I

In this paper I explore the implications of an attempt to measure "levels of acculturation" among the members of the Blackfeet Indian Tribe of northern Montana with the intent of showing how a change in the techniques of data analysis, during the process of assessing levels of ac-

Source: Reprinted by permission of the American Anthropological Association from *American Anthropologist,* Vol. 70, No. 6, 1968.

culturation, disclosed some interesting variations from the expected acculturation continuum. As one facet of a continuing research project directed toward an ethnography of these people, it follows a line of inquiry stemming from the work of Voget (1950, 1951, 1952), Bruner (1956a, 1956b), and Spindler (1955) and relates to questions examined by French (1961, 1962), Polgar (1960) and others who have stressed the heterogeneous nature of modern American Indian reservation societies and cultures. Closer examination of the variations among my data indicates that some of the concepts commonly used to assess processes of individual acculturation, or variations in bicultural experience, need further study. The questions raised can be answered only by continued research into these problems both on the Blackfeet and other reservations.

The terms used to identify levels or other categories of acculturation, such as Voget's *native, native-modified,* and *American-marginal,* Bruner's *unacculturated, marginal, acculturated,* and Spindler's *native-oriented, transitionals, lower-* and *upper-status acculturated,* describe long-term processes of tribal acculturation with reasonable accuracy. They also serve to focus attention upon the problems of individual acculturation—how people, over one to several generations, adapt to bicultural environments and learn to use cultural directives from another society. The "levels of acculturation" concept makes us aware of the differential rates of acculturation—that all segments of a tribal society do not learn and utilize concepts from another culture at the same rate and to the same degree— and provides a means for handling this differential both in description and theory.

We latecomers to the study of American Indian reservation life tend to take these categories, and the heterogeneity they handle, somewhat for granted. The cultural variation is easier to recognize now that others have pointed it out, and we can build upon these ideas and attempt refinements that appear to be called for.

This discussion will proceed in three steps: First, a brief description will be given of the Blackfeet tribal structure that represents a position along the course of tribal acculturation. This description will establish, in part, the social and cultural context within which individuals make adaptation. This will be followed by an examination of some cases of people who do not show straight-line acculturation from a more Indian to a more white position. These individual variations will be seen to relate to the statuses open in the social structure and the attendant roles, and to give some indication of how people learn these roles. I will then consider some of the implications that these cases have for studies of cultural heterogeneity on this reservation, at least, and perhaps on other Indian reservations as well.

II

The Blackfeet tribal enrollment as of February 1, 1960, was 8,456 members of which 4,850 lived on the reservation. Roughly 13 percent of this resident population was fullblood, while perhaps another 10 percent was less than one quarter Indian. Until 1962, when tribal membership was limited henceforth to those of one quarter or more Indian descent, there had been no limitation on enrollment based upon any particular degree of Indian "blood" (Blackfeet Tribal Council n.d.).

Field study (reported in McFee 1962 with data and rationale for the statements that follow) revealed a great diversity in income, occupation, schooling, and other factors among the population. Yet the tribe, as a whole, is highly acculturated. Its members participate, in varying degrees, in the economic and political life of the state and nation. All live in houses, most drive cars, watch TV, dress in Western clothes, attend the regional schools and churches. All but a few of the older people speak English. In many respects they are similar to their non-Indian, rural Montana neighbors. Indian cultural characteristics, however, persist among one segment of this population, and individual and group variations in the degree of this persistence make it possible to recognize acculturation *categories.* I stress categories because, as I hope to show later, these may or more often may not correspond to meaningful social groups. The point to be made here, however, is that in the course of tribal acculturation, a bicultural social structure has become established that provides both models and positions for varied adaptations to reservation life.

Briefly, the tribe is divided into two recognizably contrasting social groups: (1) a numerically, politically, and economically dominant group, here called *white-oriented,* that is culturally similar to any non-Indian, rural Montana community, and (2) another social grouping of tribal members who *want to be Indian* and who act in conformity with attenuated tribal traditions, persisting Indian values, and some borrowed pan-Indian symbols. I call this the *Indian-oriented group.* A man or woman who aspires to be a member of this group must value being Indian, and participate in some Indian-oriented activities, such as bundle openings, Indian dances, song services, Indian encampments, and visiting. Above all, such people must be helpful and generous to others. Display of generosity, even to the point of self-impoverishment, was highly valued in the Blackfeet past, and remains important today among this segment of the reservation population. More Indian- than white-oriented people use the Blackfeet language frequently in their homes and in conversation with their friends. Note that the criteria used to define these groups are social and cultural, not biological. While Indian orientation and greater degrees of Indian descent correlate moderately, this is not the key to Indian-oriented participation. The important factors are aspirations, values, goals and behavior.

It is this Indian behavior, and the qualities that can be inferred from it, that highlight the contrasts between these two subsocieties. To a great degree, participation in the Indian-oriented activities, and commitment to Indian values, preclude full social acceptance by the white-oriented group. These things take time that white-oriented people feel should be spent in gainful work. Generosity is fine, the latter say, but not to the point where a man and his family undermine their economic position. White-oriented people tend to be, seek to be, or think they are, more independent, acquisitive, hard-working and success-oriented than are their more Indian neighbors. Social groups form within these subsocieties, while acculturation categories may include people who have little if any social interaction.

Each of these subsocieties is stratified, providing lower and higher status positions based upon appraisals of an individual's success in conforming to the ideals of the group to which he belongs. Equivalent positions in the two subsocieties tend to contrast. A man who has achieved high status in Indian society by emphasizing Indian characteristics, by spending much time at the proper social gatherings, by his knowledge of Indian lore and ritual, and particularly by his continued generosity, may find it difficult to attain high status in the eyes of white-oriented people who measure his social worth by economic standards, scheduled work hours, formal education, and accumulated capital.

In addition, the Indian-oriented face yet another hurdle. They, more than the white-oriented, must know how to behave in terms of both cultures. Only occasionally, and usually for political purposes, do the white-oriented enter into the Indian-oriented world, but political and economic necessities require the Indian to participate at many levels within the white sphere. Here he is expected to speak English and behave according to white-oriented directives and expectations if he is to succeed in gaining the ends he seeks.

This is a culturally and socially bifurcated population held together by the legal and social implications of Indian descent, residence upon an Indian reservation, and, to a great degree, by participation in common economic and political spheres. The white-oriented segment, composed of recently acculturated persons and others from families where white socialization practices have been dominant for several generations, are assimilated, in most respects, into the general American society. The Indian-oriented group, on the other hand, consciously stands against such assimilation. This, then, sketches in some aspects of the social structure and cultural environment within which individuals make adaptation on the Blackfeet Reservation.

III

In the analysis that led to the above and following conculsions, I first attempted to sort the members of a random sample of the resident male tribal population, who had been born before 1941, into acculturation categories by analyzing their responses to a socioeconomic questionnaire. This interview material provided data on a range of activities and achievements that could be identified as either Indian or white traits. It was assumed that the cases would distribute along an acculturation continuum ranging from those who showed the most Indian characteristics to those who measured most white, which they did to some extent. Groupings along this continuum, however, did not correspond to any social units that had been observed during the course of the research. It was noted, too, that in the early assessments some individuals fell into odd positions along the line. For instance, one very successful rancher, one quarter Indian, who on the basis of the most visible criteria should have been at the highly acculturated end of the continuum, reported high competence in the use of the Blackfeet language and considerable knowledge of, and participation in, Indian activities. The rules of analysis at that point required that he be positioned near the middle of the continuum, partially acculturated, although this was an obvious misappraisal.

A second look at his case showed that this man had been socialized in white ways, had high status in the white-oriented group, but as a boy had been taught much of the Blackfeet lore, ritual, and language during a three-year residence with his Indian grandfather. This knowledge was retained and used on occasion for participation in Indian-oriented activities. These indices were pulling him back toward the more Indian end of my continuum. It was more realistic to recognize him as a white man who knew Indian ways and could participate at certain levels of Indian-oriented society. He had not become acculturated from Indian to white, but from white toward Indian. Perhaps, for this reason, he did not belong on the continuum with which I was working, yet he was a resident tribal member of minimal Indian descent.

Other cases were found where men, thus centrally located on the continuum, knew Indian culture well, learned it in their childhood homes, and took part in its modern expression. On the basis of this knowledge and the observed participation they should have measured among the less acculturated. But, in addition to all this, they had been well educated and displayed many characteristics required for successful assimilation. By these latter indices they should have fallen well into the more acculturated range of the continuum. This particular use of the continuum model was not dividing this population with sufficient accuracy. It was apparent that the model I was using rested on an assumption of cultural replacement—as a man became more acculturated he would replace Indian ways with white ways. Evidently an assumption that might hold for group acculturation could not be made about the individuals who were contributing to the group process.

The data were reexamined and some of the indices selected for further analysis. Knowledge and use of the Blackfeet language, knowledge of Blackfeet religious beliefs and lore, participation in Indian dances, singing, and give-aways, and some linguistic indices of home environment were used as measures of Indian-orientation. A comparable set of indices for white-orientation was then established from the data provided by the original questionnaire. Each man was measured by each of these standards, two continua were constructed and used as the vertical and horizontal axes of a two dimensional matrix, or scattergram, upon which the two measures of each case could be plotted.

The scattergram distribution . . . conformed reasonably well to the previous continuum, but now individuals clustered into groups that more closely fit their observed social interaction. This led to my identification of the Indian-oriented and white-oriented subsocieties as meaningful social entities. Now, too, the unusual cases appeared in better perspective.

These cases were divided into those who measured either quite low or quite high on both scales. The few who were low on both scales remain to be explained. At first glance they all appeared to be young men, and perhaps had not yet had sufficient experience in the adult roles of either group to affect the indices used. The other cases, those that measured from 45-80% on both scales were more intriguing. They were, it seemed, well-versed in both cultures. In the original sample, one man scored 35% on the Indian and 75% on the white scales; another 45% and 100% respectively. Five other people, including two women, were well known to me, however, and by less objective assessment appeared to fall in the 60-90% range on both scales.

There appeared to be two types among these highly bicultural people. One, like the rancher mentioned earlier (45% on the Indian scale and 100% on the white) represented people who had been raised in white-oriented families but had, either through some early experience like the rancher, or later in life, learned about Indian culture. Several of this type had become situationally Indian-oriented, learned the language, and participated in some Indian functions. These people retain many of the advantages of their white-oriented backgrounds, but do things with and for the Indians that gain them some respect, acceptance, and following. They neither live with, nor seek full identification with, the Indian-oriented group. Some of these people are very willing ethnographic informants; they have contributed valuable information in the past and give accurate accounts now, but some of this may be without benefit of references. They have read the books and filled out the gaps of their own experience with information from the anthropologists.

People of the second type are often full-blood, Indian-oriented men or women who have been raised in Indian homes, who speak the Blackfeet language fluently, and know about the traditions and lore. They understand the Indian-oriented culture, were raised within it, and know the requirements for leadership status within that group. In addition to their Indian training, these people have received a good education in white schools and have had a wide range of experience in parts of white culture. They speak English well. They express the ambition to be Indian, but want to do this by combining what is "best of the Indian way with the best of the white way." I have labeled these people the *Interpreters* because this is a position they frequently fill vis-à-vis the two subsocieties. The Interpreters can talk to and better understand both sides. Yet they are Indian-oriented. They live with and want to be accepted by the Indian group and to maintain their Indian identity.

The Interpreters participate in Indian ceremonies and were given parts in a Sun Dance held on the reservation in 1959. Another young man, who appears to aspire to this role, sponsored another Sun Dance in 1965. These men may not have sufficient knowledge to fill these roles in traditional ways, but they are recognized as Indian leaders who are sympathetic and "good to people." They tend to express Indian values and subscribe to Indian symbols. They often put up a tepee for the annual encampment, put on costumes, dance or sing, emphasize their Indian names, and belong to the existing Indian societies. Yet, because of their training and experience in white ways, they are capable of competing with the White-oriented and through hard work and ability have gained some economic success and the respect of the white-oriented group. These men could succeed on their own in any rural off-reservation community. But they are not wealthy. Because of their Indian-orientation, they must curb their economic ambitions in order to maintain their status. The very capabilities that make them valuable leaders within their group subject them to constant surveillance and criticism. They cannot acquire too much; they must be generous and helpful. Their knowledge of white ways is respected and seen to be useful, but they must not go too far in trying to "live like a white man."

The bicultural milieu has created the need for these mediators—Interpreters—to mesh the political forces of the two subsocieties. The Indian-oriented cannot remain economically and politically independent, but must work with the larger community in order to exist. The Interpreter role requires bilingual people, educated people, Indian-oriented people who can forward Indian goals, yet maintain the values of this group. The Interpreter understands these goals better than the well-meaning white-oriented who have learned of Indian ways. The Interpreter can use his bicultural knowledge to forward these goals and to maintain his group.

This role has been one of long standing, but the capabilities required have increased. Interpreters are called upon for greater proficiency and mobility within the white world, but retain their unique value as they learn white culture well, resist cultural and social assimilation, and maintain their identification with the Indian-oriented subsociety.

This role bears many similarities to those described in other acculturative situations; e.g., Gluckman (1940) and Fallers (1955) discuss bicultural roles in Africa, but the Blackfeet role is not as clearly defined, or firmly institutionalized, as is the case in many of these other examples. While Interpreters are often elected to the Tribal Council, they may also be B.I.A. employees and enterpreneurs. The point is they may exert their influence in a number of differing situations, but have in common a following among the Indian-oriented, a position of leadership that is achieved not ascribed, and the bicultural knowledge and experience to help the Indian-oriented minority to survive.

Once these variations from an acculturation continuum are recognized, similar trends can be noted at the lower social levels. Most Indian-oriented people know the rules of behaving in a number of social contexts within the white-oriented community. A day laborer can mix with laborers of the white group with no particular trouble. He knows the proper cultural patterns for interaction in this context. He may know, as well, the rules to follow in several other situations. He has attained a degree of acculturation that may not be reflected accurately on a straight line measure. This serves to remind us that a man is more than a culture container. If, by one measure, he scores 75% on an Indian scale, we should not expect him to be limited to a 25% measure on another scale. Contemplation of this "container" metaphor led me to call these bicultural cases the 150% men.

The experience of these people shows that there can be cultural loss at the individual level, but the retention of Indian characteristics, rather than their replacement as new ways are learned, depends upon whether or not these are seen to have continuing utility for the individual. The social and cultural milieu of the Blackfeet Reservation provides a use for both if a man wants to be Indian-oriented.

Some of the processes of learning such accommodation are implicit in the cases examined above and have been given more explicit treatment by Polgar (1960) for a bicultural situation, Crowley (1957) for a more complex plural society, and Stern (1966:227-235) for the Klamath. Stern also provides independent support for generalizing beyond the Blackfeet case: he describes a "mosaiclike" accommodation among the younger Klamath; notes that acculturation can be supplementing as well as replacing (1966:100), and has concluded that individual acculturation has been varied: "tribal members are not to be found extended along a single continuum of change" (1966:227).

IV

In summary, the continuum model has utility for assessing tribal acculturation, but may lead us into the "container" error when applied to processes of individual acculturation. The danger seems present in statements like the following: "Although there are many degrees of acculturation to be observed among the Pinon Navajo, ranging from the modern, progressively oriented high school graduate to the most traditional and unregenerate Navajo, . . . [Downs 1966:1388]." The continuum of replacement is implied even though the statement is meaningful in Downs' discussion, and perhaps unfairly lifted from that context. But, are there not many modes of individual adaptation that are overlooked by this model? Are there any 150% men among the Navajo?

I suggest that the next step in assessing individual acculturation processes and the part these play in tribal acculturation on the Blackfeet reservation, and perhaps on others as well, would be to devise a technique that would measure the numbers and kinds of situations, Indian-oriented and White-oriented, in which a person is capable of participation.[2] A matrix model of the bicultural knowledge and activities of the tribal population would result that would show categories of acculturation that should relate better to the roles provided by the tribal structure. This treatment might eliminate some of the frequently reported residual categories—marginal, transitional, etc.—that often become necessary to handle cases that do not fit the continuum. Many of the men we have considered to be "lost between two cultures" may not be lost, but happen to have been observed out of their accustomed contexts. Perhaps they were shifting their orientation, or were temporarily outside the range of their ability or experience to accommodate to some aspect of the bicultural situation. They should retain still the knowledge and skills that would allow them to return to their own group or to handle other situations.

Two points have been raised in informal discussion of these ideas with other anthropologists that should be considered. One is the statement that my division of the reservation population into two subsocieties appears to be little more than the old "Traditional-Progressive" distinction, and the second concern is that my conclusions might be explained as a consequence of the method rather than as an approximation of the real condition of the Blackfeet. My answer would be no to both possibilities. The Traditional and Progressive labels could be applied to people in both groups, but would not describe adequately the bifurcation arising from differing orientations. It is true that these terms would apply to divisions within the Indian-oriented group: the Interpreters and some others could be called Progressives in the usual sense of the term. I have, in effect, attempted to describe one kind of Progressive to show that "progressive" adaptation need not lead to cultural loss. The second point cannot be disposed of so easily. I can only plead that my original intent was to find levels of acculturation; the results were unsatisfactory and another method of analysis led to conclusions that seemed to make more sense in light of my experience among these people.

These comments and the issues discussed in this paper raise further questions. Many of the answers will come from continued research, better data, and refined analytical techniques. Much could be gained from studying the same population over a long period of time. In time, records of attempts by men to move about more widely within this bicultural, bisocial reservation environment, their successes and failures, should provide answers to some of these questions, and point up more clearly the mechanisms that are used to adapt to acculturative situations. The increasing ranges of capability developed by individuals in this context must affect both the rate and direction of tribal acculturation.

NOTES

1 This is a revised version of a paper read at the 62nd Annual Meeting of the American Anthropological Association, San Francisco, 1963. The fieldwork was conducted during the summers of 1959, 1960, 1963, and 1967.

2 David French (1962) examined the contexts in which bilingual Indians used one, both, or the other of the languages. The choices indicated their appraisal of situation and their ability to respond appropriately.

REFERENCES CITED

Blackfeet Tribal Council (n.d.), Unpublished documents. Browning, Montana.

Bruner, Edward M. (1956a), Cultural transmission and culture change. Southwestern Journal of Anthropology 12:191-199.

——(1956b), Primary group experience and the processes of acculturation. American Anthropologist 58:605-623.

Crowley, Daniel J. (1957), Plural and differential acculturation in Trinidad. American Anthropologist 59:817-824.

Downs, James J. (1966), The social consequences of a dry well. American Anthropologist 67:1387-1416.

Fallers, Lloyd A. (1955), The predicament of the modern African chief: an instance from Uganda. American Anthropologist 57:290-305.

French, David (1961), Wasco-Wishram. *In* Perspectives in American Indian culture change. E. H. Spicer, ed. Chicago, University of Chicago Press. pp. 337-430.

——(1962), What is an Indian? Paper presented at the 61st annual meeting of the American Anthropological Association, Chicago, Illinois.

Gluckman, Max (1940), Analysis of a social situation in modern Zululand. Bantu Studies 14:1-30, 147-174.

McFee, Malcolm (1962), Modern Blackfeet: contrasting patterns of differential acculturation. Unpublished doctoral dissertation. Stanford, California, Stanford University, Department of Anthropology.

Polgar, Steven (1960), Biculturation of Mesquakie teenage boys. American Anthropologist 62:217-235.

Spindler, George D. (1955), Sociocultural and psychological processes in Menominee acculturation. Berkeley and Los Angeles, University of California Publications in Culture and Society, 5.

Stern, Theodore (1966), The Klamath tribe: a people and their reservation. Seattle, University of Washington Press.

Voget, Fred (1950), A Shoshone innovator. American Anthropologist 52:53-63.

——(1951), Acculturation at Caughnawaga: a note on the native-modified group. American Anthropologist 53:220-231.

——(1952), Crow socio-cultural groups. *In* Acculturation in the Americans. Sol Tax, ed. Chicago, Univesity of Chicago Press. pp. 88-93.

CHAPTER 5

CRIME AND
DEVIANT BEHAVIOR

Despite popular stereotypes of the "drunken Indian," the "honest Indian," or "Indian giving," there is a serious lack of information about the extent to which Indian people have accepted and conform to the values and norms of American society. Sometimes glimpses of specific problems provoke public dismay, as with the reaction to reports of a high incidence of suicide among Indian youths on the Fort Hall Reservation,[1] but such glimpses are no substitute for systematic data available concerning Indian suicide, mental illness, drug abuse, crime, and juvenile delinquency. There is an abundant literature on alcohol use by Indians, but most of the forms of "deviance" among modern Indians have received little attention by researchers. In the present chapter an attempt has been made to offer at least one selection relevant to each of the problems cited above.

CRIME AND DELINQUENCY

In 1942 Hayner reported a study of crime rates on three reservations in the Northwest, and although he focused on tribal differences, he did state that for certain crimes Indians on these reservations had rates significantly higher than the national average. For example, on the Klamath Reservation between 1920 and 1930 the annual homicide rate was 16 times the national rate. Hayner concluded that Indian crime had risen with increased Indian wealth and contact with whites.[2] Von Hentig reported that in the following decade (1930-1940) the Indian arrest rate was three times as high as the national rate for whites (2,510 per 100,000 as compared to 836 per 100,000) and argued that rapid acculturation and changing norms had contributed to high rates of Indian crime.[3]

Following these two "early" studies of Indian criminality, there was a 20-year lag before Stewart published his excellent analysis based on the 1960 FBI Uniform Crime Reports. He found that the overall arrest rate of Indians was eight times that of whites, and three times greater than the arrest rate for blacks. Moreover, the pattern seemed to hold not only for alcohol-related crimes, but for other crimes as well.[4]

Of course there are extreme intertribal variations in crime rates.

A study of Indian people on the Pine Ridge Reservation in South Dakota revealed that for 1964 the homicide rate was 16.6 per 100,000 population, while the national average was 5.1.[5] On the other hand, it is reported that the homicide rates among the Navaho for the period 1956-1965 were stable and comparable with national rates.[6]

The first article in this chapter, a previously unpublished piece by Charles Reasons, goes beyond previous work in its longitudinal perspective—it examines changes in crime rates over an 18-year period (1950-1968)—and in its focus on rates for specific offenses. In general his findings substantiate Stewart's work; he finds that *arrest* rates of Indians are three times those of blacks and ten times higher than white arrest rates. On the other hand, Reasons shows that for specific non-alcohol related offenses—homicide, rape, assault, burglary, larceny, auto theft, and robbery—*blacks* had the highest rates, followed closely by Indians, with rates for both groups considerably above those of whites. The one exception was auto theft; for that offense Indians had the highest arrest rate. The trend over time indicates that Indian rates of arrest for several offenses are approaching those of blacks. Reasons' study also reveals that Indians are overrepresented as inmates in both federal and state penal institutions. Finally, he reviews several sociological and economic theories which have been offered as explaining the "high" rates of Indian crime and suggests future research in these directions.

The social-scientific literature on juvenile delinquency among Indian people is even more scanty than the literature on crime. The one exception is a 1955 interim report of the Senate Subcommittee to Investigate Juvenile Delinquency.[7] Many reservations reported the number of delinquent acts committed prior to 1955 but failed to report rates adjusted for population size, and in these cases it is impossible to ascertain how Indian juvenile delinquency compared to delinquency by non-Indians. All of the reservations—Standing Rock, Fort Berthold, United Pueblos, Hopi, and Hualapai—which did present rates or make comparisons reported that Indian juvenile delinquency was *not* as great as non-Indian delinquency.[8] However, in summarizing the results of all the testimony the subcommittee stated that "the incidence of juvenile delinquency was found in many instances to be higher among the Indian than among the non-Indian population of the United States."[9] Poverty, lack of education, unemployment, marital and family disruption and cultural conflict were suggested as probable causes of rising juvenile delinquency among Indian youth. Most spokesman reported that delinquency was on the increase and predicted that this trend would continue if significant preventive steps were not taken.

It is difficult to document what has occurred in the 16 years since the subcommittee issued its report, but there are indications that the predictions of increasing delinquency were accurate. One study revealed that on the Pine Ridge Reservation in 1968 the delinquency rate was nine times the national average (10 percent of

Indian juveniles are delinquent as compared to 2.2 percent for whites) and that 39 percent of the 17-year-olds on the reservation had been labeled as delinquent.[10] This same trend of rapidly increasing juvenile delinquency was discovered in the Minnis investigation of delinquency on the Fort Hall Reservation in Idaho, which is included in the chapter. She reports that between 1955 and 1960 the rates of crime and delinquency tripled, rising from 13 percent to 34 percent, which is considerably above the national average. The housing conditions, family structure, and land-utilization patterns of the Shoshone-Bannock Indians are identified as being directly linked to the high rates of delinquent behavior.

An issue that should be confronted when examining Indian crime and delinquency is that high rates of arrest and conviction may reflect biases in the administration of justice. Personal conversations with Indians both on reservations and in urban environments in the Northwest have revealed an almost unanimous feeling among them that the police discriminate against them. The selection by Halverson describes aspects of the judicial process which operate to the Indian's disadvantage. Once arrest has occurred, the Indian's strong distrust of government agencies, including police and courts, operates to produce differential administration of justice. Often unaware of his basic legal rights or how to exercise them, the Indian tends to plead guilty or to produce an inadequate defense. Even though public agencies such as the Public Defenders Office, Legal Aid Service, State Board Against Discrimination, Department of Human Rights, and City Ombudsman are available, the Indians' lack of trust and information prevents him from utilizing these services. Halverson provided part-time free legal assistance to persons who requested it at either of two urban Indian centers. His experience led him to conclude that the basic legal assistance needs of many urban Indians could be met if a trained paraprofessional working under the supervision of an attorney were available. The paraprofessional "would be required to have a well-developed, working knowledge of the many and various social agencies. . . . In addition this person would be required to have an understanding of fundamental legal rights in the area of contract law, consumer law, landlord-tenant relations, motor vehicle codes, welfare law and juvenile law." Halverson asserts that the services of such a paraprofessional could significantly reduce the arrest and conviction rates of Indians.

ALCOHOL ABUSE

The topic of alcohol use is the only aspect of "deviant" behavior among Indian people on which there is a substantial research literature. In part, the existence of this body of work reflects the importance of the alcohol problem among the Indians, in part it reflects federal priorities in research funding, and in part it reflects the biases of white investigators. Unfortunately, the relative abundance of studies of Indian drinking as compared to studies of other aspects of Indian life may serve to perpetuate the stereotype of the Indian as alcoholic.

Several recent works provide extensive descriptions of alcohol use among the Indians. Graves' study of a tri-ethnic (Indian, Spanish, white) community's drinking patterns revealed that alcohol intake among Indians was over three times that of persons of Spanish descent and seven times that for Anglos.[11] In addition, Indians admitted being drunk seven times as frequently as whites and nine times as often as the Spanish. Also directly relevant is Graves' paper on Navaho adjustment to life in Denver (reprinted in Chapter 6) in which arrest rates (usually for alcohol-related offenses) serve as indicators of adjustment to urban living.[12]

Two studies of Indian alcohol use have been included in this chapter: Frances Ferguson's "Navaho Drinking: Some Tentative Hypotheses," and Slater and Albrecht's "The Extent and Costs of Excessive Drinking Among the Uintah-Ouray Indians." Ferguson quotes a knowledgeable tribal member to the effect that 30 percent of the Navaho people drink excessively. In contrast, it is estimated that from 6 to 10 percent of the American population drink to excess. Ferguson also explores the association between excessive drinking and other forms of deviant behavior such as crime, delinquency, child neglect, unemployment, health problems, automobile accidents, and neglect and abuse of property. Slater and Albrecht's previously unpublished piece is an attempt to estimate the extent of drinking among those living on the Uintah-Ouray Reservation in eastern Utah, and the costs of that drinking, both to the tribe and to the agencies which provide social and financial services for the Uintah-Ouray. When the costs of alcoholic beverages, court costs and fines, wages lost because of confinement, and health costs are combined, the total economic loss to the Indian people is staggering.

SUICIDE

The extent of self-destruction by members of a particular society is often used as an indicator of the success or failure of that society to provide a physical, social, and psychological environment that permits personal self-fulfillment. The suicide rate for Indian youths is three times the national average, and on some reservations the rate is ten times the age-adjusted national rate.[13] Anomie, or a sense of normlessness, has been demonstrated to be associated with high rates of suicide for a variety of national and ethnic groups, although not specifically for Indians. Given the number of studies documenting Indians' feelings of anomie and alienation, there is reason to suspect that such feelings may be linked to the high incidence of suicide among some Indian tribes.

Bynum's "Suicide and the American Indian," is a review of government statistics and the social science literature concerning Indian suicide. The author indicates that while suicide was a part of most Indian cultures before contact with Europeans, the rate of occurrence was fairly low. National statistics on suicide indicate a gradual increase of Indian suicide to a point where it exceeds the national average and since 1967 such a dramatic acceleration that the Indian age-adjusted rates are twice as high as those for the general population. In reviewing and synthesizing five major studies on Indian suicide, Bynum concludes that the Indian suicide victim tends to be a young adult who is experiencing marriage and family discord, social disorganization in the Indian community, and personal conflict between acceptance of Indian and white culture. This, he argues, is the portrait of a "marginal man," an individual caught between two competing cultures and not fully integrated into either. His marginal status may be a factor producing anomie, aggression, and suicidal behavior.

MENTAL ILLNESS

There are very few studies of the incidence of mental illness among Indians. One of the most recent is Hellon's analysis of the admissions records of a large mental hospital in Alberta, Canada, for the period 1923 to 1962.[14] He found that the rates of diagnosis for various forms of mental illness among Indians were very similar to those for other segments of the population. The one exception to this generality was the finding that personality disorders appeared more frequently among Indian people than among whites.[15]

Studies of mental illness among American Indians tend to be examinations from a psychiatric perspective of particular cultural adaptions (or the lack of them) among a given tribe.[16] An excellent example of this type of research is the selection by Krush and his associates, which discusses mental health among Indian students at a boarding school. Statistical data and case studies are presented to illustrate the types and frequency of personality disorganization among the boarding school population. The authors conclude that the high mobility of boarding school students, that is, their transfer from one family to another and from one school to another, with the attendant exposure to differing and sometimes contradictory normative systems, creates personality disorganization.

In addition to the selection by Krush, we have reprinted the article, "Mental Health of Eastern Oklahoma Indians: An Exploration." Martin and his associates administered a personality inventory and a psychiatric interview to a sample of Indians in Oklahoma. Results showed that 29 percent of the Indians were "severely disturbed." This rate is somewhat higher than the rate for metropolitan whites reported in the 1962 Midtown Manhattan project (23 percent).[17] At the very least, the seemingly high rate of impairment among Indians would suggest that special attention, both in ameliorative programs and in research, be devoted to them.

OTHER DEVIANT BEHAVIOR

There is a dearth of systematic information on the incidence of, and factors associated with, several other kinds of deviant behavior among Indian people. We have been unable to locate empirical studies of social problems such as drug abuse, illegitimacy, or marital conflict among Indian people today. The research gap is immense; we have not even charted the dimensions of the problem, let alone experimented with ameliorative programs.

Two exceptions to the above general statements should be noted. It was reported in an article about gasoline and glue-sniffing among the Pine Ridge Sioux that 80 to 90 percent of the young Indians had experimented with sniffing gasoline and glue, and that the age of entrance into this pastime was around 9, with the average user being 13 years old.[18] A second exception is an historical analysis of illegitimacy among Indians in Canada, which traces fluctuations in rates of illegitimacy on a particular Indian reserve from 1860 to 1960 and relates the variations in illegitimacy rates to changes in the degree of social and cultural integration of the community.[19]

NOTES

1 Introductory Statement by Senator Ralph Yarborough, Chairman, Committee on Labor and Public Welfare, U.S. Senate. Indian Education Subcommittee Hearings, 90th Congress, First and Second Sessions, Part I, p. III.

2 Norman S. Hayner, "Variability in the Criminal Behavior of American Indians," *American Journal of Sociology*, 47 (January 1942), 602-613.

3 Hans von Hentig, "The Delinquency of the American Indians," *Journal of Criminal Law and Criminology*, 36 (July-August 1945), 75-84.

4 Omer Stewart, "Questions Regarding American Indian Criminality," *Human Organization*, 23 (Spring 1964), 61-66.

5 Marshall Kaplan, Sheldon Gans, and Howard Kahn, "Oglala Sioux Model Reservation Program: The Development Potential of the Pine Ridge Reservation," reprinted in Indian Education Subcommittee Hearings, 90th Congress, First and Second Sessions, Part IV, p. 1588.

6 Jerrold E. Levy, Stephen J. Kunitz, and Michael Everett, "Navajo Criminal Homicide," *Southwestern Journal of Anthropology*, 25, no. 2 (Summer 1969), 124-150.

7 Juvenile Delinquency Among the Indians," Interim Report of the Subcommittee to Investigate Juvenile Delinquency to the Committee on the Judiciary, 84th Congress, First Session, 1955.

8 *Ibid.*, pp. 15, 18, 19, 32, and 115.

9 *Ibid.*, p. 45.

10 Pine Ridge Research Bulletin, PHS Community Mental Health Program, Pine Ridge, S. Dakota, 6, December 1968. Reprinted in

Indian Education Subcommittee Hearings, 90th Congress, First and Second Sessions, Part IV, pp. 1765-1766.

11 Theodore Graves, "Acculturation, Access and Alcohol in a Tri-Ethnic Community, *American Anthropologist,* 69 (April 1967).

12 Theodore D. Graves, "The Personal Adjustment of Navajo Indian Migrants to Denver, Colorado," *American Anthropologist,* 72 (February 1970), 35-54.

13 Yarborough, *op. cit.,* p. III.

14 Alan C. Kerckhoff, "Anomie and Achievement Motivation: A Study of Personality Development within Cultural Disorganization," *Social Forces,* 37 (March 1959), 196-202; Stanton K. Tefft, "Anomie, Values and Culture Change Among Teen-Age Indians: An Exploratory Study," *Sociology of Education,* 40 (Spring 1967), 145-157; Robert L. Leon, "Some Implications for a Preventive Program for American Indians," *American Journal of Psychiatry,* 125 (August 1968), 128-132; Thomas J. Boag, "Mental Health of Native Peoples of the Arctic," *Canadian Psychiatric Association Journal,* 15, no. 2 (April 1970), 115-120; Seymour Parker, "The Wiitiko Psychosis in the Context of Ojibwa Personality and Culture," *American Anthropologist,* 62 (1960), 603-623; J. S. Slotkin, "Social Psychiatry of a Menomini Community," *Journal of Abnormal and Social Psychology,* 48 (January 1953), 10-16; L. Bryce Boyer, "Psychoanalytic Insights in Working with Ethnic Minorities," *Social Casework,* 45 (November 1964), 519-526.

15 C. P. Hellon, "Mental Illness and Acculturation in the Canadian Aboriginal," *Canadian Psychiatric Association Journal,* 15, no. 2 (April 1970), 135-139.

16 *Ibid.,* p. 136.

17 Leo Srole, et al., *Mental Health in the Metropolis* (New York: McGraw-Hill, 1962), p. 138.

18 Pine Ridge Research Bulletin, *op. cit.,* p. 1784.

19 Philip K. Bock, "Patterns of Illegitimacy on a Canadian Indian Reserve: 1860-1960," *Journal of Marriage and the Family,* 26 (May 1964), pp. 142-148.

CHARLES REASONS: CRIME AND THE AMERICAN INDIAN

Despite a long-standing interest by criminologists in the relationship between race and crime,[1] there have been few comparative studies of crime among American Indians. Early studies by Hayner and Von Hentig reported a direct relationship between crime and both extent of Indian-white contact and increased Indian wealth.[2] Subsequent studies have generally found high rates of crime and delinquency.[3]

In a recent article, Stewart analyzed the arrest rates by race for the 1960 FBI Uniform Crime Reports. He found that the Indian arrest rate per 100,000 population was eight times the white rate and three times the Negro rate, and that Indians exceeded all other races in rates of arrest for alcohol-related crimes, urban arrests, and urban non-alcohol-related arrests. Stewart also presents data from local sources which support his findings stemming from the national statistics.

Although his analysis is the most comprehensive available, it is inadequate in many respects. One important weakness is that he presents national statistics for only one year. Also, Stewart deals with gross data and thus fails to note variations by specific offenses. Finally, his population base is the entire population of each race, rather than a specific age group, for example, those 14 years of age and over.

SOURCES OF DATA

In order to gain a longitudinal perspective, arrest rates by race were computed for the 1950-1969 period from the FBI Uniform Crime Reports, which contain rates for total crimes, drinking-related offenses, non-drinking-related offenses, overall index crimes, and each of the seven specific index crimes for persons 14 years of age and older.[4] Population data were taken from the 1950 and 1960 census reports for whites, blacks, Indians, Chinese, and Japanese. In addition, statistics on federal prisoners were used when appropriate.[5]

The national arrest statistics provide only a general picture of police and criminal activity.[6] However, in the present analysis the emphasis is upon the position of the various racial groups relative to one another, rather than the absolute rates per se. Methodological problems associated with the use of national crime statistics have been discussed in detail elsewhere.[7] Here we will mention only that arrests for crimes committed on Indian reservations are not included in the FBI reports; therefore, the official Indian arrest-rate is lower than it would be if all arrests were included.[8]

FINDINGS

National arrest rates by race for the period 1950-1968 are presented in Table 1.[9] In the main, these data verify Stewart's findings: the Indians consistently have an arrest rate approximately three times that of blacks and ten times that of whites. The lowest rates are for the Chinese and Japanese populations.

Table 2 provides arrest rates for drinking-related offenses, that is, drunkenness, driving while intoxicated, and liquor violations. The disparity between the Indian rate and that of other racial groups is much wider than reported by Stewart.[10] The Indian arrest rate is generally eight times that of blacks and over twenty times that of whites, with the Chinese and

TABLE 1

Arrest Rates by Race, 1950-1968

Year	White	Negro	Indian	Chinese	Japanese
1950	572	1,957	3,492	925	261
1953	1,261	4,579	15,278	447	132
1956	1,381	6,034	19,311	259	105
1959	1,730	7,507	26,931	1,633	2,752
1962	2,638	10,512	30,647	1,298	987
1965	2,860	11,225	34,785	808	895
1968	3,271	12,256	36,584	1,041	1,261

Note: Rates are computed for 100,000 population 14 years old and older for each race, taken from the United States Census of Population, 1950 and 1960, using the FBI Uniform Crime Reports 1950-1968.

TABLE 2

Arrest Rates for Drinking-Related Offenses, by Race, 1950-1968

Year	White	Negro	Indian	Chinese	Japanese
1950	193	391	1,953	53	3
1953	682	1,631	11,888	151	67
1956	720	2,179	16,132	74	54
1959	871	2,405	22,200	415	380
1962	1,229	3,678	23,599	293	217
1965	1,229	3,539	27,143	134	189
1968	1,263	3,054	27,407	216	220

Note: Rates are computed for 100,000 population 14 years old and older for each race, taken from the United States Census of Population, 1950 and 1960, using the FBI Uniform Crime Reports 1950-1968. Drinking-related offenses include drunkenness, driving while intoxicated, and liquor violations.

Japanese again evidencing the lowest rates. The use of a different population plus the fact that Stewart never defined "alcohol-related" crimes might account for the difference.

Although much Indian crime can be explained by drinking-related offenses, rates for non-drinking-related offenses are usually at least as high as for other racial groups. The figures in Table 3 reveal that Indian and black rates generally are about four times as high as the rates for whites.

Specific information on racial differentials by type of index crime are presented in Table 4.[11] With respect to homicide, blacks manifest a rate about nine times as high as the white rate and twice the Indian rate. The Indian rate is usually at least five times that of whites. The same relative positions and disparity exists for rape.

Arrest rates for assault show a great increase for both whites and Indians during the 1960s. Until the mid-1960s the black arrest rate for assault was at least twice the Indian rate, but recently the amount of difference has decreased. Arrest rates for burglary tend to be highest for

TABLE 3

Arrest Rates for Non-Drinking-Related Offenses, by Race, 1950-1968

Year	White	Negro	Indian	Chinese	Japanese
1950	379	1,566	1,539	867	258
1953	579	2,948	3,390	296	65
1956	661	3,855	3,179	185	51
1959	859	5,102	4,731	1,218	2,372
1962	1,409	6,834	7,048	1,005	770
1965	1,631	7,686	7,642	674	706
1968	2,008	9,202	9,177	825	1,041

Note: Rates are computed for 100,000 population 14 years old and older for each race, taken from the United States Census of Population, 1950 and 1960, using the FBI Uniform Crime Reports 1950-1968. "Non-drinking-related offenses" means those other than drunkenness, liquor violation, and driving while intoxicated.

blacks, although the Indian rate is near or exceeds that of blacks from 1960 to 1964.

The Indian arrest rate for auto theft exceeded that of all other racial groups during the 1950s. It remained nearly double the black rate until 1963, when increasing auto thefts among blacks began to close the gap. During the 1960s, the black arrest rate for auto theft increased over three times. In 1968 the rate of arrest for auto theft among blacks finally exceeded the Indian rate.

Blacks have the highest arrest rate for larceny throughout the period under investigation, usually being four times the white rate. While the black rate was greater than that of the Indians during the 1950s, the difference decreased in the early 1960s, and Indians had a higher rate in 1961. After 1964 the black rate of arrests for larceny is increasingly higher than the Indian rate. Finally, the robbery arrest rate for blacks is generally 11 times that for whites, and is double the rate for Indians.

Thus, the most striking trends in American Indian crime rates by specific offense include a large increase in the arrest rate for assault, in both absolute and relative terms, and substantial increases in their burglary and larceny rates relative to the rate for blacks.

Statistics on federally sentenced prisoners provide additional insights about Indian crime. Of the confined sentenced population of *federal institutions,* Indians made up 2.2 percent, yet they comprise less than 1 percent of the general population. Comparable rates for other races in 1964 and 1966 were 25.4 percent for blacks and 72 percent for whites.[12] Thus, the American Indian greatly exceeds the other racial groups in confinement rates.

The Indian is also overrepresented in state prisons, although not so drastically as in federal institutions. In 1960, felony court commitments to *state institutions* included 64.7 percent whites, 32.7 percent blacks, and 1.2 percent American Indians. Of the year-end felony population in state institutions the proportions were, respectively, 61.9 percent, 37.1 percent, and 1 percent.[13]

TABLE 4

Arrest Rate for Each Specific Index Crime, by Race, 1950-1968

Activity and Race	1950	1953	1956	1959	1962	1965	1968
Homicide							
White	3	2	2	2	4	4	5
Black	27	15	16	18	29	35	54
Indian	17	2	2	9	19	19	34
Rape*a*							
White	6	2	3	2	4	4	5
Black	26	16	19	19	32	39	45
Indian	22	5	10	3	24	26	26
Assault*b*							
White	31	8	8	10	22	29	41
Black	263	127	152	181	265	304	385
Indian	134	32	25	54	130	175	250
Burglary							
White	32	26	32	43	93	104	138
Black	110	98	131	191	378	497	671
Indian	93	65	80	148	366	398	485
Auto theft							
White	15	16	22	25	48	57	64
Black	33	42	58	65	138	220	341
Indian	69	68	90	143	265	284	389
Larceny							
White	44	46	62	87	170	219	265
Black	197	206	273	405	691	914	1,169
Indian	146	150	244	350	688	792	913
Robbery							
White	12	6	5	7	14	15	19
Black	67	54	54	80	159	188	307
Indian	44	26	20	42	80	88	149

Note: Rates are computed for 100,000 population 14 years old and older for each race, taken from the United States Census of Population, 1950 and 1960 using the FBI Uniform Crime Reports 1950-1968.

a From 1958 the rates are for forcible rape only.

b From 1952 to 1968 only assault is used for computation.

DISCUSSION

The data presented suggest that Indian people have higher arrest and conviction rates than any other racial group in the United States. Among the factors which have been identified as determinants of Indian crime are economic status, anomie, culture conflict, and drinking.

Economic Factors

The most prevalent explanation given for the high rate of American Indian crime is essentially economic determinism. Both Von Hentig and Hayner found sudden income highly related to increased crime.[14] More recent analyses have emphasized poverty as an important determinant, although often a multiple-causation perspective has been adopted.[15] As a group, American Indians can objectively be shown to be at the bottom of the economic ladder.[16]

Anomie

Closely related to the economic status is the anomie theory of deviance.[17] The emphasis of this theory is upon differential opportunity structures to both legitimate and illegitimate means in obtaining universally-valued goals within a society. A recent study by Jessor and his associates used anomie theory as part of a scheme for explaining racial variations in deviance rates.[18] In a small community consisting of 46 percent Anglos, 34 percent Spanish, and 20 percent Indians, limited access to the legitimate opportunity structure was shown to be a major instigation to deviance. However, limited access alone was not sufficient to produce deviance; Indians in the town were in a better economic position than the Spanish, yet they exhibited a much higher rate of deviant behavior, for example, court convictions, self-reported deviance, and drinking. It was discovered that even though both had low access to opportunity structures, the Spanish had stricter attitudes toward deviance, stronger normative control, and less anomie than Indians. Among the Indians there was greater normlessness and exposure to deviant role models.

Culture Conflict

Sellin's *Culture Conflict and Crime*[19] noted that the criminal law often reflected the moral ideas of a dominant majority. Because all members of the society are not equally committed to the norms of the powerful, there is conflict which manifests itself in crime. An interpenetration of conflicting norms can occur in three ways: (1) codes clash on the border of contiguous cultural areas; (2) colonization brings imposition of one group's criminal law upon another; and (3) one cultural group migrates to another area.[20] It would seem that all three types of interpenetration have produced Indian-white conflict.[21]

The criminal law demonstrates dramatically the conflicting perspectives of the two cultures. The variance in both quantitative and qualitative aspects between tribal statutes and federal and state codes is startling. For example, within the state of Washington the most comprehensive tribal codes contain only between 40 and 60 offenses, while Washington state penal codes cover more than 2,000 offenses.[22]

Drinking

Stewart wrote that "if the reasons for the excessive use of alcohol among Indians could be understood, their excessive crime rate would be understood."[23] Although Indians have a high rate of specifically "non-drinking" offenses, the unusually high rate of drinking-related offenses merits attention. Dozier views excessive drinking by Indian people as a response to the historical, social, and cultural factors which produce a sense of inadequacy and frustration among Indians.[24] A prime example of federal paternalism is the selective prohibition against Indian use of alcohol for over a century and a half. From the passage of the general Indian Intercourse Act of 1832 until 1953, it was illegal for Indians to possess liquor. Since 1953 some tribal councils, states, and local communities have continued to attempt to impose discriminatory legal limitations on Indian drinking. Stewart suggests that such prohibition has prevented Indian people from developing norms for everyday, self-regulated use of alcoholic beverages.[25]

SUMMARY

Contemporary literature dealing with race and crime is almost exclusively of a black-white nature. Of particular interest is the fact that texts in criminology have given little, if any, attention to the American Indian, who was found to exhibit the highest crime rate of any racial group. An analysis of data on the national, state, city, and reservation levels verifies previous findings of the high incidence of crime among the American Indian in relationship to other racial groups.

In the explanation of such high rates, economic factors have been strongly emphasized. While economic factors are important, anomie and culture-conflict theories provide a more substantive basis of understanding. The unique history of Indian-white relations can be viewed in terms of continual culture conflict lending to social disorganization and anomie, with crime often resulting. As Indian-white culture contact increases, there is evidence of an increase in excessive drinking and criminal behavior among American Indians.

NOTES

1   William Adrian Bonger, *Race and Crime* (New York: Morningside Heights 1943); Marvin Wolfgang, *Crime and Race: Conceptions and Misconceptions* (New York: Institute of Human Relations Press, 1970).

2   Norman S. Hayner, "Variability in the Criminal Behavior of American Indians," *American Journal of Sociology,* 47 (January 1942), 602-613; Hans Von Hentig, "The Delinquency of the American Indian," *The Journal of Criminal Law,* 36 (July-August, 1945), 75-84.

3   Omer Stewart, "Questions Regarding American Indian Criminality," *Human Organization,* 23 (Spring 1964), 61-66; Edwin Sutherland and Donald R. Cressey, *Principles of Criminology,* 7th edition, (Philadelphia: Lippincott, 1966).

4   Federal Bureau of Investigation, Uniform Crime Reports (Washington, D.C.: U.S. Government Printing Office, 1950-1968).

5   Federal Bureau of Prisons, Statistical Tables (Washington, D.C.: U.S. Government Printing Office, 1964); Federal Prisons, Leavenworth, 1950-1957; El Reno, 1958-1959: U.S. Department of Justice, 1950-1959.

6   Federal Bureau of Investigation, Uniform Crime Reports (Washington, D.C.: U.S. Government Printing Office, 1950-1968).

7 Sutherland and Cressey, *op. cit.,* pp. 27-52.

8 *Ibid.,* pp. 145-146.

9 United States Census of Population, 1950 and 1960; FBI Uniform Crime Reports, 1950-1968.

10 Steward, *op. cit.,* p. 61.

11 FBI, Uniform Crime Reports, *op. cit.*

12 FBI, Uniform Crime Reports, *op. cit.;* Federal Bureau of Prisons, *op. cit.*

13 *Ibid.*

14 Hayner, *op. cit.,* pp. 602-613 and Von Hentig, *op. cit.,* pp. 75-84.

15 "Juvenile Delinquency Among the Indians," Subcommittee to Investigate Juvenile Delinquency, Senate Committee on the Judiciary, 85th Congress, 1956; Mhyra S. Minnis, "The Relationship of the Social Structure of an Indian Community to Adult and Juvenile Delinquency," *Social Forces,* 41 (May 1963), 395-403; Stewart, *op. cit.;* pp. 61-66; Michael J. Moyer, ed., *A Study of Spokane's Indian Population* (Spokane: American Indian Community Center, 1969); and National Prisoner Statistics: Characteristics of State Prisoners (Washington, D.C.: Bureau of Prisons, 1960).

16 Helen W. Johnson, *Rural Indian Americans in Poverty,* Economic Research Service, U.S. Department of Agriculture, Agricultural Economic Report No. 167 (Washington, D.C.: U.S. Government Printing Office, 1969).

17 Albert K. Cohen, *Deviance and Control* (Englewood Cliffs, N.J.: Prentice-Hall, 1966), p. 22.

18 Richard Jessor, et al., *Society, Personality, and Deviant Behavior* (New York: Holt, Rinehart and Winston, 1968).

19 Thorsten Sellin, *Culture Conflict and Crime* (New York: Social Science Research Council, 1938).

20 Donald R. Cressey, "Culture Conflict, Differential Association and Normative Conflict," in Marvin Wolfgang, ed., *Crime and Culture: Essays in Honor of Thorsten Sellin* (New York: Wiley, 1968), pp. 83-92.

21 Arthur S. Riffenburgh, "Cultural Influences and Crime Among Indian-Americans of the Southwest." *Federal Probation,* 28 (Summer 1964), 38-46.

22 Allen Lane Carr and Stanley M. Johanson, "Extent of Washington Criminal Jurisdiction over Indians," *Washington Law Review,* 33 (Autumn 1958), 289-302.

23 Stewart, *op. cit.,* pp. 61-66.

24 Edward P. Dozier, "Problem Drinking Among American Indians," *Quarterly Journal of Studies on Alcohol,* 27 (March 1966), 72-87.

25 Stewart, *op. cit.,* pp. 61-66.

MHYRA S. MINNIS: THE RELATIONSHIP OF THE SOCIAL STRUCTURE OF AN INDIAN COMMUNITY TO ADULT AND JUVENILE DELINQUENCY

ABSTRACT

This paper is a condensation of an empirical study of Fort Hall, Idaho, an Indian Reservation of the Shashone-Bannock Tribes. The focus of the paper is upon those areas of the social structure of the community which are reflected in, or seen as contributory aspects to, the psycho-social problems of juvenile and adult delinquency. The categories and incidence of juvenile and adult law violations are selectively presented statistically and evaluated in relation to the above conditions and characteristics within the community and in the interrelationship with the surrounding communities.

This paper is a condensation of an empirical study of the community of Fort Hall, an Indian Reservation of the Shashone-Bannock Tribes, located in southern Idaho, almost equidistant between Pocatello and Blackfoot. The data are based upon 130 completed, 18-page schedules derived from a stratified sample representing one-third of the population, families, and houses on the reservation. The field study was conducted in 1960.[1] The focus of the paper is on selected aspects of the general structure of the community, including living conditions, population characteristics, heirship of land, and family interaction which are reflected in the psycho-social problem of juvenile and adult delinquency.

The Shashone-Bannock Tribes comprise 2,135 people who occupy 522,000 acres of farm and grazing land. Unlike the surrounding development of similar land, the land utilization and cattle raising are not effective on the reservation although the land is good and water irrigation available. While much of the reservation is desert, with frequent sandstorms, there are low mountains circling the area for which the Indians express a great deal of love and attachment. The mountains not only enhance the beauty of the land but create a good opportunity for hunting. Their love of this land and homeground can be seen in the fact that a very small number of Shashone-Bannock people emigrate from the reservation, and by their fond expressions during the interviews regarding their "home land."

LIVING CONDITIONS

In spite of this close attachment, housing and living levels on this reservation are worse than on most other Indian reservations in the United

Source: Reprinted by permission from *Social Forces* 41 (May 1963), 395-403.

States. Indications of such poor conditions can be seen in a review of housing, utilities, furnishings, car ownership, and modern household conveniences. The 2,135 persons are crowded into 368 houses; or, as revealed by the sample, 792 persons are crowded into 126 houses. Table 1 indicates the type of house construction in which the Indians live.

TABLE 1

Types of Houses

Housing Type	Number of Homes Observed	Percent of Homes Observed
Type A—Log cabins	40	13.0
Type B—Box car housing	17	5.5
Type C—Small frame (substandard)	151	48.5
Type D—Frame (renovation needed)	77	25.0
Type E—Miscellaneous (tent-shack)	10	3.0
Type F—Comparable to area surrounding	16	5.0

Source: Report, p. 50 (see fn. 1).

The houses are not only sub-standard but very crowded. The median room occupancy at Fort Hall is 2.81 times as high as throughout Idaho, a predominantly rural state.[2] Furthermore, while the number of rooms per house in Idaho is 4.2, those on the reservation are 2 rooms per house, in addition to being very small in size.[3] The wide range of occupancy from the most to the least crowded is presented in Table 2.

TABLE 2

Extremes in Room Occupancy, from a Sample of 130 Households, Fort Hall, 1960

	Number of Households	Av. No. of Persons per Household	Av. No. of Rooms per Household	Av. No. of Persons per Room
Most crowded	19	8.30	1.26	6.74
Least crowded	17	2.82	4.59	.62

Source: Report, p. 51.

Dividing the 126 houses in the sample into various sizes, judged by the interviewers according to Fort Hall rather than white standards in the surrounding area, we find that only 11.5 percent are large; 29.2 percent are medium; 55.3 percent are small, and over three percent are classified as "lean-to's" and boxcars. The yards surrounding these houses are filled with refuse and tin cans which accumulate before burial since little or no collection exists on the reservation. A considerable number of the yards are littered with rusting automobiles and farm machinery. Chickens and scrawny dogs running loose all over the place complete the residential setting.

The basic means of communication with the outside world appears to be the radio and television. The television sets are old models, with dim screens, but are on continuously. It is the central place of gathering for the family and the main focus of domestic entertainment. Even those Indians who do not speak English well watch it with mesmeric attention. Table 3 shows a comparison of conditions of Fort Hall Indians, Spokane Indians and whites in Stevens County, Washington, as to levels of living and household conveniences.

TABLE 3

*Comparison of Living Levels of Fort Hall Indians; Spokane Indians;
and Whites in Stevens County on the Basis of 11 Items*

Item	Percentage of Households Possessing Item		
	Fort Hall Indians	*Spokane Indians*	*Whites*
Number of rooms 6 or more	8.5	27.5	39.9
Indoor plumbing	19.2	42.5	94.2
Bathroom	18.5	32.5	83.2
Electricity	63.8	95.0	99.1
Telephone	6.2	32.5	68.5
Television set	56.2	80.0	73.5
Daily newspaper	26.2	35.0	60.4
Weekly newspaper	30.0	19.4	73.6
Subscribe to one or more magazines	40.0	59.0	77.9
Automobile, 1953 or newer	40.0	45.0	34.5
	N = 130	N = 40	N = 620

Source: Report, p. 56; and Prodipto Roy and Della M. Walker, *Assimilation of the Spokane Indians,* Bulletin 628, Institute of Agricultural Sciences, Washington Agricultural Experiment Station, Washington State University, May 1961, p. 32.

In addition to utilities and conveniences, the pilot schedule originally included a description of the home, utilizing a combination of F. Stuart Chapin's living house scale and William H. Sewell's scale for measurement of socioeconomic status of farm families.[4] Such items as furniture, rugs, books, pictures, "original painting," etc. were listed to be observed by the interviewers with the intent of describing the interior concretely and in detail. After the pilot study of ten families, the schedule had to be considerably revised. Utilizing a graded scale as to type of furnishings, we discovered that "store purchased, comparatively new furniture" is found only in 23 of the households; 46 houses have only "old, store purchased furniture"; 36 have "very old furnishings"; and the remaining houses are furnished with "boxes," "makeshifts," and "torn and discarded pieces."

The homes are moreover sparsely decorated and reflect poverty, with calendars on walls as basic decorations in 63 and inexpensive copies of paintings in 36 of the homes. Four of the houses proudly showed the researchers obscure "original paintings" mainly of fruits, flowers, and wild life. The intimacy of family relations and attachments are to be seen in photographs of family members, displayed in more than one-fourth of the homes. Otherwise the rooms are barren; devoid of shelves (a factor which defeats some of the home economists on the reservation because they recommend large quantity buying as a measure of economy but there are no places for storage); few doors but merely cloth to divide rooms for privacy; and no closets for hanging clothes other than nails on walls or improvised hooks. These are homes that the modern gadget-proud housewife in our society would indeed find surprisingly devoid of comfort and the usually expected conveniences.

Since there exists much comment in popular conversation and literature describing Negroes riding in Cadillacs and Indians with elegant, expensive automobiles, the researchers were interested in analyzing this impression. The automobile is a very important item on the reservation since there are almost no telephones, the area is vast and sprawling, and the Indian drives many miles to attend Sun Dance Festivals, rodeos, "round-ups," to purchase daily groceries which are bought in small quantities since there is little refrigeration, and/or merely to visit with family and friends in close "gemutlichkeit." Because of this continuous daily mobility, the impression is created that there are many automobiles on the reservation. The actual enumeration of automobiles contradicts popular impression. Among the 189 families in our sample, comprising 713 persons, there are 101 cars, or approximately one car per seven persons, hardly the optimistic prediction of two cars in every family garage. There are also 42 trucks among the families in our sample. Some better situated families own a truck or "pick-up" and an automobile. As to the age and make of car, not the Cadillac but the Ford is the most predominant car, with the Chevrolet running a close second. Only two families in our sample have a Buick, and only one has a Chrysler. Some of the cars date back to 1935 although the median is about ten years old; with the interquartile range between 1949 and 1955. Only two families have a recent 1960 car. The data negate the concept of Indians riding around in fashionable cars of the latest models.

LAND UTILIZATION AND RANCHING

According to the respondents in our sample, the most important problem on the reservation is the inheritance and utilization of land. The Indians speak continuously of the "heirship problem." Owing to the original allotment law of the Federal government, giving each Indian family 160 acres of land with only 20 irrigated acres, and the subsequent inheritance of these acres, much of Fort Hall reservation is fractionized. Some Indians do not even know how many parcels of land they own and where these are located. This makes cultivation and effective utilization of land difficult. The heirship problem and fractionalization of land can be seen in chart 1.

Added to the problem of fractionalization, the Indians now face the problem which other farmers with small farms are facing today all over the world, that of a lack of farm machinery and the difficulties of competing in the agricultural market against the production of large farms. In the case

CHART 1.   Allotment of 20 Acres Farming Tract.*
(Alloted March 23, 1916)

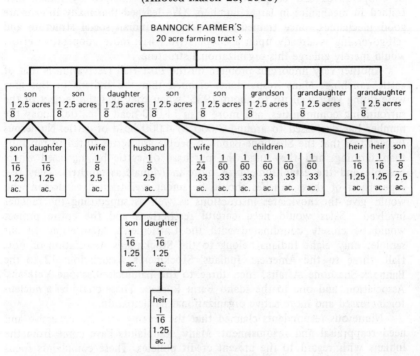

*Bureau of Indian Affairs, Fort Hall Tribal Office.
†Land remains undivided, demonstrating the problem of heirship at Fort Hall.

of the Indians the problem is compounded since they have not only small, dispersed land holdings, little agricultural machinery, and the problem of water irrigation, but the lack of well trained agricultural workers. The problem of water and irrigation was voiced by many of the Indians as a continuously disturbing factor on the reservation. There is much dissatisfaction with the canal, or ditch system, especially from those at the end of the lines of supply. Southern Idaho, however, has enough water and it is thus merely a matter of greater irrigation, better land utilization and development. Some of the respondents have suggested the more extensive use of a sprinkler system to alleviate the water shortages.

In relation to the problem of fractionalized land, the respondents made the following suggestions as possible solutions: (1) Allow greater interchange of lands which are too small and scattered to be productive. Perhaps such interchange could be done among the Indians themselves without too many official rules and regulations governing such exchanges. The official agency would merely record these exchanges. (2) The tribe buy up land, work it in large sections, creating a kind of tribal cooperative, and pay the owners a fee profit. In other words, the tribe would act as a lessee, employing Indian farm help, and pay only yearly to the owners. (3) The cultivation and sale of products upon a corporate basis, and the greater use of cooperatives and cooperative tractor stations manned by Indian men trained in mechanics in larger numbers. (We learned that many Indians are good mechanics, once trained.) Much of the Indian social structure and self-governing is already upon a cooperative basis; more cooperative effort would merely enlarge this organizational structure.

Another very important problem on the Fort Hall reservation is that of cattle ranching. Many respondents claimed that the Indians of this area were doing very well up to about 1936, when they had the respect of the surrounding communities, and more than 11,000 head of cattle. Today the number has decreased to around 3,000 to 4,000 head of cattle. Numerous Indians feel that the Shashone-Bannock people are better suited to ranching than farming, and they urge the purchase of cattle be increased where possible and the establishment of more individuals as ranchers. They feel supervision of these ranches should be under well-trained cattlemen who would give the noviciates instructions as well as supervising the ranches involved. Sales would need careful restrictions and the entire project would be closely coordinated with the Cattlemen's Association. In our sample, only eight Indians belong to the Stockmen's Association of Fort Hall, three to the American Indians' Stockmen's Association, 12 to the Bannock-Shashone Affairs, Inc., three to the Bannock-Shashone Veterans' Association, and one to the Idaho Farm Bureau. These could be a nucleus for increased and more active organizational participation.

Numerous respondents claimed that the grazing fees are excessive and need reappraisal and readjustment. Many complaints have come from the Indians with regard to the present credit policies. These complaints focus primarily upon the short duration of the loans and the preferential treatment of some of the Indians. A considerable number of the farmers and ranchers, in our sample, feel that, in order to do justice to the development of their farms or ranches, loans should be made for longer periods of time to give the farms a chance to grow, allowing for increased production. At present, some claim that they have to sell their cattle or land to meet the difficult conditions of short-term loans. Some felt that the sale of cattle should be more closely supervised, the loans restricted and specifically used for the purposes for which they are intended. (The Indians have a kind of ambivalence where they nostalgically regret the removal of governmental controls in the past and yet do not want many controls today. There is a strong feeling and fear, however, against the government's termination of federal control.) Thus while the problems of land utilization and ranching are basic to the economy of the Shashone-Bannock Tribes, the land and ranching resources are good and solutions are possible and recognized by the Indians themselves. However, at present there is the strange phenomenon of a comparatively land-rich people with levels of sub-standard living reflecting many unsolved problems, including the unemployment of many of their people and the ineffective utilization of natural and human resources.

POPULATION AND FAMILY STRUCTURE
AS RELATED TO LAW VIOLATION

The population structure of Fort Hall also indicates a problematic area for the Shashone-Bannock tribes. Utilizing a five-year cohort age distribution of the population on the reservation, we discern that, compared with the general population in the United States, the Indians of Fort Hall are heavily concentrated in the lower age groups, deficient in the middle or productive age groups, and proportionately larger in the ages 0-19. See Table 4.

TABLE 4

Percent of Population by Age Periods, Fort Hall and the United States, 1960

Age Period	Percent of Population	
	United States	*Fort Hall*
Childhood 0-9	21.73	26.04
Adolescence 10-19	16.59	22.54
Productivity 20-44	32.75	30.03
Maturity 45-64	20.34	13.73
Seniority 65-74	5.66	4.56
Old age 75 and up	3.02	2.22

Source: Report, p. 13.

It will be noted in the above table that in cohorts 0-9 and 10-19, there are 48.58 percent of the Fort Hall population as compared to 38.32 in the general population. If the cohorts 65 and above are added to the young age groups, we discover that the burden of support rests upon the productive age groups, 20-64, who comprise 43.76 percent of Fort Hall as compared to 53.09 percent of the white population. Since few women are in the labor force outside the home, the support of the tribes falls upon the shoulders of only about 25 percent of their population.

The economy is indeed one of scarcity both from the point of view of industrial development and manpower. Further, the high ratio of dependency of the young age groups is accentuated by a lack of education since many Indians, especially boys, drop out of school in the tenth grade. The reason for such "drop-outs" may be many, related to an awakening as to contrasts in clothing, spending money, language difficulties, some discrimination and, above all, the realization of "education for what?" since job opportunities are limited and land ownership postponed. Moreover, the "drop-outs" may be the result of a combination not only of the non-utilitarian aspects of education in the community but the influence of peer groups, and the attitudes of some of the Indian parents among whom the goal orientation toward an education is psychologically and socially not deeply entrenched.

While compared to other reservations the Shashone-Bannock people do not leave their homeland in great numbers, those who do migrate are usually young adults for whom there are no economic opportunities on the reservation. It is also related to the inheritance of land late in life which tends to postpone the establishment of a home. The Fort Hall male who is head of the household is, on the average three and one-half years older than the United States male in a similar capacity, and six and one-half years older than his wife.[5] A sizeable proportion of males do not establish families until they are passed 35 years of age, reflecting the lack of economic opportunities. Nearly seven percent of the population are in seasonal labor, and 11 percent are unemployed.[6]

As mentioned above, there are few women in the labor force outside the home, with the exception of a few who work in the tribal office. Some of the women make bead-leather articles and sell these privately or in a small craft shop but it is not an extensively developed craft industry as is found in the southwest. One, an unusually capable woman, serves as a member of the Tribal Council. Women, however, play a significant and, at times, dominant role in the family structure. With respect to such roles, the schedules in attempting to define the husband's, wife's, and children's participation, alone or together, in the family structure and activities, focused upon such questions as: (1) who does the large purchasing in the family; (2) the small purchases; (3) runs the house; (4) decides as to change of residence; (5) decides as to recreational places and activities; and (6) decides as to discipline of the children?

The statistical data indicate the dynamics of family interrelationships and interaction. Among the 130 schedules in our sample, the large purchases are made by 31 of the husbands and only 25 of the wives, but in 75 cases, or 58 percent, both the husband and wife decide together regarding large purchases. With respect to small purchases, the wife is the dominant decision maker, with more than 54 percent making these decisions alone, and she runs the house alone in nearly 68 percent of the households. The decision regarding change of residence is done about equally either by the husband or wife but the consensus of the husband and wife is the most characteristic action in more than half of the families. Similarly, as to recreational activities, the husband and wife, in 56 percent of the homes, make decisions together, consulting children in a few cases. In relation to discipline of the children, in only one household did the husband have the dominant role without consulting his wife. In almost 40 percent, the wife alone was the disciplinarian, and in almost 59 percent husband and wife together made decisions regarding discipline. In a few cases, 9 families or .7 percent, the children were included in disciplinary problems. The woman either alone or in consultation with her husband emerges as the dominant disciplinarian among the Shashone-Bannock families. Furthermore, as can be seen in the data above, in most of the areas the woman participates equally or dominantly in the family decisions and activities.

The important role and influence of grandparents should also be mentioned, since one-third of the families at Fort Hall still have an extended family structure, although 58 percent have the nuclear type of family.[7] Especially during festivals or trips to other reservations parents leave their children with grandparents. This also happens when the primary family is disrupted. From interviews with social welfare workers on the reservation, it was revealed that during Sun Dance festivals, "round-ups," and journeys to neighboring reservations, some parents leave even very young children with grandparents for many days or completely alone, neglected and dependent upon welfare agencies. There is a strange ambivalence toward children, with a great deal of affection for them and yet little hesitancy to desert or neglect them.

An interesting facet of child rearing was also described to the writer by a social worker who has worked with the Fort Hall people for a considerable number of years. He indicated that the Fort Hall children, to his knowledge, do not develop such nervous characteristics as nail-biting, tics, food revulsions, speech defects, etc., because of the rather relaxed family atmosphere and outward unrestrained expressions of physical affection. When the children are adopted by whites, however, the Indian children develop such nervous traits.

That these selected aspects of the social structure of the community, economic conditions, population characteristics, and family structure are seen reflected in the high rate of law violation on the reservation is the contention of this paper. We analyzed the records of the Tribal Law and Order Office for a comparatively extended period, 1934-1960, encompassing adult and juvenile law violations, felonies and misdemeanors. Of the 130 questionnaires, 75 or 58 percent have some record of breaking the law. From 1934-1960, a total of 527 offenses were committed by members of the 130 households.[8] This includes recidivism. For the year 1959, the arrest rate for 1,789 cities in the United States was 46.4 per 1,000 population whereas for Fort Hall the arrest rate was 161.[9]

Furthermore, a review of all arrests in a five-year period, 1955-1960, indicates a gradual rise in delinquency on the reservation, increasing from 13.3 percent in 1955 to 34.3 percent in 1959.[10]

A review of the offenses indicates, however, that many of the offenses are of the misdemeanor rather than the felony type, predominantly of vagrancy, drunkenness, and disorderly conduct. The offenses in broad categories, in descending order and, in parenthesis, compared with United States percentages for the year 1959, were: First, offenses involving personal demoralization (drunkenness, vagrancy, disorderly conduct, etc.) 47.04 percent (60.7); second, offenses against property, 17.65 percent (10.7); third, offenses against the person, 8.92 percent (5.7); fourth, offenses against the family (desertion, neglect, abuse, etc.), 7.97 percent (1.0); fifth, offenses related to public authority (violation of parole, flight to escape persecution, flight from institution, etc.), 5.5 percent (included under miscellaneous in United States); sixth, offenses related to operation of a motor vehicle (driving while drunk, traffic, etc.), 2.47 percent (4.2); seventh, sex offenses (rape and other sex offenses, other than prostitution since there is no commercialized prostitution on the reservation), .95 percent (2.00); lastly, miscellaneous (truancy, juvenile mischief, incorrigible, violation of fish and game laws, although the Indians are not subject to seasonal game laws as are whites, etc.), 9.50 percent (15.4).[11]

The three largest categories of offenses on the reservation are vagrancy, disorderly conduct, and grand larceny. Unlike the high rate of juvenile delinquency among the general population pertaining to auto theft, this category is rather low on the reservation, comprising only seven percent. This low rate may be explained by the close community life and strong primary controls at Fort Hall where offenders and offenses are known and easily discovered by the tribal police officers. Moreover, off the reservation, high racial visibility tends to limit and deter boys in such thefts. An important factor is also the lack of spending money which Indian youths experience making the purchase of gasoline a problem for the cars they already have. An interesting facet regarding the attitudes of treatment and punishment, which was covered extensively by the questionnaires, is that most Indians feel juveniles should be treated leniently. They draw the line, however, with cattle rustling which they consider a very serious offense since their economy is much affected by such theft.

With regard to drunkenness and disorderly conduct, especially off the reservation, persons who are interested in the Shashone-Bannock people, and social workers whom we interviewed, pointed out that many Indians are arrested for these offenses in the surrounding towns in situations where whites would not be arrested. The Indians, being of lower economic status, with different appearance, and behavior patterns characteristic of such status, drink in dingy cafes where "rot-gut" liquor is served them until their money runs out and they are pretty "pie-eyed." They are then thrown bodily out of the places and/or arrested. Such drinkers become obvious and well known. Recidivism accentuates their behavior. The few who are repeaters tend to give the whole tribe an unfair reputation. The fines given by the Tribal or Municipal courts increase progressively with each repetition thus compounding poverty with further offenses.

The significant factors of the high criminal records of these Indians must be analyzed not merely as so many cases in a police file but viewed in the perspective of the entire structure of their society. That there is such a relationship may be seen in the following table, comparing crowded home living to variables of education, economic conditions, public welfare and delinquency.

In Table 5, education refers to the highest number of years completed, representing the average for male and female; economic status to a classification of social classes developed by the interviewers, divided into rich, middle class, poor, and very poor;[12] welfare to the percentage of households with either a tribal or public welfare record; and delinquency to

TABLE 5

*Comparison of Most-Crowded with Least-Crowded Households
with Respect to Selected Factors*

	Education	Economic Status	Welfare	Delinquency Record
Most crowded	5.78	2.95	47.30	73.70
Least crowded	8.59	2.18	23.50	29.40

Source: Report, p. 52.

the percentage of households having an adult or juvenile delinquency record.

In summary, high delinquency records are interwoven with many factors—the social, economic, family, and community structure of Fort Hall. There is a kind of "lost generation" among these people. The young and vigorous who often represent the dynamic qualities of a people are here found without land, waiting for parents to die and leave them land, resulting in an unusual kind of dependency and aimlessness. Later, if they do inherit land, it is often fractionized and poorly utilized. The high porportion of the very young, as compared with the general population in our society, tends to accentuate the burden of economic production upon a small number of the Indian population. Jobs and training are not made easily available for those willing to work and this discourages those who are in school, resulting in a high "drop-out" rate. These conditions, as among whites, are creative of criminal behavior. Moreover, the disinherited youth often live with overly permissive parents, who do not set high goals for study or work. Mothers tend to be the dominant disciplinarians and fathers, when present at all, have an inferior role in the discipline of the youths. The levels of home living are usually sub-standard, highlighting the relationship of poverty to criminal arrests and records. Their contacts with near and, at times, prejudicial communities and differential treatment, especially in relation to drunkenness and disorderly conduct, points up the status of a minority group experiencing cultural clash.

They are insulated in a world of their own, psychologically and socially, imitating white neighbors in minor behavior patterns, and experiencing communication with the outside world only superficially through their old radio and television sets. Furthermore, since the tribal police work, live, and are part of the reservation, close surveillance makes escape difficult for the law violator. Off the reservation, their high visibility accentuates their presence and behavior, making even minor offenses obvious and punishment inevitable. In brief, the social, economic, and legal aspects within and around the community of Fort Hall affect and reflect the high rate of law violations of the Shashone-Bannock people.

NOTES

1 The author designed and structured the schedules and supervised the field research. The writer acknowledges indebtedness to her assistants: Alan D. Sudweeks, Charles B. Harvey, and Eloise Jane Hevewah, an Indian young woman who spoke both Shashone and Bannock. The research is part of a larger project under the aegis of the Department of Interior, Bureau of Indian Affairs and the University of Idaho. The methodology of the research and the social class stratification are reported in another journal, see Mhyra S. Minnis, "Selected Social Problems of Fort Hall Reservation," *Sociology and Social Research,* Vol. 46, No. 4, July 1962, pp. 436-445. The data for the present article are derived from a combination of the author's master charts and a preliminary report which has been issued; see Harry C. Harmsworth et al., *Human Resources, Relations and Problems of the Fort*

Hall Indian Reservation, Indian Affairs, Department of Interior, October 1961. Hereafter, the latter source will be referred to as Report.

2 Report, p. 50.
3 Ibid., p. 48.
4 F. Stuart Chapin, Contemporary American Institutions (New York: Harper, 1935), pp. 373-397; and William H. Sewell, The Construction and Standardization of the Measurement of the Socio-Economic Status of Oklahoma Farm Families, Oklahoma Agricultural Experiment Station, Bulletin 9, 1940.
5 Report, p. 14.
6 Ibid., p. 16.
7 Ibid., p. 24.
8 Ibid., p. 76.
9 Ibid., p. 75, and "Crime in the United States, Uniform Crime Report, 1959," Federal Bureau of Investigation, p. 99.
10 Ibid., p. 76.
11 Ibid., p. 78 and 79, and Uniform Crime Report, 1959, op. cit., p. 41.
12 Mhyra S. Minnis, op. cit.

LOWELL K. HALVERSON: REPORT ON LEGAL SERVICES TO THE INDIANS: A STUDY IN DESPERATION*

This report is the result of a five-week tour of various Indian centers in Seattle by an attorney of Indian extraction whose services were available without charge for anyone seeking assistance. The primary purpose of this project was to determine the need, if any, for legal counseling to Indians as a separate indigenous group, and if there was a need, to identify means by which this need could be met.

The Seattle Indian Center, the First Avenue Service Center, and the Kinatechitapi Indian Center, all in Seattle, were visited by legal counsel on a regular weekly basis for five weeks. It was hoped that with legal counsel available at a fixed time each week, Indian clients would begin to appear and make their legal complaints known. In addition, Indian center personnel were informed that legal counsel would be available on an emergency call basis as required during this five-week period.

In August, 1970, while the pilot study was still in progress, local Indian leaders requested a hearing with Seattle Mayor Wes Uhlmann regarding urban Native problems. I was invited to testify regarding the pilot study and, because those remarks fairly summarize the project findings, I have included them here.

At the risk of generalizing, it is my personal experience that the urban Natives of Seattle have a deep rooted, almost traditionalized, distrust of governmental agencies, whether federal, state, or local. Whether this arises from the urban Natives' involvement with the Bureau of Indian Affairs or is an offshoot of the "reservation mentality" or whatever, I do not know. However, he seems alienated, appears confused and uninformed about his legal rights and is being deprived of these rights every day. I wish I could say that the Legal Services Centers, the Seattle Public Defender's Office, or the ombudsman could assist these people. But I fear that, at least at present, the institutionalized distrust of government runs too deep. I noted many, many instances of Native clients who refused or failed to contact available (and free) government agencies about their problems. However, the prospective clients had no trouble conferring about their problems with an attorney of Native origins in the setting of one of the Indian centers.

While the urban Natives' involvement with the law is as substantial if not more so, than their white brethern's, their knowledge of the law is woefully inadequate. In the criminal sector many of these people do not even know the simple *Miranda* warnings; those who know them are afraid to exercise their rights for fear that things will go hard for them with the authorities. In the private sector of law, they are not aware of their rights with respect to incidents of racial discrimination, wrongful garnishments, wrongful eviction or even their rights to public assistance.

To characterize the problem in another way, the urban Native's involvement with the law is in the role of the "acted upon" rather than the "actor". Approximately ten percent of your City Jail population tonight is Indian, Your Honor. The Indian's involvement with legal process in Seattle—usually as a defendant in a vagrancy, drunkenness in public, or assault third charge—hardly instills confidence in him that justice is being dispensed equally. Typically, the First Avenue Indian caught up on one of the simpler offenses to society, public drunkenness, will spend two days awaiting trial, plead guilty on the theory that it will go easier for him, and perhaps spend another two to thirty days serving his sentence, while a rich man simply buys his freedom within hours of his arrest. Although these particular "hard core" urban Natives are afforded the form of constitutional due process, they are often denied its substance.

During the five or six weeks of this study, I came across unfair mortage foreclosures, consumer fraud, illegal evictions, serious felony charges (which, if not acted upon by legal counsel immediately, would have resulted in a waiver of constitutional rights), and the more mundane problems of driver's license suspensions, insurance cancellations, assault and drunkenness in public.

There is a plethora of available free legal services that could and should be utilized by urban Natives to meet at least some of these problems. Provided the urban Native meets certain financial requirements, he has available the Seattle-King County Public Defender's Office for felonious criminal matters and four Legal Services agencies for civil matters. In the area of consumer fraud, he can contact the attorney general's office, and if he has complaints against the local government, he may go to the ombudsman.

In all, about thirty clients were interviewed. Of these, only one had actually used any of these government agencies prior to contacting me at the Indian center. Some had legal problems which had existed for as long as two years, and yet I was the first legal counsel they had approached on the matter. This paradox, existing free legal services that are not being utilized, can be only partially explained by the institutionalized distrust of government noted previously. Many of these people simply were not aware of the availability and potential effectiveness of the services available in Seattle and King County.

I also observed that of the clients generated during this pilot study, only a few had problems of a strictly legal nature. Most required only the services of a paraprofessional, since the primary orientation of their problems was toward resolution of "social" problems. Indeed, much of the counseling actually involved referral to available free legal and social agencies.

If legal counseling is to become available to the urban Natives, perhaps the best vehicle for this counseling would be through use of a Native paraprofessional. Such a person would be required to have a well-developed, working knowledge of the many and various social agencies and, further, know how to exploit these agencies. In addition, this person would be required to have an understanding of fundamental legal rights in the area of contract law, consumer law, landlord-tenant relations, motor-vehicle codes, welfare law and juvenile law. A paraprofessional with this background could act as a conduit to the many available agencies already staffed and trained to deal with specific problems of Indians and others.

To give this paraprofessional some extra "clout," a lawyer could be retained on a strictly emergency call basis, for use in those legal problem areas where rights are lost unless action is taken immediately. Such instances might include criminal cases during that period between arrest and appointment of a lawyer; civil cases, such as foreclosure proceedings, immediately before proceedings are instituted; and cases in consumer law, within the 24-hour period following purchase of the chattel.

Except for one arrest in a murder case, which required immediate and intensive legal counseling, few of the client problems encountered by the writer could not be handled by a paraprofessional trained in social agency work and rudimentary legal principles. For example, there were a number of problems concerning motor-vehicle violations of a mundane nature (no operator's license or operation while license was suspended). The available publications for lawyers explaining the necessary steps for renewal of a license could as easily be used by a paraprofessional. These traffic matters are not included in the law school curriculum, and if a lawyer can acquire the skills to manage these cases in the course of his practice, so can a paraprofessional.

SPECIFIC RECOMMENDATIONS

Although I am not aware of any specific training program available to meet the qualifications of the sort of person needed for this paraprofessional job, it would not be difficult to develop such a program. Unless the needs of the community required more than one or two of these people, training could be obtained on a one-to-one basis right in a law office. Some field work would be required to acquaint the trainee with local social and welfare agencies. I would estimate the cost of this modest program for one year, including training and service, to be approximately $10,000 to $15,000.

Primary emphasis during training would be on acquiring a rudimentary knowledge of legal concepts so that the trainee could identify accurately those cases involving the infringement of legal rights. In order to avoid the expense of a second staff member, it would be helpful if the trainee could have basic office skills such as typing and office management. I would imagine a trainee, once qualified, would initially earn $7,200 to $8,000 per year, based on the Seattle rate for legal secretaries.

The anchor-man lawyer would be paid on an hourly basis at the standard professional rate. He would be experienced in the general practice of law, including criminal law, consumer law, landlord-tenant rights, motor-vehicle codes, welfare law and juvenile law. He should also have rapport with members of the various available social agencies.

The paraprofessional and the back-up lawyer, working together, would try to refer their clients to the available free services mentioned earlier in this report. Where this was not possible—for instance, during the time between arrest and indictment in a criminal case—they would be prepared to work together quickly and efficiently.

Assuming this proposed program could achieve some continuity, the lawyer and the paraprofessional would begin to develop other legal and social programs for the Indian population generally. Certainly, such a team could act as ombudsmen within the Native community, and when they recognized a developing social need, they would be able to rally the resources of the entire community to meet this need.

CONCLUSION

This writer is convinced that the urban Native is not utilizing available legal services furnished by the government because of institutionalized distrust of governmental agencies, impatience with the slowness of these agencies, and ignorance of their existence. Since many Indians are coming to the various urban Native centers with problems only partly legal and mostly social in nature, it would be uneconomical to maintain a lawyer on even a part-time basis to handle these problems when they can be expeditiously dealt with by a competent, experienced, and specially trained paraprofessional. This person could act as a conduit, referring clients when possible to the applicable agency or agencies for relief. A lawyer could be retained as anchor man to provide legal advice to the paraprofessional and also act as a troubleshooter on an emergency basis. In this way, the urban Natives who are not now taking advantage of the various services, could at least achieve a parity with their similarly situated white and black brethren. Such a program could be developed for a price that is modest in comparison with the results which would be achieved.

APPENDIX

First Week: July 30, 1970

A. Indian Center

One-half Tswout (British Columbia): Husband assaulted her, wants divorce immediately. Legal Aid can't give appointment for three months. Used pull and got her in the next day for divorce interview.

Full Tlingit-Haida (Alaska): Concerned about will, probations, re minor daughter. Advised a will change with her regular lawyer.

B. First Avenue Center

Full Aleut: Needed information regarding termination of probation period, and to enroll for Alaskan Federation of Natives benefits—wrote a letter for for him for information blanks.

C. Kinatechitapi

One-half Gros Ventres (Montana): Needs advice on competency of counsel defending his son for first-degree murder—conferred with his counsel and advised to stick with him.

One-half Cheyenne: Son AWOL and wanted civilian attorney. Referred to an attorney who has a grant to administer counseling on his behalf.

Muckelshoot and Cree: Desire to see greater representation on Model Cities and Urban League—called a friend in Model Cities as to availability of jobs and got them on mailing list.

Second Week: August 6, 1970

A. Indian Center

Discussed legal questions arising from participating in foundation grants, Indian Center personnel.

Full Eskimo: Cheated out of his wages by an employer who went bankrupt—called employer's attorney and offered to settle and called Millionaires Club to obtain job. Sent client to attorney to demand settlement.

B. First Avenue Center

Full Eskimo: Wanted by law for no valid operator's license, no valid registration, jaywalking. Advised to stay out of the city where he picked up the tickets until the tickets expired. Tried to raise bail amount.

C. Kinatechitapi

One-half Cree: Charged with driving while under a suspended license. Arranged appearance for personal recognizance and attempted to negotiate bail, got extension on trial date in order to arrange bail. Referred to reputable high-risk insurer for immediate insurance.

Muckelshoot: Parents deceased and children need money from guardianship but bank most reluctant to expend funds. Called bank and arranged appointment for conference with all parties; requested client to write a budget to prove increased cost of child care. Conferred with bank and got support payments increased 25 percent for each child.

Third Week: August 13, 1970

A. Indian Center

Chippewa: Purchasing a home and served with papers for foreclosure because contractor failed to make payments to bank. Conferred with bank's attorney and arranged to make payments directly to bank to protect equity; requested client to send photocopy of contract to bank. Letter to bank and copy to client sending them to Operation Equality.

B. First Avenue Center

No Indian clients.

C. Kinatechitapi

(Lineage unknown): Appears to be a transmission company's fraud upon the client; overselling goods for a worthless car—called transmission company and arranged a cash settlement to client. Client got part settlement. Called again to get balance.

Fourth Week: August 20, 1970

A. Indian Center

Full Apache and Full Eskimo (husband and wife): Concern for welfare of child whose custody was taken by court when parents left for California, parents now want child back. Called caseworker for court and arrange for parents to visit with child. Advised parents to establish a good home for child and made appointment for caseworker and guardian *ad litem* to confer with parents to change custody back to parents.

B. First Avenue Center

South American Indian (Argentina): Needs divorce. Wants to avoid draft and wants to know how to get on public assistance. Advised of legal services for divorce, draft counseling services, and sent to Public Assistance Office.

Ucluelet Tribe (British Columbia): Wants to know if needs an alien registration card in order to work in states—called U.S. Immigration who informed that Indian from Canada does not need a card but, as a practical matter, employers insist upon it and so obtained an application for client to process so he could work in U.S.

Emergency: August 21, 1970

(Lineage unknown): Arrested for fictitious plates, stolen rifle and no operator's license; now in Seattle Jail. Has three small children. Arranged for father to post bail Saturday morning and charge reduced to "no plates." Referred by Kinatechitapi Center.

Fifth Week: August 27, 1970

A. *Indian Center*

Yakima/Dwamish: Appears to have a problem of adverse possession (boundary dispute with a Japanese). Obtained a real estate man who will not charge to look over property, give appraisal, and determine if boundary line is incorrect. Surveyor too costly.

Conferred with Indian Center officials re legality of funding for a jazz festival and whether center liable for loss.

Conferred with probation officer re Indian girl who had been evicted from home. Took the girl home myself and gave her dinner. Sought job for her and enrolled her on public assistance.

B. *First Avenue Center*

Two Indians arrested for asserting fishing rights. Referred them to specialist lawyers dealing in Indian fishing right cases.

C. *Kinatechitapi*

Conferred with a man who alleges to be one-eighth Shoshone, re malpractice action.

Emergency: August 31, 1970

Received call from Indian Center that a wood-carver had been arrested for suspicion of murder. Conferred with friends of suspect, visited suspect at City Jail, arranged to have suspect examined by prison doctor to show bruises and establish legal defense of self-defense. Advised suspect not to talk to any police officers. Arranged to have his checks sent to his friend. Attempted to have a hearing for personal recognizance and early appointment of attorney. Got bail reduced to 15 percent of original bail.

September 3, 1970

Girl's license suspended for no insurance although other party was at fault; wrote Department of Motor Vehicles about apparent misunderstanding. Referred by Kinatechitapi.

September 3, 1970

Client being sued in California for vehicle accident. Assisted client in preparing an answer and defense. Referred by Kinatechitapi.

NOTES

*This study was made possible by a grant to the Seattle Indian Center from the National Endowment for the Humanities.

FRANCES NORTHEND FERGUSON: NAVAHO DRINKING: SOME TENTATIVE HYPOTHESES*

A three year treatment program for Navaho problem drinkers has produced evidence that—in the area of the relationship between treatment effectiveness and patient characteristics—the more acculturated Navahos respond less well to treatment. Such patients tend to have greater facility with English, higher than sixth grade exposure to contemporary education, and experience in military service. Furthermore, these patients are seldom satisfied with the seasonal laboring jobs that characteristically supplement traditional income: they seek instead, long-term employment in middleclass technical or white-collar jobs. Often they appear to feel pushed by the expectations of both whites and Navahos to attain higher status because of their superior education. In contrast, patients who respond well to treatment tend to be less educated and less involved in contemporary society; and they are less often rated as anxious in initial psychological examinations.

Excessive drinking among individuals from technologically underdeveloped groups confronted with severe acculturation problems has sometimes been attributed to anxiety resulting from stress.[1] Another view is that excessive drinking is not so much a reaction to stress as an indulgence in one of the new-found pleasures of town, an indulgence unstructured by any traditional patterns of control.[2]

The tendency to type the drinking patterns of certain ethnic groups persists with respect to the American Indian, even in studies which have left the "drunken Indian" stereotype far behind. Yet our study indicates that there are clearly several types of drinkers among Navaho Indians; generalizations must be made cautiously. The situation is too complex for the attribution of simple causes or the creation of facile typologies.

It does seem feasible, however, to start with the successfully treated problem drinker and work backward in an attempt to identify causes and types. Using this method, the tentative hypotheses presented here are derived from two sources: (1) observations of Navaho drinkers and Navaho drinking patterns (in conjunction with hundreds of conversations and interviews with problem drinkers and their families), and (2) more or less objectively determined results of a treatment program.

After two and one-half years of the treatment program, we are aware that we must differentiate between characteristics of patients who respond and patients who do not respond to treatment. By comparing the two groups we can attempt to predict which individuals will respond to the

Source: Reprinted by permission from *Human Organization* 27 (Summer 1968) 159-167.

kind of treatment we have to offer. The evidence suggests that patients who respond poorly to treatment fall into the category described by Horton, Hamer, and others as people suffering from the stress of severe acculturation problems with accompanying anxiety.[3] I shall call these *anxiety drinkers*. Our evidence suggests also that patients who respond well to treatment are more apt to be what I shall call *recreation drinkers*, such as those described by the Honigmanns in their account of drinking among Baffin Island Eskimo.[4] These drinkers do not seem greatly affected by acculturation difficulties. They are more likely to have taken up drinking as a new-found pleasure of town, and to have become addicted as a result of strong pressures exerted by the drinking peer group and the lack of sanctions in Navaho society against excessive drinking. The *recreation drinker* may have no deep-rooted conflicts. In treatment he acquires a new set of values with regard to drinking and begins to identify with a new, nonproblem-drinker peer group.

THE TREATMENT PROGRAM

In September 1964, a National Institute of Mental Health Grant, administered by the McKinley County (New Mexico) Family Consultation Service, established "A Community Treatment Plan for Navaho Problem Drinkers." In May 1966, the project reached its quota of 120 patients. Patients were recruited by interviewing Navahos with ten or more arrests in the jails. If they seemed motivated to quit drinking, they were offered the opportunity to volunteer for treatment over a period of eighteen months' probation. The treatment program includes the following:

1 Five days hospitalization, during which heart and liver function tests are made, and the patients are started on.
2 Antabuse, a drug which makes the person ill if he drinks.
3 Interviews with the families to prepare them for the return of the patient, or, where there is no family, the making of arrangements for temporary shelter.
4 The location of "helping persons" willing to supervise the giving of medication and keep the project staff informed of the patient's progress (for patients unable to report to the project office for Antabuse).
5 Contacting former employers when this seems advisable, or help in seeking and finding employment.
6 Psychotherapy, when this seems indicated.
7 Counseling with members of the staff who are available at any time (the project office is a place where the coffee is always hot, and patients with their friends and relatives are encouraged to come and chat with the staff or with one another).
8 Follow-up during the probation period.
9 Group discussions for those who live within reasonable distance of the project office.
10 The gathering of research data, including psychological tests, from each patient.

The U.S. Public Health Service, the Navaho Tribe, and the Bureau of Indian Affairs, in addition to community forces such as courts, police, employment and welfare offices, have all played a part in the rehabilitation of these patients. The project has seeded a Tribal Alcoholism Program now established on the Reservation and funded by the Office of Navaho Economic Opportunity. The tribal program has 24 community alcoholism workers operating throughout the Reservation. In accord with the initial NIMH proposal, patients have been treated as individuals: while Antabuse has been a part of the treatment of almost all patients, the amounts of other kinds of attention are varied according to circumstances and the patient's special need.

THE ETHNOGRAPHY OF NAVAHO DRINKING

The treatment program grew out of a very evident need, illustrated by the fact that of 600-750 drunkenness arrests per month in Gallup, New Mexico, approximately 90 percent were Navaho.[5] Gallup, a border town whose permanent population of about 17,500 is increased by many thousands during weekends, has forty or more bars. The town is a shopping center made easily accessible by the ownership of pickup trucks, which are very popular on the Reservation. Whole families pile into a pickup for the Gallup excursion. They do their shopping in town and walk up and down the streets on Saturday, greeting old friends and relatives in a jovial and affectionate manner. This is a happy occasion for people who live rather widely separated from one another on the Reservation. Inevitably drinks are offered as an expression of conviviality. One can see entire families in some of the nicer bars, with the children playing on the floor while their parents enjoy a conversation with friends. Some of these people have a drink or two, finish their shopping, perhaps picking up a couple of "six packs," and go home. That this is not always true, however, is clear from the cited high arrest rate. Many of those arrested for drunkenness have been jailed repeatedly, some as many as a hundred times.

The problem is not new, however, as is evident from historical records. The arrival of Europeans introduced alcohol to Navahos along with other innovations. By 1880, the acting Navaho agent complained that

> the crying evil that most besets this people is whisky. There are several traders at nearby points ranging from 40 to 100 miles from the Reservation where whisky of the vilest description is dealt out to these people in open violation of the law, being an incentive to crime and greatly impoverishing many of them. Decisive and prompt measures should be adopted by the Government to put a stop to this nefarious traffic, otherwise results of the most deplorable character may eventuate.[6]

Early in the 19th century the president of the United States had been enpowered to take measures controlling the sale or barter of liquor to Indians. In 1832, Congress passed an Indian Prohibition Act. More than a century later–in 1953– the law prohibiting the sale of intoxicating beverages to Indians was repealed. The new law provided for local option on Indian Reservations within the framework of state law. Both New Mexico and Arizona repealed the prohibition of sale of liquor to Indians outside the reservations.[7] The Navaho Tribe is still considering the feasibility of repeal within the Reservation, which is a 24,000 square mile area lying mainly in northeastern Arizona and northwestern New Mexico. In the meantime, contraband traffic in liquor on the Navaho Reservation continues to flourish. Very often the source is a neighbor, or a friend encountered at a ceremony. It is apparently never hard to find a bootlegger.

Although many excessive drinkers say they drink only when they go to Gallup or some other city, the number of arrests on the Reservation for "disorderly conduct" (as drunkenness is termed by the Navaho Police) was 6,565 in 1958, 8,536 in 1959, and 9,017 in 1960.[8] In a recent proposal to ONEO for funds to cope with the drinking problem, the Tribe gave an estimate of 3000 alcoholics, 10,000 problem drinkers, with 35,000 family members involved (in a total population of 100,000). One can question the reliability of such figures in any population. Navaho tribal officials state, however, that excessive drinking is one of the Tribe's greatest problems. Billy Norton, a distinguished Navaho medicine man, believes that about 30 percent of the Navaho population drink excessively. Many Navahos say that every family has some member with a drinking problem. This is not to imply that the majority of Navahos have a drinking problem, or that there is more problem drinking, with its attendant consequences, among Navahos than among members of other ethnic groups of this area or the United States in general. Navaho drinking, however, is conspicious because of its public nature. Much drinking takes place outdoors, just as do many other Navaho life activities.

Who are the excessive drinkers among Navahos? The population of this group is varied, and there is no apparent pattern of characteristics which identifies the drinkers. Their education ranges from none at all to a college degree. Occupation is represented by everything from sheepherder to tribal councilman and professional. The degree of acculturation is obviously wide, with some drinkers who speak no English and others who speak English with ease and have continual contact with contemporary society. There are veterans and non-veterans. The age range extends from the middle teens to fifty, with some tapering off among the older population. Whether this is because the heavy drinkers die young (there is an unusually high incidence of cirrhosis of the liver at the Public Health Indian Hospital in Gallup) or whether older drinkers tend to become more moderate is not known. Place of residence may be as distant as 90 miles from the treatment center in Gallup, or as near as a block or two. Both married and single men and women are found in the drinking population. Women are drinking as well as men, but are not so often arrested, although there are a few older women who go in and out of jail periodically. It is said that now many more young women are seen drinking heavily in the bars than was formerly the case. Here I shall speak mainly of Navaho men, since they volunteer for treatment far more often than the women.

Of the heavily drinking male population, some are returnees from migrant labor camps or railroad jobs, or are jobholders in Gallup or on the Reservation who spend their pay checks lavishly to treat friends. Others have sold sheep—many Navahos engage in stock raising—and are celebrating the event. The most confirmed drinkers are sometimes drinking proceeds gained from pawning their wives' or female relatives' turquoise necklaces and other jewelry—and even more often their own watches, suitcases, jewelry, hats, or other articles of clothing.

There are a number of bars in Gallup which are patronized mainly by Navahos. Some of these have small dance bands and serve as gathering places for both sexes. Navaho males, made less shy (they say) by alcohol, scrape up acquaintances with women or respond to the women's approaches. There is an air of gaiety in one such typical bar, interspersed with an occasional fight between men over women, women over men, or between a married pair or lovers. In this bar the bouncers handle the situation rather well, and only occasionally does anyone get badly hurt in a fight. Not all bars are so lively, and not all bouncers handle their customers as nicely. In some bars, drinks are sold freely to a drunk until his money is gone and he can no longer cadge drinks from companions. He then drifts into an alley where he may join another drinking group, or pass out and be loaded into the police "panel" destined for jail. On the north side of town, groups may be seen drinking behind buildings in a deserted street car. A favorite place is the "Perky," the dry steam bed of the River Puerco, which runs through town. There is a certain loss of status associated with drinking in the Perky, and few will admit to being there. Drinkers can be seen in the stream bed at all times, however.

Navaho drinkers most often congregate in small groups of three to five. The man with the money is expected to buy for others. Navaho drinkers say that even when they are penniless they are never at a loss for a drink; someone is always buying. For alleys and outside drinking the most frequently consumed beverage has been, until recently, a tokay wine that can be bought for sixty cents a pint. Lately, a synthetic fruit-flavored alcoholic beverage has become very popular. The bottle is passed from person to person, each taking as large a swig as possible. Faces are smashed with wine bottles from time to time in quarrels among the drinkers.

Drinking in pickup trucks or cars is very common, and drinkers seem to enjoy telling of past adventures while driving under the influence of alcohol. Most of those who drink excessively drink to get drunk. A little exhiliration does not interest them. The majority of excessive drinkers go on to the point of "blackout:" that is, they are still walking and talking but next day have only a vague memory of the situation. Many actually pass out, and others steal their hats and boots to be pawned for more alcohol.

When the drinking Navaho is taken to jail, he is often in the "blacked-out" condition. In this state he is able to give his name, age, census number, and address; but next morning he wakes up in the "drunk tank" and asks his friends how he got there. Residents of the drunk tank are old drinking buddies. Stories are swapped about the previous night. This is a population which has drifted in and out before. Some of the more reliable always act as trusties in the kitchen. Despite conditions that are below par and occasional cases of DT's and even deaths, this jail has its cheerful aspects. The jailers know most of the inmates by name. To some of the inmates this is a home away from home. Few people want to be in jail, however, and many eagerly wait for relatives who may bail them out. But for some, this is only one part of the circular road which traverses alley, Perky, jail and back to alley again. While this revolving-door situation is far from desirable, arrest functions not only to clear the streets of unsightly staggerers who embarrass the townspeople and shock the tourists passing through Gallup on Route 66; it also saves a good many drinkers from injury or untimely death.

The consequences of such excessive drinking are evident. When Navaho wives drink with their husbands, children tend to get lost. Spouses in a blacked-out condition may wonder off with other individuals. Babies are sometimes found in bars, or beside their mothers' unconscious bodies. The public health hospital usually has five or six such babies in what one doctor jokingly calls the "Gallup Hotel Hilton." Sometimes children left at home get hungry when parents fail to return. Hogans are without fuel in sub-zero weather. Welfare records are replete with cases of children neglected by one or both parents as a result of excessive drinking.

Twenty percent of the accident cases seen at the public health hospital are alcohol-related. Drinkers driving pickups injure themselves and others. Some freeze to death in winter, or are killed by trains. Jobs are often left or lost because of drinking. Property and stock are neglected, damaged or sold. Spouses are separated. Health is destroyed. There is a high rate of drunkenness among Navahos relocated in urban areas for training or employment, with consequent failure in these areas. Of crimes committed on the Reservation in 1960, 70 percent were alcohol-related,[9] and this seems to be a persisting trend. In a recent paper on Navaho suicide, Jerrold Levy points out the high incidence of suicide among young men as compared to the rest of the Navaho population. Forty-seven percent of contemporary suicide cases involve the intoxication of the subject at the time of or immediately prior to the act.[10]

Two characteristics seem to distinguish Navaho drinking from typical "alcoholic" drinking as described for the United States in general. One is the drinking peer group. A Navaho is seldom found drinking alone for very long. These are not individuals alienated from their fellows, as many alcoholics are said to be. Camaraderie is the essence of the Navaho drinking situation. One is reminded of drinking in neighborhood "pubs," or "the fleet's in." In the past, Navaho society tended to discourage the elevation of individuals above the group. Even today, the educated and the uneducated have close cultural and often family ties. Therefore, despite the heterogeneous character of the drinkers, various types drink together.

The pressure to drink with friends is very great. Refusing to accept or to buy a drink is an affront. The man who refuses is ridiculed, pursued, or may have wine poured on his head. His relatives sometimes tell him he does not love them any more. Refusal under such circumstances is difficult.

The enjoyments of peer group drinking are marked. There is much joking, laughter, and expression of affection; social solidarity is intensified. This solidarity seems to apply especially to men in the drinking situation. While both sexes are involved in family drinking, in public drinking groups males are in the majority.

The other outstanding feature of Navaho drinking is the absence of strong social sanctions in Navaho society against excessive drinking. To be in a white man's jail is no particular disgrace, and to get drunk is not considered shocking except by faithful members of the nondrinking Christian denominations or the Native American (peyote) Church. What *is* regarded as undesirable is the loss of property or employment, and the breaking up of families. When a man begins to cause his family trouble in this manner, there is great distress—and this is expressed verbally. But by this time the man is probably habituated to heavy drinking.

One can speculate that, given time, Navaho social controls related to alcohol may evolve in such a way as to make drinking less destructive in nature. At the same time, Navahos are apparently loath to interfere with one another's behavior. At the present time, at least, orderly drinking patterns are relatively unknown, although a few of the more acculturated Navahos are beginning to give parties at which liquor is served but drinking does not get out of hand. Excessive drinking at Navaho ceremonies such as Yeibichai and Squaw Dances is frowned upon but nonetheless common. Associated with the lack of constructively effective social controls, is the effect of the superimposed external control of prohibition which existed for so long, and which still exists on the Reservation. Prohibition has fostered the hurried gulping of alcohol to avoid being caught and arrested. As one Navaho friend explained when asked why he drank so rapidly, "I was put in jail once for having half a pint of whiskey in my pocket." This pattern of rapid drinking has been established and persists.

THE EFFECTIVENESS OF TREATMENT

The realities of the Navaho drinking patterns raise a number of questions in regard to the treatment and its effectiveness. Should the concept include more than cessation of problem drinking? Perhaps excessive drinking is a substitute for more destructive habits. Should the whole life situation be taken into consideration? If it should, then how is improvement in life situation to be assessed? For many Navahos, holding a permanent job is unusual. Part of the year is often devoted to caring for stock and farming. In assessing improvement, health and family relationships must be considered, but even these are somewhat nebulous entities. In an attempt to assess treatment effectiveness with some validity we use two measures: (1) the subjective measure that, in the opinion of the staff, there is improvement or lack of improvement in the patient's life situation; and (2) the more objective measure of whether there has been a marked decrease in the patient's arrest rate or known repetitions of drunkenness since the beginning of treatment.

It is surprising to find that some of the worst cases—men with many dozens of arrests for drunkenness, the despair of courts and police—have responded well to treatment. It would be pleasant for purposes of research to be able to say that this group had received uniform treatment, but such is not the case. Some have had a great deal of attention from the staff, and others (who live far away) have not. The overall characteristic of this group is *lack of severe acculturation problems.* Its members tend to be less well-educated and to enter modern culture only on a temporary laboring level. The following case is a good example.

A is a Navaho with 153 arrests. He is 34, married and has four children. His education did not extend beyond the third grade; he does not speak English. A had drinking companions all over town. Judges and police felt he was beyond help. A lives 40 miles away, on the Reservation, and has a minimum of attention from the staff because of distance. Since enlisting in treatment 17 months ago, he has spent his time looking after the family stock. We visit him and his family occasionally, and he comes into the office every few months. A has not been arrested nor has he been known to drink since entering treatment. He says he has no desire to drink.

On the other hand, some patients who appeared most promising at the start have responded poorly to treatment. Here again, degree of attention from the project staff is not uniform. The characteristic of this group is (apparent) high aspiration in conjunction with a good deal of involvement in modern culture. This type of person often *appears* to get along with ease in both cultures. Case B is representative of this group.

B is a college graduate, 35 years old. He had ten arrests for drunkenness when he entered the treatment program, and had lost several good jobs as a result of drinking. He is married and has four children, and the children do not speak Navaho. B takes pride in his education and goes about town hatless, wearing slacks and a white shirt, while the majority of Navaho males uniformly wear blue jeans and colored shirts, and never go hatless. Conversations with B make it clear that he feels an obligation to achieve and hold a position of some importance. He greatly reveres his traditional parents and subscribes to the old Navaho beliefs. Holding a professional job and living on the outskirts of town, he also spends considerable time at his parents' place on the Reservation and is highly skilled at roping and stock raising. As a boy B was initiated into the Yeibichai. He has a wide repertoire of traditional songs and sings outstandingly well in the prescribed Navaho manner. When he gets drunk he says such things as "I'm a drunken Indian," or taking a nickel from his pocket he points to the Indian and says, "That's my father's head." B is an outgoing, friendly fellow who loves jokes and a good time, but very often he does his drinking alone. He received a great deal of attention from the staff, but after 16 months of treatment it became evident that his drinking pattern had not altered in the least. Since enlisting in the treatment program he has wrecked three cars while intoxicated, and continues to be involved in serious marital trouble related to his heavy drinking.

This is not to suggest that most Navahos who have entered, or have become aware of the possibility of entering, modern contemporary society will have drinking problems. It is merely to say that among Navahos with a drinking problem it appears to be harder to treat this type of person effectively. He is expected to have a level of aspiration which is difficult for him to achieve. This is not due to lack of intelligence or ability. It may be that secretly he does not want to achieve such a level, but feels obligated to respond to the expectations of those who have fostered his education. Furthermore, he has to cope with the resentment of his less-educated fellows. The well-educated Navaho may suffer from conflicts between strong emotional identification with the Navaho Tribe and a desire to be a typical middle-class American male. Without undue speculation, we can at least say that it is more difficult for the Navaho male to realize his ambitions than it is for the average American male of similar education. Navaho drinker *C* is a case in point:

C is a 29-year-old high school graduate, unmarried. He attended junior college for one year, working as a psychiatric aide at the same time. He lives some of the time with his relatives on the Reservation, and at other times in town. He has also lived in such cities as Los Angeles, and has spent three years in military service. *C* danced in Navaho ceremonies as a boy, but no longer attends the dances. Like *B*, he received much attention from the staff. He too is concerned about his status and feels that he is not accomplishing what he should. He, like *B*, is ambivalent about his Indian identity. During the treatment period he married, and for the duration of the marriage he drank much less. When the marriage broke up, he went back to his familiar pattern, losing jobs, and being seen about town drunk very frequently.

The aspirations of the less acculturated are more easily realizable—or perhaps it is simply easier for them to live up to the expectations of those about them. Their identification is Navaho, and they enter modern contemporary society only on brief but frequent excursions to obtain desirable material goods and recreation. Their sojourns away from the Reservation as wage workers do not bring an identification with contemporary society. Cases *D* and *E* illustrate this pattern:

D's situation is very similar to that of *A* and a number of others. At the time of enlistment in the treatment program he had 86 arrests. Although he had fewer arrests than *A*, he was more of a legend about town. All the members of the drinking peer group, the judges, and police knew *D*. *D* is 41 years old, unmarried, has never been to school, and does not speak English. He lives over sixty miles away, and for this reason staff members have visited him and his relatives only a few times. He appears at the office about once a month. Since enlistment in the program over 18 months ago, he has given up drinking entirely and is one of the mainstays of his household, which consists of parents and a drunken brother's family. He looks after stock and also works for the Tribe in housing development.

E is 34 years old. He was married when he enlisted in the treatment plan eighteen months ago, but is now separated from his wife. He has had five years of special education, speaks fair English, but lives in the traditional manner on the Reservation, caring for stock. At enlistment in treatment he had 27 arrests for drunkenness and was well known to the Gallup drinking peer group. E has had a good deal of attention from the staff. He came to the office frequently until recently, when he got a job with the Tribe in water development. E has not been arrested nor has he been known to be drunk since his enlistment in the treatment program.

One more history illustrates an atypical but important case:

F is a 42-year-old unmarried Navaho who had 81 arrests when he entered treatment. He is one of the most interesting of our patients. F spent three years in military service during World War II, and prior to that had gone as far as the end of his junior year in high school. He lives part of the time on the outskirts of town with relatives, and part of the time with his parents on the Reservation. In spite of his exposure to eleven grades of education and his very creditable record in military service, F has no interest in assuming a position in middle-class contemporary society, but is a leader among his peers.

His identification is Navaho. He attends ceremonies frequently, participating in the singing. During his twenty drinking years he often left the region to work on a cattle ranch for three or four months, returning to Gallup to spend several hundred dollars in a few days. When he ran out of money his friends always bought wine for him. Since entering treatment he has held a steady job, which he appears to regard as a supplement to the family income from stock raising. He is building a new house for his parents and helps his brother's family when they are in need. He, like many others, has bought a pickup truck and other symbols of material prosperity such as a turquoise watchband, ring, etc.

One of the outstanding things about this patient is that through his example dozens of men have requested to enlist in the treatment program. They identify with him and seek his approval. He is, in a sense, the nucleus of the new nonproblem-drinker peer group. He has drunk with them all and been in jail with them all. F has not been known to be drunk since his enlistment in the program 18 months ago. He has had much attention from the staff. He could easily take his place in white society if he wished, but he appears to prefer the Navaho way of life, only adopting those aspects of modern contemporary culture which add convenience to the traditional way of living. This man appears to have made a successful adaptation to the culture conflict situation by retreating into the old culture while maintaining a healthy constructive contact with the new.

When each of our 120 patients joined the program, he was given a battery of psychological tests that included the Wechsler Adult Intelligence

Scale, Minnesota Multiphasic, Rorschach, Thematic Apperception, and Draw-A-Man. While some of these tests are of dubious value cross-culturally, and even the projective tests are difficult to interpret meaningfully, one can assume that the psychologists administering the tests were accustomed to recognizing anxiety in the course of an interview. To investigate the assumption that there is a correlation between treatment failure and initial anxiety, 26 patients were chosen whose success in treatment seems outstanding: 24 were chosen who have not responded to treatment. Table I—utilizing the psychologists' summary statement on each patient— shows that of the 24 unsuccessful patients, eleven (46 percent) were considered to be suffering from marked anxiety (other than situational anxiety) when they enlisted in the treatment program. Of the 26 very successful patients, only three (12 percent) were judged to be suffering from marked anxiety when they enlisted in the treatment program.

TABLE 1

*Characteristics of Successful and Unsuccessful Patients
in the Community Treatment Program*

Characteristic	Successfully Treated		Unsuccessfully Treated	
	N*	*Percent*	*N***	*Percent*
Married (at time of treatment)	13	50	11	46
Education				
High school or more	7	27	14	58
Less than 6th grade	14	54	7	29
Facility with English	15	58	19	82
Nontraditional wife	3	12	3	13
Military service	8	31	13	54
Dissatisfaction with job merely as				
supplement to traditional income	2	8	10	42
Customary living quarters nontradi-				
tional	7	27	10	42
Anxiety rating initially by psychologist	3	12	11	46
Aspirations unrealistic or demands				
overwhelming	1	4	10	42
Acculturation scale, four or more points	4	15	9	38

   *Successfully treated, N = 26.
   **Unsuccessfully treated, N = 24.

Of the 24 unsuccessfully treated patients, ten (42 percent) are rated as having aspirations beyond their reach (or being pushed to have aspirations beyond their reach). Of these ten, nine were described as anxious in the psychologists' initial evaluation. Seventeen of the unsuccessfully treated patients have six or more grades of schooling, and fourteen attended high school or beyond. Fifty percent of unsuccessful patients have more than an eleventh grade education. Of the nine unsuccessfully treated patients who were both anxious and over-aspiring, all had been as far as the sixth grade, all but one had attended high school, six had more than eleventh grade education, and seven had four points or more on the acculturation scale described below.

Of the 26 successfully treated patients, only one might conceivably be rated as having unrealistic aspirations. Twelve (46 percent) of them have had six or more grades of schooling, and seven (27 percent) attended high school. Fifty-four percent of the successful patients have less than sixth grade education.

Using a five-point acculturation scale based on (1) education, sixth grade or more; (2) facility with English; (3) military service; (4) marriage to a nontraditional wife; (5) dissatisfaction with simple job as supplement to traditional income; and (6) major living quarters not traditional, we find that 38 percent of the unsuccessfully treated patients have four or more points, while only 15 percent of the successfully treated patients have four or more points.

Variables such as marriage to a nontraditional wife, length of time in treatment, age at which drinking started, duration of drinking history, and whether the patient had a job, do not appear significant upon analysis. Age bears further investigation since the unsuccessfully treated patients' median age is 29 and their mean age 31, while the successfully treated patients' median age is 39 and mean age 37.[11] It may be that older patients are more amenable to treatment. Or perhaps the younger age of unsuccessful patients is related to the greater degree of acculturation and hence the greater anxiety.

From these very tentative figures there seems to be some indication that the anxious patient caught in an acculturational bind is less apt to respond to treatment. He tends to be more involved in contemporary culture and has aspirations (or feels pressured toward aspirations) which he is unable to achieve.

CONCLUSION

If these tenuous assumptions are correct and if continuing investigation brings further verification, it seems valid to divide excessive drinkers among the Navahos into two types. The first are *recreation drinkers* who drink because drinking is one of the pleasures of town and who have fallen or are in danger of falling, into addiction due to the strong pressures exerted by the drinking peer group and to a lack of sanctions in Navaho society against excessive drinking. These drinkers tend to be less directly involved in contemporary industrial society, although they may work away from the Reservation for several months of the year in menial jobs. The second group are *anxiety drinkers* who drink in response to stress. Frequently the most well-educated and well-employed suffer most from psychic conflict in their contacts with the dominant society. Although some attributes of both groups of Navaho drinkers—the *recreation drinkers* and the *anxiety drinkers*—are shared by all, this division seems valid.

For those patients who are successfully treated (mainly the *recreation drinkers*), it is difficult to tell which aspects of the treatment program have produced the desired results. It may be merely the "Hawthorne effect." Or it may be that, for the first time, some of these people become aware of the fact that excessive drinking is destroying their lives. Of great importance is the influence of the nonproblem-drinker peer group in the form of former drinking buddies who have embarked on a life of sobriety in the treatment program and are now wearing good hats and boots, and driving new pickup trucks. The drinkers are able to identify with these people, and many of them have enlisted in the program as a result. The new peer group operates to offset the demands of the old drinking peer group. No attempt at psychotherapy has been made with any of this group, although frequent counseling has taken place with several of them. Antabuse (which helps break up the addiction to alcohol) and other supportive measures which give structure to the patient's life have been helpful. At any rate, the current treatment spectrum can be brought to bear with some success on the *recreation drinkers,* some of whom have over one hundred arrests for drunkenness.

The *anxiety drinkers* need something more. Their trouble appears to lie at a much deeper level. Members of this group have little identification with the new nonproblem-drinker peer group with its new boots, hats, and pickups. As for awareness of the consequences of excessive drinking, the *anxiety drinkers* are usually aware of its damaging effects before enlisting in the program. Such people need help on the unconscious level where conflicts are producing the anxiety which underlies excessive drinking. Although some of the unsuccessfully treated patients have been offered psychotherapy, their response has not been impressive. It may be that present methods of psychotherapy are not readily adaptable to persons reared in a culture where concepts as revealed in the language are so different from European-American concepts.[12]

The present study has necessarily treated Navaho drinking as a special case. To what extent can the findings be generalized to drinkers in all ethnic groups? It would be interesting to investigate the possibility that people who have become addicted through recreation drinking respond readily to practical measures, such as those offered by our program, whereas the *anxiety drinkers* respond better to other modes of treatment. I would venture the conclusion that every alcohol-drinking society has both *anxiety drinkers* and *recreation drinkers* who become addicted. Anxiety drinking in Navaho society is perhaps not too different from anxiety drinking in the American public at large, where value conflicts and attempts to adjust to modern industrial life produce stress. What is distinctive about Navaho drinking is the presence of forces which promote addictive recreation drinking, without adequate counter forces to control it.

NOTES AND REFERENCES

*This paper stems from National Institute of Mental Health Project No. 5 R11 MH 01389-03, "A Community Treatment Plan for Navaho Problem Drinkers," sponsored by the McKinley County Family Consultation Service, Gallup, New Mexico.

1 Donald Horton, "The Functions of Alcohol in Primitive Societies: A Cross-Cultural Study," *Quarterly Journal of Alcoholic Studies,* Vol. 4, 1943, pp. 199-320; John H. Hamer, "Acculturation Stress and the Functions of Alcohol Among the Forest Potawatomi Indians," Ohio State University, 1964, mimeographed.

2 John J. and Irma Honigmann, "How Baffin Island Eskimo Have learned to Use Alcohol," *Social Forces,* Vol. 44, 1965, pp. 73-83; Jennings G. Olson, "Culture, Alcohol and Drinking Behavior," paper presented at the University of Utah School of Alcohol Studies, June 1966.

3 Horton, *op. cit.;* Hamer, *op. cit.*

4 Honigmann and Honigmann, *op. cit.*

5 *The Gallup Independent,* April 28, 1965, p. 1.

6 *Navajo Agency Letterbook,* Bureau of Indian Affairs Navajo Agency Files, Window Rock, Arizona, 1880.

7 Robert W. Young, "1951-1961, A Decade of Progress," *The Navajo Yearbook,* Report No. VIII, Navajo Agency, Window Rock, Arizona, 1961, pp. 274-280.

8 *Ibid.,* p. 279.

9 *Ibid.,* p. 278.

10 Jerrold E. Levy, "Navajo Suicide," *Human Organization,* Vol. 24, 1965, pp. 308-318.

11 Age range for the *total* 120 patients in treatment is 18-55, and mean age for total patients in treatment is 34. There is an implication here that patients in the middle age range tend to succeed or fail, whereas those at either end of the range tend to be in the equivocal category.

12 One assumes that core value system and habitual modes of thought acquired in early childhood are not entirely altered by acculturation.

ARTHUR D. SLATER, STAN L. ALBRECHT: THE EXTENT AND COSTS OF EXCESSIVE DRINKING AMONG THE UINTAH-OURAY INDIANS

Excessive drinking among American Indians has long been recognized as a major social problem. Non-Indian interest in the problem has been evident from the earliest attempts to outlaw the sale of liquor to Indians to the more recent concern over statistics showing that the proportion of Indians arrested for alcohol-related crimes is higher than for any other group in the nation.[1] Indian concern has been reflected in such widely diverse responses as the prohibition of liquor by various Indian tribal councils even after the repeal of federal restrictive laws, and in the growth of nativistic and messianic movements strongly emphasizing the evils of drink, such as the ghost dance and the Native American Church.[2]

Much of the concern over excessive drinking by Indian people is traceable to the sheer scope of the problem, as well as to the positive relationship often observed between drinking and various other social problems. In terms of the first point, Graves' study of drinking patterns in a triethnic community found that alcohol intake among the Navaho Indians was almost seven times that for Anglos and was over three times that for persons of Spanish descent.[3] Ferguson's study of drinking on the Navaho reservation quotes a distinguished tribal member as claiming that about 30 percent of the Navaho population drink excessively.[4] Comparable rates have been reported for various other tribes. The relationship between problem drinking and other social problems has also been widely noted. The vast majority of crimes committed by Indians are committed while the offender is under the influence of alcohol.[5] Child neglect, automobile accidents, loss of jobs, ill health, and the neglect and damage of property have also been linked to excessive drinking.[6]

The present study had a two-fold purpose: (1) to learn the extent of problem drinking among a particular Indian population—the inhabitants of the Uintah-Ouray Indian Reservation in northeastern Utah and (2) to estimate the costs of drinking, both to the tribe and to the agencies which provide social and financial services for the Uintah-Ouray. There have been many studies of the *extent* of drinking among various tribal groups, but few, if any, attempts to provide empirical documentation of *costs* of excessive drinking.

THE UINTAH—OURAY

The Uintah-Ouray Indian Reservation is located primarily in Uintah and Duchesne counties in northeastern Utah. The non-Indian population within these counties is concentrated in the three communities of Vernal, Duchesne, and Roosevelt. While some of the tribal members make their homes in these communities, the majority of them live in several smaller, outlying villages. Contact is frequent, however, as most of the Indians do their shopping and obtain their recreation in the white communities. In addition, many of them are employed by whites at various times during the year. The Indian population for the area was 1581 in 1965, with a total of 448 men and 460 women over the age of 15 included on the tribal rolls. While some Indians who are not members of the Uintah-Ouray Tribal either have employment in or are frequent visitors to the area, our statistics apply only to those included on the official tribal rolls.[7] The white population for the two-county area was approximately 17,400 in 1965.

SOURCES OF DATA

Extent of Drinking

The extent of problem drinking appeared to be most clearly reflected in the number of arrests made for drink-related offenses. Information on various arrest data was obtained by examining the police dockets of the Tribal Law and Order Office and the dockets of the justices of the peace in each of the surrounding communities. Permission to examine the dockets and to record any necessary information was granted by the tribal offices and by justices of the peace in each of the white communities. Those justices of the peace who did not have many arrests during the year were very helpful in going over their dockets with us and helping us to identify more accurately those arrests in which drinking was a factor. Where there were many arrests, and hence several books to peruse, we were left to our own devices to decide whether drink was a contributing factor in any particular arrest. As a result, it is probable that some arrests which should have been included were not because there was insufficient evidence recorded in the dockets to justify including them. The figures reported are therefore likely to be conservative.

Cost of Drinking

It was felt that the cost of drinking would be reflected in a variety of sources, including fines assessed for drink-related arrests, unemployment (both temporary during confinement and permanent loss of job), deaths, various health problems, children placed for foster care, in addition to the most obvious cost, money spent for the purchase of alcoholic beverages. While it is a relatively easy task to obtain data on some of these costs, others are more difficult to define and measure. Consequently, while we have quite accurate data on factors like arrests, fines levied, and amounts spent on the purchase of certain alcoholic beverages, estimates as to other types of costs are less definite.

Information about fines assessed and jail sentences served was obtained from the dockets of the Indian Law and Order Agency and from the dockets of each of the justices of the peace as described above. Welfare and medical data were obtained from the records of the various welfare agencies located in the two counties, including the Utah State Welfare Commission, the area office of the Department of Health, Education, and Welfare, and the U.S. Public Health Service office at Fort Duchesne, Utah. It was reasoned that most of the tribal members would go where they could get free medical treatment rather than going to private doctors, and therefore no attempt was made to seek data on medical costs from other sources.

The amount spent for the purchase of wine and hard liquors was determined through the operators of the four state-controlled liquor dispensing establishments keeping a tally of all purchases made by reservation Indians over a period of one month. This month covered the period of time from June 10 to July 9, 1966. Liquor store operators felt that the amount sold during this time was about average for all the months of the year.

Inasmuch as beer can be obtained from so many different places (i.e., grocery stores, taverns, cafes), no attempt was made to determine the quantities of beer sold by the dispensing establishments. Estimates included in this study were arrived at by questioning a number of different people on the reservation—drinkers, nondrinkers, and law-enforcement officers—and asking them to estimate the amount spent for beer in comparison to that spent for wine and whisky.

RESULTS

Extent of Excessive Drinking

Table 1 shows the distribution of arrests for drink-related offenses during the year of 1965.

The data in Table 1 indicate that an average of two people were arrested every day for drink-related offenses. In all, a total of 303 tribal members (206 men and 97 women) were arrested one or more times during the year for offenses related to the excessive use of alcoholic beverages. Since there are only 908 persons (448 men and 460 women) in the tribe aged 15 or older, this means that one-third (45 percent of the men and 21 percent of the women) of the adults and older teen-agers were arrested one or more times during the year because of drinking too much.

TABLE 1

Number of Arrests of Tribal Members During 1965 for Offenses Related to Excessive Drinking

	Male	Female	Total	Average Arrests per Month
Tribal arrests	302	102	404	33.6
Vernal arrests[a]	64	16	80	6.7
Roosevelt[b]	218	40	258	21.5
Duchesne	19	4	23	2.0
Total	603	162	765	63.8

[a] Includes arrests made by both Vernal City and Uintah County Officers.

[b] Includes records from four justices of the peace in Roosevelt plus one in the small neighboring town of Myton.

The rate of arrest for drink-related offenses among the Uintah-Ouray was almost one arrest for every two tribal members (there were 765 arrests and 1,581 tribal members). This compares with a rate for all Indians in the United States in 1960 of 11,463 arrests per 100,000 population.[8] Thus, if we were to magnify the Uintah-Ouray figures to a larger population, their arrest rate would be over four times the national rate for all Indians in 1960. Furthermore, the 1960 arrest rate for drink-related offenses for Indians was more than sixteen times that for whites and over five times the rate for blacks in the United States.[9] Not only do we find, then, that the overall arrest rate of Indians in the United States for drink-related offenses is several times the national average for other groups, but also, the rate for the Uintah-Ouray is higher than the national rate for all Indians. There can be little question, given these data, that the *extent* of excessive drinking among the Uintah-Ouray constitutes a serious social problem.

TABLE 2
Fines Assessed and Paid for Drinking-Related Arrests

Law Enforcement Agency	Fines Assessed				Fines Paid				
	Male	Female	Total	Average per arrest	Male	Female	Total	Average per arrest	Per Cent Paid
Tribe	5,163	727	5,890	14.57[a]	4,413	666	5,079	12.57[a]	86
Vernal	1,880	340	2,220	27.77	1,465	155	1,620	20.25	73
Roosevelt	9,631	1,209	10,840	42.02	5,013	950	5,963	23.11	55
Duchesne	532	335	867	37.69	386	85	471	20.47	54
Total	17,266	2,611	19,877	25.98	11,277	1,856	13,133	17.16	66

[a] Amounts given are in dollars.

TABLE 3
Days Sentenced and Served in Jail for Drink-Related Offenses

Law Enforcement Agency	Days Sentenced				Days Served				Days Suspended
	Male	Female	Total	Average per arrest	Male	Female	Total	Average per arrest	
Tribe	2,461	1,077	3,538	8.7	787	147	934	2.3	3,298
Vernal[a]	371	60	431	5.1	448	60	508	5.5	0
Roosevelt	1,476	221	1,697	6.5	611	16	627	2.4	445
Duchesne	228	30	258	11.2	185	30	215	9.3	71
Total	4,536	1,388	5,924	7.7	2,031	253	2,284	3.0	3,814

[a] The discrepancy between days sentenced and days served can be explained by the fact that parts of monetary fines were paid by serving additional time in jail.

Costs of Excessive Drinking

Fines and Jail Confinement. We can now turn to the question of the financial cost involved in these arrests, both to the individuals arrested and to the law-enforcement agencies concerned. Table 2 gives us a picture of fines assessed the problem drinkers, average amount paid per arrest, and the percent of the total amount assessed which was paid.

It can be seen from Table 2 that there is much inconsistency in the severity of the fines levied for drink-related arrests and that generally, the percentage paid declines as the amount assessed increases. The non-Indian agencies levied much higher fines on the Indians arrested than did the Tribal Law and Order agency. Unfortunately, we are unable to report fines levied by these agencies on non-Indians arrested for comparable offenses. It is very likely, considering the magnitude of fines levied against the Indians for simple public intoxication charges, that non-Indian fines would be considerably lower. Such a prediction—if it were to be substantiated—would be consistent with the findings of Lemert and Rosenberg, who report that the best predictor of differentials in length of sentence for the same offense was racial background.[10]

Returning to Table 2, note the discrepancy between fines assessed and fines paid. Only 66 percent of the fines assessed were paid. Part of the unpaid money is accounted for by the fact that some fines were paid by serving time in jail. In some of the agencies it was common practice to allow indigent individuals to work off parts of their fine in jail.

Christiansen, Clark, and Spocks[11] have reported that in 1964 the total income of the 1,581 members on the tribal rolls was $812, 635, including income from welfare payments. Thus, the $13,133 paid in fines represented 1.6 percent of the total personal income of the tribe.

Assessed fines, however, account for only a portion of the financial cost involved here. Another cost is the number of days of potential employment lost by tribal members because of confinement in jail. The figures in Table 3 indicate that tribal members were sentenced to a total of 5924 days in jail for drink-related offenses. About one-third of the total time was actually served. There was great variation among the law-enforcement agencies in proportion of sentence actually served. One agency apparently made everyone serve out his full time. On the other hand, suspended sentences were very common under tribal jurisdiction. Inadequate confinement facilities may have been a determining factor in the latter case.

The determination of the value of the days lost through confinement was arrived at somewhat arbitrarily. The authors decided that the lowest wage paid by the tribe for any of its employees would provide a good, though conservative, estimate. The lowest wage paid by the tribe is $1.25 per hour or $10.00 per day. Using this figure we arrived at a total evaluation of $22,840 lost to the individuals confined in jail because of drinking.

A final cost not included in any of the above is the fee paid the justices of the peace for each arrest handled. The standard fee is $5.00 per arrest. The 258 arrests in Roosevelt and Myton, 23 in Duchesne, 42 in Uintah County, and 38 in Vernal City cost $1,805 in justice of the peace fees for handling the arrests made off the reservation.

By even the most conservative estimates, the costs reviewed above which are related to arrests, fines, and jail confinement amount to many thousands of dollars. The combined figures of fines paid and wages lost through jail confinement amount to almost 5 percent of the total tribal income for the year.

Costs of Alcoholic Beverages. As mentioned earlier, operators of all retail outlets in Uintah and Duchesne Counties were asked to keep a tally of all wines and liquors sold to Indians during one month's time. One distributor kept a tally for a month during another season and the results were very close to the sample month. The gallonage and cost for one month, multiplied by twelve months, gave us a total of 242 gallons of hard liquor costing $10,177.44 and 1,579 gallons of wine, costing $12,823.20. These estimates are conservative, as it is certain that there was an additional amount spent for illegally produced liquor and it was possible that some purchases were made out of state or out of the two counties included in the study.

In addition to the amount spent for wine and liquor, a great amount of money was spent for the purchase of beer. Using the method previously mentioned, we received estimates of the amount spent for beer which varied from $18,000 to $23,000 per year. Such estimates of the amount spent for the purchase of beer, combined with the amount spent for wine and hard liquor, results in a yearly total of around $45,000 spent for alcoholic beverages.

A comparison was made on a per capita basis of the amount spent for wine and liquor by the Indians and that spent by the general population in the two counties. Utah State Liquor Control Commission sales in those two counties during the fiscal year 1966 (which included half of 1965 and half of 1966), amounted to $267,809. With an estimated population as of July 1, 1966,[12] of 6,700 for Duchesne County and 12,300 for Uintah County, we have a total population for the two counties of 19,000 people, and a per capita expenditure for alcoholic beverages, exclusive of beer, of $13.98. Tribal membership at the end of 1965 was 1,581. This would result in a per capita annual expenditure for alcoholic beverages (wine and liquor only) of $14.54, which is only slightly above that for the population as a whole.

Indians on the reservation have an average annual income of $514.39 per person from all sources, including welfare.[13] Their per capita expenditures for wine and liquor represent 2.8 percent of this annual figure. In contrast, the average annual per capita income for the white population of Duchesne and Uintah counties was $1,614, and the per capita expenditures for wine and liquor represents only .8 percent of this annual income. Thus, while there was little difference in per capita amounts spent for wine and liquor, due to the Indians' poverty, the *percentage* of their income spent for drinking was over three times as great as for the population as a whole.

Institutional Costs. Permission was obtained from the Utah State Welfare Commission to examine the assistance records of those tribal members who were judged to be problem drinkers. This judgment was made by the welfare directors of Uintah and Duchesne Counties, in consultation with the case workers most familiar with each case.

No claim is being made here that there is a one-to-one cause-effect relationship between problem drinking and being on welfare. Therefore, we will not suggest that all welfare payments made to families with members who are problem drinkers should be counted as an additional cost of drinking. Other factors such as lack of employment opportunities, poor education, lack of job training, and discrimination in hiring practices all contribute to the welfare rolls on the reservation. Nevertheless, it is true that many of the problem drinkers were largely dependent on welfare assistance because their drinking prevented them from holding steady jobs. In addition, a number of families who had to rely on welfare did so because they had been virtually deserted by a head of household who was a problem drinker.

In all, a total of 105 families were judged to be receiving welfare assistance because of drink-related problems. Estimating an average of 5 persons per family, the 105 families represent 525 people, or roughly one-third of the tribal membership, who were at least partially dependent upon welfare assistance for their livelihood.

We found 19 children of problem-drinker welfare recipients who had been placed in foster-care homes by the Department of Public Welfare and 11 others being cared for in other foster homes for which no foster-care money was paid. This is a total of 30 children who had been left homeless, deserted, mistreated, or neglected. The consequence of this type of treatment by parents upon the lives of their children may be a much greater cost than the $31,849 spent by the Welfare Department for their care during the year. Even though the homes in which they are placed may be very desirable, and the children may receive excellent care, desertion or mistreatment by parents can produce feelings of inadequacy, inferiority, despair, anxiety, and hostility that leave permanent scars.

Problem drinkers also received extensive financial assistance for medical care from federal sources. A total of $3,021 was spent by the U.S. Public Health Service Clinic at Fort Duchesne for clinic visits, drugs, X rays, and various treatments for a total of 69 problem drinkers. In addition, the county departments of public welfare dispensed a total of $8,099 for doctors' visits, drugs, etc., for the 105 families mentioned above. Other welfare assistance was dispensed to these families in the form of cash and various commodities.

The number of days lost from productive employment due to illnesses or injuries associated with excessive drinking was also calculated. The U.S. Public Health Clinic records reported 175 days lost. An additional 99 days were lost due to time spent in the hospital, and time lost while convalescing at home was estimated at 499 days, making a total of 773 days lost for these illnesses and injuries treated at the Public Health Service Clinic. Records from this source were quite complete, so the above figures appear to be very accurate. Placing a value of $10 per day upon the time lost as before, we arrive at an evaluation of the time lost at $7,730, not counting the actual cost for the treatment.

An additional cost is that of expense to the law enforcement agencies. The chief of police of the Tribal Law and Order Office stated to the researchers that his agency would have very little to do if there were no problem drinkers on the reservation. Similarly, the Roosevelt chief of police reported that about half of the time of his agency is devoted to problems related to excessive drinking among the Indian people. Such comments clearly indicate that a major additional expense resulting from the Indian problem drinker is the amount it costs the tribe and other law enforcement agencies in surrounding communities to hire personnel to enforce the laws, to feed and care for arrested prisoners, and to maintain confinement facilities.

By prorating the total budget for the Tribal Law and Order Agency according to the percentage of total arrests which were associated with problem drinking and by obtaining figures for cost of food, maintenance of confinement facilities, and personnel expenses for the other law enforcement agencies concerned, we obtained an estimate of $109,491 for expenses which appear to be directly related to problem drinking. The cost of feeding arrested prisoners alone amounts to several thousand dollars.

In summary, the *extent* of problem drinking among the Uintah-Ouray was clearly reflected in an arrest rate for drink-related offenses that is many times the national average.[14] By even the most conservative estimates, combined figures of fines paid and wages lost through jail confinement amount to almost 5 percent of the total tribal income. An additional amount, equaling over 5 percent of total income, is spent on the purchase of alcoholic beverages. Total costs incurred by agencies who must deal with the problem are even higher.

NOTES

1 Edward P. Dozier, "Problem Drinking Among American Indians," *Quarterly Journal of Studies on Alcohol,* 27 (March 1966), 72-87; Omer C. Stewart, "Questions Regarding American Indian Criminality," *Human Organization,* 23 (Spring 1964), 61-66.

2 Dozier, *op. cit.*

3 Theodore D. Graves, "Acculturation, Access, and Alcohol in a Tri-Ethnic Community," *American Anthropologist,* 69 (April 1967), 306-321.

4 Frances N. Ferguson, "Navaho Drinking: Some Tentative Hypotheses," *Human Organization,* 27 (Summer 1968), 159-167.

5 Theodore D. Graves, Tri-Ethnic Research Report No. 29, Institute of Behavioral Sciences, University of Colorado, 1966; Dozier, *op. cit.*; Stewart, *op. cit.*; Ferguson, *op. cit.*; p. 161; Dwight B. Heath, "Prohibition and Post-Repeal Drinking Patterns Among the Navaho," *Quarterly Journal of Studies on Alcohol,* 25 (March 1964), 119-135.

6 Ferguson, *op. cit.*

7 The rates are calculated from figures reported in the Federal Bureau of Investigation Uniform Crime Reports (Washington D.C.: U.S. Government Printing Office, 1960 and 1965), and in Statistical Abstracts of the U.S. Bureau of the Census (Washington D.C.: U.S. Government Printing Office, 1965). The drink-related offenses reported include arrests for drunkenness, driving while intoxicated, and liquor violations.

8 Federal Bureau of Investigation Uniform Crime Reports, and Statistical Abstracts of the U.S., 1960 and 1965.

9 *Ibid.*

10 E. M. Lemert and J. Rosenburg, *The Administration of Justice to Minority Groups in Los Angeles County* (University of California Publications in Culture and Society, 1948).

11 John R. Christiansen, James R. Clark, and Cynthia Spocks, "Social and Economic Characteristics of the Ute Indians on the Uintah-Ouray Reservation," *Social Science Bulletin,* No. 4, Brigham Young University, 1965.

12 Population figures were taken from the Utah Economic and Business Review, 26, No. 12, December 1966.

13 Christiansen, Clark, and Spocks, *op. cit.*

14 It should be cautioned that *direct* comparisons would be valid only with other groups who have been studied in the same detailed manner as has been undertaken here.

JACK BYNUM: SUICIDE AND THE AMERICAN INDIAN: AN ANALYSIS OF RECENT TRENDS[1]

The report of explorers and early settlers indicates that prior to the arrival of the Europeans the knowledge and practice of self-destruction existed in the cultures of most Indian tribes. For example, one student of suicide summarizes the historical evidence:

> Instances of suicide are reported in history from among the Chippewa Indians, from among the Dakotas and Omahas and from among the Indians of Oregon and Western Washington. Of the Delaware and Iroquois Indians we are told as early as 1789 that some of them grieving unto death on account of the infidelity of their wives, ate poisonous roots, which infallibly cause death after a few hours. The women of these tribes resort to the same means of self-destruction, when they become angry or depressed over the unfaithfulness of their husbands.
>
> Among the Dakotas, we learn that suicide is a common resort after every disappointment. In every season girls hang themselves because of jealousy, or from fear of marriage to those whom they do not love. A beautiful instance of this kind of 'love suicide' is contained in the well-known story of Winona. . . .
>
> The Chippewas never kill their old parents, but sometimes these abandon themselves to death. . . .
>
> The report of another early expedition assures us that suicide among the men of this tribe is not common, but occurs sometimes from disappointment or from shame after capture. Among the

women it is much more frequent from the motives of jealousy, disappointed love or loss of children.[2]

Although evidence that suicide was known and practiced among the American natives is most convincing, there is little support for the traditional view of many whites that Indians have always had a high propensity to suicide.

For the years 1896 to 1906, the suicide rate for American Indians was 6.9 per 100,000, which is fairly low.[3] Undoubtedly this low rate reflects inadequate reporting of Indian suicides, but even after more reliable reporting techniques were applied in 1920, the suicide rates were not unusually high. For example, in 1921 the Indian suicide rate was 10.2, a figure comparable to the national rate for that year.

In recent years the dramatic increase in the Indian suicide rate has become a major source of concern to Indian people, federal agencies charged with responsibility for Indian health and welfare, and many social scientists. The present paper is an attempt to assemble and interpret the available data on this topic.

Table 1 contrasts the trends in Indian suicide from 1959 to 1967 with the average rates for the United States as a whole. During the first eight years of this period, the crude rate of Indian suicides fluctuated around a mean of 11.5 per 100,000 population. But in 1967, the rate rose to 17 per 100,000, an increase of over 36 percent in one year. In direct contrast to

TABLE 1

Suicide Deaths and Death Rates for Indians in 24 Reservation States and U.S., All Races, Calendar Years 1959-1967, Rates per 100,000 Population

| | | | Rates[b] and their Ratios | | | | | |
| | Number | | Crude | | | Age-Adjusted[c] | | |
Year	Indian[a]	U.S.: All races	Indian[a]	U.S.: All races	Ratio: Indian to U.S.	Indian[a]	U.S.: All races	Ratio: Indian to U.S.
1959	57	18,633	11.7	10.6	1.1	17.0	10.6	1.6
1960	57	19,041	11.7	10.6	1.1	16.8	10.6	1.6
1961	61	18,999	11.7	10.4	1.1	16.7	10.5	1.6
1962	59	20,207	12.1	10.9	1.1	16.9	11.1	1.5
1963	66	20,825	11.4	11.0	1.0	15.6	11.3	1.4
1964	52	20,588	11.6	10.8	1.1	15.8	11.0	1.4
1965	65	21,507	11.3	11.1	1.0	15.3	11.4	1.3
1966	64	21,281	13.6	10.9	1.2	18.6	11.2	1.7
1967	94	21,325	17.0	10.8	1.6	23.1	11.1	2.1

Source: United States Department of Health, Education, and Welfare, Indian Health Service, *Suicides and Homicides Among Indians* (Silver Springs, Maryland, 1969), p. 5.

[a]Includes Aleuts and Eskimos.

[b]Indian rates are three-year averages through 1966. All other rates are based on single year data.

[c]Adjusted to 1940 U.S. total resident population

the sudden increase in Indian suicides, the annual rate of suicides for the United States (11 per 100,000) has shown only slight variations over the entire nine-year period. The age-adjusted rates (columns 6 and 7 in Table 1) place Indian suicide even higher in relationship to that of the general population; prior to 1967 the Indian rates were about one and one-half times as high as the general rates, and in 1967 over twice as high.

Thus, figures on Indian suicide show a pattern comparable to the national average until a sudden and alarming increase in Indian suicides occurred in 1967. It must be recognized that sizable annual fluctuations in Indian suicide rates are expected because of the relatively small numbers involved, but the sharp increase noted in 1967 is too large to be considered a random fluctuation. Reviewing the social science literature on Indian suicide revealed five recent articles which discussed the rates and correlates of Indian suicide. Each of these studies will be reviewed briefly.

PREVIOUS STUDIES ON INDIAN SUICIDE

The first study to be considered is George Devereux's, "Mohave Ethnopsychiatry and Suicide: The Psychiatric Knowledge and the Psychic Disturbances of An Indian Tribe."[4] Devereux's work was conducted in the traditional anthropological style, with heavy emphasis on case studies, informants, and intensive interaction with the Mohave people. Using these methods he was able to describe in detail the suicide patterns of the Mohave Indians in 1961.

One reviewer of Devereux's study assessed it as a very positive contribution, "throwing much light on the frequency and motivations of suicide in a representative primitive population."[5] A closer examination may indicate that such praise is unwarranted. First, Devereux sheds no empirical light on the "frequency" of Mohave suicide. His obvious commitment to nonquantitative methods of data collection make it impossible to calculate rates from his data.

Furthermore, to consider Devereux's study an analysis of suicide in a "representative primitive population" is a misconception. To describe any Indian tribe as "representative" is to ignore vast and complex cultural variability among American Indian tribes. In addition, technical or statistical representativeness is impossible without an acceptable random-sampling procedure, and Devereux did not employ sampling in any form.

Devereux's description of Mohave suicide and list of motives and causal factors are his most important contributions. He begins by examining the history of Indian-white relations, and suggests that the switch from a nomadic, warring way of life to a reservation existence increased the suicide rate: "... a wave of suicides occurred among a great many Indian tribes when they were placed on reservations and were denied access to their traditional means for directing aggression against outsiders."[6]

This hypothesis suggests the "fatalistic suicide" which, according to Durkheim, occurs under conditions of intense regulation.[7] Devereux also argues that increased contact with the dominant, complex white society resulted in considerable disorganization of the Mohave culture which accelerated suicide behavior.

Additional manifest motives for Mohave suicide enumerated by Devereux are desire to reunite with a deceased loved one, marital and romantic discord, and illness. These motives are very similar to the determinants of suicide among non-Indian populations. However, their methods of suicide are more "Indian": In addition to the modern methods such as shooting and hanging, there was the old-fashioned use of poisonous plants and herbs found in abundance on the reservation.

In 1965 Jerrold E. Levy completed a thorough and well-organized study of Navaho suicide.[8] With the aid of Wyman and Thorne,[9] and Navaho police records, Levy was able to obtain data for the entire reservation period of Navaho history (1890 to 1965). While acknowledging that the accuracy of suicide statistics was very poor on the reservation until 1952, Levy does report a consensus among his informants that suicide was remarkably rare during the first sixty years of Navaho reservation life.

For the 1954-1963 decade, tribal police records show a dramatic change from the previous near-zero suicide rate to an incidence of suicide approaching the national rate. The ten-year national average during the years 1950-1959 was 10.3 per 100,000, and the Navaho average for the years 1954-1963 was 8.3.

Levy reports that Navaho males commit suicide 13 times as often as females, and the ratio for attempted suicides is 28 to 1 in favor of males. These rates are quite different from national rates for males, which shows that males commit suicide 4 times as often as do females, but that females make more unsuccessful attempts. Levy suggests that unusual sex differentials in suicidal behavior among the Navahos may be related to their matrilineal clan system and matrilocal residence patterns, which provide greater social support and integration for females than for males.

One of the most startling findings of Levy's study has to do with the age of suicide victims. The long-standing pattern in the United States is that there are very few suicides among children, adolescents, and young adults, and the incidence of suicide progressively increases with advancing age. This pattern is reversed among the Navahos, where a majority of victims were young adults, and the rates decline with advancing age. However, according to Wyman, in earlier times the Navaho pattern was more comparable to the national pattern.

Levy lists marital trouble as the most frequent motive for suicide. He also found that 47 percent of Navaho suicides involved alcoholic intoxication of the victim. He concludes that the Navaho's spontaneous and rapidly executed suicide is indicative of violent aggression turned inward upon himself, perhaps because of his inability to cope with or harmonize conflicting roles and cultures. As evidence, Levy cites the New Mexico Apache groups living on small reservations, surrounded and dominated by white communities. These Apaches have an annual suicide rate of 20.8, almost twice the national average. On the other hand, remote Pueblo Indian reservations in New Mexico have rates of suicide far below the national average. Thus, the argument is that suicide rates are related to levels of acculturation and the concomitant integration or disintegration of tribal society as it comes in contact with the culture of white America.

Two recent articles about suicide among the Cheyenne Indians derive from a virtual epidemic of suicide *attempts* among Cheyenne Indians in 1966. In fairly rapid succession, 15 episodes were reported, 13 of which involved young people between the ages of 15 and 21. Ten of these 13 were girls. None of these attempts was successful. The two studies attempted to identify causes of Cheyenne suicidal propensities by examining the historical background and present situation of the Cheyenne.

The first study "Suicide Among the Cheyenne Indian" was conducted by Larry H. Dizmang, M.D., a special assistant at the Center for Studies of Suicide Prevention of the National Institute of Mental Health.[10] Dizmang appears convinced that the high incidence of suicide attempts among the Cheyenne is directly related to blockage of traditional means of handling aggression without the provision of acceptable alternatives. He gives a detailed historical account of Cheyenne war parties, buffalo hunts, and the ritualistic, self-tortures of the sun dance, and makes the point that little suicide occurred during the prereservation period of Cheyenne history. "Suicide among Northern Cheyenne males is reported to have been rare in the early history of the tribe. . . . Suicide among the Cheyenne women, however, was a more frequent occurrence although still relatively rare."[11]

The traditional aggressive activities, now outlawed, "form a baseline," according to Dizmang, "from which we can see the kinds of changes that have evolved up to the present time." His main thesis is that these changes form a context in which we can find some of the clues to the present suicide problem.

Dizmang moves from his historical-cultural setting rather quickly into his theory, without taking into account that it has been over seventy years since these "traditional means of handling the aggressive impulse" were terminated. Several generations of new Cheyenne have been born and socialized. Dizmang fails to explain why suicidal tendencies are just now manifesting themselves after the passage of all these years since the Cheyenne was able to vent his aggressive feelings in a good old-fashioned war party.

Moreover, according to his own records, the earliest historical accounts of the Cheyenne Indians depict them as a peaceful, agricultural people. The reservation life of the Cheyenne might be viewed as a return to a way of life comparable to their patterns prior to the aggressive adventures that followed their acquisition of the horse.[12]

Finally, Dizmang suggests that high suicide and alcoholism rates are symptons of cultural deterioration among the Cheyenne. Young Cheyenne Indians, in particular, encounter the "push-pull crisis"—the push to leave the reservation for the white world on the outside, and the conflicting pull to remain a part of Cheyenne culture. The resulting effect on the young Cheyenne is that he is poorly integrated in both societies. Suicide may be seen as a solution to the alienation that usually accompanies such marginality.

A second article on recent Cheyenne suicide, "Suicide and Self-destructive Behavior on the Cheyenne River Reservation," was written by Wilson V. Curlee of the Public Health Service Indian Hospital at Eagle Butte, South Dakota.[13] He begins his study with a vivid description of the Cheyenne River Reservation and the style of life of approximately 3700 Indians living there.

> ... the reservation is predominantly rural, with much of the population living in small communities ... many of which are isolated....
>
> There is virtually no industry... and most of the jobs are temporary.... For this reason, the Indian is forced to leave the reservation in search of a job or to stay and accept low-paying jobs or relief. If he stays ... he is likely to be caught in a crippling web of dependency....
>
> On the ... reservation the housing and the living conditions are very poor. Alcoholism and violence rates are high. There is not the feeling of closeness and helpfulness among the Indians.[14]

Unfortunately Curlee presents no quantitative indicators of the frequency of the phenomena he discusses, so comparisons to other reservations or communities are not possible. His theory of the causes of Cheyenne suicide stresses the effects of the social environment. Curlee draws a parallel between Indian suicide and the research which has consistently reported social isolation and suicide as correlates of urban life: "People suffer from the same feeling of isolation in the small Indian communities that is prevalent in the larger cities across the United States. Social disorganization is rampant, and the family is not the source of strength and comfort it might be."[15]

Like Dizmang, Curlee sees Cheyenne suicides as acts of aggression, turned inward on the actors, but he identifies a different origin for the aggression. Whereas Dizmang views suicide as aggression due to thwarted traditional ways of expressing hostility, Curlee interprets Cheyenne Indian suicide as aggression resulting directly from extremely low self-concept. And the Indian's feeling of inferiority and worthlessness is seen as a consequence of his being caught between two conflicting cultures, unable to identify fully with either.

A fourth study of Indian suicide is the report of Carl Mindell and Paul Stuart on self-destructive behavior on the Pine Ridge Indian Reservation.[16] Their paper begins with a detailed case study. Unlike Devereux, however, who relied heavily on qualitative case studies, Mindell and Stuart use their single case study as an illustrative model of their detailed statistical tabulations. In conjunction with their professional positions in the Community Mental Health Program on the reservation, they were able to collect data on 25 suicide attempts (no fatalities) and 5 serious threats to commit suicide between July, 1966, and June, 1967. "Using a population base of 10,000 (estimated), this gives an attempted suicide rate of 250/100,000 (for the Oglala Sioux), or somewhat more than twice the rate reported by Shneidman and Farberow in Los Angeles."[17]

These investigators began by recording the three demographic variables of age, sex and marital status of their subjects. Of those Oglala Sioux attempting suicide, 96 percent were under 40 years of age. 60 percent were single. The sex of those attempting suicide on the reservation corresponds well with the national statistics: 80 percent were women.

The inclusion of those persons making suicide threats as part of the total number of attempted suicides seriously weakens their analysis. For example, when such "attempts" were coded as to method, they appeared as "suicide attempts by thoughts." "Thoughts," when compared to hanging, overdose of drugs, and wrist-slashing, present logical difficulties which weaken the conclusions based on such data.

Of special interest is their assessment of "most common precipitating stresses."[18] Fifty-two percent of their subjects felt rejected by an important person in their milieu, and another 16 percent blamed "interference in family by relatives moving in" as a precipitating factor. Thus, personal relationships and family discord are again identified as major precipitants of suicide among Indian people.

Mindell and Stuart conclude from their research that attempts at suicide by the Oglala Sioux represent aggression turned inward. They summarize the dominant characteristics of the average suicide attempt among the Sioux in the following profile:

> The patient will be a young woman, under 29 and quite likely under 19, who is single and of mixed blood. The suicide attempt is mild and most likely accomplished by taking an overdose of medication . . . Diagnostically the patient will have a neurosis. The attempt will probably be precipitated by a felt rejection of a person important and meaningful to the patient, who probably was involved in an intense hostile-dependent or symbiotic relationship with this other person. The suicide attempt is then used, usually, to reestablish the old relationship.[19]

In both this study and the previous one on Cheyenne suicide, Indian child-rearing practices are identified by the authors as possibly contributing to suicide propensity. It is clear in both reports that many Indian parents do not impose their will upon their children, except in very minimal ways. The child is socialized to become autonomous and self-willed. It seems conceivable that this is a form of excessive individualization described by Durkheim as central to "egoistic suicide."[20]

Larry H. Dizmang, who produced the Cheyenne suicide study in 1967, has more recently concluded an analysis of seven years of suicidal behavior among the Shoshone-Bannock Indians near Fort Hall, Idaho.[21] His report includes case studies, a review of Shoshone-Bannock history and culture, a psychological perspective, use of a control group for comparison purposes, and a fairly extensive statistical treatment.

Between 1960 and 1970 there were 15 suicides among 2600 Indians at Fort Hall. This rate is approximately ten times the national average. Thirteen of the 15 suicides were male, and, in keeping with the typical Indian pattern elsewhere, the great majority were young (only 2 were over the age of 35). There were also 88 known suicide attempts during this period. The dominant method of suicide was by hanging, with 8 of 11 hangings occurring in Idaho County Jails and the Idaho State Prison. This astonishing discovery must suggest that some review of incarceration procedures is in order.

In no other report does Indian suicide emerge so dramatically as part of a cluster of stress and maladjustment symptons. In convincing style, Dizmang correlates acute alcoholic intoxication, family instability, social and emotional deprivation, multiple-arrest record, youthfulness, low self-esteem, culture conflict, social disorganization, accident-prone tendencies, and overwhelming personal tragedies into a patterned network of social death as a prelude to physical death.[22] The new element in this cluster, unmentioned heretofore in Indian suicide studies, and containing the seed of "new theory" is the history of successive calamities present in nearly every case on record. These include an almost unbelievably high frequency of death of family members, accidents, family strife, rejection, poverty, financial setbacks, and cruelty—both physical and mental—inflicted on the suicide victim prior to his attempt.

SUMMARY OF FACTORS ASSOCIATED WITH INDIAN SUICIDE

The data presented in the five studies reviewed above were synthesized in an attempt to create an overall profile of the American Indian suicide victim. Indicated on the two-dimensional chart below are those character-

TABLE 2

Summary of Factors Associated with Indian Suicide

Characteristics of Suicides:	Mohave	Navaho	Cheyenne	Sioux	Shoshone-Bannock
High rate of alcoholism		*	*		*
Poverty		*	*		*
Marriage and familial discord	*	*		*	*
Low self-esteem		*	*		*
Social disorganization	*	*	*		*
Unmarried		*	*	*	*
Male (attempts and successes)	*	*			*
Spontaneity of act	*	*		*	
Hanging and shooting	*	*		*	*
Youthful		*	*	*	*
Suicide as inward aggression	*	*	*	*	*
Suicide rare in early history of tribe		*	*		*
Cultural conflict (Indian-white)		*	*	*	*
Cultural transition		*	*	*	*
Cultural approval or suggestion of suicide (in myths or religion)	*		*		

istics of suicides identified in the studies reviewed. It should be kept in mind that a failure to indicate positive findings for a given characteristic in a particular tribe does not always imply negative findings, but may mean only that the characteristic was not mentioned.

Although the five tribes are widely separated geographically (two from the Southwest, one from the Northwest, and two from the Northcentral section of the country), and while the persistent problem of cultural variability is recognized, a definite pattern of variables emerges for the five tribes under discussion. In four of the five tribes, a majority of suicide victims are young people, and marriage and familial discord, social disorganization, and culture conflict are concomitants of suicidal behavior. At least three of the five tribes show agreement on *every* variable. It is especially interesting that all the researchers involved agree that suicide among the Indians of these five tribes is a manifestation of aggression, turned inward. Their general consensus is that this psychological phenomenon springs from sociocultural causes. The young Indians, especially, suffer the social disorganization concomitant with the clashing values and norms of competing Indian and white cultures. "The material would seem to suggest that the young male is bearing the brunt of the stresses in the society due to his immediate involvement in the economic and role changes taking place at present and perhaps due to the lesser degree of stability or integration afforded him in his society."[23]

It appears that the young American Indian represents an almost classic example of the "marginal man."[24] In brief, the marginal man is a person who participates in two different cultures without being totally committed to, or accepted by, either. Tension and maladjustment is often the result of bicultural loyalties. Originally, the concept was applied to the acculturation problems of migrant foreigners, the second generation, or children of foreign migrants; Jews or other ethnic groups newly emancipated from the ghetto; and persons of mixed racial backgrounds. However, the concept and theory of the "marginal man" offers a framework for the understanding of Indian suicide. The American Indian, especially the younger generations, have become "marginal men." This condition has been caused by inadequate acculturation and assimilation of Indians into the ways and society of the white man. His marginality, in turn, has led to isolation, alienation, anomie, aggression, social disorganization of the minority subculture, and suicidal behavior.

In 1947, before rapidly rising Indian suicide rates came to the attention of government agencies and social scientists, Clyde Kluckhohn and Dorothea Leighton, in their excellent treatise on the Navaho, warned of the desperate dilemma of the Navaho Indian, caught between two conflicting cultures:

> They are torn between their own ancient standards and those which are urged upon them by teachers, missionaries, and other whites. An appreciable number of Navahos are so confused by the conflicting precepts of their elders and their white models that they tend, in effect, to reject the whole problem of morality (in the widest sense) as meaningless or insoluble. . . . The absence of

generally accepted standards of behavior among individuals constitutes, in fact, a definition of social disorganization.

There tends to be a distortion of the whole cultural structure which makes it difficult to preserve harmonious personal relationships, and satisfying emotional adjustments. Widespread exercise of escape mechanisms, especially alcohol, is the principal symptom of that resultant friction and decay....[25]

Proliferating Indian problems of the past twenty years, specifically mounting suicide rates, give their statement additional authority and predictive value.

NOTES

1 Appreciation is extended to Bruce A. Chadwick and Howard M. Bahr for their assistance in the preparation of this paper.

2 Adolph Dominic Frenay, *The Suicide Problem in the United States* (Boston: Richard G. Badger, Publisher, The Gorham Press, 1927), pp. 152, 153.

3 *Ibid.*, p. 153.

4 George Devereux, "Mohave Ethnopsychiatry and Suicide: The Psychiatric Knowledge and the Psychic Disturbances of An Indian Tribe," Smithsonian Institute, Bureau of American Ethnology, Bulletin 175 (Washington, D.C.: U.S. Government Printing Office, 1961).

5 Louis I. Dublin, *Suicide, A Sociological and Statistical Study* (New York: Ronald, 1963), p. 84.

6 Devereux, *op. cit.*, p. 86.

7 Emile Durkheim, *Suicide: A Study in Sociology,* trans. by John A. Spaulding and George Simpson (New York: Free Press, 1951).

8 Jerrold E. Levy, "Navajo Suicide," *Human Organization,* 24 (Winter 1965), 309.

9 L. C. Wyman and B. Thorne, "Notes on Navajo Suicide," *American Anthropologist,* 47 (1945), 278-288.

10 Larry H. Dizmang, M.D., "Suicide Among the Cheyenne Indians," Bulletin of Suicidology (Washington, D.C.: U.S. Government Printing Office, July 1967).

11 *Ibid.*, p. 8.

12 Larry H. Dizmang, M.D., an expanded and unpublished account of "Suicide Among the Cheyenne Indians," delivered as an address at the Los Angeles Suicide Prevention Center, August 12, 1966, p. 1.

13 Wilson V. Curlee, "Suicide and Self-Destructive Behavior on the Cheyenne River Reservation," *Suicide Among the American Indians* (Washington, D.C.: U.S. Government Printing Office, 1969).

14 *Ibid.*, p. 34.

15 *Ibid.*, p. 35.

16 Carl Mindell, M.D., and Paul Stuart, "Suicide and Self-Destructive Behavior in the Oglala Sioux: Some Clinical Aspects and Community Approaches," *Suicide Among the American Indians,* a publication of the United States Department of Health, Education, and Welfare (Washington, D.C.: U.S. Government Printing Office, June 1969), pp. 25-33.

17 *Ibid.*, p. 29.

18   *Ibid.*
19   *Ibid.,* p. 30.
20   Durkheim, *op. cit.*
21   Larry H. Dizmang, M.D., "Observations on Suicidal Behavior Among the Shoshone-Bannock Indians," presented at the First Annual National Conference on Suicidology in Chicago, Illinois, March 20, 1968.
22   *Ibid.,* pp. 1-5, 7.
23   Levy, *op. cit.,* p. 310.
24   Robert Park and Herbert A. Miller, *Old World Traits Transplanted* (Chicago: University of Chicago Press, 1925); Everett V. Stonequist, *The Marginal Man: A Study in Personality and Culture Conflict,* (New York: Scribner's, 1937); and Aaron Atonovsky, "Toward a Refinement of the 'Marginal Man' Concept," *Social Forces,* 35 (October 1956), 57-62; Tamme Wittermans and Irving Kraus, "Structural Marginality and Social Worth," *Sociology and Social Research,* 48 (April 1964), 348-360.
25   Clyde Kluckhohn and Dorothea Leighton, *The Navaho* (Harvard University Press, 1947), pp. 114, 217.

THADDEUS P. KRUSH, JOHN W. BJORK, PETER S. SINDELL, JOANNA NELLE: SOME THOUGHTS ON THE FORMATION OF PERSONALITY DISORDER: STUDY OF AN INDIAN BOARDING SCHOOL POPULATION[*]

Much has been said on all sides as to culpability incurred in the actions of larger groups as they interact with smaller groups and vice versa. Mistakes are made and become historic. Witness thereof is given in the two-hundred-year cycle—of inhumane custody, humane isolation, distant treatment, dehumanizing penury, community concern, humanization—in our chosen field of psychiatry. A series of parallel problems has occurred in the same period, and this paper will attempt to explore some of their complexities.

For the moment let us imagine that several roistering, quarreling brothers traveling from the East chance upon a homestead of great plenitude, but already occupied in part by brothers about whom they were unaware. All are frightened of each other. All have a need for the land. All are disdainful of the rights of others until their own are secured. A fight ensues, but the resources and weapons are different and the strongest wins.

This brother, unlike Cain, has developed a code which stays his hand so that he does not destroy his conquered rivals. Having partially disposed

Source: Reprinted from *The American Journal of Psychiatry,* volume 122, pp. 868-876, 1966. Copyright 1966, the American Psychiatric Association.

of them, he assumes the prerogative of the head of the family. He makes contracts with these "younger" or subsidiary brothers which he breaks, usually describing such breaches as being in the best interest of the younger brothers. They in turn at first rebel, then grudgingly accept. The strongest brother makes plans for the subsidiary brothers and then entices, cajoles, threatens and occasionally forces them to do it his way. That the plans might not be applicable to the younger brothers' way of life only fleetingly enters his mind. Only occasionally will he consult with them prior to instituting change because it causes such a fuss.

Plans are made to educate the younger brothers' children to the "better" way of older brother. But the younger brothers find that by seeming to agree, they are left to themselves with more time to do as they see fit. A contest for the minds of the children ensues in which each is accorded equal time to undo the work of the other—all the while averring that they are acting in accord with previous agreements made to last for as long "as the grass shall grow, the waters flow, and the sun shall shine."

"WARRIORS WITHOUT WEAPONS"

In the thirties, Gordon MacGregor and his associates(11) described the setting and conditions of the relatively isolated "warriors without weapons" of the great plains. Our study will begin to describe the composition of the off-reservation Indian boarding school population which has evolved since that time and will suggest trends of development in the mental health of the children so managed.

The background of health services for American Indians is set forth in a comprehensive report by the Public Health Service. Special attention was given to the statement: "Further mental health studies, beyond the scope of this survey, are called for, not only with respect to mental illness as such, but in relation to the problems of intercultural conflict, alcoholism, child delinquency and truancy, and accidents and crimes of violence"(4).

At the request of the Aberdeen Area Medical Officer of the Division of Indian Health, a pilot project was started at the Flandreau Indian Vocational High School in 1957. Material obtained by this small project team(1, 8, 9, 10, 22) served as the basis for a National Institute of Mental Health grant to study intensively and extensively three off-reservation boarding school populations of the northern plains.

The study was designed to serve as a problem-defining effort that would stimulate a variety of alternative efforts in the management and prevention of mental illness. It is necessary to approach the problem of mental illness systematically and with operationally effective definitions. Mental illness is time- and culture-bound. For the purposes of this study mental illness may be said to exist in an individual when that individual repeatedly demonstrates by his behavioral pattern that he cannot solve his problems with his own resources.

The approach we used was to attempt to define and describe disorder from the viewpoint of different disciplines. The clinical research team consisted of a psychiatrist, social work supervisor, social worker, anthropologist and sociologist based at Flandreau, with field social workers located at Pierre and Wahpeton. A social worker, anthropologist and four psychologists served as consultants.

The areas of concern of the project team were as follows. The psychiatrist performed individual diagnostic interviews with selected cases. The social workers used individual and group casework techniques and visited the reservations to do selected family interviews. The anthropologist lived in the boys' dormitory for a year gathering data on student-staff interaction and, with the Kluckhohn Value Orientation Scale, studied the student population and staff. The sociologist did classroom teaching and used social-educational devices to study the teachers and the students. The psychologists did testing in the classroom setting using a variety of devices: the Minnesota Multiphasic Personality Inventory, California Psychological Inventory, Quay-Peterson Delinquency Scale, Time Factor Examination, Student's Sentence Completion Test, Semantic-Differential Examination and Bower-Lambert Screening Scale. A great deal of material has been gathered by these workers and this paper will present some of the preliminary findings.

One of the primary aims of the project team was to effect an epidemiological study of mental illness incident in a boarding school population of 1200 and encompassing the first twelve grades. Selected for this study were two grade schools (grades 1 to 8) located in Pierre and Wahpeton, and a high school (grades 9 to 12) located in Flandreau. Both grade schools have an annual enrollment of approximately 300 each; Flandreau's annual enrollment is approximately 600. This paper will concentrate on the material gathered at the latter school.

The Flandreau school obtains its enrollment from an area generally consisting of the Billings and Aberdeen areas of the Bureau of Indian Affairs. Five states, Montana, Wyoming, North Dakota, South Dakota, and Nebraska, 21 reservations, and 18 tribes are represented in the school. Of the aggregate enrollment, approximately 33 percent are freshmen, 30 percent sophomores, 20 percent juniors and 17 percent seniors.

The facilities of a boarding school are usually looked upon from the standpoint of providing housing and accommodations for the student to live in a location where conventional academic or vocational schooling may be obtained. In this sense, the boarding facilities are secondary to the school or classroom services. The student lives at the boarding school rather than home due to the fact that he is unable to go to such a school in his natural home area.

However, at this school the reverse is the case. Here the boarding facilities are frequently looked upon as a means of removing a student from a socially complicated or disorganized environment to a setting where attention must be given not only to the traditional educational program but to every phase of social development as well.

What follows, then, is an attempt to narratively set forth the mental health problems encountered in a boarding school attempting to effect acculturation and ultimately assimilation of its charges. Certain impressions stand out and can to some degree be validated.

Several standardized objective psychological tests were used to assess the personality characteristics of the Flandreau students and to compare the findings with non-Indian normative groups(12, 14). The testing was done in the regular classroom period of 55 minutes.

Juniors and seniors were administered the Minnesota Multiphasic Personality Inventory. This is mainly a pathology-orientation test, with the subscales largely attempting to measure psychiatric diagnostic samples of various categories of disorder. In every case the scores earned by the Flandreau sample are higher than the scores earned by the ninth grade Minnesota (3) normative sample. While there is a difference in the elevation of the profile, the shape of the profile is highly similar. The results indicate that on all of the categories, with the exceptions of hysteria and hypomania, the Flandreau sample was higher. These students are more pathological. The MMPI also contains "neurotic" and "psychotic" triads. Here the difference for the Flandreau sample is the "psychotic" end of the scale. This does not mean that these persons are literally trending toward a psychotic configuration, but the movement is in the direction of disturbance in adjustment. The t test, an examination of differences of means, indicated an extremely high p value—.001 in eight of the 13 scales for the boys and seven for the girls. Two items for both sexes showed a p value of .01 and three items were not significant.

The California Psychological Inventory was given to sophomores, juniors and seniors. The CPI attempts to measure traits associated with normal functioning. The same results were evident, but in reverse. The Flandreau sample, in 15 out of 18 items, showed significant differences from Gough's normative high school groups(2). The t test indicated a p value of .001 in 12 of the 18 scales for both sexes. The Flandreau sample was lower on positive traits. The difference is in intensity, although again the profile was highly similar in shape to the normative groups. In effect the results appear to show that these youngsters are tending toward distress.

All four grades were given the Quay-Peterson Three Factor Scale. This test measures the three personality constellations associated with juvenile delinquency. The factorial content of the scales was studied in samples of both institutionalized delinquents and normal adolescents. Only limited norms are as yet available. The scales are: 1) psychopathic-delinquency scale to measure attitudes and behavior associated with a tough, amoral, aggressive and impulsive syndrome; 2) neurotic-delinquency scale to measure items associated with guilt, depression, concern, but coupled with impulsiveness and poor control; and 3) subcultural-delinquency scale to measure attitudes and behaviors associated with the adoption of a pattern of behavior dictated by a delinquent subculture but not accompanied by personality maladjustment. The mean scores of the Flandreau sample indicate they are similar to the neuroticism and psychopathy scores of the institutionalized delinquents. Taken in all, the group psychological testing reaffirms the position that we are dealing with a high-risk population regardless of which parameter is applied.

CULTURE AND MENTAL CONFLICT

It is difficult to discern what constitutes abnormal behavior in an abnormal setting. While cultural conflict can be observed, it does not appear to be primary in the causation of mental conflict. Rather, the cultural trappings offer a rationalistic cloak for the basic problems, which are three in number: 1) heightened mobility or "psychosocial nomadism," 2) shifting standards, and 3) superficiality of response, or the "chameleon response."

Heightened Mobility

Our studies show a marked "psychosocial nomadism"—a condition which obtains when the child is exposed not only to repeated changes in loci but to repeated changes in the constellation of his meaningful persons. Further, each new locus necessitates the formation of relationships different from that of the past. Thus a child in a family which shows heightened mobility for cause, but has no distortion of his relations with his critical loved persons, may be anxious in each new locus but not disorganized to the point of profound reaction in the form of aggression or withdrawal(13).

Heightened mobility must be examined in the light of relationships and the reason for the movement if it is to serve as the indicator of disturbance. There is a marked tendency on the part of disturbed youngsters, or others intervening on their behalf, to take the lines of least resistance. Psychologically, whenever stress occurs, the individual repeatedly backs off and moves to another situation.

We have attempted to trace disturbance and the formation of personality disorder through movement and substantiate this with the student life careers of individuals showing increased maladaptation at the school and on the reservation. The high incidence of mobility has been documented from the medical-social case histories, with special emphasis on examining the manifest and covert reasons for movement.

"Psychosocial nomadism" can be documented in many instances by the everlengthening comet's tail of records of administrative decisions made in an attempt to keep a roof over the head of the child and at the same time provide him an education. As might be expected, records become sketchy with increased movement and the reasons advanced have more to do with administrative regulation than the actual reason for the move.

An illustrative example is that of a girl, now 19 years of age, who was observed by various members of the project team and followed for the duration of the project. Admitting that all the moves could not be logged, such as leaving home and spending days and weeks with relatives, the official log still shows an impressive number of situational changes. In all, there were no less than 30 changes of locus. She has been exposed to the ministrations and competitions of her father and mother, five siblings, seven half-siblings, maternal grandparents, paternal grandparents and serial stepfathers, not to mention her contacts with orphanage, boarding school and boarding home staff, teachers and dormitory personnel.

The first move was to grandmother's home at age two with the advent of a sister and parental dissension. The most stable period of her life as far as domicile was concerned was a three-year period from 1956 to 1959. Two years later, there were six runaway episodes terminating in jail.

She had 19 placements in five different education settings, with return usually necessitating change in adult relationship with both teachers and dormitory staff. Education from the eighth grade through the tenth grade required five years and was punctuated by no less than ten interruptions in schooling, varying from a few weeks to several months.

This girl has been variably diagnosed as acute anxiety reaction, acute and chronic schizophrenia, psychosomatic disorder, depressive reaction and adolescent adjustment reaction.

A 19-year-old Indian student was referred to the boarding school during the summer of 1960. The specific reason for referral is not clear, but a brief summary reports a history of gasoline sniffing, social movements and family ill health. He was placed on the waiting list and accepted for the 1961-62 term.

According to official records, this student's paternity is in doubt; two names are reported in the records and two different names are used by the boy and his mother. There is almost no official social history information available; however, a recent autobiography completes missing links and describes his movements so adequately for our purposes that it will be reported here completely:

> I was born in the year 1946 (on an Indian Reservation). I grew up in the home in which both my parents and grandparents lived.
>
> When I reached the age of five I was placed by my parents in the Indian Mission. I lived and went to school from there for four years, at the public school.
>
> When I was nine my brothers, little sister, and parents went along with my grandparents to spend the summer in Minnesota. Everything had gone good all summer when one day my mother and father had an argument. My mother left my dad with my little sister and brothers.
>
> During the last part of October my mother and I left Minnesota and went to Wisconsin. My mother wanted to go up and see her brother, my uncle, who lived in a small town. When we arrived there we found out that he had moved to Milwaukee. So we stayed with relatives in the town, where I attended a country school. We stayed there from October until late February then returned back to the reservation.
>
> When we got back (to the reservation) my mother put me back up at the Mission where I stayed for three more years. When I was in the seventh grade I enrolled myself at the Catholic school where I went to school for a year and a half. After that year and a half I ran away and enrolled back into the public school. During the last six or seven weeks of school I got sick and was in the hospital, in Omaha, for about two months.
>
> That summer was mostly trouble for me. I was in and out of jail. And the county judge had given me break after break. The last time I was placed on probation and said that I would go to

Flandreau Indian School for the next four years. Right then I hadn't realized that I flunked the eighth grade and made out an application for Flandreau. I was accepted and was all ready to leave for school when I got into more trouble. I was taken to court and the judge sentenced me until the age of twenty-one at the state Boys' Training School.

I arrived at the Training School thirty days after my trial. When I got there I was treated nice by both counsellors and boys. For the first thirty days I did nothing, about all I did was peel potatoes along with the rest of the new boys. Then I was transferred out to another company, and then I began school. That's when I found out that I hadn't completed the eighth so I had to do it over again. I was graduated from junior high school the following spring (1961). I was in the Training School for eleven months. Then I was paroled, I think, for a year and during that time I was to attend school and Flandreau.

When I was finished with my first year I didn't plan to come back for the rest of the three. But I liked the school and returned every year, now I am a senior.

In January 1963 he was referred to the project when vocational teachers complained of his uncooperative, defiant attitude. During that school year and the next he was seen eight times by a project social worker, once by the psychiatrist.

Teachers considered him secretive, impudent, sullen, restless, quarrelsome, slovenly, cowardly, irresponsible, resentful of criticism and a daydreamer. He was said to be guilty of lying and stealing. Work habits were poor and intellectual curiousity was lacking. He was not interested in or sought out by others. He has maintained a "D" average in most subjects and, although a senior, he will not graduate. Dorm staff have reported occasional incidents of lighter-fluid sniffing and, during the summer of 1960, he was hospitalized two months for lead poisoning associated with sniffing. Roommates assumed many housekeeping tasks because he refused to do these chores.

The clinic nurse reported his frequent visits for facial acne, injuries from fighting and other minor physical complaints. He bites his nails severely and he was considered to be a stutterer by the Speech and Hearing Clinic. Training school reports indicate that he had similar problems there. He learned to conform, but his personal habits and interpersonal relations improved less noticeably. It was also reported that his parole was delayed until the start of school because his mother was drinking heavily and "having unacceptable relations with many men."

Project staff noted that the student's closest ties have been with maternal family members. He understands the importance of proper behavior, but he has had little opportunity for identification with adequate males. The marked hostility for adult authority and the fact that the boy is a loner were also emphasized. Whenever possible he was interviewed on his own ground, i.e., in the dormitory or on the campus.

Shifting Standards

The second basic problem appears to be confusional cultural values or shifting standards. It is evident that there are distinct variations in the value orientations of the students, their relatives, the teachers, dormitory personnel and the administrative staff. It is not uncommon for the youngsters to be exposed to individuals of the lower three classifications (according to Hollingshead and Redlich [5]) on a daily, even hourly, basis. This necessitates the youngsters' meeting the standards of individuals of varying cultural backgrounds and value systems that are at variance with their own.

The following vignette is illustrative of the confusion of the child as he tries to determine who he is, where he is and what he is doing. Three Sisseton Sioux youngsters, ranging from 10 to 12 years of age, were traveling from the Pierre Boarding School to the reservation located in northeastern South Dakota. This conversation was overheard by the social worker:

> First Child: Did you know Sisseton was a reservation?
> Second Child: Sure, I knew that last year.
> Third Child: Did you know that real Indians live there?
> Second Child: Of course, we're real Indians—we can't be play Indians.

Students and staff at Flandreau were given the Kluckhohn Value Orientation Scale (6, 7, 16, 17). This technique measures the variant value orientations in four dimensions: Relational, Man-Nature, Time and Activity. The primary theoretical focus is on acculturation.

In the Relational orientation, Kluckhohn sees the adult middle class as dominantly Individualistic, preferring this orientation significantly to the Collateral and Lineal alternatives. In man's relationship to nature or supernature, the dominant American preference is for Mastery-over-Nature, preferred significantly to Subjugation-to-Nature and Harmony-with-Nature. In the Time orientation, Future is ranked first, Present second and Past third; all at statistically significant levels. In the preferred mode of Action, Americans prefer Doing in contrast to Being.

A recent study of 52 teachers and 68 social workers, using Kluckhohn's device, yielded data on their value orientations which "coincided almost perfectly on all four orientations with the Kluckhohn analysis of general United States culture"(15).

Flandreau students were tested with this instrument in the regular classroom period. Of the 544 students then enrolled, 92 percent or 503 were tested. Preliminary analysis of the data shows that student value orientations as a whole are as follows. The girls differ significantly from the middle class in two orientations. They prefer the Subjugated-to-Nature alternative significantly to Master-over-Nature and to Harmony-with-Nature, as well as preferring Over to With significantly. This is a statistically significant one-order reversal from the dominant middle-class preference for Mastery-over-Nature. The girls also have a significant reversal in the Time Orientation, preferring Present to Future and Past.

Although the boys have moved away from the girls' position toward the middle class in the Man-Nature orientation, they have not achieved a statistically significant first-order preference for Mastery-over-Nature. The boys rank Over first, Subjugated second and With third. In the Time orientation, again the boys seem to be transitional; they do not prefer Present statistically to Future, although they still prefer Present and Future to Past significantly. Therefore, the boys have a position between that of the girls and the middle class.

In the Relational orientation both sexes differ from the middle-class pattern of dominant Individualism. The boys and girls both prefer Collateral nonsignificantly to Individual and prefer both of these to Lineal significantly. Neither the boys nor the girls differ from the middle class in the Activity orientation: all prefer Doing significantly to Being.

Thus, both boys and girls differ from middle-class value preferences in the Relational, Man-Nature and Time orientations, and the girls are much further from middle-class values than the boys. These differences support the Spindlers' hypotheses (19, 20) on female conservatism in cultural change.

Class and tribe are not very powerful discriminating factors in themselves, but when paired with sex do reveal many significant differences. The freshmen girls and the Sioux stand out sharply as less acculturated. There is also evidence that the seniors, particularly boys, are more acculturated. It is reasonable to describe the boys as transitional, not highly acculturated to the middle class, but closer than the girls, whose choices resemble those of the urban lower class as studied by Schneiderman.

The staff of the school was also given this instrument and 70 protocols were completed, giving us a 90 percent sample. Staff value orientations coincide almost exactly with those found by both Schneiderman and Kluckhohn. The staff as a whole displays a middle-class pattern of value orientations, with some ambivalence in the second-order preference in the Man-Nature dimension and in their choice of Future over Present.

Taking just the 29 teachers, we see they are essentially middle class in their order of preferences, with the same ambivalence as the whole staff showed.

The dormitory staff, a total of 21 persons, differs from the staff as a whole and the teachers in the Man-Nature dimensions and they show a one-order reversal with Subjugation-to-Nature nonsignificantly preferred to Mastery-over-Nature.

Comparing the preferences of the students to those of the staff as a whole and to the choices of the teachers and dormitory staff, we see great differences. The students differ from the staff and teachers in the direction of the lower-class value orientations. The staff as a whole and teachers chose the Individualistic, Mastery-over-Nature and Future alternatives as their first-choice preferences, in contrast to the students' first choices of Collateral, Subjugated-to-Nature and Present. The dormitory staff has a much weaker commitment to middle-class value orientations than the staff as a whole or the teachers as a group. Although three of the four first-order choices of the dormitory staff are the same as the middle class, only one of these differs significantly from the first choice of the students. The fourth choice, Subjugation-to-Nature, is the same as that of the students. All four groups prefer Doing over Being, but the teachers and the staff prefer Doing more strongly, according to the statistics.

Kluckhohn postulates that nonsignificant preference indicates that the population is in a state of cultural transition. In light of this view it is extremely useful to have the analyses of variants, which indicate that a statistically significant gap still exists between the students and the staff as a whole and the teachers, and very few significant differences between the dorm staff and the students.

Evidence that value orientations influence one's responses to others has come from many sources—Spindler (18) and others. From the above results, we can predict that biases in cultural transmission occur. Certainly the teacher's class background and values may unconsciously distort his perceptions and expectations of the students.

Walter Taylor says, "All the brilliant teachers and all the most modern methods of teaching are powerless to insure transfer of the most elementary idea, unless the pupil himself places a value upon that idea or upon learning in principle." He feels that "the educator and the educational planner must know the values which are characteristic of the culture and which motivate the pupil"(21). He also feels that the teacher should work through the values of the pupil to make him want to learn.

Superficiality of Response

A "chameleon-like" response results as the youngsters attempt to match their values to the values of the people they face. Superficiality of response is encouraged with acquiescence to the exigencies of the situation only so long as is necessary to get by. Obviously, value systems could not then be deeply held but rather are used for the particular moment. Validation of this point is difficult, but the two following illustrations are advanced to suggest its existence.

A home economics teacher desired to impress upon the girls of her class the necessity for cleanliness. Since they were soon going to have a formal dance she asked each of the girls to pay $2.00 for the rental of the formals. Those who returned clean formals would receive 50 cents in change; those who returned dirty formals would forfeit the two dollars. Having second thoughts on this procedure, she had the girls write their answers to the question: "What should be the punishment if a girl returns a soiled gown?"

The answers elicited went like this: 1) She should be made to kneel on the floor for an hour. 2) She should be made to stand with her nose up against the blackboard. 3) She should scrub the floor with a toothbrush.

Another home economics teacher decided to check the same group of girls and asked the same question: "What should be the punishment if...."

The group responses she got ran something like this: 1) You should take the girl aside and talk with her. 2) You should sit down and find out the reason that it happened. 3) You should tell the girl not to do it again.

CONCLUSION

The authors contend that frequency of movement and the necessity to conform to changing standards can only lead to confusion and disorganization of the child's personality. The frequency of movement further interfers with and discourages the development of lasting relations in which love and concern can permit adequate maturation.

This is approached as though it were an Indian problem. But it begins to appear that these are problems common to individuals who are dependent and/or neglected. It is our contention that "psychosocial nomadism" and shifting value systems result in inward disturbance. These findings are applicable to groups other than the population being studied as the patterns are similar to youngsters of different and deprived cultures.

Thus, the dilemma in approaching individuals who have disordered homes and disordered behavior is how to get them to relinquish the dependency that we, ourselves, create in trying to get them well or educated. It is evident that if our findings are substantially correct, there will be serious logistical problems in altering ignorance and poverty.

ACKNOWLEDGEMENTS

The authors wish to acknowledge the help of the following colleagues: Dr. William A. Hunt, Northwestern University; Dr. Herbert C. Quay, University of Illinois; Dr. Sol L. Garfield, Teachers College, Columbia University; Dr. Malcolm L. Helper, Nebraska Psychiatric Institute; Mrs. Virginia Bellsmith, New York School of Social Work, Columbia University; Dr. Frank A. Miller, University of Minnesota; and project social workers Mr. Paul Felix, Flandreau, S.D.; Mr. Cyrus Behroozi, Pierre, S.D.; Mr. Donald Blashill, Wahpeton, N.D.; and sociologist Mr. Donald Nugent, Flandreau, S.D.

NOTE

*Read at the 121st annual meeting of the American Psychiatric Association, New York, N. Y., May 3-7, 1965.

This work was supported in part by Public Health Service grant MH-00967 from the National Institute of Mental Health.

REFERENCES

1 Bogard, H., Warner, B. B., Krush, T. P., and Jones, M. First Project Report, 1957 (processed).

2 Gough, H. G. California Psychological Inventory Manual (Palo Alto, Calif.: Consulting Psychologists Press, 1956-1957).

3 Hathaway, S. R., and Monachesi, E. D., eds. Analyzing and Predicting Juvenile Delinquency with the MMPI (Minneapolis: University of Minnesota Press, 1953).

4 Health Services for American Indians. U. S. Department of Health, Education, and Welfare, Public Health Service Publication No. 531, Washington, D. C., 1957.

5 Hollingshead, A. B., and Redlich, F. C. Social Stratification and Psychiatric Disorders, Amer. Sociol. Rev. 18: 163-169, 1953.

6 Kluckhohn, F. R. Variations in Value Orientations as a Factor in Cultural Change, 1964 (processed).

7 Kluckhohn, F. R., and Strodtbeck, F. L. Variations in Value Orientations (Evanston: Row, Peterson and Co., 1961).

8 Krush, T. P., and Bjork, J. W. Fourth and Fifth Annual Reports of the Mental Health Clinic at the PHS Indian School Health Center, Flandreau Indian Vocational High School, 1961 (processed).

9 Krush, T. P., and Bjork, J. W. Mental Health Factors in an Indian Boarding School, Ment. Hyg. 49:94-103, 1965.

10 Krush, T. P., Lello, A. J., and Bjork, J. W. Third Annual Report of the Mental Health Clinic at the Flandreau Indian Vocational High School, 1959 (processed).

11 MacGregor, G. Warriors Without Weapons (Chicago: University of Chicago Press, 1946).

12 Mental Health Project for Indian Boarding Schools. Proceedings of conference, 1964 (processed).

13 Pederson, F. A., and Sullivan, E. J. Relationships among Geographical Mobility, Parental Attitudes and Emotional Disturbances in Children, Amer. J. Orthopsychiat. 34:575-580, 1964.

14 Quay, H. C., Hunt, W. A., Krush, T. P., Bjork, J. W., and Slavin, D. Personality Patterns of Plains Indian Adolescents Attending an Off-Reservation Boarding School, undated (processed).

15 Schneiderman, L. Value Orientation Preferences of Chronic Relief Recipients, J. Social Work 9:13-19, 1964.

16 Sindell, P. S. Cultural Transmission and Social Learning in an Indian Boarding School, 1965 (processed).

17 Sindell, P. S. Flandreau Student Value Orientations, 1965 (processed).

18 Spindler, G. D. The Transmission of American Culture. (Cambridge: Harvard University Press, 1960).

19 Spindler, L. S. Menomini Women and Culture Change, Memoir 91, American Anthropological Association, 1962.

20 Spindler, L. S., and Spindler, G. D. Male and Female Adaptations in Culture Change, Amer. Anthropologist 60:217-233, 1958.

21 Taylor, W. The Role of Anthropology in Educational Planning, 1963 (processed). Reprinted from Jacobs, R., Wiegand, G. C., and Macomber, F. G.: Developing Institutional Resources to Assist with Educational Planning with Particular Focus upon the Interdisciplinary Team Approach to Educational Planning (Carbondale: Southern Illinois University, 1963).

22 Warner, B. B., Krush, T. P., Bjork, J. W., and Jackson, K. Second Annual Report of the Mental Health Pilot Project at the Flandreau Indian Vocational High School, 1958 (processed).

HARRY W. MARTIN, SARA SMITH SUTKER, ROBERT L. LEON, WILLIAM M. HALES: MENTAL HEALTH OF EASTERN OKLAHOMA INDIANS: AN EXPLORATION*

North American Indians have attracted a great deal of research interest, particularly on the part of anthropologists; yet relatively little is known about their mental health.[1] Intelligence tests and other instruments such as the Rorschach[2] have proved most popular in attempts to assess the Indian's intellectual ability and personality. Havighurst's[3] review of intelligence studies indicates that the innate capacity of Indian children is equivalent to that of non-Indians. He concludes that because of differences in culture and life conditions, Indian children are at a disadvantage compared with white children. Kerchoff's[4] study of *anomie* and achievement motivation among Chippewa children supports Havighurst's conclusions with social psychological data.

The Spindlers,[5] from their own research and that of others, conclude that American Indians *probably* exhibit a common core of psychological features.[6] They point out that Hallowell's[7] Rorschach data on the Ojibwa gives no evidence of psychological change consonant with the adoption of white culture; psychological shifts appearing in protocols reflected regressive and disintegrative tendencies. Essentially the same pattern appeared among "native-oriented" Menominee studied by the Spindlers; however, those Menominee with occupational and social positions equivalent to high status whites in the same locale did not exhibit the regressive tendency. Various sources of acculturative stress impinging upon Indians have been reviewed by Sasaki,[8] and in recent years mental health problems among Indian children attending boarding schools have attracted attention.[9]

THE STUDY AIMS

In spite of a massive body of research and general literature on North American Indians, major information gaps remain regarding the mental health of these various people. For example, epidemiological studies estimating either prevalence or incidence of mental illness are entirely lacking.[10] The present study takes one step toward closing this gap. It had two principal aims: (1) to explore the usefulness of a psychiatric screening device, standardized on a non-Indian population, as an instrument for assessing the mental health of Indians; and (2) to compare results obtained on Indians with those obtained on white and Negro subjects of comparable socio-economic status.

Source: Reprinted by permission from *Human Organization* 27 (Winter 1968), 308-315.

THE SUBJECTS

Forms were completed by 640 persons attending medical outpatient clinics operated by the Division of Indian Health, U. S. Health Services, at Shawnee and Claremore, Oklahoma. This number included 42 non-Indian spouses; these were eliminated from this analysis. Also deleted were all forms with four or more items unanswered, as well as those forms requiring an excessive amount of interpretation. This procedure reduced the number of usable forms on Indian subjects to 571. The 278 white and Negro subjects—208 and 70, respectively—were persons attending outpatient medical clinics at the University Medical Center[11] in Oklahoma City during the first two months of 1963. Data on the Indian subjects were collected during the preceding summer.[12]

Women outnumbered men in all three racial groups; they accounted for 67, 74, and 89 percent of the whites, Indians, and Negroes, respectively. Median ages were 25, 34, and 40 for Negroes, Indian, and white women; 43 and 49 for Indian and white men. The median years of schooling for Indian men and white men and women was in the 7-9 year range; the medians of Indian and Negro women were in the 10-11 year range.

Occupationally, housewives accounted for a majority of subjects: 50, 55, and 46 percent of the whites, Indians, and Negroes, respectively. Table 1 gives the occupational distribution of all persons, excluding housewives, reporting an occupation. Differences between Negroes and whites are all less than five percentage points except in the case of students. The proportion of laborers and service workers among Negroes was almost twice that of Indians and whites; there were no skilled or semiskilled persons among the Negroes; the proportion of Negro students was half that of Indians, and slightly lower than that of whites.

TABLE 1

Occupation by Race (Housewives Excluded) in Percent

Occupation	Indian N = 247	White N = 91	Negro N = 21
Owners and professionals	14.6	15.4	14.3
Skilled and semiskilled	17.4	22.0	0.0
Service workers and laborers	28.3	31.8	57.1
Retired and unemployed	10.5	13.2	14.3
Students	29.2	17.6	14.3

The Indian subjects were characterized by considerable diversity with respect to tribe and Indian inheritance as indexed by degree of Indian blood. Among the twenty-six tribes represented, the five Civilized Tribes—Cherokee, Choctaw, Creek, Chickasaw, Seminole—accounted for 51 percent of the total. Each of the remaining tribes was represented by eight or fewer persons. Seventy percent were fullbloods; approximately one-fifth of these were children of Indian parents with different tribal identification. The remaining 30 percent were persons of Indian and non-Indian parentage. The possible influence which these factors may have for psychological adjustment is not considered in this paper.

Although the primary aim of the study was to explore the use of a psychiatric screening device among Indian subjects, the question of how well the subjects represent the Indian population from which they were drawn is relevant. Table 2 compares the study population by age and sex with approximations[13] of the age-sex distribution of Oklahoma Indians as of 1960. Four of the six comparisons among males are close, but only two of the six among females. Male subjects 20-29 are underrepresented and those 50-59 overrepresented in the study. Females in the 20-29 and 40-49 age groups are overrepresented while those in both older categories are underrepresented.

TABLE 2

Age-Sex Distribution of Oklahoma Indians,[a] Age 15 and Over as of 1960, Compared with Age-Sex Distribution of Indian Subjects, in Percent

	Males		Females	
Age	Total Indian population N = 19,395	Study population N = 160	Total Indian population N = 19,917	Study population N = 411
15-19[b]	16.7	16.3	13.8	16.1
20-29	19.2*	13.7	18.7**	25.3
30-39	17.5	13.7	19.0	19.0
40-49	15.8	13.7	17.5*	21.9
50-59	15.3**	26.3	14.9**	9.7
60 +	15.5	16.3	16.1**	8.0

[a] *Source:* U.S. Bureau of the Census, *U.S. Census of Population: 1960,* Final Report PC(1)-38D, Detailed Characteristics, Table 96.

[b] The study population in this age group contains persons 14-19 years of age.

*P = .05.

**P = .01 or less. Probabilities computed after removal of the number of subjects in each age-sex category from the respective population category.

THE INSTRUMENT

The Cornell Index (N2), containing 100 questions to be answered "yes" or "no" by subjects, was developed from an earlier instrument for screening military inductees.[14] The Index is simple to administer either individually or in groups, and has enjoyed extensive use in research. Scores are determined by the number of responses given in specified directions. Three cut-off levels are recommended: Method A employs scores of 23 or more as a cut-off point; Method B, a score of 13 or more; and Method C, a score of 13 or more plus one or more "stop" items.[15] This paper employs cut-off points of 13 and 23 as well as mean scores for purposes of analysis.

ADMINISTRATION OF THE INDEX

The instrument was administered by nurses at Shawnee and by the social worker at Claremore. Usually two to ten persons at a time completed the form while waiting to see a doctor. The general attitude was serious and cooperative; refusals to complete the form were considerably less than one percent. At times younger persons would giggle or make remarks about some question; on rare occasions a patient would ask, "Is this a mental test?" or "Will the doctor see it?" If anxiety or resentment were generated, these feelings were well concealed. In spite of the serious cooperation given, very few persons evidenced further interest in the matter. One physician suggested that the subjects may have assumed that the Index was just another form the government wanted them to fill out.

Use of an instrument standardized on one cultural group for research in a different cultural setting poses certain problems regardless of whether translations are used.[16] In the present case, except perhaps for persons literate in Cherokee, translations were impossible, and to a certain extent unnecessary. Reference to Table 6 shows that approximately 80 percent of the Indian men and 90 percent of the women had seven or more years of schooling. Thus, on the basis of education, the vast majority of the Indian respondents were relatively well-acculturated. Those persons unable to read (about five percent of the total) had the items read to them.[17]

The words and phrasing of a few items in the Index presented difficulty for some of the more literate persons. Items which occasioned the most frequent questions were item 18 ("Do you have an uncontrollable need to repeat the same disturbing actions?"), item 96 ("Do you always do things on sudden impulse?"), and item 99 ("Is the opposite sex unpleasant to you?"). These items were altered to read, respectively, "Are there things you can't help doing?"; "Do you always do things without thinking?"; "Do you dislike the opposite sex?"

Other substitutions included "boss" for "superior," and "trouble" for "difficulty." The adverbs "usually" and "always" bothered some subjects;[18] reading the question aloud or emphasizing the adverb in question usually resolved these problems.

Reliability

The Index was given a second time to 55 of the Indian subjects at least four weeks following the first administration. The product moment correlation between the first and second set of scores was .90, and a coefficient of .86 occurred between the 12 "stop" items. The first coefficient compares favorably with the .95 reported by the developers of the Index. These coefficients suggest that the language bias, whatever it may have been, was consistent. Moreover, the coefficients indicate a high order of test/retest reliability in measuring whatever the Index measures. What the Index measures is, of course, a crucial question. Arensten[19] maintains that it contributes little to psychiatric examinations, but remains a useful research tool. Indeed, as the developers of the Index point out, it is an adjunct to the psychiatric interview, not a substitute.

Validity

Some eight months following completion of the study, persons in the Shawnee area with scores in the upper and lower 20 percent range[20] were requested to return to the clinic during a three-day period. Thirty-six returned[21]—14 high-scorers and 22 low-scorers—and agreed to an interview. This constituted a total return of 30 percent, or less than a quarter of the high-scorers and just over a third of the low-scorers. Three psychiatric residents, working only with the knowledge that the subjects were in one or the other of the score extremes, conducted 30 to 60 minute interviews. Each person was seen by only one resident who gave an opinion as to whether a psychiatric disturbance was present or not. The overall agreement between the Index and the residents was better than 66 percent.

No disturbance was indicated for 17 (77 percent) of the low-scorers, and present for 7 (50 percent) of the high-scorers. On the basis of psychiatric judgment, then, 23 percent of those persons with low scores had some impairment, and 50 percent of those with high scores had no impariment. These results of case-to-case comparisons between scores and psychiatric opinion are disappointing from one set of expectations. This procedure assumes that one psychiatric interview is more valid than the Index—which, of course, is not necessarily true. An increasing order of case-to-case agreement can be attained only as completely valid instruments[22] and psychiatric opinions are approached.

Although such agreement is desirable, it may not be necessary for estimating the amount of psychiatric impairment in a population. For example, according to the Index, 14 (38.9 percent) of the 36 subjects examined had some psychiatric impairment, and 12 (33.3 percent) of the total group were considered impaired to some extent by psychiatric interviews. Thus, the overall estimate of the presence of psychiatric impairment by both methods is in relatively close agreement.[23]

One additional check on the validity of the Index should be described. At the time of the psychiatric interviews, 34 of the subjects completed[24] the 22-item screening instrument developed by the Midtown Study of mental disorders in Manhattan.[25] A cut-off score of four or more points on this instrument is suggested for selecting cases for further examination. Comparisons of scores on this scale with those made by the 34 subjects on the Index some eight months earlier showed that 95.2 percent of the low-scorers on the Index had scores of less than four on the Langer scale, and 92.3 percent of those with scores above 24 on the Index scored above four on the Langer scale. Although these subjects were persons scoring at the extremes on the Index, it appears that the Index and the Langer scale may give essentially the same results.

THE FINDINGS

Scores by Race and Sex

The mean Index scores and standard deviations for each race and sex are given in Table 3. Since rather marked age, sex, and occupational

TABLE 3

CI Scores for Indians, Whites, and Negroes by Sex

	N	X̄	S.D.
Indians (total)	571	17.7	13.40
Men	160	16.2	13.32
Women	411	18.2	13.41
Negroes (total)	70	19.1	11.72
Men	8	27.1	12.59
Women	62	18.4	11.21
Whites (total)	208	23.0	14.85
Men	69	21.4	14.90
Women	139	23.9	14.81

Indian vs. white males: t = 4.17, P. < .01.
Indian vs. white females: t = 2.60, P. = .01.
Negro vs. white females: t = 2.59, P. < .02.

distributions appeared among the three racial groups, we restrict the report on racial comparisons to those given in this table and in Table 4. Disregarding sex, the mean scores are in descending order by race: whites, 23.0; Negroes, 19.1; and Indians, 17.7. This pattern tends to hold with sex controlled; however the means of Indian and Negro females differ by a slight amount, and the mean of the eight Negro males[26] is far in excess of that of whites. Except in the case of Negroes, the mean scores of women exceed those of men. Higher scores among women appear to be a general result in the use of the Index.[27]

Degree of Presumed Impairment

Felton,[28] employing cut-off points of 13 and 23, designated persons with CI scores of less than 13 as "normals," persons in the 13 to 22 range as "mildly neurotic," and those scoring 23 or more as "severely neurotic." The percentage of our subjects in each of these categories is shown in Table 4. As can be seen in the table, whites have the largest percentages in the severe category and the smallest percentages of normals; Indians have the highest percentages in the normal category; and Negro women are most heavily represented in the "mildly neurotic" category. Negro women also fall between whites and Indians in the normal and severe categories. These distributions, as shown in Table 4, differ significantly for all race/sex comparisons, except for that between Indian and Negro females.

One report from a recent national conference on Indian health estimates that *possibly* 20 to 25 percent of the Indian population is affected by some type of mental illness ranging from major psychoses to personality disorders.[29] If scores of 23 or more only are considered, then almost 30 percent (see Table 4) of all the Indians have some psychiatric impairment. Employing scores of 13 and above, the percentage indicated as having some impairment approaches 60 percent. Earlier we showed that the Index and psychiatric interviews suggest some degree of impairment in approximately one-third of the Indian population, although the two procedures did not agree on which individuals belonged in that third. If we

TABLE 4

Degree of Presumed Impairment by Race and Sex (Percentage)

	Number	Normal (0-12)	Mildly Neurotic (13-22)	Severely Neurotic (23 +)
Men				
Indian	.160	50.0	26.3	23.7
White	69	31.9	26.1	42.0
Women				
Indian	411	40.6	27.7	31.7
Negro	62	33.9	37.1	29.0
White	139	24.5	24.5	51.0
Both sexes				
Indian	571	43.3	27.3	29.4
White	208	26.9	25.0	48.1

	X^2	df	P
Indian *vs.* white males	9.016	2	.02
Indian *vs.* white females	18.598	2	.001
Indian *vs.* Negro females	2.321	2	.30
White *vs.* Negro females	8.418	2	.02

include only those cases on which the Index and interviews agreed as to the presence of disturbance, (7 of 36), then only 20 percent are affected. Thus, we have two estimates between which the true proportion may fall: that is, either between 20 and 30 percent or between 20 and 60 percent. The most conservative estimate would be 25 percent, or the midpoint of the first two percentages. This is the upper limit of the estimate reported by the national conference on Indian health cited above.

It should be noted that the Indian respondents in this study do not reside on reservations; Oklahoma has no reservations as such. Place of residence—on or off reservations—may have important mental helath consequences for Indians;[30] however, a discussion of these conditions leads too far afield. We now turn briefly to the relationship between Index scores, age, and education.

Scores by Sex and Age

Table 5 gives the mean scores for Indians, by sex and age. Among men, the average score rises abruptly in the 50-59 year age bracket, but drops about three points from that high for age 60 and over. An increase in average score also occurs among women, but this is less abrupt than that for men and does not occur until age 60 and over. The relationship between age and Index scores was examined by dichotomizing each sex at its median age and Index scores at the cut-off point of 13. By this method, age and scores were positively and significantly[31] related among men but not among women.

Scores and Education

Index scores by sex and years of education are displayed in Table 6. The CI means decline from a high of 22 among men with six or fewer

TABLE 5

TABLE 5

Mean CI Scores by Sex and Age

	Men			Women		
Age	N	$\bar{X}$	S.D.	N	$\bar{X}$	S.D.
14 to less than 20	26	13.9	10.00	66	18.2	11.85
20-29	22	15.1	14.65	104	17.3	12.46
30-39	22	13.1	9.27	78	17.8	13.94
40-49	22	13.0	10.76	90	18.5	13.93
50-59	42	20.6	15.66	40	18.3	13.22
60 +	26	17.4	10.16	33	21.2	15.91

TABLE 6

Mean CI Scores and Level of Education by Sex

	Men				Women			
Years of Schooling	N	%	X	S.D.	N	%	$\bar{X}$	S.D.
0-6 years	29	18.7	22.2	14.55	42	10.6	29.2	12.60
7-9 years	55	35.5	17.6	15.65	124	31.3	19.0	13.77
10-11 years	31	20.0	13.7	8.66	101	25.5	19.3	11.67
High school graduate	32	20.6	9.9	9.36	101	25.5	13.8	11.66
Some past high school	8	5.2	11.9	7.53	28	7.1	14.7	11.31

years of schooling to a low of just under ten for high school graduates, and rises toward twelve among those with more than high school training. A similar pattern may be noted for the women. With the Index scores dichotomized at the cut-off of 13, 60 percent of the men with nine or fewer years of schooling scored over 13 while only 35 percent of those with ten or more years of schooling scored this high.[32] Among the women, 62 percent of those with nine or fewer years of schooling had an Index score of 13 or more, and 42 percent of those completing ten or more years scored 13.[33]

DISCUSSION

On the basis of these findings, we tentatively conclude that the Cornell Index and the Langer 22-item screening device are relatively effective means for estimating the prevalence of emotional disturbance in the Indian population. Since the Langer scale contains about one-fifth as many items as the Index, and appears to produce similar results, its brevity affords certain advantages. On the other hand, the Index contains a number of subscales which may prove useful for making distinctions not possible with the Langer scale. Further explorations with both of these instruments seem warranted.

In spite of this favorable conclusion, the discrepancy between the

Index results and the psychiatric interviews cannot be ignored. Use of the Index in several smaller studies[34] has suggested that, in addition to identifying some persons with psychiatric problems, the instrument taps a social psychological dimension of "pathology" or a sense of disturbance not captured by current psychiatric concepts.[35] We are inclined to think that many high scorers reflect an internal disquietude resulting from sociocultural stress and inadequacy which does not, from a clinical point of view, constitute psychopathology in the traditional sense. This is not to say that these persons are not sick, but to suggest the existence of psychosocial dynamics which do not in all cases produce classical psychiatric symptoms. Our psychiatric interviews failed to take this hypothesis into consideration. The discrepancy between the Index and psychiatric interviews and the possibility of pathogenetic dynamics which contribute to this discrepancy call for intensive theoretical and methodological research. Ideally, psychiatric diagnosis and screening instruments would, with high comparability, identify and differentiate between classical psychopathologic states and states which, though they appear as psychiatric symptoms, stem primarily from different sources.

Finally, the most conservative estimate indicates that 25 percent of the Indian population as represented by our subjects is psychiatrically impaired. The Midtown Manhattan study,[36] to report one comparison with findings from an urban, non-Indian population, considered 23.4 percent of its subjects as impaired. This percentage is six points smaller than our severe category in Table 4. Combining our mild and severe categories (Table 4) and the Manhattan categories of moderate to incapacitating symptoms, the proportions are almost identical—56.7 percent for Indians and 52.2 percent for Manhattanites. This suggests that the prevalence of psychiatric problems does not differ markedly between Indians and non-Indians. However, the comparisons with low socioeconomic status whites and Negroes indicate that psychiatric problems may be less severe and less widespread among Indians than among whites and that Negroes place somewhere between the two.

NOTES AND REFERENCES

*The research was supported by U. S. Public Health Service Funds, National Institute of Mental Health.

1 For recent reports on Indian health and economic conditions see: *Illness Among Indians.* DPHEW, PHS, Indian Health Service, November, 1963; "Indian Poverty and Indian Health," *Indicators,* no volume indicated (March 1964); E. E. Hagen and L. C. Shaw, *The Sioux on Reservation: The American Colonial Problem,* preliminary edition (mimeographed), Massachusetts Institute of Technology, May 1960; H. Rusk, "They Still Die Young," *Congressional Record,* Jan. 23, 1962; John Adair, Kent Deuschle, and Walsh McDermott, "Patterns of Health and Disease Among the Navaho," *The Annals,* Vol. 311 (May 1957), pp. 80-94.

2 Gardner Lindzey, *Projective Techniques and Cross-Cultural Research* (Appleton-Century-Crofts, Inc., New York, 1961), p. 2 ff.

3 Robert J. Havighurst, "Education Among American Indians," *The Annals*, Vol. 311 (May 1957), pp. 110-113.

4 Alan C. Kerchoff, "Anomie and Achievement Motivation: A Study of Personality Development Within Cultural Disorganization," *Social Forces*, Vol. 37 (March 1959), p. 261.

5 George D. and Louise S. Spindler, "American Indian Personality Types and Their Sociocultural Roots," *The Annals*, Vol. 311 (May 1957), pp. 147-157.

6 *Ibid.*, pp. 148-149. Among the common psychological characteristics listed by the Spindlers are nondemonstrative emotionality, high control over interpersonal aggression, ability to endure pain and deprivation, positive valuation of bravery and courage, a generalized fear of the world as dangerous, and tendency toward practical joking, These features are said to function differently within variant tribal areal cultures. A question may be raised here: Are the above features only a "corps" of common psychocultural features peripheral to the basic personality "core"?

7 A. T. Hallowell, "Ojibwa Personality and Acculturation," in Sol Tax (ed.), *Proceedings and Selected Papers of the 29th International Congress of Americanists* (University of Chicago Press, Chicago, Illinois, 1951), p. 112 (cited by the Spindlers, *ibid.*, note 13).

8 Tom T. Saski, "Sources of Mental Stress in Indian Acculturation," in John C. Cobb (ed.), *Emotional Problems of the Indian Students in Boarding Schools and Related Public Schools*, Workshop Proceedings, Albuquerque, New Mexico, April 11-13, 1960.

9 For example, see Cobb, *op. cit.* and Elizabeth E. Hoyt, "Young Indians: Some Problems and Issues of Mental Hygiene," *Mental Hygiene*, Vol. 46 (January 1962), pp. 41-47.

10 "The presence of mental disturbance among Indians can be estimated only on the basis of known prevalence among certain other segments of the [U. S.] population." Agnes Fahy and Carl Muschenheim, M.D., "Third National Conference on American Indian Health," *Journal of the American Medical Association*, Vol. 194 (December 6, 1965), p. 191.

11 At the University of Oklahoma Medical Center, we are particularly indebted to: Dr. Carl W. Smith, Miss Edna Keefe, Mrs. Mary Hall, and Mrs. Esther Henderson.

12 We are indebted to the following persons of the Indian Health Service: Dr. Robert A. Hudgins, former Area Medical Officer, Mrs. Elizabeth Silcott, Area Social Work Consultant; at the Shawnee Health Center: Dr. John Rinehart, Mrs. Ruby Neaddeau, R.N., Mrs. Beulah Walker, R.N., and Miss Joan Marshall, R.N.; at Claremore: Mrs. Frances Paxson, M.S.W. We are also heavily in debt to all those patients who cooperated in the study at the three health facilities.

13 Census data include Indians with all "other" races. Non-Indians, for the most part Orientals, account for approximately four percent of the total. Age/sex breakdowns were not available for the non-Indians, thus they could not be removed without assuming an equal distribution over the age/sex categories.

14 Arthur Weider, *et al.*, *Cornell Index* Manual (The Psychological Corporation, New York, 1949) revision.

15 There are twelve "stop" items which refer to "crucial symptoms," e.g., "Have you ever had a fit or convulsion?"

16 These problems have been discussed by Laufer in the use of the Cornell Index (N2) among Okinawan natives, and by Chance for the Cornell Medical Index in this work with Eskimos. (The Medical Index is a 195-item instrument to collect information on both medical and psychiatric problems.) See Ludwig G. Laufer, "Cultural Problems Encountered in Use of the Cornell Index Among Okinawan Natives," *The American Journal of Psychiatry,* Vol. 109 (May 1953), pp. 861-864; and Norman A. Chance, "Conceptual and Methodological Problems in Cross-Cultural Health Research," *American Journal of Public Health,* Vol. 52 (March 1962), pp. 410-417.

17 These persons were, on the average, older by ten years, and had less schooling—half completed six or fewer years. Index scores for the men averaged two points higher than the total, and those of the women were nine points higher. Elimination of these persons would have reduced average scores for each sex by .5 or less.

18 Laufer encountered similar problems with adverbs and qualifying adjectives among Okinawans. *Op. cit.,* p. 862.

19 Kaj. Arentsen, "An Investigation of the Questionnaire Method By Means of the Cornell Index (Form N2) I," *Acta Psychiatrica et Neurological Scandinavica,* Vol. 32 No. 3 (1957), pp. 41-44.

20 Low-scorers requested to return had an Index mean of 3.0; high-scorers a mean of 38.7. Men accounted for 26 percent of the study group, and 21 percent of the low- and high-scorers. The men in this group had an education median of 10-11 years as compared with 7-9 years of the total. Age and education medians of the women were identical to those of the total study group.

21 The group which returned for validation interviews contained only three men—aged 17, 30, and 37 years. Their Index scores were three or less. Among the women, age and education medians did not differ from those of the total women.

22 The Cornell Index, for example, like many other instruments, has no means for checking "test-taking attitude." It is quite likely that some persons shape their responses to Index items according to whether they want to make a "good" or "poor" showing. This, in turn, is related to the definition under which the form is completed and what subjects hope to obtain or avoid on the basis of test results.

23 This conclusion may not be generalizable, on the grounds that the 36 subjects were all extreme scorers who volunteered for an interview.

24 We are indebted to Dr. John H. Gladfelter for administering this test. No serious language problems arose for the subjects who completed this form.

25 Thomas S. Langer, "A Twenty-Two Item Screening Score of Psychiatric Symptoms Indicating Impairment," *Journal of Health and Human Behavior,* Vol. 3 (Winter 1962), pp. 269-276.

26 Because of their small number, Negro males are deleted from further consideration.

27 See Weider, *et al., op. cit.,* for a comment on this difference.

28 Jean Spencer Felton, "The Cornell Index Used As An Appraisal of Personality by an Industrial Health Service," *Industrial Medicine,* Vol. 18 (April 1949), pp. 133-144.

29 Fahy and Muschenheim, *loc. cit.*

30 A considerable literature is developing on the Indian's transition to an urban environment. For example, W. R. Hurt, Jr., "The Urbanization

of the Yankton Indian," *Human Organization,* Vol. 20 (Winter 1961-62), pp. 266-231; H. W. Martin, "Correlates of Adjustment Among American Indians in an Urban Environment," *Human Organization,* Vol. 23 (Winter 1964), pp. 290-295; J. Ablon, "Relocated American Indians in the San Francisco Bay Area," *Human Organization,* Vol. 23 (Winter 1964), pp. 296-304; R. L. Leon, "Maladaptive Interaction between Bureau of Indian Affairs Staff and Indian Clients," *American Journal of Orthopsychiatry,* Vol. 25 (July 1965), pp. 723-728; W. R. Hurt and R. M. Brown, "Social Drinking Patterns of the Yankton Sioux," *Human Organization,* Vol. 24 (Fall 1965), pp. 222-230.

31 The chi-square for men was 11.77 (P $<$ .001, 1 d. f.), but zero for women.

32 Chi-square = 7.96 (P $<$ .01, 1 d. f.).

33 With education of women grouped by years of schooling, i.e., less than 9, 10-11, and 12 or more years, chi-square = 20.92 (P $<$ .001, 2 d. f.).

34 Data on most of these studies are unreported; however, see: R. L. Leon, *et al.,* "The Cornell Index and Social Dependency," *Texas Reports on Biology and Medicine,* Vol. 21 (Spring 1963), pp. 12-15.

35 There are no doubt other plausible explanations. For example, some high-scorers may have made "good" social adjustments by internalizing their psychological conflicts which are experienced somatically. These symptoms call for a "yes" response on the Index which elevates the score. Brief psychiatric interviews, not specifically directed to detect such symptoms, will pick up only gross pathology.

36 Leo Srole, *et al., Mental Health in the Metropolis* (McGraw-Hill Book Company, Inc., New York, 1962), p. 138.

CHAPTER 6

THE URBAN INDIAN

Urban Indians have been invisible men. Their migration to the cities is decades old, although now they come in increasing numbers. As with almost all migrations, many of them have returned to their homes after a short time in the cities. But others have stayed and been "lost," statistically as well as, at times, psychologically.

Steiner has described the plight of the urban Indian in "The Cement Prairies." His account of their statistical invisibility is relevant:

> The U.S. Census Bureau counts Indians only when they so identify themselves, or are identifiable. And the city Indians often "pass" as whites. . . . Those who don't "pass" have been usually counted as "nonwhite"—a nearly invisible shade, it seems, when they happen to be Indians.
> The statistics of the Bureau of Indian Affairs have been as equalitarianly invisible, for the Bureau's concern has traditionally been the reservation Indian, and the cajoling of him to leave the reservation. Once he goes, however, the Bureau no longer counts him.
> So the city Indian has been an invisible man.[1]

Now there are indications that the invisibility of the urban Indian is coming to an end. Statistical information on them may remain fragmentary and inaccurate, but they are coming to be visible in other ways. Part of their new visibility is a consequence of "Red Power" movements and Pan-Indianism; part of it may derive from a late-awakening interest in Indian people by persons other than academic anthropologists. At least there is evidence that an increasing number of sociologists are joining the anthropologists as students of the Indian,[2] and the sociologist's traditional concern with the city bodes well for increased attention to city Indians by social scientists.

The first selection in this chapter, Bahr's "An End to Invisibility," is a discussion of the factors which have contributed to and sustained the long-term invisibility of the city Indian, and of the processes which have operated to increase the visibility and the political power of urban Indians. It is suggested that the federal relocation programs, designed to "submerge" the Indians in "mainstream" America, have had the unintended consequence of creating conditions which have fostered Pan-Indianism and provided the beginnings of a power base for Indian people.

Most of the research on Indian people in the cities has been concerned with their "adjustment" or "assimilation," with a primary, though not exclusive, focus on persons relocated under the BIA Employment Assistance programs. The second selection in this chapter, Joan Ablon's study of social interaction and Indian identity among relocatees in the San Francisco Bay area, emphasizes the role of the city in promoting "Indianness," and of Pan-Indianism as a device for maintaining Indian identity rather than a passing stage in the assimilation of Indian people into white society. Despite the fact that the Indian "community" maintained a somewhat tenuous identity (less than one-sixth of the adults she interviewed participated in the activities of Indian organizations), the "psychological awareness of Indian identity" is described as ever-present; the Indians tolerate whites but rarely form intimate relationships with them; and although the option to assimilate is open to them, few pass into white society. If jobs were available on the reservation, most would return there.

Ablon's work was limited by a relatively small sample (53 cases) and by a concentration upon Indian people who were relocated by the BIA; only five of her cases were "self-relocated." John Price's "The Migration and Adaptation of American Indians to Los Angeles" is the report of a study which avoided both these limitations. Price obtained basic data from a sample of 3000 Indians, supplemented by detailed "subjective" information from a subsample of 158 heads of households. Because his sampling universe included all identifiable Indians in the city, he is able to contrast the characteristics of persons relocated under BIA auspices with those who have come to the city on their own. Like Ablon, he sees Pan-Indianism as an enduring rather than transitional part of Indian life in urban America. But he also reports that acculturation and assimilation are taking place, with children much less likely than their parents to speak Indian language well, marriage rates with non-Indians increasing with each succeeding generation, and most respondents stating a preference for a mixed neighborhood including both whites and Indians over either all-white or an all-Indian neighborhood. Moreover, there are indications that as length of residence in the city increases, the pattern of adaptation to urban life becomes increasingly congruent with that of the general population. Price's analysis of tribal differences in urban adaptation leads him to conclude that over time Indian people whose present adaptation to the city is "weak" will come to manifest the "relatively full" adaptation which now characterizes members of the Five Civilized Tribes in Los Angeles, Indian people who "take their Indianness lightly" as only one of the several facets of their identity.

The most ambitious study of the adjustment of Indian migrants in cities that has been undertaken thus far is the Navajo Urban Relocation Research Project, directed by Theodore Graves. Using a variety of data-gathering techniques, including formal interviews with Indians and their employers, analysis of BIA records, participant observation and in-depth studies of selected individuals, Graves and his associates have carefully charted and evaluated the experience of Navaho migrants in Denver. In the article we have selected to represent that body of work, Graves uses a single indicator of adjustment—the frequency with which Indian migrants are arrested— and shows how variations in adjustment may be explained by a combination of factors including the Indian's marginal economic position, the nature of his parental role models, education and vocational training, his personal goals and future expectations, and the social pressures exerted by friends and family members. The conclusion he reaches is that problem drinking among Navahos is "an adaptive response to structural conditions" not necessarily linked to racial factors; thus, most Navaho drunkenness ". . . can be accounted for without recourse to the fact that our subjects are Indians." It is maintained that the most fundamental problem is the Indian's economic marginality; more than anything else, the migrant needs better jobs.

The selection by Sorkin is an analysis of certain aspects of Indian migration from a national perspective. He documents the educational selectivity of the migration to the cities, demonstrates that relocation results in economic and educational advancement, and projects an increasing need for relocation among reservation Indians. BIA relocation programs have not had much impact on unemployment among reservation Indians because they have been operated on a relatively small scale. If the economic status of Indian people is to be improved significantly, either the pace of industrialization of the reservations must be quickened or funding of the Employment Assistance Programs must be substantially increased.

The rapid growth of urban centers in the United States has created a situation in which some Indians become urbanites simply by remaining on the reservation. As the city expands, it may come to include all or part of a nearby reservation, and some of the cultural and legal problems attending this kind of urban sprawl have recently been summarized.[3] John Dowling's "A 'Rural' Indian Community in an Urban Setting" describes a related situation in which an Indian community has become part of Green Bay, Wisconsin. For the Oneidas in Green Bay, social distance has replaced territorial distance as a device for maintaining the integrity of the Indian community. Unlike most other cities, Green Bay did not show a dramatic increase in the number of Indians between 1940 and 1960. According to Dowling, the population remained fairly stable because young people migrated to other metropolitan centers to avoid the prejudice they perceived among Green Bay employers.

NOTES

1   Stan Steiner, *The New Indians* (New York: Harper & Row, 1968), pp. 176-177.

2   Examples of the relatively recent interest in Indian people by
     sociologists are the special session of the 1970 Rural Sociological
     Society Meetings devoted to "rural and urban adaptations of
     American Indians" and an extensive study of the development of
     indigenous leadership in American Indian communities conducted
     by Columbia University's Bureau of Applied Social Research. See
     Elisabeth Gemberling and Margaret Nelson, in collaboration with
     Sam D. Sieber, "The Role of Secondary Education in the
     Development of Indigenous Leadership in American Indian Com-
     munities," mimeographed (New York: Bureau of Applied Social
     Research, Columbia University, 1970).
3   Joe P. Sparks, "The Indian Stronghold and the Spread of Urban
     America," *Arizona Law Review*, 10 (Winter 1968), 706-724.

HOWARD M. BAHR: AN
END TO INVISIBILITY

To speak of "the urban Indian" is almost a contradiction in terms and
creates disturbing dissonances among cherished American stereotypes.
Usually, however, these dissonances are kept manageable by a fiction ably
and sometimes unwittingly fostered by the scriptwriters, cartoonists, and
even by many of the anthropologists to whom academia has relegated
matters Indian, the fiction that urban Indians are not "real" Indians, and
therefore their existence, when noticed, need not negate our stereotypes
about basic Indianness. To the general public, the anthropologists—we do
not speak of sociologists because most of them have impartially ignored
both rural *and* urban Indians—and even Indian people themselves the
realization that a very substantial proportion of the nation's Indian
population now dwell in cities has been slow coming.

ACCOUNTING FOR THE INVISIBILITY
OF URBAN INDIANS

Among the reasons for the late arrival of the social scientists on the
urban Indian scene is the informal but very real division of labor between
sociology and anthropology with respect to American racial minorities. It is
almost as if representatives of the two disciplines had agreed, "Anthropologists will take the American Indians, sociologists can have the American blacks." Anyone wishing to examine the real consequence of this
division of labor has only to spend a few minutes counting articles about

Indians in the major sociological journals, comparing their number with articles about American blacks in the same journals, and then watching the ratio "flip-flop" when he turns to the anthropological journals. Thus the sociologist, student of modern man and the metropolis, when confronted by the anomaly of the Indian in the city, has turned away ("Beware: you are about to encroach upon the sacred hunting ground of the anthropologist"), and the anthropologist has done the same thing, but for a different reason ("Beware: the culture you are about to observe is so adulterated by the ways of the white man that its study can only produce confusion").

The anthropologists have been absorbed in the study of the American preliterate, the traditional Indian whom they feared would soon vanish, and documenting his current "process of becoming," especially when that "becoming" included extensive involvement in modern metropolitan life, has been somehow less important than recording and analyzing the details of his unique past. Anthropological research on the Indian was based on the premise that Indian culture would change and disappear, a premise that lent urgency to the study of traditional Native American culture before it was too late.[1] The anthropologists focused on what was "really Indian" and tended to avoid the complications of the modern community "polluted" by extensive contact with representatives of white society.

Thus, the culture of the modern Indian has been ignored as "transitional," and to the extent that it is "modern," it is usually defined as un-Indian. Rosenthal asserts that the concept of culture is no longer a working tool, but a "sacred cow"—culture has become the traditional way of life, not the current pattern for living[2]—and culture as sacred cow so limits the field that the modern Indian community, especially the urban one, is largely outside the pale of legitimate interest. She illustrates the resulting confusion: "If most of the people in an Indian community speak English, if 80 percent are on relief, if we see alcoholism and wife-beating, if Elmer Comes-a-Flying goes to college, if the medicine bundle is in the basement of the council hall, and the tribal chairman is in town having dinner with a lawyer—what is there to see?"[3] The situation is even more unsettling if stated in terms of life in the metropolis. If the people ride the subway, work in downtown offices, and shop at Macy's, and their children attend P.S. 109, then surely there is nothing worth observing.

The results of this perspective have been remarked by several writers. The sociologist Murray Wax, after noting the dearth of studies on the urban Indian, concludes: "In the elegance and precision of our sociological tools, we have progressed far beyond Charles Booth, but—ironically—these tools prove most efficacious in surveying the stable elements of our nation (whose lives are bounded by home ownerships and jobs), while the poor in their desperate migrations continue to elude our chartings."[4] Similarly, Ablon notes the curious blindness of her anthropological colleagues: "Although American anthropologists have examined problems of urbanization in Latin America, Africa, and Asia, they have had little interest in following their native aborigines who leave the traditional cultural trappings of reservation life."[5]

One consequence of this research gap is an ignorance that impedes the planning and execution of programs aimed at ameliorating many of the negative consequences of urban migration. The social worker searches for leads and insights in a literature frequently irrelevant to his current problems:

> The anthropological literature is helpful background information, but much of it is not directly useful to Bureau of Indian Affairs program planners because the literature discusses the Alaskan native culture as it existed several decades ago. It is important to investigate the present problems of Eskimo and Indian cultures, particularly as they relate to the dominant white culture.[6]

Another negative outcome is that both Indian and white children are deprived of information about increasingly important aspects of Indian life. Textbooks tend to reflect the dominant interests of professional academicians. Hence, they have ignored the urban Indian. Striner's recent review of the status of Indian education included the recommendation that factual material about current Indian life was important for both Indian and non-Indian children if they were to achieve a balanced perspective.[7]

Another reason for the discrimination by academics against the urban Indian is his low profile. One of the factors attracting social scientists (as well as foundations, boards, citizens' councils, and other funding agencies) to a research topic is the extent to which a problem or population is readily visible, needs something done about it, is capable of being studied, and is "interesting" (read sexy, unusual, exotic, immoral, full of human interest, timely, threatening, unthinkable, or profitable). Where matters of "human interest," scholarly salience, and availability of subjects intersect, we may expect academic interest far out of proportion to that shown topics lacking such "triangulation" of theoretical and methodological advantages. An example of such an intersection of favorable factors is the skid-row man. There are more urban Indians than skid-row men (in 1960 the two populations were of comparable size[8]), but the former have been virtually ignored by students of urban life while the research literature on the latter seems far out of proportion to the importance of skid row as a social problem. The presence of the extensive literature on skid-row men may be explained by several facts: The homeless man evokes wonder, sometimes envy, certainly interest; he tends to be conveniently concentrated in one or more well-known sections of the city, so that, as Caplow puts it, "for the price of a subway ride he [the researcher] can enter a country where the accepted principles of social interaction do not apply";[9] and the very ecological concentration which makes the skid-row man readily available to the tourist, slummer, and social researcher also tends to make him obnoxious to his more orthodox neighbors, with the result that there are periodic attempts to "clean up" skid rows and to "relocate" the homeless men. Consequently, ready funding has been available to scientists who promised to provide useful insights or solutions.

In contrast, the urban Indian is not particularly visible, having "passed" into the white population to a considerable extent, and usually he does not dwell in large ecological concentrations. In fact, his residential dispersion is remarkable. Recently, anthropologists in Colorado established a theoretical definition of an ethnic enclave, observed the residential distribution of Navahos in Denver, their social interaction frequencies and acquaintance with other Navahos in the city, and concluded that the Navaho in Denver could not be described as living in an enclave.[10] A similar situation has been shown to exist in major cities in the state of Washington, where Indians are far more dispersed than any other nonwhite minority,[11] and in Albuquerque.[12] Even if researchers want to study Indians in cities, their dispersion makes field work difficult and expensive, and consequently, studies have tended to concentrate on Indians hooked into a particular agency, usually a BIA relocation office. Even then, since the BIA has had little research money,[13] the researcher has had to be self-motivated enough to secure funds from somewhere on his own, and hence studies have tended to have small samples.

Moreover, the urban Indian is not particularly good journalistic copy. Lacking headdress and beads, he seems "just like anyone else" and attracts no special attention. Besides, the unspoken argument goes, he lacks a future. The urban Indian is on his way to assimilation, is a "vanishing Native American," and to study him in the city is to catch him "in process" between identities and in fact neither traditional Native American nor assimilated modern man, so what have you? Conceptually hard-to-define, lacking human interest (now, if only he would riot or liberate some federal property . . .), not clustered for ready observability, and not posing a particular problem for anyone (his problems tend to be his own, since to a great extent he hasn't known how to "lean on" city bureaucracies to make his problems their's[14]), the Native American in the city has been a stranger, his influence diminished by his invisibility to the public, and his plight (whatever it is) accorded a low priority by city, state, and federal agencies.

FEDERAL RELOCATION PROGRAMS

In 1947, federal funds were appropriated for a Labor Recruitment and Welfare program for the Navaho and Hopi reservations. Indians seeking employment opportunities were to be relocated in Denver, Los Angeles, Phoenix, and Salt Lake City. A national program of relocation assistance was undertaken in 1952 and expanded in 1957. In 1962 the "Voluntary Relocation Program" was renamed the "Employment Assistance Program," and its activity was broadened to include job placement on or near reservations, as well as in certain metropolitan areas.[15] BIA employment assistance centers are maintained in Chicago, Cleveland, Dallas, Denver, Los Angeles, Oakland, San Jose, Tulsa, Oklahoma City, and Seattle. As currently administered, the program helps Indians find jobs (direct employment assistance) or to acquire training to increase their employability (adult vocational training). A recent report from a BIA area office lists the several goals of the Employment Assistance Program:

(1) Develop employment opportunities for Indian people with some degree of skill who are employable but unable to find jobs. (2) Make available institutional training for all Indian boarding school and public school graduates who do not plan to or cannot go on to higher education. (3) Provide on-the-job training for the unskilled to meet the labor demands of the increased industrial development occurring on or near Indian reservations. (4) Provide vocational counseling and guidance to the unemployed or under-employed reservation Indians. (5) Participate in community development programs on the reservation and provide work orientation and motivation.[16]

Although writers about the program stress its voluntariness,[17] this is a fiction to the extent that the white man has structured the alternatives in such a way that economic pressures force the Indian to relocate. The incentives might just as well be structured the other way, and at a time when welfare burdens in the city are already too high, such a restructuring would seem appropriate. If the Indian people truly are to have freedom of choice, they must have the option of remaining on or near the reservation and still being able to support themselves. The current BIA program, in effect, says to the Indian, "either conform to the Anglo way and move several hundred miles away from the reservation or stay . . . and live at substandard levels."[18]

DIMENSIONS OF THE MIGRATION

The BIA estimates that in the past decade about 200,000 Indian people have moved to urban areas.[19] Over half of these migrants came on their own, continuing the "rurban" life style that had become part of Indian culture even before relocation to the cities became federal policy.[20] The remainder were assisted in some way by BIA programs.[21] Many of these migrants were only temporary urbanites who "raided" the city without becoming a permanent part of it (a custom not peculiar to Indian people, and practiced with notable success by numerous white city-haters, who venture into the city only long enough to "take" whatever city resource they seek, and then return to the quiet countryside or rustic suburbia to "live" again).

Census data on Indians are notoriously unreliable, and estimates by agencies or informed individuals frequently are not much better; but, as students of suicide have demonstrated, fairly reliable indications of trends can be derived from comparisons of figures whose absolute validity is questionable. The trend toward Indian residence in the cities is readily apparent in statistics from individual cities. For example, the number of Indian people in Minneapolis (Hennepin County) increased fivefold between 1950 and 1960, rising from 426 to 2,391; by 1967 the total was near 5,000, and in December, 1969, there were about 10,000 Indians in Minneapolis.[22] In 1965 the Milwaukee Indian population was estimated at 2,000; by 1969 that figure had doubled.[23] The Indian population of Los

Angeles doubled between 1960 and 1966;[24] that of Seattle increased from about 2,000 in 1960 to an estimated 6,000 *families* in 1969.[25] Thus, viewed either from the perspective of the Indian population as a whole or with reference to changes in the number of Indian people who reside in a particular metropolitan area, the conclusion is the same: A spectacular population shift is under way.

If in the past decade one-third of the nation's Indian population has moved to urban areas, it is obvious that Indian culture is now, in part, urban culture. Even if a large proportion of the urban Indian people eventually leave the city, it cannot be denied that the urban experience has become a major, if not dominant, element determining the attitudes, behavior, and values of Native Americans. In fact, it seems probable that in terms of long-term consequences for Indian culture, the movement of Indians to cities that began in midcentury may be as significant as their earlier forced removal to reservations.

AN END TO INVISIBILITY

All indications are that the rate of migration will continue and perhaps increase. BIA relocation programs already operate on such a scanty budget that a sizable proportion of applicants are denied assistance, and it is projected that "unless industrialization of the reservation occurs at a far more rapid pace than it has in recent years, the need for relocation of American Indians to secure their economic advancement will likely grow more urgent."[26] Expansion of the relocation program will place the government in the paradoxical position of continuing to foster the migration of disadvantaged minority individuals to metropolitan centers at a time when the government leaders have endorsed a policy of rural development which is aimed at halting the tide of immigration to the cities and encouraging industrial and population dispersion.[27]

Even more ironic is the apparent consequence for Indian political power of the urban relocation. Government officials have abetted relocation under the assumption that it would bring Indians into the "mainstream." In the words of the late Senator Watkins of Utah, "The sooner we can get the Indians into cities the sooner the government can get out of the Indian business."[28] But the unintended consequence appears to be the creation of conditions which have fostered Pan-Indianism. In cities bordering on reservations the ready accessibility of Indian companions and the proximity of the reservation may operate to dilute the impact of the urban environment. It is hard for the urbanite Indian to "drown in the mainstream" when the reservation is only a half-hour away. In contrast, for the relocatee in cities like Los Angeles or Chicago, "home" is a long way off, and the Indian who comes directly from the reservation may experience severe culture shock and a direct threat to his identity. A normal response to feelings of being "lost" in an alien culture is to seek out others like oneself and to reaffirm a threatened identity by celebrating common elements of the threatened culture. Thus the relocation of relatively unassimilated Indians to major urban centers far removed from reservations has tended to increase their sense of Indian identity, as well as teaching them the ways of the city.

Urban Indians, like most immigrants, are younger and better educated than nonimmigrants, and they are more willing to fight "the system" than their brothers on the reservation. Formerly hopelessly divided, they have begun to overlook tribal differences in the face of their common antagonist, the white man. They have established their own urban centers in most major cities, and numerous pressure organizations representing all shades of political orientation have established programs aimed at achieving justice for Indian people. These organizations are in a position to exert pressure in ways that separate tribes never could.

The existence and vitality of Indian organizations in urban areas suggests that Indian people have recognized that they are in the cities to stay. This recognition is reflected in the request by the militant American Indian Movement (AIM) that the Department of the Interior redesign BIA to serve urban Indians as well as reservation Indians, and that sizable sums be allocated to urban Indian programs.[29]

Thus the migration of Indian people to cities, rather than "submerging" them in the mainstream, has created conditions which have enhanced Indian identity and have led to the establishment of a Pan-Indian power base. The recent emergence of a genuine Indian press,[30] combined with the proliferation of Indian organizations and the increasing sophistication and numerical strength of urban Indians, portends a situation in which the federal government will have to "do business" with an increasingly powerful antagonist. It seems probable that as a consequence of pressures exerted by these "new" Indians, the level of federal outlays for Native Americans will increase substantially rather than decline.

NOTES

1 Elizabeth Clark Rosenthal, "'Culture' and the American Indian Community," in Stuart Levine and Nancy Oestreich Lurie, eds., *The American Indian Today* (Deland, Florida: Everett/Edwards), p. 48.

2 *Ibid.*, p. 51.

3 *Ibid.*, p. 50.

4 Murray L. Wax, "The White Man's Burdensome 'Business': A Review Essay on the Change and Constancy of Literature on the American Indians," *Social Problems*, 16 (Summer 1968), 113.

5 Joan Ablon, "Relocated American Indians in the San Francisco Bay Area: Social Interaction and Indian Identity," *Human Organization*, 4 (Winter 1964), 296.

6 Robert L. Leon, Harry W. Martin, and John H. Gladfelter, "An Emotional and Educational Experience for Urban Migrants," *American Journal of Psychiatry*, 124 (September 1967), 383-384.

7 Herbert E. Striner, "Toward a Fundamental Program for the Training, Employment and Economic Equality of the American Indian," a paper from *Federal Programs for the Development of Human Resources,*

submitted to the Subcommittee on Economic Progress of the Joint Economic Committee, Congress of the United States, Vol. 1, Part II, Manpower and Education, March 1968, p. 302.

8 Donald J. Bogue, *Skid Row in American Cities* (Chicago: University of Chicago Community and Family Study Center, 1963), pp. 5-8.

9 Theodore Caplow, "The Sociologist and the Homeless Man," in Howard M. Bahr, ed., *Disaffiliated Man: Essays and Bibliography on Homelessness, Vagrancy, and Skid Row* (Toronto: University of Toronto Press 1970), pp. 1-8.

10 Peter Zane Snyder, "The Social Assimilation and Adjustment of Navaho Indian Migrants to Denver, Colorado," (doctoral dissertation, University of Colorado, 1968).

11 Calvin. F. Schmid, Charles E. Noble, and Arlene E. Mitchell, *Nonwhite Races State of Washington* (Olympia: Washington State Planning and Community Affairs Agency, 1968), pp. 57-76.

12 William H. Hodge, *The Albuquerque Navajos,* Anthropological Papers of the University of Arizona, no. 11 (Tucson: University of Arizona Press, 1969), p. 43.

13 Striner, *op. cit.,* p. 324, has characterized as "shocking" the "total absence of research demonstration funds in the BIA budget." This absence is particularly troublesome in view of two other deficiencies he documents, namely the "grossly inadequate" available socioeconomic data about Indians and the BIA's limited access to consultants.

14 For example, Ablon reports that Indians receive little aid from community agencies because few of them are "sufficiently aggressive to pursue assistance" and because they are only "dimly aware" of existing agencies. Instead, the Indian family reacts to chronic problems by leaving the city. See Joan Ablon, "American Indian Relocation: Problems of Dependency and Management in the City," *Phylon,* 26 (Winter 1965), 370.

15 William Metzler, "Relocation of the Displaced Worker," *Human Organization,* 22 (Summer 1963), 142-145.

16 Arizona Commission of Indian Affairs, "Annual Report, 1967-1968," mimeographed, 1968, p. 27.

17 For example, see Stanley Weber and Virginia S. Hart, "Vocational Programs for American Indians," *School Shop,* 24 (May 1965), 17-18; Alan L. Sorkin, "Some Aspects of American Indian Migration," *Social Forces,* 48 (December 1969); and Metzler, *op. cit.*

18 Donald F. Harvey and Bernard E. Anderson, "The Navajo: The Widening Cultural Gap," unpublished manuscript, Navajo Employment Adjustment Project, Northern Arizona University, p. 26.

19 Bureau of Indian Affairs, United States Department of the Interior, *Answers to your Questions about American Indians* (Washington, D.C.: U.S. Government Printing Office, 1968), p. 23.

20 Levine has characterized the migration of Indians to cities early in this century:

> Indian people seemed to . . . find their way to industrial employment in the cities in a manner reminiscent of hunting, trading or war expeditions. They drifted back home periodically to seek help from relatives if they were broke or to share the spoils of the 'hunt' with their kinsmen until it was necessary to forage again. They took to automobiles as enthusiastically as many had taken to ponies at an earlier time, becoming commuters to cities or other palces where they could find work, returning to their tribesmen upon retirement. And these

patterns persist today. Unlike the usual migrants, Indian people do not seem to perceive urban work as a break with the rural past, but merely as an extension of the peripheries of the territory which can be exploited economically. It is difficult to escape the conclusion that Indian people were "rurban" long before anyone coined the term or saw the industrial blending of city and country life as the direction in which the nation as a whole was to move.

Levine and Lurie, *op. cit.*, p. 40.

21 Sorkin, *op. cit.*, p. 244.
22 Dean A. Crawford, Avid L. Peterson, and Virgin Wurr, *Minnesota Chippewa Indians: A Handbook for Teachers* (St. Paul: Upper Midwest Regional Education Laboratory, 1967), p. 89; Hilda Bryant, "Loneliness is the White Man's City," *Seattle Post Intelligencer,* December 14, 1969.
23 Joyce M. Erdman, *Handbook on Wisconsin Indians* (Madison: Governor's Commission on Human Rights), p. 50; and Nancy Oestreich Lurie, "Wisconsin Indians: Lives and Lands," *Wisconsin Magazine of History,* 53 (Autumn 1969), 3.
24 John A. Price, "The Migration and Adaptation of American Indians to Los Angeles," *Human Organization,* 27 (Summer 1968), 169.
25 Schmid et al., *op. cit.*, p. 68; Bryant, *op. cit.*
26 Sorkin, *op. cit.*, p. 249.
27 See, for example, The President's Task Force on Rural Development, *A New Life for the Country* (Washington, D.C.: U.S. Government Printing Office, March 1970).
28 Bryant, *op. cit.*
29 *Ibid.*
30 See Jeannette Henry, "The Indian Press, A Slow Development," *The Indian Historian,* 1 (Winter 1968), 15-17.

JOAN ABLON: RELOCATED AMERICAN INDIANS IN THE SAN FRANCISCO BAY AREA: SOCIAL INTERACTION AND INDIAN IDENTITY*

INTRODUCTION

The urbanization of American Indians has been occurring on a small scale for many years as individuals and families have quietly slipped into city life. The process has been intensified in the past decade through official government relocation programs. This recent influx of large numbers of Indians into metropolitan areas represents the formation of a new urban ethnic group that holds special research interest for the anthro-

Source: Reprinted by permission from *Human Organization* 23 (Winter 1964), 296-304.

pologist. Although American anthropologists have examined problems of urbanization in Latin America, Africa and Asia, they have had little interest in following their native aborigines who leave the traditional cultural trappings of reservation life. There are few published statements in the anthropological literature dealing with American Indians who have settled in cities.[1]

This article will focus on the nature of the new relationships that are conceived and maintained by persons coming from kin-oriented, relatively closed communities to large metropolitan centers. Early sociological studies of rural-urban migrations emphasized the breakdown of primary social bonds and the problems that resulted from ensuing social alienation. Recent urban studies have highlighted strengthened kindred bonds and new forms of social interaction that develop in the metropolitan setting. The factors of background, class, and ethnicity all appear to contribute to the form and nature of new relationships on the individual and formal group levels.

The present article will attempt to show that American Indians who have come to the Bay Area have chosen to associate primarily with other Indians of their own or differing tribes in both informal and formal social interaction. The fact of self-conscious Indianness appears to determine the choice of Indian relationships—a choice that usually precludes intermingling with non-Indians either in social groups or on an individual intimate friendship basis. The ever-present psychological and social awareness of Indian identity comprises an important positive factor in the maintenance of the urban pan-Indian activities of Indian social centers, dance groups, churches, and other Indian organizations in the Bay Area.

American Indians bring to the city a diversity of tribal and accultura-tive backgrounds, but a common heritage of participation in small rural folk communities with a basis of aboriginal tradition, and a dependent relationship with the white world as symbolized by their long and often painful association with the Bureau of Indian Affairs. The reservations they leave are economically underdeveloped areas, but constitute communities which have provided some degree of security and social control for the individual, and have acted as buffers against the immediate encroachments of white culture. The peculiarity of the position of American Indians as an ethnic group stems from a number of facts which are crucial to their potential adjustment in white urban life. The most important of these is a basic antagonism to white society that has developed from a history of rejection and discrimination. American Indians perforce have had their traditional cultures decimated in one way or another, and have been drawn often unwillingly into the mainstream of American life. Highly important also is the fact that many fundamental Indian values are not only incompatible with those of American culture, but work directly in opposi-tion to the principles on which the modern competitive capitalistic order is based. Indians generally do not want to compete with others. They would rather share money or material goods than budget and save. They will not often speak out to complain or to demand their rights. A basic tribal world view defining the interrelationships of man with his society and the world around him, and the paternalistic nature of Bureau administration of Indian community affairs have helped produce complex and deeply entrenched attitudes of dependency which greatly hinder adjustment to the practical demands of urban life.

THE SAN FRANCISCO BAY AREA

Current estimates by Indian organizations and by white agencies which deal with Indians place the number of Indians in the San Francisco Bay Area at about 10,000, representing some one hundred tribal groups.[2] The majority of these persons have relocated through government relocation programs but about one-third have come on their own resources. Formal aids to Indian migration have been Indian school placement, Santa Fe Railroad employment, and the current Bureau of Indian Affairs Employment Assistance Program (formerly called Voluntary Relocation Program) and the Adult Vocational Training Program. The Bureau operates field relocation centers in San Francisco, Oakland, and San Jose to administer these programs.

The Bay Area has long been an attractive destination for Indians who have relocated on their own initiative. The three metropolitan centers offer a diversity of employment opportunities, vocational schools, social groups, and varied amusements for relocatees. Indians are only one of a number of ethnic groups in the area, and they generally encounter little of the open discrimination that they traditionally have faced near their reservations. Many Indians who were stationed here during World War II chose to return after the war, often bringing their families with them. Others migrated to the area in the war years to work in defense industry and remained.

The data on which the present paper is based were drawn from those gathered for a broader study of the nature and persistence of cultural tradition and identity of relocatees who have settled in the Bay Area.[3] Traditional anthropological techniques of observation, participant-observation, and interviewing were used over a period of about 18 months in 1961-1962. Intensive study was carried out with two groups of relocatees: Families who were brought in through the federal Voluntary Relocation Program in the first year of its operation in the area, 1954-1955, and who had remained here until the time of the study were of special interest. Thirty-four persons or families of the first 200 who relocated were traced and interviewed. Informants were highly skeptical that many more remained in the area from the pioneer group. A second general group of nineteen additional families was studied. Fourteen of the latter came through government-sponsored programs in the years following 1955, and five families were self-relocated, some having come to the Bay Area as early as 1941. Seventeen tribes were represented within the two groups, with the largest numbers of persons coming from the Navaho, Sioux, and Turtle Mountain Chippewa tribes. These tribes have consistently contributed large numbers of families from their reservations to relocation centers across the country. During the course of the study more casual and incomplete information was gathered for about 25 other families.

Individual situations varied, but a commonality of process and Indian response to the relocation program became readily apparent. From a consideration of the Bureau of Indian Affairs files on those individuals and families who returned, it appears that the education, acculturation experiences, and economic and social backgrounds of those who remained were similar to the backgrounds of those who returned. During the early years of the Voluntary Relocation Program more than three-fourths of the persons who relocated returned home. The current return figure is estimated by the Bureau at 35 percent.

The relocatees (single persons and family heads) exhibited a wide variety of educational experiences and former contacts with whites. About half were veterans, and most had interacted with whites in some form of previous work experience. Most persons came on relocation because they could not find steady employment on their reservations. The incentive to find employment often was compounded by a variety of personal and family problems which contributed to the decision to leave the reservation area. Most had the majority of their close relatives still living on their home reservations, although a great many have had some of their own or their spouses' siblings in the Bay Area at some time since their arrival.

Indians are employed in a very wide range of unskilled, semi-skilled, and skilled positions in both large and small industrial enterprises and in service fields in all three relocation centers. Most Indians, however, come to the city as unskilled or semi-skilled workers, and encounter a shifting job market that requires more and more skilled persons each year. Lay-offs are common, and hit the unskilled worker particularly hard. Personal attitudes toward work often appear to be more important in the retention of jobs than previous training or sophistication in the complexities of unions or of the job market. For this reason many unskilled and uneducated persons are able to retain jobs they consider "dirty" or unpleasant that the more educated and acculturated Indians would reject, because the former with a desire for job security well realize their disadvantage in employment competition.

Such domestic problems as the drinking and violence common to many Indian families do not appear to be peculiar results of the shift from rural to urban life, but rather characteristic features of reservation family and social disorganization which are carried to the city and intensified by new pressures and the departure from the stability of immediate family and community. In some instances the move to the city which takes a family away from dependent or heavy-drinking relatives improves the domestic situation.

The stated Bureau housing policy is to disperse Indians among the general population to further the goal of assimilation. Most of the families contacted in the course of my research lived in Oakland because the first field relocation office was set up in this area. About one-fifth of the cases in the two groups studied lived in other metropolitan areas around the Bay. Most relocatees live in typical working class housing, and many have taken advantage of low-rent housing projects. One large housing project in Oakland has continually attracted a relatively large number of Indian families. Most families in the groups studied have moved at least three or four times since their arrival in the area. A few relocatees are buying their own homes, but this does not necessarily reflect a definite intent or commitment to remain in the area. Indeed, common responses suggest that most relocatees now living in the Bay Area would return home to their reservations immediately if they could find employment there. The absence of employment opportunities and the associated social problems characteristic of most reservations preclude the presentation of legitimate alternatives in the choice of whether to attempt relocation or to be satisfied with an impoverished welfare-based existence in the home community.

SOCIAL INTERACTION AMONG INDIANS IN THE BAY AREA

Informal Social Interaction

Informal interaction consists of visits to the homes of other Indians, and of contacts with persons in bars or in other public places. Each of the major relocation centers has several "Indian bars" in the central districts where many Indian men and women of a variety of tribes congregate and meet new friends and sexual partners. Others visit bars only on payday, or stop by on holidays for a few drinks. Many Indians begin friendships with persons of other tribes whom they meet in the Bureau offices or spot as being Indian and approach in stores, clinics, or on the street. Such chance encounters may lead to invitations for home visits.

Home visiting occurs chiefly among persons related through the ties of kinship, tribal affiliation, or prior acquaintance on the reservation, or among persons who have met as a result of contacts in Indian groups, through common church attendance, proximity of residence, or association at work. Persons who have siblings, parents, or cousins in the area usually see them with some frequency, and feel obliged to give them help when needed. In general all Indians and especially the Sioux tend to feel the responsibility of helping their kinsmen or tribesmen when asked, and will give money, food, or lodging to a needy family. The flexibility of the Indian household often seems to be infinite, and most Indian families assume that there is always room for five or six additional persons at their table or for lodging, no matter how small the actual living quarters may be. Some families have been known to leave town or to keep their place of residence secret because they were burdened with responsibilities for aiding others, and did not feel they could refuse assistance if asked for it.

Informal gatherings of a number of families of one tribe occur infrequently. The most regular informal gatherings occurred in the groups observed among the Turtle Mountain Chippewas who meet in couples groups in homes, for spring and summer baseball games, and in larger parties, such as at annual New Year's gatherings. At New Years most of the families in the Oakland area converge on several generous hosting families, and over spreads of food and drink converse animatedly in Chippewa, Cree, French, and English and many of the men dance a lively jig when sufficiently intoxicated. A common activity is to go to the home of the oldest relocatee in the area and pay him respect in a traditional French-Canadian manner. In the early years of relocation Turtle Mountain families gathered more frequently for bar parties and picnics. The parties have diminished because most of the original relocatees have returned to the reservation, and the heavy drinking and ensuing quarrels and fights served to discourage many wives from attendance. Although some families speak of the *esprit de corps* of the Turtle Mountain people and of their aid to one another in times of hardship, many complain that their old friends and relatives did not help them when they needed it, nor were people fulfilling their godparent obligations. Most Turtle Mountain relocatees are lively and verbal. They are universally the mixed-bloods from that reservation, of French Canadian and Salteaux descent, and they are relatively well acculturated.[4] They often comment that because they are mixed-bloods, they are not like other Indians and do not maintain traditional customs or dances. They associate largely with other Turtle Mountain families or with whites. Few have established relationships with Indians of other tribes.

Navahos most frequently tend to associate almost exclusively with other Navahos, usually persons of their own age group who are relatives or whom they have met through common housing or at formal events. Navahos are more restricted socially than persons from other tribes, chiefly because of their sheltered tribal background, a reserved manner that quickly becomes intensified when among non-Navahos, and by a strong fear of English language inadequacy. Many Navahos began school at a relatively late age and went through hasty accelerated programs. Even those who have worked outside of the reservation often limited their association to their Navaho workmates and spoke to whites as infrequently as possible. Their sensitivity about their halting speech often generates a pervading anxiety about dealing with non-Navaho speakers. A Navaho Club has recently been formed in Oakland but the attendance has not exceeded a dozen persons and the small group has already been paralyzed by factions. Most of the hundreds of Navahos in the area do not appear to take an active interest in any kind of formal activity, Navaho, pan-Indian, or white.

Sioux families usually engage in frequent home visiting with relatives or tribesmen. Several annual all-Sioux events have been held, but little formal organization has materialized despite attempts of several families to unite the many Sioux of the area into a social or political group.

Formal Interaction

Any formulation of a viable definition of an "Indian Community" in the sense of an organized, visible body of persons who interrelate with regularity in socially meaningful ways must turn to the many active social, religious, and political Indian organizations of the Bay Area, rather than to any network of relationships encompassing individuals or families. Some sixteen specific organizations which were organized for Indian participation (although often sponsored and staffed by whites) existed in the three relocation centers at the time of my study. The activities of a number of Indian baseball and basketball teams were also focal points for social interaction. Since the conclusion of the study, Navaho, Eskimo, Chippewa, and Tlingit-Haida clubs are in the process of organization. The following groups existed in 1961-1962:

Oakland	San Francisco
Intertribal Friendship House	American Indian Center
Four Winds Club	American Indian Baptist Church
American Indian Baptist Church	Methodist Baptist Interdenomina-
Santa Fe Indian Village	tional Fellowship
	Indian Holiness (Pentecostal) Church
	Native American Church

San Jose	General Area Groups
San Jose Dance Club	American Indian Council of the Bay
American Indian Council of Santa	Area
Clara Valley	American Indian Youth Council of
American Indian Alcoholics Anony-	the Bay Area
mous	Haskell Institute Alumni
American Indian Baptist Church	Indian Baseball and Basketball Teams

The most influential organizations are the Intertribal Friendship House, the San Francisco American Indian Center, the Four Winds Club, The Oakland American Indian Baptist Church, the San Jose Dance Club, and the American Indian Council of the Bay Area. The Santa Fe Indian Village was for many years a unique self-contained social entity.[5]

Indian Dancing and Pow-wows

Pow-wows, social gatherings where Indian traditional dancing and singing are featured, are sponsored monthly by the San Jose Dance Club and recently, by the American Indian Council of the Bay Area each month at the San Francisco Indian Center. Occasionally other groups will sponsor pow-wows, and several times a year a special pow-wow is held by a Kiowa or Sioux family to commemorate a personal occasion such as a birthday or the arrival or departure of visiting relatives. There are usually from twenty to forty costumed dancers, some of whom may have come from Los Angeles or Nevada for the event. The core group of drummers and singers are mostly men from Oklahoma Plains tribes and Sioux. Many of the dancers and singers did not participate in pow-wows at home because of lack of interest or religious prohibitions. The audience at local pow-wows usually numbers from 100 to 200 persons, almost all Indians. Perhaps a grand total of some 300 or 400 persons will attend pow-wows in the area throughout a year. In contrast to dancing activities on the reservations, local pow-wows are usually free from drinking.

"The Indian Community"

The reality of an actual Indian community is indeed tenuous when considered in the perspective of the total Indian population in the area, notwithstanding the number and frequency of activities sponsored by Indian organizations. Less than one-sixth of the adult Indians are effectively touched by the activities. Probably not more than thirty adults are regularly active in more than one club. It is no coincidence that the stable core of planners of most of the organizations is often the same persons. Indeed, the continuing existence of the groups and the number of functions which are held attest to the vigor and abilities of the small group of planners.

Characteristic of the operation of the groups are a lack of authoritarian leadership, a general practice of group participation in planning, and a frequent absence of concrete pre-event duty assignment (with much complaining afterward about the often resulting confusion). The planning group for the most part appears to receive obvious personal gratification through the arranging of functions, and from the "busy work" of the planning sessions and the actual events. However, few of these persons are personal friends, nor have their years of mechanical association given them a strong friendship solidarity. It may be observed that the majority of the planners moved away from their reservations long ago, and are accustomed to participation in Indian center activities, and to relating to Indians of other tribes and to whites with some degree of ease. Although actually exhibiting more white patterns of aggressiveness and action than many Indians exhibit, they are not "white man's Indians," i.e., ones who accommodate themselves in order to win approval from whites. To the contrary, they often are the most vocal in expressing belligerency against whites, and extolling a fierce pride in Indian identity. These planners, however, seem more able to form close personal ties with individual white friends than many Indians are able to do.

Many persons have noted ironically that they had to move to the city before they developed a real interest in Indian affairs or Indian dancing. On the other hand, many persons who participated in these activities at home before relocation or who participate when they return for visits do not take part in activities here. No pow-wow activities include Navaho singing or dancing, and the few Navahos who dance here have accustomed themselves to Plains music and dance forms. It would seem that many Indians do not care for an artificial pow-wow without benefit of home community, relatives, friends, and the serving of traditional foods. Although many do care to join in pan-Indian dancing, others find no necessity to recharge or reify their Indianness nor do they think of pan-Indian activities as relevant to their personal Indian identity or tribal interests. The subject of pan-Indianism will be discussed in a later section of this paper.

SOURCES OF SOCIAL INTERACTION

First Social Interaction

The following responses were given by the two groups interviewed in the course of my study to questions asking where first or early social contacts in the Bay Area were made. Some broadly interpreted this to mean the first year after their arrival. Most gave more than one response. "Early cases" are those 34 family heads or individuals who arrived in the first year of the Relocation Program in the Bay Area, 1954-1955. "Additional cases" refers to the group of 19 families who came in later years on the Relocation Program or who relocated through their own initiative and resources.

	Early Cases	Additional Cases
Intertribal Friendship House	23	13
San Francisco Center	3	0
San Jose early groups	2	2
Four Winds Club	2	1
Church groups	5	8
Bureau sponsored events or through the relocation process	6	3
Neighborhood	3	4
Public Housing projects	7	2
Work	9	2
"Around" (stores or public places)	2	2
Bars	3	2
Through known Indians	4	0
Knew from home	10	10
Relatives	2	11
No formal Indian activities	2	3

The early relocatees arrived when there were few formal Indian organizations or channels for expressly meeting Indian people. The setting up of the now existing centers was in progress in 1955. It appears there occurred in the early pioneering days of the relocation program a first searching for social contacts and friendship relations in places where one could find other Indians.

Continuing Social Interaction

The following responses were given to questions asking about the sources of continuing social contact during years of residence in the area:

	Early Cases	Additional Cases
Intertribal Friendship House	6	5
Intertribal Friendship House infrequently	13	4
San Francisco Indian Center	2	2
San Francisco Indian Center infrequently	3	1
San Jose social groups	1	2
San Jose social groups infrequently	2	1
Four Winds Club	2	2
Four Winds Club infrequently	7	2
Church groups	5	8
Neighborhood	13	9
Public housing projects	4	4
Work	18	5
"Around" (stores or public places)	8	1
Bars	2	1
Knew from home	6	12
Relatives	18	15
Never attended Indian events	3	3
Rarely attended Indian events	8	9

After the seeking-out period, the pattern for attendance at group functions shifted and the social interaction developed along diverse lines. As many persons changed jobs and places of residence they took on new friendships in these activity areas. Some began attending church services and made contacts there. Many had large families who settled in the area, and thenceforth free time was given to visiting and recreation with relatives. As the nuclear families of many young relocatees grew they stopped attending formal community functions and became "homebodies" as many labeled themselves. The hiring of paid babysitters is almost unknown to Indians, unless they are the babysitters being hired. Some families may have a relative living in to babysit if the wife works. Unless there is such a relative or a friend to help with the children, most spend their evenings at home. Sunny weekends may be given to outings or home visiting if all the family are well, the car is running, and there is money for gas.

Most families leveled their formal social interaction to attendance at only the largest Indian events such as Christmas parties, the annual Indian Day picnic, or more rarely a Four Winds dance or a pow-wow. Some supplemented these with an occasional look-in at the Intertribal Friendship House or the San Francisco Center. Thus the formal groups often served to stabilize many wobbly new relocatees and allow them the security of an Indian meeting place and an opportunity to interact with others like themselves with the same problems as they adjusted to their new city life.

Although it has been frequently stated in the literature that participation in voluntary formal groups is an important part of urban social intercourse, research among lower status groups points out that formal social interaction is more generally characteristic of the educated, upper classes.[6] Dotson reported that among the working class urban families he studied in New Haven, formal social groups were relatively unimportant areas of social interaction. The most frequent and regular interaction occurred among small cliques which were frequently composed of kindred.[7] Bell and Boat also concluded from their research in San Francisco that kindred are more likely to provide close personal friendships than neighbors and co-workers.[8] Among the Indian families that I interviewed, those who had relatives in the area usually spent a great deal of their free time with them.

Zimmer, who studied the participation of migrants in urban structures in a Mid-Western town found the chief factors affecting speed of participation in formal groups of the community to be the length of residence, the nature of prior life experience of the migrant, education, and type of work.[9] He found that rural manual laborers and those of the lowest education entered community activities at the slowest rate. While Indians ideally would be expected to enter formal activities at the slowest rate, then, because most are of rural background, are manual laborers, and generally have a low level of education, the majority of cases in my study approached Indian social centers soon after their arrival. The decisive factor in determining this pattern which differs from the urban working class norm appears to be that of ethnicity.

SOCIAL INTERACTION WITH WHITES

The proportion of Indian as opposed to white friendships maintained by the adults in the cases studied are presented in the following tabulation:

	Early Cases	Additional Cases
Associate only with other Indians	7	4
All Indian with exception of one or several special dependency relations with older whites	3	2
Mixed Indian and white, mostly Indian	15	10
Mixed Indian and white, about equal	7	2
All white with exception of one or two Indians	2	0
All white	0	1
	34	19

Although many Indians responded that they had white friends as well as Indian, I soon determined that most relationships established with whites were relatively superficial ones, consisting of those with workmates along side of whom they worked or ate lunch, and with white neighbors with whom they sometimes exchanged pleasantries or had a cup of coffee. Usually such relationships with whites could be classified more accurately as acquaintances as one relocatee suggested when he talked about the relationships he had made on the job. Another type of white friendship was enjoyed by several young Navaho couples and several Sioux families who developed a form of highly functional dependency relationship with older white couples who loyally responded to the obvious emotional, practical, or financial needs of the Indians.

True friendship relations as used here would be characterized by an egalitarian quality, reciprocal home hospitality, and exchanges of confidences concerning personal affairs or problems. This kind of relationship most often occurred only between Indians. The determinants of Indian-white relationships are a complex blending of positive personal desires, and negative inhibitions shaped by background cultural and personal experiences with whites. Most Indians, particularly full-bloods, have had little opportunity to enjoy an egalitarian relationship with a white. Indians have experienced such constant economic and social rejection from whites who live around the peripheries of their reservations or who lease reservation lands, that they often are suspicious of white overtures of friendship, and suspect some objective of white gain to Indian disadvantage.[10]

While the friendly white may be viewed with suspicion, at the same time, because of the characteristic white role as a government official or as a local health or welfare worker, whites are viewed functionally as persons to be used and relied upon in specific situations. Dependent relationships with whites are the typical pattern. When a white refuses to help an Indian when asked, the suspicion with which any white generally is viewed as well as the constant fear of rejection come to the fore, and the Indian then quickly relegates this particular white to the usual province of all whites—

persons who look down on Indians and only help them when it is to their own advantage. Also many Indians never can feel secure with whites because they fear that no white will ever really respect or understand them if he finds out certain fundamental facts about them—particularly the details of their poverty-stricken background and their mystical beliefs. The Indian's own confusion between two belief and value systems contributes to his insecurities and makes him ashamed within himself of reservation poverty and primitive beliefs. Thus three characteristic attitudes of Indians toward whites are: suspicion, potential dependency, and fear of white rejection. To struggle beyond these to gain an egalitarian relationship with an Indian requires great sensitivity on the part of the white. The relationship must be worked out through a continuous give and take process. Some basic personality differences between Indians and whites that are relevant to this subject have been discussed by Wax and Thomas.[11]

I have found it useful to consider Indian-white relationships in terms of two potential limits of interaction that will be allowed by Indians: a line of tolerance of whites by Indians, and an area of intimacy, which has the potential for full friendship responsibilities. The latter, if allowed by the Indian, who himself ultimately sets the tone of the relationship, can result in a true egalitarian friendship. In general, those persons coming from less acculturated tribes such as Navahos, tend to be able only to tolerate the presence of whites, and rarely can open themselves to more intimate egalitarian relationships. Some more acculturated Indians, as exemplified by many Sioux, appear to allow an area of intimacy because of their verbal abilities and readiness to talk to whites in specific situations. However, it soon becomes apparent that their easy conversation may be deceptive and most Sioux bear sharp antagonistic feelings toward whites which are manifested in varying levels of verbal hostility or in aggressive actions toward other Indians.

In the larger scheme of social interaction Indians in the Bay Area usually will be accepted wherever *they* choose to go. The facts that there are not great numbers of Indians going into white groups, and that Indian-white relationships usually occur on a private and often superficial level reflect that Indians are very hesitant about committing themselves to these relationships, even when invitations are extended and doors are open to them. It would appear that there is a combination of inhibitions in relating to whites, some, which are negative as outlined above, and some of which are the counterpart of positive forces—the qualities of Indianness and Indian social identity—which make for voluntary in-group interaction. I would not consider a main aspect of any Indian marginality problem in the Bay Area to be social frustration. Indians generally do not strive for white relationships or for positions in white organizations. Those looking for formal social activity turn to Indian organizations.

Most chose to go to the Indian centers when they first arrived, and even though the majority of these have stopped attending group events regularly, they rarely have joined any white organizations. Exceptions are membership in unions and occasional visits to white churches or P.T.A. groups. Most who attend white churches attend only the Sunday morning services, and they have not formally joined congregations nor participated in church social activities. Even those who have never attended formal Indian social functions have still tended to mingle with Indians on an informal level. Rarely have they sought relationships in white formal groups.

Indian Identity and Pan-Indianism

Almost every Indian I encountered in the course of my research was impressed with an unmistakable stamp of identity of which he always seemed to be acutely aware. The personal dimension of identity frequently is manifest in manner as well as by constant references to the fact of one's Indianness or to stories about the home reservation. Among most Indians the "Indian" manner was a certain reserve mixed with individual personal, and tribal cultural characteristics. This identity dimension of Indianness does not appear to be destroyed by the impact of intermarriage, profession, life style, or diverse social preferences, nor by the absence of such frequently considered indicators of Indianness as retention of native language, exhibition in the home of Indian crafts or possessions, or participation in Indian activities.

Many persons emphasized to me that their children were *really* Indians. Some made a point of saying that although they had lived in towns away from the reservation for many years, their children were Indians, had been raised as Indians, and that there was no getting around this fact. When asked what being "raised as Indians" meant, they usually could not be more explicit.

Many Indians who come to the city often exhibit a neo-Indian social identity which is pan-Indian in its orientation. It may be noticed that alumni of Haskell Institute[12] well illustrate the pan-Indian social focus by associating more easily with persons of other tribes than do most Indians. The fact of a common Haskell background often is of more importance to them than common tribal identity. By and large the neo-Indians are often relatively well educated and well dressed. Many have the social skills and comparable material possessions to allow them to pass into white society if they so wished, but they consistently choose to mingle almost exclusively with Indians. I would suggest that a positive continuing sense of personal and social identity is the chief factor in the self-segregation of Indians. The fact of Indian identity seems to determine the choice of looking to Indian groups to find one's friends. Time and time again the idea was expressed to me that "Because we are Indians it is just *the* (or the natural) thing to do—that we should want to go places where we can find other Indians." One young and verbal mixed-blood Sioux who has lived in cities all of his life expressed his attitudes this way: "Maybe psychologically I am afraid of being rejected; I don't know, but I don't think so. I just don't go to any group that is not Indian. I prefer to be around Indians."

Discussions of pan-Indianism in the anthropological literature have tended to explain this phenomenon as a defensive manuever of Indian tribes as a way of responding to white dominance, rather like a giant parallel ethnic institution within which Indian people may maintain a sense of identity and integrity because as a group they are regarded as sub-ordinate.[13] James has stated "The key to pan-Indianism, in other words, appears to lie in social relations between Indians and Whites rather than in relations between tribes."[14] Howard described it as a degenerative cultural phase and has called it "one of the final stages of progressive acculturation just prior to complete assimilation."[15] It would appear from my data that pan-Indian activities in the city have a positive reason for developing and continuing. The pan-Indian movement cannot be written off as a disappearing and faltering last kick, despite the painful appearance of dance costumes often reduced to dyed blue ostrich plumes over leopard skin bikinis, and 49-er songs which were made up the night before.

In the city the alternative of passing into white society is often an easy one, but still it appears that not many take that course. To the contrary, many become more positive of their Indianness after they arrive. Perhaps the self-image of Indianness stands out more sharply in the white world for people who come from reservations where the old ways are dying out and no meaningful new identity-action patterns have developed for the individual. In the city a person may dramatically realize that he is an *Indian*, because for the first time his identity stands in high relief in the midst of his all-white neighbors and workmates. As a result he begins to seek out Indian groups, to "dance Indian" for the first time or to take pride in his children's dancing. Perhaps he will take an active interest in Indian political problems. Thus a neo-Indian type on a new level of self- and group identity with a pan-Indian as well as tribal orientation may be born from the necessity of mingling with members of other tribes.

CONCLUSIONS

The adjustments most Indians make in learning the cues for living successfully in the white world seem to be superficial to their established basic personality structures. Such basic qualities of Indianness—as Indian identity and continuing belief in early teachings and values—are strongly resistant to change, despite efforts of the Bureau of Indian Affairs and the dominant white society to effect fundamental changes during the process of adjustment. In the course of my study in the Bay Area I did not encounter any persons I could consider to be assimilated. The psychological awareness of Indian identity was ever-present and seemed to vary little in relation to intermarriage, profession, or diverse social preferences.[16]

Most Indians prefer to associate socially with other Indians, and most frequently these are relatives and members of their own tribal group. Their strong feeling of identity motivated most of the Indians I interviewed to go to Indian centers of interaction in their early years here. Ultimately it seems to be the Indian himself who makes the choice of association. In the Bay Area Indians live in an open society of open associations, yet they have tended largely to limit their contacts to other Indians.

Likewise, few have aspirations of social mobility, although they may wish to obtain some of the same sort of material possessions as are owned by those who are obviously of a higher social status than themselves. The general lack of the kind of motivation that first generation European ethnics have exhibited toward climbing the social ladder or even toward the amassing of money and social skills to prepare themselves or their children for this climb appears to be due partially to Indians thinking of themselves in a unique Indian social niche which is alien to the community social hierarchy, and partially to Indian basic inhibitions against economic planning for the future and the amassing of personal wealth or material goods.[17]

The existence of a pan-Indian orientation and activities among some Indians appears to be connected with a neo-Indian identity and emerging awareness of the meaning and implications of being Indian in a white city. I suggest that the social and psychological imperatives of Indian identity have led to an enforced mingling of tribes in the city, i.e., if one cannot be surrounded by members of his home community, at the least, it is more comfortable to associate with Indians of other tribes than with whites. Thus I see the need of Indians to be with other Indians as a cohesive force for the development and maintenance of pan-Indianism in the city, in contrast to the views in the literature which emphasize pan-Indianism as a structural defensive mechanism or as a terminal phase in the assimilation process. The importance of Indian identity as a maintaining device can begin to be evaluated empirically in the coming years by observing the generational progression in retention or loss of values, attitudes and behavior in second and third generation Indian city dwellers.

NOTES

*The research for two years during 1961-1963 was financed by a pre-doctoral research fellowship of the National Institute of Mental Health.

1 Wesley R. Hurt, "The Urbanization of Yankton Indians," *Human Organization,* XX (Winter 1961-62), 226-231; E. Russell Carter, "Rapid City, South Dakota; Institute on American Indian Assimilation," *The American Indian,* VI (Summer 1953), 29-38; Robert Ritzenthaler and Mary Sellers, "Indians in an Urban Situation," *The Wisconsin Archeologist,* XXXVI (December 1955), 147-161. An unpublished summary report by Paula Verdet of the only study that dealt with cross-tribal cases in large cities was distributed in mimeographed form at the American Indian Chicago Conference in 1961. This report can be ordered from Dr. Sol Tax, Department of Anthropology, University of Chicago.

2 Of this number approximately 4000 are estimated to be in the Oakland-larger East Bay Area, 4000 in San Francisco, and 2000 in the San Jose area. There are no accurate agency figures on this subject. The 1960 Census figures are very low and of little value because of their racial classification criteria. The Bureau of Indian Affairs will not attempt to give exact figures for the number of relocatees in the area because they cannot follow up relocatees and usually do not know when persons have returned to their reservations.

3 Joan Ablon, *Relocated American Indians in the San Francisco Bay*

Area: Concepts of Acculturation, Success and Identity in the City, unpublished Ph.D. Dissertation, University of Chicago, 1963.

4   See James H. Howard, "The Turtle Mountain Chippewa," *The North Dakota Quarterly,* XXVI (Spring 1958), 37–46; David P. Delorme, *A Socio-economic Study of the Turtle Mountain Band of Chippewa Indians and a Critical Evaluation of Proposals Designed to Terminate Their Federal Wardship Status,* unpublished Ph.D. Dissertation, University of Texas, 1955.

5   The Intertribal Friendship House, supported by the American Friends Service Committee, and the San Francisco American Indian Center, supported since its inception by the Society of St. Vincent De Paul but recently turned over to the American Indian Council of the Bay Area, are Indian social centers with regular programs of social-recreational activities. Both were set up in the early years of the Relocation programs to meet the needs of the incoming relocatees. The Four Winds Club is sponsored by the Oakland Young Womens Christian Association and offers varying monthly social events. The Oakland American Indian Baptist Church is a local church of the Southern Baptist Convention and has a vigorous religious and social program. Many tribes are represented in the church, but the majority of regular members and attenders are from Oklahoma tribes who have long been associated with SBC churches. The San Jose Dance Club is a small core group of primarily Kiowas who organize monthly pow-wows in San Jose. The American Indian Council of the Bay Area is a cross-tribal political group working for the general betterment of relocatees. The Council has traditionally sponsored the Annual Indian Day Picnic, and in recent years come into national notice by their widely publicized criticisms of the Relocation programs. The Santa Fe Indian Village is a community of railroad laborers and their families from Laguna and Acoma pueblos brought to Richmond in the early years of World War II. In its prime years the village functioned as two microcosms of pueblo communities operating on a simple level, maintaining their own governors and officials and calendars of religious events. Now the population has dwindled from forty families to about eight and there are few activities.

6   Floyd Dotson, "Patterns of Voluntary Association Among Urban Working Class Families," *American Sociological Review,* XVI (October 1951), 687–693; W. Lloyd Warner *et al., Democracy in Jonesville,* First Ed. (Harper and Brothers, 1949), pp. 141, 143.

7   Floyd Dotson, *op. cit.*

8   Wendell Bell and Marion D. Boat, "Urban Neighbors and Social Relations," *American Journal of Sociology,* LXII (January 1957), 395.

9   Basil G. Zimmer, "Participation of Migrants in Urban Structures," *American Sociological Review,* XX (April 1955), 219–224.

10 Many Indians tend to relate more easily to Mexican-Americans, Hawaiians, Filipinos, and other persons who share a minority group status and common poverty, than they do to Anglo-American whites. However, most Indians express very negative feelings about having to associate with, work, or live side-by-side with Negroes. Many persons from northern tribes who had never seen Negroes before they arrived in California are the most vehement about the race issue. Their attitudes appear to be born largely from a jumping on the lower class pecking-order band wagon, rather than from any pragmatic evaluation

of actual Negro behavior, or from memories of oral tradition about
Negro troops sent in to pacify various tribes in the last century.

11 Rosalie H. Wax and Robert K. Thomas, "American Indians and White
People," *Phylon,* XXII (Winter 1961), 305-317.

12 Haskell Institute in Lawrence, Kansas generally is considered to be the
superior Indian boarding school of the country. Haskell offers academic
and vocational high school curriculums and post-graduate vocational
training. Many Haskell graduates take jobs in the Bay Area each year.

13 Evon Z. Vogt, "The Acculturation of American Indians," *The Annals
of the American Academy of Political and Social Sciences,* CCCXI
(May 1957), 146; Bernard J. James, "Social-psychological Dimensions
of Ojibwa Acculturation," *American Anthropologist,* LXIII (August
1961), 721-746; James H. Howard, "Pan Indian Culture of Oklahoma," *The Scientific Monthly,* LXXXI (November 1955), 215-220.

14 Bernard J. James, *op. cit.,* 744.

15 James H. Howard, *op. cit.,* 220.

16 Robert Ritzenthaler and Mary Sellers, *op. cit.,* 160; and Paula Verdet,
op. cit., likewise came to this conclusion concerning Indians they
interviewed in urban situations. A. I. Hallowell investigated the problem of whether changes in the personality structure necessarily take
place during the process of acculturation in "Ojibwa Personality and
Acculturation," in *Acculturation in the Americas,* Sol Tax (ed.)
(University of Chicago Press, 1952), 105-112. Hallowell reported a
general persistence of Indian "psychological characteristics." For a
discussion of the importance of early cultural training see Edward M.
Bruner, "Primary Group Experience and the Processes of Acculturation,"
American Anthropologist, LVIII (August 1956) 605-623.

17 Contrast with the description of European ethnic groups in Yankee City
in W. Lloyd Warner and Leo Srole, *The Social Systems of American Ethnic
Groups,* Yankee City Series, Vol. 3 (Yale University Press, 1945), pp. 78 ff.

JOHN A. PRICE: THE MIGRATION AND ADAPTATION OF AMERICAN INDIANS TO LOS ANGELES*

The city of Los Angeles has the largest population of American Indians
in the United States. In this city, the Indians are actively creating a
pan-Indian subculture which accommodates their aboriginal history and
reservation culture to the newer world of urban living. Athletic leagues,
Christian churches, and other institutions Euro-American in character are

Source: Reprinted by permission from *Human Organization* 27 (Summer 1968),
168-175.

focusing on their Indian membership and identity with such activities as social centers annual fairs and yearly Christmas parties. Tradition-oriented dance clubs flourish.

But along with these changes expressive of Indian association or identity, are equally extensive changes toward the assimilation, acculturation, and adjustment or adaptation of Indians to the white society and culture of Los Angeles.

Such adaptation as a process for enhancing survival in new circumstances is reflected in the U.S. Census data given below.[1] This data is followed by a brief history of Indian migration to Los Angeles. The adaptation of the migrants is then outlined in terms of assimilation (the incorporation of a minority into the social relations network of the greater society), acculturation (the change of cultural characteristics of the minority in response to those of the surrounding majority), and adjustment (social and psychological health). Finally, variations of urban adaptation according to tribal background are considered.

Table 1, based on the 1960 census, illustrates some of the demographic and cultural patterns of the Indians in California in contrast to non-Indians. It also indicates that in selected areas whites are more adapted to urban living than Indians, and suggests the extent of the potential adaptive shift for Indians.

The table indicates that in California, Indians more than whites are rural residents, are younger, come from larger families, have less schooling, are more often unemployed, and have lower incomes. Indians are rarely

TABLE 1

Comparison of Indian and White Males in California
(1960 U.S. Census Figures)

	Indian	White
Urban residence	53.0%	86.0%
Under 20 years of age	45.0%	38.0%
Families of six or more persons*	37.0%	12.0%
Median school years completed†	9.7	12.0
Unemployment rate†	15.1%	5.5%
Median annual income in 1959†	$2,694	$5,109
More Whites		
Professional, technical & kindred	3.8%	14.0%
Managers, officials & proprietors	2.0%	12.5%
Sales workers	1.1%	8.0%
Clerical & kindred	3.1%	7.9%
More Indians		
Laborers, nonfarm	17.3%	5.6%
Farm laborers & foremen	10.2%	3.1%
Private household workers††	0.4%	0.1%

*Refers to population of the thirteen western states. All other data refer to California alone.

†Men 14 years of age and older.

††About 40 percent of both Indians and whites are "craftsmen, operators and kindred workers." Because of lack of contrast, these are omitted.

entrepreneurs, even in small businesses; they tend to work for others in manufacturing, agriculture, and personal services. Only those occupations are given which reveal sharp contrasts between Indians and whites. These contrasts hold when only Los Angeles is considered, although Los Angeles Indians have shifted closer to the white pattern than Indians in California generally. A statistical outline as sparse as this does not reflect the rich and diverse cultural heritages of Indians or the wide individual variations, which do in fact include college graduates and a few professionals and entrepreneurs.

MIGRATION TO THE CITY

In the sixty years between 1890 and 1950, the population of California identified for census purposes as Indian increased numerically from 16,624 to 19,943, but declined proportionately from 1.4 percent to 0.2 percent of the total California population.

In the following decade, the Indian population underwent a dramatic doubling, increasing to 39,014 in 1960. California's total growth for the period was a very high 49 percent, and Indians had the highest growth rate of any ethnic group for which the Census Bureau compiled data.

While the total number of Indians doubled, the number of Indians in the various *urban* areas was from three to four times greater in 1960 than in 1950. In 1960, 12,405 Indians were recorded for greater Los Angeles (32 percent of the state total), 3,883 for San Francisco-Oakland (10 percent), and 3,293 for San Diego (9 percent). Indications are that this influx has continued; in 1966 Los Angeles had about 25,000 Indians—double the figure of six years earlier.

The great majority of these Los Angeles Indians are migrants from other states. (In our survey of 3,000 Indians, only six Gabrielino are descendants of the aboriginal occupants of Los Angeles, and 3 percent—77 persons—are descendants of aboriginal Californians.) The first wave of migrants came largely from nonreservation areas outside of California. Many came in the 1930's from Oklahoma, and then from widely scattered areas during the 1940's and early 1950's.

Los Angeles County had a population of 6,000 Indians in 1955, composed mainly of Cherokee, Creek, Choctaw and Seminole who had come from Oklahoma. In 1960, Oklahoma had 12 percent of all U.S. Indians,[2] but our survey revealed that of the Los Angeles Indians, 25 percent have come from Oklahoma, over twice the national proportion in that state.

The second, more massive migration began around 1955, the majority coming from reservation areas. They came particularly from Arizona (15 percent in Los Angeles *versus* 15 percent nationally), New Mexico (8 percent *vs.* 10 percent) South Dakota (9 percent *vs.* 5 percent), North Dakota (6 percent *vs.* 2 percent), and Montana (7 percent *vs.* 4 percent). Including those born in California (6 percent *vs.* 7 percent), some 76 percent came from these seven states. In addition to the great migration from Oklahoma noted above, a disproportionate number of Indians came from the states of the Northern Plains.

These Los Angeles proportions roughly reflect the national distribution of Indians. A similar correlation is found for tribal representation.

Indians are invariably precise about their tribal identity, often specifying a tiny tribelet or reservation. The original 101 "tribes" listed by our respondents were condensed into 76 categories (Table 2). Since this sample is about 12 percent of the total number of Indians in Greater Los Angeles, it is possible to approximate the total population of any relatively large tribal population by multiplying by eight the sample size given in Table 2. For example, there are roughly 3,000 Navaho, 2,800 Sioux and 1,400 Cherokee. The margin of possible error in this technique increases with the decrease in sample size. Thus, instead of eight Washo as predicted, there could in fact be any number from one individual to possibly twenty or thirty.

The increasing geographical mobility of Indians is reflected in the fact that only 19 percent of our respondents were born in the same state as their fathers. Recent arrival in Los Angeles is also a factor: since the later wave of migration was about three times greater than the earlier one, the median arrival data of our sample is only 1961.

TABLE 2
Tribal Membership of 2,945 Indians in Los Angeles, 1966

Navaho (14.1%)	417	Arapaho	25	Eskimo	4
Sioux (12.0%)	354	Omaha	23	Mohican	4
Cherokee (6.3%)	185	Crow	19	Athabascan	3
Creek (6.0%)	183	Ponca	19	Klamath	3
Pueblo (5.1%)	151	Shoshone	19	Kutenai	3
Choctaw (4.5%)	134	Assiniboin	18	Pomo	3
Seminole (3.7%)	108	Osage	18	Aleut	2
Cheyenne (3.3%)	97	Yakima	18	Caddo	2
Chippewa (3.1%)	92	Chickasaw	14	Chickahominty	2
Apache (3.1%)	92	Colville	14	Coeur d'Alene	2
Kiowa	85	Ute	13	Powhatan	2
Papago	74	Mohave	10	Quapaw	2
Gros Ventre	65	Nanticoke	10	Quechua	2
Kickapoo	64	Shawnee	9	Chumash	1
Comanche	59	Yavapai	9	Haida	1
Pima	55	Mandan	8	Huron	1
Blackfoot	47	Pawnee	8	Lillooet	1
Mexican Indians	45	Tlingit	8	Maricopa	1
Iroquis	42	Flathead	7	Ottawa	1
Winnebago	42	Oto	7	Peoria	1
Mission	38	Potawatomi	7	Salish	1
Arikara	35	Cree	6	Shasta	1
Yuma	34	Sac-Fox	6	Spokane	1
Paiute	33	Wea	6	Umatilla	1
Delaware	31	Cocopa	4	Umpqua	1
Nez Perce	31			Washo	1

A key to the great size of the post-1955 migration is the Employment Assistance ("Relocation") Program of the Bureau of Indian Affairs (BIA). In 1952, the BIA began to place Indians from reservation areas in jobs in western industrial centers. In 1958, it added the Adult Vocational Program to coincide with relocation. By 1962, the BIA had trained over 5,000 Indians and had relocated more than 40,000. Both programs have been intensified since 1962, and have been a massive stimulant to the growth of the Los Angeles Indian community. The BIA office in Los Angeles has, in recent years, been assisting about 1,300 Indians annually.

The relocation process begins at the reservation with an application, supplemented by data collected from police, health, welfare, and educational agencies. A physical examination is required of all applicants. An accepted applicant is then assisted in moving to the city of his choice. Once he reaches his destination, several days of orientation begin.

He is assigned a social worker who assists him in solving immediate problems such as temporary housing, receiving shipped items, and use of the city buses. He also attends at least two group orientation meetings: the first to explain medical plans, and the second to deal with the geographical area and its social attitudes, and the specific skills needed in urban living. Our survey revealed that some 42 percent of the Indians coming to Los Angeles have received this brief course on how to live in the city.

After employment is obtained or school enrollment is completed, the BIA assists the relocatee in finding permanent housing and in the solution of such personal problems as budgeting. Ideally, contact is maintained with individuals after employment through visits scheduled at intervals of one, three, and six months.

Compared to those who came to Los Angeles on their own, the relocatees in our survey tend to (1) be younger (median age, 25 years); (2) have resided in Los Angeles a shorter time (median, just less than 2 years); (3) have a lower income (median, $4,000); (4) live in the central Los Angeles area more often (59 percent); (5) associate with other Indians more often; (6) speak an Indian language more often (86 percent) and better (84 percent of those who speak an Indian language speak it "quite well"); and (7) more often would return to their reservation if they could get a job at their current rate of pay (56 percent).

We analyzed the subjective side of this migration by asking the heads of 158 households a series of questions about life on the reservation, life in the city and what led individuals to migrate. The pattern of responses was not significantly different for that which could be expected from Euro-Americans who had migrated to a large city from a rural or small town background. The incentive for migration is primarily economic: to find jobs, higher wages, and improved physical living conditions. Indians tend to dislike the smog, urban density, transportation problems, the high cost of living in the city; and they look with fondness at the social contacts and activities they had on the reservation. As the years in the city go by, they increasingly withdraw from previous reservation contacts (fewer returns to the reservation, fewer letters, etc.), while at the same time they increasingly tend to idealize the physical and cultural aspects of reservation life. Many older urban Indians talk of retiring to their reservations, where they own property or where as members of the tribe they have a right to reside.

The Navajo Agency has compiled information on relocation and returns to the reservation.[3] Of the 3,273 Navahos who relocated between 1952 and 1961, 37 percent later returned to the reservation. This rate has been fairly constant over the years. The causes for returning most commonly given by the 115 returnees who specified reasons were illness (23 percent), alcoholism (16 percent), military service (8 percent). That is, illness, excessive drinking, or military service dislocated them from the city and they returned to the reservation. In addition, about 25 percent of the responses can be summarized as social and emotional reasons, 19 percent as economic, and 3 percent each on language difficulty and climate discomfort. Compared to those who return, Navaho relocatees who remain in the city tend to be between 20 and 40 years of age; have a greater fluency in English; and have attended a public school, rather than a mission or government school (although level of education was not determinative in either staying or leaving).

ASSIMILATION

Our findings tend to validate the statement of Nancy Lurie that "the option to assimilate is far more open for Indians than for almost any other minority."[4] The movement from a reservation, where Indians are virtually the total society, to a city, where they are a tiny minority, is a major step toward assimilation into white society. But the Indian also has the option to continue to relate to other Indians in the city. The city contains a variety of Indian social groups (kinship, tribal, pan-Indian clubs or centers, etc.) with which Indians affiliate in varying degrees. Our study explored three aspects of assimilation: marriage, formal associations, and informal associations.

Marriage

We found a significant decline with successive generations in the rate of marriage within the race and tribe. Sixty-four percent of marriages in the generation of the respondent's parents were within the tribe; only 39 percent of marriages in the respondent's generation were within the tribe. About one-third of the married respondents had married whites.

Formal Associations

Although formal Indian associations (athletic leagues, churches, clubs, and centers) have extensive mailing lists of nominal members, only about 20 percent of Los Angeles Indians are active in such associations. Church preferences can be classified as follows: Roman Catholic (29 percent); fundamentalist Protestant (27 percent); general Protestant (18 percent); Latter Day Saints (5 percent); various nativistic Indian churches (3 percent); 18 percent had no religious preference. While 23 percent said they went to church once a week, the median attendance rate is about once a year. More Indians go to church in the city (70 percent) than did on the reservation (53 percent).

Nine fundamentalist Protestant churches and one Latter Day Saints church in Los Angeles have predominantly Indian memberships. A special survey sample of 74 persons was taken in the largest Indian church, the Indian Revival Center (Assembly of God). Approximately 250 persons attend services at the church; three-fourths of these are young children. The beautiful new church, located in the low-income district of Bell Gardens, was built largely by the Indians themselves. The largest tribal group in the church is the Navaho. They conduct their own Sunday school class in Navaho and have a separate choir which sings Christian hymns in Navaho. Some 54 percent of this sample were born in Arizona or New Mexico, with the others coming primarily from Oklahoma and Montana. Compared to the rest of the survey respondents, these Revival Center Indians have (1) more children (3.8 average *versus* 3.2 for the total sample); (2) a higher rate of relocation through the BIA program (58 percent); and (3) a higher rate of intratribal marriage in both the respondent's (52 percent) and the parents' (84 percent) generations. Of all the large Indian social groups in Los Angeles, this is one of the least assimilated.

Informal Associations

Some 29 percent of our total survey sample reported their usual association as being only with Indians, 67 percent with Indians and whites, and 4 percent with whites exclusively. With residence considered as an aspect of informal association, 5 percent preferred an all-Indian neighborhood, 45 percent preferred a mixed neighborhood, and 8 percent preferred an all-white neighborhood (42 percent had no preference or did not reply).

Three patterns of residence were discernible: a primary concentration (46 percent) in the low rental district of central Los Angeles City; a secondary concentration in a low-class suburban southeastern extension of the City (28 percent); and a wide distribution throughout the remaining cities and suburbs of greater Los Angeles (26 percent). Indians are much more widely scattered than Negroes or Mexican-Americans in Los Angeles. There is a tendency for recent arrivals (particularly for the first two years) to reside in the central city; longer-term residents move outward to the suburbs. This outward movement is considered indicative of a shift toward assimilation, although some who are major Indian leaders live in the farthest suburbs.

ACCULTURATION

Urban acculturation for the Indian involves replacing or modifying his reservation culture, as well as acquiring new traits. It is not simply the learning of financial budgeting, industrial skills, or driving on the freeways, but the changing of a whole range of behaviors and attitudes.

For example, Indians tend to retain the attitude that one should not spend much on clothes or housing. On the reservation a few work clothes and a single set of dress clothes are sufficient; housing is of course inexpensive. Hence the Los Angeles Indians on the average spend a relatively small portion of their income on clothes and housing, while relatively large amounts go toward travel and entertainment. Although most of the surveyed households have a television set, Indians probably watch television somewhat less than whites. When asked, "What do you usually do for recreation?" 46 percent said sports; 16 percent mentioned TV, movies or plays; 9 percent said powwows (Indian dances); 7 percent said they go to bars. A wide variety of other activities received briefer mention.

Other indices of acculturation are level of formal education, occupation, and the loss of ability to use an Indian language (with its reciprocal implication of increasing ability to use English). We found a median of 11.2 years of education; 5 percent were in professional occupations, with 31 percent in skilled occupations. The educational level comes close to that of Los Angeles whites, although the occupational level is still very low. There are also indications that the quality of education is lower on the reservations where most of the Indians went to school. It may be that nine or ten years of education in Los Angeles is equivalent to eleven years schooling on the reservation.

Some 54 percent speak one or more Indian languages. Since language retention is a useful index of the lack of acculturation, we went into the subject in detail with a sample of 158 household heads. Forty-one percent said they spoke their Indian language "quite well." In 57 percent of the married households the spouse spoke an Indian language, in 22 percent an Indian language was spoken in the house "usually" (13 percent) or "always" (9 percent). Twenty-nine percent of those with children said their children speak an Indian language, but only 3 percent said their children speak "quite well," and only 11 percent said their children speak to each other in an Indian language.

ADJUSTMENT

Adjustment—as the dimension of psychological and social health—can be measured by such maladjustive factors as rates of suicide, internment in mental hospitals, crime rates, and unemployment rates. Drunkenness is also maladjustive. Nationally, "drunkenness alone accounts for 71 percent of all Indian arrests."[5] Drunkenness was seen by 32 percent of our respondents as their major problem. The very high unemployment rate (15.1 percent for Indians in the 1960 California census) is another indication of maladjustment.

A recent incident in Los Angeles highlights the problem of adjustment. A newly-arrived Navaho, who spoke no English, became quite ill, and on the street approached a woman wearing a white uniform, in the belief that she was a nurse. The woman, a beautician, thought she was being attacked and had the Indian arrrested. Unable to communicate with the man, the police placed him in a hospital where he was classified as an insane Mexican-American. Clearly, sudden exposure to an alien context, emphasizing the lack of assimilation and acculturation to white society and culture brought a maladjusted reaction from this man, just as a white man might react maladjustively on the Navaho reservation.

Acculturation and adjustment are not always correlated positively. Military service, for example, seems to have a negative effect on Indian adjustment to white society, but a positive effect on acculturation to white culture. In an unnamed urban center, Martin found the Navaho better adjusted to urban life, in terms of fuller employment and lower arrest rates, than Sioux or Choctaw.[6] This kind of passive adjustment to urban life can take place with minimal acculturation. According to Kluckhohn and Leighton, "Navahos are distinguished among American Indians by the alacrity, if not the ease, with which they have adjusted to the impact of white culture, while still retaining many native traits and preserving the framework of their own cultural organization."[7] Martin indicates that Navaho men are less *adjusted* than Navaho women, while our data shows Navaho men to be more *acculturated* than their women.

The high geographical mobility of Indians within the city, while difficult to analyze, may be another indication of maladjustment. The addresses of members of the Los Angeles Indian Center change about 10 percent per month, indicating that the average member moves at least once a year. Such an address list is virtually useless a year after it is compiled. That this mobility clearly is not due to discrimination in housing is shown by the finding that only 4 percent felt that prejudice or discrimination was the "Number One problem of Indians in Los Angeles," while 73 percent said they thought that Indians are treated fairly in Los Angeles.

TRIBAL DIFFERENCES IN URBAN ADAPTATION

For the analysis of tribal differences in adaptation, the survey forms were initially divided into six groups according to tribal location in the United States. Individuals from tribes located in the northeastern part of the country were found to be closest to the expected pattern of direct adaptation to urban life: high on educational level, but low on use of an Indian language, intratribal marriage, and use of the relocation program.

A comparison of individual tribal groups indicated that the three major tribal groups in the city of Navaho, Sioux, and the Five Civilized Tribes represent three degrees of adaptation to the city—from the weak adaptation of the Navaho to the relatively full adaptation of the Five Civilized Tribes (See Table 3). Our study indicates that Indians fresh from strongly rural or reservation backgrounds tend, like the Navaho, to shift over time to patterns of life exemplified by the Five Civilized Tribes. Also, as the Indian community in Los Angeles matures, we may expect tribal groups such as the Navaho to shift toward tribal groups like the Five Civilized Tribes. The latter in turn is culturally close to the general population of Los Angeles, except for the particular ethnic identity.

Compared to the total sample the Navaho (primarily from Arizona and New Mexico) are more involved in reservation life. More voted on the

TABLE 3

Movement in Urban Adaptation

	Weak ⟶		Strong
	Navaho	Sioux	Five Civil.
Survey			
1. Sample size	417	354	618
2. Years education	10.4	10.3	10.9
3. Median year of arrival	1964	1964	1959
4. Speak an Indian language	89%	46%	40%
5. Intratribal marriage	46%	25%	14%
6. Came on B.I.A. relocation	49%	53%	32%
7. Residence in city center	55%	34%	30%
Detailed Interviews			
1. Sample size	25	22	35
2. Sports for recreation	18%	38%	49%
3. Belong to clubs	4%	36%	49%
4. Lived on a reservation	88%	82%	23%
5. Are on a tribal roll	80%	91%	43%
6. Plan to live on a reservation	52%	50%	11%
7. Write or phone reservation	68%	55%	20%
8. Associate entirely or mostly with Indians	64%	33%	26%

reservation, more plan to live on the reservation some day, and more visit the reservation frequently. A very high percentage of the Navaho speak their native language. The Navaho turn more often to television, sight-seeing, or "nothing" for recreation; tend not to join clubs; and associate predominantly with other Indians, especially with other Navaho.

The Navaho stand out as distinct and sometimes despised within the general ethnic group of Indians. Other Indians resent what they see as the clannishness and foolish pride of the Navaho. In the joking among Indians which often involves tribal stereotypes, the Navaho are a frequent target. For example, a group of Sioux were playing pool when one player missed a very easy shot. Another player said, "You're shooting like a drunken Navaho now," and everyone burst into laughter.

The Five Civilized Tribes are represented in Los Angeles by Cherokee, Creek, Choctaw, and Seminole—primarily from eastern Oklahoma. Fewer of these Indians have lived on reservations or are on tribal rolls. They have resided in Los Angeles longer than most Indians. Only about one-third have come on the BIA relocation program. People of the Five Civilized Tribes are more involved with sports for recreation, particularly with the local Indian athletic leagues. These Indians tend to take their Indianness lightly: it is only one of the several components of their identity. Their various occupations, religious and political involvements, and residential neighborhoods contribute heavily to their social associations and identities.

CONCLUSIONS

Urban adaptation involves changes that enhance the survival and expansion of a minority population in the city. These changes are reflected in training in new and appropriate occupations, and in learning to function according to as well as alongside of the impersonal, legalistic standards of the city. As a factor in such adaptation, one-fifth of the Indians in Los Angeles have found in social enclaves a security against the impersonality of the city, and a new and wider identity in pan-Indian associations.

There are several conditions which support the pan-Indian enclave rather than tribalism in the city. Common and exclusive occupation of a reservation gives a tribe a unity and stability which cannot be maintained as its members scatter across a city. Lack of discrimination in housing for Indians in Los Angeles leads them to scatter widely from each other and to live close to their work. Thus individuals, even members of tribes with over one thousand members in Los Angeles, rarely see other tribal members except their own kinfolk and a few friends. One acculturated Navaho told me that although he goes looking for other Navaho in the Indian bars about twice a year—so that he can enjoy speaking his native language again and hear the latest news of the reservation—he is often unable to find a single member of his tribe.

Conditions in the city lead the Indian away from tribal patterns. The reservation offers a very narrow range of occupational, religious, political, and recreational alternatives. The range of possible choices is vastly increased in the city. This, together with a new relative social anonymity, and the high-pressure selling of the city, lead the Indian into making choices he would never make on the reservation.

The physical appearance of the Indian invariably conditions many of the choices he makes. The majority of Indians "look Indian" and are defined and treated by the majority population of Los Angeles simply as Indians (or Mexicans) rather than specifically as Navaho, Sioux, or Creek. While Indians themselves are enabled to make judgments of the physical appearance of other Indians that approximate major tribal physical types, the larger population cannot do this. However, an Indian can "pass" as a white more easily than a white can "pass" as an Indian, because Indian society is much smaller and less diversified than the white. One outcome of this is that those Indians who, although reared on a reservation, do not physically reflect their Indianness, have difficulty operating in pan-Indian associations. One "white-Indian" who is active as a master of ceremonies for local powwows seems continually to need to establish his Indianness by telling newcomers about his reservation days, yet they persist in defining him as "a nice guy, but not really an Indian."

As an ethnic group, Indians do have a common history and a shared heritage. But many individual Indians are not really aware of this until they leave their reservation, with its narrow concerns, and in the city meet Indians from other parts of the country. An awakened pan-Indianism then often becomes an additional dimension to, and sometimes a substitute for, their tribal affiliations. Although only one-fifth of our respondents are socially active in pan-Indian associations, the great majority of Indians in the city clearly are ideologically and emotionally affiliated with pan-Indianism. Pan-Indianism thus seems to emerge as a stabilizing element—and perhaps a permanent part—of the adaptation of the Indian migrant to the metropolitan areas, and a significant facet of the ethnic diversity of the American city.

NOTES AND REFERENCES

*This article is based on a city-wide sample survey during the spring of 1966 in cooperation with the Los Angeles Indian Center, and detailed interviews with the heads of selected households in December 1965, and July 1966, in cooperation with Alice Maloney of the National Council of Churches of Christ. Also utilized were topical reports by members of the U.C.L.A. ethnographic Summer Field School of 1966, directed by the author. Support for the analysis of data came from a University of California Faculty Research Grant.

1 California Department of Industrial Relations, *American Indians in California* (San Francisco, 1965).
2 California State Advisory Commission on Indian Affairs, *Indians in Rural and Reservation Areas* (Sacramento, 1966), p. 53.
3 Navajo Agency, *Navajo Yearbook,* Window Rock, Arizona, Report No. VII, 1958, pp. 367-9 and Report No. VII, 1961, p. 236.
4 Nancy O. Lurie, "The Enduring Indian," *Natural History,* 1966, Vol. 75, No. 9, pp. 10-22.
5 Omer Stewart, "Questions Regarding American Indian Criminality," *Human Organization,* 1964, Vol. 23, No. 1, p. 61.
6 Harry W. Martin, "Correlates of Adjustment Among American Indians in an Urban Environment," *Human Organization,* 1964, Vol. 23, No. 4, pp. 290-5.
7 Clyde Kluckhohn and Dorothea Leighton, *The Navaho* (Doubleday and Co., New York, 1962), p. 17.

THEODORE D. GRAVES: THE PERSONAL ADJUSTMENT OF NAVAJO INDIAN MIGRANTS TO DENVER, COLORADO[1]

ABSTRACT

Urban migration creates many adjustment problems for those American Indians who find economic opportunities on their reservations inadequate. Their extremely high rate of arrest in comparison with other urban groups, almost all for drunkenness or drinking-related offenses, is testimony to the extent of their difficulties and the inadequate resources that they possess for coping with them. A systematic investigation of 259 male Navajo Indian migrants to Denver over the last ten years reveals a number of economic, social, and psychological pressures and constraints bearing on them, which account in large part both for intragroup differences in adjustment among them, and for their high arrest rates in comparison with other minority groups. The interaction among these determinants, as well as feedback from the migrant's behavioral response, is analyzed as a system of mutually interlocking and reinforcing variables through time. Practical implications of this study are briefly explored, including the apparent primary role played by the migrant's marginal economic position in the city.

INTRODUCTION

One Wednesday morning in mid-September a young Indian stepped off the bus at the Trailways depot in downtown Denver, Colorado. Like most Navajo migrants, Harrison Joe[2] was in his early twenties and single. He had graduated two years before from the Special Navajo Program at Intermountain School in Brigham City, Utah. This program, now discontinued, was a five-year course for Navajos with little or no prior educational experience. It emphasized basic language skills and vocational training and was all the education Harrison Joe had ever had. Nor had experience served as a substitute. The majority of Navajos who come to Denver have never been in a city before, and neither had Harrison Joe. Other than boarding school his only off-reservation experience was two months picking potatoes in Idaho, at $120 per month.

At Intermountain, Harrison Joe received vocational training in upholstery. But this didn't help him find a job near his reservation home. During the two years following graduation his only wage labor work was ten days for the tribe at $10 per day. So he decided to try relocation. Denver was his first choice because he had a relative there and it was close to home. The Bureau of Indian Affairs (BIA) which "sponsors" most

Source: Reprinted by permission of the American Anthropological Association from *American Anthropologist,* Vol. 72, No. 1, 1970.

Navajo migrants, agreed to pay his way to the city and to help him find a job there, under a special government program in operation since 1954.

And so on arrival in Denver, the first thing Harrison Joe did was to ask his way to the BIA Office of Employment Assistance. There he was given intake interviews and a haircut and was taken to a rooming house where several other Indian relocatees lived. His first weekly subsistence check was isued: $30, which after paying $21 for room and board still left him with a bit of pocket money. On Friday and Saturday the Office also gave him job counselling and sent him out on three nonproductive job interviews.

Though unsuccessful at finding a job those first few days, Harrison Joe had no difficulty finding friends. The first morning in town he met another Navajo at the Bureau office, and his new roommate at the boarding house was also Navajo. Thursday evening he went looking for his "uncle," a young man about his age with a couple of years of urban experience in both Chicago and Denver. But he had moved. Friday, Harrison Joe tried again, and this time found him sitting in the park with some other migrants. So the whole group spent the evening together. On Saturday afternoon another Navajo took him out to see the town, and later to watch TV at his apartment. Sunday, Harrison Joe struck up an acquaintance with a former Navajo roomer at his boarding house who was to become his closest friend. Together they went to the "Pink Elephant," a popular Navajo bar where they spent the evening with his "uncle" and other friends. Though this was fun, the evening was marred on his way home by a fight with another group of Navajos, who taunted the shy stranger.

During his next week in Denver, a temporary five-hour job as a brickyard laborer and another day heaving cinder blocks were Harrison Joe's only work. All of his job interviews were unsuccessful, and he was beginning to feel discouraged. That Saturday, BIA subsistence funds again in his pocket, he set out to explore the town. Meeting no one he knew, he again dropped into the Pink Elephant, where he spotted his "uncle" chatting with another clan brother from Gallup. This fellow, also a new migrant, had found no work and had been beaten up. He, too, was getting discouraged and talked of returning home.

Harrison Joe's third week in the city was equally unsuccessful. By Tuesday the BIA had given up trying to get him work in upholstery, and instead got him hired as a cinch maker in a saddle shop. The next day he was fired because he was too slow and came to work two hours late. Thursday he tried to get a job on his own at the Colorado State Employment Office. Because the lines were so long, however, he didn't even get to fill out an application form. By this time he was so discouraged that after he picked up his BIA subsistence check he packed his bag and decided to return home. But instead he spent the evening talking with one of our researchers. Friday morning, when he stopped at the BIA office, they got him a job as a trainee leather trimmer, to begin the following week, so he decided to stick around and give the city another try.

Saturday was an eventful day. He earned $3 cutting lawns and, with this added to the $9 left from his subsidy check after paying room and board, he felt quite flush. He decided to wander down to Larimer Street, Denver's skid row, where other Navajos had pointed out a friendly bar. "Navajos, two of them, were around," he reported later, "and they bought some beers for me, and we started drinking." In typical fashion, each bought drinks for the others, and they moved from one bar to the next. Exactly what transpired during the evening is unclear. At some point Harrison Joe got into a fight and was badly bruised and cut on one arm. He may also have been slipped a Mickey and rolled (his perception of the events), or perhaps he and his friends simply drank up his $12. "I don't know how much I drink," he admitted.

In any event, there were some "police standing there and me drunk. One Navajo took off. And I just sit there, don't know if I had been passed out. And I was in jail." Because it was his first offense he was released Sunday morning, but was required to return to court Wednesday. Broke, tired, and hung-over, he hiked to the house of a friend, who took him out for a couple of beers to sober him up. Then he went home to bed.

Monday, Harrison Joe began work as a leather cutter trainee. Tuesday he was fired. Wednesday he went to court and was given a $10 suspended sentence. Thursday he picked up his $30 maintenance check from the BIA and without a word to anyone, left town.

Harrison Joe is fairly typical of the majority of Navajos who come to Denver in search of better employment opportunities. Migration to the city creates for them a difficult emotional conflict. On the one hand they want the material goods their Western education has taught them to value but that limited job opportunities on the reservation prevent them from attaining. On the other hand they retain a deep emotional attachment to their kin and the reservation for which the city offers few substitutes (Graves and Van Arsdale 1966). The average migrant arrives in Denver with other handicaps. He has limitations of language, race, and culture, and Indian education still lags behind that of the American public at large. It is therefore not surprising that over half the migrants remain in the city less than six months. But often the migrant is equally ill-equipped to compete back home. The better educated Navajos who remain on the reservation command the best available jobs. Thus the migrant is apt to slip into a cycle of urban migration and return, each phase of which ends in personal failure. Small wonder that large numbers of these "marginal men" seek release from frustration and failure in drunken stupor.

Research on the personal adjustment problems of Navajo migrants in Denver has been in progress at the University of Colorado since 1963. The present paper reports some of the economic, social, and psychological factors associated with the quality of their adjustment. It is a distillate from a book-length manuscript (Graves, in preparation) and can present only highlights from our findings, with emphasis on but one of the three theoretical "models" that guided our work (Graves 1966).[3] But even in this brief summary our multi-dimensional, "concatenated" approach to explanation will emerge.

THE PROBLEM OF INDIAN DRUNKENNESS

One index of the psychic difficulties these migrants experience is the frequency with which they are arrested in Denver, almost always for a drinking-related offense. The high rate of Indian arrests in comparison to other U.S. minority groups and to the dominant white community has been documented by several researchers (Graves, in preparation; Honigmann and Honigmann 1968; Stewart 1964; Ferguson 1968; Whittaker 1962). Tables 1 and 2 present figures based on official FBI statistics and census data for the nation at large and the city of Denver, Colorado, as summarized by Stewart (1964:61, 65). Note that Indian arrests are ten or more times·those for whites, and at least three or four times those for other minority groups.

Figures of this kind, however, are subject to the criticism that the population base on which these rates are calculated may be badly distorted. This problem is particularly acute in an urban area such as Denver. Rapid Indian turnover in the city makes accurate census-taking nearly impossible, nonresident Indians temporarily in the city for recreational purposes may account for many arrests, and the urban Indian population is made up predominantly of young, single males in the lowest strata of the

TABLE 1

Comparative Rates of Arrest of Various Ethnic Groups
in the United States—1960

	Total Arrests	Alcohol Related Arrests	Official % Alcohol Related
Total population	2,200	940	43
White	1,700	780	47
Negro	5,900	2,000	33
Indian	15,000	11,000	76
Chinese-Japanese	1,100	270	24

*Taken from Stewart 1964, Table 2, p. 61. Rates shown are per 100,000 population.

TABLE 2

Comparative Rates of Arrests of Various Ethnic Groups
in the City of Denver, Colorado—1960 *

	Total Arrests	Alcohol Related Arrests	Official % Alcohol Related
Total population	5,300	2,700	51
White	4,800	2,500	53
Anglo	3,500	2,000	57
Spanish	15,000	7,000	46
Negro	12,000	3,600	30
Indian	60,000	51,000	86
Chinese-Japanese-Filipino	1,100	470	41

*Taken from Stewart, 1964, Table 14, p. 65, as corrected by Graves. Rates shown are per 100,000 population.

population, who are disproportionately liable to drunkenness and arrest.
Their racial distinctiveness, furthermore, and their pattern of public
drinking makes their drunkeness particularly conspicuous, regardless of any
latent prejudice some police officers may harbor.

To control for such factors in our study, individual police records of
488 migrant Navajo males were collected, representing 94% of the known
Navajo migrants in Denver over the last ten years. In addition, we collected
similar records on 139 Spanish-American male migrants (Rendon 1968) and
41 lower-class Anglo males who occupied jobs in the city similar to the
Navajo (Weppner 1968). Since Denver police consider Spanish their major
problem-group, these subjects served to control for possible police bias in
arrests, as well as for any problems of unfamiliarity with the city which a
new migrant might suffer. The lower-class Anglo group served to control
for the possible effects of reputed lower-class drinking "culture."

Despite these controls against bias, the Indian group exhibited an arrest
rate of 104,000 per 100,000 man-years in the city, which is more than
twenty times the Anglo rate (5,000) and over eight times the migrant
Spanish rate (12,500). At least 93% of the Navajo arrests were for
drinking-related offenses, far higher than for the other two groups. Even
this figure may be too low, however if a careful follow-up were made of
each arrest to check the possibility of alcohol involvement. In exactly such
a study of 610 Indian arrests in San Francisco, for example, Swett found
that "consumption of alcohol was a contributing factor, either to the
offense or to the arrest, in every case" (1932:2). Furthermore, when we
examined the *types* of crimes for which our migrant subjects were being
arrested, it appeared that the rate of arrest for serious crimes, whether
against persons or against property, was clearly *lower* than for the
population at large. Obviously it is not that Indians are more "criminal"
than other minority groups, as Stewart (1964:65) implies, they are simply
more drunk. It is to an explanation of this phenomenon that we must now
turn.

THE STRATEGY OF EXPLANATION

An explanation of these gross group differences can be sought in either
of two ways. The typical anthropological approach is to examine factors in
the history of the Navajo, or of American Indians in general, to discover
aspects of their cultural tradition, particularly with respect to alcohol use,
that might explain their apparent low threshold for drunken excess (Heath
1964; Stewart 1964; Ferguson 1968). For example, most North American
Indian groups lacked aboriginal intoxicants; they acquired a taste for hard
liquor within the context of a "frontier" society; their long history of
prohibition gave them little opportunity to learn and practice patterns of
"moderate" social drinking; and so forth (Dozier 1966).

The poverty of culture as an explanatory concept is apparent, however,
on two counts. First, despite the depressing overall picture of migrant
drinking just presented, about half the Navajo who came to Denver never

have a run-in with the police and appear to be keeping their drinking within tolerable limits. Yet all are products of this same cultural tradition. Recourse to specific features of a culture's development or to limitations in its adaptive behavioral repertoire simply fail to help us understand these significant *intra*group differences.

Second, even if we were able to achieve some satisfactory level of explanation of migrant Indian drinking through an appeal to unique features of Indian "culture," our general understanding of drunkenness as a behavioral phenomenon would be relatively little advanced. Each "cultural" explanation of group differences is ideographic, an explanation that can apply only to that group (or very similar groups) in that place and time. But how then are we to explain drunken excess among American Indian groups such as the Apache and those south of the border who *did* possess intoxicants aboriginally, or among half-breeds whose socialization to Indian tradition is often attenuated, or among the Eskimo whose cultural tradition and contact history are quite different? And won't the American Indian experience have anything to contribute to an understanding of the growing problem of drunkenness among their Spanish-American neighbors, or stepping farther afield, among educated South African Bantu?

The strategy of explanation adopted in the present study is quite different, and I believe far more fruitful in the long run. All analyses have been conducted within a single ethnic group, the Navajo, thus controlling for effects of cultural heritage. Drawing on more general social science theory about the social-psychological etiology of excessive alcohol use, analytic variables have been selected on which individual Navajo migrants may differ. Thus whatever empirical relationships we find between indices of drunkenness and other structural or psychological variables among Navajo migrants have potential explanatory significance for other groups with drinking problems as well.

This strategy does not imply that Navajo culture is irrelevant for understanding excessive drinking among them. For example, the modal position of Navajo subjects on the analytic variables we have investigated results in large part from the way their culture patterns the typical learning experiences of the Navajo child and subsequently conditions his likely position within the wider American society. Furthermore, the typical *form* that Navajo drinking takes (Heath 1964; Ferguson 1968), its social and public nature, makes it particularly susceptible to notice by the police, so that arrest rates can be used as a convenient and objective index of drunkenness rates, something that could not be done if Navajo drinking were generally more covert.

Finally, drunkenness has come to occupy a prominent place in the adaptive repertoire of many Indian people: its narcotizing effects are leaned on heavily as a way of coping with, by temporarily escaping from, feelings of personal inadequacy and failure. This is only one of many functions of alcohol use, of course, and one that most drinkers, Indians and non-Indians alike, are aware of and depend on from time to time (Jessor, Graves, Hanson, and Jessor 1968; Jessor, Carmen and Grossman 1968). It is possible, however, that in the typical response hierarchy of Indian people drunkenness has a lower threshold for selection when adjustment problems arise than alternative, more constructure adaptations.

Such a response tendency, if it exists, could be ascribed to the peculiarities of Indian culture tradition. Alternatively, however, it may also be explained in terms of the typical structural conditions within which their problems of adaptation occur. This is my own reading of the facts. I find no convincing empirical evidence that there is something unique about the way Indians use alcoholic beverages, or that other people in similar circumstances would not behave in a similar fashion (Jessor, Graves, Hanson, and Jessor 1968). In fact, it is my contention that the vast majority of Indian drunkenness can be explained purely in terms of structural and psychological variables relatively independent of their particular cultural tradition and that any residue of difference between them and other minority groups that remains may as well be accounted for by the limitations of our theory and measurement as by some Indian "cultural predisposition."

THEORY AND METHODOLOGY

The theoretical orientation adopted in this study is a synthesis of two major intellectual traditions. One embodies theories of psychopathology, which treat drunkenness as one of many "neurotic" responses to conditions of psychic stress. Critical elements in these theories are such things as *conflicts* between competing but mutually incompatible goals, or the *disjunctions* that result from unfulfilled aspirations. The other is made up of socialization theories, which treat drunkenness as learned behavior. Critical elements are the social *models* provided, and the pattern of social *reinforcements* and *punishments* by which behavior is socially modified and directed.

These two bodies of theory are complementary: each explains exactly what the other leaves out. Disjunction-conflict theories of psychopathology provide powerful psychological *motives* for drinking, social learning theories account for the *channeling* for these motives into specific behavioral form. Their synthesis results in a true social-psychological or "field" theory of urban Indian drunkenness (Yinger 1965).

My approach has been to treat drinking as a rational and purposive act, an adaptive maneuver in a migrant's continuing efforts to achieve personal satisfaction. The determinants of this act are hypothesized to lie in the interaction between a particular set of objective conditions and a particular set of personal attributes for perceiving, evaluating, and coping with these conditions. Such a simplified "decision-theory" framework is straight-forward enough when applied to specific choices such as whether to return home to the reservation (Graves and Van Arsdale 1966). But drunkenness is a *recurring* act; our interest is not in whether a migrant drinks, but how often he drinks to excess. This requires us to search for explanatory variables that can be related to group differences in *rates* of drunkenness by increasing or decreasing the probability that a drinking response will be displayed by a variety of actors in a variety of situations through time.

Finally, a word must be said about the nature of alcohol itself. People drink for many reasons. An adequate theory of drinking behavior should therefore provide room for a diversity of individual motives, such as the many social-convivial ends consumption frequently serves. But drunkenness is a peculiarly attractive response to conditions of frustration and conflict. Its narcotizing effects provide a simple, inexpensive, and readily available means for temporary escape from psychic misery. When trying to account for high rates of drunkenness within any group, therefore, these physical properties of alcohol must certainly be recognized.

Based on these theoretical considerations, four general hypotheses have been formulated concerning sources of intragroup variations in Navajo migrant drinking behavior:

Hypothesis I: *Those Navajo migrants who are least successful in obtaining the economic rewards of urban life will display the highest rates of drunkenness.*

A migrant may come to Denver for many reasons. But the main thing he is seeking is a good job, one better than the limited reservation resources can provide. Failure to obtain steady, well-paying work in Denver should therefore prove to be a major source of disappointment and frustration, which alcohol could help him to forget.

Hypothesis II: *Those Navajo migrants with the greatest opportunity for acquiring skills for successfully holding down good jobs will display the lowest rates of drunkenness.*

Failure on a job may occur either because it is too difficult or because the migrant has limited personal resources for coping with its demands. One source of their urban difficulties, therefore, should be found in the poor training and limited experience that many migrants bring to the city.

Hypothesis III: *Those Navajo migrants who experience the greatest disjunction between their personal goals and their expectations of achieving them, or the greatest conflict between competing, mutually incompatible goals, will display the highest rates of drunkenness.*

Although a marginal economic position should be the major structural source of migrant motives to drink, they may differ in the way they perceive and evaluate their marginality. And material things are not the only goals toward which migrants aspire. For a more complete understanding of reasons they may seek drunken escape, therefore, a direct assessment of these psychological variables is also required.

Hypothesis IV: *Those Navajo migrants experiencing the weakest social pressures to drink and the strongest social controls against drinking will display the lowest rates of drunkenness.*

In Denver the major social pressures and constraints relevant to a migrant's drinking stem from his wife and his fellow Navajo peers. This fourth hypothesis directs us to examine the effect of these social relationships on migrant drinking behavior. In interaction with strong psychological motives to drink, these factors should provide substantial understanding of the high rates of Navajo drunkenness and arrest observed.

To bring empirical evidence to bear on this decision model, data were collected on 259 male Navajo migrants and former migrants, including essentially all who were living in Denver during 1963–1966 ($N = 135$), as well as a one-third random sample of all former Denver migrants who had returned to the Navajo Reservation ($N = 124$).[4] Our main instrument was a lengthy formal interview of about two hours duration, which included background information, complete job histories, and a battery of psychometric and sociometric tests. In addition, interviews and ratings were collected from most employers of Navajo Indians in Denver (Weppner 1968), all migrant records from the Bureau of Indian Affairs were abstracted, participant observation of Navajo recreational activities in Denver was conducted (Snyder 1968), and case studies in depth were made of representative migrant individuals and families (McCracken 1968; McSwain 1965; Ziegler 1967). From this wealth of data, findings of substantial internal consistency and reliability are now emerging.

In the present paper arrest rates in the city will serve as our major criterion measure. These have the virtue of being "nonreactive" (Webb et al. 1966) and extend over the entire period each migrant remained in the city. Self-report data on drinking rates and drinking-related problems were also collected, but for a number of reasons these have not proved to be as useful. Not the least of these is that half the self-reports were collected after the migrant returned to the reservation and therefore may reflect a post-migration adaptation.

The use of arrest rates places some limitations upon the analysis, however. In the case of the Navajo (and probably all urban Indians) the assumption that the greater the drunkenness the greater the arrest rate is not unreasonable, given the high percentage of arrests that are for drinking-related offenses and the predominantly public form that Indian drinking takes. But because the relationship between drunkenness and arrest is probabilistic rather than mechanical, *group* rates will be more dependable than *individual* rates, making correlations between a migrant's personal attributes and his frequency of arrest unstable. This problem is exacerbated by the fact that many migrants, like Harrison Joe, remain in the city only a few weeks or months, so that the temporal base on which individual rates might be calculated is often very small.

As a results of such considerations, our analytic procedure has been as follows. To relate arrest rates to various "independent" variables, these are dichotomized at the median, or in some cases at a natural break in the distribution or at some psychologically significant point. Then we estimate the arrest rate for those migrants with high and with low scores. First we count the number of arrests among those "highs" interviewed on the reservation, multiply this figure by three (since we have a one-third sample) and add it to the number of arrests acquired by "highs" interviewed in Denver (where we had essentially a total sample). The same procedure is then followed for estimating the number of man-years the "highs" spent in the city, and arrests are divided by man-years, rounded to two significant decimal places, to yield an estimated rate per man-year for the "highs." These steps are then repeated for migrants falling in the "low" category as well. In standard form these two figures are then converted to rates per 100,000 man-years in the city (simply multiplying each by 100,000) to permit direct comparison with data such as were presented in Tables 1 and 2.

This procedure may sound complicated, perhaps even a bit under-handed. It is not. Nevertheless, since it will be used throughout this paper and is critical to the argument, it is essential that credibility not be lost at this point. The following demonstration may help to illustrate and clarify the procedure and perhaps allay suspicions of mathematical legerdemain as well.

The arrest rate for our migrant population in Denver has already been presented; it was based on actual records from almost the entire group. Suppose we were to estimate this same rate from our interviewed sample. How would this estimate be calculated, based on the procedure outlined above, and how would it compare with the actual rate?

The 135 migrants inverviewed in Denver had 245 arrests, while the 124 interviewed on the reservation had 137. Since this reservation group is a one-third sample of all returnees, we multiply their arrests by three to get an estimate of the total returnee arrests: 411. When these are added to the Denver group we obtain an estimate of 656 arrests for the total population. The actual number by count was 665, giving us an error in estimate of about 1½%. Similarly for man-years in the city. The group interviewed in Denver account for 352½ man-years, while the group interviewed on the reservation account for 86-1/3. Multiplying the latter figure by three and adding the two we obtain an estimate of 611½ man-years in the city for the total migrant group. This compares with 639 man-years by actual count, or an error in estimate of about 4%. Finally, to calculate the arrest rate, we divide the estimated number of arrests, 656, by the estimated number of man-years in the city, 611½, and multiply by 100,000. This yields a figure of 107,000 arrests per 100,000 population, as compared with the actual rate of 104,000, for an error in estimate of less than 3%.

Also worth mentioning at this point is the question of the "statistical significance" of the data to be presented subsequently. Since arrests are not independent events, i.e., the same person may be arrested more than once, there is no statistical procedure by which the "significance" of a difference between the arrest rates of two groups can be tested. This problem is exacerbated by the unequal sampling ratios employed in the Denver and returnee strata, since data from the latter subjects must be multiplied by three to provide population estimates, introducing further nonin-dependence. As a consequence, no tests of statistical significance will be presented in this paper. Instead, we will be forced to apply far more stringent criteria to an evaluation of our results: (1) is the magnitude of the group differences in arrest rate found large enough to have *social* significance, and (2) is the *pattern* of associations found consistent and in line with a reasonable set of theoretical expectations? If these two criteria are met, then the issue of statistical significance would be irrelevant anyway. For those still concerned with the problem, however, some evaluation of the results can be based on the error in estimate of group rates just presented. If group differences in arrest rates are no larger than 3,000 to 5,000 per 100,000 man-years in the city, for example, they are probably not large enough to be stable, and therefore not worth interpreting. But almost all of the differences to be presented here are of the order of 20,000 or more. It is therefore very unlikely that our interpretations are empirically unfounded despite our inability to demonstrate the formal statistical significance of our results.

ECONOMIC FACTORS

As I have emphasized in a different research context, the major structural pressure to drink experienced by Indians in U.S. society derives from their marginal economic position. The theoretical basis for this statement is to be found in the work of Merton (1957) and others. When goals are strongly held for which society provides inadequate means of attainment, in the view of these theorists, the resulting means-goals "disjunction" produces pressures for engaging in allternative, often nonapproved adaptations, of which excessive drinking is one common form. In decision theory terms what this means is that the anticipated rewards (goals) for engaging in socially approved behavior (means) are relatively low. The resulting disappointment and frustration leads to the selection of *other* courses of action (such as drunkenness) that may not be so highly approved but provide substitute rewards. Using a rural sample of both Indians and Spanish-Americans, I found that among those strongly oriented toward the dominant society and its material values, those with poor and irregular jobs consistently had higher rates of drinking and associated problem-behavior, as well as stronger psychological *feelings* of deprivation and alienation, than those holding down relatively steady jobs. By contrast, among those with relatively little commitment to the dominant group values, the kind of jobs they held had practically no relationship to drinking rates or associated psychological feelings (Graves 1967a. See also Jessor, Graves, Hanson, and Jessor 1968 for the more general situation among nonacculturating groups as well).

Among migrant Indians, the situation is different than among these rural-reservation groups. Essentially all migrants are strongly attracted to economic goals, which is a major source of their dissatisfaction with reservation life and motivation to migrate. Furthermore, those who remain in the city longest display the strongest economic value orientation (Graves and VanArsdale 1966). We therefore hypothesized that any index of economic failure in the city would be associated with higher rates of drunkenness and arrest among all migrants.

This hypothesis was repeatedly supported, regardless of what measures of economic success we employed (Tables 3 and 4). Wages have great psychological salience for these migrants, and the reader should particularly note the association between arrest rates and an indirect measure of

TABLE 3

Initial Economic Experiences in the City Versus Denver Arrest Rates

	Percentage of All Migrants	Arrest Rate per 100,000 Pop.
Initial % employed		
more than 85%	50	73,000
85% or less	50	128,000
Starting wage		
more than $1.25 per hour	38	77,000
$1.25 or less per hour	62	93,000
Starting wage relative to highest premigration wage		
same or higher than premigration	48	54,000
lower than premigration	52	116,000
Combined pattern of variables		
favorable on all three of the above	11	34,000
favorable on two out of three	32	85,000
favorable on only one indicator	41	88,000
unfavorable on all three of the above	16	214,000

TABLE 4

Subsequent Economic Experiences in the City Versus Denver Arrest Rates

	Percentage of All Migrants	Arrest Rate per 100,000 Pop.
Subsequent % employed		
full employment	66	66,000
some unemployment	34	179,000
Present wage		
more than $1.35 per hour	45	57,000
$1.35 or less per hour	55	167,000
Present wage relative to highest premigration wage		
higher than premigration	51	43,000
same or lower than premigration	49	165,000
Combined pattern of variables		
favorable on all three of the above	22	44,000
favorable on two out of three	32	55,000
favorable on only one indicator	33	157,000
unfavorable on all three of the above	13	448,000

feelings of *relative deprivation* that we derived from this fact. When the migrant's starting wage was *lower* than the highest wage he had received before migrating, as was true for slightly over half of all migrants, it is probably fair to assume that he might well begin to wonder if the many sacrifices associated with migration were worthwhile. This structurally based psychological situation is associated with a subsequent arrest rate of 116,000 per 100,000 man-years in the city, more than double the rate of

54,000 among those migrants whose starting wages were at least as high as they had experienced before migration.

But absolute levels of economic achievement are also associated with arrest rates; jointly these form an even more powerful predictor. Those who experienced unemployment rates of 15% or more during their first few months in Denver and who had a starting wage of no more than $1.25 per hour, which was also as low or lower than they had experienced before migration (16% of all migrants), had an arrest rate of 214,000 per 100,000 man-years in the city. By contrast, those with less unemployment and higher starting wage in both relative and absolute terms (11% of all migrants) had an arrest rate of only 34,000 per 100,000, about one-sixth that of their less fortunate brethren.

Although these initial economic experiences in Denver are powerful predictors of a migrant's subsequent drinking problems, the association between economic position and arrest rate deepens with time in the city (Table 4). For example, those who continued to have periods of unemployment during their last few months in Denver and who were making less than $1.50 per hour, which was a wage no higher than they had received before coming to Denver (13% of all migrants), had an appalling arrest rate of 448,000 per 100,000 man-years in the city!

In part this depressing relationship between economic position and arrest rate probably results from the fact that continuing deprivation is more psychologically disturbing than initial deprivation, when hopes may linger for better times to come. But it also derives from the effect of the migrant's drinking on his economic position. Complaints about their drunkenness is the major factor that differentiates employer ratings of Indian employees from those of whites in comparable jobs, and these complaints are clearly related to lower Indian wages or dismissal (Weppner 1968). As one employer put it, describing his experience with one of our subjects, "He'd take off three or four days at a time because of drinking. We took him back three or four times but hell, there's no use putting up with it." This feedback from the migrant's drinking behavior to the structural and psychological "determinants" that in turn give rise to it is a theme we have tried to pursue in this study wherever our time-linked data permit. Thus we can trace the development of a vicious cycle between structural position, personality, and behavior that is difficult to break once it has been set in motion.

BACKGROUND FACTORS

This developmental cycle does not begin in the city, however. Background preparation for urban life also contributes to economic success in Denver, and thereby to a better personal adjustment. We were particularly fascinated by the possible influence of a migrant's father (or father surrogate) in providing both direct and indirect training for successful wage-labor, via now familiar processes of social learning and "modeling" (Bandura and Walters 1963). Our hypothesis was that

TABLE 5

Economically Successful Parental Role Models Versus Denver Arrest Rates

	Percentage of All Migrants	Arrest Rate per 100,000 Pop.
Father's occupation		
father has nontraditional occupation (wage-labor)	39	75,000
father has traditional occupation (farming-herding)	61	97,000
Economic position of family or orientation		
perceived as better off than neighbors	60	75,000
perceived as worse off than neighbors	40	117,000
Combined pattern of variables		
nontraditional occupation *and* family was better off	26	62,000
mixed pattern	48	83,000
traditional occupation *and* family was worse off	26	135,000

successful parental wage-labor role models would be associated with better economic performance in the city by their sons, and therefore better personal adjustment. All the links in this chain of inference cannot be presented here, though this hypothesis received support at each point examined. Table 5 presents the end product, the association between parental models and subsequent urban arrest rates. As can be seen, those migrants whose fathers provided economically successful wage-labor role models had arrest rates of 62,000 per 100,000 man-years in Denver, less than half the rate for migrants whose fathers were engaged in more traditional reservation occupations and were economically unsuccessful as well (135,000 arrests per 100,000 man-years).

Education and vocational training provide even more direct preparation for successful economic performance and were therefore also expected to be associated with a better urban adjustment. The evidence in support of this hypothesis is presented in Table 6. Migrants with eight or more years of formal education that included skilled vocational training also had arrest rates of less than half those with less education and no skilled vocational training (51,000 versus 145,000 arrests per 100,000 man-years in the city). Note, however, that a small amount of education or training is associated with higher arrest rates than almost none at all! Perhaps this results from raising the migrant's aspirations higher than this level of preparation can help him achieve. Commonly these migrants, like Harrison Joe, who came to the city with semiskilled training for which there is a limited market, expected to receive good jobs in their chosen field right away and are disappointed when they don't.

Other forms of premigration experience were also implicated, but not always in the manner one might anticipate. For example, premigration wage labor experience, though it usually resulted in better urban jobs, was

TABLE 6

Education and Vocational Training Versus Denver Arrest Rate

	Percentage of All Migrants	Arrest Rate per 100,000 Pop.
Years of education		
11 years or more	14	33,000
8-10 years	31	75,000
5-7 years	45	128,000
4 years or less	10	87,000
Vocational training		
skilled	41	66,000
semiskilled	45	117,000
none	14	83,000
Combined pattern of variables		
8 or more years of education *and* skilled vocational training	21	51,000
mixed pattern	43	77,000
less than 8 years of school *and* no skilled vocational training	36	145,000

also associated with higher arrest rates. From other data it appears likely that favorable premigration experience raises migrant aspirations farther than the reality of urban life can satisfy, thus producing a sense of "relative deprivation" among many otherwise "successful" migrants.

In sum, if we were to look at no other variables than a migrant's economic position in the city, we would still have achieved a major understanding of his drunkenness and arrest problems.

PSYCHOLOGICAL FACTORS

The finding already reported that urban wages relative to premigration wages are a better predictor of arrest rates than absolute wage level indicates the importance of *psychological* processes in mediating this empirical relationship. Two types of psychological variables are of focal importance: personal *goals* and future *expectations* concerning one's ability to achieve these goals.

Our most successful technique for getting at migrants' values involved a content analysis of four open-ended questions:

(1) What are the things you like best about living in Denver?
(2) What do you *not* like about living in Denver?
(3) What do you like best about living on the reservation?
(4) What do you *not* like about living on the reservation?

The answers to these questions did two things for us simultaneously: (1) they helped us define the *opportunity structure* of the city and the reservation *as perceived by these migrants,* and (2) they provided us with a basis for distinguishing those migrants whose personal goals are most compatible with that the city can provide. The results of this content analysis have been reported elsewhere (Graves and VanArsdale 1966), and demonstrate the overwhelming significance of *economic* opportunities in the city, whereas the reservation is characterized by the variety of *social* and *traditional* goals it can provide. From this sharp distinction in the perceived opportunity structure of the city and the reservation the following hypothesis was derived:

> *Those migrants who have a personal goal structure least in line with urban opportunities will experience the greatest psychological conflict about remaining in Denver and will therefore drink the heaviest.*

To test the hypothesis, migrant responses to these four open-ended questions were sorted into categories, and the proportion of economic-material goals mentioned was calculated for each subject. When the resulting distribution was divided at the median, those migrants with the weakest commitment to economic-material goals did indeed have higher arrest rates in Denver (Table 7).

To get at the other end of the value continuum, and to provide a second, operationally distinct measure of migrant goals, a semiprojective measure of Navajo "traditionalism" was used, which Goldschmidt, Edgerton, and Nydegger originally developed and kindly loaned us (see a related test by Goldschmidt and Edgerton 1961). Subjects were shown pictures that contrasted traditional and modern scenes, and their responses to these scenes were again content analyzed. Those subjects who displayed a strong orientation toward the goals of traditional reservation life also had higher arrest rates in Denver (Table 7). Neither of these two value measures, moreover, bore any relationship to *actual* economic achievement in the city. Thus a correlation between material values and good jobs could not account for the lower arrest rates, adding weight to the value conflict interpretation. And when combined, these two value measures yield a substantial degree of association with arrests: those migrants whose goals

TABLE 7
Personal Values Versus Denver Arrest Rates

	Percentage of All Migrants	Arrest Rate per 100,000 Pop.
Economic value orientation		
high economic values	50	84,000
low economic values	50	96,000
Navajo traditionalism*		
low traditional values	37	82,000
high traditional values	63	95,000
Combined pattern of personal values		
high economic values *plus* low traditional values	17	61,000
mixed patterns	49	86,000
low economic values *plus* high traditional values	34	117,000

*Based on a sample of approximately two-thirds of the protocols available.

are most compatible with urban opportunities have an arrest rate of 61,000 per 100,000 man-years in Denver; those migrants whose goals are least appropriate have arrest rates almost double, 117,000 per 100,000 man-years.

The source of this particular type of psychic distress, and thus of migrants' drunken response, resides in the fact that the pursuit of one set of goals (economic-material) through urban migration leads to inadequate satisfaction of another set of goals (social-traditional) that are often equally strong. Another way to measure this conflict and its consequences is through a self-anchoring scale of migrants' future expectations (Graves and VanArsdale 1966). Those migrants who expect to do well in the city in the future but have no hope for success on the reservation have few doubts about migrating. They remain in the city longest and have the lowest arrest rates: 75,000 per 100,000 man-years (Table 8). Those who expect to·do well back home but not in Denver also have relatively low arrest rates: 81,000. What conflict they feel is quickly resolved by a return to the reservation. Those who feel they could do well in either location are in a "double-approach" conflict reflected in an arrest rate of 93,000 per 100,000 man-years. Those in the more devastating "double avoidance" conflict who cannot anticipate personal success in either location have a far higher arrest rate: 179,000. This analysis provides strong empirical support for a "conflict theory" of drunkenness.

Also of interest to us were three personality traits at a fairly high level of abstraction that we believed would serve both to promote economic success and to control against selection of escapist behavior such as drunkenness (Graves 1966). These included feelings of personal control (versus fatalism), an extended future time perspective, and high achievement motivation. The first two were measured using modifications of techniques developed for the Tri-Ethnic Research Project (Jessor, Graves, Hanson, and Jessor 1968: Graves 1967b). The third was measured by a TAT-type test of our own construction, with the assistance of a Navajo artist (Michener 1965).

TABLE 8

Future Expectations Versus Denver Arrest Rates

	Percentage of All Migrants	Arrest Rate per 100,000 Pop.
Future expectations if in Denver		
will improve in next 5 years	65	82,000
will stay the same or get worse	35	113,000
Future expectations if on reservation		
will improve in next 5 years	48	90,000
will stay the same or get worse	52	95,000
Interaction between future expectations for		
Denver and reservation		
will improve in Denver but not on reservation	35	75,000
will improve on reservation but not in Denver	18	81,000
will improve in either location	30	93,000
will not improve in either location	17	179,000

TABLE 9
Need-Achievement Versus Denver Arrest Rates

	Percentage of All Migrants	Arrest Rate per 100,000 Pop.
Achievement motivation		
low	49	64,000
high	51	86,000
Interaction between this need and economic pressures		
present wage higher than highest premigration wage *and*		
a. low need-achievement	27	33,000
b. high need-achievement	23	39,000
present wage same or lower than highest pre-migration wage *and*		
a. low need-achievement	21	97,000
b. high need-achievement	29	176,000

Space does not permit me to report here all the fascinating surprises this analysis revealed. Contrary to expectations, these attributes of "industrial man" proved completely *unrelated* to economic success in the city, and for two the relationship with drunkenness and arrest was in the *opposite* direction anticipated. Need-achievement will serve as an illustration. Those with high achievement motivation actually had *higher* arrest rates than those with low achievement motivation (Table 9). In interaction with our most potent measure of economic failure the dynamics of this process are revealed more clearly. Among those migrants who probably perceived themselves as doing relatively well in the city (those making more money than they ever had before), high or low achievement motivation appears to be almost unrelated to arrest rates. But among those who probably felt economically deprived, such aspirations become critical: migrants with low need-achievement have arrest rates of 97,000 per 100,000, but those in similar economic circumstances with high need-achievement have arrest rates of 176,000. Achievement striving is apparently not the adaptive trait teachers working with Indian students may believe; instead, for those with limited marketable skills it makes the inevitable frustrations of urban living that much harder to bear.

SOCIAL FACTORS

For a more complete understanding of migrant drinking, however, social pressures and constraints from peers and wives should also be taken into consideration. The social-recreational nature of Navajo drinking (Heath 1964; Ferguson 1968), common to most American Indian groups, was observed in Denver as well. In fact, recreational activities among migrants almost always involve some drinking, more often than not heavy drinking and drunkenness (Snyder 1968). It is not surprising, therefore, that pressures from buddies to join them is the single most common explanation of their drinking problems given by Navajos themselves both on and off the reservation. That this is not the whole explanation is obvious from the associations already presented between arrest rates and economic deprivation. But the Navajo's excuse cannot be dismissed as pure rationalization, as was amply illustrated by the case of Harrison Joe. To a young migrant alone in the city, the social rewards for deciding to drop into a bar with his friends may be very high indeed.

The empirical support for the influence of peer group members on migrant drinking is strong (Table 10). Those with exclusively Navajo friends in the city have arrest rates of 131,000 per 100,000 man-years, substantially higher than those who spend at least part of their spare time with non-Navajos (62,000 arrests per 100,000 man-years).[5] Furthermore, this influence apparently begins as soon as the migrant arrives in Denver: those with any kin or freinds in the city on arrival (other than wife) have a subsequent arrest rate of 107,000 per 100,000, as compared with a rate of only 69,000 arrests for those who arrived knowing no one. The case of Harrison Joe illustrates how this relationship comes about. Whatever positive function a Navajo reference group may serve in helping a new migrant adjust to a strange urban environment, it also serves to socialize him to a pattern of recreational drinking that is likely to get him into trouble and make his adjustment more difficult.

TABLE 10

Informal Social Relationships in the City Versus Denver Arrest Rates

	Percentage of All Migrants	Arrest Rate per 100,000 Pop.
Kin and friends at arrival		
none	47	69,000
some	53	107,000
Friendship pattern in the city		
some non-Navajo friends	51	62,000
exclusively Navajo friends	49	131,000
Navajo sociometric score (those interviewed in Denver only)		
relatively few Navajo friends	$N = 56$	38,000
many Navajo friends	$N = 56$	66,000
Interaction between peer group pressures and economic pressures		
present wage higher than highest premigration wage *and* some non-Navajo friends	28	32,000
present wage higher than highest premigration wage *and* exclusively Navajo friends	24	77,000
present wage same or lower than highest pre-migration wage *and* some non-Navajo friends	24	113,000
present wage same or lower than highest pre-migration wage *and* exclusively Navajo friends	24	207,000

The establishment of Navajo drinking groups, and the powerful influence that they apparently have on members' behavior, can be understood, I believe, in terms similar to the formation and maintenance of other types of "deviant subcultures" (Cohen 1955, Cloward and Ohlin 1960). Given the manifold pressures on many migrants to drink as an escape from the frustrations and problems generated by their marginal socioeconomic position, a pattern of drinking to oblivion is established and continues to be strongly reinforced among core participants and others with similar psychological needs who may be drawn to the group. Such drinking groups are an attractive adaptation for migrants not only because of the escape that drunkenness may yield, but also because of the social solidarity that they create among participants. Furthermore, by flaunting the mores of the dominant community, group drunkenness provides an outlet for hositility toward the white reference group many would like to join, but which has failed to accept them fully (Berreman 1964; Parker 1964). Once a pattern of group drunkenness becomes normative, however, it also serves as a standard of behavior for some participants who may not have the psychological needs that generated the pattern in the first place. Thus the existence of the pattern itself, as mediated by the social pressures exerted by core participants, becomes a sufficient cause for the drinking behavior of others who come in contact with it.

This interpretation gains support, from the interaction between economic pressures and peer pressures. When migrants are doing relatively well in the city economically, even if their friendships are drawn exclusively from the ranks of other Navajos, their arrest rate is only 77,000. The peer group pressures to get drunk are apparently *far greater*, however, when migrants are doing poorly in the city and therefore have a personal, psychological motive to get drunk as well. Those with relatively poor wages evidently find the enticements of their Navajo drinking companions far more attractive and have an arrest rate of 207,000 per 100,000 man-years in the city, almost three times the rate of their economically more fortunate comparisons.

Counteracting these peer pressures are the constraints being applied by a migrant's wife. Keeping her husband's drinking within bounds is one of her major responsibilities (McSwain 1965). Some wives are obviously more successful at this task than others, but all that we spoke with on this matter at least try. A measure of their success is seen in an arrest rate of only 56,000 per 100,000 man-years among those married throughout their stay in the city (Table 11). This rate rises to 73,000 among those married during only part of their stay, and jumps to 124,000 among the three-quarters of all Navajo migrants who are single their entire time in Denver. The fact that only 20% of the Navajo migrants are married when they arrive is a major structural difference between them and other minority groups in Denver, which also helps to account for part of the radical difference in arrest rates between them. For example, 88% of the Spanish migrant comparison sample are married, though many first came to the city alone and then called their family to join them after they found a job (Rendon 1968).

Since married migrants might be assumed to be older and more experienced, the alert reader may wonder if this relationship between marriage and low arrest rates is not simply a matter of better jobs. But somewhat surprisingly, marital status is *unrelated* to economic success in the city. As with many other variables we investigated, however, the migrant's economic position is highly important for understanding the points at which wifely controls become most critical. When migrants receive relatively good wages, those who are married have arrest rates only about 10,000 lower than those who are single. By contrast, when migrants are receiving relatively poor wages, those who are married have arrest rates 100,000 lower than those who are single (bottom of Table 11). The influence of a migrant's wife as an agent of social control appears to be far more important when he is badly off, and therefore highly motivated to get drunk, then when he is doing well.

Finally, the joint influence of social pressures and controls, in conjunction with a migrant's economic position in the city, reveals the powerful value of a field-theoretical approach to an explanation of urban Indian drunkenness. For a migrant who is single throughout his stay in the city, associates exclusively with other Navajos, and earns no more than he had received previously, both the pressures and the temptations to drink heavily are great. Eighteen percent of all Navajo migrants to Denver fell into this pattern, and their arrest rate was 243,000 per 100,000 man-years in the city. At the other end of the scale we have a handful of stable migrants (8%) who were married throughout their stay in Denver, did not spend their spare time exclusively in the company of other Navajos, and were receiving the highest wages they had ever enjoyed. Their arrest rate

TABLE 11
Marital Status in the City Versus Denver Arrest Rates

	Percentage of All Migrants	Arrest Rate per 100,000 Pop.
Marital status at arrival		
married	20	60,000
single	80	106,000
Marital status during entire migration		
married throughout stay	19	56,000
married part of stay	6	73,000
single throughout stay	75	124,000
Interaction between marital controls and economic pressures		
present wage higher than highest premigration wage and married any time in city	14	39,000
present wage higher than highest premigration wage *and* single throughout stay	37	55,000
present wage same or lower than highest premigration wage *and* married any time in city	13	120,000
present wage same or lower than highest premigration wage *and* single throughout stay	36	228,000

was only 26,000, or approaching the range found among Spanish-Americans and Negroes. In the interaction between social variables and economic variables, therefore, it appears that most of the difference in arrest rates between Navajo migrants and other urban minority groups can be accounted for.

CONCLUSIONS

Generally speaking, recourse to a group's "culture" for explaining their behavior simply serves to conceal our ignorance of the underlying processes in operation. In this study we made a deliberate attempt to seek an explanation of excessive Indian drunkenness in terms of structural and psychological variables that are also relevant to non-Indian drinkers. For example, our focus was on the type of parental role models, premigration training for successful urban employment, martial status, and so on. After showing that better prepared Indians have far fewer drinking problems than less well prepared Indians, we can then understand their high drinking rates in comparison to other urban groups by virtue of the fact that their preparation for successful, unstressful urban living is far poorer. Almost a third of the Spanish migrants' had fathers who were employed as semiskilled wage laborers or better (Rendon 1965); most Navajo wage labor of the last generation was purely unskilled manual work. A third of the Spanish migrants also had essentially high school training (eleven years or more), whereas only 14% of the Navajo migrants got this far in school. Eighty-eight percent of the Spanish migrants were married; only 20% of the Navajo were married. The first job in Denver for 15% of the Spanish migrants was skilled, whereas only 6% of the Navajo were able to do this well. And so on.

Our analysis of Navajo drinking groups also has this type of analytic generality, even though in some respects these groups appear culturally specific. The typical Navajo social drinking group is here seen as an adaptive response to structural conditions that give rise to similar groups within other tribes and among many non-Indian peoples as well. In addition, its "deviant" form, which helps us to understand its dynamics, provides theoretical linkages with such well-studied phenomena as delinquent gangs and drug-use circles. Furthermore, when we define groups of Indian migrants who are peculiarly susceptible to the social pressures exerted by members of these drinking cliques—single Navajos whose marginal economic position in the midst of affluence generates strong feelings of relative deprivation and whose friendships are drawn exclusively from the ranks of their fellow Navajos—arrest rates are more than twice as high as for Navajo migrants in general. By contrast, married migrants with stable urban adaptation who are not socially mapped into these groups have arrest rates close to those of other minority groups in the city and only a fraction as high as the overall Navajo rate.

Thus it would appear that the vast majority of Navajo drunkenness, at least in Denver, can be accounted for *without recourse to the fact that our subjects are Indians.* Although this conclusion will displease some of my anthropological colleagues, these findings have greater theoretical and applied implications as a result. Particularly significant is the fact that many of the critical determinants examined in this paper are structural variables over which society can exercise some measure of control.

Even though this is a statistical analysis, it has potential policy implications for persons working with individual migrants, as long as the *probablistic* relationship between variables is borne in mind. This may be illustrated by returning to the case of Harrison Joe, the migrant with whom I began this essay. A summary of his background attributes and urban experience is presented in Table 12. On five of the six "predictors" discussed in this paper, Harrison Joe appears poorly equipped for success in the city. Only the fact that his father was a silversmith, a marginal case of "wage labor" at best, might possibly suggest success.

If funds for the relocation program were limited, discouraging such "poor risks" from coming to the city might be advocated purely on the basis of a cost-benefit analysis. One might also argue, however, that encouraging people to migrate despite a poor prognosis may be doing them a disservice. Resulting failure may have serious long range psychological and social consequences, setting them on an endless spiral of migration and return, marked by frustration, failure, and drunkenness at every turn.

As in all statistical decision-making, one must consider both the cost of letting a migrant come to the city and being wrong versus keeping him away and being wrong. Some applicants with poor qualifications *do* succeed in the city, and the Bureau quite properly is reluctant to cut them

TABLE 12
Harrison Joe's Profile on Key Variables

	Prognosis
Predictors	
Father was a silversmith (considered wage labor)	+
But family perceived as worse off than neighbors	−
5 years of education (Special Navajo Program)	−
Semi-skilled vocational training (upholstery)	−
Unmarried	−
Had friends and relatives in Denver on arrival	−
Initial urban experience	
62% initial unemployment	−
Starting wage was only $1.25 per hour	−
But this was higher than he had earned before migration	+
Subsequent urban experience	
Continued high unemployment rate throughout stay	−
Wages never rose above $1.25 per hour	−
Though this was higher than premigration wages	+
Maintained an exclusive Navajo friendship circle	−
Was arrested for drunkenness within 3 weeks of arrival	−
Returned home almost immediately thereafter	−

off from the chance. It would be far better to encourage such applicants first to take advantage of BIA sponsored basic educational and vocational training before embarking on direct employment assistance. At the very least, special counseling and follow-up should be provided for high risk applicants after their arrival.

Our work has many other obvious applied implications. The role of economic marginality in the migrant's adjustment problems is fundamental, as it was for another tribe and their Spanish-American neighbors in a rural-reservation setting as well (Graves 1967a). Repeatedly factors such as marriage, peer pressures, and a variety of personality variables make their primary contribution to the migrant's drinking problems, whether this contribution be positive or negative, when the migrant has a poor and unstable income. If these economic hardships could be solved, other factors would assume minor importance. What the migrant needs is not more psychological counseling (Ferguson 1968) or more wholesome recreational outlets (Dozier 1966), but better jobs. Any limitation in his personality or cultural repertoire for coping with his adjustment difficulties becomes irrelevant if the economic basis for these difficulties can be dealt with. But it is also clear from our research that urban migration is not the best way to solve economic limitation of reservation life. Our experience with migrants indicates that most would prefer to live and work near their reservation homes. Forcing them to seek employment in large urban centers only adds to their adjustment problems in the many ways this paper has documented.

Finally, we must always acknowledge that every research project, no matter how ambitious, is in many respects incomplete. The migrant Indian's tendency to turn to alcohol when adjustment problems arise is not fully explained by the variables we have dealt with here. Obviously there are additional factors that also contribute to the differences between Indians and other minority group migrants in drunkenness and arrest. For example, certain group variables typical of Indians, such as low normative concensus, the prevalence of deviant Indian role models and relative absence of successful ones, and a self-fulfilling image of themselves as "drunkards" also undoubtedly contribute to their problems. By operationalizing terms such as these an imaginative researcher might successfully account for a significant portion of the remaining variance.

Furthermore, the empirical success of our decision model does not rule out the possibility that other explanatory models may also be relevant. For instance, some Indian drinking may better be understood not as the product of rational choice but as patterned role behavior or a type of symbolic communication by which the drinker tells other Indians that he's one of them and tells the white man that he's not. But rather than argue about which variable or which model is more appropriate simply on grounds of disciplinary loyalty, I would welcome an empirical demonstration of how much variance in Indian drinking behavior each can account for. For this, after all, is the true challenge of social science.

NOTES

1 The research reported in this paper was undertaken with the Program of Research on Social Processes, Institute of Behavioral Science, University of Colorado. The research has been supported by the University's Council on Research and Creative Work and the National Institute of Mental Health grant nos. 1-R 11 MH 1942-01, 02, and 03. Much of the present analysis was completed while at the Makerere Institute of Social Research, Kampala, Uganda, and I wish to thank the director, Dr. Derryk Belshaw, his colleagues and staff for their generous and gracious support.

   Because this research was designed in part to serve as a training laboratory for social science graduate students at Colorado, a great many people have participated in the data collection and analysis: Drs. Braxton M. Alfred, Robert D. McCracken, Romola McSwain, Duane Quiatt, Peter Z. Snyder, O. Michael Watson, C. Roderick Wilson, and Robert S. Weppner, Messrs. Avery G. Church, William Hozie, Kenneth L. Kuykendall, Bryan P. Michener, George Oetinger III, Carl Shames, and Minor Van Arsdale; Mesdames Mary Collins and Suzanne Ziegler. My debt to all these students is great. Under the same title an abridged draft of this paper was presented at the International Congress of Anthropological and Ethnological Sciences, Tokyo, Japan, September 7, 1968.

2 The case material presented in this section was collected in weekly interviews by Bryan Michener, supplemented by records from the Bureau of Indian Affairs and the Denver Police Department. The important role of police records in this research enterprise will become increasingly apparent to the reader, and I wish to acknowledge my profound debt to former Denver Police Chief Harold A. Dill for his cooperation and to Police Captain Doral E. Smith for the time he devoted to search his records for us. I am also grateful to Dr. Philleo Nash, former Commissioner of Indian Affairs, and to the former and present director of the Denver Office of Employment Assistance (BIA), Dr. Solon G. Ayers and Mr. Maynard Gage and their staffs, for the many ways in which they facilitated our work. I hope that what we have learned will be of value to administrators such as these, as well as to many "Harrison Joes" whose patience and cooperation made the research possible.

3 Two dissertations, Weppner 1968 and Snyder 1968, bring data to bear on the other two models used in this study. A book is planned in which all three models will be examined simultaneously, including a study of systematic linkages between models.

4 Actually, only about half of these "returnees" were selected on a truly random fashion from a total list derived from BIA records. During our first summers of fieldwork we had no idea how difficult it might be to locate specific returnees on the reservation. Consequently, we simply divided up the reservation into areas and attempted to locate what returnees we could from each on a "quota sampling" basis, making an effort not to select only the most readily available. On dozens of economic, social, and psychological variables these two returnee samples differed significantly no more often than would be expected by chance. They have therefore been combined and all treated as a single random sample.

5 The use of sociometric data to define the strength of peer group influence reveals similar results, but the measure is restricted to the subsample of migrants interviewed in Denver who remained in town long enough to develop stable friendship patterns.

REFERENCES CITED

Bandura, Albert, and Richard H. Walters (1963), Social learning and personality development. New York: Holt, Rinehart & Winston.

Berreman, Gerald D. (1964), Aleut reference group alienation, mobility, and acculturation. American Anthropologist 66:231-250.

Cloward, Richard A., and Lloyd E. Ohlin (1960), Deliquency and opportunity: a theory of delinquent gangs. New York: Free Press.

Cohen, Albert K. (1955), Delinquent boys: the culture of the gang. New York: Free Press.

Dozier, Edward P. (1966), Problem drinking among American Indians: the role of socio-cultural deprivation. Quarterly Journal of Studies on Alcohol 27:72-87.

Ferguson, Frances N. (1968), Navajo drinking: some tentative hypotheses. Human Organization 27:159-167.

Goldschmidt, Walter, and Robert B. Edgerton (1961), A picture technique for the study of values. American Anthropologist 63:26-47.

Graves, Theodore D. (1966), Alternative models for the study of urban migration. Human Organization 25:295-299.

———(1967a), Acculturation, access and alcohol in a tri-ethnic community. American Anthropologist 69:306-321.

———(1967b), Psychological acculturation in a tri-ethnic community. Southwestern Journal of Anthropology 23:337-350.

———in preparation, There but for grace: a social-psychological study of urban Indian drunkenness.

Graves, Theodore D., and Minor Van Arsdale (1966), Values, expectations and relocation: the Navajo Indian migrant to Denver. Human Organization 25:300-307.

Heath, Dwight B. (1964), Prohibition and post-repeal drinking patterns among the Navajo. Quarterly Journal of Studies on Alcohol 25:119-135.

Honigmann, John J. & Irma Honigmann (1968), Alcohol in a Canadian northern town. Paper presented at the annual meeting of the Canadian Sociology and Anthropology Association.

Jessor, Richard, Roderick S. Carmen, and Peter H. Grossman (1968), Expectations of need satisfaction and drinking patterns of college students. Quarterly Journal of Studies on Alcohol 29:101-116.

Jessor, Richard, Theodore D. Graves, Robert C. Hanson, and Shirley Jessor (1968), Society, personality, and deviant behavior. A study of a tri-ethnic community. New York: Holt, Rinehart & Winston.

McCracken, Robert D. (1968), Urban migration and the changing structure of Navajo social relations. Unpublished Ph.D. dissertation, University of Colorado (mimeographed).

McSwain, Romola, (1965), The role of wives in the urban adjustment of Navajo migrant families to Denver, Colorado, Unpublished MA thesis, University of Hawaii (mimeographed).

Merton, Robert K. (1957), Social structure and anomie. *In* Social theory and social structure. Glencoe: The Free Press, pp. 131-194.

Michener, Bryan P. (1965), The development and scoring of a test of need achievement for Navajo Indians. Navajo Urban Relocation Research Report No. 6 (mimeographed).

Parker, Seymour (1964), Ethnic identity and acculturation in two Eskimo villages. American Anthropologist 66:325-340.

Rendón, Gabino, Jr. (1968), Prediction of adjustment outcomes of rural migrants to the city. Unpublished Ph.D. dissertation, University of Colorado (mimeographed).

Snyder, Peter Z. (1968), Social assimilation and adjustment of Navajo migrants to Denver. Unpublished Ph.D. dissertation, University of Colorado (mimeographed).

Stewart, Omer C. (1964), Questions regarding American criminality. Human Organization 23:61-66.

Swett, Daniel H. (1963), Characteristics of the male Indian arrest population in San Francisco. Paper presented at the annual meeting of the Southwestern Anthropological Association.

Webb, E. J., D. T. Campbell, R. D. Schwartz, and L. Sechrest (1966), Unobtrusive measures; Nonreactive research in the social sciences. Chicago: Rand McNally & Co.

Weppner, Robert S. (1968), The economic absorption of Navajo Indian migrants to Denver, Colorado. Unpublished Ph.D. dissertation, University of Colorado (mimeographed).

Whittacker, James O. (1962), Alcohol and the Standing Rock Sioux tribe. I. The pattern of drinking. Quarterly Journal of Studies on Alcohol 23:468-479.

Yinger, J. Milton (1965), Toward a field theory of behavior: personality and social structure. New York: McGraw Hill.

Ziegler, Suzanne (1967), An urban dilemma: the case of Tyler Begay. Unpublished manuscript. To be published as an appendix in Graves (in preparation).

ALAN L. SORKIN: SOME ASPECTS OF AMERICAN INDIAN MIGRATION*

ABSTRACT

This paper is a study of federally assisted American Indian migration from the reservations to urban areas. The education of the migrants, their earnings before and after relocation, and the change in the degree of antisocial behavior after leaving the reservation are analyzed.

It is found that while relocation can enhance the standard of living of those participating in federal programs, budget limitations prevent these programs from assisting enough applicants to markedly reduce the level of surplus labor on the reservations.

The purpose of this paper is to present information on the magnitude and character of migration of American Indians from the reservations to urban areas, and its effect on the reservation economy.

There are approximately *380,000* American Indians residing on or adjacent to reservations (U.S. Public Health Service, 1966:10). These individuals comprise the most poverty-stricken minority group in the United States. The median family income for reservation Indians is *$1,800* per annum, with *76* percent of all reservation families earning incomes below the poverty threshold (U.S. Bureau of Indian Affairs, 1967). Unemployment of reservation males in 1967 was *37.3* percent of the labor force, or *50* percent higher than in the United States as a whole during the worst part of the Great Depression (U.S. Department of Labor, 1968:68). In 1966, according to a task force on Indian housing, over *75* percent of all reservation homes were substandard, with over *50* percent needing to be replaced (U.S. Bureau of Indian Affairs, 1966:5).

In order to ameliorate the problems of poverty and surplus labor on the reservations, the Bureau of Indian Affairs operates two separate relocation or employment assistance programs for reservation Indians. The first is a direct employment program; the second, known as Adult Vocational Training, provides training and subsequent employment in an off-reservation setting. Each of these programs will be described briefly.[1]

An Indian desiring to enter the direct employment program simply files an application for employment assistance with a Bureau of Indian Affairs employment assistance officer located on the reservation. After aptitude testing and counseling, the Indian and his family are transported at government expense to one of seven urban areas in which the B.I.A. has employment assistance centers.[2] When the family (or single individual) arrives at the center, they are given low-cost temporary housing, additional

Source: Reprinted by permission from *Social Forces* 48 (December 1969), 243-250.

counseling and advice in job seeking. Later, the family is aided in moving into permanent housing. After the individual is placed in a position, he generally receives follow-up services for one year.

Partly as a result of the fact that so few Indians are employed in positions above the unskilled category, the Indian Vocational Training Act was enacted in 1956. This Act made available a wide variety of courses which permit the Indian to upgrade his vocational skills. In 1966, vocational training courses in *125* different occupations had been approved at accredited schools in *26* states. These schools are located in both urban centers and near Indian reservations. However, whether or not the training is taken at an urban center, most graduates obtain employment (utilizing B.I.A. placement services) in urban off-reservation areas. The Bureau of Indian Affairs pays the trainee's and his family's (1) transportation to place of training and subsistence en route; (2) subsistence during the course of training (including clothing); (3) tuition, books, supplies and tools utilized in training.

Table 1 indicates the number of individuals relocated or trained under the two programs, by fiscal year.

Thus, between 1952 and 1968, over *100,000* Indians participated in these programs, which have as their principal objective, the relocation of American Indians from the reservations to urban areas.

THE FOLLOW-UP SAMPLE

During 1963, there were *1,678* participants in the direct employment program and *2,885* adult vocational trainees (these numbers include heads of households only). Samples of *6* percent from each category were ran-

TABLE 1

Number Entering Direct Employment and Adult Vocational Training (Plus Dependents) 1952-68

Fiscal Year	Direct Employment	Adult Vocational Training
1952	868	–
1954	2,553	–
1956	5,119	–
1958	5,728	873*
1960	3,674	1,809
1962	3,494	2,500
1964	4,097	3,054
1966	3,747	5,502
1967	5,599	5,545
1968	5,881	4,491
Total	67,522	36,047

Source: Unpublished tabulation computed by Branch of Employment Assistance, Bureau of Indian Affairs, entitled "Statistical Summary of Activities from Inception of Individual Program Through June 30, 1968."

*First year of program operation.

domly selected by the Bureau of Indian Affairs, and these individuals were interviewed during 1966 and 1968 in order to ascertain their success in adjusting to life off the reservation. (Sample size was determined through consultation with specialists at the Bureau of the Census and the Bureau of Labor Statistics.)

By utilizing the information compiled during these interviews, it is possible to determine demographic characteristics of these relocatees, their earnings before and after migration, their tendency to obtain additional education *after* participating in these programs, and their level of antisocial behavior before and after leaving the reservation.

THE EDUCATIONAL SELECTIVITY OF AMERICAN INDIAN MIGRATION

Hamilton (1959) and Fein (1965) have shown that the migration of American Negroes from the South to the North has been selective; that is, there is a tendency for the better-educated Negroes to have higher rates of net out-migration than less educated Negroes.

It appears that American Indian migration from the reservations to urban areas follows a similar pattern. Table 2 presents data on the educational distribution of a sample of relocatees and adult vocational trainees, and compares it with the educational distribution of all reservation Indians (primarily nonmigrants) of similar age.[3]

It is evident that the Indians participating in the direct employment and adult vocational training programs are better educated than all reservation Indians of comparable age. The difference between the median years of schooling for those participating in the direct employment program and all reservation Indians is nearly three years; while the difference between the median years of schooling of the trainees and all reservation Indians was more than four years. However, it must be pointed out that about 75

TABLE 2

Educational Distribution, Sample of Relocatees, Vocational Trainees and All Reservation Indians 18-35

Direct Employment Recipients (Relocatees)		Adult Vocational Trainees		All Reservation Indians (18-35)	
Years of school	*Percent*	*Years of school*	*Percent*	*Years of school*	*Percent*
0-8	31	0-8	9	0-8	55
9-11	33	9-11	23	9-11	26
12 or more	36	12 or more	68	12 or more	19
Median	10.6	Median	12.0	Median	7.8

Source: U.S. Bureau of Indian Affairs, Branch of Employment Assistance, "A Follow-up Study of 1963 Recipients of the Services of the Employment Assistance Program" (October 1966) mimeo., p. 16, 26. U.S. Bureau of the Census. U.S. Census of Population: 1960; *Subject Reports. Nonwhite Population by Race.* Final Report PC(2)-1C (Washington, D.C.: Government Printing Office, 1963), Table 20, p. 43.

percent of the courses taken by adult vocational trainees require a mini-mum of high school graduation.[4] Thus, the relatively high educational level of the trainees reflects the requirements of the program as well as the tendency for the better-educated Indian to avail himself of training and employment opportunities.

A recent study of American Indian migration to Los Angeles confirms these results. The Los Angeles study indicated that the median years of schooling of the migrants was *11.2* years, or about three years more than that of nonmigrants of similar age from the same tribes.[5]

RETURNEES

Although no statistics have been maintained on the number of adult vocational trainees who return to the reservation, the Bureau of Indian Affairs maintained statistics on the number of relocatees participating in the direct employment program who returned to the reservation *during the fiscal year in which they were sent.* These data are reproduced in Table 3.

These data indicate that three out of ten relocatees returned home the same year in which they were located. What these data do not indicate is how many Indians eventually returned home. The figure is no doubt much higher.[6]

TABLE 3

Number of Returnees and Nonreturnees by Fiscal Year in Which Initial Relocation Was Made, 1953-57

Fiscal Year	Relocated Persons	Returned Persons	Percentage of Nonreturnees	Percentage of Returnees
1953	1,191	379	68	32
1954	1,263	362	71	29
1955	2,557	567	76	24
1956	4,191	1,113	73	27
1957	6,335	1,952	69	31

Source: Indian Relocation and Industrial Development Program, Report of a Spe-cial Committee on Interior and Insular Affairs, House of Representatives, 85th Con-gress, 1st session, p. 3.

In 1958, the Comptroller General's annual report criticized the Bureau of Indian Affairs for maintaining inadequate statistics on various phases of its activities, including the relocation program. In 1959, in response to the criticism, the Bureau *eliminated* its statistical series on the status (returnee or nonreturnee) of relocated Indians. The Bureau felt that statistics on returnees were giving too much ammunition to critics of the program.[7]

Most of the research on the characteristics of Indian migrants who return home has been done by anthropologists. Martin (1964) has shown that Indians who are younger in age, higher in level of educational attain-ment, and of mixed blood, are more likely to make a successful adjustment to an urban environment than older, less educated, full-blooded Indians. Graves and Van Arsdale (1966:283), have shown that the principal factor causing Indian migrants to leave Denver and return to the reservation is their economic success. Since older, less-educated Indians may have more difficulty finding and holding a job, Martin's finding is not surprising.

In a study of Navajo relocation, Cullum (1957:8), pointed out: "The only sharply positive findings related to attendance at public school and previous occupational experience at school trades. Definitely negative findings emerged with regard to families containing five or more children, to heads of families over forty, and in lesser degree to persons completing less than four grades of school."

Thus, not only is there a greater tendency for the better-educated reservation Indian to participate in these programs, as compared to his less-educated counterpart, but considering only the participants in the direct employment program, it is the better educated who are more likely to remain away from the reservation.

CHANGES IN EARNINGS

One would expect that since the marginal productivity of the adult vocational trainees has been enhanced by training, their earnings would be increased over pretraining levels. Moreover, the marginal productivity of those relocated without training is also increased, since labor is being transferred from an area of superabundance (an Indian reservation) to one of relative shortage (an urban area).

In addition, not only would one expect the earnings of these relocatees to be enhanced because of their increased productivity (usually measured by an increase in hourly wages), but because of more regular employment (as indicated by an increase in hours worked per year).[8]

Table 4 presents data on the changes in earnings for the sample of those participating in the direct employment and adult vocational training programs in 1963. Data on average earnings for three years before and three years after participation is presented.

As Table 4 indicates, incomes of participants in the program were sharply higher after participating in the two programs even after adjustments taking account of what these individuals would have earned had they remained on the reservation during 1964-66.

Although impossible to measure, the standard of living of these relocated Indians may not have increased as much as the income changes would indicate. First, reservation Indians receive free medical services if they are one quarter or more Indian blood. Second, many reservation Indians live rent-free on allotted land, but usually must pay rent for off-reservation housing. Third, reservation Indians pay no state income tax and no federal income tax on income derived from trust property, but are subject to these taxes when they leave the reservation. However, prices in trading posts and other small retail establishments located on the reservations are generally higher than they are in urban areas for goods of comparable quality.

TABLE 4

Changes in Earnings After Participating in Bureau of Indian
Affairs Manpower Programs (1963 Sample)

Type of Program	Average Earnings 1960-62	Average* Earnings 1964-66	Unadjusted Differential (column 3– column 1)	Adjusted† Differential
Direct employment	$1,039	$2,694	$1,655	$1,238
Adult vocational training	1,281	3,120	1,839	1,392

Source: Data on participants' incomes from U.S. Bureau of Indian Affairs, "A Follow-up Study of 1963 Recipients of the Services of the Employment Assistance Program," mimeo., pp. 18, 44. Age-earnings profiles used for adjusting earnings from 1960 Census of Population, *Nonwhite Population by Race,* Table 33, p. 104.

*These earnings data include *all* of the individuals in the sample whether they were regularly employed or remained in the labor force during 1964-66 or not.

†This adjustment takes into account an estimate of what the migrant would have earned had he remained on the reservation in 1964-66. Age-earnings profiles of reservation Indians, based on the 1960 Census of Population permit an estimate of earnings increase due to increasing age. Moreover, it is assumed that the *4* percent per annum increase in reservation incomes, which prevailed in the 1950-60 period took place in the 1964-66 period. Thus, adjusted earnings consider what the migrant would have earned if he had remained on the reservation by taking into account his increasing age and the secular growth of reservation income.

It is significant that those individuals who returned to the reservation earned lower incomes than those who remained in the field office centers where they were relocated (initially or after training). However, even those who returned to the reservation earned more than they would have had they not left the reservation (see Table 5). This results from the fact that many of the returnees were able to use their newly acquired skills on the reservation.

Moreover, many returnees did not go back until they were fairly certain that they would be able to secure employment when they returned.[9]

FURTHER INVESTMENT IN HUMAN CAPITAL

Economists have termed migration and technical training as well as education as investments in human capital. One of the more interesting aspects of investment in human capital is that an initial investment often stimulates an additional investment. For example, Mincer (1962) found that on-the-job training is positively associated with the level of educational attainment.[10] It appears that participation in B.I.A. manpower programs stimulated the participants to obtain further schooling.

Table 6 presents data on the educational distribution of a sample of program participants in 1966 and 1968.

Regarding the direct employment participants, the above data indicate a decline of *8* percent in the number of program participants with eight years of school or less, and an increase of *5* percent in the number of high

TABLE 5

Average Earnings, 1964-66 of Sample of Program
Participants, by Location, in 1966

	Direct Employment	Adult Vocational Training
Field office areas	$3,017	$3,277
Near reservation	2,382	3,218
On reservation	2,466	2,906
Earnings 1960-62	1,039	1,281

Source: U.S. Bureau of Indian Affairs, "A Follow-up Study of 1963 Recipients of the Services of the Employment Assistance Program," October 1966 and revised version July 1968.

TABLE 6

Educational Distribution Sample of Relocatees and Trainees, 1966, 1968

Direct Employment			Adult Vocational Training		
Years of school	1966	1968	Years of school	1966	1968
0-8	31	23	0-8	9	9
9-11	33	36	9-11	23	21
12 or more	36	41	12 or more	68	70
Median	10.6	11.1	Median	12+	12+

Source: Bureau of Indian Affairs, "A Follow-up Study of the Recipients of the Employment Assistance Program," revised version, July 1968, mimeo.

school graduates between 1966 and 1968. The median level of schooling of the sample of program participants increased by one-half year. In 1966, it was reported that *14* percent of the relocatees were attending night school or had attended since relocation in 1963; by 1968, this figure had increased to *39* percent.[11]

Considering the adult vocational trainees, at first glance it appears that there has not been much change in their educational distribution. However, this is due to the fact that data were not collected on the amount of *post-high school training* attained in 1966 or 1968. In fact, in 1966 *17* percent of the sample were attending night school, and by 1968, *36* percent of all vocational trainees in the 1963 follow-up sample had attended or were attending night school.

DECLINE IN ANTISOCIAL BEHAVIOR

One of the important benefits of a manpower program is the decline in the antisocial behavior of the participants. One method of measuring a change in antisocial behavior is to examine an individual's arrest record.[12] Thus, if the program participants (partly as a result of higher earnings and more regular employment) show a decrease in arrests after participating in a manpower program, as compared with the level prior to participation, it seems reasonable to conclude that a decline in antisocial behavior has taken place. Table 7 presents information on the level of arrests of the sample of direct migrants and adult vocational trainees in 1960-62 and 1964-66.

The data in Table 7 indicate that there was a greater decline in the level of arrests for those participating in the direct employment program, as compared to the adult vocational training program. This difference is likely not due to economic factors since the vocational trainees earned *more* money than the relocatees (see Tables 4 and 5). Perhaps the pressure placed on the vocational trainees in their skilled and semiskilled positions (as compared to the higher proportion of direct migrants in unskilled positions) caused the trainees to turn to alcohol and subsequent arrest.[13]

TABLE 7

Level of Arrests Prior to and after Participation in Bureau of Indian Affairs Manpower Programs (1963 Sample)*

Type of Program	Number of Arrests 1960-62	Number of Arrests 1964-66	Percent Decline
Direct employment	51	21	59
Adult vocational training	48	30	38

Source: U.S. Bureau of Indian Affairs, "A Follow-up Study of 1963 Recipients of the Services of the Employment Assistance Program," October 1966, mimeo., pp. 21, 47.

*No distinction was made between misdemeanors and felonies.

IMPACT ON THE RESERVATION ECONOMY

Although one of the main purposes of the two relocation programs described above is to improve the standard of living of the participants, a second purpose is to reduce the level of surplus labor on the reservations. Table 8 indicates the recent change in the reservation unemployment rate as compared with the overall national unemployment rate.

In spite of the large number of Indians that have participated in these programs (see Table 1), the impact on the reservation unemployment rate is small. In fact, between 1958-67, unemployment declined by only one-fourth as much for reservation Indians as for non-Indians.[14]

The principal reason that these relocation programs have failed to substantially reduce the level of surplus labor on the reservations is simply because the programs are being operated on too small a scale (relative to the need) to have a major impact.

For example, during 1967 and 1968, about *25-30* percent of those applying for adult vocational training were turned away.[15] On virtually all reservations visited during 1968, budget limitations prevented anyone from being sent to vocational training centers after January. Thus, from January until the end of the fiscal year (June 30), no one from these reservations was sent for training. As a result, six to nine months backlogs of potential trainees developed. Employment assistance officers informed the author that a large number of these potential trainees soon lose interest, and are no longer available for training when it is possible to send them.[16] At

TABLE 8

Male Unemployment Rates, Reservation Indians and National Average*

Year	Reservation Indians	National Average
1958	43.5	6.8
1959	48.2	5.3
1960	51.3	5.4
1961	49.5	6.4
1962	43.4	5.2
1965	41.9	4.0
1966	41.9	3.2
1967	37.3	3.1
Percent decline 1958-67	−14.2	−54.4

Source: Reservation unemployment rates for 1958-62, computed and seasonally adjusted from data contained in *Indian Unemployment Survey,* a publication of the U.S. House of Representatives, Committee on Interior and Insular Affairs, 88th Congress, First Session, 1963.

Data on reservation Indians for subsequent years from unpublished tabulations, Bureau of Indian Affairs, entitled "Selected Data on Indian Reservations Eligible for Designation Under Public Works and Economic Development Act September 1965, December 1966, and December 1967."

Data for labor force as a whole from U.S. Department of Labor, *Manpower Report of the President,* 1968, p. 234. Table A-11.

*Data for reservation Indians include males 14 and over. Data for labor force as a whole include males 16 and over.

present levels of funding, this problem will grow worse as increasing numbers of Indian high school graduates complete high school and become eligible for most of the adult vocational training courses offered.

A similar situation exists with respect to the direct employment program. There are more applicants for direct relocation than can be handled with existing funding. Lack of money not only limits the number of Indians that can be relocated, but also prevents the field employment assistance centers from having sufficient staff to provide needed levels of counseling and follow-up services.

Unless industrialization of the reservations occurs at a far more rapid pace than it has in recent years, the need for relocation of American Indians to secure their *economic advancement* will likely grow more urgent.[17] In spite of a *net* out-migration of *7,000* a year from the reservations, the population is increasing about *.8* percent per annum (Bureau of Indian Affairs, 1966).[18] Broadening the opportunity for American Indian migration *for those who wish to relocate* would not only mitigate the increasing population pressure, but allow more of the first Americans a chance to participate in the American dream.

CONCLUSIONS

1 As in the case of southern Negroes, the migration of reservation Indians to urban areas is educationally selective; that is, there is a greater tendency for the better educated to migrate in comparison with the less educated.

2   Earnings data indicate that a sample of participants in these programs earn on the average more than twice as much (even after adjustment for increasing age and the secular rise in reservation income) for the three years after initial training and relocation, as compared to the three years before participation.

3   Earnings of relocatees who remained in the urban areas in which initial employment was secured earned somewhat more than those who returned to the reservation.

4   By 1968, over one-third of a sample of Indians relocated or trained in 1963 had furthered their education by attending night school.

5   A significant decline in antisocial behavior, as measured by the number of arrests was observed for a sample of participants in these programs.

6   Lack of funds prevents these programs from being operated on a sufficiently large scale to accomodate all applicants and markedly reduce the level of surplus labor on the reservations.

NOTES

*This study was in part financed by funds provided by the William H. Donner Foundation, Inc., to the Brookings Institution where the author was a Research Associate.

1   It must be emphasized that these are *voluntary* programs. The Bureau of Indian Affairs does not pressure Indians in any way to apply for relocation or training.

2   The centers are located in Chicago, Cleveland, Dallas, Denver, Los Angeles, Oakland, and San Jose. In addition within the last year, two smaller centers have been opened in Tulsa and Oklahoma City.

3   Since virtually all of the participants in the two programs are between 18-35 years of age, their educational achievement is compared with 18-35 year-old reservation Indians (primarily non-participants).

4   There is no educational requirement for participation in the direct employment program.

5   There were approximately *20,000* Indians in Los Angeles in 1965 compared to *6,000* ten years earlier. The data on education of Los Angeles migrants are from John A. Price (1968) and include all migrated Indians and not just those who participated in Bureau of Indian Affairs relocation programs.

6   Joan Ablon (1965) estimates that *50* percent of the Indians relocated eventually return home.

7   Interview with Employment Assistance Officer, Branch of Employment Assistance, Washington, D.C., July 1968.

8   The unemployment rate for the combined sample of participants in the direct employment and adult vocational training programs was an estimated *40* percent in 1963 (before relocation and training) but had declined to *9* percent by 1966.

9   In addition, since those individuals who had returned to the reservation by 1966, had, in most cases, spent part of 1964-66 in an off-reservation setting, their 1964-66 income would reflect the likely higher earnings which accrued to them while in the latter location.

10 Weisbrod (1962) points out that one of the "benefits" of achieving a certain level of schooling is that it permits one to take advantage of even more schooling. This point could be applied to other types of human capital.

11 This latter figure seems quite high when one considers the relatively low incomes in comparison with non-Indians, and the fact that the schooling expenses are borne by the Indians themselves.

12 Indians apparently have a very high tendency toward being arrested. For example, police records in Denver indicated that about half of the Navajo migrants are arrested at least once during their stay in the city, with about *95* percent of the arrests alcohol-related (Graves, 1966).

13 Nationally, drunkenness alone accounts for *71* percent of all Indian arrests (Stewart, 1964).

14 Moreover, if it wasn't for a modest reservation industrialization program, which by 1968 employed *4,000* Indians in reservation industry, it is unlikely that the reservation unemployment rate would have declined at all between 1958-67. However, it must be pointed out that without the direct employment and vocational training programs, even on their present scale, the problem of surplus labor on the reservations would be even worse.

15 Based on interviews with employment assistance officers located on the Rosebud, Navajo, Blackfeet, Crow and Standing Rock Indian reservations.

16 Typical reasons given for nonavailability include: entered military service, found a job, or got married.

17 According to data provided the author by the Branch of Industrial Development, Bureau of Indian Affairs, the number of Indians employed in reservation industry increased from about *600* in 1960 to *4,000* in 1968. This latter figure represented *3.2* percent of the reservation labor force.

18 Birth rates on Indian reservations are *2* to *2½* times the national average. Moreover, rapid improvement in Indian health due to the efforts of the Public Health Service has lowered the death rate on Indian reservations to approximately the national average.

REFERENCES

Albon, J. (1965), "American Indian Relocation, Problems of Dependency and Management in the City." *Phylon* 26 (Winter): 362-368.

Cullum, R. (1957), *Assisted Navajo Relocation, 1952-56.* Mimeographed.

Fein, R. (1965), "Educational Patterns in Southern Migration." *Southern Economic Journal* 34 (July): 106-124.

Graves, T. (1966), "Alternative Models for the Study of Urban Migration." *Human Organization* 25 (Winter): 295-299.

Graves, T., and Van Arsdale, M. (1966), "Values, Expectations and Relocation: The Navajo Migrant to Denver." *Human Organization* 26 (Winter): 300-307.

Hamilton, C. Horace (1959), "Educational Selectivity of Net Migration from the South." *Social Forces* 38 (October): 33-42.

Martin, H. (1964), "Correlates of Adjustment Among American Indians in An Urban Environment." *Human Organization* 23 (Winter): 290-295.

Mincer, J. (1962), "On the Job Training, Costs, Returns and Some Implications." *Journal of Political Economy* 70 (October): 50-79.

Price, J. A. (1968), "The Migration and Adaptation of American Indians to Los Angeles." *Human Organization* 27 (Summer): 168-175.

Stewart, O. (1964), "Questions Regarding American Indian Criminality." *Human Organization* 23 (Winter): 61-66.

U.S. Bureau of Indian Affairs (1966), "Indian Housing, Needs, Alternatives, Priorities and Program Recommendations." Mimeographed.

——(1967), "Selected Reservations Eligible for Designation Under Public Works and Economic Development Act." Unpublished tabulation.

U.S. Department of Labor (1968), *Manpower Report of the President*

U.S. Public Health Service (1966), *Indian Health Highlights.*

Weisbrod, Burton (1962), "Education and Investment in Human Capital." *Journal of Political Economy* 70 (October): 110-113.

JOHN H. DOWLING: A "RURAL" INDIAN COMMUNITY IN AN URBAN SETTING*

Rural communities in Wisconsin, like rural communities throughout the United States, have a demographic curve which contrasts sharply with that of urban areas. Relative to urban areas, rural areas generally have more children and young people, fewer people in the working age range (18 to 64), and more elderly people. In general, the degree of contrast varies directly with physical distance from urban centers, with the demographic curve of remote communities contrasting most markedly with that of urban centers. As a single index of demographic variation, median age generally reflects the demographic curves involved, with median age declining as territorial distance from urban centers increases.

The dynamic social forces involved in the distinctively rural demographic patterns are well known. For a variety of reasons rural families are, in general, larger than urban families, producing more offspring than are necessary to replenish the local population. This expansion is usually offset by a migration of young adults to urban centers for economic reasons. As a result, the local rural population often remains relatively constant despite the high rate of reproduction. Many elderly people also return to or migrate to rural communities on retirement, drawn by low rent, lower prices, a slower pace of life, and other less tangible factors. Rural communities have been aptly termed "America's Old Folks' Home."[1]

Given the model just outlined, it is rather surprising to discover a distinctive community adjacent to and, indeed, extending into an urban center which has the demographic attributes of a hinterland, rural community. Such is the case with the Oneida Indian community of east-central Wisconsin. Territorially, half of the Oneida community (and, in terms of

Source: Reprinted by permission from *Human Organization* 27 (Fall 1968), 236-240.

population, more than half) is within the Green Bay Standard Metropolitan Statistical Area which has a total population of 125,000 people. Yet the median age of the Oneida Indian community is only 17 years,[2] while that of the city of Green Bay is 25 years.

The present paper is concerned with the demographic attributes of the Oneida community and with some of the historical and contemporary forces which have structured the community demographically in a way which conforms to the model appropriate for hinterland communities. To anticipate, the data suggest that in the Oneida community social distance is the functional equivalent of territorial distance in remote communities.

THE COMMUNITY SETTING

Overlapping with and extending southwest from the city of Green Bay is a roughly rectangular area of some 65,000 acres which sixty years ago formed the Wisconsin Oneida Indian reservation. The present-day Oneida are the descendants of two groups who left upper New York state in the 1820's and, in accordance with an agreement made with the Wisconsin Menomini and Winnebago, settled along Duck Creek in this area. In 1838, a 65,000-acre reservation was established by treaty for the Oneida. In 1892, under the provisions of the Dawes allotment act of 1887, the Oneida reservation was divided into lots and allocated among the population. Fourteen years later, in 1906, the Indians acquired fee simple title to their alloted lands and lost their tax-exempt status. As with many Indians then and now, the Oneida were unprepared for detribalization. Through ignorance of tax laws and the obligations of general citizenship, general poverty, and occasional unscrupulous dealings, they soon began to lose their land.

By 1930, all but about 1,000 acres of original 65,000 acres were in the hands of non-Indians. Under the provisions of the Wheeler-Howard act of 1934, the Oneida formed a constitution and by-laws and elected officials to a formal tribal organization. The federal government purchased approximately 1,900 acres of the old reservation which is now held in trust either for individuals or for the tribe. For the most part, tribal lands have been assigned to individuals, the size of the assignments ranging from one to 90 acres. Most of the assignments are between ten and 26 acres, however. Thus today the Oneida Indians on the former reservation live on individually-owned land, land held in trust for individuals and their descendants, tribally-assigned land, and land rented either from other Indians or from whites. The Indian population density increases toward the center of the old reservation and is focused in the unincorporated village of Oneida five miles from Green Bay. The village contains a Post Office, two grocery stores, a filling station, a laundromat, four churches and as many taverns, as well as several streets of houses.

East-central Wisconsin is dominated economically by dairy farming, an activity which not only requires considerable land but also considerable capital in livestock, equipment, and buildings. The acreages owned or operated by Oneida families, however, are generally too small for effective dairying. Most Oneida do not have, nor are they able to acquire, the necessary capital. There are, in fact, only three Oneida families who make their living by dairying. Most of the acreages are also too small for effective nondairy farming and most Oneida do not even have kitchen gardens.

The Oneida population is dispersed over the former reservation on relatively small land holdings and is geographically interspersed with whites, many of whom are successful dairy farmers while others commute to jobs in urban, industrial, business, and service industries. There are, in fact, two communities in the same geographical area, one white and the other Indian. There is little communication of any kind between them. Even when Indians and whites are in the same store or tavern they typically ignore one another. Similarly, neighbors generally ignore one another if they are of different races. Both populations are largely endogamous.

DEMOGRAPHIC CHARACTERISTICS

In the summer of 1939, Robert Ritzenthaler carried out an ethnographic survey of the Oneida Indians near Green Bay and at that time counted approximately 1,500 Indians in the area of the former reservation.[3] According to the census figures for 1950, there were 1,423 Indians in the area; the vast majority of these were Oneida, but there were a few Stockbridge and Menomini spouses of Oneida Indians. In 1965, the Oneida tribe carried out an Office of Economic Opportunity survey of 75 percent of the Indian households in the community. Based on this survey, the present-day population is estimated at approximately 1,600.

The Oneida population on the former reservation seems, according to these figures, to have remained fairly stable for the past 25 years. This has been a period during which both the rural and urban areas of Brown and Outagamie counties (the counties in which the Oneida community is located) have had an accelerating population growth. The apparent Oneida stability is misleading; it has, in fact, been the end result of two dynamic demographic processes. The Oneida population has been expanding through the past quarter-century period, but the expansion has been fairly consistently offset by a counter process of out-migration.

Oneida families today tend to be relatively large. The average Oneida household has 4.13 persons in it as compared with the state average of 3.36. The largest family which came to the author's attention was one with 18 living children. A further indication of the population productivity of the community is the "effective fertility ratio," a census bureau statistic based on the number of children under five years of age per 1,000 women between the ages of 15 and 49. The Oneida EFR is 689.6 as compared with a general Wisconsin EFR of 542.4. All of the data available thus indicate that the Oneida community is characterized by a high rate of reproduction. Yet the total population in the Oneida community has remained relatively constant.

Expansion of the local population has been offset consistently by emigration. Each year a significant number of Oneida leave the community. Interviews indicate that the majority of those who leave do so when they are in their late teens or early twenties; this is further supported by the median age for the community of 17 years. Some of these Oneida migrants move to Green Bay, DePere, Appleton, Kaukauna, Neenah, Oskosh and other urban areas in the general vicinity of the Oneida community. But the majority move to Milwaukee, Chicago, Detroit, Minneapolis, and other, more heavily industrialized cities. In Milwaukee, the Oneida form not only the oldest Indian population but the largest such population as well.[4]

While many Oneida leave the natal community, there are still many social and emotional bonds which connect the emigrants with those who remain behind. There is a considerable amount of two-way visiting and other communication between those who go and those who stay. Many of those who live in Milwaukee and Chicago return to Oneida for weekends, pow-wows, and holidays. Many also return to be married in Oneida churches and later return to have their children baptised or christened there. Again, many return for the various life-crisis rites of their kinsmen on the former reservation. And, when they die, the bodies of many of those who have moved out are returned for burial in the local cemeteries. Finally, many who emigrate return to the Oneida community to retire in their late fifties and sixties, a pattern which has important economic consequences for the community.

The general demographic picture which emerges, then, is that of a community with a relatively large number of young people, a relatively large number of elderly people, and relatively few people in their economic "prime," i.e., relatively few who can make a contribution to the economic well-being of the community. This is the demographic pattern expectable of a hinterland community, not of an urban and urban fringe community.

In the 1965 survey of 298 households carried out by the tribe, 42 percent of the households had an earned income of more than $3,000 while 31 percent had no earned income at all. These are household figures and consequently many of the household incomes that exceed $3,000 reflect several employed people rather than relatively high rates of pay. The median household income for the community is somewhat less than $3,000.

Approximately half of the men in the employable age range (18 to 64) and well over half of the women in the employable age range were either underemployed or unemployed during the year preceding the 1965 survey. Some of the people in the community are employed in permanent jobs, of course; but the majority are employed in seasonal occupations, working primarily in the summer and living off savings, unemployment compensation, and welfare during the winter. The major seasonal occupations include construction work, road maintenance, apple and cherry picking, work as longshoremen on the Green Bay docks, canning factory and paper mill work, and caddying at nearby golf courses. Although the pay scale for some of these occupations is good (e.g., longshoremen), the majority have low rates of pay. Thus for the employed of the community, income is generally low and frequently periodic. The income data, added to the demographic pattern of the community, produces a picture of general and extensive poverty.

BARRIERS TO LOCAL EMPLOYMENT

The Oneida poverty and demographic pattern could be broken if the young people remained in the community and contributed to the economic base of the community. Interviews with those nearing completion of their high school training indicate that many would like to remain in the community. Furthermore, interviews with young Oneida who have migrated away from the community indicate that many of these would like to return. Yet many of the young people in Oneida are now planning to leave and those who have already left are not returning except for short visits. Most informants give as their reasons for leaving the fact that they cannot get good, steady jobs in Oneida or anywhere in the near vicinity but can get such jobs elsewhere.

At the same time, the city of Green Bay, less then ten miles away from well over half of the people in the Oneida community, is a rapidly expanding industrial and commercial city and is now experiencing an acute labor shortage. Furthermore, the Oneida Indians have the skills necessary for filling many of the Green Bay positions now open. Their median educational attainment, for example, is the 9th grade; 75 percent of the potential labor force has completed elementary school (8th grade) while one out of four has completed high school. For younger members of the potential labor force the educational average is even higher.

According to the Oneida interviewed, the major obstacle to employment in Green Bay is the prevalent anti-Indian prejudice of that city's employers. The Oneida say that they do not experience such prejudice in Milwaukee, Chicago, Detroit, and elsewhere. Consequently they continue to leave the community despite a preference for living in Oneida.

People in Green Bay are divided on the question of anti-Indian prejudice. The Green Bay Voluntary Commission on Human Rights, a group which includes a number of knowledgeable civic and business leaders, affirms the prevalence of anti-Indian prejudice. Similarly, some city officials who have been involved in city affairs for years have stated that prejudice is a bar to the employment of Oneida Indians. On the other hand, members of the State Employment Bureau in Green Bay question the existence of significant prejudice against the Indian and state that they can place an Oneida who wants a steady job. About ten years ago the Oneida community hired a survey team to analyze the economic and employment problems of the community. The report from this survey also denied the existence of significant prejudice among Green Bay employers.[5] The interviews on which this conclusion was based, however, consisted mainly of asking employers about past and possible future employment of Oneida laborers and apparently lacked the sophistication required for research on prejudice. Until an adequate study of Green Bay firms is carried out, the presence and extent of anti-Indian prejudice must remain unclear.

Regardless of the actual situation, prejudice is perceived by the Oneida as being both present and extensive. Most Oneida can cite anecdotal cases of prejudice which have occurred either to themselves or to their kinsmen. Such anecdotal, non-statistical data cannot validate the generalization that extensive prejudice exists in Green Bay, of course. But such data do prove the generalization as far as the typical Oneida is concerned.

Having defined the social environment as one containing much anti-Indian prejudice, the Indian has employment expectations consonant with that prejudice. The typical Oneida Indian expects to find only seasonal jobs in Green Bay. Where permanent employment is available, it is expected to be relatively menial and low paying. Furthermore, the Indian with a steady job does not usually anticipate promotion to higher positions. Consequently, the upward-oriented Oneida looks elsewhere for employment. Thus prejudice increases the social distance between people: it reduces interaction and communication between them in the same way that territorial distance would. The fact that the perceived prejudice may be an illusion is irrelevant. A cognitive orientation which posits the existence of prejudice generates social distance in the same way actual prejudice would, and it is consequently just as effective a bar to employment.

CONCLUSION

Like the member of a remote, rural, white community, the Oneida Indian experiences difficulty in finding satisfactory employment opportunities in the neighborhood of his home. But where the member of a remote, rural community has difficulty because of the physical distance between home and potential job, the Oneida has difficulty because of the social distance between himself and the employment market. The social result is the same: the job-seeker leaves his natal community and finds work elsewhere. Again, the consequences for the home community are the same in both instances: a demographic pattern reflecting a high proportion of dependent, non-productive people. In this situation social distance becomes the functional equivalent of territorial distance.

NOTES AND REFERENCES

*The summer field work (1966) for this study was supported by a research grant from the Graduate School of the University of Wisconsin—Milwaukee. The present study, while self-contained, is also part of a larger study of Indians and Spanish-speakers in selected urban areas of Wisconsin. The larger study was supported by research grants from the Graduate School, University of Wisconsin—Milwaukee and the Institute for Research on Poverty at the University of Wisconsin—Madison.

An earlier draft of this paper was read and critized by Edward Wellin, Nancy Lurie, James Silverberg, and Irwin Rinder, to whom the author is indebted for their many helpful comments.

1   T. Lynn Smith, "The Role of the Village in American Rural Society," *Rural Sociology,* Vol. 7, 1942, pp. 10-21.

2 Unless otherwise noted, statistics on the Oneida community derive from the Office of Economic Opportunity survey of 75 percent of the households in the Oneida community, which was carried out by the tribal council in 1965. "Spot-checking" of the 1965 survey data by the author in the summer of 1966 uncovered no discrepancies.

3 Robert E. Ritzenthaler, "The Oneida Indians of Wisconsin," *Bulletin of the Public Museum of the City of Milwaukee,* Vol. 19, No. 1, 1950, p. 7.

4 Robert Ritzenthaler and Mary Sellers, "Indians in an Urban Situation," *The Wisconsin Archaeologist,* Vol. 36, No. 4, 1955, pp. 147-61.

5 Douglas Thorson, *Report on the Labor Force and the Employment Conditions of the Oneida Indians,* Department of Economics, University of Wisconsin—Madison, 1958 (mimeographed).

CHAPTER 7

RED POWER, ACTION PROGRAMS, AND THE FUTURE

AUGUST, 1953:

House Concurrent Resolution 108, 83rd Congress, 1st Session:

Whereas it is the policy of Congress, as rapidly as possible, to make the Indians within the territorial limits of the United States subject to the same laws and entitled to the same privileges and responsibilities as are applicable to other citizens of the United States, to end their status as wards of the United States, and to grant them all of the rights and prerogatives pertaining to American citizenship; and

Whereas the Indians within the territorial limits of the United States should assume their full responsibilities as American citizens: Now, therefore, be it

Resolved by the House of Representatives (the Senate concurring), That it is declared to be the sense of Congress that, at the earliest possible time, all of the Indian tribes and the individual members thereof located within the States of California, Florida, New York, and Texas, and all of the following named Indian tribes and individual members thereof, should be freed from Federal supervision and control and from all disabilities and limitations specially applicable to Indians: The Flathead Tribe of Montana, the Klamath Tribe of Oregon, the Menominee Tribe of Wisconsin, the Potowatamie Tribe of Kansas and Nebraska, and those members of the Chippewa Tribe who are on the Turtle Mountain Reservation, North Dakota. It is further declared to be the sense of Congress that, upon the release of such tribes and individual members thereof from such disabilities and limitations, all offices of the Bureau of Indian Affairs in the States of California, Florida, New York, and Texas and all other offices of the Bureau of Indian Affairs whose primary purpose was to serve any Indian tribe or individual Indian freed from Federal supervision should be abolished. . . .

JUNE, 1961:

National Indian Chicago Conference: Declaration of Indian Purpose:

We, the majority of the Indian people of the United States of America, . . . have the inherent right of self-government . . . and the same right of sovereignty. . . .

It is a universal desire among all Indians that their treaties and trust-protected lands remain intact and beyond the reach of predatory men. . . .

... When we ask that our treaties be respected, we are mindful of the opinion of Chief Justice John Marshall on the nature of the treaty obligations between the United States and the Indian tribes.

Marshall said that a treaty "... is a compact between two nations or communities, having the right of self-government. ... The only requisite is, that each of the contracting parties shall possess the right of self-government, and the power to perform the stipulations of the treaty."

And he said, "We have made treaties with (the Indians); and are those treaties to be disregarded on our part, because they were entered into with an uncivilized people? Does this lessen the obligation of such treaties? By entering into them have we not admitted the power of this people to bind themselves, and to impose obligations on us?"

The right of self-government, a right which the Indian possessed before the coming of the white man, has never been extinguished; indeed, it has been repeatedly sustained by the courts of the United States. ...

Our forefathers could be generous when all the continent was theirs. They could cast away whole empires for a handful of trinkets for their children. But in our day, each remaining acre is a promise that we will still be here tomorrow. Were we paid a thousand times the market value of our lost holdings, still the payment would not suffice. ...

When we go before the American people, as we do in this Declaration, and ask for material assistance in developing our resources and developing our opportunities, we pose a moral problem which cannot be left unanswered. ...

With that continent gone, except for the few poor parcels they still retain, the basis of life is precariously held, but they mean to hold the scraps and parcels as earnestly as any small nation or ethnic group was ever determined to hold to identity and survival.

What we ask of America is not charity, not paternalism, even when benevolent. We ask only that the nature of our situation be recognized and made the basis of policy and action.

In short, the Indians ask for assistance, technical and financial, for the time needed, however long that may be, to regain in the America of the space age some measure of the adjustment they enjoyed as the original possessors of their native land.

These two documents, House Concurrent Resolution 108 of August, 1953, heralding the resurgence of "termination" as Congressional policy, and the "Declaration" of June, 1961, calling for self-determination and continued federal aid for Indians, serve to summarize the United States governmental policy and the subsequent Indian response that set the stage for the emergence during the 1960s of a new form of militant Indian activism and assertiveness referred to by many Indians as "Red Power."

The "Declaration of Indian Purpose" of 1961 summarized the ideas about Indian goals developed during one year of conferences among the leaders of a majority of the nation's tribes and bands. It also represented the achievement of a relative consensus between the youthful militants of the newly formed National Indian Youth Council (NIYC) and the older moderate leaders of the National Congress of American Indians (NCAI). The Chicago Conference was sponsored by Sol Tax, an anthropologist with the University of

Chicago, as an opportunity for Indians from all regions to gather and build a national consensus on priorities and goals that could then be used to confront the newly elected presidential administration. Perhaps the most central issue for conference participants was the termination policy of the Eisenhower administration. By 1959 the drastic effects of termination on several tribes, in particular, the Menominees of Wisconsin and the Klamaths of Oregon, had become evident, and many Indian leaders realized that much more was being dissolved than the guardian-ward relationship. It was obvious from the experience of the tribes involved that above all else termination meant the extinction of the tribes as viable groups with unique cultures. It thus became evident, especially to the members of the Youth Council and certain leaders of the NCAI, that new organization and tactics were going to be needed if tribal groups and cultures were to survive. The emergence of Indian activism during the 1960s is one of the responses to that need.

The primary purpose of this chapter is to provide an overview of the process of emergence of militant Indian activism during the 1960s, including details about the ideas, goals and tactics of several leaders in the movement. Secondarily, the chapter offers several selections about topics related to the crystallization of collective political and social action among Indian people.

The first article reprinted in this chapter is a description of the tactics employed by one Indian activist to promote the cause of Indian rights and tribal survival. Roy Bongartz's article, "The New Indian," does an admirable job of portraying not only the tactics but, more importantly, the tone and spirit of the challenges to the white establishment mounted by Wallace "Mad Bear" Anderson, the Tuscarora merchant seaman turned activist. The tactics employed by Mad Bear have been most imaginative and innovative. His early exploits in leading protest served as models for the collective actions of the Youth Council in the mid-1960s and after. At 29 years of age, he helped lead the Mohawk's fight against the New York income tax on the grounds of Indian sovereignty. He marshaled nearly 400 Indians from a reservation and led them into a courtroom to tear up summonses issued for refusal to pay taxes. The next year, using a combination of physical and legal tactics, Mad Bear mounted a successful campaign to block construction of a reservoir on Indian land. On a later occasion he attempted a citizen's arrest on the U.S. Commissioner of Indian Affairs in Washington, D.C., and put up a picket line around BIA offices. Mad Bear even went to Cuba in 1958 with a group of Florida Indians to gain Castro's sponsorship for a petition to the United Nations urging acceptance of the Iroquois into the body as an independent sovereign nation.

The major dimensions of Mad Bear's tactics become evident in this review of his projects. He is accomplished at challenging and blocking power plays by whites which violate old, forgotten treaties with Indians, and is skillful in gaining publicity and support for such treaty rights in the process. His tactics remain nonviolent, with a few minor exceptions, and often humorously and symbolically ridicule the white system while effectively protesting a specific violation of Indian rights. Mad Bear manifests little of the deep bitterness and hostility toward whites which is more common in the statements of black militants.

The combination of nonviolence, symbolic ridicule, and legal challenge to the activities of white corporations or government agencies has proven to be very effective in gaining desired changes in white institutions and practices. Moreover, Mad Bear has pointed the way to an international perspective on Indian problems which has led many Indian leaders to perceive their reservations as "internal colonies" monitored by the BIA and to identify with other nations around the world struggling to become self-sufficient after colonial domination.

One of the most influential spokesmen of the Indian movement toward collective activism in support of tribal nationalism is Vine Deloria, Jr. His article, "This Country Was a Lot Better Off When the Indians Were Running It," is included as a sample of the perspective and style which have characterized his statements. Deloria has become one of the dominant Indian leaders by virtue of his past leadership of the National Congress of American Indians and the influence and effectiveness of his articles and books. His incisive analysis of white power plays and institutional racism is combined with skillful ridicule, sarcasm and biting wit, and the effect is impressive. Some of the basic ideas developed in his two books, *Custer Died for Your Sins* and *We Talk, You Listen*,[1] are discussed briefly in the article reprinted. He sees the occupation of Alcatraz by young Indian activists in November, 1969, as an effective way of gaining attention and support for the nationalist Indian goals of independent self-determination and cultural and political survival with the support of continued, focused federal aid. He contrasts the extreme deprivation and discouragement of reservation existence prior to World War II with the current mood and activities of the NCAI and various regional intertribal councils, noting that "There is an increasing scent of victory in the air in Indian country these days." He points out that "everyone is watching mainstream America," to see how whites will handle the problems of pollution, poverty, crime, and racism when they do not understand the issues. Deloria says that whites very clearly need the advice and counsel of Indians to understand and resolve urban problems. The religious value placed on the environment, the political technique of the "open council" to develop community consensus, and reduced emphasis on competitive striving for material success are recommended by Deloria as Indian cultural elements desperately needed by whites. He briefly mentions the "tribalizing process" occurring among various subgroups within current white society (e.g., the "Woodstock Nation," the "Blackstone Nation," etc.) as analogous to the tribal nationalism movement among Indians.

Before turning to the next article in this chapter, the reader should be reminded that Peter Collier's "The Red Man's Burden," (reprinted in Chapter 2) also discusses the meaning and importance of the Alcatraz project. In that piece Collier describes the personal experiences, frustrations and some of the social factors that combine to create in LaNada Means, a 22-year-old Shoshone-Bannock girl, the basic urge to join the struggle to alter white institutions and Indian self-conceptions in projects like the occupation of Alcatraz.

The third selection, "The Emergence of Indian Activism as a Social Movement," by Robert C. Day, is an original article designed to portray the historical events and the social influences operating among various Indian leaders to produce the "Declaration of Indian Purpose" and the activist organization the National Indian Youth Council during 1960-1961. In the second section of the piece, there is an analysis of the subsequent emergence between 1961 and 1970 of the multiple forms of more sophisticated collective actions by Indians in every region of the country. Day finds that Indian activism is essentially nonviolent, though it has revolutionary implications of a peaceful sort for the United States. Collective Indian activities may be divided into two broad categories, including (1) tactics that obstruct, delay or halt elements of the white "system," (e.g., government practices, commercial operations) and (2) projects designed to promote benefits to Indians from the operation of the white establishment, or from exchange with it. Day's analysis of the development of Indian activism during the past decade reveals an increasing reliance on obstructive challenges to white political and economic institutions. The article concludes with a review of the details and implications of the Nixon administration policy favoring the long-term goal of tribal nationalism.

The chapter concludes with a piece by Edward M. Kennedy, which summarizes a liberal politician's point of view about federal Indian policy and its negative consequences. Kennedy rejects all forms of white paternalism and control in favor of self-determination for Indians as declared congressional policy. Having noted with optimism this apparent trend toward convergence of policy recommendations from white politicians and Indian leaders, we terminate this book.

NOTE

1   Vine Deloria, Jr., *Custer Died for Your Sins: An Indian Manifesto* (New York: Macmillan, 1969), and *We Talk, You Listen* (New York: Macmillan, 1970).

ROY BONGARTZ:
THE NEW INDIAN

A massive brown man sits at a table in the doorway of a small cinder-block garage, writing a letter in a bold, florid hand: "Dear Mr. President." It is a modest setting indeed for a leader about to set up a new American nation. At the sight of a visitor, he bounces to his feet and reaches out a welcoming hand, a broad grin on the wide, heavy-featured face with the slashing scar on one cheek. This is the indomitable Mad Bear, main arrow of a new movement to find a true American Indian identity.

The key word is: Unite. The fact that Indians, routed and demoralized by the white man, have never before joined together in any sort of continent-wide alliance doesn't worry Mad Bear a bit. All over the U.S. and Canada he spreads word of an Indian rebirth: as the white man destroys his own world with guns and garbage, the Indians will inherit the land once again. And sympathetic nationalist revolutionaries in India, in South Africa, in Aden, in Brazil, in Cuba, in Yugoslavia, in Taiwan, in Japan have been amazed to hear this forty-two-year-old, 284-pound Tuscarora merchant seaman, while on shore visits in port cities, assure them that the traditional solidarity of the Iroquois Confederacy—the Six Nations of New York State and eastern Canada—is reaching out, someday to become fifty or a hundred Indian nations in one.

Last summer he organized a caravan of Indians from some sixty tribes that barnstormed through Iroquois reservations like a traveling circus, encouraging the locals to see a wide, bright future for themselves and their distant brothers, in spite of the fact that the outside world still insists there cannot be *real* Indians in the East anymore. All day, in the traditional longhouses, in an atmosphere heavy with emotion, they poured out their hearts to one another, arguing about Red Power and their No. 1 problem, the White Man; with a rare exception, non-Indians, especially government "spies," were kept out. Mad Bear, a prophet honored "save in his own country," is not a chief of his own Tuscarora nation, but he says this just gives him more freedom to act, and he wears the deer antlers of a chief anyway. In any case, he is the acknowledged leader of tradition-minded Iroquois who hope their way of life may survive, and elsewhere his influence is growing fast; Western Indians accept the leadership of the Iroquois (Onondaga, Mohawk, Seneca, Oneida, Cayuga, and Tuscarora), with their advanced political organization and written constitution. Mad Bear, articulate and sparkling with imagination and humor, is able to deal with the white man on his own terms, yet he remains sensitive to the central peacefulness of the Indian mind, which, despite his rambunctious nature, he shares.

This goal of a separate, unified Indian nation has come out of hundreds of battles to defend Indian rights, mostly involving land grabs; the Indian is fast realizing that with those last remaining bits of real estate goes his identity. In the past two decades, Mad Bear has been in an awful lot of those fights. In 1957 he helped the Mohawks fight the New York State income tax on the grounds of Indian sovereignty by leading some four hundred Indians from the St. Regis reservation into court at Massena, and tearing up summonses issued to Indians for tax refusal. When a trooper tried to arrest him for contempt, Indian women shoved the lawman out of the courtroom and knocked him down a flight of stairs, then made off safely with Mad Bear, to meet later at the longhouse for a ceremonial burning of the tattered summonses.

Then, in 1958, back home on the Tuscarora reservation outside Niagara Falls, there came a greater threat. Without consulting the Indians, Robert Moses, chairman of the Power Authority of the State of New York, had condemned 1383 Indian acres for a reservoir in a $705,000,000 power project. Says Mad Bear, "The land is your mother. You cannot sell your mother." Indians blocked surveyors' transits and deflated their car tires. When they returned the next day, escorted by over a hundred state troopers and sheriff's deputies, some two hundred Indians fought them. Women scratched, and children as young as four years tackled the invaders. Mad Bear, with another, was jailed for unlawful assembly; released the next day, they kept up the resistance. Guns were fired over surveyors' heads; kids threw firecrackers at them. An eighty-three-year-old woman shoved a marshal into a creek. The Authority tapped Indian leaders' telephones; the Indians promptly switched to the Tuscarora language. The Authority sent out false news for television that the Indians had given up, but nobody believed it. When bulldozing began, Mad Bear called thirty Indian operators off the job. "We have no more time for stalling and debate," said Moses, and made a final offer of $3,000,000 to the one hundred seventy-five Indians involved. The not very rich Indians knew perfectly well that this was Moses' final offer, and they turned it down. And in a new ruling in early 1959, the Federal Power Commission said the Indians could not be compelled to sell. At the .time, the Buffalo *Courier-Express* commented that "Mad Bear, more than anyone else, was responsible for the tribe's decision."

A month later, Mad Bear was up at the Six Nations Reserve in Brantford, Ontario, fomenting a week-long revolution in which the traditionalists captured and occupied the Council House—a one-story government and administration center built something like an old-fashioned schoolhouse—that had been seized by Mounties in 1924 and turned over to government-appointed Indians who were working toward assimilation of all Indians into the general population. The rebels ousted the "official" Iroquois and rounded up, arrested, and disarmed a dozen Mounties—Mad Bear had issued "I.P." ("Iroquois Patrol") armbands to a number of young insurgents. Mad Bear likes to follow a certain protocol, so had warned

Ellen Fairclough, the Canadian commissioner for Indian affairs, beforehand of the coming attack; according to the press, she had laughed and told them to go ahead, that she would keep order anyway. Seven tractable Mounties were released on their promise to get off the Indian land, and were given back their guns at the border. Five defiant ones were kept half a day in a damp basement awaiting a hearing before the chiefs upstairs; then they were let go, too. Mad Bear and his junta held out for a week. Then at three o'clock one morning some fifty armed Mounties surrounded the Council House with fifteen cars, cleared out the rebels, and clubbed and jailed three of the Indian patrol. More stimulated than dismayed by this defeat, Mad Bear went home. (Mad Bear operates as freely in Canada as he does at home in the U.S.; since Iroquois lands extend to both sides of the border, he's in his own territory in either country, and has the treaty of 1784 to prove it.)

Fired up, Mad Bear next joined Indians from all over the U.S. in a march on the Bureau of Indian Affairs in Washington protesting a termination bill that was to do away with reservations. (Several tribes were "dumped" this way before the law was changed; now Canada is threatening the same move, which traditional Indians plainly call genocide because it does away with tribal rolls, with Indian identity altogether.) With a posse of some three hundred Indians, Mad Bear tried to make a citizen's arrest on the Indian Commissioner, but officials cleverly reminded them that they had been denying their citizenship, thus making a "citizen's" arrest doubtful. So the Indians got a cooperative retired U.S. Army general to try to make the arrest for them, but they failed. "The commissioner hid under his desk," says Mad Bear. Picket lines surrounded the Bureau, and when one Indian, Chief Ray Johnson, of Canby, California, dropped dead of a heart attack, Mad Bear saw a rare opportunity for bringing public sympathy to the Indian cause. Johnson's body was paraded in a U-Haul trailer with a sign reading: "Administrative Murder." Bureau officials told the Indians they couldn't drive around with a body like that, and offered to handle funeral arrangements, but the Indians refused, and Mad Bear found a cut-rate Negro undertaker who would embalm Johnson's body for sixty dollars. When this was done, the Bureau offered to fly the body back to California, agreeing to take along Johnson's wife and his four dogs as well—officials were anxious to see the last of Chief Johnson. Instead of accepting the offer, Indians formed a twelve-car caravan to drive the chief across the country, ignoring warnings that transporting a corpse was illegal. They set off, Mad Bear among them, and he says, "Nobody wanted to stop us; in fact most towns gave us a police escort to get rid of us as fast as they could." Police in an Oklahoma town met the Indians at the city limits with box lunches ready for them so they would have no excuse to stop on their way through, but they made headlines all the way across the country anyway.

In order to punish the government for denying these Washington protests, all the Indians had to do was to let the *prophecy* do its work: There were to be many gates closed to America. Mad Bear says the Iroquois little people, who up to a dozen years ago had extended their spiritual protection to U.S. leaders, withdrew it, with the result that Nixon was attacked in Venezuela, Eisenhower had to cancel a trip to Japan, and a long spate of attacks on American embassies and libraries began. This prophecy is an elusive, unwritten, changeable series of predictions and explanations of world events by myth that the Iroquois recite every ten years in a special longhouse ceremony that takes from sunrise to noon of exactly four days to complete; it is due again next summer. Some Hopi prophecies seem to agree with those of the Eastern Indians, but since they are all kept orally only, they cannot be frozen into a single version. Yet Mad Bear and the other Indians refer to "the prophecy" in the same taken-for-granted way they talk about a supply of bread and corn ordered for the summer caravan's kitchen tent. One part of it now says that the white man will soon blow himself off the face of the earth.

When Mad Bear accompanied some Florida Indians to Cuba, hoping for moral support from Fidel Castro and Ché Guevara, they were grandly received in public ceremonies, but Castro later went at the Indians statistically, wanting to know the exact percentage of the U.S. population they represented. Returning rather empty-handed from Cuba, Mad Bear was threatened by Miami immigration officials with loss of citizenship for overstaying his travel permit to Cuba, but he denied that they could touch his Iroquois nationality and refused to be interrogated about his Cuba trip. Two F.B.I. agents followed him home on the plane and tried to grill him in the two-hundred-year-old log cabin, built by a French trapper, he was then living in—its chimney has since crumbled and Mad Bear has moved into a new one-car garage down the road. Mad Bear ordered the G-men off the reservation, but they claimed they could go anywhere within the continental limits of the U.S. Mad Bear showed them a treaty signed by George Washington specifying that U.S. territory ended at the Tuscarora border, and one G-man said, "They told me you were a fanatic, and now I really believe it." Mad Bear brandished his .40-.22 combination rifle; the G-men were armed, too, but a number of other Indians, also with guns, circling the cabin outside, finally persuaded the F.B.I. to retreat, and they never came back.

The Thomas E. Dewey Thruway was another challenge. When, during the Revolution, George Washington asked the Six Nations to leave off demanding tolls of guns and blankets from his impoverished troops moving through Iroquois lands, they agreed on condition that the U.S. guarantee forever a free right-of-way for Indians along the main pathway between Albany and Black Rock (now Buffalo). Mad Bear found out that this agreement had since been put into New York State law, so one day in 1960, when he and five other Indians were driving east to visit the Onondaga reservation, they refused to pay any toll at the Syracuse exit. They wouldn't sign a bill for unpaid toll, either, and showed a hundred-dollar bill to prove they were solvent. For two hours the toll taker put in a lot of telephone calls until finally the state attorney general sent word to the tollbooth that the Indians could pass without payment until a legal study could be made. For eight months the Indians drove free on the toll road; then the state withdrew the special status on the ground that the

Thruway had not been foreseen by the original treaty makers. Mad Bear intends to try refusing the toll again one of these days.

A hint as to why Mad Bear is not always universally admired by his fellow Indians may be seen in his scheme to sabotage the annual Tuscarora dance festival that brought out thousands of admission-paying non-Indians and made certain Tuscaroras a good deal of money. To Mad Bear it was phony un-Iroquois dancing, with all kinds of flamboyant Western feathered headdresses, done by Indians hired from Ontario; there wasn't a Tuscarora in the bunch. Mad Bear telephoned the dancers to tell them it was immoral and un-Indian to take money for dancing and to pretend to be local Tuscaroras, and asked them to cancel their appearance. When he warms up to an issue of Indian tradition, Mad Bear can be persuasive, and the dancers agreed not to show up, leaving the festival with five scheduled perform-ances and no performers—none of the Tuscaroras knew any dances. Mad Bear to the rescue: he had, waiting in the wings, some sixty members of the Wanka Tanka dance troupe from Buffalo—just great, except that these enthusiasts of Indian dancing were all *whites*. As they came onstage in the outdoor arena, Mad Bear jumped up and grabbed the microphone, shout-ing, "Shame on you Indians! We should all bury our heads, that we have to hire whites to dance for us!" His message got through, and soon afterward Indian parents were sending their children to lessons in traditional Tuscarora dancing that Mad Bear organized in the reservation school on Sundays, starting just as nearby church bells rang.

A certain Niagara Falls judge has also been treated to a sample of Mad Bear's wiles. After Mad Bear got a summons from a game warden for illegally catching a sturgeon (Indians claim exemption from restrictions on hunting and fishing on their own lands), before the case came up he invited the judge to a picnic. The Indians brought on the fresh sturgeon and began eating it with gusto until the judge asked for a taste. They gladly gave him a plateful and then took his picture, his mouth full of sturgeon, with a grinning Mad Bear right beside him. Then Mad Bear showed him the summons. The case was dropped. This winter Mad Bear plans to attend Indian fish-ins in the state of Washington, demonstrations of Indian sovereignty of the kind Dick Gregory and Marlon Brando have joined. The fishermen are also supported by a sort of brown-skinned Paul Bunyan, Bigfoot, who shows his anger with white man's authority by stomping around in the mountains, causing great storms and thunder at times the Indians are demonstrating. Mad Bear says Bigfoot is sometimes fifteen feet tall, thirty feet tall at others; at meetings last summer a California Indian displayed a yard-long plaster cast of a Bigfoot footprint he said he's taken from a path on Lonesome Ridge in the northwestern California mountains. Bigfoot's message to Indians is: Return to the traditional life.

For some years, since he took part in the Council House revolution, Mad Bear has had standing against him a deportation order from Canada, but he regularly ignores it. Recently, however, on a trip to Canada to get brother Iroquois to agree to the hiring of an Egyptian lawyer to represent the Indians before the United Nations, Canadian officials lowered a gate in front of his car and tried to question him. He smashed through the gate and went on his way. Returning home a few days later, U.S. border officials, generally more willing than the Canadians to admit to Indian rights of unmolested passage across the line, told him that the Canadians had asked them to stop him. "They're sore because you broke their gate," they said. Mad Bear cheerfully suggested they send him a bill for the damage, and drove on. "If I get one I'll just send it on to the Indian Bureau," he says. Again last summer, when the unity caravan headed into Canada, Mad Bear was on hand—his jalopy had to be pushed through customs by friends in a newer-model car behind him, but officials did not notice him. Newsmen did, however; banner front-page headlines read: *Mad Bear Slips Into Canada.*

Other border trouble had broken out last winter on the international bridge at Cornwall, Ontario, when Canadian customs began charging duty on goods that Mohawks were taking from one part of their reservation, which is in New York State, to another part, which is in Canada. The Indians assert that this is a direct violation of the Jay Treaty; Canadians say that the treaty was between the U.S. and England and does not concern them. Indians blocked the bridge with stalled cars; forty Mohawks were arrested and dragged off. That night a bullet tore into the customs house and bounced lightly off an officer. Tension kept up through the summer; one night, Indians sneaked past an armed guard into the customs house, which is on Indian land, and turned on the water in an upstairs bathroom. The resulting flood ruined the ceilings. Thus the arrival at the bridge of a caravan of some hundred Indian cars—including Mad Bear's, being pushed—one day last August was not designed to calm the jittery nerves of Canadian police and border agents, especially when the Indians all demanded to be let over the bridge without paying the dollar toll (they were). A good number of the cars had Western license plates, and all sported bumper stickers: *I Support the North American Indian Unity Caravan, If Ur Indian Ur In, We Remember the Wounded Knee Massacre,* or *Custer Died for Your Sins.* But there were no incidents.

Besides his skirmishes with the Canadians and with Robert Moses' surveyors, Mad Bear has been put under house arrest in Capetown after publicly advising black South Africans to burn their identity cards, and he was arrested in Taiwan for associating with "recalcitrant" aboriginals and for photographing graves of Taiwan-for-the-Taiwanese activists executed by the government. But except where a roadblock or tollgate may have to suffer, Mad Bear follows a basic philosophy of nonviolence which is central to Indian philosophy. All his protests are marked by a certain sense of wit combined with impeccable logic and an extremely stubborn, if passive, resistance. "Getting arrested is not important," he says. "Indian unity *is* important." Mad Bear is fascinated by any new way of advertising Indian independence; when a Passamaquoddy Indian in the caravan told how ninety members of his tribe had formed a human barrier across highway U.S. 1 in Maine in July, and charged travelers a dollar per car to pass, Mad Bear's eyes sparkled with admiration. "Hey, maybe we ought to try that!" he exclaimed.

Among Mohawks especially in the East and with many young Western

Indians the tenet of nonviolence has hard going; they want action. Many young Mohawks are workers in high steel, building skyscrapers and bridges all over the U.S. and Canada. They are well-paid, and proud, and they feel like using their strength on Indian grievances. In this Mad Bear showed himself as a bridge between young and old, between brash activists and stolid chiefs who like to give weeks of meditation on any question. This difference—it never came to an actual split—came up once with the pretty twenty-six-year-old Indian-rights campaigner Kahn-Tineta Horn, a Mohawk known for her fiery speeches in colleges from coast to coast. Facing trial on a concealed-weapons charge in the bridge blockade, she demanded help from the chiefs, who, she said, had let her down. "I'm all alone! I don't want to go to jail!" she said loudly. Mad Bear assured her that she was not alone, and then Seneca Chief Beeman Logan told her rather severely, "A chief does not give a reply in fifteen minutes!" It transpired that the girl had spurned the legal counsel hired by the other Indians and had gone off on her own, but with great tact Mad Bear brought the two sides (the girl and her brother Taio Tekane Horn, another activist, both feeling a bit abandoned and unloved by their elders; and the chiefs, feeling they were being pushed too fast by loud, ungrateful youngsters) slowly together. The young brother and sister agreed to meet with the chiefs before the trial and to accept their advice; in return, the chiefs promised to provide plenty of moral support in person at the trial. (Fifty Indians did show up in the Cornwall court, ready to carry Kahn-Tineta off by force, at her trial a week later, but she was acquitted.)

The differing approaches were apparent, too, in a debate on the wording of a statement to government leaders, including Prime Minister Trudeau (Smart Snake). Protesting unemployment, loss of children to religious schools, alcoholism as a result of Indian disgust with white society, and police brutality, the suggested wording was that unless conditions changed the Indians "feared a violent reaction against law-enforcement agents." Strong protests against the word "violent" came—this was not the Indian way. Then a stocky young woman in a buckskin dress, an Ojibway from Upper Slave Lake in Alberta named Rose Ojek, cried out in an emotional burst, "The violence is here already! Changing the word won't stop it. There are young Indians in Alberta who are going to burn the schools and the churches. They're not criminals in their hearts, but one of them says he's going to get a huge Caterpillar tractor and go to High Prairie and bulldoze the liquor store, pretend he's drunk. The police arrest them when they get drunk; a girl was arrested for that, and when her brother tried to touch her hand, that she was reaching out of the police car, they arrested him, too, and he got *six months!* I can't stand it when I hear of talking peace!" The Indians crowded along the benches in the Council House muttered the approving, "Huh!" And again Mad Bear brought about the amazing Indian unanimity that followed every disagreement: this time, he said, Indians must not be too timid to use a word; it was not a threat of violence, but only a warning, and anyway, "It's only a word in the white man's language—what are you worried about?"

As chairman, Mad Bear also led stormy sessions on the question of letting government-employed Indians into the Council House. So that the Indians could express themselves freely, all non-Indians, with the exception of a magazine writer, had already been excluded from most of the meetings. When an Indian couple known to be employed by the Canadian government showed up and asked to be admitted, the local chief—this happened on the Maniwaki Reserve, north of Ottawa—refused them, and sent them away. But at the meeting he was having second thoughts. Shouldn't *any* Indian be received here as a brother? This was a *unity* convention. "No!" shouted Taio Tekane Horn. Glaring, he clenched his teeth angrily. "They're spies, traitors, and they deserve to be put to death." But the others wanted unity. The peaceful atmosphere they had built here could only be a help to Indians who had strayed from the path. Mad Bear thought that mixing with the traditional-minded Indians would be good for the soul of any lost brother, and thus it was decided that the convention should welcome any Indian who might like to come in. The Indians also decided to impeach Secretary of the Interior Walter Hickel for "his high-handed, inconsiderate and illegal theft of native Alaskan, Eskimo and Indian tribal lands," and to denounce the South Dakota death sentence upon a twenty-one-year-old Rosebud Sioux named Thomas White Hawk. They want to issue identity cards to all North American Indians who want one, as soon as a properly "Indian-looking" design can be made, so as to take the business of saying who is and who is not an Indian away from white men's governments. As a further token of unity, tribal delegates would in the future go from various areas to join in local demonstrations involving Indians. And the unity caravan will ride again: next year to Oklahoma and Alberta.

After a dinner of traditional corn soup and roast beaver with beans baked in sand, the Indians straggle off toward a blazing campfire, where soon the dancing begins, to last all night—the stomp dance, the rabbit dance, the welcome dance, the duck dance. A trio of tireless young Mohawks pounds on drums and sings a hoarse, sharp, and haunting accompaniment from out of a lost and distant time. In the shadows along the edge of the field, where cars and tents line the way, Mad Bear sits talking to friends. Shadows from the horns of his headdress bob in the firelight against a canvas wall as he relates some of the prophecy; the white man's money will soon be worthless; his society is crumbling. "We don't want to be a part of it," he says. "We don't want to have to hate the black man." But the Indians don't want the help of black activists, either—"We have our own power," says Mad Bear. The roguish delight he'd shown in recounting his many forays against the enemies of traditional Indians now becomes subdued as he speaks of the perishable Indian identity, the Indians' most precious possession, that still survives amid the blithe ignorance of the white man, who assumes the Indian must want to become white too. The Indian's hardest job is to fight the indifference all around him, the idea that he is cute and amusing, his story a subject fit only for children, or worse, the belief that he does not exist at all. Boxed in by white men's religions no less based on articles of faith than are the longhouse legends, he sees his myths and spirits derided. But the longhouse faith is growing fast; where only a dozen Indians showed up for a ceremony five years ago, now all the benches are full. They're leaving the white society's edges. Mad Bear put in his time, too; he joined the Navy at sixteen (by using his brother's birth certificate; when the brother joined the same unit, there was hell to pay). He piloted a landing craft in the Seventh Amphibious Fleet at Saipan and Okinawa; since his discharge, at twenty-one, he's been a merchant seaman, and while at sea he reads—mainly lawbooks. He has never married.

But he has really found his calling as a leader. For his next berth, he would dearly love to ship out on the Indian Bureau ship *Northern Lights,* that takes supplies to Alaskan natives, so that he can get in a little aboriginal propaganda along the way. Before that, he has hopes to travel out West and drape a heavy chain around a customs house that stands, as Mad Bear says, in a tow-away zone of a certain Indian reservation that we'll be reading about in the papers before long. He intends to hire a bulldozer to take it away. "I don't really know if it will move or just fall apart," he says with a look of pleased innocence. That earlier moment of easy, contemplative silence, as he considered the possible future luck of the Iroquois, sitting there quietly in the firelight, is now forgotten. Mad Bear is cooking up schemes again.

In his excellent book, *Apologies to the Iroquois,* Edmund Wilson quoted one of these Indians' true friends among upstate New York whites, the scholar William Fenton: "The Indians are like a boiling pot. From time to time somebody comes along and takes off the lid and looks in. Then he puts it on again and goes away."

VINE DELORIA, JR.: THIS COUNTRY WAS A LOT BETTER OFF WHEN THE INDIANS WERE RUNNING IT

On Nov. 9, 1969, a contingent of American Indians, led by Adam Nordwall, a Chippewa from Minnesota, and Richard Oakes, a Mohawk from New York, landed on Alcatraz Island in San Francisco Bay and claimed the 13-acre rock "by right of discovery." The island had been abandoned six and a half years ago, and although there had been various suggestions concerning its disposal nothing had been done to make use of the land. Since there are Federal treaties giving some tribes the right to abandoned

Source: From the *New York Times Magazine,* 8 March 1970. ©1970 by The New York Times Company. Reprinted by permission.

Federal property within a tribe's original territory, the Indians of the Bay area felt that they could lay claim to the island.

For nearly a year the United Bay Area Council of American Indians, a confederation of urban Indian organizations, had been talking about submitting a bid for the island to use it as a West Coast Indian cultural center and vocational training headquarters. Then, on Nov. 1, the San Francisco American Indian Center burned down. The center had served an estimated 30,000 Indians in the immediate area and was the focus of activities of the urban Indian community. It became a matter of urgency after that and, as Adam Nordwall said, "it was GO." Another landing, on Nov. 20, by nearly 100 Indians in a swift midnight raid secured the island.

The new inhabitants have made "the Rock" a focal point symbolic of Indian people. Under extreme difficulty they have worked to begin repairing sanitary facilities and buildings. The population has been largely transient, many people have stopped by, looked the situation over for a few days, then gone home, unwilling to put in the tedious work necessary to make the island support a viable community.

The Alcatraz news stories are somewhat shocking to non-Indians. It is difficult for most Americans to comprehend that there still exists a living community of nearly one million Indians in this country. For many people, Indians have become a species of movie actor periodically dispatched to the Happy Hunting Grounds by John Wayne on the "Late, Late Show." Yet there are some 315 Indian tribal groups in 26 states still functioning as quasi-sovereign nations under treaty status; they range from the mammoth Navajo tribe of some 132,000 with 16 million acres of land to tiny Mission Creek of California with 15 people and a tiny parcel of property. There are over half a million Indians in the cities alone, with the largest concentrations in San Francisco, Los Angeles, Minneapolis and Chicago.

The take-over of Alcatraz is to many Indian people a demonstration of pride in being Indian and a dignified, yet humorous, protest against current conditions existing on the reservations and in the cities. It is this special pride and dignity, the determination to judge life according to one's own values, and the unconquerable conviction that the tribes will not die that has always characterized Indian people as I have known them.

I was born in Martin, a border town on the Pine Ridge Indian Reservation in South Dakota, in the midst of the Depression. My father was an Indian missionary who served 18 chapels on the eastern half of the reservation. In 1934, when I was 1, the Indian Reorganization Act was passed, allowing Indian tribes full rights of self-government for the first time since the late eighteen-sixties. Ever since those days, when the Sioux had agreed to forsake the life of the hunter for that of the farmer, they had been systematically deprived of any voice in decisions affecting their lives and property. Tribal ceremonies and religious practices were forbidden. The reservation was fully controlled by men in Washington, most of whom had never visited a reservation and felt no urge to do so.

The first years on the reservations were extremely hard for the Sioux. Kept confined behind fences they were almost wholly dependent upon Government rations for their food supply. Many died of hunger and malnutrition. Game was scarce and few were allowed to have weapons for fear of another Indian war. In some years there was practically no food available. Other years rations were withheld until the men agreed to farm the tiny pieces of land each family had been given. In desperation many families were forced to eat stray dogs and cats to keep alive.

By World War I, however, many of the Sioux families had developed prosperous ranches. Then the Government stepped in, sold the Indians' cattle for wartime needs, and after the war leased the grazing land to whites, creating wealthy white ranchers and destitute Indian landlords.

With the passage of the Indian Reorganization Act, native ceremonies and practices were given full recognition by Federal authorities. My earliest memories are of trips along dusty roads to Kyle, a small settlement in the heart of the reservation, to attend the dances. Ancient men, veterans of battles even then considered footnotes to the settlement of the West, brought their costumes out of hiding and walked about the grounds gathering the honors they had earned half a century before. They danced as if the intervening 50 years had been a lost weekend from which they had fully recovered. I remember best Dewey Beard, then in his late 80's and a survivor of the Little Big Horn. Even at that late date Dewey was hesitant to speak of the battle for fear of reprisal. There was no doubt, as one watched the people's expressions, that the Sioux had survived their greatest ordeal and were ready to face whatever the future might bring.

In those days the reservation was isolated and unsettled. Dirt roads held the few mail routes together. One could easily get lost in the wild back country as roads turned into cowpaths without so much as a backward glance. Remote settlements such as Buzzard Basin and Cuny Table were nearly inaccessible. In the spring every bridge on the reservation would be washed out with the first rain and would remain out until late summer. But few people cared. Most of the reservation people, traveling by team and wagon, merely forded the creeks and continued their journey, almost contemptuous of the need for roads and bridges.

The most memorable event of my early childhood was visiting Wounded Knee where 200 Sioux, including women and children, were slaughtered in 1890 by troopers of the Seventh Cavalry in what is believed to have been a delayed act of vengeance for Custer's defeat. The people were simply lined up and shot down much as was allegedly done, according to newspaper reports, at Songmy. The wounded were left to die in a three-day Dakota blizzard, and when the soldiers returned to the scene after the storm some were still alive and were saved. The massacre was vividly etched in the minds of many of the older reservation people, but it was difficult to find anyone who wanted to talk about it.

Many times, over the years, my father would point out survivors of the massacre, and people on the reservation always went out of their way to help them. For a long time there was a bill in Congress to pay indemnities to the survivors, but the War Department always insisted that it had been a "battle" to stamp out the Ghost Dance religion among the Sioux. This does not, however, explain bayoneted Indian women and children found miles from the scene of the incident.

Strangely enough, the Depression was good for Indian reservations, particularly for the people at Pine Ridge. Since their lands had been leased to non-Indians by the Bureau of Indian Affairs, they had only a small rent check and the contempt of those who leased their lands to show for their ownership. But the Federal programs devised to solve the national economic crisis were also made available to Indian people, and there was work available for the first time in the history of the reservations.

The Civilian Conservation Corps set up a camp on the reservation and many Indians were hired under the program. In the canyons north of Allen, S.D., a beautiful buffalo pasture was built by the C.C.C., and the whole area was transformed into a recreation wonderland. Indians would come from miles around to see the buffalo and leave with a strange look in their eyes. Many times I stood silently watching while old men talked to the buffalo about the old days. They would conclude by singing a song before respectfully departing, their eyes filled with tears and their minds occupied with the memories of other times and places. It was difficult to determine who was the captive—the buffalo fenced in or the Indian fenced out.

While the rest of America suffered from the temporary deprivation of its luxuries, Indian people had a period of prosperity, as it were. Paychecks were regular. Small cattle herds were started, cars were purchased, new clothes and necessities became available. To a people who had struggled along on a $50 cash income per year, the C.C.C. was the greatest program ever to come along. The Sioux had climbed from absolute deprivation to mere poverty, and this was the best time the reservation ever had.

World War II ended this temporary prosperity. The C.C.C. camps were closed; reservation programs were cut to the bone and social services became virtually nonexistent; "Victory gardens" were suddenly the style, and people began to be aware that a great war was being waged overseas.

The war dispersed the reservation people as nothing ever had. Every day, it seemed, we would be bidding farewell to families as they headed west to work in the defense plants on the Coast.

A great number of Sioux people went west and many of the Sioux on Alcatraz today are their children and relatives. There may now be as many Sioux in California as there are on the reservations in South Dakota because of the great wartime migration.

Those who stayed on the reservation had the war brought directly to their doorstep when they were notified that their sons had to go across the seas and fight. Busloads of Sioux boys left the reservation for parts unknown. In many cases even the trip to nearby Martin was a new experience for them, let alone training in Texas, California or Colorado. There were always going-away ceremonies conducted by the older people who admonished the boys to uphold the old tribal traditions and not to fear death. It was not death they feared but living with an unknown people in a distant place.

I was always disappointed with the Government's way of handling Indian servicemen. Indians were simply lost in the shuffle of 3 million men in uniform. Many boys came home on furlough and feared to return. They were not cowards in any sense of the word but the loneliness and boredom of stateside duty was crushing their spirits. They spent months without seeing another Indian. If the Government had recruited all-Indian outfits it would have easily solved this problem and also had the best fighting units in the world at its disposal. I often wonder what an all-Sioux or Apache company, painted and singing its songs, would have done to the morale of elite German panzer units.

After the war Indian veterans straggled back to the reservations and tried to pick up their lives. It was very difficult for them to resume a life of poverty after having seen the affluent outside world. Some spent a few days with the old folks and then left again for the big cities. Over the years they have emerged as leaders of the urban Indian movement. Many of their children are the nationalists of today who are adamant about keeping the reservations they have visited only on vacations. Other veterans stayed on the reservations and entered tribal politics.

The reservations radically changed after the war. During the Depression there were about five telephones in Martin. If there was a call for you, the man at the hardware store had to come down to your house and get you to answer it. A couple of years after the war a complete dial system was installed that extended to most of the smaller communities on the reservation. Families that had been hundreds of miles from any form of communication were now only minutes away from a telephone.

Roads were built connecting the major communities of the Pine Ridge country. No longer did it take hours to go from one place to another. With these kinds of roads everyone had to have a car. The team and wagon vanished, except for those families who lived at various "camps" in inaccessible canyons pretty much as their ancestors had. (Today, even they have adopted the automobile for traveling long distances in search of work.)

I left the reservation in 1951 when my family moved to Iowa. I went back only once for an extended stay, in the summer of 1955, while on a furlough, and after that I visited only occasionally during summer vacations. In the meantime, I attended college, served a hitch in the Marines, and went to the seminary. After I graduated from the seminary, I took a job with the United Scholarship Service, a private organization devoted to the college and secondary-school education of American Indian and Mexican students. I had spent my last two years of high school in an Eastern preparatory school and so was probably the only Indian my age who knew what an independent Eastern school was like. As the program developed, we soon had some 30 students placed in Eastern schools.

I insisted that all the students who entered the program be able to qualify for scholarships as students and not simply as Indians. I was pretty sure we could beat the white man at his own educational game, which seemed to me the only way to gain his respect. I was soon to find that this was a dangerous attitude to have. The very people who were supporting the program—non-Indians in the national church establishments—accused me of trying to form a colonialist "elite" by insisting that only kids with strong test scores and academic patterns be sent east to school. They wanted to continue the ancient pattern of soft-hearted paternalism toward Indians. I didn't feel we should cry our way into the schools, that sympathy would destroy the students we were trying to help.

In 1964, while attending the annual convention of the National Congress of American Indians, I was elected its executive director. I learned more about life in the N.C.A.I. in three years than I had in the previous 30. Every conceivable problem that could occur in an Indian society was suddenly thrust at me from 315 different directions. I discovered that I was one of the people who was supposed to solve the problems. The only trouble was that Indian people locally and on the national level were being played off one against the other by clever whites who had either ego or income at stake. While there were many feasible solutions, few could be tried without whites with vested interests working night and day to destroy the unity we were seeking on a national basis.

In the mid-nineteen-sixties, the whole generation that had grown up after World War II and had left the reservations during the fifties to get an education was returning to Indian life as "educated Indians." But we soon knew better. Tribal societies had existed for centuries without going outside themselves for education and information. Yet many of us thought that we would be able to improve the traditional tribal methods. We were wrong.

For three years we ran around the conference circuit attending numerous meetings called to "solve" the Indian problems. We listened to and spoke with anthropologists, historians, sociologists, psychologists, economists, educators and missionaries. We worked with many Government agencies and with every conceivable doctrine, idea, and program ever created. At the end of this happy round of consultations the reservation people were still plodding along on their own time schedule, doing the things they considered important. They continued to solve their problems their way in spite of the advice given them by "Indian experts."

By 1967 there was a radical change in thinking on the part of many of us. Conferences were proving unproductive. Where non-Indians had been pushed out to make room for Indian people, they had wormed their way back into power and again controlled the major programs serving Indians. The poverty programs, reservation and university technical assistance groups were dominated by whites who had pushed Indian administrators aside.

Reservation people, meanwhile, were making steady progress in spite of the numerous setbacks suffered by the national Indian community. So, in large part, younger Indian leaders who had been playing the national conference field began working at the local level to build community movements from the ground up. By consolidating local organizations into power groups they felt that they would be in a better position to influence national thinking.

Robert Hunter, director of the Nevada Intertribal Council, had already begun to build a strong state organization of tribes and communities. In South Dakota, Gerald One Feather, Frank LaPointe and Ray Briggs formed the American Indian Leadership Conference, which quickly welded the educated young Sioux in that state into a strong regional organization active in nearly every phase of Sioux life. Gerald is now running for the prestigious post of chairman of the Oglala Sioux, the largest Sioux tribe, numbering some 15,000 members. Ernie Stevens, an Oneida from Wisconsin, and Lee Cook, a Chippewa from Minnesota, developed a strong program for economic and community development in Arizona. Just recently Ernie has moved into the post of director of the California Intertribal Council, a statewide organization representing some 130,000 California Indians in cities and on the scattered reservations of that state.

By the fall of 1967, it was apparent that the national Indian scene was collapsing in favor of strong regional organizations, although the major national organizations such as the National Congress of American Indians and the National Indian Youth Council continued to grow. There was yet another factor emerging on the Indian scene: the oldtimers of the Depression days had educated a group of younger Indians in the old ways and these people were now becoming a major force in Indian life. Led by Thomas Banyaca of the Hopi, Mad Bear Anderson of the Tuscaroras, Clifton Hill of the Creeks, and Rolling Thunder of the Shoshones, the traditional Indians were forcing the whole Indian community to rethink its understanding of Indian life.

The message of the traditionalists is simple. They demand a return to basic Indian philosophy, establishment of ancient methods of government by open council instead of elected officials, a revival of Indian religions and replacement of white laws with Indian customs; in short, a complete return to the ways of the old people. In an age dominated by tribalizing communications media, their message makes a great deal of sense.

But in some areas their thinking is opposed to that of the National Congress of American Indians, which represents officially elected tribal governments organized under the Indian Reorganization Act as Federal corporations. The contemporary problem is therefore one of defining the meaning of "tribe." Is it a traditionally organized band of Indians following customs with medicine men and chiefs dominating the policies of the tribe, or is it a modern corporate structure attempting to compromise at least in part with modern white culture?

The problem has been complicated by private foundations' and Government agencies' funding of Indian programs. In general this process, although it has brought a great amount of money into Indian country, has been one of cooptation. Government agencies must justify their appropriation requests every year and can only take chances on spectacular programs that will serve as showcases of progress. They are not willing to invest the capital funds necessary to build viable self-supporting communities on the reservations because these programs do not have an immediate publicity potential. Thus, the Government agencies are forever committed to conducting conferences to discover that one "key" to Indian life that will give them the edge over their rival agencies in the annual appropriations derby.

Churches and foundations have merely purchased an Indian leader or program that conforms with their ideas of what Indian people should be doing. The large foundations have bought up the well-dressed, handsome "new image" Indian who is comfortable in the big cities but virtually helpless at an Indian meeting. Churches have given money to Indians who have been willing to copy black militant activist tactics, and the more violent and insulting the Indian can be, the more the churches seem to love it. They are wallowing in self-guilt and piety over the lot of the poor, yet funding demagogues of their own choosing to speak for the poor.

I did not run for re-election as executive director of the N.C.A.I. in the fall of 1967 but entered law school at the University of Colorado instead. It was apparent to me that the Indian revolution was well under way and that someone had better get a legal education so that we could have our own legal program for defense of Indian treaty rights. Thanks to a Ford Foundation program, nearly 50 Indians are now in law school, assuring the Indian community of legal talent in the years ahead. Within four years I foresee another radical shift in Indian leadership patterns as the growing local movements are affected by the new Indian lawyers.

There is an increasing scent of victory in the air in Indian country these days. The mood is comparable to the old days of the Depression when the men began to dance once again. As the Indian movement gathers momentum and individual Indians cast their lot with the tribe, it will become apparent that not only will Indians survive the electronic world of Marshall McLuhan, they will thrive in it. At the present time everyone is watching how mainstream America will handle the issues of pollution, poverty, crime and racism when it does not fundamentally understand the issues. Knowing the importance of tribal survival, Indian people are speaking more and more of sovereignty, of the great political technique of the open council, and of the need for gaining the community's consensus on all programs before putting them into effect.

One can watch this same issue emerge in white society as the "Woodstock Nation," the "Blackstone Nation" and the block organizations are developed. This is a full tribalizing process involving a nontribal people, and it is apparent that some people are frightened by it. But it is the kind of social phenomenon upon which Indians feast.

In 1965 I had a long conversation with an old Papago. I was trying to get the tribe to pay its dues to the National Congress of American Indians and I had asked him to speak to the tribal council for me. He said that he would but that the Papagos didn't really need the N.C.A.I. They were like, he told me, the old mountain in the distance. The Spanish had come and dominated them for 300 years and then left. The Mexicans had come and ruled them for a century, but they also left. "The Americans," he said, "have been here only about 80 years. They, too, will vanish, but the Papagos and the mountain will always be here."

This attitude and understanding of life is what American society is searching for.

I wish the Government would give Alcatraz to the Indians now occupying it. They want to create five centers on the island. One center would be for a North American studies program; another would be a spiritual and medical center where Indian religions and medicines would be used and studied. A third center would concentrate on ecological studies based on an Indian view of nature—that man should live with the land and not simply on it. A job-training center and a museum would also be founded on the island. Certain of these programs would obviously require Federal assistance.

Some people may object to this approach, yet Health, Education and Welfare gave out $10 million last year to non-Indians to study Indians. Not one single dollar went to an Indian scholar or researcher to present the point of view of Indian people. And the studies done by non-Indians added nothing to what was already known about Indians.

Indian people have managed to maintain a viable and cohesive social order in spite of everything the non-Indian society has thrown at them in an effort to break the tribal structure. At the same time, non-Indian society has created a monstrosity of a culture where people starve while the granaries are filled and the sun can never break though the smog.

By making Alcatraz an experimental Indian center operated and planned by Indian people, we would be given a chance to see what we could do toward developing answers to modern social problems. Ancient tribalism can be incorporated with modern technology in an urban setting. Perhaps we would not succeed in the effort, but the Government is spending billions every year and still the situation is rapidly growing worse. It just seems to a lot of Indians that this continent was a lot better off when we were running it.

ROBERT C. DAY: THE EMERGENCE OF ACTIVISM AS A SOCIAL MOVEMENT[1]

"Custer Had It Coming!" "Red Power!" "Indians Discovered America!" "Kemo Sabe Means Honky!" The slogans on bumpers, telephone poles, and student notebooks announce to white Americans that after more than a century of silent anger and hostile passivity, the original American is astir, seeking new ways of solving the "white problem."[2] The new voices of Indian militancy make it clear that Indians are fed up with silence, poverty, and the agencies of white power that have made the Indian an alien in his own land.

During the last 25 years, two major national Indian organizations have emerged, the National Congress of American Indians (NCAI) and the National Indian Youth Council (NIYC). The NCAI, more than any other organization, is the voice of approximately three-fourths of the 650,000 Indians in the nation. This "United Nations of the tribes," representing as many as 100 groups, was organized by young Indian intellectuals in November, 1944. It was the first broad-scale attempt by Indian people to develop intertribal consensus and to influence national and state Indian policy. The NCAI has been the principal Indian power group to grapple with the shifting goals and tactics of the Bureau of Indian Affairs and the Department of the Interior, especially during the termination and relocation policies of the 1950s.

The National Indian Youth Council was organized in August, 1960, by ten young Indians who combined university education with varying degrees of political activism or militancy. The factors which led to its organization included general impatience and frustration with shifts in national Indian policy, with the continued paternalism of the BIA and with the limited goals and cautious tactics of NCAI leaders. Members of the Youth Council subsequently developed a broad new policy of self-determination and self-help, and it has become a genuine social movement led by militant youth but supported in varying degrees by a significant number of reservation elders.

According to one account, the term *Red Power* was first uttered on a public rostrum during the 1966 convention of the National Congress of American Indians. Said Vine Deloria, the Executive Director of the NCAI that year: "Red Power means we want power over our own lives. . . . We do not wish power *over* anyone. We are only half a million Indians. We simply want the power, the political and economic power, to run our own lives in our own way."[3]

By 1970 "Red Power" had become a movement to achieve a reservation-based "tribal nationalism," and its proponents used a full range of instrumental or symbolic tactics of protest to gain public support and exert political pressure. Among the specific tactics were fish-ins, the closing of beaches, rivers, bridges, and highways on reservation land, the occupation of land areas such as Alcatraz or Ft. Lewis (Washington), demands for financial aid or legal protection, blockage of dam construction, and occupation of BIA or other government offices. The remainder of this paper is an attempt to describe the origins and supportive factors in the emergence between 1960 and 1970 of vigorous Indian activism (i.e., "Red Power") and several other strategies ultimately aimed at creating self-reliant, Indian-controlled, tribal "nations" within the boundaries of the United States.

THE INITIAL PROJECT IN DIRECT ACTION: THE FISH-INS IN THE NORTHWEST

The first protests led by the National Indian Youth Council were a series of illegal fish-ins on the Quillayute, Puyallup, Hoh, Yakima, Nisqually and Columbia rivers in the state of Washington.[4] The actions were organized with the support of local tribes in the Spring of 1964. The immediate crisis that triggered the fish-ins was a state supreme court decision in December, 1963, which in effect nullified the Treaty of Medicine Creek signed in 1854 by the United States and several tribal groups in the state of Washington. By this and ten other treaties the Indians of Puget Sound had signed over most of their land and had been left with little more than the right to fish in the traditional fishing grounds. The Supreme Court of Washington argued that none of the treaty signatories contemplated fishing with 600-foot gill nets which endangered the spawning and survival of the species, and on that ground nullified the century-old agreement.[5]

The director of the state fisheries stated that in breaking the treaty he was simply obeying the law, and "that's what happens when progress pushes forward." It was not the first violation of Indian fishing rights by the state of Washington. The state earlier had denied fishing rights to Indians at a point on the Columbia River, subsequently leasing those rights to a commercial concern for $36,000 a year. Three months after the December, 1963, court decision the Makah tribe decided to ask members of the Youth Council to lead the small and scattered tribes of Washington in taking direct action to protest the situation.[6]

Protest efforts were initially blocked by the disunity, apathy, and traditional values of many tribal leaders (i.e., going to jail was perceived as undignified). Some questioned whether direct action was "the Indian way." Many worried about negative repercussions, but in the end there was no choice; the tribal leaders knew that if they lost their fishing rights, they could not survive as a cultural unit.[7]

The first fish-in occurred on the Quillayute River in March, 1964. Several hundred Indians had gathered on the banks and watched in silence and growing hostility as the Indians rowed out to fish and the game wardens and state police moved in with warrants. Mel Thom, the president of the Youth Council, described the scene:

> The tone of the crowd was rather tense. You could feel the hostility build up against the game wardens. The authorities, the people with the law, were really mad at us for being there.
> We knew the game wardens would make arrests. They did. . . . And then a funny thing happened. The Indians began to enjoy it. They were happy to see some direct action. Then the tenseness broke.[8]

The fish-in tactic was expanded to half a dozen other rivers. Some of the tribes that initially opposed the fish-ins later began their own direct action, and women and children threw sticks and rocks at the wardens arresting their men. Several men were arrested at each of the demonstrations along the Quillayute, Nisqually and Green rivers, and these arrests hardened the Indians' resolve to fight. They subsequently enlarged their protest to include "treaty treks" on city streets, "canoe treks" through Puget Sound, and a series of war dances on the steps of the capital rotunda in Olympia terminating with a "Proclamation of Protest" and consultation with Governor Rossellini.[9]

The fish-ins had far-reaching effects. Indian groups from all over the country had traded and tested ideas about organizing and running protests. The Youth Council with support from tribal elders had taken the risk of leading direct action in the use of civil disobedience, arrests and jailings to create an issue, to gain press coverage for a cause, to get ingroup support and organization, to alter the passive image of the "vanishing Indian" and to start a long, complex social and legal process of court tests, discussion, and consensus building in the white community.

The fish-ins initiated a legal battle to nullify the effects of Public Law 280, but they had much broader implications. Mel Thom was explicit about this: "Our whole interest was to build communities, Indian communities. The Youth Council is dedicated to modernizing and preserving tribal society. Not only for today, but for the future."[10]

On May 31, 1966, two years later, the fish-ins netted the biggest catch of all. The federal Department of Justice agreed to "uphold the solemn obligations of the government" and to defend the fishing rights of the tribes of the Northwest. Justice Department lawyers appeared before the Supreme Court of the State of Washington as *amicus curiae* to defend the Puyallups who had been enjoined from exercising their treaty fishing rights. This unprecedented event, a vindication of the leaders and participants of the fish-in, illustrated for Indian people across the nation the value of direct collective action. The court cases and demonstrations over fishing rights have continued intermittently to the present time without clear resolution of the issue,[11] but the Indian groups involved have become fully aware of the value of nonviolent demonstrations to develop social pressures to achieve institutional changes in the direction of civil and treaty rights. On May 27, 1968, the United States Supreme Court handed down its decision on the Nisqually and Puyallup cases, confirming the treaty rights of Indians to fish off reservation but giving the state the right to regulate "provided the regulation meets appropriate standards and does not discriminate against Indians."[12] In the fall of 1968, renewed demonstrations and violence on the lower Nisqually led to an investigation by the Governor's Advisory Committee on Indian Affairs and a statement by the BIA supporting off-reservation fishing by Indians and questioning the necessity of the state regulation outlawing Indian net fishing. The controversy continued into 1969 and 1970 with increasing public awareness of Indian economic deprivation as a partial consequence of violated treaty rights.

ORIGINS OF DIRECT COLLECTIVE ACTION BY INDIANS: ANTECEDENTS OF THE FISH-INS OF 1964

It was only after months of traveling around the nation, getting to know the participants, talking things over, and reviewing written notes on prior conferences and meetings that Steiner was able to assemble a relatively complete account of the emergence of collective protest among

Indian groups during the past 15 or 20 years.[13] From his narrative it becomes evident that the early stages of the movement involved a gradual process of personal exploration and growth which seems to have occurred primarily on university campuses and at intermittent meetings and conferences, beginning in Santa Fe in 1954.

Between 1954 and 1960, broad new tribal goals and alternate strategies to achieve them were worked out in formative discussions and conferences involving a core of fewer than 100 persons. The Native American college students discussed and reviewed their ideas with reservation leaders in order to remain realistic and practical in their task and to gain relief from the ego-shaking confusion and alienation of operating within white organizations and white culture.   The discussions and conferences between 1954 and 1960 served to produce a fairly cohesive group with well-defined issues and goals and the leadership skills to promote a significant social movement when a congenial combination of environmental factors occurred.

In the early summer of 1960, Sol Tax, an anthropologist at the University of Chicago, organized a conference of Indian leaders to develop guidelines for the new Presidential administration. The American Indian Chicago Conference and the election of John F. Kennedy to the Presidency combined to trigger the emergent social movement of Indian activism which became visible to the white community for the first time in the 1964 fish-ins.

Though it usually violates the realities of a social process to choose some moment in time as the "starting point," Steiner suggests that the gathering in Santa Fe in 1954 can legitimately be used as one of the important initial events in the long social and cultural process culminating in Indian activism. World War II and the Korean War had provided new experiences and perspectives for Indians that stimulated changes in veterans' attitudes about personal goals, the chances for achieving expanded objectives, and the value of education for obtaining newly defined occupational goals. The children of World War II veterans had been encouraged to finish high school, or even to try some college. Korean War veterans entered universities at an accelerated rate: In 1950 there were 24,000 Indian high school students; a decade later there were 57,000. At the same time the number of Indian college students increased from 6,500 to 17,000.[14]

In addition to the complex identity crisis derived from being caught in the cultural "no-man's-land" halfway between the reservation and Anglo society, the termination policy of the Eisenhower administration put students in a double bind. This policy encouraged students to become educated and to reject "Indianness" and melt into the Anglo mainstream. Among the students who had experienced the tensions and ambiguities in the Indian student's role was a Navaho named Herbert Blatchford. Blatchford and others had serious questions about the apparent goals of Indian education, and they organized a conference of university students and reservation leaders to attempt to resolve some of their anxieties and to develop needed consensus on specific goals for the educational enterprise.[15] The conference was held in Santa Fe in 1954. At the meeting Blatchford phrased the problem in this way: "How can we, as young people, help to solve conflicts between cultures?"[16] The outcome of the conference is not reported in any detail, but a degree of consensus about the necessity for education seems to have been developed. Periodic visits to university campuses by reservation adults helped to bridge the cultural gap for the students. The elders' basic message was that the students were welcome in the Indian community when their education in the white man's world was completed.[17] Thus the Santa Fe meeting of 1954 produced a partial resolution of the uncertainties of the student role, a general expression of community support from adult reservation leaders, and the impetus for the organization of interuniversity Indian clubs for further discussions of goals, priorities and strategies. Both Blatchford and the leaders of the National Congress of American Indians stress that from the earliest days of the Indian youth movement, there has been continuous mutual sharing of ideas, values and goals with reservation elders so that for the most part a disruptive "generation gap" has been avoided.[18]

The organizing process started at the Santa Fe meeting eventually led to the formation of the Southwestern Regional Youth Conference (SRYC). At the early spring conference of the SRYC in 1960, 350 Indian youths from 57 tribes held serious discussion about tribal nationalism as a model and goal. But the initial concrete written expression of Indian nationalism as a policy goal first appeared in the "Declaration of Indian Purpose" developed at the 1960 Chicago Conference sponsored by Sol Tax. The conference brought together the largest and most varied group of modern Indians that had ever gathered independently of the influence of the BIA or other government agencies to consider policies and goals. Members of "lost" tribes from the eastern states, such as the Haliwa and Houma, were present along with unaffiliated urban Indians and representatives of the powerful western tribes.[19] Opinions ranged from the views of the de-tribalized assimilationists who advocated participating freely in white organizations and culture to those of the extreme nativists or traditionalists who denied that they were American citizens and focused exclusively on tribal nationalism.[20]

A group of young Indians just out of college, including Herbert Blatchford, Mel Thom, Clyde Warrior and others, attended the initial meeting in the summer of 1960, though they had not been invited. For a time the college Indians listened to the routine rhetoric of the official Indian leaders, but soon they became very impatient and restive. Twelve of them formed a "youth caucus" to voice their own opinions, and some became chairmen of a number of conference committees.[21]

The Youth Caucus asserted itself in a "statement of purpose" which was used extensively in the final declaration of the conference. That declaration, stressing self-government, sovereignty, and nationalism, made it clear that Indian people wanted complete autonomy to protect their land base from expropriation and to make their own plans and decisions in building an economic system to rid themselves of poverty while reasserting traditional cultural values.[22]

After the initial meeting of the Chicago Conference in June, 1960, the twelve members of the youth caucus separated but continued to communicate. The group assembled the following August at the Inter-Tribal Ceremonial in Gallup, New Mexico, to form their own organization to foster the youth movement in support of tribal nationalism and the subsidiary goals developed after the Chicago meeting. The result was the National Indian Youth Council (NIYC). Its central purpose was defining the nature of the "new tribalism" and creating strategies for developing it.[23]

The Youth Council agreed on a number of related goals and principles in this initial session. While moving into direct action to achieve their ends with regard to treaty rights, civil rights and control of federally financed projects, the group felt it was vital to remain, where possible, within tribal values of dignity, fairness and reverence for tribal counsel and tribal service. "Political climbing" within the organization was labeled as an Anglo tactic and rejected. Learning how to use political action, propaganda, and power within an overall plan was stressed.[24]

The American Indian Chicago Conference, at the University of Chicago, was probably the most important single event in the emergence of tribal nationalism as a social movement. Despite gloomy predictions by many observers of Indian affairs that the conference would fail because Indians were too factionalized to achieve intertribal cooperation, a public consensus on a revolutionary new concept (i.e., tribal nationalism) was achieved among both the aggressive, educated youth and the elder leaders in the conference. The Chicago Conference likewise precipitated the formation of the American Indian Youth Council which, in turn, led to the first direct-action fish-ins of the State of Washington a few years later and fostered innumerable subsequent protest actions of various kinds.

Though the point has not been developed in any of the accounts of the early meetings of the Youth Council, it may be that Wallace "Mad Bear" Anderson significantly influenced the type of militant tactics eventually used by the group. Mad Bear's tactics for civil disobedience, as described in the article by Roy Bongartz in this chapter, provided a notable example to the Youth Council concerning the tangible, beneficial results that can be achieved with creative disruptiveness.

In 1957 Mad Bear helped lead the Mohawks' fight against the New York state income tax on the grounds of Indian sovereignty. He organized a group of 400 Indians from the St. Regis Reservation to go into court and tear up summonses issued for tax refusal. Then in 1958 on his own Tuscarora Reservation Mad Bear successfully blocked the activities of surveyors and others trying to build a large reservoir on the reservation without Indian permission, by fighting, deflating tires, tossing firecrackers, and shooting guns over workers' heads. Robert Moses, chairman of the state power authority, offered three million dollars for the land, and was refused. In 1959 the Federal Power Commission ruled that the Indians could not be compelled to sell their land for the reservoir.[25]

A month later Mad Bear participated in another challenge to the Establishment's legal decisions, this time by occupying a Canadian government council house for a week of turmoil. His tactics fall into a clear pattern of using various laws and old treaty agreements to challenge existing white efforts to encroach upon Indian rights and land. Mad Bear's protests are "marked by a certain sense of wit combined with impeccable logic" (with regard to the legal status of his activities) and a stubborn, if passive, resistance. In many cases he successfully "puts the Establishment on" in an essentially nonviolent way while at the same time gaining unsurpassed publicity, sympathy and support and achieving the protection of legal victories and altered government policy.[26]

Mad Bear Anderson had one other extremely significant project in 1968 which had continuing ramifications for the tribalism movement. He decided to lead a delegation of Indians from the Six Nations of the Iroquois to Cuba to ask Fidel Castro to sponsor their admission to the United Nations as a sovereign independent state. Castro did not follow through, but the project was brilliantly conceived and provided a model for taking an international perspective in sharing ideas and resources in the anticolonial movement of tribal nationalists. Mad Bear's employment as a merchant seaman during the 1950s had provided him with the opportunity to compare national forms of social organization, and he soon came to see how "colonial" the United States' treatment of Indians was and to talk of alliances of the Iroquois with nationalist revolutionaries in India, Taiwan, Japan, Yugoslavia, Brazil, and Cuba. Other Indian leaders such as Deloria are now using the colonialism analogy and incorporating the international perspective into their thinking and planning.[27]

Though little direct evidence is available to support the argument, another factor that probably contributed significantly to the urgency and impetus, if not the planning and organization of the Youth Council during the summer of 1960, was the rapidly spreading sit-in movement among black college youth which was triggered by four black students at North Carolina A and M, in Greensboro, North Carolina, on February 1, 1960.[28] Black youth had long been frustrated with the seemingly unspectacular pace of NAACP legal battles and had been searching for a vehicle for fuller participation and involvement in the civil rights movement. Use of sit-ins as a tactic spread rapidly during the spring and summer and produced some immediate, publicized successes in "moving the Man's system" which almost certainly impressed the impatient university Indian leaders.[29] The observer cannot help but note the parallel between the black case and the growing impatience of Indian youth with their own lack of direct action and involvement, as well as their frustration with the efforts of adult reservation leaders.

The choice of the term *Red Muslims* clearly suggests Indian awareness and acceptance of some of the elements of activism provided by the Black Muslims. All comparisons with black perceptions and models of organized response, however, must be drawn with some caution because Indian leaders have generally shown very little "borrowing" of tactics from either white or black culture without substantial innovation and alteration in "the Indian way." There is as yet little documentation of actual teamwork or alliances between blacks and Youth Council leaders in the formative years between 1960 and the 1964 fish-ins, in which Dick Gregory, the black comedian, participated.[30]

One of the more aggressive militants of the founders of the NIYC, Clyde Warrior, spent the summer of 1961 working with SNCC's voter-education project in the rural Black Belts of Georgia, Alabama, and Mississippi.[31] Subsequently, Warrior was one of the first Indian activists to shift from reformist goals and begin using revolutionary rhetoric.

In a press conference in Washington, D.C., after his assumption of the leadership of the NIYC, Warrior labeled BIA officials as "white colonialists, racists, fascists, Uncle Tomahawks, and bureaucrats."[32] Thus, a major Indian leader publicly used the terms of revolutionary rhetoric so often used by blacks: "exploiters," "oppressors," "colonialists," and "fascists." Perhaps Warrior's thinking was influenced by the more militant members of SNCC.

THE TRIBALISM MOVEMENT AND SUPPORTIVE COLLECTIVE ACTIONS: 1961 TO 1970

As described above, the "Declaration of Indian Purpose," issued in final form in June, 1961, by participants in the Chicago Conference soon became a kind of challenge and mandate to the Youth Council members who were searching around for new, more aggressive tactics, not only to resist termination, but to foster the resurgence of a modern, adaptive tribalism. Activism and social protest was a very new role for Indians, engendering varying degrees of role conflict for college youth and sub-sequent searching discussions over cultural values and new roles with the older traditional reservation leaders. The search for suitable situations for direct action and the related discussions of values and strategies with reservation leaders continued from June, 1961, to March, 1964. It required a crisis over fishing rights with the survival of several tribes in the state of Washington at stake to precipitate the first collective action of the direct-confrontation variety. That crisis occurred in December, 1963, when the Supreme Court of Washington made the decision to restrict the commercial fishing activities of several coastal tribes, and the Makahs responded by asking the Youth Council to enter the situation and organize the fish-in demonstrations.

Indians have utilized many forms of collective action, however, and focusing exclusively on the confrontation tactics used during the fish-ins ignores other important related activities. Consideration of protests alone would lead to gross stereotyping and oversimplification of the tribalism movement. Analysis of news releases in the *New York Times* between 1961 and 1970 reveals that collective actions used by Indians in the last decade fall into roughly two broad clusters of tactics, namely, those that block and obstruct the social system and those that promote and facilitate it.

Obstructive tactics include challenges of government laws and practices (i.e., federal, state, or local) and violations of organizational rules and procedures by blocking or halting ongoing activities in some way, or by violating laws, regulations or strongly held norms and values. Specific obstructive tactics used by the Indians have included: (1) Delaying or halting dam construction, logging operations, customs collection, beach or island use, and use of negative stereotypes in advertising; (2) seizing control of, occupying, or obstructing use of government offices, military installations, border customs facilities, off-reservation fishing sites and "government surplus" islands; (3) nonviolent picketing, speeches, sit-ins, marches and boycotts to pressure policymakers and gain public support; and (4) strong public verbal attacks against government officials or policies, such as jeering a Secretary of the Interior's speech and calling for his resignation. All of these actions involve violations of laws, organizational practices, or informal norms.

In applying their obstructive tactics, the Indians have carefully attempted to avoid all forms of violence, except an occasional fight, while tenaciously demonstrating against the law, rule, or practice in question. Accordingly, in describing the Indians' use of obstructive tactics, the customary terms "confrontation," "disruptive protest," and "civil disturbance" have purposefully been avoided so that the special characteristics of Indian "protest" will be highlighted.

The term "facilitative tactics" refers to all nonobstructive forms of collective action. It includes the following types of activity: (1) Promoting economic development of reservation resources such as timber and minerals with the aid of white professionals and BIA staff, and encouraging white corporations to locate industrial plants on or near reservations; (2) sponsoring public relations projects designed to alter white people's stereotypes about Indians; (3) holding conferences to form new regional associations, to explore ways to exert pressure upon the Department of Interior or BIA officials, or to organize urban community centers; (4) organizing new educational institutions under Indian guidance and control; (5) initiating legal proceedings to maintain or reassert land rights, mineral, timber, and grazing rights, fishing and water rights, civil rights, or to seek control over valued artifacts now in white museums (e.g., wampum belts); and (6) initiating complaints and government investigations of reservation or urban living conditions. None of these facilitating actions involve violations of laws, agreements or broadly held norms. In each case existing legitimate channels of influence in the white social structure were employed to gain a desired result.

After this typology had been developed, reports in the *New York Times* of collective action by Indians were analyzed in a search for trends. The goal was to use news releases in an assessment of the approximate rate and nature of collective Indian actions each year between 1961 and 1970, and thus to reveal the overall pattern of development in collective action by Indian people.

In using an "incident count" to assess the development of the Red Power movement, we followed the rule that each specific incident was counted only once, despite continued press coverage of its consequences. Thus, even though two or more articles were published about a single event, only one "incident" was recorded. The only exception to this policy was the series of incidents on Alcatraz during 1970. Several very different episodes occurred on the island and they were counted as distinct collective actions.

As a method for tracing the development of a movement, the procedure of counting separate incidents reported in a single paper is subject to several sources of bias. The *Times* editors failed to print accounts of a number of the earliest fish-ins in 1964, for example, because for a brief period they were not aware of the importance of this new type of Indian activity. However, many of the obstructionist activities thereafter were covered by special correspondents on the *Times* staff. Undoubtedly, other types of biases and errors of omission occurred in the *Times'* information gathering process. In assessing the growing rate of news releases on any topic, it is impossible to standardize for the effect of growing sensitivity to an issue by newspaper editors which influences their decisions on coverage. We have simply used the raw rate of releases in the *New York Times* from year to year as a rough indicator of growing Indian activism. But since our purpose was to ascertain trends rather than to compile a definitive list of all collective actions, use of a single source as a standard over the entire period can be justified.

The overall annual rate of collective actions is presented in Table 1. It

TABLE 1

The Rate of Collective Actions by Indians Reported
in the New York Times, 1961-1970

| | Type of Collective Action | | | | |
| | Obstructive Tactics | | Facilitative Tactics[a] | | Total |
Year	Number	Percent	Number	Percent	Actions
1961	0	0	4	100	4
1962	0	0	8	100	8
1963	0	0	4	100	4
1964	2	17	10	83	12
1965	2	18	9	82	11
1966	2	13	13	87	15
1967	4	17	20	83	24
1968	9	38	15	62	24
1969	16	33	33	67	49
1970 (9 mos.)	18	42	25	58	43
1970 (Annual)[b]	24	42	33	58	57

[a] All news releases pertaining to suits of the Indian Claims Commission were omitted from this analysis.

[b] Annual figures projected on the basis of the first nine months.

is clear from the annual figures shown there that during the decade there was a steady increase in the use of both obstructive and facilitative tactics. Obstructive activities were not started until 1964 and remained at the low rate of 2 per year for three consecutive years before doubling in 1967 (4 incidents), doubling again in 1968 (9 incidents) and again in 1969 (16 incidents). It should also be pointed out that the use of obstructive tactics began slowly but during the last four years increased at a faster rate than did the use of facilitative activities. Evidently the results of nonviolent disruptiveness and blocking tactics have been perceived as substantially more rewarding, all told, than the outcomes of promotion and facilitation.

Having reviewed the trends in the yearly counts of collective action, it is now pertinent to take a look at the specific obstructive and facilitative activities for each year to gauge the qualitative alterations in tactics and the growth in sophistication developed by participants in the movement. As is apparent in Table 1, the tactics used during 1961-1963 were entirely of the facilitative, promotional variety, including a few nonobstructive complaints to facilitate new investigations by whites of living conditions on reservations. The four incidents recorded in the *Times* during 1961 included an appeal for aid for 2500 persons suffering from malnutrition and starvation at Ft. Hall, Idaho, an account of the Pueblos' efforts to gain full rights to their Blue Lake religious shrine, details about the Chicago Conference, and a public blast against the termination of the Menominee tribe.[33] It should be noted that the Blue Lake issue was not settled until President Nixon's policy statement in 1970 which also, by coincidence, was the first time that a United States President overtly supported major themes of the Chicago Declaration.[34]

In 1962, eight facilitative actions were reported, including four public complaints against violations of civil or land rights (e.g., police brutality, loss of land rights in Alaska),[35] a suit to end a ban on the use of peyote in religious ceremonies, an NCAI convention to unify policy which initiated an antibias drive, and the proclamation of "American Indian Day" by the Iroquois.[36] Thus, the shift from the policy of silence about violations of Indian rights to a policy of activism was well under way in the 1961-1962 period, but the initial activism was kept strictly within legitimate channels. The public relations projects of the NCAI leaders such as the antibias drive and the institution of American Indian Day marked another new but "safe" departure from past policies.

During 1963 the rate of facilitative actions reported in the *Times* dropped to the original 1961 level, four incidents. Perhaps the debate between NIYC militants and NCAI moderates over whether and how to shift to "system blocking" tactics was so prevalent and time-consuming that little attention could be focused on facilitative or promotional activity. In March, 1963, President Kennedy was petitioned to shift his policy toward more self-determination for Indians, but no direct pressure was applied.[37] Later the Sioux of South Dakota were active within the state system in getting petitions signed to achieve a referendum on a bill giving the state courts jurisdiction over civil and criminal cases occurring on reservations.[38]

In 1964 the rate of collective actions picked up with a total of 12 reported incidents, 2 of which constituted the first cases of nonviolent, "illegal" challenges to white regulations. A group of Mohawks claimed free entry into the New York World's Fair on the basis of an agreement contained in a 1684 deed conveying the Flushing Meadows section of New York City to English settlers. On the basis of a statement allowing Indians to collect bullrushes in this area forever, free access to the fair was demanded and allowed. The news release does not mention who led the group but the skillful use of ancient legal agreements certainly suggests that Mad Bear Anderson might have had a part in the operation. A few days later a Matinnecock Princess, Sun Tamo claimed the right of free entry for her group of 200 tribal members still living in the Flushing Meadows area.[39]

The promotional and facilitative actions of 1964 represent a rapid expansion of the ideas applied in the previous years. NCAI representatives visited President Johnson and stimulated an announcement that the War on Poverty would be directed at Indian problems too. Indians also sat down with actor Marlon Brando to plan a drive to inform the public of the injustices against Indians, and Brando demonstrated in Olympia and joined the Washington fish-ins in March.[40] An Indian arts and artifact exposition was opened in Anadorko, Oklahoma, and an Indian Hall of Fame was announced in New York City. Indian commercial projects were initiated, including a tourist attraction at Window Rock, Arizona, and a resort at Kah-nee-ta, Oregon. Finally, perhaps the most significant new facilitative event of the year was the election of two Navahos (Democrats) to the state legislature of New Mexico.[41]

During 1965, members of the Youth Council either participated in the various fish-ins and issue-building "treaty treks" or discussed and evaluated the developing court cases and appeals. It was a year for assessment of tactics and for organizational work around the nation, a time to prepare for further collective action. In 1965, 11 news stories related to Indian activism were printed in the New York Times. In June a Catholic priest was evicted from the Isleta pueblo near Albuquerque, New Mexico, for interfering with and ridiculing several Indian traditions and practices. In December, several urban Indians in Milwaukee, Wisconsin, complained of fraudulent impersonators who performed at local ceremonial functions, thereby depreciating the ceremonies. The issue of termination cropped up in only one release that year; in April a Times article reported about the opposition of Vine Deloria and other leaders of the NCAI to a termination bill for the Colville Reservation in the state of Washington.[42]

In contrast to the restrained quality of Indian activism in 1965, 1966 showed an increase in collective activity, including 15 reported incidents that were extremely significant in terms of their effects on the consolidation and growth of the Indian movement. Actions of Secretary of the Interior Udall and other important federal officials at a high-level "reorganization meeting" in Santa Fe demonstrated to the Youth Council and the NCAI the surprising degree of benign paternalism in the Secretary's approach, permitted the Indian leaders to label that approach a subtle form of modern "colonialism," and made it possible for them to develop a powerful consensus in opposition to Udall's initial, termination-oriented proposals. The net result was to thoroughly imbue many of the older leaders of the NCAI with the new concept, goals, and strategies of the more assertive Youth Council leaders, and to further broaden the base of support for "tribal nationalism."

The whole process started in April, 1966, when Secretary Udall met in Santa Fe, New Mexico, with the newly appointed Commissioner of Indian Affairs, Robert Bennett, and other Interior and BIA officials.[43] Two hundred Indian leaders from 62 tribes around the country, including Vine Deloria, John Belindo, Anne Wanneka, and Youth Council leaders Mel Thom, Bruce Wilkie, and Clyde Warrior, gathered to participate in the policy discussions for the Johnson administration and found themselves barred from the meeting.

Udall's recommendations were even more appalling than his exclusion of Indian leaders at the beginning of the conference. He announced a "crucial turning point" in Indian affairs, a "new era for the BIA" with "reorganization at the top," and "new opportunity." His proposals contained in an omnibus bill included upgrading the educational program, giving the tribal councils a larger voice, removing curbs on tribal business enterprises, and allowing tribes to mortgage their land to secure loans for new economic ventures. Udall said, ". . . the big thing is to get the Indians into the money markets of the country—to the banks—into the economic mainstream. . . . Forget the past. . . . Get a smile on your faces. . . ."[44]

Udall's recommendations and phrasing angered the young Indian leaders, and the older leaders could see their point. The proposals reflected a lack of homework on the Indian side of the issues and a gross insensitivity to Indian feelings about paternalism. The proposal on mortgages reminded both BIA officials and Indians of the infamous Allotment Act of 1887, which had facilitated the loss of 90 million of a total of 140 million acres of Indian land. The emphasis on getting the Indian into the "economic mainstream" of America and thereby abandoning all tribal ties was simply a reassertion of the termination goal actively opposed by NCAI leaders all during the 1950s and early 1960s. Udall's proposal indicated that he had never taken the time either to talk to leaders of the NCAI or NIYC or to read the "Declaration of Indian Purpose" of the Chicago Conference of 1960-1961. The final insult, especially to the educated youth, was the benevolent paternalism and implicit sense of superiority feelings carried in the Secretary's remarks. The Indians began to refer to the Interior Department as the "Colonial Office." Even some of Commissioner Bennett's remarks were paternalistic.[45]

The surprising thing is that paternalism is so thoroughly internalized by white legislators, BIA officials, and even the "Uncle Tomahawks" that they repeatedly fail to recognize it in their own policy decisions and statements. As white people have become aware of their discrimination against Indians and have taken steps to welcome them to compete with whites "on an equal basis" for education, jobs, or other things, they have been surprised to hear that Indians don't want to melt away into the "mainstream" with its technological superiority and social alienation. Instead, a growing number of them are determined to revitalize their cultural traditions while remaining on and developing their reservations. At the same time, they hope to provide some guidelines to whites with respect to matters such as pollution control and religious values.

At the 23rd annual convention of the NCAI in the late fall of 1966, the delegates ridiculed the omnibus bill as the "Ominous Bill," the "Anonymous Bill" and the "Ambush Bill." Former Commissioner Philleo Nash, the Kennedy appointee who had been forced to resign by Udall to facilitate his "new" policy, said the omnibus bill had the "signs of trouble."[46] The Cherokee anthropologist Robert Thomas added to the drama of the developing struggle by writing a professional analysis of the "hidden colonialism" in the BIA methods of governing the reservations.[47]

In February, 1967, the government attempted to muster support for the omnibus bill before submitting it to Congress by inviting the leaders of 30 tribal groups to a conference in Washington, D.C. After four days of debate and voting the group voted 44 to 5 to turn down the omnibus bill and submit their own "Resolution of the Thirty Tribes" calling for an extensive "foreign aid program" for Indian people.[48]

The "Resolution of the Thirty Tribes," reiterating the principles and goals of the "Declaration" from the 1960 Chicago Conference, compares in significance with the white revolutionaries' "Declaration of Independence" of 1776. In the course of debating general policy, the elders of the reservation tribes had publicly equated their status with that of colonial nations. Moreover, the resolution had broad implications for other minority groups in the United States, as well as for the white establishment. Yet the event was not covered at all by newspapers and television networks.[49]

Nationalism is an ancient concept among the Indians, and the concept of "nationhood" had been applied repeatedly by the Congress and the courts.[50] But although the government had consistently applied the term "nations" to Indian tribal groups, it strongly resisted the demand that Indians be treated as bona fide nations within reservations needing "foreign aid" to develop resources. Commissioner Bennett rejected the resolutions of the 30 tribes, and Vice-President Humphrey reiterated the administration's support of the Commissioner.[51]

Another major event in the spring of 1966 was the international conference of tribal religious leaders in Washington, D.C., organized by Wallace "Mad Bear" Anderson. Representatives of tribes from 18 countries of the Eastern Hemisphere met to share common problems and consider ways of cooperating in their resolution. The real significance of the project was that it demonstrated to United States Indians and colonial tribes on both continents that conferences on common problems were possible and useful. Mad Bear's 1966 conference thus added a pragmatic international perspective to the growing movement of tribal nationalism that probably influenced the thinking and arguments of the leaders who subsequently wrote the "Resolution of the Thirty Tribes" calling for "foreign aid" to United States Indians commensurate with aid currently given to new nations in Asia, Africa, and Latin America.

Another important event supplying an additional model for later action was the request by one of the fish-in leaders, Hank Adams, during the summer months of 1966, for $100,000 in federal aid to Washington tribes for technical assistance in building a commercial and sports fishing industry to put the tribes on a firm economic footing. Adams proposed to have qualified Indians run the program. He supported his request by pointing out two things. First, on the local scene, he showed that nearly twice the requested amount was available from the Federal Bureau of Commercial Fisheries to local non-Indian commercial fishermen. Secondly, Adams found that the Civic Action Program in Vietnam was assisting the Vietnamese in a massive fisheries development program costing many times the $100,000 he sought. He commented that "while the State of Washington was confiscating hundreds of fishing nets and scores of boats and motors of the Indians, the United States was supplying nearly 10,000 outboard motors, 50,000 sets of fishing gear, 27,000,000 fingerlings for stocking purposes, and building 16 fishing piers for the Vietnamese."[52] Adams thus provided another concrete example of a program backed with an argument from the international perspective which was used and expanded in the "Resolution of the Thirty Tribes" in February, 1967.

During 1967, the total news releases jumped to 24 and the percent of these activities that were obstructive also increased over the level of the prior year. Eight new types of collective activity emerged during the year, apart from the Washington, D.C., conference of the 30 tribes. Two disputes involved the mass media. A Chippewa leader, Roger Jourdain, of Red Lake, Minnesota, objected to a General Electric advertisement in the *Saturday Evening Post* reading: "When you decide to shoot wild Indians, you can't afford to miss."[53] General Electric decided to terminate the ad. In a second dispute, a Kiowa Indian, A. Hopkins-Duke, protested the treatment of Custer in an ABC television program. ABC refused to stop showing the program, however, saying that its portrayal was both "sympathetic and realistic."[54]

Another type of dispute with far-reaching implications arose in Nedrow, New York, where the Chief of the Iroquois League demanded return of a number of wampum belts dating back to 1570. The altercation became rather complicated, and the legal maneuvering continued into 1970 without resolution. The belts remain, as yet, in the New York State Museum of Albany.[55]

In other action, two Rosebud Sioux came to Washington, D.C., in March to announce the formation of a new national organization, the American Indian Civil Rights Council. The council, it was stated, would employ the tactics used by blacks to gain support for issues and to pressure the U.S. Civil Rights Commission to spend more of its resources on the civil rights of Indians. Three months later, a member of the Matinnecock tribe produced old maps and documents to support a claim that most of

Flushing, New York, was illegally taken from the Matinnecocks and sold to whites for 52¢ per acre without the consent of the Indians. Return of a former burial ground was demanded by the tribal group. Later in the year, the Oglala Sioux reached an agreement with the Department of the Interior, in which 200,000 acres in South Dakota were returned to the tribe.[56]

In terms of the thrust toward tribal nationalism, all forms of land acquisition and development by Indians are very significant and important. During 1967, two stories pertaining to timber and housing developments appeared in the *New York Times*. Near Warm Springs, Oregon, several tribes, including the Paiutes, decided to develop a lumber and plywood industry around 915 square miles of forest land, using professional advice from university staff and industrial consultants. In Oklahoma, Cherokee and Choctaw Indians in four townships arranged to build 56 low-cost houses with federal loans and private support.[57] Such industrial and housing developments, created and maintained by the Indians themselves, probably are more important in the long run for tribal nationalism than are many types of narrowly oriented, local protests.

The *New York Times* covered 24 separate Indian-initiated collective actions during 1968, exactly the number counted the previous year. The most significant new type of activism took place in a metropolitan area, far from the reservations. In Seattle a new national organization, American Indians United, Inc., was formed in October, 1968, to organize, support and protect recently migrated urban Indians in their search for jobs, housing, recreation, and personal security. In New York City, which may contain as many as 15,000 Indians, new social and cultural-support organizations were initiated, including the Indian League of the Americas, the American Indian Arts Center, the American Indians Women's League and the Thunderbird American Indian Dancers. During the year, several of those urban groups registered protests against current fashion trends which used Indian cultural themes without providing economic benefits to Indians.[58]

In June, up to 300 Indians participated in the "Poor Peoples' Campaign" led by the Reverend Ralph Abernathy of the Southern Christian Leadership Conference.[59] The whole group marched on the BIA central office one day under Mad Bear Anderson's leadership and attempted a citizens' arrest of the Commissioner in protest against a termination bill. As related by Bongartz, when Chief Ray Johnson of Canby, California, dropped dead of a heart attack while picketing the BIA office, Mad Bear decided to publicize the event by driving Johnson's body across the nation to his California burial ground in a twelve-car caravan, ignoring warnings that transporting a corpse was illegal.[60]

In another new type of dispute, a delegation of Sioux mothers from North Dakota came to Washington, D.C., to protest the extraordinary behavior of local welfare workers who allegedly took children away from their reservation homes, using coercion and threats of starvation if the parents didn't cooperate. The mothers had finally decided to fight against the welfare workers who were attempting to impose the standards of white middle class suburbia on the reservation children.[61]

Later in the year the Mohawk Indians of the St. Regis Reservation on the New York-Canadian border, again under Mad Bear's skillful leadership, blocked the International Bridge to protest customs duty charges in violation of the Jay Treaty of 1794. Forty-seven Indians were arrested and a gun shot was fired into a nearby Canadian government customs house. A few days later, however, Mad Bear and his colleagues gained an unofficial agreement letting Indians pass duty free, as well as release of all arrested Indians.[62]

The choice between retaining land or selling was again placed before an Indian community, the Taos Pueblos, in May, 1968, and the group voted to keep the land even though the Claims Commission had already voted to pay $297,684 for the 48,000-acre parcel. Choosing undeveloped land in lieu of an immediate monetary payment was an unusual choice, considering the relatively deprived living conditions that pervailed in the community. The explanation for the choice lay in the sacred and religious value of the land in question, as well as its new meaning in terms of the ideology of tribal nationalism.[63]

In July of 1968 there was another timber dispute, this time between the Passamaquoddy Indians around Indian Township, Maine, and the Georgia Pacific Company. After a long-term dispute over control of logging of 19,000 acres, forty Indians stopped the logging operation by squatting in front of company logging tractors. After only five days Georgia Pacific agreed to give control of the disputed area back to the Indians and to man all operations on Indian land with Indian crews.[64] Such successful protest tactics against the economic exploitation of Indian land become models for similar projects across the nation.

Another long dispute between Indian people and private industry was settled by the United States Supreme Court in favor of the Indians in March, 1968. The pattern of decision-making by various courts in this case reflects a national pattern wherein the local state Supreme Court decides in favor of white economic interests and then is reversed by the United States Supreme Court in favor of the Indians. The Comanches had filed suit against Skelly for having allowed natural gas to escape in their drilling operations instead of containing and marketing it. The Oklahoma Supreme Court upheld Skelly Oil on technical legal grounds, but was promptly reversed by the United States Supreme Court.[65] The same pattern was identified earlier in the judicial process over treaty fishing rights in the state of Washington, in which a state Supreme Court decision favoring local white commercial interests was reversed at the federal level.

Let us cite one more example of innovative collective action by reservation Indians in 1968. In May, the NCAI sponsored a group of 49 Indians from 15 reservation tribes who toured Manhattan, talking to executives of various firms and offering social and economic incentives to attract industry to the reservations. It was pointed out that under similar conditions several of the firms involved had already risked projects in Puerto Rico, with successful outcomes, and that many companies, such as Allis Chalmers, Fairchild, Semi-conductor, Kaiser Gypsum, and General Dynamics, had already located plants on reservations, after successful pilot operations.[66] The economic payoffs of such vigorous tactics by the NCAI can have tremendous social and economic consequences for the nationalist Indian movement.

During 1969 the rate of direct collective action more than doubled the rate of the previous year and also expanded into new institutional areas. Forty-nine separate projects, including 16 that were obstructive in nature, were reported in the *New York Times* during the year. The provocative new types will be reviewed. In January, the opening of Navaho Community College—a two-year junior college at Many Farms, Arizona, funded with support from OEO, tribal money, and the Donuner Foundation—was announced.[67] It was the first college to be established and controlled by Indians, and its program contained several significant innovations designed to facilitate education for older adults as well as for college-age youth. The college accepts any Navaho over 18 who applies, even adults with no past educational experience. The initial enrollment was 357 students. The program is modeled in some ways after that of the Rough Rock Demonstration School (elementary) started with OEO and BIA support in 1966; the usual academic courses are to be supplemented with units in Navaho language, history, arts, and culture, as well as with vocational subjects. The school's leaders are confident that it will create a labor force, thus attracting industry and reducing the 70 percent unemployment rate while raising substantially the $680 annual family income on the reservation.[68]

The impact of the Navaho Community College stretched to every large reservation in the nation. Plans for several similar projects are underway. A few months after the school opened, a group of Chippewas from Minnesota visited it, and eight Pueblo tribes in New Mexico moved to establish their own college.[69] Though no militant protest was involved in the establishment of the school, it represents a constructive spin-off of the growing vigor of Indian assertiveness and can be related in a number of ways to the movement toward tribal nationalism.

In March, 1969, the NCAI announced that it would launch a national public relations campaign designed to create a "new and true picture" of the American Indian. The organization identified a number of ways Indians might improve their image to white society, including the imparting to whites of Indian values, appreciation and reverence for nature.[70] While the public relations effort may have altered stereotypes harbored by whites, a more significant outcome may have been a sense of accentuated self-worth and adequacy among the Indians in contact with the message.

An effective facet of the program was the new Miss Indian America pageant. After winning the contest in the fall of 1968, Miss Thomasine Ruth Hill from Crow Agency, Montana, embarked on a one-year national tour, making talks to various civic groups on Indian values, arts, and social and economic goals. Her activities enhanced public awareness and acceptance of the new Indian presence. When questioned by middle-aged whites, she denied that Indians having true native values would resort to violent tactics to achieve special goals.[71]

The Pyramid Lake Paiutes of Nevada achieved wide coverage of their long-standing controversy over the water level and ecology of their beautiful lake without an overt demonstration. The manipulations of various white interest groups, including irrigating ranchers and commercial power groups, to control the flow of the Truckee River out of Lake Tahoe is a complex and rather appalling story, considering the clear treaty rights of the destitute Paiutes, whose economic well-being has been ignored throughout the proceedings. The end result of all the power plays is that the Indians are stymied in developing a resort area on the lake until they know whether any water will be left in their basin and whether its level will remain high enough for recreational purposes.[72]

During the summer of 1969, a number of collective projects representing new variations of prior tactics were carried off with added sophistication. In June the NCAI presented another promotional exhibit and luncheon in Manhattan, and the 150 industrialists who attended learned the economic advantages of locating new plants on Indian reservations. Wendell Chino, President of the NCAI, described the successful operations among many of the 159 plants that had been started on reservations since 1964.[73]

Later that summer, 50 Passamaquoddy Indians set up a roadblock on U.S. Highway 1 in Maine, exacting tolls from motorists to protest the state legislature's failure to provide funds for child care. The roadblock was called off when conferences between officials indicated the state was taking the issue seriously. In a similar move in August the Quinault Indians closed to white tourists 25 miles of beaches around Taholah, Washington, to protest littering, theft of fishing nets drying on the beach, destruction of commercial clam beds by white land developers and the defacing of Indian petrogliphs on Point Grenville rocks.[74]

Two new organizations, one regional and one national, emerged toward the end of the summer. Four tribes from southeastern states, including the Choctaws, Seminoles, Miccosukee, and eastern Cherokees, formed a regional alliance, the United South Eastern Tribes.[75] In August, the Citizens' Advocate Center, a Washington-based nonprofit organization, sponsored a conference in Denver of 40 of the most highly trained Indian professionals in the nation, including professors, doctors, lawyers, community organizers, economic development specialists and students. Non-Indians and "Uncle Tomahawks" were excluded. This study group formulated a policy statement calling emphatically for Indian self-determination as a replacement for white paternalism and manipulation of Indian resources.[76] While these professionals did not specifically set their sights on the tribal nationalism espoused by the Chicago Conference of 1960 and the "Resolution of the Thirty Tribes" in 1967, their statement in no way disputes the general goal of sovereignty.

The most significant and interesting event of 1969, however, was the vigorous, negative response to the new Nixon administration appointees Walter Hickel and Louis R. Bruce. Interior Secretary Hickel had angered many NCAI and NIYC leaders earlier in the year by ignoring their desires in appointing the new Commissioner of Indian Affairs and choosing a man (Bruce) with all of the stereotypes of an Uncle Tomahawk (i.e., affluent, urbane, a New York City-dweller with no recent activism in his record). Early in October, Commissioner Bruce began making public statements rejecting the termination policy and lack of consideration of Indian views during the 1950s,[77] but a number of Hickel's decisions and remarks led Indians to view the Secretary as an exploitive terminationist and they were forceful in their response. Representatives of 46 tribes attending the Traditional Indian Unity Convention on the Onondaga Reservation issued a statement calling for Hickel's immediate impeachment because he had "destroyed the faith of all Indians toward the U.S. Department of the Interior by his high-handed, inconsiderate, and illegal theft of native Alaskan, Eskimo and Indian tribal lands, rivers, hunting and fishing rights, timber, oil, gas and mineral resources."[78]

Prior to the 1969 NCAI convention, Commissioner Bruce issued a general statement in support of Indian self-determination and control, a greater voice for youth in the BIA, which was being "reorganized," and opposing termination until Indians achieve better social, educational and economic opportunities.[79] The message failed to have the desired effect. Four days later in a speech to 1500 members of NCAI convening in Albuquerque, Secretary Hickel was loudly and repeatedly jeered with calls of "shut up" and "go home, white honky," an unprecedented and significant event. He could not have finished his speech if President Wendell Chino had not repeatedly called for order.[80]

Vice President Agnew was subsequently applauded for a speech stressing Indian leadership and fewer words, less tokenism, and more action. Agnew, as the leader of the National Council on Indian Opportunity, has direct responsibility within the Nixon administration for making good on these statements. Most Indian leaders at the convention agreed that "this may have been a turning point for the Indians. You heard new voices here and there was a new attitude."[81]

The new voices belonged to the original "Red Muslims" of the NIYC and a range of even younger leaders such as Lehman L. Brightman of Berkeley, Gerald Wilkinson, Cherokee leader of the NIYC, and Michael Benson, a 19-year-old Navaho leader of the Organization of Native American Students. Some of the older, conservative Indians who traditionally have been the spokesmen for their groups were openly branded as "sellouts" and "Uncle Tomahawks" by the newly emergent militants of the NIYC. "Its time that we realize that white people can't do a damn thing for us," said Brightman. "The time has come for Indians to get up and do something for themselves." Publicly officials of the NCAI were critical of the abuse aimed at Hickel, but in private conversations both young and older leaders agreed that it was probably a good thing, all told, for NCAI delegates to show their feelings to white leaders as vigorously and bluntly as possible.[82] The Albuquerque meeting marked the first occasion in which the emergent trend toward expressive, direct action had exploded in open public rejection of a top white government official at a major Indian convention or conference.

As if to signal the rest of the Indian and white communities that their convention words would in fact be backed up with action, a number of additional collective responses were initiated in the closing months of 1969, the most publicized and provocative of which was the occupation of

Alcatraz Island in San Francisco Bay on November 9. The landing on the notorious 13-acre "Rock," the claim of ownership "by right of discovery," and the offer to purchase the island for "$24 in glass beads and cloth, a precedent set by the white man's purchase of a similar island about 300 years ago," gained instant world-wide publicity and a good deal of sympathy and tangible support for the Indian cause.[83] The initial landing of 14 Indians led by Richard Oakes, a 27-year-old Mohawk student at San Francisco State College and Adam Nordwall, a Chippewa from Minnesota, had its precedent in a similar attempt that took place in 1964 when a group of Sioux residing in the Bay Area made a landing and filed a claim after the United States had declared Alcatraz "excess property" in March of that year.[84]

When the San Francisco American Indian Center serving the needs of 30,000 Indians in the immediate area burned down on November 1, 1969, however, the young militant leaders in the area, just back from the NCAI convention in Albuquerque, decided to channel their frustrations in symbolically powerful, direct action, and to occupy the island as a future site for cultural activities.[85] The mood of the moment was well portrayed in a bitter parody of frequently broken United States treaties and offensive paternalism which the invaders of Alcatraz wrote into their proposal for caring for the white caretakers encountered on the island:

> We will give to the inhabitants of this island a portion of that land for their own, to be held in trust by the American Indian Government—for as long as the sun shall rise and the rivers go down to the sea—to be administered by the Bureau of Caucasian Affairs. We will further guide the inhabitants in the proper way of living. We will offer them our religion, our education, our life-ways, in order to help them achieve our level of civilization and thus raise them and all their white brothers up from their savage and unhappy state.[86]

Rupert Costo, a noted Indian historian, has identified several factors contributing to the decision to occupy Alcatraz, in addition to the frustrations of the fire at the community center. Indian students at San Francisco State College, for example, were very frustrated with the constraints of college life and with the irrelevant curriculum that whites had built into a new Native American Studies Program. The thoroughly militant actions of other minority group leaders in the Bay Area, such as the Black Student Union, the Black Panthers, the Chicano groups and the Third World Movement, were both disappointing in their lack of focus on Indian problems and tempting models for Indian action, so the decision to act was made. The settlers' goal is to develop an institute of Native American studies, an ecological research center, a medical center, and a museum, but the estimated costs are high and many argue that the money for new facilities would go substantially further on other sites in California.[87] Thus far, the main effect of the Alcatraz caper has been broad publicity for the new Indian movement and its activist posture. The whole event has become a national symbol of successful assertiveness and challenge to the white system of controls, and thus has served to focus new group pride and identity. Curiously enough, the occupation of Alcatraz was the first Indian challenge to white power to reach a broad enough segment of the white public to trigger real discussion of Red Power and its implications. Whether the Indians eventually gain control of the island and build new facilities on it is not important, in view of the immense value that the whole affair has had as a symbol of the new Indian and his movement toward self-determination, group pride, and self-respect.

As shown in Table 1, the total rate of Indian demonstrations, legal tests, and promotional activity not only accelerated in 1970, but generally shifted toward greater emphasis on obstructive but nonviolent protests and demonstrations. In 1969, 33 percent of the collective actions reported in the *New York Times* were of the militant type, while in 1970 the proportion rose to 42 percent. Apparently the shift toward militancy noted in the NCAI Albuquerque convention did not trigger a successful effort by older conservatives to control the actions of youthful militants, because the end result was a real surge of provocative but nonviolent activity to challenge legitimated white institutional practices. Without a thorough survey it is impossible to assess the relative support in the Indian community for varied degrees of militancy in collective actions. Steiner, Hilda Bryant, and others have collected statements for and against militant action from a variety of elder and younger leaders, but valid group trends cannot be deduced without systematically collected data.[88] The superficial indicators suggest to this observer, however, that the accelerated Indian militancy of 1970 had the tacit, if not the explicit, support of most leaders of the NCAI and NIYC organizations.

It also should be noted that no Indians have been identified as participants in urban civil disturbances. Very few of the Indian protests have produced any property damage or personal injuries. On a number of occasions, Indian demonstrators have actually withdrawn from situations that were escalating into overt violence without "losing face," but they have in almost all cases reached an agreement which embodied desired changes in the institutional system. The overall "score" in using nonviolent protest to gain beneficial changes in the established system has been exceedingly high for Indian "actions." Therefore it appears to be valid to conclude that future militant protests will remain nonviolent in terms of property damage and personal injury as long as the rate of positive outcomes per demonstration remains relatively high.

We will not take the time to review all the specific promotional or obstructive actions in 1970. Almost all of them resemble one of the prior types of tactics already identified. Suffice it to say, however, that each year since the fish-ins of 1964, the tactics have become more instrumental and effective in gaining desired institutional change, and 1970 is no exception.

One 1970 innovation worth noting, however, is the creation of a corps of Indian observers to monitor police actions. Borrowing an idea from blacks, Clyde Bellecourt, a tough Chippewa with 14 years' experience behind bars, has organized an "Indian Patrol" to reduce police harassment in the Indian ghetto of Minneapolis. Dressed in red jackets, the patrol learns of Indian disturbances from police radios and arrives on the spot to observe silently while white police do their job. The result of this nonviolent surveillance has been a drastic reduction in Indian arrests and subsequent altercations with police.[89]

The most significant and startling event of 1970, in terms of long-term consequences, was the July announcement by President Nixon of the Indian policy and program of his administration.[90] It is not an overstatement to call his speech to Congress a revolutionary reversal of prior policy toward the Native Americans. Ten short years after the formation of the American Indian Youth Council and only nine years after the "Declaration of Indian Purpose" of the Chicago conference, a Republican President of the United States formally renounced the Eisenhower policy of termination and specifically urged Congress to give operational control of existing Indian aid programs (educational, housing, medical, public works, and economic development) to tribal leaders. If enacted by Congress, such legislation will greatly facilitate achievement of the goal of tribal self-determination and sovereignty.

President Nixon's message to Congress was explicit, frank and unequivocal in its review of past Indian-white relations. He stated that as a result of "centuries of injustice" the Indians were the most "deprived," "brutalized," and "oppressed" minority group in the nation. He continued:

> But the story of the Indian in America is something more than the record of the white man's frequent aggression, broken agreements, intermittent remorse and prolonged failure. It is a record also of adaptation and creativity in the face of overwhelming obstacles. It is a record of enormous contributions to this country—to its art and culture, to its strength and spirit, to its sense of history and its sense of purpose. The time has come to break decisively with the past and to create the conditions for a new era in which the Indian future is determined by Indian acts and Indian decisions.[91]

The President's statement provided a thrust of moral leadership which will pay off in concrete institutional change if it persists. He explicitly labeled and identified federal paternalism and its disastrous psychological and social consequences. He noted that "termination" falsely implies that the trusteeship responsibility for Indians of the United States government is an "act of generosity" that may be unilaterally discontinued at any time, rather than a "solemn obligation" written into formal treaty agreements with Indians. "These agreements continue to carry immense moral and legal force," said Nixon. "To terminate this relationship would be no more appropriate than to terminate the citizenship rights of any other American."[92]

The President sent legislation to Congress that would give Indian groups authority to assume control over federally administered programs in education, housing, medical services, economic development and public works totalling $400 million annually. He called for establishment of tribal boards of education to replace federal control of BIA schools. He urged changes in existing law to allow funds for education to go directly to

Indian groups as well as to public school systems. It was proposed that, among other incentives, the current revolving fund for economic development be raised from $27 million to $77 million annually. Plans for expanded health programs and new urban centers to aid dislocated Indians in Los Angeles, Denver, Phoenix, Omaha, Minneapolis, and Fairbanks also were announced, and the President proposed an independent new agency, the Indian Trust Counsel Authority, to represent Indian groups in future legal disputes, thus resolving the "inherent conflict of interest" of having the Departments of Interior and Justice defend the needs of both the nation and the Indians. The new agency clearly bolsters the Indian concept and goal of tribal nationalism. Finally, to facilitate the enactment of the new programs, Nixon proposed to create a new post of Assistant Secretary for Indian and Territorial Affairs in the Department of the Interior. Indians know better than anyone else that it takes a long time and much active pressure to move a Presidential program through Congress and that many worthy ideas can be dropped in the debate and maneuvering. Nevertheless, Vine Deloria, Jr., says, "There is an increasing scent of victory in the air."[93] The Indian movement has gathered momentum and Indian leaders are now exceedingly skilled in all the pressure tactics required for success in their modern battle for freedom and self-determination.

NOTES

1 The author is indebted to Howard M. Bahr for his criticisms and thoughtful comments and to Ronald Halfmoon and Rudolph Ryser for guiding suggestions.
2 *New York Times,* December 7, 1969, p. 47; February 9, 1970, p. 15.
3 Stan Steiner, *The New Indians* (New York: Dell, 1968), p. 269.
4 For detailed accounts and background information on the fish-ins, see American Friends Service Committee, *Uncommon Controversy: Fishing Rights of the Muckleshoot, Puyallup and Nisqually Indians* (Seattle, Washington: University of Washington Press, 1970); and Steiner, *op. cit.*
5 Steiner, *op. cit.,* p. 55-56.
6 *Ibid.,* pp. 53, 56.
7 *Ibid.,* p. 54.
8 *Ibid.,* p. 50.
9 *Ibid.,* pp. 57-58.
10 *Ibid.,* pp. 58-59.
11 American Friends Service Committee, *op. cit.,* pp. 111-113.
12 *Ibid.,* p. 111.
13 Steiner, *op. cit.,* pp. 290-297.
14 *Ibid.,* p. 31.
15 *Ibid.,* p. 32.
16 *Ibid.,* p. 33.
17 *Ibid.*
18 *Ibid.,* p. 34.
19 Nancy O. Lurie, "What the Red Man Wants in the Land That Was His," *Saturday Review,* October 4, 1969, p. 40.
20 *Ibid.*

21 Steiner, *op. cit.,* p. 36.
22 *Ibid.,* pp. 37-38.
23 *Ibid.,* pp. 39-47.
24 *Ibid.,* pp. 40, 43.
25 Roy Bongartz, "The New Indian," *Esquire,* August 1970, p. 107.
26 *Ibid.,* p. 126.
27 Vine Deloria, Jr., *We Talk, You Listen* (New York: Macmillan, 1970).
28 Donald R. Matthews and James Prothro, *Negroes and the New Southern Politics* (New York: Harcourt, Brace & World, 1966).
29 Marvin Rich, "The Congress of Racial Equality and Its Strategy," *The Annals of the American Academy of Political and Social Science,* 357 (January 1965), 115-117.
30 Hilda Bryant, "Indians Battle Fishing Rights Versus Conservation," *Seattle Post-Intelligencer,* December 8, 1969, p. 11.
31 Steiner, *op. cit.,* p. 69.
32 *Ibid.,* p. 72.
33 *New York Times,* March 16, 1961, p. 24; April 18, 1961, p. 42; June 13, 1961, p. 6; June 15, 1961, p. 20.
34 *New York Times,* July 8, 1970, p. 1.
35 *New York Times,* July 10, 1962, p. 29; August 24, 1962, p. 16.
36 *New York Times,* July 27, 1962, p. 6; September 3, 1962, p. 23; September 6, 1962, p. 35; September 17, 1962, p. 1.
37 *New York Times,* March 6, 1963, p. 7.
38 *New York Times,* June 2, 1963, p. 8.
39 *New York Times,* March 19, 1964, p. 26; March 30, 1964, p. 35.
40 *New York Times,* January 21, 1964, p. 15.
41 *New York Times,* June 14, 1964, p. 27; October 15, 1964, p. 36; May 3, 1964, p. 39; October 11, 1964, p. 17; November 6, 1964, p. 20.
42 *New York Times,* June 28, 1965, p. 57; December 10, 1965, p. 38; April 7, 1965, p. 87.
43 *New York Times,* April 14, 1966, p. 1; Steiner, *op. cit.,* pp. 250-267.
44 *New York Times,* April 14, 1966, p. 1; Steiner, *op. cit.,* pp. 250-253.
45 Steiner, *op. cit.,* p. 253.
46 *Ibid.,* p. 271.
47 *Ibid.,* p. 254.
48 *Ibid.,* pp. 283-285.
49 *Ibid.,* p. 285.
50. *Ibid.,* p. 272.
51 *Ibid.,* p. 286.
52 *Ibid.,* p. 62.
53 *New York Times,* January 13, 1967, p. 65.
54 *New York Times,* July 24, 1967, p. 55.
55 *New York Times* March 25, 1967, p. 25; April 17, 1970, p. 40.
56 *New York Times,* May 27, 1967, p. 33; August 2, 1967, p. 3.
57 *New York Times,* August 13, 1967, p. 10.
58 *New York Times,* September 18, 1968, p. 34.
59 *New York Times,* June 21, 1968, p. 24.
60 Bongartz, *op. cit.,* p. 108.
61 *New York Times,* July 17, 1968, p. 86
62 *New York Times,* December 19, 1968, p. 2.
63 *New York Times,* May 23, 1968, p. 40.
64 *New York Times,* July 5, 1968, p. 13.
65 *New York Times,* March 19, 1968, p. 20.

66 *New York Times,* May 19, 1968, p. 15.
67 *New York Times,* January 21, 1969, p. 29.
68 *New York Times,* January 21, 1969, p. 29; April 11, 1969, p. 67.
69 *New York Times,* April 11, 1969, p. 67.
70 *New York Times,* March 16, 1969, p. 36.
71 *New York Times,* February 4, 1969, p. 30.
72 *New York Times,* February 25, 1969, p. 45.
73 *New York Times,* June 19, 1969, p. 59.
74 *New York Times,* July 8, 1969, p. 85; August 26, 1969, p. 43.
75 *New York Times,* July 3, 1969, p. 16.
76 *New York Times,* August 24, 1969, p. 29.
77 *New York Times,* October 5, 1969, p. 39.
78 *New York Times,* August 24, 1969, p. 87.
79 *New York Times,* October 5, 1969, p. 39.
80 *New York Times,* October 9, 1969, p. 24.
81 *Ibid.*
82 *New York Times,* October 12, 1969, p. 41.
83 *New York Times,* November 21, 1969, p. 49; December 7, 1969, p. 140;
    December 10, 1969, p. 37; December 26, 1969, p. 15.
84 Rupert Costo, "Alcatraz," *The Indian Historian,* 3 (Winter 1970), 7.
85 *New York Times,* March 8, 1970, pp. 32, 48, 50, 52, 54, 56.
86 *New York Times,* January 5, 1970, p. 20.
87 Costo, *op. cit.,* p. 12.
88 Steiner, *op. cit.,* pp. 44-46, 59-61, 261-262, 268-289; Hilda Bryant,
    Seattle Post-Intelligencer, November 26, 1969, p. 8; November 27, 1969,
    p. 18.
89 *Time,* February 9, 1970, p. 14.
90 *New York Times,* July 8, 1970, p. 1.
91 *New York Times,* July 8, 1970, p. 18.
92 *Ibid.*
93 *New York Times,* March 8, 1970, p. 56.

EDWARD M. KENNEDY: LET THE
INDIANS RUN INDIAN POLICY

As chairman of the Senate Subcommittee on Indian Education, I issued last year a report based on more than 1700 pages of testimony. It includes statements from Federal officials, United States senators, professors, doctors, tribal chairmen, and members of Indian tribes across the country.

Source: Reprinted by permission of the publisher from "Let the Indians Run Indian Policy," by Senator Edward M. Kennedy, Look Magazine © 1970.

It also includes a statement from Margaret Nick, a young native girl from Alaska. She gave us no statistics, no charts, no case studies, no classroom results. She said, very simply, this: "... I can't predict how I should educate my children. I can't predict how they should be educated, but one thing I know is, if my children are proud, if my children have identity, if my children know who they are and if they're proud to be who they are, they'll be able to encounter anything in life. I think this is what education means. Some people say that a man without education might as well be dead. I say, a man without identity—if a man doesn't know who he is—he might as well be dead."

Add Margaret Nick to the list of Americans standing up to be recognized. Add the American Indian and Alaskan native to the list of minorities who want to take part in the decisions that affect their lives.

From a history of neglect and despair, the Indian is beginning to emerge and to demand his own identity and share of American life. It has been a long time in coming, this new Indian self-consciousness. But it is here, and America must pay attention.

Indians have already begun their move for self-reliance. They have filed legal suits in various parts of the country, involving trespass, employment discrimination, misuse of school funds, unauthorized taking of water rights and breach of treaty agreements. Many of these suits have been filed against the Federal Government itself.

Tribal councils travel weekly to Washington, bringing their grievances and proposals directly to the Congress and the Interior Department, rather than using the local Bureau of Indian Affiars, as had been the custom.

And perhaps most dramatically, Indians have begun to adopt the confrontation tactics that have marked the dramatic emergence of other minorities in this decade. As the world knows now, a group of Indians has occupied Alcatraz Island in San Francisco Bay, demanding the island be turned over to them for educational facilities. Another Indian group has attempted to establish Alcatraz number two at Fort Lawton in the State of Washington. Indians have occupied BIA offices in Denver, Cleveland, Chicago and Minneapolis. In many cases, their efforts have been rebuffed. But they have begun to tell us that our long-standing policies toward the Indians in this nation amount to abject failure:

And what they are telling us is true. Before I became chairman of the Indian Education Subcommittee, that post was held by my brother, Robert Kennedy. He traveled America extensively in that role, exposing the severity and degradation of Indian poverty and the failure of this nation to help the Indian people.

He saw, as I have seen, the resilience of the Indian way of life, a way of life that has for many generations resisted destruction despite Government blunders that almost seem designed to stamp it out. My brother called America's treatment of the Indian "a national tragedy and a national disgrace."

I second that opinion. And I think it is past time to end this disgrace.

In the course of my work on the Indian Education Subcommittee, I have seen statistics reflected in the faces of thousands of Indians. Their lives are hard and often filled with despair. Their average income is about $1,500 a year. Their teen-agers are three times as likely to take their own lives as are young people outside the Indian community. They have 12.2 times the chance of an alcohol-related arrest as the average white American. Their children are plagued with disease. (One Indian leader told our committee he had lost eight children to disease: ". . . it is a lot of kinds of sickness they die from. Not only one kind. Mostly with whooping cough and measles all together. It hit them one at a time and that way they die.") And their pride decays into a passive wariness of the white man and his misguided attempts to help.

America has been frustrated by the "Indian problem" since the dawn of the nation. This despite the high regard that early leaders such as Thomas Jefferson and Benjamin Franklin held for the Indians' political institutions. This despite the contributions that Indians made to our society—their early brand of federalism among their nations; their concept that elected leaders are the servants and not the masters of the people; their insistence that society must respect individual diversity.

With all this as part of our common heritage, we have still given the Indian the back of our hand.

First, we embarked on a policy of isolation, marching entire Indian nations to desolate reservations. Later, we turned toward assimilation, but for the wrong reason—to exploit and expropriate Indian land and Indian resources. We shouldered the "white man's burden" initially by herding separate Indian nations together against their will—then turned around and plunged them headlong into the white man's society, thereby helping to tear them apart. But in any case, so the feeling went, the Indians would be off our conscience, off our land, out of our pocketbooks.

Well, it hasn't worked. Our casual paternalism has done more to hurt than to help. It has disorganized or destroyed this country's Indian communities. It has created a severe and self-perpetuating cycle of poverty for most Indians. And it has brought about an enormous, ineffective bureaucracy that seems to treat the elimination of Indian poverty as a gross waste of Federal funds.

The work of our committee was confined to an examination of how the Federal Government is carrying out its responsibility to educate Indian children. The Government assumed this responsibility through treaties and other agreements with Indian peoples in exchange for land relinquished by them. It was our task to assess the Government's performance.

Children are mirrors of their environments. By studying the educational systems, we learned much more about the Indian communities than simply the ABC's of the classrooms. We saw the statistics I have mentioned etched in the faces of these children.

Yet even if we had learned nothing more than our subcommittee's mandate required, we would have been appalled enough. For even in the classroom—and perhaps most importantly there—the American Indian is a poor relation.

The average educational level for Indian children under Federal supervision is five school years—and the Indian dropout rate is twice the national average. Only 18 percent of the students in Federal Indian schools go on to college, against a much higher national average. And only three percent of these Indians graduate. The BIA spends only $18 per year per child on textbooks and supplies—compared to a national average of $40.

And when this same agency began a crash program to improve education for Navajo children in 1953, it emerged 14 years later with a budget that showed supervisory school positions increased by 144 percent, but actual teaching positions increased by a mere 20 percent.

So it is clear that the Indian child is being shortchanged. It is clear that the American Indian has the cards stacked against him. And it is clear as well that the BIA isn't doing much to help.

Throughout the 1960's, the Federal Government groped toward a more enlightened national policy. The results can be measured largely in terms of words rather than action. Numerous studies, reports and commissions have come forth with their "solutions" for the Indian problem. But the crucial ingredient that has always been missing is the concept that the Indian can speak for himself, can say what is wrong, what he wants and needs, and what our policies should be in his regard.

On numerous occasions, the Federal Government has suffered the embarrassment of putting forth grand schemes to solve Indian problems without really permitting the Indian to determine the policies and programs for himself. This is not only a hypocritical charade that breeds cynicism and frustration on both sides, it is also, more importantly, a perpetuation of our cumulative failures.

The vast Federal bureaucracy charged with "managing" Indians for the United States can never, as presently structured, be expected to change our tragic Indian policies. This is a harsh conclusion. It brings no satisfaction to Americans who believe that ours is a land of equality and justice for all. It brings no solace to Americans who believe that the special attention given to Indians in this country is beneficial in practice as well as theory. But it is true nonetheless. Even two of the recent Commissioners of Indian Affairs have expressed their frustration at the lack of sensitivity to the Indian problem all through the Government. It is this lack of national will that keeps American Indians prisoners of wars long past.

So, is there anywhere to turn? We might try turning to the American Indian himself.

That's what he is asking. That's what he is demanding. And ultimately, that's what we must recognize as the best solution.

Just in the area of schools, our subcommittee has discovered that the rule of self-determination is the most just and the most effective. Consider the Rough Rock Indian School on the Navajo Reservation in Chinle, Ariz.

Established in July, 1966, the Rough Rock School is a private, nonprofit organization. It is run by a five-member Navajo school board. Only two of the schoolboard members have had any formal education, and the weekly meetings of the board are conducted in the Navajo language.

Yet this—the only Indian-controlled school in the United States—is also the most innovative Indian school in the nation. It carries on extensive community and parental participation in school affairs. It uses Navajo teachers and teachers' aides in the classroom. It employs bilingual instruction and course material reflecting the richness of the Navajo culture. Rather than extinguishing Navajo traditions, it enhances them; and its staff has been trained to respect, understand and respond to the community it serves.

The Rough Rock School, as a demonstration project, has played a noteworthy role in the overall reform movement in Indian education. But beyond that, it has become a symbol of the value and indeed the absolute necessity of Indian participation in and control over their own programs and their own lives.

And its success has spawned further advances of this particular tribe. In early April, the Navajo School Board in Ramah, N.M., completed negotiations with the Bureau of Indian Affairs to bring the community's children home from boarding school to an Indian-controlled high school. With additional private and governmental commitments, the school board expects the school to open by September. How far this principle is extended depends on the continued support and commitment of the BIA, the Congress and the Indian community.

Similar gains are being made in other areas of Indian life. Major economic development plans are being put forward by the Zuñi in New Mexico and the Seneca in New York State. The Crow tribe in Montana is moving toward extensive development of its mineral resources; the Lummi in Washington are experimenting with advanced agriculture; and natives at Bethel, Alaska, continue their cooperative fishing ventures. So, progress is possible—if the Indians manage their own affairs.

The Subcommittee on Indian Education, in its report issued late last year, made 60 recommendations to the Congress. They are diverse and comprehensive, but perhaps best summed up by this statement from the Subcommittee:

"The Federal Government must commit itself to a national policy of educational excellence for Indian children, maximum participation and control by Indian adults and communities, and the development of new legislation and substantial increases in appropriations to achieve these goals."

In other words, we must help the Indian people take an active and vigorous part in managing their own lives. And, because they are starting with so little, they will need a great deal of help.

INDEX

Abel, Annie H., 8, 9, 20
Abenaki Indians, 15, 200, 216-217
Aberle, David, 64
Abernathy, Ralph, 522
Ablon, Joan, 241, 402, 405, 412-428
Acculturation, 5, 11, 13, 14, 17, 24, 30
  definition of, 193, 205, 239-240
  identity and, 193-312
  levels of, 303-312
  urban Indians and, 434-435
Achievement, academic, 133-135, 146, 159
  motivation for, Navaho students and, 130, 172-177
Ackerknecht, Erwin, 213
Activism, Indian, 485-536
  emergence of, 506-532
Adams, Hank, 521
Adamson, Representative, 122
Adaptation, urban, tribal differences in, 436-437
Adjustment, urban Indians and, 435-436, 440-466
Adoption, of whites by Indians, 200, 203, 208, 209, 211-213, 217
Agnew, Spiro, 526
Agriculture, U. S. Department of, 5
Agua Calientes, 59
Alabama Empire (Kelley), 205
Alakanuk, Alaska, 263, 264-265, 267-274
Alaska, University of, 263
Albrecht, Stan L., 316, 358-367
Alcatraz, 51-53, 488, 489, 498-499, 505-506, 507, 516, 527-528, 533
Alcohol problem, 315-316
  crime and, 324-325
  Navajos and, 316, 345-358, 359, 440-463
  Uintah-Ouray Indians and, 358-367
Aleut Indians, 25, 26, 159, 368
Algonquin Indians, 15, 216
Alienation, Indians and, 4, 156
Allotments, 60, 117-118
Amalgamation, 195, 225, 227-228, 233-

235, 236, 239, 240, 242, 243, 244, 245, 247
American Indian Arts Center, 522
American Indian Chicago Conference, 510, 511-512, 514, 517
American Indian Civil Rights Council (proposed), 521
"American Indian Day," 517
American Indian Leadership Conference, 503
American Indian Movement (AIM), 410
American Indians and the Federal Government, 3
American Indians United, Inc., 522
American Indians Women's League, 522
Anderson, Bernard E., 241
Anderson, James G., 46, 69-80
Anderson, Wallace "Mad Bear," 52, 487-488, 490-498, 504, 512-513, 518, 520, 522, 523
Angulo, Jaime de, 35
Anomie theory of deviance, 324
Antisocial behavior, decline in, manpower program and, 473-474
Apache Indians, 5, 39, 135, 370
Apologies to the Iroquois (Wilson), 498
Arapaho Indians, 4
Arrest rates, 313, 314, 315, 316, 320-323, 335, 347, 351, 440, 448-461
Arrow in the Hill (Cooper), 203
Aspinal, Wayne, 65
Assault, arrest rates for, 314, 321, 322
Assimilation, 4, 24, 81-84, 116-118, 195, 196, 213, 220
  definition of, 239
  measurement of, 225-249
  stages of, 239-240
  urban Indians and, 239-249, 402, 407, 433-434
Assimilative Crimes Act, 119, 125
Atkinson, John W., 172
Auto thefts, 314, 322, 336

"Back to the Blanket" (Marriott), 220
Bahr, Howard M., 401, 404-412

Bahr, Rosemary S., 49, 110-114
Bandura, Albert, 452
Bannocks, 60, 315, 327-338, 373
Banyaka, Thomas, 68, 504
Barbeau, Marius, 208
Beals, Ralph, 226
Beard, Dewey, 500
Beckwourth, Jim, 205
Behavior, deviant, 311-400
Behavior patterns, comparison of Indian
　　and white, 31-41
Belindo, John, 519
Bell, Wendell, 421
Bellecourt, Clyde, 528
Bennett, Emerson, 202
Bennett, Robert, 519, 520
Benson, Michael, 526
Bereiter, Carl, 162, 168, 169, 170
Berelson, Bernard, 111
Berkhofer, Robert, Jr., 9, 11, 13, 21
Bernstein, B., 170
Berreman, Gerald D., 459
Berry, Don, 218
Beston, Henry, 219
Biculturalism, 193, 194, 198
Bjork, John W., 377-388
Blackfoot Indians, 4, 159, 160, 161, 198
　　acculturation among, 303-312
Blackfoot, Idaho, 53, 54, 63
Blackfoot Indian Reserve (Alberta), 156
Blacks, stereotyping of, in cartoons,
　　110-114
　　treatment of, in textbooks, 101-110
　　　　See also Negroes
Blatchford, Herbert, 510-511
Blood Indians, 159, 160, 161
Blue Lake issue, 517
Boat, Marion D., 421
Bogardus, Emory S., 44-45, 46, 50
Bongartz, Roy, 487, 490-498
Bopp, John, 63
Bowers, J. L., 164
Bowker, Lee H., 47, 101-110
Boyer, Edward, 61
Braddock, Edward, 217
Brando, Marlon, 494, 518
Bridges, Al, 52
Briggs, Ray, 503
Brightman, Lehman, 52, 526
Bruce, Louis R., 525, 526
Bruner, Edward M., 304
Bryant, Hilda, 528
Bryde, John F., 156
Budget, Bureau of, 184, 185
Burgess, Ernest, 226
Burglary, 314, 321-322
Bushnell, John H., 196, 249-261
Bynum, Jack, 317, 367-377

Cahn, Edgar, 3-4, 6
California, University of, 56
California Indian Legal Services, 60
California Intertribal Council, 504
California v. Arizona, 65, 66
Campbell, Ernest Q., 70
Canada, education for Indians in, 129,
　　155-161
Caplow, Theodore, 406
"Carbonate City," Colorado, Navajos in,
　　47, 89-101
Carmen, Roderick S., 445
Carnegie Foundation, 58
Cartoons, stereotyping of Indians and
　　blacks in, 49, 110-114
Cass, Lewis, 17
Castro, Fidel, 487, 493, 513
Cattle, Indians and, 62, 280-282, 332,
　　336
Central Arizona Project, 65-66
Century of Dishonor (Jackson), 8, 20
Cervantes, Lucius F., 156
Chadwick, Bruce A., 128, 195, 239-249
Chamber of Commerce of the United
　　States, 30
Chapin, F. Stuart, 329
Charlestown, New Hampshire, 217
Cherokee (Tracy), 203
Cherokee Nation v. Georgia, 116
Cherokee Indians, 4, 6, 18, 47, 80-89.
　　116-117, 139, 198, 204, 291-303,
　　390, 430, 437, 522, 525
　　attitude toward education, 298-301
　　health practices among, 293-298
Chesky, Jane, 47
Cheyenne Indians, 4
　　suicide among, 371-372
Chicasaw Indians, 81, 204, 390
Child, Lydia Maria, 201
Child-rearing practices, Indian, 37-38,
　　40-41, 129, 146-147, 335
　　suicide propensity and, 373
Chilocco, Oklahoma, 54, 58
Chino, Wendell, 525, 526
Chippewa Indians, 4, 178, 367, 389,
　　414, 416-417, 418, 485, 524
Choctaw Indians, 4, 81, 204, 390, 430,
　　436, 437, 522, 525
Christiansen, John R., 363
Cities, Indians and, see Urban Indians
Citizens' Advocate Center, 525
Civil Rights Act (1964), 69
Civilian Conservation Corps, 501
Clark, Burton, 70
Clark, James R., 363
Clark, William, 17
Cloward, Richard, 156, 459
Cohen, Albert K., 459

Coleman, James S., 46, 50, 70, 133, 134, 135, 136, 137, 140, 143, 144, 145
Collier, Peter, 44, 51-68, 489
Colonialism, 513, 519
Colorado River, 65-66
Colville Reservation, 518
Colville Indians, 68
Comanche Captives (Cook), 203
Comanches, 523
Combs, A. W., 70
Community Action Program, 180, 183
Confederacy of American Indian Nations (proposed), 52
Confrontation tactics, 514, 533
Cook, Lee, 504
Cook, Will, 203
Cooper, James Fenimore, 201, 202, 212
Cooper, Jefferson, 203
Costo, Rupert, 527
Cotterill, R. S., 15
Cowboys, as model for Navajo boys, 282-288
Crane, Verner, 218
Creek Indians, 81, 204, 214, 216, 218, 390, 430, 437
Crèvecœur, J. Hector St. John de, 209, 219, 220
Crime, 331-400
  causal factors, 323-325
  family structure and, 333-337
  population structure and, 333
  on reservations, jurisdiction over, 118
Croghan, George, 219
Cronemeyer, Hoskie, 90
"Crossover effect," 134
Crow Indians 536
Cultural deprivation, 130, 138-139, 146, 162
Cultural survival, Indians and, 53
Culture, Indian, 1-3
  conflict with white culture, 1-3, 324
  contributions to other cultures, 194-195, 200-225
  crime and, 324
  disintegration of, 1, 9, 11, 14, 16
Culture, integral, concept of, 9-10, 20
Curlee, Wilson V., 372
Curriculum, of Indian schools, 137
Custer, George Armstrong, 521
Custer Died for Your Sins (Deloria), 488

Dakota Indians, 367
Dancing, 418
Dartmouth College, 213, 216-217
Davis, Isaac, 206
Dawes Act, *see* General Allotment Act
Day, Gordon M., 217
Day, Robert C., 489, 506-532

"Declaration of Indian Purpose," 485-486, 489, 511-512, 514, 519, 520
Deerslayer, The (Cooper), 202
Delaware Indians, 367
Delinquency, 313-315, 319
  causes of, 337
  social structure and, 327-338
    See also Juvenile delinquency
Delinquency and Opportunity (Cloward and Ohlin), 156
Deloria, Vine, Jr., 47, 488, 498-506, 507, 513, 518, 519, 530
DeMille, Cecil B., 203
Demonstrations, 494, 528
Denver, Colorado, adjustment of Navajos to, 440-466
Dependency, Indians and, 4, 15, 28-29
Deprivation, 45
  cultural, 130, 138-139, 146, 162
  educational, causes of, 136-143
  language, 162-171
Desertion, 313, 335
Deshayes, Louis, 219
Deutsch, Martin, 78
Devereux, George, 369-370
Deviant behavior, 313-400
  anomie theory of, 324
De Vorsey, Louis, Jr., 11
Discrimination, 43-127, 406, 520
  against Navajos, 89-101
Disorder, personality, 377-388
Disorderly conduct, 335, 336, 348
Divorce, 313, 343
Dizmang, Larry H., 371, 373, 374
DNA, 66
Dodge, Ernest S., 207
Donuner Foundation, 524
Dornbush, Sanford M., 226
Dorson, Richard M., 219
Dotson, Floyd, 421
Double Man, The (Pryor), 203
Dowling, John H., 403, 478-484
Downs, James F., 196, 197, 275-291
Dozier, Edward P., 324, 463
Drinking, *see* Alcohol problem
Dropout: Causes and Cures (Cervantes), 156
Dropouts, school, 128, 129, 132, 135-136, 146-161, 333
Drug abuse, 313, 318
Durkheim, Émile, 369
Dustin, Hannah, 217
Dysentery, 45

Earnings, changes in, vocational training and, 471-472
Eaton, Joseph W., 226
Economic Opportunity, Office of, 180, 191

Economics, 15
  crime and, 323-324
Edgerton, Robert B., 455
Education, Indian, 46-47, 58-59, 97,
    128-192, 253, 254, 534-536
  achievement motivation in Navajo and
    white students, 172-177
  as measure of degree of acculturation,
    230, 240, 242, 246-247
  attitude of Indian's toward, 131, 160,
    298-301
  Bureau of Indian Affairs and, 3
  Canada and, 129, 155-161
  causes of failure of, 136-143
  cultural deprivation and, 130, 138-139
  curriculum and, 137
  equal opportunities for, 69-80
  facilities, inadequacy of, 136
  factors related to academic failure of
    Indian students, 129
  improvements in, suggestions for, 141-
    143, 179-180
  language problem and, 139-140, 160,
    162-171
  migration and, 469-470
  reading program, 162-171
  self concepts and, 140
  teachers and, 137-138
    See also Schools
Education, U. S. Office of, 69, 133
Educational deprivation, causes of, 136-
    143
Employment, off-reservation, 90-91
Engelmann, Siegfried, 162, 168, 169,
    170
Equal Employment Opportunity Com-
    mission, 45
Equality, Indian's belief in, 14
Erikson, Erik H., 40
Eskimos, 25, 26, 42, 133, 159, 196, 197,
    368, 406, 418
  drinking among, 346
  ethnic identity and acculturation
    among, 261-275
Ethnic identity, acculturation and, 261-
    275
Ex Parte Crow Dog, 118

"Facilitative tactics," 515, 516, 517, 518
Facilities, educational, inadequacy of,
    136
Fairchild, Hoxie Neal, 220
Fairclough, Ellen, 492
Family of Outcasts (Rubenfield), 156
Family structure, crime and, 333-337
Federal aid, 521
Federal policy, 67, 486, 489, 517, 529-
    530, 534-536

Fein, R., 469
Felonies, 322, 335, 339
Fenton, William N., 10, 14, 21, 22, 498
Ferguson, Frances Northend, 316, 345-
    358, 359, 443, 445, 457, 463
Fiedler, Leslie A., 194
Fisher, A. D., 129-130, 135, 155-161
Fisher, Vardis, 203, 217
Fish-ins, 507-509, 514, 516, 518
Five Civilized Tribes, 81, 89, 204, 390,
    402, 436, 437
"Five County Northeast Oklahoma Cher-
    okee Organization," 86
Five Nations, 15
Flathead Indians, 485
Flexner, James T., 206, 218
Flint, Timothy, 202
Ford Foundation, 505
"Foreign aid," 520, 521
Foreman, Grant, 9, 21
Fort Hall Reservation (Idaho), 53-54, 55,
    56, 60-63, 132, 373, 517
  relationship between social structure
    and delinquency on, 315, 327-
    338
  suicide on, 313
Fort Lawton, 533
Fort Mojaves, 66
Foster, Laurence, 214
Franklin, Benjamin, 8, 14, 534
Freedom, Indian's belief in, 14
French, Elizabeth, 173
French Test of Insight, 173
Friedenberg, Edgar Z., 154
Frontier, 210
Frontiersmen, 18-19
Furnas, J. C., 215

Galloway, Charles G., 130, 139, 162-171
Gaston, Fort, 252
Gates Reading Test, 166
General Allotment Act (1887), 60, 117,
    124, 479, 519
General Electric, 521
Georgia Pacific Company, 523
Giles, Janice Holt, 203
Gill, Joseph-Louis, 200
Girty, Simon, 220
Godfrey (Indianized Negro), 205, 218
Gold, Joel W., 130, 139, 172-177
Goldschmidt, Walter, 455
Gonneville, Captain de, 220
Gordon, Caroline, 203
Government, tribal, 186-187
Grandparents, role and influence of, 334-
    335
Graves, Theodore, 240, 316, 359, 402-
    403, 440-446

Gray v. United States, 115, 118, 119-123
Green, Arnold W., 226
Green Bay, Wisconsin, Oneidas and, 478-484
Green Centuries (Gordon), 203
Gregory, Dick, 494, 514
Grossman, Peter H., 445
Guevara, Che, 493

Hagan, William T., 15, 18, 22, 23
Hiliwas, 511
Hallowell, A. Irving, 194-195, 200-225, 389
Halverson, Lowell K., 315, 338-344
Hamer, John H., 346
Hamilton, C. Horace, 469
Hanson, Robert, 445, 446, 450, 456
Harrison, Ira E., 154
Harvey, Donald F., 241
Haskell Institute, 172, 174, 175
Havighurst, Robert, 158, 389
Hawkin, Benjamin, 214
Hayner, Norman S., 313, 319, 323
Head Start projects, 131, 180-184
Health, Education and Welfare, Department of, 4, 26, 506
Health, Indian, 26-27, 45-46
    mental health, 317, 377-400
    Public Health Service and, 3, 26-27
Health practices, Cherokee, 293-298
Heath, Dwight B., 445, 457
Hellon, C. P., 317
Helpers, professional, 188-189, 190
Henry, Jeannette, 48
Henry, Jules, 154
Hentig, Hans von, 313, 319, 323
Hentz, N. M., 202
Herskovits, Melville J., 193, 195, 205, 218, 229
Hickel, Walter, 51, 68, 497, 525-526
Hill, Clifton, 504
Hill, Thomasine Ruth, 524
Hoar, Senator, 121-122
Hobomok: A Tale of Early Times (Child), 201
Homicide, 313, 314, 321, 340, 342, 344
Honigmann, Irma, 346, 443
Honigmann, John J., 346, 443
Hope Leslie (Sedgwick), 201
Hopis, 283, 493
Hopkins-Duke, A., 521
Horan, James D., 203
Horn, Kahn-Tineta, 496
Horn, Taio Tekane, 496, 497
Horsman, Reginald, 10, 17-18, 21, 22, 23
Horton, Donald, 346

Houma Indians, 511
Housing, 3, 5, 45, 65, 94, 146, 293-294, 327-330, 415-416, 467, 522
Houts, Kathleen C., 49, 110-114
Hubbard, William, 208
Hudson Bay Company, 60
Hughes, Everett Cherrington, 31, 178, 188
Hughes, Helen MacGill, 31
Humphrey, Hubert, 520
Humphrey, Norman D., 226
Humphrey Clinker (Smollett), 217
Hunt, George T., 14, 22
Hunter, Robert, 503
Hupa Indians, 196, 249-261
Huron Indians, 15, 216

Ibsen, Henrik, 177-178
Idaho State College, 55
Identity, acculturation and, 193-312
    Pan-Indianism and, 424-425
    social interaction and, 412-428
Illegitimacy, 313, 318
Income, 4, 45, 56, 533
    family (reservation Indians), 467
    family (rural Indians), 25-26
Indian, The: America's Unfinished Business (Brophy and Aberle), 3
Indian Affairs, Bureau of, 3-4, 44, 54, 55, 57-62, 64, 66, 67, 253, 255, 264, 265, 266, 275, 276, 278, 279, 285
    activities of, 3
    attitude of Indians toward, 4, 44
    criticism of, 3-4, 6
    employment assistance programs, 402, 407-408, 432, 441, 467
    housing policy, 415
    paternalism of, 57
    rehabilitation of alcoholics, 347
    relocation programs, 90-91
    schools operated by, 132, 136, 143
"Indian Americans," vs. term "American Indians," 249-261
Indian Citizenship Act (1924), 117
Indian Claims Commission, 59
Indian Country (Johnson), 218
Indian Hall of Fame, 518
Indian Health Service, 26
Indian Historical Society, 48
Indian Intercourse Act (1832), 325
Indian League of the Americas, 522
"Indian Patrol," 528
Indian Prohibition Act (1832), 347
Indian Trust Counsel Authority (proposed), 530
Indian Reorganization Act (1934), 118, 254, 499, 500, 504

Indian Vocational Training Act (1956), 468
Indian-white relations, conflict between cultures, 1-3, 7-23
    early America and, 1-3, 7-23, 200
    present-day, 6, 31-42, 177-192, 412-428
    process of, 1, 2, 9
Indianization, 194, 195, 200-225
Infant mortality rates, 5, 27, 28, 46, 56
Influenza, 46
Instability, family, 313
Integral culture, concept of, 9-10, 20
Integration, social, 195, 225, 227, 232-233, 236, 239-244, 416-417
Interaction, social, Indian identity and, 412-428
Interior, Department of, 3, 57, 64, 65, 66, 67, 255, 410, 519, 522, 526, 530, 533
Intermarriage, see Miscegenation
Intermountain Indian School (Utah), 58
Iroquois Indians, 14, 15, 216, 367, 487, 490-498, 513, 517, 521
Irrigation, 59, 65, 89

Jackson, Helen Hunt, 8, 20
Jacobs, Wilbur R., 10, 12, 14, 21
Jacobson, Lenore, 140
Jacoby, Harold S., 195, 226
Jaguar Queen, or the Outlaws of the Sierra Madre (Whittaker), 202
James, Bernard J., 425
Janissaries, 207
Jay Treaty, 495, 523
Jefferson, Thomas, 209, 534
Jersild, A. T., 70
Jessor, Richard, 324, 445, 446, 450, 456
Jessor, Shirley, 445, 446, 450, 456
Jesuits, Indians and, 211, 216
Johnson, Dorothy M., 218
Johnson, Helen W., 5, 24-30
Johnson, J. Hugh, 218
Johnson, Lyndon, 518
Johnson, Ray, 492, 522
Johnson, Sir William, 206, 217
Josephy, Alvin M., Jr., 14
Jourdain, Roger, 521
Justice, U. S. Department of, 509, 530
Juvenile delinquency, 313, 314
    causes of, 314, 315, 337
    social structure and, 327-338

Karok Indians, 251, 258
Keller, A. G., 210-211, 220
Kelley, Wellbourn, 205
Kelly, William, 134
Kennedy, Edward, 489, 532-536

Kennedy, John F., 510, 517
Kennedy, Robert F., 533
Kentuckians, The (Giles), 203
Kerchoff, Alan C., 389
King's Rebel (Horan), 203
Klamath Reservation, homicide rate on the, 313
Klamath Indians, 68, 132, 485, 487
Kluckhohn, Clyde, 47, 172, 375, 379, 436
Kotzebue, Alaska, 263, 265-274
Kroeber, A. L., 226
Krush, Thaddeus P., 317, 377-388
Kupferer, Harriet J., 139, 197-198, 291-303
Kwakiutl Indians, 159, 160

Labor, U. S. Department of, 45
Laird, Charlton, 203
Land, Indian-white conflict over, 13-14
    utilization by Indians, 330-332
Land Management, Bureau of, 66
Language, problem of, education and, 139-140, 160, 162-171
Language deprivation, 162-171
LaPointe, Frank, 503
Larceny, 314, 322, 336
Law, federal Indian, 116-123
Law violation, see Crime
Leach, Douglas Edward, 12, 18
Leadership, Indian, need for, 29
Lee, Dorothy, 40, 41
Legal assistance, 60, 315, 338-344
Leighton, Dorothea, 47, 172, 375, 436
Le Jeune, Father, 211
Le May, Alan, 203
Lesser, Alexander, 260
Letters from an American Farmer (Crèvecœur), 209
Lev, Joseph, 174
Levy, Jerrold E., 350, 370
Life expectancy, 5, 27, 28, 46, 56
Light in the Forest, The (Richter), 203, 212
Linton, Ralph, 193, 195, 205, 229, 276
Living, level of, 327-330
    as measure of acculturation, 230, 241, 245
    Cheyenne Indians and, 372
Logan, Beeman, 496
London Missionary Society, 206
Los Angeles, California, migration and adaptation of Indians to, 402, 428-439
Lowell, Edgar, L., 173
Luebben, Ralph A., 47, 89-101
Lummi Indians, 536
Lurie, Nancy, 433
Lynd, Robert, 87

McClelland, David C., 172, 173
McCloud, Janet, 57
McCoy, Isaac, 216
McCracken, Robert D., 448
McFee, Malcolm, 198, 303-312
McGillivray, Alexander, 205
MacGregor, Gordon, 33, 47, 378
McKenney, Thomas L., 17
MacMeekin, Daniel H., 49, 115-127
McSwain, Romola, 448, 459
Major Crimes Act (1885), 118, 119, 121, 125
Makah Indians, 514
Maniwaki Reserve, 497
Manpower program, 467-476
Maricopas, 134
Mariner, William, 206-207, 215
Marriott, Alice, 220
Marshall, John, 116-117, 118, 486
Martin, Harry W., 317, 436, 470
Mather, Cotton, 201
Matinnecock Indians, 521-522
Mead, Margaret, 226, 260
Means, La Nada, 53-58, 60, 489
Menominee Indians, 67, 389, 485, 487, 517
Mental health, 317, 377-400
Mental illness, 313, 317-318, 377-400
Merton, Robert, 197, 450
Metis Indians, 161
Metropolitan Water District of Southern California, 66
Mexican-Americans, 44
Miccosukee Indians, 525
Michener, Bryon P., 456
Migration, Indian, adjustment problems and, 428-439, 440-466
   to Denver, Colorado, 440-466
   education and, 469-470
   to Los Angeles, 402, 428-439
   to San Francisco Bay area, 412-428
   to urban areas, 408-409
   vocational training and, 467-478
Militancy, Indian, 528
Miller, S. M., 154
Mills, Sid, 52
Mincer, J., 472
Mindell, Carl, 372-373
Minnis, Mhyra S., 315, 327-338
Miscegenation, 22, 82, 195, 227-228, 233-235, 239, 242
Miss Indian America pageant, 524
Missionaries, Indians and, 11, 13, 213, 253
Moberly, John Henry, 217
Models, acculturation and, 275-291
Mohave Indians, 369-370
Mohawk Indians, 495, 496, 497, 518, 523

Mood, Fulmer, 219
Mooney, James, 211
Morbidity rate, 5, 28
Morse, Wayne, 132
Mortality rates, 5, 27, 28
Morton, Sarah Wentworth, 201
Moses, Robert, 491, 513
Motivation, achievement, in Navajo and white students, 130, 172-177
Murad I, 207
Myths, 3, 83-86, 88

Nash, Manning, 33
Nash, Philleo, 520
National Congress of American Indians, 86, 486, 487, 488, 503, 504, 505, 506-507, 511, 517, 518, 519, 520, 523, 524, 525, 528
National Council on Indian Opportunity, 526
National Indian Chicago Conference, 485-486
National Indian Youth Council, 486, 487, 489, 504, 506, 507, 508, 509, 512, 513, 514, 517, 518, 519, 525, 526, 528
Nationalism, tribal, 520, 522
Native American Church, 351, 358
Navajo Community College, 65, 524
Navajo Cowboy Association, 282
Navajos, 4, 47, 57, 58, 63-66, 89-101, 196, 197, 240, 242, 262, 275-291, 414, 417, 418, 436-437, 524, 535-536
   acculturation among, 275-291
   achievement motivation in students, 172-177
   adjustment to Denver, Colorado, 407, 440-466
   alcohol problem among, 316, 345-358, 359, 440-463
   education and, 130, 139, 172-177
   homicide rates among, 314
   prejudice and discrimination against, 89-101
   relocation information, 433
   suicide among, 370
Negroes, Indians and, 204-205, 211, 213, 214, 216, 218-219, 220
   See also Blacks
Nelle, Joanna, 377-388
Nevada Intertribal Council, 503
Nick, Margaret, 533
Nixon, Richard, 517, 529-530
Noble savage concept, 12-13, 14
Noninterference, policy of, 6, 35-41
Nonviolence, 515, 517, 518
Nordwall, Adam, 498, 499, 527
Norris, Rep., 122

Oakes, Richard, 52, 53, 498, 527
Obstructive tactics, 515, 516, 517, 524, 528
Occum, Samson, 213
Occupation, as measure of degree of acculturation, 230-231, 240-241, 242-243
Occupational patterns, 27-29, 160
Oglala (South Dakota) Community High School, 149
Ohlin, Lloyd, 156, 459
Ojek, Rose, 496
Ojibwa Indians, 262, 389
Oklahoma, Cherokees in, 80-89
Old Hicks the Guide (Webber), 202
Old White Boy, 213, 216
Omaha Indians, 367
Omnibus bill, 520
One Feather, Gerald, 503, 504
Oneida Indians, 403, 478-484
Organization of Native American Students, 526
Ortiz, Fernando, 205
Osceola, 214
Ottoman state, transculturization in, 207, 208, 216, 219
Ouâbi (Philena), 201
Our Brother's Keeper: The Indian in White America (Cahn), 3, 57

Pacific Islands, transculturization in, 206-207, 214-215, 216
Paiute Indians, 522, 524-525
Pala Reservation (California), 59
Pan-Indianism, 52, 142, 401, 402, 410, 438, 439, 490
    Indian identity and, 424-425
Papagos Indians, 41, 47, 133, 505
Park, Robert Ezra, 178, 226
Parker, Seymour, 158, 160, 196-197, 261-275, 459
Parkman, Francis, 14
Parliament, H. E., 164
Passamaquoddy Indians, 523, 525
Paternalism, 57, 519, 529, 534
Patten, Lewis B., 203, 212
Peach War (1655), 15
Pearce, Roy Harvey, 194, 210
Pemmican (Fisher), 203
Pequot Indians, 16
Personality disorder, 377-388
Philena, see Morton, Sarah Wentworth
Philion, William L. E., 130, 139, 162-171
Philip, King, 16
Pima Indians, 133, 134
Pine Ridge Reservation (South Dakota), 129, 146-155, 372, 499-502

homicide rate on the, 314
juvenile delinquency on the, 314-315
Pit River Indians, 35
Pocahontas, 220
Pocatello, Idaho, 53, 60
Political History of the Cherokee Nation, A (Wardell), 84
Politics, Indians and, 14, 15
Pontiac, 14
Poor, federal programs for rehabilitation of the, 184-189
"Poor Peoples' Campaign," 522
Population statistics, 25, 28, 43-44, 333, 478
Potowatamie Indians, 485
Poverty, 4-5, 45, 56-57, 63, 146, 534
    crime and, 324
    rural Indians and, 24-30
Pow-wows, 418
Prejudice, 43-127
    against Navajos, 89-101
    against Oneidas, 483
Price, John A., 402, 428-439
Private enterprise, 63
Prophecy, 492-493
Protests, 514-530
Prucha, Francis Paul, 13, 15, 17, 18, 22, 23
Pryor, Elinor, 203
Public Health Service, U.S., 3, 347, 378, 390
Public relations campaign, 524
Pueblo Indian, 4, 370, 517, 523, 524
Puritans, Indians and, 15-16, 208, 212, 215
Puyallup Indians, 509
Pygmalion in the Classroom (Rosenthal and Jacobson), 140, 145

Quinault Reservation (Washington), 132
Quinault Indians, 525

Radin, Paul, 226
Ranching, 332
Rape, 49, 115-127, 314, 321, 335
Ray, Charles, 158, 160
Reading program, Indian children and the, 162-171
Reasons, Charles, 314, 319-326
Reboussin, Roland, 130, 139, 172-177
Recidivism, 335, 336, 347, 352
Red Muslims, 514, 526
Red Power, 142, 401, 486, 490, 506, 507, 516, 528
Redfield, Robert, 193, 195, 205, 229
Reeder, T. A., 70
Rehabilitation programs, 184-189
Reina, Ruben, 205

Relativism, 9-10, 11-12
Relocation, changes in earnings and,
    471-472
  federal programs and, 407-408
  programs, 467-476
  San Francisco Bay area and, 412-428
  vocational training and, 467-476
Removal, Indian, 8-9, 17-18, 23
Rendon, Gabino, Jr., 459, 461
Renegade, The (Bennett), 202
Reservations, Indian, 186-187
  crimes committed on, jurisdiction
    over, 118, 517
  impact of relocation programs on,
    474-475
  returnees, 470-471
  termination of, 67-68, 487, 492, 517,
    518, 522, 526, 529
Resettlement communities, 89-101
Resighini rencharia, 59
"Resolution of the Thirty Tribes," 520,
    521
Returnees, 470-471
Richter, Conrad, 203, 212
Rights, human, Indians' belief in, 14
Ritzenthaler, Robert, 480
Roadblocks, 525
Roakoke Renegade (Tracy), 203
Robbery, 314
Robinson, Rubin, 133, 142
Rodeos, Indians and, 282-284
Rolfe, Thomas, 220
Rolling Thunder, 504
Rosenthal, Elizabeth Clark, 405
Rosenthall, Robert, 140
Ross, John, 84
Ross Party, 81-82
Rossellini, Governor (Washington), 509
Rough Rock Indian School, 524, 535-
    536
Round Valley Reservation, 252
Rovillian, Eugene E., 217
Rowlandson, Mary, 208
Roy, Prodipto, 195, 225-239, 241
Royle, E. M., 202
Rubenfield, Seymour, 156
Rural Indians, demographic character-
    istics, 25
  income of, 25-26
  occupational patterns of, 27-29
  poverty and, 24-30
Rustling, cattle, 336
Ryan, Joan, 158, 160

Safar, Dwight, 46, 69-80
St. Mary's School for Indian Girls (Spring-
    field, South Dakota), 54
Salter, Patricia J., 111

San Francisco, California, 55
  relocated Indians in, 412-428
Sasaki, Tom T., 47, 389
Saturday Evening Post, 49, 110, 111,
    112, 113
Schoenfeld, Amram, 110
Schoolcraft, Henry R., 205
Schools, 128
  curriculum of, 137
  defined as a rite of passage, 157
  dropouts, 128, 129, 132, 135-136,
    146-161, 333
  operated by the Bureau of Indian Af-
    fairs, 132, 136, 143
  teachers, 137-138, 146, 147
  underenrollment in, 128, 133
    See also Education
Searchers, The (Le May), 203
Seattle, Washington, legal services avail-
    able to Indians in, 338-344
Sedgwick, Catherine M., 201
Self-conception, 70
  assimilation and, 239-260
  education and, 140
Self-consciousness, Indian, 533
Self-determination, 489, 517, 525, 526,
    530, 535
Self-realization, Indian's attempts at, 3-4
Sellin, Thorsten, 324
Seminole Indians, 81, 204, 214, 390,
    430, 437, 525
Senate Subcommittee on Indian Educa-
    tion, 532-536
Senate Subcommittee to Investigate Ju-
    venile Delinquency, 314
Seneca Indians, 536
Sequoyah, 84
Sewell, William H., 329
Sheehan, Bernard W., 1-2, 7-23
Sherman Institute (Riverside, California),
    58
Shoshone Valley (Flint), 202
Shoshone Indians, 60, 315, 327-338,
    373
Siegel, Bernard J., 226
Silence, Indians and, 6, 31-33
Simpson Timber Company, 59
Sindell, Peter S., 377-388
Sioux Indians, 5, 40, 41, 51, 53, 57,
    129, 135, 146-155, 156, 159, 161,
    178, 318, 414, 417, 436, 499-504,
    517, 522, 527
  suicide rate among, 372-373
Skelly Oil, 523
Slater. Arthur D., 316, 358-367
Smith, Henry Nash, 210
Smith, Redbird, 83
Smollett, Tobias G., 217

Snyder, Peter Z., 448, 458
Snygg, D., 70
"Social distance scale," 44-45
Social integration, 195, 225, 227, 232-233, 236, 239-244, 416-417
Social interaction, Indian identity and, 412-428
Social structure, delinquency and, 327-338
Societal Evolution (Keller), 210
Sons of the Shaking Earth (Wolfe), 20, 23
Sorkin, Alan L., 403, 467-478
Southwestern Regional Youth Conference, 511
Spaniards, Indians and the, 20
Spanish-Americans, equal educational opportunities and, 69-80
Speck, Frank G., 200, 214, 216
Spencer, Oliver, 220
Spicer, Edward H., 193, 195
Spicer, Joseph, 47
Spindler, George, 160, 291, 304, 389
Spindler, Louise S., 277, 389
Spocks, Cynthia, 363
Spokane Indians, 195, 225-249, 329
Spokane Reservation, 195, 229
Squaw Man, The (Royle), 202
Stark, John, 217
Steiner, Stan, 47, 401, 509, 510, 528
Stereotypes, 48-49, 110-114, 313, 316, 345, 404, 515, 524
Stevens, Ernie, 504
Stevens, P. H., 70
Stewart, Omer, 313, 314, 320, 324, 325, 443
Stewart Institute (Carson City, Nevada), 55, 58
Stones, E., 166
Striner, Herbert E., 406
Stuart, Paul, 372-373
Suicide, 46, 63, 132, 313, 316-317, 367-377, 534
    alcohol and, 350, 370, 374
Sun Tamo, Princess, 518
Supreme Court, U. S., 523
Swamp and Overflow Act (1850), 66
Swanton, John R., 205, 212, 213, 216

Tadeukund, the Last King of the Lenape (Hentz), 202
Taho, Lake, 525
Tax, Sol, 486, 510, 511
Teachers, 137-138, 146, 147
Technical assistance, 521
Teedyuscung, 10, 21
Termination, of reservations, 67-68, 487, 492, 517, 518, 522, 526, 529

Textbooks, treatment of Indians and blacks in, 47-48, 101-110
Thom, Mel, 5, 508, 509, 511, 519
Thomas, Robert K., 6, 31-42, 47, 57, 80-89, 291-292, 294, 295, 301, 428, 520
Thorne, B., 370
Thorpe, Joseph "Frank," Jr., 61-63
Thrashing Buffalo Reservation, 183
Thunder on the River (Laird), 203
Thunderbird American Indian Dancers, 522
Timber disputes, 523
Tracy, Don, 203
Traditional Indian Unity Convention, 526
"Trail of Tears," 81
Training, vocational, 467-476
Transculturalization, 194-195, 200-225
Trask (Berry), 218-219
Treaties, violation of, by whites, 8, 507-508, 527
Treaty Party, 81, 82
Trelease, Allen W., 14, 15
Tribal government, 186-187
Tribalism movement, 514-515
Truckee River, 525
Tuberculosis, 5, 27, 45
Turner, Frederick Jackson, 210, 211, 219
Tuscarora Indians, 494

Udall, Stuart, 65, 518-519, 520
Uhlmann, Wes, 338
Uintah-Ouray Indians, alcohol problem among the, 316, 358-367
Underachievement, academic, of Indian children, 133-143
Underenrollment in schools, 128, 133
Unemployment, 4-5, 45, 56, 129, 155-156, 332, 467, 475, 524
United Bay Area Council of American Indians, 499
United Native Americans, 52, 56
United South Eastern Tribes, 525
United States v. *Kagama*, 118, 125
United States Code, 115, 119, 123
University Agriculture Extension Service, 61
Urban Indians, 316, 401-484
    acculturation and, 434-435
    adjustment and, 435-436, 440-466
    assimilation and, 239-249, 402, 407, 433-434
    invisibility of, 401, 404-410
    legal services available to, 338-344
    relocation and, 407-409, 412-428
    plight of, 401
    San Francisco Bay area, 412-428
    tribal differences in adaptation, 436-437

Vagrancy, 335, 336
VanArsdale, Minor, 446, 450, 455
Van Doren, Carl, 202
Van Every, Dale, 205
Vaughan, Alden T., 11, 15-16
Violence, 8, 12, 14, 16, 34, 44, 58
VISTA, 131, 178, 181-183, 188, 189
Vocational training, 467-476
  decline in antisocial behavior through,
    473-474
Vogel, Virgil J., 48
Voget, Fred, 304
Vogt, Evon Z., 227-228, 236, 242
Voltaire, F. M. A., 217
Volunteers in Service to America, 178
Voyagers, The (Van Every), 205

Wahrhaftig, Albert L., 47, 80-89
Walker, Della M., 329
Walker, F. A., 221
Walker, Helen M., 174
Walker, Roy, 329
Wallace, Anthony F. C., 10, 21
Walters, Richard H., 452
Wampum belts, demand for return of,
  521
Wanneka, Anne, 519
"War on Poverty," 5, 178, 184, 185, 518
Wardell, Morris, 84
Warner, W. Lloyd, 87
Warrior, Clyde, 511, 514, 519
Washburn, Wilcomb E., 12, 21, 22, 204
Washington, D. C., conference of the 30
  tribes, 520
Washington, George, 19, 493
Water rights, 65
Watkins, Senator (Utah), 409
Wax, Murray L., 131, 139, 147, 156,
  159, 161, 177-192, 194, 405
Wax, Rosalie H., 6, 31-42, 129, 131,
  135, 146-155, 156, 159, 161, 177-
192, 194, 423
We Talk, You Listen (Deloria), 488
Webb, E. J., 448
Webber, Charles, 202
Weppner, Robert S., 241, 452
Wept of Wish-ton-Wish, The (Cooper),
  202, 212
West, W. A., 164
Wheeler-Howard Act (1934), 479
Wheelock, Eleazar, 217
Whetten, Nathan L., 226
White, Lynn C., 195, 239-249
White Deerskin Dance, 252, 256, 260
White Hawk, Thomas, 497
White Warrior (Patten), 203, 212
Whittaker, Frederick, 202
Whittaker, James O., 443
Wilkie, Bruce, 519
Wilkinson, Gerald, 526
Williams, Eunice, 208
Wilson, Edmund, 194, 498
Winters Doctrine, 65, 66
Wissler, Clark, 210
Wolcott, Harry, 160
Wolfe, Eric R., 20, 23
Women, Navajo, 275-290
  role of, 334
Worcester v. *Georgia,* 117, 125
World War II, 255, 257, 501
Wounded Knee, Battle of, 53, 500
Wyman, L. C., 370

Yinger, J. Milton, 446
Young, John, 206
Young, Mary Elizabeth, 13
Young, Robert W., 90
Yurok Indians, 251, 258

Ziegler, Suzanne, 448
Zimmer, Basil G., 421
Zuñi Indians, 536